Textbook of

Highway Engineering

Textbook of

Highway Engineering

R Srinivasa Kumar

Department of Civil Engineering
University College of Engineering
Osmania University, Hyderabad

Universities Press

TEXTBOOK OF HIGHWAY ENGINEERING

UNIVERSITIES PRESS (INDIA) PRIVATE LIMITED

Registered office
3-6-747/1/A & 3-6-754/1, Himayatnagar, Hyderabad 500 029, Telangana, India
e-mail: www.universitiespress.com

Distributed by
Orient Blackswan Private limited

Registered office
3-6-752 Himayatnagar, Hyderabad 500 029, Telangana, India

Other offices
Bengaluru / Bhopal / Chennai / Guwahati / Hyderabad / Jaipur
Kolkata / Lucknow / Mumbai / New Delhi / Noida / Patna / Vijayawada

First Published 2011
Reprinted 2012, 2013, 2016, 2018

ISBN: 978-81-7371-681-2

Cover and book design
© Universities Press (India) Private Ltd 2011

501425

Typeset in Palatino 10/12 *by*
Techastra Solutions Pvt. Ltd., Hyderabad 500 029

Printed at
Sri Balaji Graphics
Hyderabad 500 044

Published by
Universities Press (India) Private Limited
3-6-747/1/A & 3-6-754/1, Himayatnagar, Hyderabad 500 029, Telangana, India

I dedicate this book to
all my teachers

Content

Preface

The demand imposed on the transportation system in India, especially the highway network, is increasing at a rapid rate due to the increase in traffic volumes and axle loads. To meet this ever increasing demand, the Government of India has initiated different schemes to construct new highways and to widen and rehabilitate existing highways. Ambitious plans have been drawn up to narrow the gap between the demand on the highway system and the capacity of the highways to carry the traffic at an acceptable level of service. The major plans comprise of various phases of the National Highway Development Project (NHDP), the Jawaharlal Nehru National Urban Renewal Mission (JNNURM), Pradhan Manthri Gram Sadak Yojana (PMGSY) and Bharath Nirman. Apart from these major schemes, a number of other projects have also been undertaken by the central and different state Governments for the rehabilitation of the existing road network with assistance from funding agencies such as the World Bank, the Asian Development Bank, OECF and NABARD.

Considering the magnitude of the task undertaken, it is obvious that vast sums of money will be spent and large-scale construction and maintenance activities will be taken up. Along with the realisation of the need to quickly upgrade the highway transportation infrastructure, the level of awareness about the necessity of using the latest approaches/methodologies for testing materials, design, construction and evaluation of highways have also increased significantly.

In view of the importance to cater to the above needs, the author has undertaken the task of writing a comprehensive text on highway engineering incorporating existing and latest methods/techniques on pavement materials testing, design and evaluation. Though the text is basically meant to meet the academic needs of civil engineering students at undergraduate and postgraduate levels, the incorporation of elaborate content on important recent research work related to highway pavements will be of interest to the practicing highway/transportation engineers also.

The text comprises different topics on highway engineering and is presented in ten chapters. The basic approach of the text is intended to explain the fundamental concepts and principles in a simple elegant manner yet refer to their wider applications. Towards this purpose, the author has presented different types of solved example problems with neat sketches wherever necessary. Typical exercise problems are also given at end of the each chapter. This is intended to evaluate the students in their ability to grasp the underlying fundamental concepts and apply them for solving problems related to their professional career.

R. Srinivasa Kumar
Hyderabad

Acknowledgements

To accomplish the enormous task of bringing out this book, the author is indebted to Dr. D. Venkateshwar Rao, Rtd., Professor of Civil Engineering. He has been a source of inspiration and has guided me at every stage of improvement of the text.

The author is grateful to the American Association of State Highway Officials (AASHTO), the Asphalt Institute (TAI), Indian Roads Congress (IRC) and National Rural Roads Development Agency (NRRDA) for providing prompt written permission to reproduce a few excerpts from their publications.

The author wishes to express his gratitude to his teachers, Dr. B. B. Pandey, Rtd. Professor, Dr. Mayajit Mazumdar (late), Rtd., Professor and Dr. K. Sudhakar Reddy, Professor of Civil Engineering, IIT Kharagpur, for providing basic training in transportation engineering.

The author is thankful to all the researchers cited in the list of references, and who have contributed to the development of the subject around the globe.

The author thanks the publisher, M/s. Universities Press, Hyderabad, for accepting this project and for the co-operation offered during various states of publication of the text.

Thanks are also due to his colleagues, Dr. N. Suresh Kumar and others in the Department of Civil Engineering, UCE, OU. The author also wishes to thank Dr. P. Ramamohan Rao, ex-colleague and Mr. C. S. Rao, VNRVJIET, for providing necessary encouragement.

Last but not least, the author is thankful to his parents and wife Saritha, for their cooperation and patience during the writing stage of the manuscript.

Although efforts were made to check and improve the text while writing, editing and proof reading, there still may be a few omissions and errors. The author will be very grateful for any positive and constructive suggestions from the readers for further improving the text.

R. Srinivasa Kumar
Hyderabad

Organisation of Text

The text comprises ten chapters. The details are as follows.

Chapter 1: This chapter presents an introduction to the historical, latest and proposed developments in the highway infrastructure of India. Focus is also on highway location surveys.

Chapter 2: It covers topics related to the geometric design of highways including a few basic concepts of surveying.

Chapter 3: This chapter discusses various test methods/principles related to characterisation of pavement materials such as soil and mineral aggregates. Permissible test values are presented for each test referring to codes of standard institutions viz. Indian Roads Congress (IRC), Bureau of Indian Standards and AASHTO.

Chapter 4: It contains the details of testing paving bituminous materials.

Chapter 5: This chapter covers topics related to characterisation of hardened cement concrete and mix design procedures used for cement concrete pavement.

Chapter 6: Factors considered for design of flexible and rigid pavements are presented.

Chapter 7 and 8: These chapters present different analysis and design methods of flexible and rigid pavement respectively.

Chapter 9: Various aspects of structural evaluation of flexible and rigid pavements are presented. In this context, the focus in on the use of falling weight deflectometers, as it is the latest technological development in recent practices of structural evaluation methods of pavements.

Chapter 10: The use of dynamic cone penetrometers for evaluating unbound granular layers and sub-grade soil have been presented. Research findings related to estimation of sub-grade strength are well covered in this last chapter.

Note: The techniques presented in Chapter 9 and 10 are widely used all over the world for structural evaluation of different layers of highway pavements.

1

Highway Development Programmes and Surveys

A good transportation system facilitates the mobility of persons and goods to different places. If rural and urban areas were connected by a systematic network of roads, it would give an additional boost to developmental activities in the civil, military and recreational fronts. Trade of agricultural and industrial products and interchange of human resources take place rapidly with increased road transportation. Thus, with a good network of road systems, the nation prospers. Keeping this relationship between good roads and prosperity in mind, Indians and Indian rulers through the years have considered road development works as an important part of administration. The evolution of Indian roads through the ages is discussed in this chapter.

1.1 Road Development in Ancient India

The first Indian civilisation flourished in the Indus valley region from about 3300 BCE to 1300 BCE. Well planned towns were constructed with wide roads, colonies of houses and ports. Sophisticated sanitary and drainage systems were also observed in some of the excavations. Straight streets in rectangular patterns were found in excavations at Mohenjodaro. Based on archaeological evidences gathered, it is learnt that even carts and chariots existed during this period.

The period of the Mauryan empire (300–180 BCE) was a period of great consolidation in Indian history. Agriculture, art, cultural and economic activities, all thrived and flourished across India because of the creation of a single and efficient system of finance, administration and security. The road system too thrived, especially during the rule of Chandragupta Maurya. Towns were established with well planned roads and good drainage and sanitation systems. From the documented records of Kautilya, in *Arthashastra*, durable roads were laid with separate specifications for civilian and military purposes. During this period, most of the important places of the northern region of the Indian continent were connected by roads with strategically placed arboriculture, wells and rest-houses. Ashoka the Great (304–232 BCE), the Mauryan emperor, was also responsible for improving the road network for political and socio-economic purposes. Roads were built with suitable shelters, water-wells and avenue trees on either side.

The establishment of a good road system was well-documented by Hiuen-Tsang, Fa-hien of China, Megasthenes of Greece and others who visited India during the period.

Durable roads were constructed and maintained properly during the rule of the Mughals (early 1500 CE till about the end of the 18th century).

1.2 Road Development in India During the British Rule

After the decline of the Mughals, the road network in India was severely damaged. They deteriorated beyond compare. During the British rule, only those roads which were considered of strategic military use were built and maintained for their political advantage. The modern Grand Trunk Road (the Grand Trunk Road already existed during the Mauryan era) was built from Delhi to Kolkata by William Bentinck. Lord Dalhousie took many steps to improve the service condition of roads. He formulated an organisation called the Public Works Department (PWD) in 1885, which is similar to the present PWD in India. After the introduction of railways in India, major road development works ceased, except work on feeder roads from port, harbours, railway stations and other important places.

1.3 The Jayakar Committee

In 1927, based on the recommendation of the Indian Roads and Transport Development Association (IRTDA), a committee chaired by Dr M. R. Jayakar was instituted by the central government. The committee studied the existing conditions of roads, the probable increase in volume of mixed traffic and the anticipated needs of road development. They prepared a report (1928) which delineated the methodology for the future development of roads in India. The following recommendations were made.

- Road development in India should be considered a national interest. Major initiatives should be taken by the central government in this regard.
- An extra tax should be levied on petrol charges, and the money collected should be used for road development.
- A technical advisory organisation has to be formed to collect technical knowledge related to design, maintenance and other aspects related to road development, and to disseminate the knowledge.
- An institution is to be set up to conduct research and offer consultancy services related to the development of road networks.

The central government accepted and implemented the above recommendations as,

- In 1929, an extra tax of 2 annas/gallon of motor fuel was collected and termed the Central Road Fund (CRF). The CRF account was maintained by the Accountant General of the Central Reserve, New Delhi. Twenty per cent of the CRF collected was set apart as Central Reserve. It was used for administrative purposes; maintenance and dissemination of technical data; research; and related purposes of road development. The remaining 80 per cent of the CRF was allotted to different states for the development of their respective roads based on the petrol/fuel consumption of the state.

  In 1999, a CRF of about Rs 55 billion was collected by charging cess on petrol and high speed diesel (HSD) oil (India Vision 2020; 2004; RDPV 2001). This fund has been legitimated under the Central Road Fund Act which was enacted in December 2000 (MORTH 2006). In the period 2007–2008, two rupees per litre of petrol and HSD was collected as cess (India 2008). The cess fund collected during that period was about Rs 6,542 crores (Indiabudget 2008). This fund may increase with increased consumption of fuel.

  The breakup details of the collected cess (Rs. 2/litre) are as follows.

  1. Rs 0.5/litre is allocated exclusively for the development and maintenance of national highways.
  2. The balance amount of Rs 1.5/litre is allocated as follows:
     a 50 per cent of the cess collected on HSD is allocated for development of rural roads (on an average, Rs 4000 crore annually).
     b The balance amount (50% on HSD) plus any other cess collected on petrol is distributed by the central government for the development and maintenance of the national highways, bridges, safety works at unmanned railway crossings; for the improvement of state roads of economic importance; and for financing interstate road connectivity schemes and R&D in the roads sector.

- In 1930, the Central Road Organisation (CRO) was established.
- In 1934, a semi-official technical body named the Indian Roads Congress (IRC) was set up to act as a platform for providing all technical knowledge and experience related to road construction, materials, design specifications, maintenance, economics and overall development of roads within the country.
- In 1935, the Transport Advisory Committee was formed.
- In 1939, the Motor Vehicle Act was passed in the parliament to set standards for traffic rules, vehicle standards, driver characteristics and regulations. This act was revised in 1988.
- Long-term road development programmes were also planned for 20-year periods.
- In 1950, the Central Road Research Institute (CRRI) was set up at New Delhi by the Council of Scientific and Industrial research (CSIR) to carry out research and consultancy works related to road planning, construction, design, evaluation, traffic, maintenance, economics, financing, instrumentation and use of alternative materials for roads.

- In 1956, the National Highway Act was approved by the central government. According to the act, the central government reserves all rights to develop, maintain and designate any road as a national highway (NH) or declare an NH as any other type of road. In 1995, the act was amended to permit the central government to collaborate with any state government or private organisation for the development and maintenance of NHs. This amendment allows private participation in building any required road infrastructure.

1.4 Initial Major Road Development Plans in India

The major plans evolved since 1943 to 2001 for the development of road networks in the country are given below.

1. Nagpur Road Plan: The First 20-Year Road Development Plan (1943–1963).
2. Bombay Road Plan: The Second 20-Year Road Development Plan (1961–1981).
3. Lucknow Road Plan: The Third 20-Year Road Development Plan (1981–2001).

1.4.1 The Nagpur Road Plan: The First 20-Year Road Development Plan (1943–1963)

After the Second World War, i.e., after 1938–45, the roads in India had deteriorated significantly since the responsibility of maintaining them was confined to provincial or local governments. It was not possible to satisfy the increased traffic needs due to the poor condition of the roads. Therefore, in 1943, at Nagpur, the central government and IRC convened a meeting of the chief engineers of all the states and provinces. The aim of the meeting was to chalk out a comprehensive plan for the development of a sophisticated road network. Following were the recommendations made by the conference for the target period, 1943 to 1963.

- A target road density of about 16 km/100 sq. km is to be achieved by the end of the plan period.
- A long-term plan is desired for road development work to facilitate greater communication and mobility all over the country.
- Deteriorated roads should be maintained routinely on a short-term basis.
- Growth in economy of the country is related to enhanced road development. The central government should initiate and coordinate road development work programmes in each state and also take up intrastate projects.
- Roads are to be classified as
    1. National highways (NH)
    2. Provincial highways or state highways (SH)
    3. Major district roads (MDR) or other district roads (ODR)
    4. Village roads (VR)

- The above classes of roads should be developed adequately and no class of road should be developed at the cost of other classes.
- The central government should take the responsibility of planning, constructing, designing and maintaining national highways.
- The NH, SH and MDR should be constructed with well designed pavement principles and should be able to serve the traffic in all weather conditions without any interruption of traffic flow.
- The ODR and VR should be constructed with gravelly soils.
- Bridges should be suitably constructed in places on the NH, SH and MDR, where submergence of a road section for more than, 12 hours at a time or 6 times per year may cause interruption to traffic.
- Required widths and lengths of NH, SH, ODR and VR are to be formulated based on the coverage of agricultural areas, non-agricultural areas and number of habitations within the area, existing length of railway tracks. An allowance of 15 per cent must be kept for future developments in the next 20-year period.

During the post-war period and as well as during the five-year plans, the above recommendations were implemented strictly by the central government. The central government also took total responsibility for the development and maintenance of the national highways.

The first 20-year road development plan (1943–1963) was systematically implemented during the first two five-year plans from 1951 to 1961 and attained the target road density of about 16 km/ 100 sq. km two years before the end of the plan period. Therefore, it was decided that the second 20-year road development programme start from 1961.

1.4.2 The Bombay Road Plan: The Second 20-Year Road Development Plan (1961–1981)

In 1959, a meeting of the chief engineers of all the states was convened at Bombay, under the aegis of the IRC, to formulate the second 20-year road development plan; the plan was approved by the central government. The experience gained while implementing the Nagpur Road Plan was reviewed and a strategy for future road development was conceived based on the increased growth volume of traffic, agriculture, industries, population and anticipated traffic necessities for the next 20 years. The following recommendations were made in this plan.

- A target road density of 32 km/100 sq. km is to be achieved by the end of the plan period.
- Due emphasis should be placed on the rural road communication system to provide effective connectivity of rural villages to nearby towns. This will discourage migration to urban areas.
- The proposed road development should be properly linked with agricultural areas, well-developed, under-developed and un-developed areas.
- Roads used for military purposes are to be considered for other strategic requirements too.

- Following are the maximum allowable distances prescribed for different areas.

Sl. No.	Type of area	Maximum distance (km) from	
		Metalled road	Un-metalled road
1	Any developed or agricultural area	6.5	2.4
2	Semi-developed area	12.8	4.8
3	Undeveloped area	19.2	8.0

- Separate equations were prescribed for length calculation of different road classes, namely, NH, NH + SH, NH + SH + MDR, NH + SH + MDR + ODR and NH + SH + MDR + ODR + VR, based on the type of developed area, the number of towns with their population count and allowance for future developments.

- Stage construction of roads is to be considered in case of limited financial resources.

By 1981, the density of road length achieved was of the order of 34.8 km/100 sq. km, which was more than the targeted value of 32 km/100 sq. km. The third 20-year plan was delayed due to change in policies from the 5th to the 6th five-year plans (1974–1985). During this period, the Highway Research Board (HRB) and the National Transport Policy Committee (1978) were established.

1.4.3 The Lucknow Road Plan: The Third 20-Year Road Development Plan (1981–2001)

To finalise the recommendations for the third 20-year road development plan covering the period 1981 to 2001, the IRC convened a meeting in 1985 at Lucknow. It constituted the chief engineers of all the states along with road experts from different organisations. During the formulation of the plan, due consideration was given to road infrastructure requirements for cities, towns and villages. The economic growth pattern of the country, economical usage of fuels, improvement of living standards and safety aspects related to traffic operations were also taken into account. The policies and goals set up in the plan are mentioned below (RDPI 1984; RDPV 2001).

- A target length of road density 82 km/100 sq. km by the end of the plan period was set up.
- All villages with a population of 500 and above should be connected with all-weather roads by the end of the plan period.
- Long-term master plans were prepared to realise the required length of road network at the national, state, district and village levels.
- Due encouragement should be given to less industrialised areas by suitably developing the road network.
- Construction of roads should generate employment, ensuring growth of industries, and agriculture covering hilly, coastal, desert and remote areas.
- Balanced road development should be made in rural and urban regions.
- More length of NH should be constructed to form a NH square-grid of size 100 km.

- On main traffic routes, expressways should be constructed to facilitate faster movement of vehicles.
- During road development, aspects related to environmental quality, road safety and conservation of energy should be thoroughly studied.
- All towns and villages having a population above 1500 should be connected by MDR of length 300000 km.
- It was proposed that all towns with a population of 5000 and above should be linked by national and state highways. The target length was 66000 and 145000 km respectively.
- All villages having population ranging from 1000 to 1500 should be connected by ODR and VR of a target length of 2189000 km.
- The existing roads should be maintained properly.

The following formulae may be used to calculate different classes of road lengths under this plan.

$$\text{Length of NH} = L_{NH} = (\text{area in sq.km})/50 \tag{1.1}$$

$$\text{Length of SH} = L_{SH} = (\text{area of a state in sq.km})/25 \tag{1.2a}$$

or

$$L_{SH}\ (\text{km}) = (63\times \text{ No. of towns in the state}) - L_{NH}\ (\text{km}) \tag{1.2b}$$

Choose the maximum value of L_{SH} from the above relationships.

$$\text{Length of MDR} = L_{MDR} = (\text{area of a state in sq.km})/12.5 \tag{1.3a}$$

or

$$L_{MDR}\ (\text{km}) = 100\times \text{ No. of towns in the state} \tag{1.3b}$$

Choose maximum value of L_{MDR} from the above relationships.

Total road length: L_{Total}

$$L_{Total}\ (\text{km}) = 4.74\times \text{ Total number of villages and towns} \tag{1.4}$$

Length of (ODR + VR): L_{ODR+VR}

$$L_{(ODR+VR)}\ (\text{km}) = L_{Total} - (L_{NH} + L_{SH} + L_{MDR}) \tag{1.5}$$

Q. *Calculate the length of different classes of roads according to the Lucknow Road Plan based on the 2001 census data.*

Area of Andhra Pradesh (AP): 275,068 sq. km; No. of villages = 28123; No. of towns = 210; Population: 757 lakhs; Density: Approx. 275 per sq. km.

A.

Length of NH = L_{NH} = Area/50 = 275,068/50 = 5501.36 km

Length of SH:

L_{SH} = Area/25 = 275,068/25 = 11002.7 km

or

$$L_{SH} = 63\times \text{ No. of towns in AP} - L_{NH}$$
$$= 63 \times 210 - 5501 = 7729 \text{ km}$$

Therefore, take the maximum value of $L_{SH} = 11002$ km

Length of MDR:

$$L_{MDR} = \text{Area}/12.5 = 275{,}068/12.5 = 22005.4 \text{ km}$$

or

$$L_{MDR} = 100\times \text{ No. of towns in AP}$$
$$= 100 \times 210 = 21000 \text{ km}$$

Therefore, take maximum value of $L_{MDR} = 22005$ km

$$L_{Total} = \text{Total length of NH + SH + MDR + ODR + VR}$$
$$= 4.74\times \text{ No. of villages + towns} = 4.74 \times (28123 + 210)$$
$$= 134581.75 \text{ km}$$

Length of ODR+VR $= L_{(ODR+VR)}$

$$= L_{Total} - (L_{NH} + L_{SH} + L_{MDR})$$
$$= 134581 - (5501 + 11002 + 22005)$$
$$= L_{(ODR+VR)} = 96073.75 \text{ km}$$

Summary:

$$L_{NH} = 5501.36 \text{ km};\ L_{SH} = 11002 \text{ km};\ L_{MDR} = 22005 \text{ km}$$
$$L_{(ODR+VR)} = 96074 \text{ km};\ L_{Total} = 134582 \text{ km}$$

1.5 Organisations/Institutions Involved with Road Development in India

1.5.1 The Ministry of Shipping, Road Transport and Highways (MORTH)

Formerly, the MORTH was known as the Ministry of Surface Transport (MOST). MORTH works under the control of the central government in close collaboration with HRB, IRC, CRRI, NHAI, NIHTEE and other institutions of road development in the country. It plays a critical role in strategic planning and policy for developing and maintaining national highways (RDPV 2001). The Department of Road Transport and Highways (DORTH) is a part of MORTH which deals with all types of activities related to road policies (the planning, design, construction, formulation of transport related legislations in the country). The aim is to fulfill the following objectives (MORTH 2006).

- To plan, initiate, formulate and administer various policies related to road transport, road research and national highways of the country for safe and efficient operation of traffic flow.
- To call tenders; provide documentation and support (financial, technical and other required resources); take responsibility for execution and maintenance of all national highways in the country.
- To provide technical and financial aid for road network development of state, interstate and other essential roads.
- To develop and prepare various specifications of design, quality control standards, standard drawings for the construction of bridges, culverts and road intersections.
- To legislate and administrate the Road Transport Corporations Act 1950, the Motor Vehicles Act 1988 and the Carriage Byroad Act 2005.
- To implement the National Highways Act 1956, the National Highways Authority of India Act 1988, the Central Road Fund Act 2000, and the Control of National Highways (Land and Traffic) Act 2002.
- To explore and pave way for present and future trends of technological adaptations (CNG, LPG, anti-braking systems etc.) and private sector participation in various developmental activities related to national highways (the new Model Concession Agreement (MCA), annuity and BOT schemes).
- To monitor and guide various developmental activities related to the national highways in the country, viz. the National Highway Development Project (NHDP), the Golden Quadrilateral (GQ), the North South–East West (NS–EW) Corridors, expressways and grade-separated structures.
- To pool and analyse accident data for evolving policies on road safety in the country.
- To disseminate information related to various aspects of roads and bridges; and recommend standard specifications for design, construction, quality control and maintenance of the same.
- To compile and publish information-rich books on statistics of motor transport, basic road statistics, and pocket books on transport in the country.
- To conduct and aid various activities related to road safety, viz. road safety weeks, seminars, exhibitions, advertisements, training programmes, distribution of printed and multi-media material, safety awareness campaign, National Road Safety Council and Transport Awards.
- To implement the National Highways Accident Relief Service Scheme (NHARSS) by financially assisting in the purchase of ambulances for immediate medical assistance to victims of road accidents; and cranes for removal of damaged vehicles from the accident site. The recurring expenditure is to be borne by the state government, a NGO or the concerned authority.
- To administrate associated institutions, viz. NHAI, NITHE etc.

- Other activities involve up-gradation of road and transport technology in the country, highway linkages with neighbouring countries in Asia and taking care of Memorandum of Understanding (MOU) agreements with similar international organisations.

The entrusted activities of the MORTH are integrated/ pursued by every state headquarter through regional offices (RO) which continuously coordinate with the state PWDs. They are examined and reviewed by Preliminary Committees, the Planning Commission, the Ministry of Finance (MOF) and the Prime Minister's Office (PMO).

1.5.2 The Indian Roads Congress (IRC)

The IRC was established in December 1934 by the Government of India to collect, organise and disseminate all information related to the development, design, construction and maintenance of roads and bridges in the country. It is registered as a society under the Act of Registration of Societies and is funded by contributions collected from members, the sale of publications, and financial support from the central and various state governments. A few salient objectives of the IRC are given below:

- To provide a scientific platform and repository of database for anything road related.
- To act as a centre for national-level collection and dissemination of all kinds of road experiences and the latest methods in the development of roads, bridges and other connected elements in the country including various issues related to organisational and institutional aspects.
- To prepare standard specifications for the design, construction and maintenance of roads and bridges.
- To reveal research findings in the road and transport sector by publishing journals, magazines and research bulletins.

Every year, the IRC conducts a national conference in any one state in order to discuss road problems and make policy decisions.

1.5.3 The Indian National Group of IABSE

The Indian National Group (ING) was set up in May 1957 by DORTH after consultation with various state governments. It works as the Indian arm of the International Association for Bridge and Structural Engineering (IABSE) which was established in Zurich in 1929. The IABSE comprises different subject experts and engineers from 14 countries across the globe. Its objective is to share and exchange technical and scientific knowledge, research work and information collected across respective national borders.

The Indian arm of IABSE conducts research, seminars and workshops; it promotes all aspects of infrastructure development activities related to roads and bridges.

1.5.4 The Highway Research Board (HRB)

To promote road research and related developmental activities in the country, the HRB was set up in October 1973 with the assistance of IRC (MORTH 2006). The following are the objectives of the HRB.

- To identify need-based research areas for the development of roads in the country using innovative methods and technologies.
- To cooperate with other bodies for the promotion of road research and other related matters.
- To collect, organise and disseminate various road research findings in the country and exchange published information with other countries as well.
- To coordinate various research activities on projects related to roads conducted by DORTH, IRC, CRRI, universities and other institutions.
- To act as a science and technology advisory committee for MORTH.

1.5.5 The National Highways Authority of India (NHAI)

The NHAI, which was constituted by the Parliament under the Act of the National Highways Authority of India 1998, has been operational since February 1995. It is entrusted with the task of implementing all projects that are related to the development, maintenance and management of the national highways in the country, viz. NHDP (all phases), the Golden Quadrilateral, NS–EW Corridors, port connectivity to road networks under the NHDP, special purpose vehicles (SPV) for funding road projects, the Naini Bridge (across Yamuna on the NH-27), the Hapur Bypass, the Durg Bypass and some selected projects.

1.5.6 The National Institute of Training for Highway Engineers (NITHE)

The NITHE is also a registered society like the IRC. It works under the administrative control of DORTH and was set up as a collaborative body in 1983 to cater to the needs of the road and transport sector. It provides training to highway and bridge engineers and consultants of private institutions, and central and state governments, at the entry level and for working engineers by charging a reasonable course fee. Training programmes are organised at the state, regional, national and international levels to provide up-to-date knowledge related to highway and bridge engineering in India and foreign countries, viz. Canada, UK, Australia, Bhutan, Ghana, Malawi, Nepal and Thailand.

Apart from the development of software packages and training manuals, the NITHE is actively involved in the following activities.

- Training new highway engineers by conducting training programmes, workshops etc.
- Taking part in research work related to various road research projects of DORTH.

- Planing and outline specific needs of projects undertaken by different institutions in the private sector and central and state governments.
- Preparing multi-media presentations on various elements of infrastructure, viz. roads, ports, shipping, inland water transport, telecommunications and power etc. to educate and effectively train engineers.

1.5.7 Border Roads Organisation (BRO)

In May 1960, the BRO was established to develop roads which are used by the military in the northern, northeastern and other border areas (India 2004; 2008) for strategic purposes. The BRO not only links up border areas with the country, it also develops road infrastructure in various states, viz. Andhra Pradesh, Andaman and Nicobar Islands, Bihar, Chattisgarh, Karnataka, and Rajasthan. Through the years, it has evolved into an important organisation for the construction and maintenance of roads as well as runways, bridges and buildings for various puposes.

So far, about 31,061 km length of formation works and 37,077 km of surfaced roads with various permanent bridges have been constructed and are well maintained. A few important development works of the BRO are listed below:

1. Work on the 9 km Rohtang Tunnel which would make the Rohtang Pass, located on the highway between Manali and Leh, accessible throughout the year is in progress. The BRO is also constructing approach roads and a 292 km alterante route to Leh. The project is targetted to be completed by 2014.
2. As a part of a scheme of the NHDP, four-laning of the NH-1A from Jammu to Vijaypur has been taken-up by the BRO.
3. Under the Special Accelerated Road Development Programme for the Northeast Region, the BRO has started constructing new roads and widening existing roads of length 492 km to two-lane highways.
4. Rehabilitation of roads effected by the 2004 Indian Ocean Tsunami in Andaman and Nicobar Islands.
5. A re-construction plan for Jammu & Kashmir announced by the Prime Minister of India, to upgrade:
   (a) 94 km length of the NH-1A from Srinagar to Uri,
   (b) 17.25 km long road from Uri to LoC,
   (c) the two-lane road of 260 km length (NH-1B) along Batote, Kishtwar and Ananthnag,
   (d) widening of 14.14 km length of NH-1C from Domel to Katra and
   (e) two-laning of 422 km length of NH-1D along Srinagar, Kargil and Leh.

The above approved road development works in J & K are scheduled to be completed by 2012.

Apart from the execution of several other road development projects on the border, the BRO has been involved in the construction of roads and improving the road infrastructure to help inter-state connectivity for the North Eastern Council (NEC). The NEC was enacted by the Parliament for coordinating the socio-economic development of the northeastern states. All the schemes of the NEC are funded by the Ministry of Home Affairs and its activities are controlled and administered by the North Eastern Council Secretariate, Shillong (RDPV 2001).

1.6 Classification of Roads

The roads in India can be classified into different categories based on the seasonal use, purpose, plan, location and materials used for road construction. Figure 1.1 (a–c) shows how roads can be classified according to plans and seasonal use.

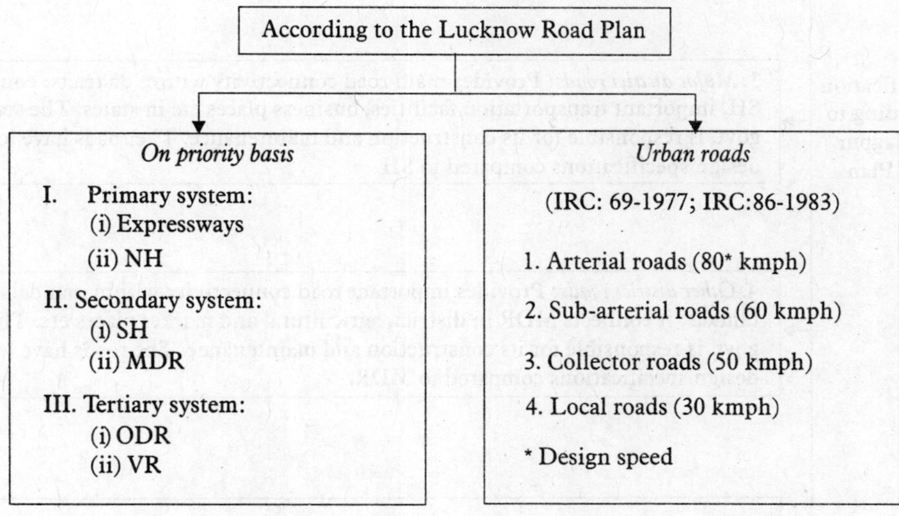

Figure 1.1(a) *Classification of roads*

1.7 Road Network in India

India has the second largest road network in the world with a total length of about 3.34 million kilometres. For better connectivity, both the central and state governments have taken up steps to further develop the road network in urban and rural areas.

The details of the road network in India are presented in Table 1.1. It can be observed that the length of the national highways consists of about 2% of the total length of the road network, but carries 40% of the total traffic in the country which is alarming and requires immediate attention. It calls for further development of the road network on a priority basis. The details of the national highway in each state is presented in Table 1.2.

Road classification according to the Nagpur Road Plan

- 1. *National highways*: Connects the capital and all important cities of the states, important transportation facilities; business places; important boarder places etc. The central govt. ministry is responsible for the development, construction and maintenance of NHs through NHAI, state PWDs and BRO (India 2008).
- 2. *State highways*: Provides important road connectivity in the state; connects NH, important transportation facilities, business places etc in states. The state govt. is responsible for its construction and maintenance. The design specifications are similar to NH.
- 3. *Major district roads*: Provides main road connectivity within districts; connects SH, important transportation facilities, business places etc in states. The state govt. is responsible for its construction and maintenance. The roads have lower design specifications compared to SH.
- 4. *Other district roads*: Provides important road connectivity within mandals and talukas; it connects MDR in district, agricultural and market places etc. The state govt. is responsible for its construction and maintenance. The roads have lower design specifications compared to MDR.
- 5. *Village roads*: Connects ODR and villages in rural areas, local markets and agricultural places. The state govt. is responsible for construction and maintenance. The roads have lower design specifications compared to ODR.

Figure 1.1(b) *Classification and details of roads*

Based on seasonal use

- *All weather roads*: The roads are serviceable throughout the year including the monsoon period, except at a few locations of major river crossings.
- *Fair weather roads*: The roads are not in a serviceable condition during monsoon season due to inundation and overflow of streams.

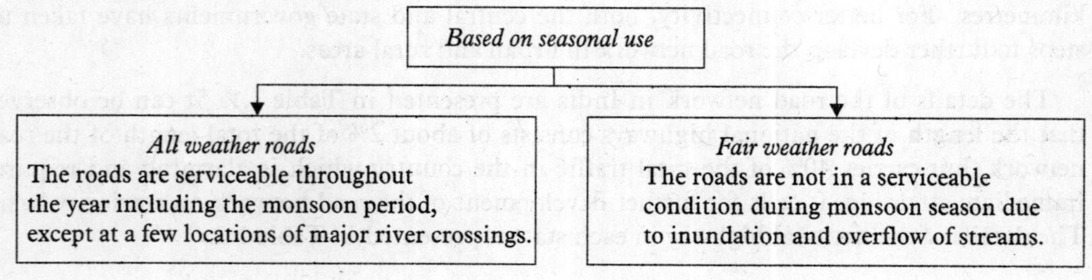

Figure 1.1(c) *Classification of roads*

Table 1.1 *Details of the Indian road network (India 2008; www.nhai.org/roadnetwork.htm, accessed on 1-8-2008)*

Sl.No.	Description of road		Length ★ (km)	Percentage of	
				Total road length	Total road † traffic carried
1		Expressways	200	–	–
	NH	4/ 6/ 8 lane: 12% of length			
		Double and intermediate lane: 56% of length	66,754 ‡	≈ 2%	≈ 40%
		Single lane: 32% of length			
2	SH	4 lane: 1% of length			
		2 lane : 19% of length	1,31,899	≈ 4%	≈ 40%
		Single lane: 80% of length			
3	MDR		4,67,763		
4	VR and ODR		26,50,000		
		Total	= 3,316,616×		

★ NOTE: The latest and more detailed Indian road network with maps can be obtained from http://www.nhai.org and http://morth.nic.in

‡ At the time of independence (1947), the national highways length was 21,440 km (Manorama 2008).

† The Indian roads carry about 80% of passenger traffic and 65% of the frieght traffic (Manorama 2008). Vehicles average growth rate was reported as 10.1% per annum during the last five years, 1999–2000 to 2003–2004 (Annual Report 2007–08, DORTH).

× Road density can be determined if we know the area of India (Total = 32,87,590 km^2; land = 29,73,190 km^2)

Table 1.2 *State-wise list of national highways in India (from morth.nic.in, accessed on 1-8-2008)*

Sl. No.	Name of state	National highway number	Total length (in km)
1	Andhra Pradesh	4, 5, 7, 9, 16, 18, 43, 63, 202, 205, 214, 214A, 219, 221, 222	4472
2	Arunachal Pradesh	52, 52A, 153	392
3	Assam	31, 31B, 31C, 36, 37, 37A, 38, 39, 44, 51, 52, 52A, 52B, 53, 54, 61, 62,151,152,153, 154	2836
4	Bihar	2, 2C, 19, 28, 28A, 28B, 30, 30A, 31, 57, 57A, 77, 80, 81, 82, 83, 84, 85, 98, 99, 101, 102, 103, 104, 105, 106, 107, 110	3642
5	Chandigarh	21	24
6	Chhattisgarh	6, 12A, 16, 43, 78, 200,202, 216, 217, 111, 221	2184
7	Delhi	1, 2, 8, 10, 24	72
8	Goa	4A, 17, 17A, 17B	269
9	Gujarat	NE1, 6, 8, 8A, 8B, 8C, 8D, 8E, 14, 15, 59, 113, 228	3245
10	Haryana	1, 2, 8, 10, 21A, 22, 64, 65, 71, 71A, 72, 73, 73A , 71B, NE2	1512
11	Himachal Pradesh	1A, 20, 21, 21A, 22, 70, 72, 88, 73A	1208
12	Jammu & Kashmir	1A, 1B, 1C, 1D	1245
13	Jharkhand	2, 6, 23, 31, 32, 33, 75, 78, 80, 98, 99, 100	1805

continues...

Table 1.2 continued.

Sl. No.	Name of state	National highway number	Total length (in km)
14	Karnataka	4, 4A, 7, 9, 13, 17, 48, 63, 67, 206, 207,209, 212, 218	3843
15	Kerala	17, 47, 47A, 47C, 49, 208, 212, 213, 220	1457
16	Madhya Pradesh	3, 7, 12, 12A, 25, 26, 26A, 27, 59, 59A, 69, 75, 76, 78, 86, 92	4670
17	Maharashtra	3, 4, 4B, 4C, 6, 7, 8, 9, 13, 16, 17, 50, 69, 204, 211, 222	4176
18	Manipur	39, 53, 150, 155	959
19	Meghalaya	40, 44, 51, 62	810
20	Mizoram	44A, 54, 54A, 54B, 150, 154	927
21	Nagaland	36, 39, 61, 150, 155	494
22	Orissa	5, 5A, 6, 23, 42, 43, 60, 75, 200, 201, 203, 203A, 215, 217, 224	3704
23	Puducherry	45A, 66	53
24	Punjab	1, 1A, 10, 15, 20, 21, 22, 64, 70, 71, 72, 95	1557
25	Rajasthan	3, 8, 11, 11A, 11B, 11C, 12, 14, 15, 65, 71B, 76, 79, 79A, 89, 90, 113, 112, 114, 116	5585
26	Sikkim	31A	62
27	Tamil Nadu	4, 5, 7, 7A, 45, 45A, 45B, 45C, 46, 47, 47B, 49, 66, 67, 68, 205, 207, 208, 209, 210, 219, 220, 226, 227	4462
28	Tripura	44, 44A	400
29	Uttarakhand	58, 72, 72A, 73, 74, 87, 94, 108, 109, 123, 119, 121, 87 Ext., 125	1991
30	Uttar Pradesh	2, 2A, 3, 7, 11, 12A, 19, 24, 24A, 24B, 25, 25A, 26, 27, 28, 28B, 28C, 29, 56, 56A, 56B, 58, 72A, 73, 74, 75, 76, 86, 87, 91, 91A, 92, 93, 96, 97 , 119, NE2	5874
31	West Bengal	2, 2B, 6, 31, 31A, 31C, 31D. 32, 34, 35, 41, 55, 60, 60A, 80, 81, 117	2524
32	Andaman & Nicobar	223	300
		Total	**66754**

1.8 Recent Road Developmental Schemes/Activities in India

1.8.1 The National Highway Development Project (NHDP)

The central government of India has taken the initiative to develop the road network under various schemes. One of the objectives of the 9th plan period (1997–2002) was the coordinated and balanced development of the road network in the country. The National Highway Development Project (NHDP) was evolved to realise this objective. Under the schemes of NHDP-I and -II, 14,357 km of national highways will be converted to high quality four/six lanes at an estimated cost of Rs. 64,639 crore at 2005 prices. They were planned to be completed by the end of the 10th Plan (December 2007).

According to the central government decision taken on April 2007, the NHDP consists of 7 phases, with an estimated cost of Rs. 2,35,690 crore and is scheduled to be completed by 2015 (Annual Report 2007–2008, DORTH). It has been decided to implement all the NHDP programmes from phase III onwards and a part of phase II by the PPP (public–private partnership) route, first through BOT (toll), failing which, by BOT (annuity). If all else fails, the projects will be completed through EPC (engineering, procurement and construction) contracts with the approval of the ministry. The NHAI is responsible for implementation of the projects. The NHDP is the largest and most prestigious road development project undertaken in India so far (Figure 1.2).

The scheme NHDP consists of following major components.

NHDP Phase-I

Golden Quadrangle (GQ) Comprising a total national highway length of 5,846 km. It connects four metropolises of India, viz. Delhi–Kolkata–Chennai–Mumbai–Delhi. Most of the above length of highway network is completed.

Port connectivity and other projects To enhance accessibility and improve connectivity to the existing ten major ports in the country, viz. Haldia, Cochin, Jawaharlal Nehru Port, Kandla, Mormugao, Mangalore, Visakapatnam, Chennai and Ennore, other projects include building 380 km of 4-lane national highways and upgradation of 831 km length of other important national highways. The responsibility of implementation of this scheme is entrusted to NHAI.

NHDP Phase-II

The North–South and East–West (NS–EW) Corridors The north–south regions are connected by a national highway running from Srinagar to Kanyakumari including the Kochi–Salem spur. The East–West Corridor comprises a national highway running from Silchar to Porbandar. These two corridors cover a total length of about 7,300 km.

NHAI's main source of finance for the implementation of the NHDP phase-I and -II is the cess collected on petrol and diesel (Spectrum 2008).

NHDP Phase-III

Another major initiative is the formerly known, Pradhan Mantri Bharath Jodo Pariyojana (PMBJP) which will link up important places to the network of NHDP highways.

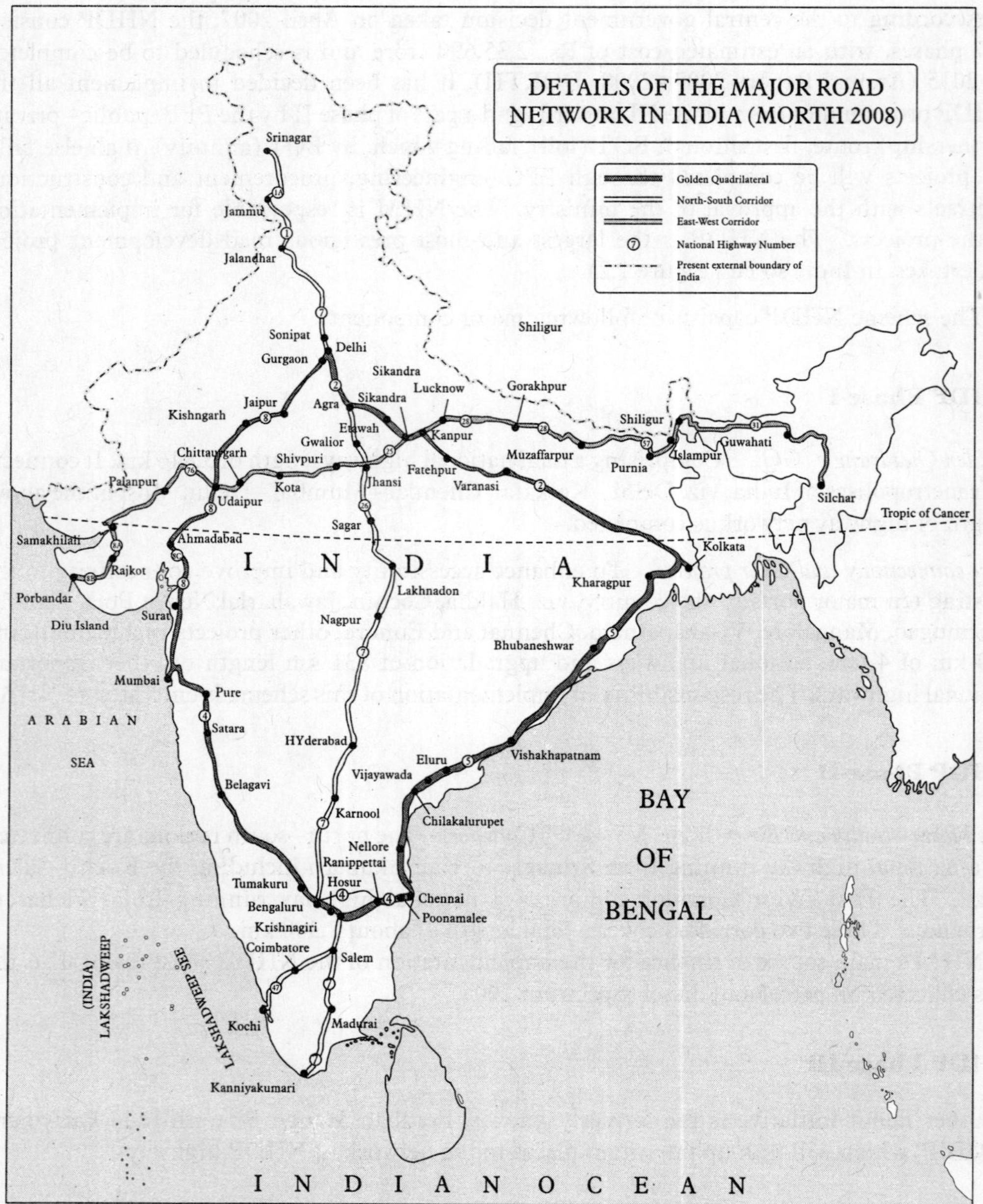

Figure 1.2 *Details of the major road network in India (MORTH 2008).*

Under the NHDP phase-III, the central government has approved the upgradation of 12,109 km of existing national highways by widening the existing two-lane road to four /six lane/paved-shoulder roads. This is to connect state capitals, high density corridors, tourist places and other places of economic importance to the network of NHDP highways that were not earlier considered under the NHDP phase I and II (www.nhai.org. 2006; MORTH 2006).

The NHDP phase-III is divided into two phases, viz. phase-IIIA and IIIB. Under NHDP phase-IIIA, the central government has approved the upgradation of 4,815 km of national highways to four or six laning through the PPP-BOT method. The balance length of 7,294 km of four or six-lane national highways has to be developed by the BOT method under phase-IIIB. The cost of the NHDP Phase III project is estimated as Rs. 80,626 crore and is targetted to be completed by December 20013 (MORTH 2006; 2008).

The government has also initiated a programme called Improvement of Riding Quality of National Highways (IRQ-NH) in 1999 to improve the riding quality of all national highways in the country.

NHDP Phase-IV

About 20,000 km length of existing single/intermediate/two-lane national highways are proposed to be upgraded to two-lane national highways with paved shoulders at an estimated cost of Rs.27,800 crore through the PPP route based on BOT (toll/ annuity).

NHDP Phase-V

In 2006, the central government has approved widening of existing 6,500 km of four-lane national highways to six-lane national highways at an estimated cost of Rs. 41,210 crore through PPP and BOT (toll) mode using the DBFO (design, build, finance and operate) methodology. The approved highway length includes 5,700 km of GQ and other selected stretches of national highways. The NHDP phase-V is scheduled to be completed by December 2012.

NHDP Phase-VI

Under this scheme, full access-controlled four/six-lane expressways of length 1000 km have been approved for construction at an estimated cost of Rs.16,680 crore through PPP and BOT (toll) mode using the DBFO pattern. The government/NHAI has agreed to contribute Rs. 7,680 crore towards expenditure for land acquisition, utility, shifting etc. The NHDP phase-IV roads are scheduled to be constructed by December 2015.

NHDP Phase-VII

To remove or ease bottlenecks on the national highways, the central government has approved the construction of 700 km length of stand-alone bypass roads, ring roads, underpasses, flyovers, tunnel roads etc at an estimated cost of Rs.16,680 crore through PPP and BOT (toll) modes. This is scheduled to be completed by December 2014.

Apart from these schemes, a number of other projects for the development of new as well as upgradations of existing road networks have also been undertaken by the central and different state governments. Funds for the schemes have been borrowed from domestic markets through bonds that provide capital gain tax exemption and by loans from various financial international institutions, viz. World Bank, Asian Development Bank (ADB), Overseas Economic

Cooperation Fund, Japan (OECF), National Bank for Agriculture and Rural Development (NABARD) and Japan Bank for International Cooperation (JBIC) (Spectrum 2008).

In order to increase the development of the road network, the Indian government has announced numerous incentives for the active participation of the private sector—these incentives are meant not only to induce the industry to invest in road construction but also help in the maintenace operations. Several road projects were taken up for implementation on BOT (build, operate and transfer) basis and a few are considered on an annuity basis. Apart from NHDP, a few more new projects are in the pipeline to be awarded soon (www.nhai.nic.in, accessed on 1-8-2008).

During the 10th plan (2002–2007) period, the development of a road network in the country was considered as an integral part of the total transport system. Due emphasis was made on strengthening the road network in India under the following three functional groups.

1. Primary system
   - National highways (NH)
   - Expressways
2. Secondary system
   - State highways (SH)
   - Major district roads (MDR)
3. Rural roads (RR)
   - ODR
   - VR

It is envisaged that implementaion of the objectives set under the NHDP scheme as well as rehabilitation, widening and maintenance of the existing network of national highways will make a significant contribution to the economic growth of the country.

1.8.2 Special Accelerated Road Development (SARD) Programme for the Northeastern Region

MORTH initiated the SARD-NE programme for improving road connectivity to remote places from strategically important places of the northeastern region. The plan was to use budgetary support and private–public participation (PPP) on BOT (annuity) mode (MORTH 2006; India 2008). Under the SARD-NE programme, it is proposed to widen two/four-laning of about 3,228 km length of national highways; to two-lane or improve about 2,500 km of state highways and 1,888 km length of roads that are strategically important. With this development, road connectivity will be ensured to 34 out of 85 district headquarters which are not yet connected to the national highways in the eight N-E states, viz. Arunachal Pradesh, Assam, Manipur, Meghalaya, Mizoram, Nagaland, Sikkim and Tripura.

1.8.3 Rural Roads (India 2004)

Roads are a key component of rural development. They provide connectivity to various business places, improve accessibility to various facilities like education, health, security, and foster the economic well being of the region.

It is expected that in India by the year 2020, the urban population will rise from 28 per cent to 40 per cent (India Vision 2020 2004). To discourage this migration of population from rural to urban areas for employment, it becomes necessary to develop adequate rural transport infrastructure. Comprehensive planning is needed to balance and distribute the development of road network, and to narrow disproportion between urban and rural areas.

During the process of planning, the government of India has formulated various schemes, viz. Minimum Needs Programme, National Rural Employment Programme, Command Area Agency and Employment Assurance; the objective was to construct earthen roads to connect clusters of villages in rural areas and nearby all-weather roads (AWR) that are negotiable throughout the year. At present, these schemes are clubbed together and allocated under the scheme of Sampurna Grameen Rozgar Yojana (SGRY).

In 2000, the government of India constituted a National Rural Roads Development Committee (NRRDC) to identify the total road length required for rural connectivity, specifications of AWR, sources of funds, and to construct and maintain rural roads. The recommendations of the NRRDC were accepted by the Ministry of Rural Development (MORD) and the ministry launched a scheme called the Pradhana Manthri Gram Sadak Yojana (PMGSY) in December 2000 to provide rural connectivity in a phase-wise manner and on priority basis. The MORD is looking after 12 divisions—one of them is PMGSY. Following were the objectives of the PMGSY programme (India Vision 2020 2004).

- To provide all-weather road (AWR) connectivity to all unconnected villages with a population of more than 1000 by the year 2003 and villages with population between 1000 and 500 by the year 2007.
- To connect, by all-weather roads (AWR), all unconnected habitations with a population of 250 persons and above, in desert areas, tribal areas and hill states of the northeast, Sikkim, Himachal Pradesh, Uttaranchal, Jammu and Kashmir.
- To build all-weather roads (AWR) and bring connectivity to all villages with population below 500 by the year 2010 (RDPV 2001).

PMGSY is sponsored (100%) by the central government. The aim was to attain the above first two objectives in all the states and six union territories by the end of the tenth plan (2007), with an estimated amount of Rs.58,200 crore (in the year 2005). It is not fully realised yet.

The PMGSY works for upgradation/new connectivity are assessed by preparing (i) core network and (ii) district rural roads plans (DRRP), also known as district master plans for rural roads. The core network provides information about AWR-connectivity between villages/habitations and essential nearby services. Details of habitations, the existing core network, existing and proposed roads are sketched on to a map for each block. Such maps of all blocks are integrated at the district level to form the DRRP, which is necessary for getting the approval from the district panchayat. Only such approved works are considered under PMGSY (Sikdar 2007). Detailed guidelines can be obtained from MORD.

National Rural Roads Development Agency (NRRDA)

The National Rural Roads Development Agency (NRRDA) works under the guidance of MORD to provide managerial and technical support for the implementation of PMGSY. Its major activities consists of preparation of DRRPs, identification of the core network (CN), project scrutiny, programme monitoring, quality management and financial management. The NRRDA has taken active initiatives to develop a separate set of specifications and a standard data book for rate analysis of rural roads in India. PMGSY works are implemented and monitored through the World Wide Web, on a site termed as On-line Management, Monitoring and Accounting System (OMMAS). Steps were taken to train the concerned engineers and technicians at all levels. Few R&D activities are also in progress for developing traffic growth models and performance-based designs.

Bharath Nirman

Another scheme termed as Bharat Nirman has also been started. It is a time-bound business plan under the framework of the PMGSY intended to accelerate and further develop/upgrade rural roads. Under this programme, the construction of 1,46,185 km length of rural roads is planned to benefit 66,802 unconnected eligible habitations at an estimated cost of Rs. 48,000 crore. The above projects are not only funded by the CRF but also by multinational financial institutions, viz World Bank, Asian Development Bank, NABARD etc. More and latest details about the different schemes related to rural connectivity are available elsewhere on the Internet (pmgsy; pmindia; planningcommission; cag).

1.9 Highway Alignment Surveys

Various surveys are required for the alignment of a new highway to decide the precise location of its centre line—this is in order to minimise cost of construction, maintenance, transportation, vehicle operating cost and to have the least impact on the surrounding environment. Horizontal and vertical controls of the proposed highway play a vital role in fixing the centre line alignment to suit terrain conditions. Before a new highway project is started, the feasibility of the proposal should be assessed with the following factors in mind—the spatial conditions prevailing in the locality, economic considerations, environmental impact, availability of materials and various other engineering aspects. New highways as well as stage-wise upgradation of existing highways should be planned by adopting a systematic approach (Figure 1.3). The following important elements should be kept in mind during preliminary planning of a project.

- Standard design specifications should be adhered to as much as possible.
- There should be no alteration of the finalised alignment at later stages as it may be difficult and expensive to alter completed work (Losh 1932).

Process of highway planning

↓

Data collected by surveys

- *General:* Details of existing road network, agricultural area, non-agricultural areas, number of towns, cities and villages to be served with census data, per capita income, length of existing railway lines, current and future developments envisaged.
- *Financial:* Available and anticipated revenue from vehicle registration, taxes, govt. fees, other sources of income by private participation, loan from banks; cost of living etc.
- *Engineering:* Various surveys to collect data related to traffic volume, growth rate, desired road links; existing transport facilities, anticipated traffic demands; soil characteristics, topography, drainage, river crossings, materials availability and climatic conditions.

↓

Graphical presentation of above data

- Topographic sheets showing all existing and spatial features of the terrain in the area under consideration and market facilities.
- Spatial distribution of habitation, industries, offices, agricultural areas, existing transport network, proposed or desired road network.

↓

Study of the above data and preparation of alternate routes in exigency.

↓

Master plan

- Analyses, comparison and prioritisation of the alternative routes based on productivity, density of population with number of villages, intensity and demand of traffic, road development targets and funds allotment made available in annual and five-year plans.
- Calculation of desired length of different classes (NH, SH, MDR, ODR and VR) of roads based on latest information available from road development plans; maximum utility by the locality or utility of road/ km.
- Final selection of a route and prioritisation or stage-wise construction of different links of the selected route based on funds availability, population, villages, industrial and agricultural productivity to be served by the proposed link or a part of the selected route.

Figure 1.3 *An outline of the highway planning process*

1.9.1 Factors Considered for Alignment of a New Highway

- Places and towns that are to be connected should be listed.
- Shortest route length is to be proposed.
- Gentle ground slopes or easy gradients to be chosen to facilitate safe movement of animal-drawn and motor vehicular traffic.
- Both, horizontal and vertical bends should be by gentle curves or with large radii curves without hampering design speeds.
- Adequate sight distance to avoid collisions.
- Favourable sub-grade soil and foundations for culverts and bridges.
- Good drainage conditions along the alignment to drain off surface run-off and seepage flow.
- Minimum earth work; balanced excavation and embankment fill along the alignment.
- Availability of adequate right of way.
- Appropriate locations at crossings of rivers, roads and railway lines.
- Availability of constructional materials at reasonable and economical distances.
- Free from land slides, avalanches and other natural hazards.
- Minimum cost of construction, maintenance and operational cost for roads especially in mountainous and desert areas.
- Direction of sand dunes or ridges, terrain of the country and adequate space of land along alignments in case of desert roads.
- Anticipated annual interest, maintenance and operations costs (Kerr 1932).
- Second-stage planning for construction of bypass roads due to paucity of funds or need-based highway construction (Giffin 1932).
- Economically feasible with ground improvement techniques (Rao 2008).

The concept of minimum or shortest distance between any two places is always difficult to decide but suitable diversions are to be conceived for the following cases (Bishop 1932).

- Marshy and swampy areas
- Location of river meanderances and multiple crossings
- Wider and high-altitude river banks
- Archeological and historical monuments
- Religious places such as temples, mosques, churches, graveyards etc.

- Well-developed areas such as agriculture, industrial, schools, hospitals, business places and residential areas
- Hills and valleys, where huge tunnelling work is needed
- Forest and other natural valuable resources
- Mining areas and other prohibited areas viz. military and nuclear hazardous places
- Watershed and liquefaction zones. (Rao 2008).

1.9.2 Control, Mandatory and Obligatory Locations

The following locations along a new highway alignment are to be strictly connected to avoid inconvenience (Losh 1932).

Terminal and intermediate points Main terminal points should be connected using suitable alignments taking into account intermediate places such as towns, villages and places of productivity. For example, a typical area showing two terminal places and a few intermediate points (Figure 1.4 (a)) may be connected by alternate alignments as shown in Figure 1.4 (b) and (c).

Crossings At crossing points of canals, streams, rivers and railway lines, the alignment of the road should be carefully decided to avoid difficulties in design, construction, maintenance and operational costs of structures. Multiple crossings are avoided as far as possible. Also, generally, skew crossings are avoided and perpendicular crossings with straight approaches are preferred. A typical river crossing is shown in Figure 1.4 (d).

Developed areas Built-up areas such as agricultural, industrial, residential areas, valuable natural resources, graveyards and religious places should be avoided or the alignment should be averted from these areas. In case of ponds (Figure 1.4 (e)), the alignment should be at a safe embankment height above maximum water level. Near hillocks, the alignment should be at a safe distance from the toe to avoid points of slips and rock falls. Figure 1.4 (f) presents a typical road diversion from the shortest route at religious places to avoid disturbances and prohibitive compensation costs. Also public sentiment must be given due consideration (Carpenter 1932) and a minimum safe distance should be left from religious places for maintaining zones of silence.

Easy gradient Vertical alignment for undulating, rolling grounds, hills, valleys should be carefully studied to avoid hairpin bends with steep gradients. Length of the highway may be increased to get suitable gradient as shown in Figure 1.4 (g). Generally, a gentle gradient of 1 in 40 for flat areas and 1 in 20 for hill roads is provided as a standard gradient. But for shorter distances, these gradients may be slightly relaxed and modified.

Location to prevent snow drifting Regions subject to heavy snowfall should be avoided (Bishop 1932).

Tunnels As far as possible tunnel operations should be avoided (Rao 2008).

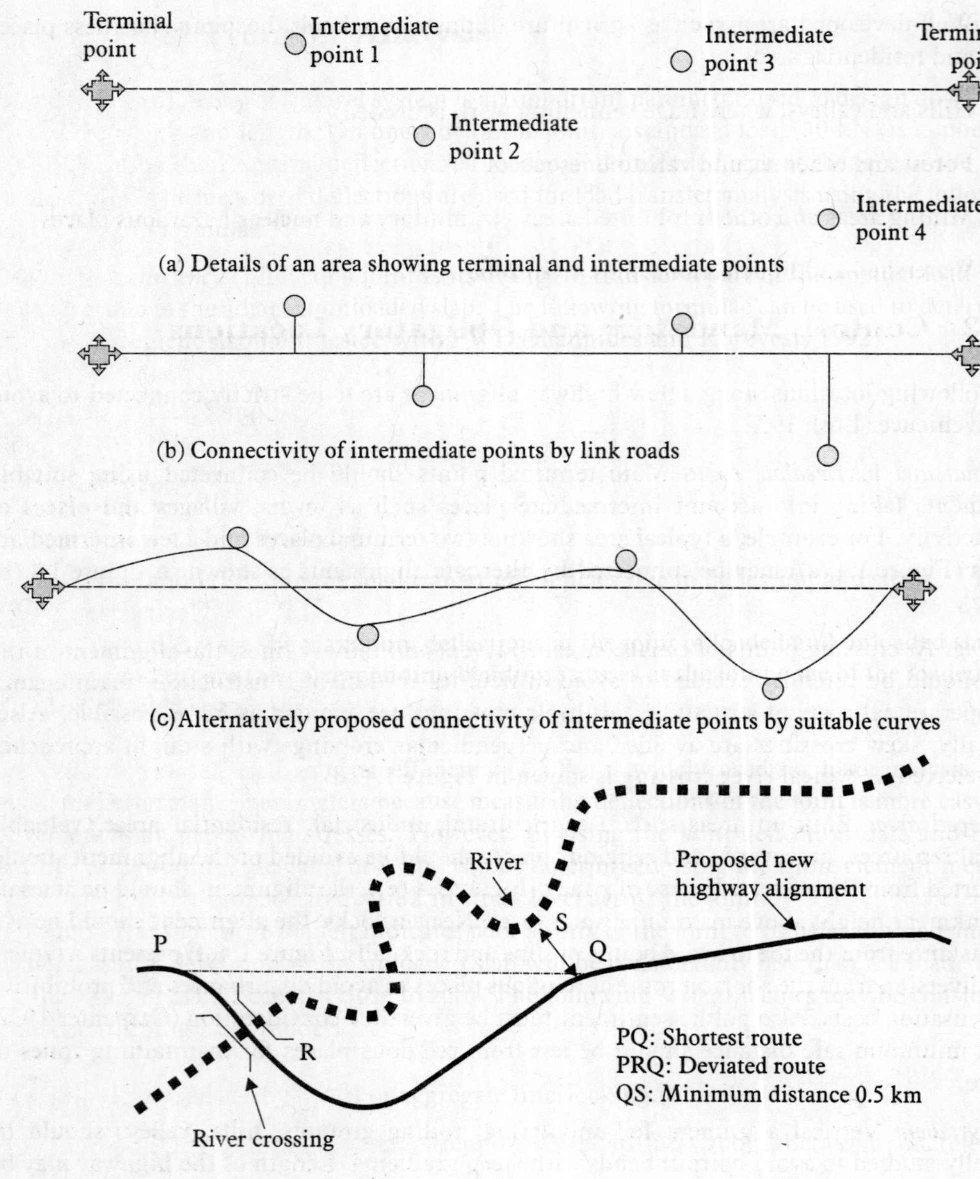

Figure 1.4 *Typical deviations of alignment from shortest route*

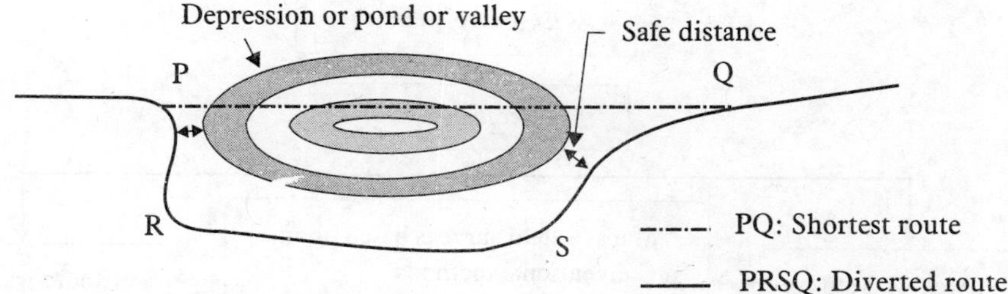

(e) Diverted alignment due to intermediate natural elements

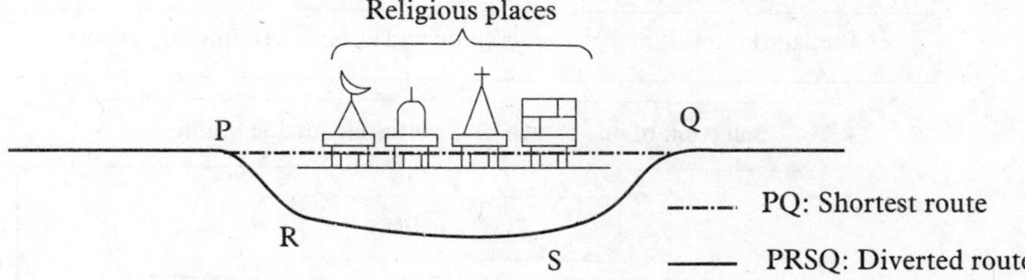

(f) Alignment avoiding elements of religious important places

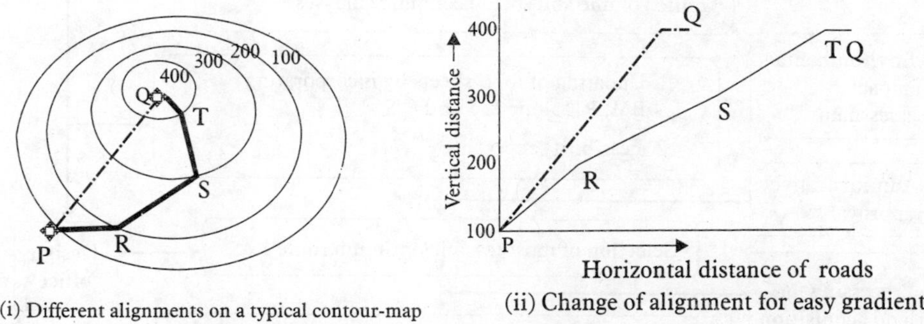

(i) Different alignments on a typical contour-map

(ii) Change of alignment for easy gradient

(g) Influence of gradient on alignment

Figure 1.4 *continued*

1.9.3 Highway Location Surveys

A systematic approach is required for alignment of a new highway. The data required is collected in three different stages, viz. reconnaissance, preliminary and final location surveys. The sequence of surveys to be carried out and activities associated with alignment of a new highway are presented in Figure 1.5.

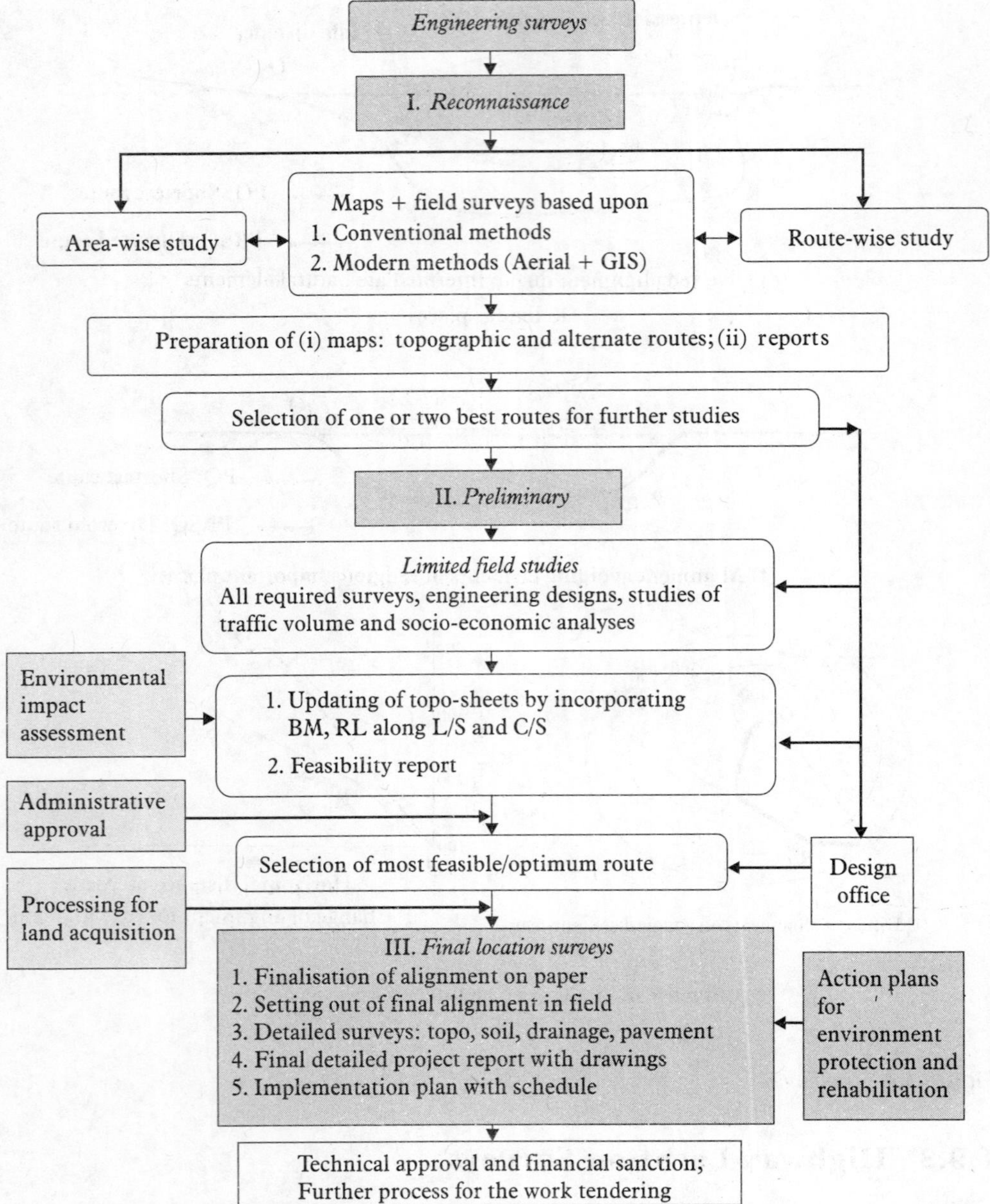

Figure 1.5 *Details of highway location surveys*

Reconnaissance Survey

Information related to the existing geographical features of ground and all man-made structures in the study area is to be collected during reconnaissance survey. Such data is used for further detailed study of the proposed route(s). Following are the objectives of the survey.

- To explore the possibilities of constructing a road in between two given terminal points.
- Identification and marking of the best routes on map and its verification on ground.
- Preparation of a report incorporating various related issues about the alignment with approximate estimated cost.

The reconnaissance should also cover areas and proposed alternate routes with the help of the topographic maps available (to scale 1:250000 or smaller) from Survey of India, aerial photographs of similar scale or resolution (to any scale between 1:5000 to 1:20000), satellite remote sensing imagery (on scales of 1:12500, 1:25000 and 1:50000) from the National Remote Sensing Agency (NRSA), Hyderabad and small format aerial photographs (on original or enlarged scale of 1:1000 to 1:10000) from NRSA or the Indian Air Force or Air Survey Company, Kolkata. Some ground and aerial studies are to be carried out in addition to the study by maps. During field studies, existing features of ground and environmental factors such as vegetation cover, land use and terrain characteristics should be verified with the details presented on the map. New features are to be marked in accordance to the field observations. Some traditional surveys using minor instruments like the Abney level, clinometer, binoculars, pedometer, ghat tracer etc may be carried out. Advanced instruments, like the geographic positioning system (GPS) or differential GPS may be used based on the importance of the work/ project. Any other previous reports which might have required information should also be noted down. Finally, the information collected should be reported. The report should contain the following information to aid further investigations in finalising route(s).

Reconnaissance survey report	Date:
• Title of the project • The existing ground features and proposed different routes connecting the terminal points should be shown in a topographic map of scale at least 1:50000 • Possible number of proposed routes explored with a brief detail about the alignments should be shown on the map • Approximate lengths of each route • Discussion about the merits and demerits of each alternate route along with their estimated cost • Details of pegs inserted on the ground at some salient locations of the alignments for further identification • Geometric features like sight distances at curves, radius of curves, level crossings, river crossings, gradients, right of way availability etc. • Data related to rain, temperature, humidity, soil drainage conditions, soil type and hydrological data • Approximate cost of compensation for acquisition of land • Availability of road building material and workmen at reasonable distances • Locations of crossing points at rivers, railways and existing roads with proposed alternatives • Details of affected forest and wild life sanctuaries • Connectivity of villages, towns, agricultural areas and other business places • Impact on environment due to proposed highway construction	
	Officer-in-charge

Based upon the above investigations, the concerned engineer-in-charge, selects one or two best routes from the available alternate routes and recommends them for further detailed surveys.

Preliminary Surveys

Detailed surveys are conducted on the selected best routes explored in the reconnaissance survey. The reconnaissance report and maps should be enriched further by incorporating detailed geometric alignment features and inputs for design of the highway components. Detailed surveys are conducted in a systematic and scientific manner using all minor and major tools and equipment. Accurate field work is to be carried out along the alignment(s) proposed in the reconnaissance survey. The following data is collected during the preliminary surveys and used as basis for determination of the final centre line of the highway.

Establishment of benchmarks (BM) Permanent or temporary BM should be established along the traversing line at intervals of 250 to 500 m and intermediate BM at not more than 30 m intervals.

Placement of pegs Pegs should be fixed along the selected best routes at not more than 100 m intervals.

Measurement of geometric details Longitudinal sections (L/S) at every 50 m intervals, cross-sections (C/S) for plain terrain should be at intervals of 100 to 250 m, for rolling terrain 50 m and for hilly terrains up to 20 m intervals (IRC:SP:19-2001). Other geometric details are taken along the alignment by using a plane table and levels to obtain data just sufficient to estimate the earth work quantities and approximate cost of the road per each km.

Hydrological data Data regarding rain fall, flood levels, number of cross-drainage works with their geometrical details must be taken.

Soil data Classification and distribution of soil types along the alignment; surface and sub-surface condition of the area; estimation of earth work quantities; ground water table levels; forest and vegetation covered.

Spatial data All existing spatial features along the alignment such as buildings, ponds, agriculture area, communication lines, river crossings, fencings, rock strata.

Traffic surveys Origin and destination survey data, traffic volume, type of traffic, axle load, traffic projection etc.

Environmental impact In order to mitigate the harmful effects of road building projects on the environment and the surrounding areas of the proposed projects, it was made mandatory to have an Environmental Impact Assessment (EIA) for 32 categories of development activities (India 2008). The EIA study includes

- Environmental analysis dealing with protective measures, the positive and negative impacts of the project with reference to cost-effective preventive measures
- Environmental design for reducing the adverse impact of the proposed road such as erosion of soil due to floods; submergence of surrounding area by accumulated water; loss of vegetation, reserve forest, wild life etc. Implementation of cost-effective measures to maintain environmental quality in terms of reduction of air pollution, water pollution, soil pollution due to spillages from automobiles, and reduction of noise pollution
- Environmental management action plan for execution of the schedule prepared under this category

- Resettlement and rehabilitation action plan to quantify loss sustained by tribes and habitation surrounding the project, further formulation of an action plan or policy of rehabilitation, employment and compensation package to the people effected. More details about EIA are available elsewhere (IRC: 104-1989; http://envfor.nic.in; UNEP 2002).

The above surveys may be conducted by using different procedures.

By conventional method Theodolite, chain, steel tap, clinometer, plane table, staves, compass and in case it is a hilly area, ghat tracers are used for detailed surveying of the alignments with respect to longitudinal and cross-sectional view of the proposed routes.

By modern method Aerial and satellite maps are used to supplement the available topographic maps. Remote sensing, geographic positioning system (GPS), geographic information system (GIS) and total stations are also used for three-dimensional modelling and precise quantification of various ground features. These soft copies of maps are suitably converted into AutoCad format or similar files and the proposed route's alignment with respect to the longitudinal section and cross-section is plotted.

The following details are reported in the preliminary survey:

Report of the preliminary survey or feasibility report	Date:
• Title of the project • Location of terminal and intermediate points. • Drawings showing all existing topographic, spatial features, L/S and C/S along the alignments; they are to be prepared for a contour interval of 1 to 3 m • Required number and locations of cross-drainage works along L/S • Soil and hydrological data • Traffic details with anticipated grow rate • Proposed pavement type with approximate thickness of the pavement crust • Location and approximate transport cost of the road building materials • Available and required road width along the alignments • Details of cost estimate of each alternate route with economic justification. Economic analysis can be made with reference to IRC: SP:30 of India or HDM-IV of the World Bank or RTIM III of TRL UK • A discussion of the merits and demerits of each route. • Special factors affecting the final location of the alignment. • Hydrological data • All drawings (Table 1.4)	
	Officer-in-charge

A comparative statement of the routes surveyed has to be prepared and the most appropriate and economical route selected. The following major impact factors may be considered for evaluation of the alternatives (Kulkarni et al. 1993).

- Land use
- Relocation impact
- Agricultural production
- Biological/ natural resources
- Cultural resources (with potential historic importance)
- Air quality
- Noise

The details given in the above feasibility report are used as a basis by competent authority to accord administrative approval for further detailed surveys.

After obtaining approval, the final selection of the alignment is marked on the map with details of earth work and costs involved. A team of engineers are then deployed for field verification and comparison with the alignment marked on the map. During the field inspection, an assessment is made to identify the possible problems and difficulties during construction, maintenance and operation of the highway. Based upon the examination in the field with reference to the map, required alterations are marked on the map for further survey purposes. The process for land acquisition should be immediately started at this stage since it will take time to get approval from the private owners and government officials concerned.

Final Location Survey

As we observed in the earlier sections, comprehensive investigations are made in the selection of the final alignment during the preliminary surveys. The centre line of the final alignment should be marked in the field by fixing stakes at intervals of 20 m in hilly terrains and 50 m in plain and rolling terrains (IRC: SP:19-2001). Further studies are made along the centre line to precisely work out and document the following data.

- Executive summary and socio-economic profile of the locality
- Availability of the required right of way along the centre line
- List of the associated problems for land acquisition and compensation costs
- Data required for:
  Geometric design of the highway Right of way, design speed, minimum sight distances, overtaking sight distances, radius of curves, super elevation, side drains and cross-drainage works
  Pavement design Traffic data, sub-grade soil support, foundation strength, soil type, surface and sub-surface drainage details
  Preparation of drawings Cross-drainage works, evaluation of earth work quantifications, preparation of working drawings for construction, scheduling of the project work
  Cost calculations/evaluation Item-wise cost estimate, overall cost, average cost per km of the highway, economic and financial analyses and construction programming
- Action plans for mitigating environmental impacts and related issues such as rehabilitation and resettlement of effected people and habitat.
- Construction materials, equipment, labour and related issues.

- Miscellaneous and petty work
- Conclusions and recommendations for successful implementation and maintenance of the project.

Field work All required instruments used for marking and driving pegs on the final alignment in field, as well as instruments for marking boundaries of the highway along the alignment should be available. During driving of pegs, offsets, salient points, important permanent structures or points of BM (at every 250 m interval) are taken as reference. Offset distance from these reference points should be 10 m in case of straight and 20 m for curved paths along the centre line. If any alterations or modifications are to be made during pegging the centre line, they should be immediately marked on the map. Permanent reference poles and wooden pegs are fixed firmly on the ground at an interval of 100 m and 30 m respectively along the centre line by using any precise angle-measuring instrument (such as total station) with a steel tape. Cross-sectional details should be preferably taken at intervals of 50–100 mm, 50–75 m, 50 m and 20 m in plain terrain, rolling terrain, built-up areas and hilly terrains respectively (IRC: SP:19-2001). In addition to this, cross-sectional details should also be taken at abrupt changes in alignment, starting and ending point of curves and at other geometrically significant locations.

Precise levelling survey has to be performed along the reference poles and wooden pegs with reference to the permanent and temporary BM established during the preliminary survey. Cross-sections should be taken at right angles to the centre line. The desired width of right of way should be taken on both sides of the wooden pegs at an interval of not more than 20 m. If there are any considerable changes in the direction of the centre line or ground profile, additional sets of cross-sections should be taken.

Soil explorations should be made to collect data related to bearing capacity, soil classification, level of water table, rock strata and drainage conditions. Soil samples are collected by using an auger or any other tool and tested in the laboratory for determination of gradation (as per IS: 2720, Part IV), liquid and plastic limits (as per IS: 2720, Part V), density and optimum moisture content (as per IS: 2720 Part VII and VIII), contents of deleterious materials (as per IS: 2720, Part XXVII), and to determine soil engineering properties (as per IS: 2720, Parts XV and XI). Based on the project requirement, information should be collected for low embankments (as per IRC: 10 and IRC: SP: 13), high embankments (as per IRC: 75), land slide prone areas (as per IRC: SP: 15), flexible pavement design (as per IRC: 37), rigid pavement design (as per IRC: 58 and IRC: SP: 17). Non-destructive tests such as the electrical resistivity method or nuclear tests are to be conducted to assess the suitability of the site for construction of highway or foundation for construction of cross-drainage works.

In case of upgradation or strengthening of existing highways, additional information such as road inventory, road riding quality condition, toll collection (for BOT projects) and future economic growth in the area effected by the project are required to be documented.

Location of crossings through reserved forest areas are to be specifically marked on the map of the final alignment. Similarly, the locations of hazardous areas and water logged areas are also be marked.

Any other data required for the estimation of the proposed project should be collected and suitably reported in the detailed project report (DPR) with detailed drawings. The list of drawings to be appended to the report of the final location survey is given in Table 1.3

Table 1.3 *Details of drawings to be prepared during highway alignment surveys (Details summarised from IRC: SP: 19-2001)*

Sl. No.	Title of the drawing	Purpose/salient feature	Prescribed convenient scale
1	Locality map	Location of the construction area with existing and proposed road alignment along with important towns and economically important centres	1:250000 (1 cm = 2.5 km)
2	Site map or index map	Special information at and around the project road	1:50000
3	Land acquisition plans	Existing village map or similar map is used for detailing the final centre line of the alignment, property boundaries with survey numbers and related special information along the alignment	1:2000 to 1:8000
4	Plan and longitudinal section	Every 1 km length of the alignment should be shown on a single sheet consisting of all geometric features of the road with necessary drainage details	For plain and rolling terrain: 1:2500 horizontal and 1:250 vertical scales For built-up areas and hilly terrain: 1:1000 horizontal and 1:100 vertical scales
5	Cross-section map	Existing and proposed ground levels; all cross-section elements of road; detailed cross-sections should be drawn at salient locations such as at curves, cuts, fills etc.	~1:100
6	Cross-drainage structures	Standard designs of culverts, small bridges etc.	1:50
7	Road junction	Junction details showing existing and proposed roads, road markings, sign boards etc.	1:500 to 1:600
8	Drawings for retaining structures, roadway amenities, location of sign boards and others	Relevant information should be shown at appropriate locations	Suitable scale, large enough to show the required details

The following manuals and codes may be referred to for obtaining more information about surveys conducted for road-related projects.

- IRC:SP:19-2001 for NH, SH and MDR
- IRC:SP:20 for ODR and RR
- IRC:52-2001 and IRC:SP:48 for hill roads and road tunnels
- IRC:SP:13 for cross-drainage works where the span does not exceed 6 m
- IRC:SP:54 for bridges

Exercises

1.1 Write a short note on road development in Ancient India.

1.2 Briefly explain how roads were developed during the British Rule in India.

1.3 State the significance of the Jayakar Committee for the development of the road network in India. What were its recommendations? Name the institutions set up and the road-related developments that took place.

1.4 What is the Central Road Fund and state how the fund is being distributed for different schemes of roads development activities?

1.5 Enumerate along with the year of establishment the different institutions/organisations related to road development in India.

1.6 What are the major initial road development plans evolved since 1943? Briefly explain the salient features of each road network development plan in India.

1.7 In detail, discuss the salient features of the Nagpur Road Plan or the First 20-Year Road Development Plan (1943–1963).

1.8 In detail, discuss the salient features of the Bombay Road Plan or the Second 20-Year Road Development Plan (1961–1981).

1.9 In detail, discuss the salient features of the Lucknow Road Plan or the Third 20-Year Road Development Plan (1981–2001).

1.10 State the formulae prescribed in the Lucknow Road Plan for determination of different classes of road lengths.

1.11 What is the role of the Ministry of Shipping, Road Transport and Highways (MORTH), in the development of road networks and road related activities in India?

1.12 State the objectives of the Department of Road Transport and Highways (DORTH).

1.13 What are the objectives and activities of the Indian Roads Congress (IRC)?

1.14 Discuss the role of CRRI in road development related activities.

1.15 Write a short note on the Indian National Group of IABSE.

1.16 What are the major activities of the Highway Research Board (HRB)?

1.17 Write a short note on the National Highways Authority of India (NHAI).

1.18 What is the main purpose of establishing the National Institute of Training for Highway Engineers (NITHE)? Discuss its activities related to road development in India.

1.19 Write a short note on the Border Roads Organisation (BRO). Discuss a few major contributions of the Border Roads Organisation (BRO) to road development activities since its inception.

1.20 What are the different types of classification of roads in India?

1.21 Write a short note on the scenario of the present road network and road carried traffic.

1.22 Discuss the National Highway Development Project (NHDP) in India. State its objectives.

1.23 In detail, explain the NHDP phases I and II. Also state the ten major ports of India.

1.24 In detail, explain the NHDP phases III to VI. State how these phases of road development activities are planned to be funded.

1.25 Write a short note on the SARD-NE programme of road development in India?

1.26 State the significance of rural roads development in India?

1.27 What is the PMGSY programme of rural road development? State its objectives.

1.28 What is the need for systematic planning in highway alignment surveys? State the important elements of planning that should be kept in mind during preliminary planning of a new road project.

1.29 State the factors affecting alignment of a new highway.

1.30 At what locations is the concept of minimum or shortest distance between two terminal stations not to be considered and why?

1.31 What are the control, mandatory and obligatory locations to be considered for alignment of a new highway project? Draw figures wherever applicable.

1.32 Draw a flow chart describing the process of activities involved in highway location surveys.

1.33 What is the significance of reconnaissance survey in locating a new highway's centre line? Discuss the different types of reconnaissance surveys.

1.34 Discuss the different maps (with scale) used for reconnaissance surveys.

1.35 In detail, explain the surveys required at the preliminary stage.

1.36 State the significance and detail of surveys required under the Environmental Impact Assessment (EIA) for a new highway/ road project.

1.37 State the major impact factors considered for evaluating alternative routes of road proposals.

1.38 Discuss in detail the surveys required for the final location of a new highway.

1.39 Discuss in detail the drawings with scales to be prepared during highway alignment surveys.

2

Highway Geometric Design

Introduction

Developing a highway geometric design consists of determining the physical dimensions of the various elements needed for the highway based upon scientific and practical requirements. A geometric design is deemed to be excellent if it allows the safe, smooth and economic movement of pedestrians and vehicles—both motorised and non-motorised. If the layout of different geometric elements and their dimensions are defective, it poses serious problems which may be impossible to rectify at later stages due to developments along the roadside (Losh 1932). Therefore, the need for a good geometric design becomes more pressing. Appropriate specifications and recommendations of various standard institutions should be suitably implemented in the design.

In this chapter, design details of various geometric elements of a highway are discussed. A good highway geometric design should take into account the following aspects.

1. Cross-sectional elements
2. Vehicle dimensions and permissible axle loads
3. Sight distances
4. Elements in horizontal alignment
5. Elements in vertical alignment
6. Intersection layout
7. Cross-drainage works, viz. causeways, culverts, bridges etc
8. Accommodation of important utility services within the right of way. The utility services include sewers, drainage and water pipelines, cables, transmission towers, telephone lines and gas pipelines and those carrying combustible materials (IRC: 98-1997)

9. Location of new road–rail level crossing (IRC: 39-1986)
10. Noise and light barriers
11. Minimum width of land to be acquired keeping in view future developments
12. In hilly areas, alternate routes are to be provided in case of road blockages due to land slides, rock fall etc. (IRC: 52-2001)
13. Road safety measures
14. Miscellaneous other issues such as markings, lighting, channelisation, flyovers, road arboriculture, and roads for military use to cater to special vehicles.

Following are the factors considered while planning the geometric design of highways.

- The design should, at all times, situations and environment, be safe, economical and compatible.
- Vehicle dimensions such as length, width and height should be taken into consideration.
- Suitable provisions should be made to accommodate future increased traffic intensity and for developments in the locality along the road network.
- The design should be consistent and conform to the standard specifications of IRC or other international institutions (for e.g., the AASHTO—American Association of State Highway and Transportation Officials).
- Factors related to humans and vehicles are suitably considered.
- Minimum total costs, which include construction, maintenance, operational and user costs should be calculated (often termed as life cycle cost analysis).
- The design should be comprehensive and complete with drainage systems, signs, markings, arboriculture, medians, footpaths, signals and lighting systems.

2.1 Vehicle Dimensions

Vehicle dimensions such as length, width, height and gross weight play an important role while designing various geometric elements of highways (Table 2.1).

Table 2.1 *Vehicle parameters useful for designing geometric elements of highways*

Sl. No.	Vehicle parameter	For design of
1	Width	Width and number of lanes or lane capacity Width of shoulder and design of signals Parking area, cross-drainage works Lateral placement of vehicles
2	Height	Location of electric and other cables Flyover and underpasses

Table 2.1 *continued.*

Sl. No.	Vehicle parameter	For design of
3	Length	Bridges and underpasses Highway junctions, hill roads, curves and hairpin bends Overtaking zones, highway capacity
4	Engine capacity	Design speed, skid resistance and braking distance Gradient, grade compensation and length of vertical curve Super elevation on curve Safety measures at salient locations

Table 2.2 lists the standard vehicle dimensions according to the IRC.

Table 2.2 *Vehicle parameters useful for designing geometric elements of highways (IRC: 86-1983 and IRC: 3-1983)*

Sl. No.	Vehicle parameter	Maximum allowable value (m)
1	Width	2.44
2	Height	For single deck: 3.81 For double deck: 4.72
3	Length†	With 2 axles: 10.67 More than 2 axles: 12.19 Tractor with semi-trailer: 15.24 Tractor with trailer: 18.29

† Maximum allowable length of vehicles in USA = 31 m and in Canada = 25 m (Wang and Cartmell 1998)

Standard weights of axles and their configuration are discussed in Chapter 6.

2.2 Terrain Classification

The geometric design of highways is based upon the topography of the terrain (general nature of the ground slope) on which the highway is to be laid and the corresponding design speeds specified. The cost of construction and maintenance of highways mainly depends upon the type of terrain. For example, the cost of road construction in a mountainous area is higher than that on flat or rolling ground. The cross slope of a terrain may be classified into four types. A typical terrain classification along with the general ground slopes encountered is presented in Figure 2.1.

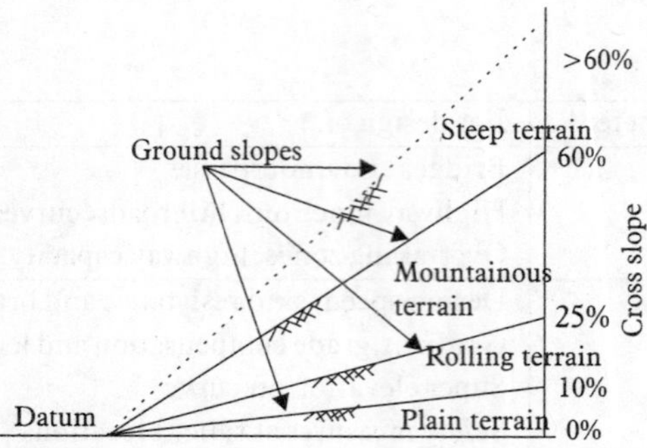

Figure 2.1 *Terrain classification based on cross slope (IRC: 73-1980)*

2.3 Design Speed

Design speed may be defined as the maximum average safe operating speed of vehicles that is either specified or maintained by most drivers travelling through all features of the roadway. It is one of the prime parameters that dictate the overall geometry of highways in plain as well as hilly areas.

Dimensioning and layout of most geometric elements are basically derived from design speed considerations. Field observations are made to correlate different speeds with the location of various highway geometric elements. Based upon field observations and scientific analysis, IRC, AASHTO and other institutions have recommended certain minimum acceptable geometric standards. The design speeds are prescribed by IRC (Table 2.3) depending on the type of cross slope of the country, the terrain classification and the importance of the highway. According to IRC (IRC: 73-1980), the ruling design speed is generally considered as a design criterion and taken as a primary input parameter for the design of various geometric elements of highways. The minimum design speed is considered if adopting the ruling design speed is not possible for practical reasons and other considerations. Appropriate design speeds may be selected based upon site conditions, feasibility, economics of construction and for traffic operations. But care should be taken to maintain uniform vehicular speed throughout the length of the road even when terrain conditions differ.

Table 2.3 *Design speeds (IRC: 73-1980 and IRC: SP: 48-1998)*

Road class	Design speed (km/h)							
	Plain terrain		Rolling terrain		Mountainous terrain		Steep terrain	
	Ruling	Minimum	Ruling	Minimum	Ruling	Minimum	Ruling	Minimum
NH and SH	100	80	80	65	50	40	40	30
MDR	80	65	65	50	40	30	30	20
ODR	65	50	50	40	30	25	25	20
VR	50	40	40	35	25	20	25	20

If the design is according to the British and German design practices, estimates of 85th percentile operating speeds should be adopted (Kanellaidis 1996). This means that on any given segment of roadway, the design speed should not be less than the estimated 85th percentile operating speed (Nicholson 1998). To design horizontal curves, the operating speed (at 85 percentile) is generally used as a parameter for controlling speed (Bonneson 1999). If the proposed design speeds is to be assumed, it should be a logical one, determined primarily by considering natural terrain, land use and highway classification (AASHTO 1990). But design of highway geometric elements based on assumed design speed is no longer considered adequate, especially for lower design speed (Hirsh et al. 1986).

2.4 Cross-Sectional Elements

Cross-sectional elements include all visible physical features of a highway (Figure 2.2). A few of the important ones considered for highway geometric design are briefly discussed in the following sections.

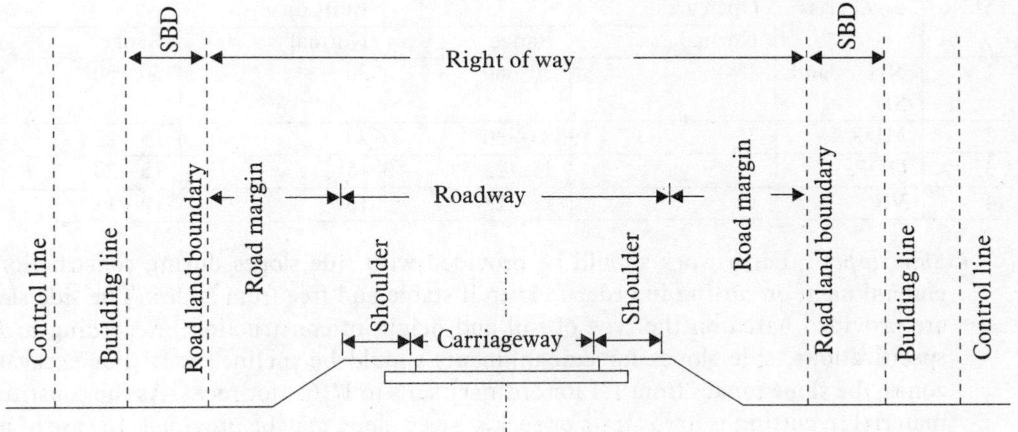

Figure 2.2 *Salient cross-sectional details of a highway (IRC: 73-1980)*

For more details on cross-sections of urban roads please refer to IRC:69-1977.

2.4.1 Boundary Lines

Boundary lines can be classified into road boundaries, building lines and control lines. Each boundary line serves a particular purpose (Figure 2.2). No construction should be made within the limits of the building lines to ensure uniformity of the road width. Within the control lines, the government has limited control over construction of structures. Based on the terrain and type of road to be laid, IRC: SP:15-1974 recommends standard overall widths between these respective lines. These widths of land should be specified for new highway alignments to help during land acquisition. They should also be monitored to prevent illegal developments along the highways. The land width between the road boundary and the building line is called the set back distance (SBD). The standard values of SBD recommended for NH and SH are 3 to 6 m in plain and rolling terrain and for the remaining classes in all terrains, 3 to 5 m (IRC: 73-1980).

2.4.2 Right of Way or Road Land Width

Right of way is the width of land acquired to accommodate the width of the carriageway, the shoulders and road margins. It is generally acquired for at least five decades of the service life of a highway. Necessary provision has to be made for future road-widening or anticipated developments along the alignment. This is because, land acquisition, especially in the case of built-up or urban areas, is very difficult and leads to legal problems and payment of a heavy compensation (Losh 1932).

The required right of way for different terrain and road classes as recommended by the IRC is furnished in Table 2.4.

Table 2.4 *Desirable right of way (m) for different road classes (A partial table from IRC: 73-1980)*

Sl.No	Road class	Plain and rolling terrain			
		Open areas		Built-up areas	
		Normal	Range	Normal	Range
1	NH and SH	45	30–60	30	30–60
2	MDR	25	25–30	20	15–25
3	ODR	15	15–25	15	15–20
4	VR	12	12–18	10	10–15

- ***Side slopes*** Earth work should be provided with side slopes during construction of embankment or cutting in order to keep it stable and free from slides. The side slopes are provided based on the type of soil and height of construction. According to IRC specifications, side slopes for embankments should be inclined 2:1. For excavation zones, the slope ranges from 1:1 for ordinary soils to 1/16:1 for rocks. As the constituent material in cutting is hard strata or rock, a steep slope may be provided. In case of high embankments, to restrict the land width, reinforced earth techniques are adopted to eliminate occupation of land for side slopes.

- ***Curbs*** It is a raised structure or a step-like component. A series of cut stones, pre-cast cement blocks, brick masonry walls are provided along the edges of a carriageway. Generally, curbs are provided along footpaths in urban roads to separate or restrict the movement of vehicles and provide firm support to the footpath. About 100 mm to 200 mm depth of curbs are constructed at carriageway edges.

- ***Road margin*** It is the width (or strip) of land provided along the side of shoulders to accommodate side slopes, berms, side drains, spoil banks and arboriculture (if any).

- ***Side drains*** Side drains are provided within the width of the road margin on either side of the alignment to drain off surface water to a safe distance. Suitable longitudinal gradients are provided according to the terrain. Side drains are designed to carry away storm water and also control the ground water table (GWT) at a safe depth below the sub-grade by preventing capillary rise.

2.4.3 Carriageway Width and Roadway

It is the main width of the road responsible for providing a strong, stable and smooth riding surface. The carriageway (CW) is based on traffic volume, design life, lane capacity, vehicle dimensions and clearance to be maintained between adjacent vehicles and the road edge. The IRC specifications regarding widths of carriageway and roadway based on the number of lanes are given in Table 2.5 and 2.6 respectively.

Table 2.5 *Width of carriageway (IRC: 73-1980)*

Sl.No.	Lane	Width of carriageway (m)
1	Single lane	3.75
2	Double lanes (without raised curbs)	7.0
3	Double lanes (with raised curbs)	7.5
4	Double lanes of less important roads	5.5
5	Multi-lanes	3.5 m per lane
6	Single lane (less important or village roads)	3.0

Table 2.6 *Width of roadway or formation (IRC: 73-1980)*

Sl.No.	Road class		Roadway width (m) for terrain*	
			Plain and rolling	Mountainous and steep
1	NH and SH	Single lane	12.0	6.25
		Double lane	12.0	8.8
2	MDR	Single lane	9.0	4.75
		Double lane	9.0	
3	ODR	Single lane	7.5	4.75
		Double lane	9.0	
4	VR (Single lane)		7.5	4.0

*The above values may vary subject to site conditions as recommended by IRC: 73-1980.

2.4.4 Shoulder

Shoulder is the width of paved surface which is laid along both sides of the carriageway to facilitate overtaking, temporary parking, walking and for emergency halting. Shoulders provide a lateral edge support to the carriageway along its length, a level surface during overtaking operations and facilitate draining the surface water to side drains. The width of the shoulder should be equal to one-half the difference between widths of the roadway and the carriageway. According to IRC, minimum width of shoulder should not be less than 2.5 m.

Depending upon requirements, shoulders are paved using earthen surfaces, mechanically compacted gravel–soil mix, stabilised soil using bituminous materials, cement or lime. According to Indian practice, the outward minimum slope of shoulders for earthen surfaces is 0.5% steeper than the pavement camber (which should be a minimum of 3%). For paved shoulders, a suitable value is selected from Table. 2.7. On super elevated pavement sections, the same value of cross-fall is provided as that of the pavement (IRC: 73-1980).

2.4.5 Camber

The cross-slope or slope in the transverse direction provided to the carriageway surface on either side of its centre line is called a camber or cross-fall (Figure 2.3). With reference to the level of carriageway edges, the middle portion of the carriageway surface is raised. This cross-fall or transverse slope of the carriageway surface facilitates the quick drain-off of rain water on to the shoulders and prevents stagnation on the carriageway.

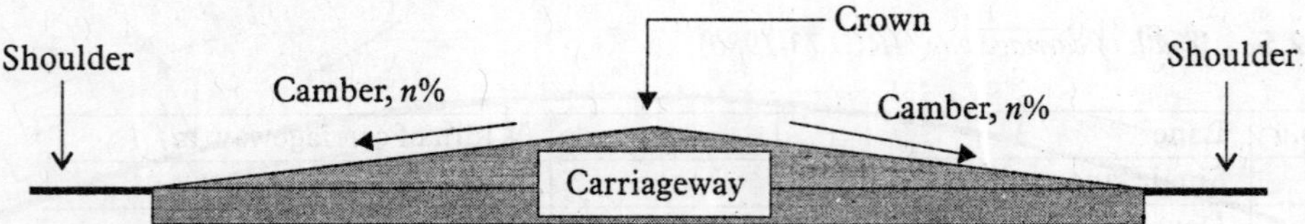

Figure 2.3 *Details of transverse slope or camber*

Sufficient camber should be provided for safe surface drainage. The value of camber is to be carefully specified based on rainfall intensity, type of materials used for construction, required smoothness and imperviousness of the carriageway. Generally, more camber is provided for unpaved or earthen surfaces than for paved surfaces. This is because, paved surfaces are smooth and do not allow rain water to percolate beneath the layers. At the same time, care should be taken not to provide more camber than is required for unpaved surfaces. It may create erosion, rutting or potholes.

The classification of cambers based upon the shape of the sloped surface is given in Figure 2.4(a). Table 2.7 shows the maximum allowable camber for different surfaces of pavements recommended by the IRC.

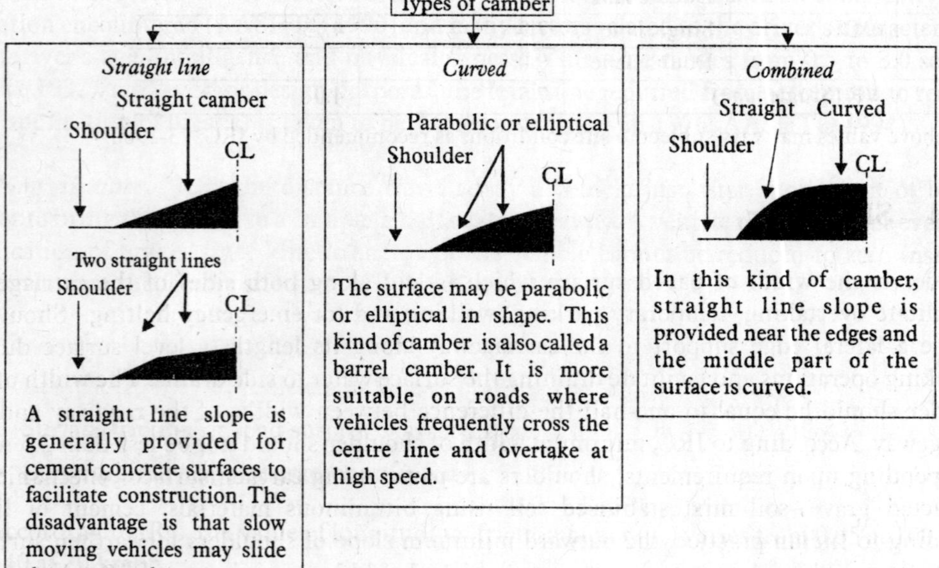

Figure 2.4(a) *Types of camber*

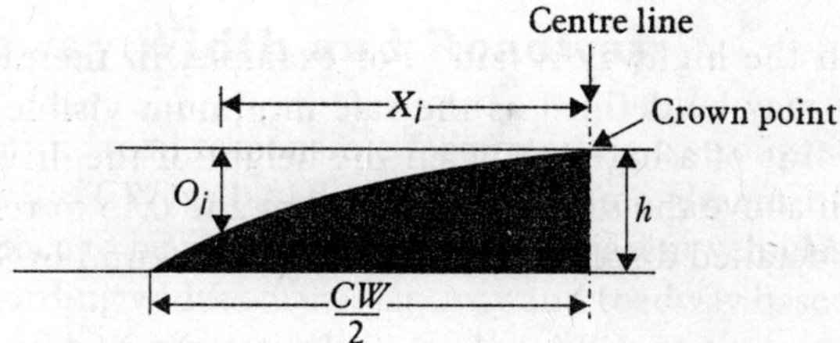

Figure 2.4(b) *Details of the offset for a parabolic camber surface. CW = width of carriageway; h= depth at crown point; O_i = offset at distance X_i from the centre line.*

Table 2.7 *Values of camber for different surfaces of pavements (IRC: 73-1980).*

Sl. No.	Type of pavement surface	Range of camber for rainfall intensity: Light to heavy	
		in per cent	1 in N
1	High-type bituminous surfacing and cement concrete	1.7 to 2.0	1 in 60 to 1 in 50
2	Thin bituminous surfacing	2.0 to 2.5	1 in 50 to 1 in 40
3	Water bound macadam (WBM) and gravel	2.5 to 3.0	1 in 40 to 1 in 33
4	Earthen road	3.0 to 4.0	1 in 33 to 1 in 25

If the camber is provided with a parabolic curved surface, the following relationship may be used to determine the offsets from the centre line at the crown point of a carriageway (Figure 2.4(b)).

$$\frac{O_i}{(X_i)^2} = \frac{h}{\left(\frac{CW}{2}\right)^2} \tag{2.0}$$

2.5 Sight Distance

Sight distance is the maximum distance visible to the driver along the centre line of a highway. The desirable length of sight distance depends on many factors, e.g., characteristics of the driver and vehicles, design speed, super elevation, horizontal and vertical curvatures. Driver characteristics include physical and perception capabilities to react to eventualities during driving. Vehicle characteristics consist of efficiency of the braking system, engine capacity and dimensions (Table 2.2). Sight distance is classified into the following types.

1. Safe-stopping sight distance (SSD) or non-passing sight distance
2. Overtaking sight distance (OSD) or passing sight distance
3. Intersection sight distance (ISD)

2.5.1 Safe-stopping Sight Distance (SSD)

The minimum distance travelled by a vehicle after the driver perceives an obstruction (distance travelled during perception time), acts on his observation; applies the brakes and the vehicle stops is called the safe-stopping sight distance. The distance and definition varies depending on the terrain on which the highway is laid. For example, in the case of a summit curve, according to IRC, SSD may be defined as the safe minimum visible straight distance of a driver along the centre line of a highway when the height of the driver's eye and an object in the opposite direction above the road surface is 1.2 m and 0.15 m respectively (Figure 2.5) (IRC: 66-1976). A more detailed discussion on curves can be found in Section 2.11.2.

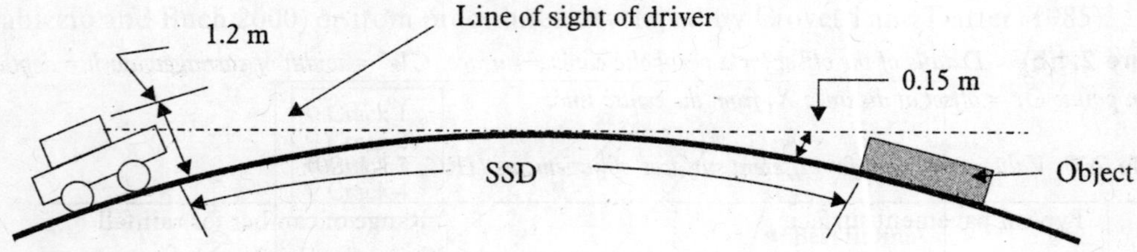

Figure 2.5 *Safe-stopping sight distance on summit curve*

Perception time It is the time required for a driver, while driving the vehicle, to observe, notice, assess and mentally analyse a given situation—the driver will then decide whether to react, apply the brake or steer away. In other words, during driving, it is the minimum time required for a driver to react instantly and exercise control. Perception time may be explained by the PIEV theory.

PIEV theory According to this theory, the driver *p*erceives a situation on the road, analyses it using his *i*ntelligence, *e*motionally feels it and reacts with *v*olition.

$$\text{Stopping sight distance (SSD)} = \text{Lag distance (LD)} + \text{Braking distance (BD)} \quad (2.1a)$$

Lag distance It is the distance travelled by a vehicle from perception of a situation to application of brakes by the driver. Perception–reaction time varies based on complexity of the situation encountered (AASHTO 1990) and many factors related to the driver's characteristics, viz. driver's age, intelligence and physical fitness. This time ranges from 0.5 to 3.0 seconds (Bruce 1932). However for design purposes, the total time required from perception to reaction (say application of breaks) is taken to be 2.5 seconds (IRC: 66-1976; AASHTO 1994).

Braking distance It is the distance travelled by a vehicle just after application of brakes, either to bring the vehicle to a complete halt or steer it away. A vehicle moves further even after application of brakes since kinetic energy of the vehicle cannot be reduced to zero instantly. Following are the factors affecting braking distance.

- Velocity of the travelling vehicle and its inertial force
- Brake efficiency of vehicle and type of braking system
- Surface friction or road surface characteristics
- Longitudinal slope or gradient of a road

According to IRC, the value of longitudinal friction factor (f_S) varies from 0.35 at 100 kmph to 0.40 at 20 kmph.

The following are the two methods of calculating SSD on different terrains.

CASE 1: On a level road surface (Figure 2.6)

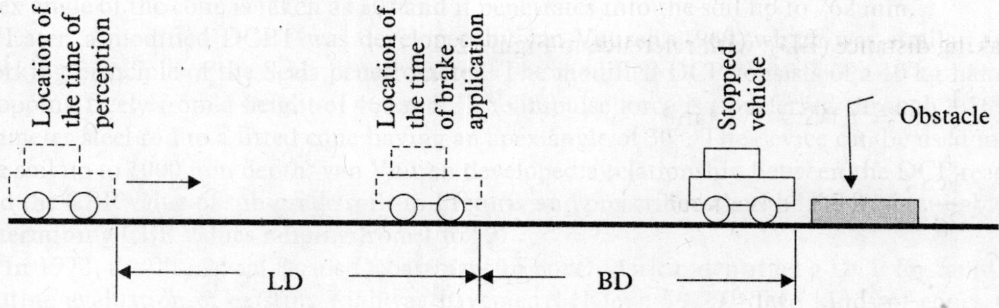

Figure 2.6 *Safe-stopping sight distance on plain road*

Lag distance $(LD) = v \times t$

Braking distance (BD) It may be derived by equating the kinetic energy of the moving vehicle to the work done by the frictional force (F) of the road surface to stop the vehicle.

$$\frac{1}{2}mv^2 = f_s WL$$

$$\frac{W}{2g}v^2 = f_s WL \qquad \left(\because W = mg;\ m = \frac{W}{g}\right)$$

$$L = \frac{v^2}{2gf_s}$$

$$SSD = vt + L$$

$$SSD = vt + \frac{v^2}{2gf_s} \tag{2.1b}$$

where, L = braking distance, m;
v = speed of vehicle, m/s;
f_s = coefficient of surface friction, 0.35 to 0.40 for speed range of 100 to 2 kmph;
g = acceleration due to gravity, 9.81 m/s^2

CASE 2: On a sloped road surface (Figure 2.7)

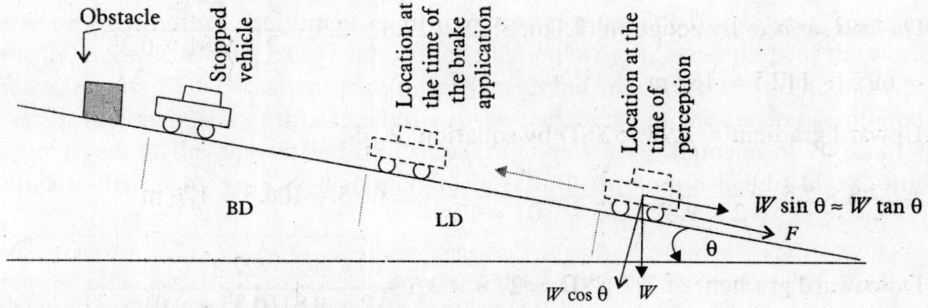

Figure 2.7 *Safe-stopping sight distance on a sloped road*

Lag distance (LD) = vt

Braking distance (BD): with reference to Figure 2.7,

$$\frac{1}{2}mv^2 = f_s WL + WL\tan\theta$$

$$\frac{W}{2g}v^2 = f_s WL + WL\tan\theta$$

$$\frac{v^2}{2g} = L(f_s + \tan\theta)$$

$$L = \frac{v^2}{2g(f_s + \tan\theta)}$$

$$L = \frac{v^2}{2g(f_s + 0.01n)}$$

(since, $\tan\theta = +0.01n$, if ascending gradient is taken as $+n\%$ or 1 in n)

$$L = \frac{v^2}{2g(f_s - 0.01n)}$$

(since, $\tan\theta = -0.01n$, if descending gradient is taken as $-n\%$ or 1 in n)

$$\text{SSD} = \text{LD} + \text{BD} = vt + L$$

$$\text{SSD} = vt + \frac{v^2}{2g(f_s \pm 0.01n)} \tag{2.1c}$$

Q. *A vehicle is travelling at an average speed of 100 km/h under the following conditions: (i) level surface, (ii) upward gradient of 1.98% and (iii) downward gradient of 2%. Assume perception and brake reaction time = 2.5 seconds and coefficient of longitudinal friction between vehicle tyres and road surface = 0.35. Determine safe-stopping sight distances.*

A: Vehicle velocity = 100 km/h = 0.278 × 100 = 27.8 m/s

(i) *On level surface:* By equation (2.1b), SSD $= 27.8 \times 2.5 + \dfrac{27.8^2}{2 \times 9.81 \times 0.35}$

$= 69.5 + 112.5 = 182$ m

(ii) Upward gradient = 1.98%: SSD by equation (2.1c),

$$= 27.8 \times 2.5 + \frac{27.8^2}{2 \times 9.81(0.35 + 0.01 \times 1.98)} = 69.5 + 106.5 = 176 \text{ m}$$

(iii) Downward gradient of 2%: SSD $= 27.8 \times 2.5 + \dfrac{27.8^2}{2 \times 9.81(0.35 - 0.01 \times 2)}$

$= 69.5 + 119.5 = 189$ m

2.5.2 Overtaking Sight Distance (OSD) or Passing Sight Distance (PSD)

Under mixed traffic conditions, different vehicles travel at different speeds. However for comfortable travelling, vehicles travelling at design speed frequently need to overtake slow moving vehicles. During this process, the fast moving vehicle enters into the opposite lane for a distance until it overtakes the slow moving vehicle and re-enters the original lane. For safe overtaking, the driver should be provided sufficient long sight distance ahead in order to avoid collision with vehicles coming in the opposite direction.

Overtaking sight distance may be defined as the minimum distance on an undivided highway required by a vehicle/driver to overtake a slow moving vehicle that is travelling in the same direction safely against approaching traffic in the opposite direction. The minimum required OSD for different design speeds and vehicles have been obtained by AASHTO (1994) based upon extensive field studies (Prisk 1941) and empirical formulas (AASHTO 1990).

The following standard conditions are assumed (AASHTO 1994). An average speed differential between impeding and overtaking vehicle passing at design speed is assumed to be 16 km/h. That means, if an overtaking vehicle is travelling at 100 km/h, the impeding vehicle is assumed to be travelling at 100 – 16 = 84 km/h. The maximum allowable difference of 16 km/h between design and operating speeds is taken as a widely used assumption in highway design in order to achieve operational consistency and improve driving comfort and safety (Kanellaidis 1991).

Let three vehicles travel on a two-lane undivided straight road as shown in Figure 2.8. The fast moving vehicle F is travelling at design speed and the slow moving vehicle S is travelling at a uniform speed slower than F. The third vehicle O is travelling at design speed in the opposite direction on the opposite lane.

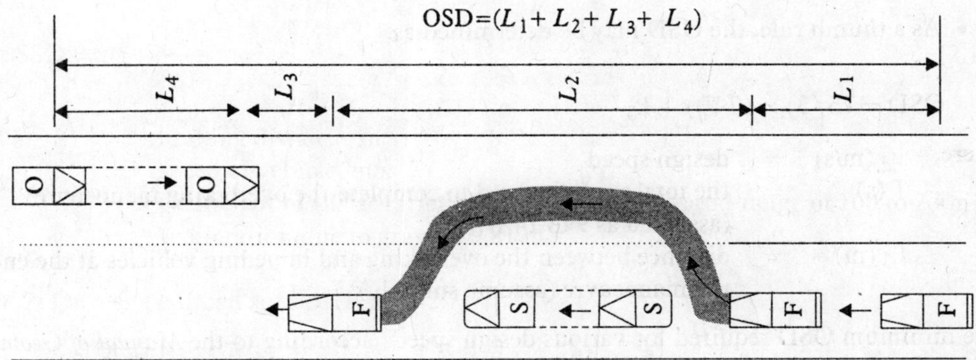

Figure 2.8 *Details of overtaking on two-lane undivided carriageway*

L_1 = Distance travelled during the perception–reaction time of t_1 seconds and during the initial acceleration to the point of encroachment on the right lane. The perception time is the duration of time required for the driver of the vehicle F to make the decision to overtake the slow moving vehicle S.

L_2 = Total distance travelled by the vehicle F from the time it overtakes S, enters onto the opposite (right) lane, accelerates while travelling along the side of vehicle S for some distance and re-enters onto the left lane after finishing overtaking.

L_3 = distance between the vehicle F and the vehicle O at the end of its manoeuvre. It usually ranges from 30 to 90 m (AASHTO 1994).

L_4 = the distance travelled on the right lane by the opposing vehicle O at design speed during 2/3rd of the time the vehicle F occupies the right lane or equal to $2L_2/3$.

$$OSD = L_1 + L_2 + L_3 + L_4 \tag{2.2}$$

Minimum required OSD may be determined using standard values or empirical equations of AASHTO (1994) (Table 2.8).

Usage of the values given in Table 2.8 $L_1 = t_1(s) \times$ speed of impeding vehicle (m/s); $L_2 = t_2$ (s) × design speed (m/s); L_3 = as given or suitably assumed; and L_4 = 2/3rd of L_2.

For example, if design speed = 70 km/h, $L_1 = 4.0 \times (70 - 16) \times 0.278 = 60$ m; $L_2 = 10 \times 70 \times 0.278 = 195$ m; $L_3 = 55$ m; and $L_4 = (2/3) \times 195 = 130$, OSD = 60 + 195 + 55 + 130 = 440 m.

The IRC method (IRC: 66-1976) assumed the following conditions and recommended safe OSD values (Table 2.9).

- About 9 to 14 seconds of time duration is taken for completion of an overtaking manoeuvre.
- The time taken for the initial manoeuvre is about one-third the total time required for overtaking. The remaining 2/3rd of the time is accounted for by the opposing vehicle that is travelling at design speed.
- OSD is the unobstructed distance between two points on the carriageway which are 1.2 m above the road surface—one point represents the position of the driver's eye and the other point represents the height of the object.
- As a thumb rule, the OSD may be determined as,

$$OSD = (5/3) \times (TV_d) + L_3$$

where, V_d (m/s) = design speed

T (s) = the total time required to complete the overtaking manoeuvre (assumed as 9 to 14 s)

L_3 (m) = distance between the overtaking and impeding vehicles at the end of the manoeuvre (assume suitably)

The minimum OSD required for various design speeds according to the *Manual of Geometric Design Standards for Canadian Roads*, Transportation Association of Canada (TAC) (Sparks et al. 1993) is listed in Table 2.9.

Table 2.8 *Elements of safe OSD on undivided two-lane two-way carriageways*

Speed group (km/h)	50–65	66–80	81–95	96–110
Average overtaking speed (km/h)	56.2	70.0	84.5	99.8
Initial manoeuvre				
Average acceleration (km/h/s)†	2.25	2.30	2.37	2.41

continues...

Table 2.8 *continued*

Speed group (km/h)	50–65	66–80	81–95	96–110
t_i = Time (s)†	3.6	4.0	4.3	4.5
L_1 = Distance travelled (m)	45	65	90	110
Occupation of right lane				
t_2 = Time (s)†	9.3	10.0	10.7	11.3
L_2 = distance travelled (m)	145	195	250	315
Clearance length				
L_3 = distance travelled (m)†	30	55	75	90
Opposing vehicle				
L_4 = distance travelled (m)	95	130	165	210
OSD = $(L_1 + L_2 + L_3 + L_4)$	315	445	580	725

†For a consistent speed relation, the observed values have been adjusted slightly.

Table 2.9 *Overtaking sight distance*

Speed (km/h)	Safe OSD (m) according to the Indian Roads Congress (from IRC: 66-1976)	Minimum OSD‡ (m) according to the *Manual of Geometric Design Standards for Canadian Roads*, Transportation Association of Canada (TAC) (from Sparks et al. 1993)
40	165	
50	235	340
60	300	420
65	340	
70		480
80	470	560
90		620
100	640	680
110		740
120		800
130		860

‡TAC recommends that the operating speed be 10 km/h less than the highway design speed.

The following factors/salient features are considered to be helpful for determining the minimum OSD (Wang and Cartmell 1998).

- Longer the passing and/ or impeding (slow moving) vehicle, longer the OSD. It has been shown that the increase in the impeding vehicle length has the same affect on OSD as that of the increase in length of the passing vehicle.
- The greater the acceleration of the overtaking vehicle, the smaller the OSD. This means that if the overtaking vehicle has an engine of greater capacity, it requires shorter OSD.

- If the speed of the impeding vehicle is greater, the required OSD is much larger and extra care should be taken.
- As the speed of the opposing vehicle increases, there is a linear increase in OSD.
- It was observed by another study (Sparks et al. 1993) that the values of OSD are significantly (≈ 40%) greater when overtaking a long truck (23–25 m) than when overtaking a car (4.5 m) at an operating speed of 100 km/h. It was also noted that whether a truck is 23 or 25 m, it does not have a significant impact on the OSD requirements.
- The differential speed between the overtaken and the overtaking vehicles has the greatest influence in determining the required OSD (Sparks et al. 1993).

Apart from the above cited references, there are other sources where the reader may obtain information on the determination of OSD according to the generalised versions of models (Lieberman 1982; Glennon 1988) and the models based on probability (Sparks et al. 1993).

Intermediate Sight Distance

At approaches of intersections between the main highway and intermediate or single or unimportant roads, intermediate sight distance is provided. Intermediate sight is also used when provision of OSD is not possible due to economic reasons or space limitation at site. According to Indian practice, intermediate sight distance is taken as two times the value of safe stopping sight distance (SSD). It is measured between two points on the carriageway which are 1.2 m above the road surface—one point represents the position of the driver's eye and the other point represents the height of the object (IRC: 66-1976). Because of practical reasons, intermediate sight distances, are not provided on summits and horizontal curves. If there is no space for SSD, restrictive pavement markings (IRC: 35-1970) or 'no overtaking' sign boards should be installed at appropriate places along the road.

2.5.3 Intersection Sight Distance (ISD)

Estimation of intermediate sight distance becomes more crucial at intersections where no traffic control devices are installed. At such locations, minimum sight distance (xz) should be provided with a suitable margin or limit beyond which buildings should not be constructed, to avoid obstruction of vision along the xy line (Figure 2.9). The area covered by the xyz triangle is called the *sight triangle*. As stated before, there should not be any obstruction to vision in this area. The sight distance (xz) is a function of the time gap (t_g) needed for a stopped vehicle on a

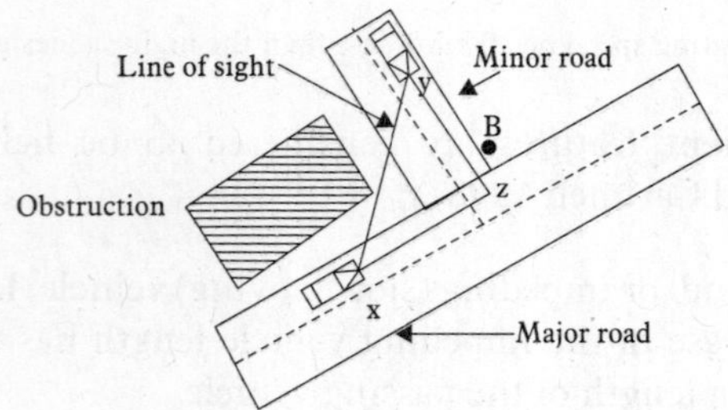

Figure 2.9 *Details of intermediate sight distance*

minor road to turn or pass through a major road (Harwood et al. 2000). At point B, a total stop board is provided for vehicles approaching the junction from the minor road. The time gap acceptance method is specified by AASHTO (2001) for determination of ISD based on the assumptions that (i) the time gap is independent of the approach speed on the major road, (ii) the intersection angle is 90° and (iii) both major and minor roads are straight and have no curvature in the horizontal and vertical planes. The required sight distance (xz) is calculated by the following relationship.

$$\text{Sight distance (xz)} = v \times t_g \tag{2.3}$$

where, v is the design speed on the major road (m/s) and t_g is the time gap (s) required for a vehicle on the minor road to proceed. The value of t_g for different type of vehicles, may be obtained from *A Policy on Geometric Design of Highways and Streets*, AASHTO, 2001.

Adequate sight distance should be provided at intersections to view vehicles approaching and decide whether to stop, reduce speed or cross the main road smoothly without collision (in case of un-controlled intersections). According to Indian practice (IRC: 66-1976), the minimum visibility distance (yz) along the minor road is taken as 15 m and the average time gap to travel the distance (xz) along the major road is assumed to be 8 seconds. For example, for a vehicle standing on a minor road 15 m before approaching a major road, the minimum visibility distance required along the major road (xz) is equal to $v \times 8$, where v is the design speed in m/s on the major road.

2.5.4 Sight Distance at Medians

In case of median crossing, vehicles generally stop adjacent to the median and cross or take a U-turn when sufficient distance is available from the vehicle coming opposite (B) (Figure 2.10). For crossing a median, the minimum required sight distance (SD) may be determined from the relationship, SD $= v \times T$, where $v =$ design speed of the vehicle on the opposite lane (m/s); $T = t_p + t_c$; $t_p =$ perception time (s) and $t_c =$ time (s) required to cross or U-turn around a stopped vehicle adjacent to the median.

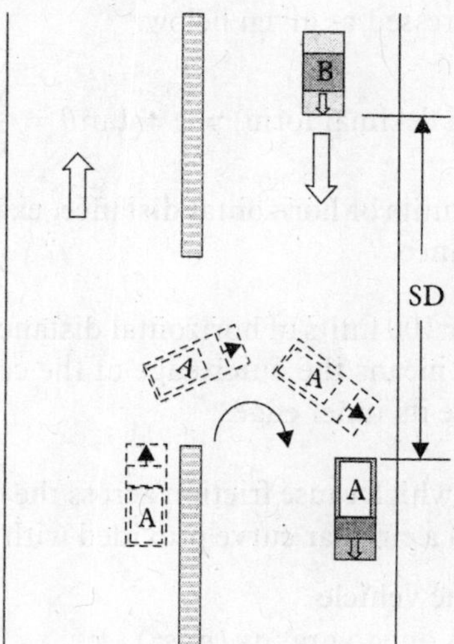

Figure 2.10 *Sight distance at a median turning*

2.6 Super Elevation

If a vehicle is travelling along a horizontal curve, there is a chance that it may fall either by overturning or skidding due to centrifugal force. The intensity of the centrifugal force depends on the radius of the curve, the weight and velocity of the travelling vehicle. To counter-act the centrifugal force acting on the vehicle while travelling on the horizontal curve, the outer edge of the carriageway surface is elevated with respect to the inner side. This elevated outer edge of carriageway or the provision of a slope in the transverse direction of the carriageway along a horizontal curve is called super elevation (*e*) or by the terms 'cant' or 'banking'. The different forces acting on a vehicle travelling on a curved path with respect to its centre of gravity (cg) are presented in Figure 2.11.

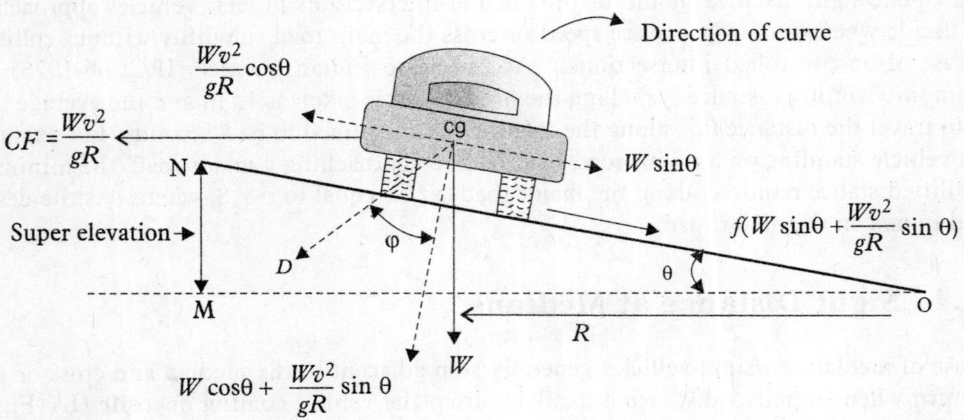

Figure 2.11 *Forces acting on a vehicle travelling on a circular curve provided with super elevation (not to scale)*

The super elevation may be expressed as given below.

1. Rate of super elevation (in decimal form) $= e = \tan\theta = \frac{\text{MN}}{\text{ON}}$

2. 1 in n = 1 unit rise for n units of horizontal distance, example: 1 in 700 = 1 cm rise for 700 cm of horizontal distance.

3. n per cent = n unit rise for 100 units of horizontal distance, example: 7% super elevation for 7 m wide carriageway means the outer edge of the carriageway is raised by [(7/100) × 700 cm)] = 49 cm above its inner edge.

The relation between the forces which cause friction across the carriageway and the centrifugal force of the vehicle travelling on a circular curve provided with super elevation is given below.

Let, W = weight of the vehicle
g = acceleration due to gravity (m/s^2)
v = velocity of the vehicle (m/s)
R = radius of the curve (m)

θ	=	angle of carriageway surface or transverse slope of carriageway
D	=	resultant of the weight of the vehicle and the centrifugal force
f	=	$\tan(\phi) =$ co-efficient of the side friction between the tyres and the road surface or side-friction factor, (a non-dimensional value)
CF	=	centrifugal force which pushes the travelling vehicle outward from the centre of the horizontal curve. It is perpendicular to the force of gravity. The centrifugal force is inversely proportional to the curve radius. As the radius of the curve becomes smaller, the CF becomes greater and vice versa.

In highway design, the CF is counter-acted by side friction and the component of the weight of the vehicle which is caused by super elevation (Awadallah 2005).

Consider the super elevated surface (Figure 2.11),

CF = Horizontal component of the weight of the vehicle + force caused due to surface friction of the carriageway against sliding.

$$\frac{Wv^2}{gR}\cos\theta = W\sin\theta + f\left(W\cos\theta + \frac{Wv^2}{gR}\sin\theta\right)$$

$$\frac{v^2}{gR}\cos\theta = \sin\theta + f\cos\theta + f\frac{v^2}{gR}\sin\theta$$

$$\frac{v^2}{gR}(\cos\theta - f\sin\theta) = \sin\theta + f\cos\theta$$

Dividing with $\cos\theta$ on both sides,

$$\frac{v^2}{gR}(1 - f\tan\theta) = \tan\theta + f$$

$$\frac{v^2}{gR}(1 - f \times e) = e + f \qquad \text{(since } \tan\theta = e\text{)}$$

$$\frac{v^2}{gR}(1 - 0) = e + f \text{ (since } f \times e \approx 0 \text{ when max. allowable values of } f \text{ and } e \text{ are taken)}$$

$$e + f = \frac{v^2}{gR} \tag{2.4}$$

From the above relationship (2.4), for a selected design speed, the minimum required radius of horizontal curve can be determined by substituting the maximum values of super elevation and side friction factor.

2.6.1 Design of Super elevation

According to the IRC, the centrifugal force produced due to 75 per cent of the design speed is taken care of by super elevation and the rest of the 25 per cent is counter-acted by the surface friction of the carriageway. Based on the above assumption, the rate of super elevation (e) is designed using the following formula (IRC: 73-1980).

$$e = \frac{(0.75\,v)^2}{gR} \tag{2.5}$$

According to Indian (IRC: 73-1980) and US guidelines (AASHTO 1984), design speeds are used for limiting the super elevation whereas in German guidelines, operating speeds are used (Kanellaidis 1991). Operating speeds are usually expressed as the 85th percentile of passenger cars under free-flow conditions (Lamm and Choueiri 1987).

2.6.2 Design Rate of Super Elevation

Five maximum super elevation rates (12, 10, 8, 6 and 4%) are considered according to US guidelines (AASHTO 1984). However, a maximum super elevation rate (e_{max}) of 8% is taken as the US mean representative value and it is suggested that 4 or 6% be taken for urban areas. Equation (2.4) is used to determine the minimum radius of curve. According to German guidelines, 7% rate in general and 8% rate for exceptional conditions are considered (Kanellaidis 1991). In Australia and New Zealand, the e_{max} is generally taken as 0.1% (Nicholson 1999). In India, the permissible e_{max} values recommended by IRC (IRC: 73-1980 and IRC: 86-1983) are given below.

- In plain and rolling terrain including snow bound areas : 7% (1 in 16)
- In hilly areas not bounded by snow : 10% (1 in 10)
- Urban area with frequent intersections : 4% (1 in 25)

When the super elevation determined from equation (2.5) is less than the road camber, the normal camber should be provided along the curved section; super elevation need not be provided (IRC: 73-1980).

The above differences in limiting values of super elevation may be because of variability in speed behaviour of drivers, climatic conditions (warm or cold), carriageway characteristics and terrain conditions prevailing in different countries. Lower values of e_{max} are suitable in cold and snow falling areas. This is because heavy vehicles travelling on curves even at low speeds tend to slide down due to low coefficients of side friction offered by snowy surfaces (Awadallah 2005). The above differences in limiting values of super elevation may be because of variability in speed behaviour of drivers, climatic conditions (warm or cold), carriageway characteristics and terrain conditions prevailing in different countries. Lower values of e_{max} are suitable in cold and snow falling areas. This is because heavy vehicles travelling on curves even at low speeds tend to slide down due to low coefficients of side friction offered by snowy surfaces (Awadallah 2005).

Q: *Determine the curve radii beyond which no super elevation is provided when the design speed is 70 km/h and the camber is of 2%.*

A: $v = 0.278 \times 70 = 19.46$ m/s

Use equation (2.5), $e = \dfrac{(0.75v)^2}{gR}$ and substitute the value of e as equal to camber value.

$$R \geq \frac{(0.75\,v)^2}{g \times (\text{camber})} = \frac{(0.75\ \times 19.46)^2}{9.81 \times \left(\dfrac{2}{100}\right)} = 1085.7\ \text{m}$$

$\therefore$ For the given conditions, no super elevation is required when the radius is greater than 1086 m.

2.6.3 Design Side Friction Factor

The optimal design side friction factor ($f_{\max}$) is one that assures safe driving on a horizontal curve having minimum permissible radius, maximum super elevation and design speed (AASHTO). $f_{\max}$ is generally used to define the minimum radius available for the design of horizontal curve. The friction factor depends on many parameters and can vary spatially and temporally (prevailing weather conditions). Variations in the available values of friction and the friction demanded by different vehicles travelling at different speeds lead to variations in the margin of safety (Nicholson 1998). Due to these reasons, the $f_{\max}$ should be carefully selected. For various design speeds, different values of $f_{\max}$ recommended by several highway agencies are shown in Figure 2.12 (Bonneson 1999).

According to AASHTO (2001), for design of low speed facilities (where the design speed is taken as $\leq$ 70 km/h), the value of the side friction factor varies from 0.16 to 0.31—when a minimum design speed of 30 km/h and a maximum design speed of 70 km/h is taken respectively. In a study it was observed that on horizontal curves, drivers accept higher side friction factors with higher speed reductions (Bonneson 1999). This means that when there is an increase in speed reduction, there is a greater demand for side friction. Therefore, for the design of low speed facilities such as rural roads and urban streets, appropriate values of side friction factor should be taken to avoid exceeding the intended design speed on curves (Gattis et al. 2005).

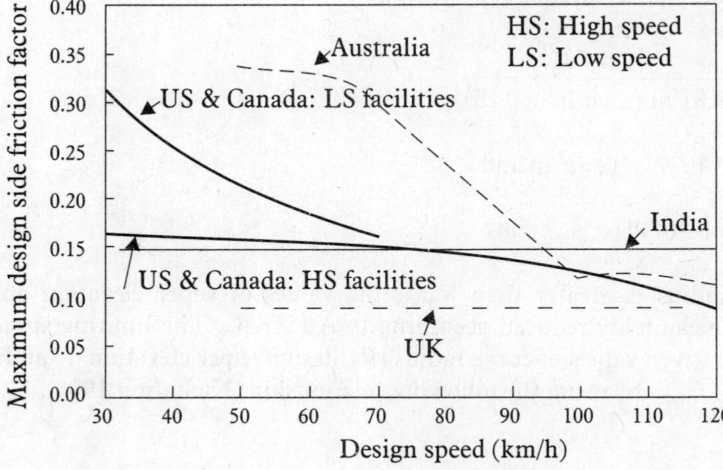

Figure 2.12 *Maximum design side fraction factors recommended by several highway agencies (developed from Bonneson 1999)*

In India, the value of f_{max} recommended for all design speeds is 0.15 (IRC:73-1980). From Figure 2.12, it can be observed that in most countries, (UK and India are exceptions where the values are insensitive to speed), the values of f_{max} vary with speed.

2.6.4 Analysis of Curve Radii

Ruling and minimum curve radii can be determined using ruling and minimum design speeds respectively. Depending on the type of terrain and design speed (Table 2.3), suitable equations may be used (either (2.6) or (2.7) given below). The IRC has recommended radii beyond which no super elevation is required and also R_{min} for different terrain conditions (IRC:73-1980).

We have, $R = \dfrac{v^2}{g(e+f)}$

The above equation may be expressed as below.

$$R_{min} = \frac{v^2}{g(e_{max} + f_{max})} \tag{2.6a}$$

For plain, rolling terrian and hilly areas including snow bound locations as,

$$R_{min} = \frac{(v\,\text{m/s})^2}{9.81\ \text{m/s}^2(0.07+0.15)}$$

$$R_{min} = 0.46335(v_{min})^2\ \text{m and} \tag{2.6b}$$

$$R_{ruling} = 0.46335(v_{ruling})^2\ \text{m} \tag{2.6c}$$

Similarly, for hilly areas unbounded by snow:

$$R_{min} = \frac{(v\,\text{m/s})^2}{9.81\ \text{m/s}^2(0.10+0.15)}$$

$$R_{min} = 0.40771(v_{min})^2\ \text{m and} \tag{2.7a}$$

$$R_{ruling} = 0.40771(v_{ruling})^2\text{m} \tag{2.7b}$$

If the curve radius is greater than R_{min}, the values of super elevation and side friction factor should be suitably reduced according to AASHTO. The limiting speed (V_L), may be determined for given values of curve radius (R), design super elevation (e) and maximum side friction factor (f_{max}) by using the following relationship (Nicholson 1998).

$$V_L = \sqrt{gR(e+f_{max})} \tag{2.8}$$

The difference between limiting speed (V_L) and design speed (v) can be considered as the design margin of safety. It is also called design speed margin of safety (DSMS). Variations in safety margin arise on horizontal curves mainly due to variations in available friction and the friction demanded by drivers. When we fix the design criterion of horizontal curves, the maximum allowable coefficient of side friction ($f_{\max}$) is generally considered because, at this critical condition, overturning/or sliding of vehicles is sufficient to cause discomfort to drivers and thereby restrict higher speeds (Dabbour et al. 2004).

Values of variance and mean of DSMS are determined for a given section of highway consisting of horizontal curves. If variance of DSMS is small, it indicates that the design consistency is good. If the mean value is large, it indicates that the available safety is better (Nicholson 1998 and Easa 2003).

Conditions Assumed

1. When $f = 0$, $e = v^2/gR$. This means that the total centrifugal force is counter-acted by super elevation only because it is assumed that there will be no frictional forces. By providing this calculated value of super elevation (e) at design speed, the pressure distribution under both wheels will be equal. This condition is termed as equilibrium cant (Figure 2.13).

2. If $e < v^2/gR$, the total centrifugal force is not counter-acted by the provided super elevation. It is assumed that frictional forces will come into play to compensate for the same.

3. If $e = 0$, $f = v^2/gR$. Here it is assumed that surface frictional forces are entirely responsible for counter-acting the total centrifugal force. If the f value provided is less than the calculated value, the vehicle may slide down.

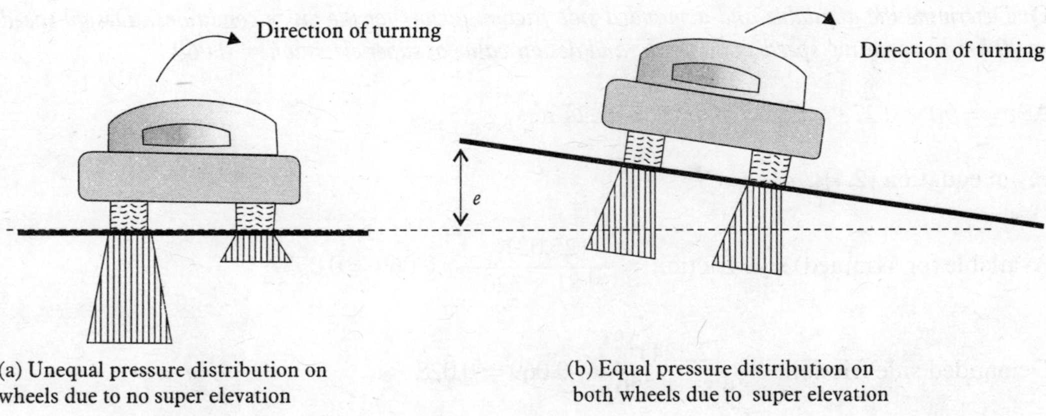

Figure 2.13 *Variation in wheel-load distribution on the road surface at curves*

Q: *For a proposed NH, determine the minimum required value of radius when the design speed = 100 km/h, $f_{\max} = 0.15$ and $e_{\max} = 0.07$.*

A: Let $v = 100 \times 0.278 = 27.8$ m/s

Minimum radius required for the curve corresponding to v is determined by equation (2.6b).

$$R_{\min} = 0.46335(v)^2 = 0.46335(27.8)^2 = 358 \text{ m}$$

Q: *Determine the design speed margin of safety (DSMS) when the design speed = 90 km/h and the horizontal circular curve radius = 520 m. Assume suitable required values.*

A: Assume, $f_{\max} = 0.15$ and $e_{\max} = 0.07$. Let $v = 90 \times 0.278 = 25.02$ m/s. From equation (2.5),

$$e = \frac{(0.75 \times 25.02)^2}{(9.81 \times 520)} = 0.069 < e_{\max}; \text{ provide } e = 6.9\%$$

From equation (2.4), the actually needed or demanded value of f is determined as,

$$f = \frac{v^2}{gR} - e = \frac{(25.02)^2}{9.81 \times 520} - 0.069 = 0.0537$$

Friction utilisation ratio $= 100 \times f/f_{\max} = 100 \times 0.0537/0.15 = 35.8\%$

It is determined that the required side friction is less than the assumed value of maximum side friction. Therefore, the design is safe. The corresponding limiting speed may be determined by equation (2.8),

Therefore, design speed margin of safety (DSMS) $= V_L -$ design speed (v)

$$= 120.23 - 90 = 30.32 \text{ km/h}$$

Q: *Determine the available and demanded side friction factors for the given conditions: Design speed = 90 km/h; operating speed = 80 km/h; and design value of super elevation = 0.069.*

A: $v_d = 90 \times 0.278 = 25.02$ m/s; $v_o = 22.24$ m/s

From equation (2.4),

$$\text{Available (or assumed) side friction} = \frac{(25.02)^2}{(9.81 \times 520)} - 0.069 = 0.0537$$

$$\text{Demanded side friction} = \frac{(22.24)^2}{(9.81 \times 520)} - 0.069 = 0.028$$

The above values and their difference may be used to evaluate the performance of horizontal curves against recommended standard driving safety criteria (Lamm et al. 1991).

Q: *A national highway (NH) is passing through plain, rolling and hilly areas. According to IRC guidelines, design a super elevation for the given conditions:*

(i) For plain terrain: Ruling design speed = 80 kmph and horizontal curve radius = 215 m.

(ii) For rolling terrain: Ruling design speed = 80 kmph and horizontal curve radius = 300 m.

(iii) For hilly area: Ruling design speed = 100 kmph and horizontal curve radius = 137 m.

(i) *For plain terrain:*

$v = 80 \times 0.278$ kmph $= 22.24$ m/s

From equation (2.5),

$$e = \frac{(0.75 \times 22.24)^2}{(9.81 \times 215)} = 0.1319 > e_{max}$$

Therefore, provide $e = e_{max}$ and check the value of f_{max}.

From equation (2.4),

$$\text{Available } f = \frac{v^2}{gR} - e_{max} = \frac{(22.24)^2}{(9.81 \times 215)} - 0.07 = 0.164 > f_{max}$$

Therefore, determine maximum allowable speed when $e = e_{max}$ and $f = f_{max}$ values are taken,

$$V_L = \sqrt{9.81 \times 215(0.07 + 0.15)} = 21.54 \text{ m/s} = 77.48 \text{ kmph}$$

(ii) *For rolling terrain:*

$v = 80 \times 0.278$ kmph $= 22.24$ m/s

From equation (2.5),

$$e = \frac{(0.75 \times 22.24)^2}{(9.81 \times 300)} = 0.094 > e_{max}$$

Therefore, take $e = e_{max} = 0.07$ and check the value of f_{max}. From equation (2.4),

$$\text{Available } f = \frac{v^2}{gR} - e = \frac{(22.24)^2}{(9.81 \times 300)} - 0.07 = 0.098 < f_{max}$$

Provide $e = 0.07$ for the given speed.

(iii) *For hilly areas:*

$v = 100 \times 0.278$ kmph $= 27.8$ m/s

From equation (2.5),

$$e = \frac{(0.75 \times 27.8)^2}{(9.81 \times 137)} = 0.080 < e_{max}$$

where $e_{max} = 0.1$.

Therefore, provide super elevation rate = $0.08 \times 100 = 8\%$.

Q: *For achieving the best surface drainage conditions, economy in construction and environmental compatibility with surroundings, it was proposed to provide negative super elevation on a horizontal curve of a multi-lane highway. Determine the minimum radius of the horizontal curve given the following conditions: Operating speed of vehicles = 60 km/h, $e_{max} = -2.4\%$ and $f_{max} = 0.08$.*

A: $v = 60 \times 0.278 = 16.68$ m/s; $e_{max} = -2.4\% = -0.024$ and $f_{max} = 0.08$.

From equation (2.6 a),

$$R_{min} = \frac{(16.68)^2}{9.18 \times (-0.024 + 0.08)} = 506.4 \text{ m}$$

2.6.5 Attaining Super Elevation

Super elevation may be attained by adopting any one of the methods given in Table 2.10. The choice of the method depends on the site condition.

Table 2.10 *Suitability of different methods for attaining super elevation*

Sl.No.	Method of attaining super elevation*	Remarks
1	Rotation of roadway surface about its inner edge Inner edge taken as axis of rotation	• Facilitates drainage when the inner edge level of the roadway is required to be unaltered. • Provides uniform appearance of the super elevated curve. • Used more often in earth filling operations. • Centre line of carriageway may have to be shifted along the length of the curve. • Suitable for multi-lane highways having medians and ramps with baseline.
2	Rotation of roadway surface about its outer edge. outer edge taken as axis of rotation	• Used more often in earth cutting operations. • Care should be taken to drain off accumulated rain water at the inner portion of the curve. • Centre line of the carriageway may have to be shifted along the length of the curve. • Suitable for multi-lane highways having medians and ramps with baseline.
3	Rotation of a roadway surface about its centre line (as illustrated in Figure 2.14 (b)).	• Most frequently adopted method since the least distortion occurs to the construction centre line of the roadway. Thus the vehicle maintains stability while manoeuvering the curve.

* Reference: IRC: 73-1980 and IRC:86-1983.

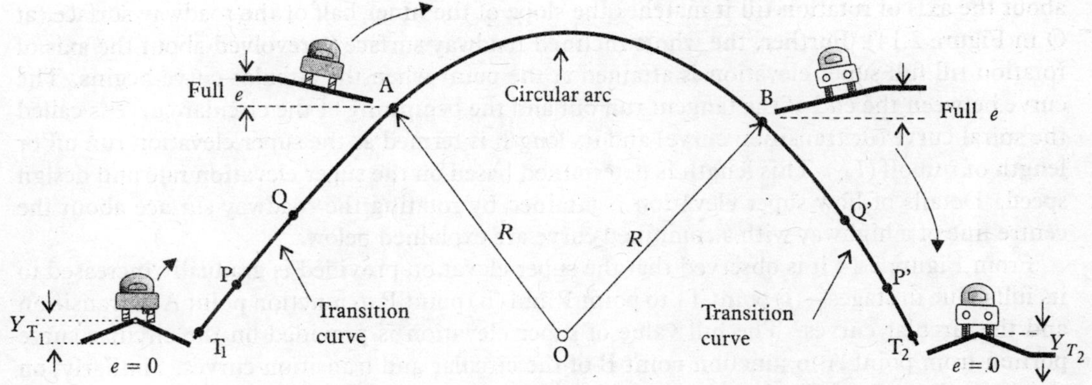

(a) Plan view of a highway with a combined curve

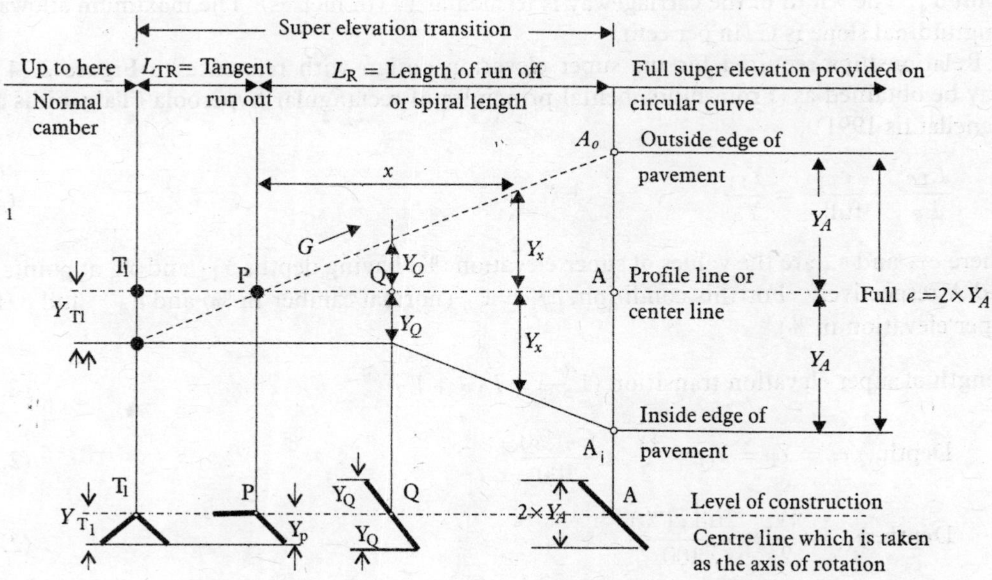

(b) Profile of the roadway along the highway as given in (a).

Figure 2.14 *Super elevation design by rotating the roadway about the centre line (not to scale)*

A reference line or axis of roadway along the inner edge or outer edge or centre line is considered as the datum line or axis of rotation. The respective points of the roadway surface are revolved about the axis of rotation, in two stages. At the first stage, the outer half of the cambered roadway surface is gradually rotated to the horizontal (i.e., normal cross slope = 0) and the inner half of the roadway surface is kept at the normal camber. This means that the normal camber on the outer half of the roadway is removed (Hinkle 1930) and gradually made horizontal over a length of the road. This length is termed as tangent run out (L_{TR}). In the second stage, the horizontally placed outer half of the roadway surface is gradually rotated about the axis of rotation till it matches the slope of the inner half of the roadway surface (at Q in Figure 2.14). Further, the whole inclined roadway surface is revolved about the axis of rotation till full super elevation is attained at the point when the circular curve begins. The curve between the end of the tangent run out and the beginning of the circular curve is called the spiral curve (or transition curve) and its length is termed as the super elevation run off or length of run off (L_R). This length is determined based on the super elevation rate and design speed. Details of how super elevation is attained by rotating the roadway surface about the centre line of a highway with a combined curve are explained below.

From Figure 2.14 it is observed that the super elevation provided is gradually increased to its full value in stages—(i) point T_1 to point P and (ii) point P to junction point A of transition and the circular curves. The full value of super elevation is provided on the circular curve portion from point A to junction point B of the circular and transition curves. Similarly, on the down slope, the full value of super elevation (at B) is decreased to zero from point B to T_2.

Let us consider the combined curve (Figure 2.14) where a circular curve is augmented with similar spiral curves at either ends. A normal camber of C (in per cent) is provided up to the point T_1. The width of the carriageway is termed as W (in metres). The maximum allowable longitudinal slope is G (in per cent).

Relationships required for the super elevation design with reference to Figure 2.14 (b) may be obtained as (From fundamental principles of rectangular hyperbola (Taiganidis and Kanellaidis 1991)),

$$\frac{L_{TR}}{L_R} = \frac{e_{T1}}{\text{full } e} = \frac{Y_{T1}}{Y_A} \qquad (2.9)$$

where e_{T1} and e_A are the values of super elevation (%) having depths Y_{T1} and Y_A at points T_1 and A respectively. For this condition, $e_{T1} = C_n$ (normal camber in %) and e_A = full e (full super elevation in %).

$$\text{Length of super elevation transition } (L_{ST}) = L_{TR} + L_R \qquad (2.10)$$

$$\text{Depth, } Y_{T1} = Y_P = Y_Q = \frac{W}{2} \times \frac{C_n(\%)}{100} \qquad (2.11)$$

$$\text{Depth, } Y_A = \frac{W}{2} \times \frac{\text{full } e(\%)}{100} \qquad (2.12)$$

At any horizontal distance x units from the point P, the super elevated depth Y_x can be determined based on the principle of similar triangles by considering the triangle PAA_0.

$$\frac{Y_x}{Y_A} = \frac{x}{L_R} \qquad (2.13)$$

The depth values between points T_1 and P may be determined in a similar fashion.

2.6.6 Rate of Change of Super Elevation

While attaining super elevation, there should be no abrupt change in the longitudinal gradient of the curve. Abrupt changes create inconvenience to passengers. It may also cause slow moving vehicles to slide and the inner side tyres of the vehicles to undergo greater wear than the tyres on the outer side. Sufficient curve length, especially in the case of the transition curves, should be maintained in order to keep the desired gradient along the curves. According to the IRC, the rate of change of super elevation should not be more than 1 in 150 ($\approx 0.67\%$) for plain and rolling terrain ($G_{P\&R}$) and 1 in 60 ($\approx 1.67\%$) for hilly or mountainous terrain ($G_{H\&M}$). The above criteria may be checked by equations (2.14 a and b) and (2.15 a and b). If these conditions are not satisfied, the lengths of run off or/ and tangent run out should be suitable increased.

$$\left(\frac{100}{L_R} \times Y_A\right) \leq G_{P\&R}\% \tag{2.14a}$$

$$\left(\frac{100}{L_{TR}} \times Y_{T1}\right) \leq G_{P\&R}\% \tag{2.14b}$$

$$\left(\frac{100}{L_R} \times Y_A\right) \leq G_{H\&M}\% \tag{2.15a}$$

$$\left(\frac{100}{L_{TR}} \times Y_{T1}\right) \leq G_{H\&M}\% \tag{2.15b}$$

where $G_{P\&R}$ and $G_{H\&M}$ are longitudinal grades in plain and rolling, hilly and mountaneous terrains respectively.

According to normal practice, the length of the transition curve is provided longer than the length of the run off. However, the length of the super elevation transition (L_{ST}) should be long enough to make the pavement rotation from the normal crown to the full super elevated rate imperceptible to drivers (Medina and Tarko 2007).

Where no transition curve is provided, the super elevation (e) should be attained gradually over a length—2/3rd the value of super elevation should be attained on a straight section before the beginning of the circular curve and the remaining 1/3rd value of super elevation should be attained on the curve (AASHTO and IRC:52-2001). For better speed operating conditions near circular curves, 70 to 90% of the run off length should be placed over the tangent length (AASHTO 2004). To find out super elevation designs for multi-lane divided highways, readers may refer to AASHTO recommendations.

Q: *Determine the minimum length of the tangent run out, when camber* = 2%, *rate of design super elevation* = 7% *and length of spiral* = 90 m.

A: From equation (2.9), let us assume

length of spiral = length of super elevation run off (L_R)

$$\frac{L_{TR}}{90\,\text{m}} = \frac{2\%}{7\%}; \quad \therefore L_{TR} = 25.7\,\text{m}$$

Q: *Determine the values of super elevation at salient locations along a combined curve with reference to Figure 2.14(a) and check for maximum allowable longitudinal gradient acording to the IRC guidelines.*

The pavement consists of an undivided dual lane in rolling terrain and has a width of 7.0 m. The other conditions are the same as given in the above problem.

A: From the above problem, we get, $C = 2\%$; full $e = 7\%$; $L_R = 90$ m and $L_{TR} = 25.7$ m. Assume that full super elevation should be provided throughout the length of the circular curve. The notations followed will be as given in Figure 2.14 (a) and (b). From equation (2.10),

$$\text{Length of super elevation transition } (L_{ST}) = 25.7 + 90 = 115.7 \text{ m}$$

$$\text{Depth, } Y_{T1} = Y_P = Y_Q = \frac{7.0}{2} \times \frac{2\%}{100} = 0.07 \text{ m} = 7 \text{ cm}$$

From equation (2.12),

$$\text{Depth, } Y_A = \frac{7.0}{2} \times 0.245 \text{ m} = 24.5 \text{ cm}$$

As an example, let us take a point at a horizontal distance of 50 m from the point P. The depth $Y_{@50m}$ can be determined by equation (2.13).

$$\frac{Y_{@50m}}{0.245 \text{ m}} = \frac{50 \text{ m}}{90 \text{ m}}; Y_{@50m} = 0.136 \text{ m} = 13.6 \text{ cm}$$

Similarly, other depths at required intervals may be determined. Check for maximum allowable longitudinal gradient limit: As the highway is in rolling terrain, the value of $G_{P\&R} \approx 0.67\%$. From equations (2.14 a and b),

$$\left(\frac{100}{90 \text{ m}} \times 0.245 \text{ m}\right) \leq G_{P\&R}; \quad 0.272\% \leq G_{P\&R}; \text{ or}$$

$$\left(\frac{100}{25.7 \text{m}} \times 0.07 \text{ m}\right) \leq G_{P\&R}; \quad 0.272 \leq G_{P\&R};$$

For the given conditions, the calculated longitudinal gradient value is less than the maximum allowable limit. Hence, the design is safe.

2.7 Widening of Carriageway on Curves

There are many reasons why carriageways are widened on curves.

1. When a four-wheeled vehicle turns along a horizontal curve, the rear wheels do not pass exactly over the same path as traced by the front wheels because the rigid-based axle assembly of the rear wheels tracks along the inner side of the curve. Therefore, extra width of carriageway is required on curves to accommodate this deviated path of the rear wheels.

2. As a safe margin on curves, drivers try to keep an offset distance on both sides of the vehicles. This extra space is maintained while travelling on curves—the extent of the extra space depends on the driver's psychological characteristics.

Let us consider the right angled triangle ABC in Figure 2.15. Interior angle at B is 90°.

$d \approx$ BC = wheel base length (m)

R_{out} = AC = radius of path traced by the outer front wheel (m)

R_{in} = AB = radius of path traced by the outer rear wheel (m)

$X_m = R_{out} - R_{in}$ = mechanical widening of carriageway (m)

R_c = radius of the curve with respect to the centre line of the carriageway or mean radius of the curve (m)

From triangle ABC,

$$AB^2 = AC^2 - BC^2$$

$$R_{in}^2 = R_{out}^2 - d^2$$

$$(R_{out} - X_m)^2 = R_{out}^2 - d^2$$

If $R_{out} = R_{in} = R_c$, and we simplify the above equation, X_m = mechanical widening = $0.5d^2 / R_c$ (approximately).

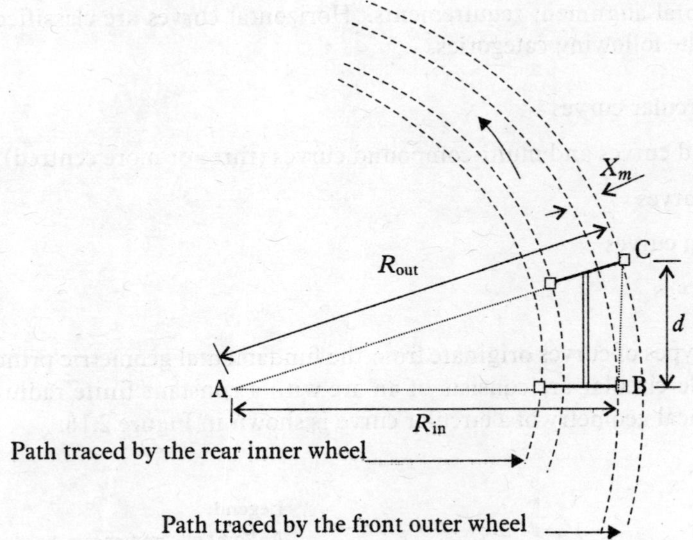

Figure 2.15 *Widening of carriageway on curves*

If the number of traffic lanes is n, the above equation can be rewritten as

$$X_m = 0.5nd^2 / R_c \tag{2.16}$$

In addition to the mechanical widening of curves, it is practical to increase the value of widening to allow margin space during steering and overtaking operations. This extra widening of carriageway on curves is termed as psychological widening (X_p). Based on field studies and experience, IRC has suggested the following formula for determination of X_p.

$$X_p = 0.36v / \sqrt{R} \tag{2.17}$$

where v = design speed in m/s.

Total widening, X_e (in meters) = Mechanical widening (X_m) + Psychological widening (X_p)

$$X_e = 0.5nd^2/R_c + 0.36v/\sqrt{R_c} \tag{2.18}$$

According to the IRC: 73 guidelines, extra widening of curves is not required if the curve of the radius is longer than 60 m and 300 m for single and double lane carriageways, respectively. In case of hill roads with curves having sharp radius, additional extra width may be provided along the inner side of the curve. The extra width should be equally provided on both sides of the carriageway. The full width of extra widening is attained gradually; starting from zero at the beginning of the curve and reaching its full value in the middle of the curve—from there it is gradually reduced to zero at the end of the curve.

2.8 Horizontal Curves

Horizontal curves are used to divert highway alignments from the straight route to any other path. The length and type of curve will be decided depending upon the location of the site and the horizontal alignment requirements. Horizontal curves are classified based on their geometry into the following categories.

1. Simple circular curves
2. Compound curves and multi-compound curves (three or more centred)
3. Reverse curves
4. Transition curves
5. Mixed curves

The first three types of curves originate from the fundamental geometric principles of circular arcs. The simple circular arc consists of an arc with a constant finite radius throughout its length. The typical geometry of a circular curve is shown in Figure 2.16.

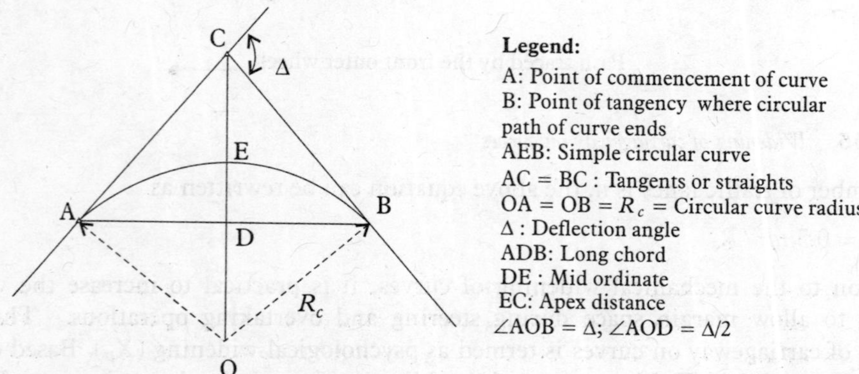

Figure 2.16 *Elements of a simple circular curve*

Well-known standard relationships for determination of various geometric elements of circular curves are given below.

$$\text{Tangent length} = AC = BC = R_c \tan\left(\frac{\Delta}{2}\right) \tag{2.19}$$

$$\text{Length of long chord} = ABD = 2R_c \sin\left(\frac{\Delta}{2}\right) \tag{2.20}$$

$$\text{Mid-ordinate} = DE = R_c\left(1 - \cos\left(\frac{\Delta}{2}\right)\right) \tag{2.21}$$

$$\text{Apex distance} = CE = R_c\left(\sec\left(\frac{\Delta}{2}\right) - 1\right) \tag{2.22}$$

$$\text{Length of circular curve} = AEB = \frac{\pi R_c \Delta}{180^\circ} \tag{2.23}$$

Circular curves are generally adopted for slow moving traffic whereas compound curves are used where deviation of alignment is inevitable.

A compound curve consists of a combination of two or more circular arcs having different radii, joined together in the same direction. Their curve centres fall in same side of the curves. In case of reverse curve, the circular arcs of different (or same) radii are connected with their centres lying in opposite directions (Figure 2.17 (d)).

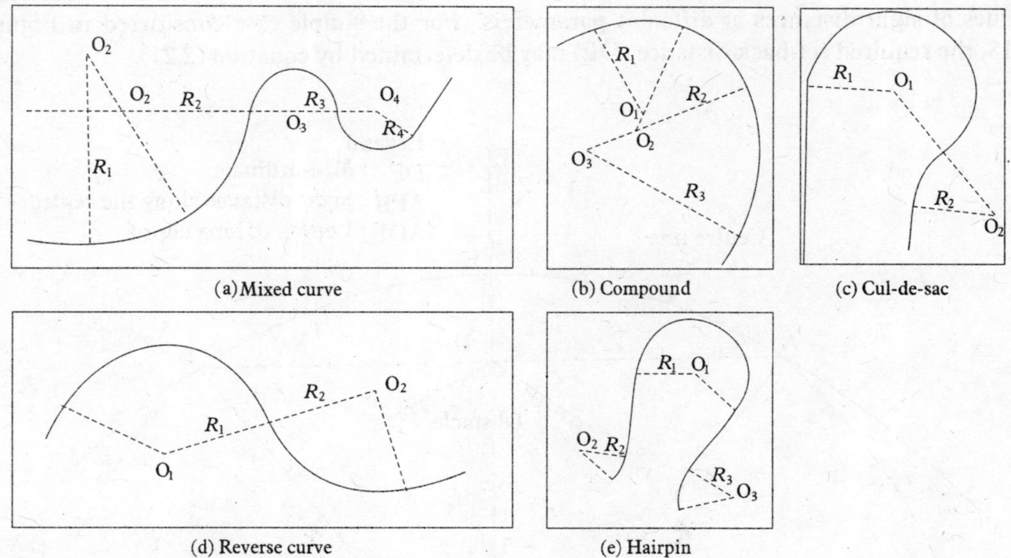

Figure 2.17 *Typical horizontal curve alignments*

Use of reverse curves in highway alignment is favourable for alignment of mainline or freeway interchange ramps where there is minimal need for acquiring land (Dabbour et al. 2004). In case of sharp curves, sudden change of direction results in arduous steering where available sight distance is also insufficient. To satisfy the demand for high driving speeds and automatic drives, transition spiral curves are used in alignment of high-speed highways such as national highways and expressways.

2.8.1 Sight Distance on Horizontal Curves

When a vehicle is travelling on a horizontal curve, the driver's eye sight is limited by obstructions, such as a building or any immovable structure, which are situated inside of the curve. Therefore, for horizontal curves, as a safe geometric design criterion, the sight distance provided along the curve should always be longer than the actual distance required for stopping a vehicle or performing a further action. The sight distance availability is governed by the following parameters (Easa 1993).

- Geometric features of the horizontal curve such as R_c, Δ etc.
- Location of the obstacle causing vision obstruction
- Location of the driver with respect to the obstacle and an approaching object considered on the curve.

The sight distance also depends on the design speed, characteristics of the vehicle, the driver and complexity of the location (AASHTO).

When an obstacle is located at the mid-point of the long chord of a circular curve on a single-lane carriageway, clear visibility in the lateral direction is obtained by providing a set-back distance (DE) between the centre line of the carriageway and the point of obstruction (Figure 2.18). The IRC: 52-2001 has recommended different setback distances for different values of sight distances at different parameters. For the simple case considered in Figure 2.18, the required set-back distance (DE) may be determined by equation (2.21).

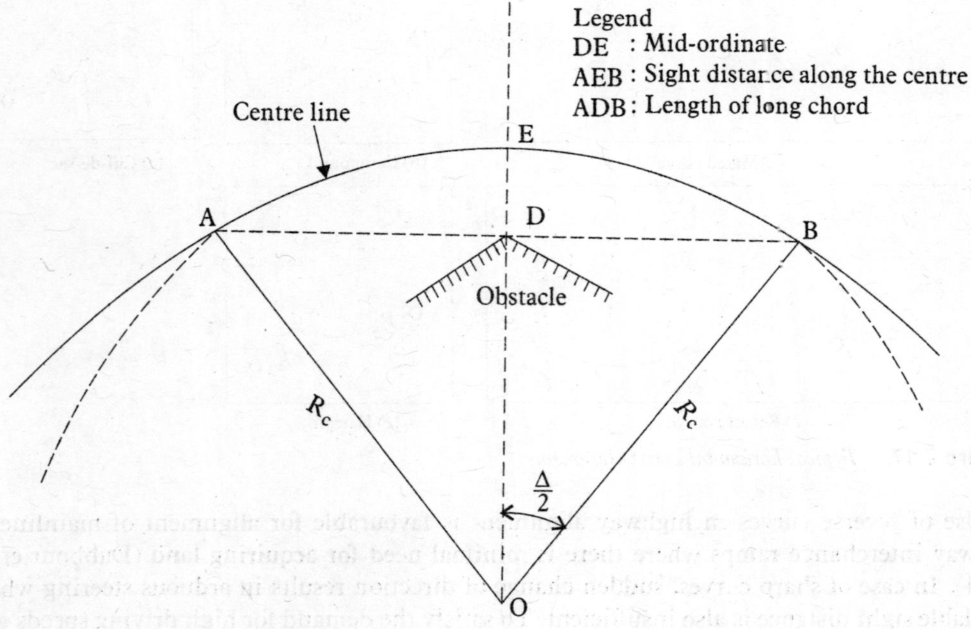

Figure 2.18 *Sight distance along a circular curve*

The available sight distance along circular curves for different locations of obstacles may be evaluated according to the AASHTO geometric design guidelines. Available and minimum sight distances on circular curves may also be obtained by exact solutions (Easa 1991). Sight distances at intersections which are controlled by a stop sign may be determined by using Design Aids—software which help to design and evaluate transportation systems (Easa 2004).

Minimum sight distances on compound horizontal curves having different radii and for obstacles at different positions may be determined using relationships and design tables available in literature (Easa 1993). In extreme cases, it is preferable to change the alignment, so as to avoid obstructions altogether. A few examples of compound curves are presented in Appendix A.

Q: *Determine the required set-back distance when a 2-lane wide carriageway road has a curve radius of 550 m along its centre line and minimum stopping sight distance of 180 m.*

A: With reference to Figure 2.18, the given values are interpreted as follows: $R_c = 550$ m; Sight distance, $S =$ Curve length (AEB) $= 180$ m; EB $= R_c \times \Delta/2$

Therefore,

$$\Delta/2 = \text{EB} / R_c = 90/550 = 0.1636 \text{ radians} \times (180°/\pi) = 9.373°$$

From equation (2.21), the required set-back distance from the centre line of the road

$$= \text{DE} = 550(1 - \cos(9.373)) = 7.34 \text{ m}$$

Otherwise, the following equation may be used to calculate the set-back distance from the centre line of the road.

$$\text{DE} = R_c\left(1 - \cos\left(\frac{28.647 \times S}{R_c}\right)\right) = 550\left(1 - \cos\left(\frac{28.647 \times 180}{550}\right)\right) = 7.34 \text{ m}$$

2.8.2 Transition Curve

A transition curve is inserted between diverse alignments of highways to ease the change in centripetal acceleration experienced by drivers traveling along the curve. The transition curve may be in different forms of a mathematical curve, viz. clothoid, cubic parabola, spiral or lemniscate. As an example, a transition curve inserted between the tangent point of a straight alignment and a circular curve is shown in Figure 2.19. The radius of the transition curve decreases at a uniform rate from an infinite value at the tangent point to a finite value at the junction between the transition and circular curves. At this junction point, the radius of the transition and circular curves are equal. Transition curves are used to align the centre line of highways by assuming the following conditions (Despotopoulos 1947).

1. The essential property of changing the curvature or radius of the transition curve at a uniform rate facilitates comfortable driving at a constant linear velocity (v) within the transition.

2. While traversing on a transition curve, the steering wheels and consequently the front wheels of the vehicle turn at a constant angular velocity (ω).

By considering points A and B on the transition curve (Figure 2.19), the following conditions holds good (Despotopoulos 1947).

$$R_1 \times \omega \times t_1 = R_2 \times \omega \times t_2 = \text{Constant} \tag{2.24a}$$

$$\text{and } R_1 \times \frac{L_1}{v} = R_2 \times \frac{L_2}{v} = \text{Constant} \tag{2.24b}$$

where R_1 and R_2 are the radii of curvature at points A and B respectively. L_1 and L_2 are the lengths from the beginning of the transition curve corresponding to times t_1 and t_2. However, the above relationships do not satisfy the given condition at the beginning point (or tangent point) of the transition curve.

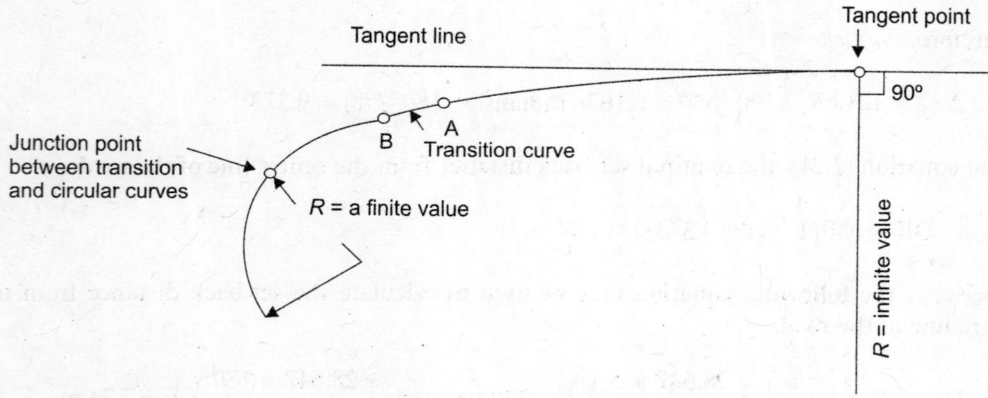

Figure 2.19 *A typical combined curve*

Transition curves with spirals are preferred in highways alignments due to the following reasons (Craus and Polus 1977; Lipičnik, 1998).

- Super-elevation on the curved path can be increased at a uniform rate which is the same as the rate of decrease of radius of the transition curve.
- They help to avoid the sudden impact of the centrifugal force by providing smooth change consistent with the vehicles path.
- Centrifugal force is reciprocal to the change in alignment curvature. When the speed of vehicles is assumed as constant, non-uniform change in the magnitude of the side pressure takes place due to abrupt changes in curvature. The differential side pressure (or thrust) causes detrimental effects on the surface of the road as well as the vehicle performance. In such alignment locations, transition curves should be inserted suitably.
- They facilitate gradual change in turning angle of steering wheels.
- They provide safe and comfortable travel on the curve even at high speeds.

Following are the possible (or favourable) cases where transition curves can be inserted in alignment of highways (Lipičnik 1998):

- Between two straight parts of an alignment.
- Between circular curves aligned in the same and apposite directions having the same or different radii.
- Between the alignment of a straight part and a circular curve.

2.8.3 Length of Transition Curve

There are two important considerations which are needed to calculate the required length of a transition curve—the rate of change of radial acceleration and the rate of change of super elevation. Based upon these, the length of the transition curve can be calculated by these two methods and the longer length of transition curve is recommended.

Method 1: By Maximum Allowable Rate of Change of Radial Acceleration

Assume that the design speed and the rate of increase of centripetal acceleration are constant (Greenstein 1976). Let the maximum radial acceleration at the end of the transition curve (i.e., at the beginning point of the circular curve) be equal to v^2/R_c, where v is the velocity of the vehicle in m/s. The radial acceleration will be zero at the tangent point when R value becomes infinite.

Time taken to travel on a length of transition curve $= t = L_t/v$

Rate of change of radial acceleration (A_R) = radial acceleration/time taken to travel the distance

$$A_R = (v^2/R_c)/(L_t/v)$$

Therefore,

$$L_t \geq v^3/(R_c \times A_R) \tag{2.25}$$

For design purposes, the value of the maximum permissible rate of radial acceleration (A_R) that does not impart any kind of jerk or discomfort during travelling on the transition curve is selected. The value of A_R depends on the speed of the vehicle tracing the transition curve. It can be taken as a maximum of 0.8 m/s^3 and a minimum of 0.5 m/s^3 (IRC: 73). The permissible value of A_R may be calculated by using the formula given below.

$$A_R = 80/(75+3.6v) \tag{2.26}$$

Method 2: By Maximum Allowable Rate of Change of Super Elevation

To determine the minimum required length of the transition curve (L_t) according to the guidelines of IRC: 73 and as discussed in Section 2.6.6, the following relationships may be used.

$$L_t \geq \left(\frac{100}{G_{P\&R}\%} \times Y_A\right) \tag{2.27}$$

$$L_t \geq \left(\frac{100}{G_{H\&M}\%} \times Y_A\right) \tag{2.28}$$

The above notations carry the same meaning as explained before in Section 2.6.6. The relations hold good when the super elevation is attained by rotating the surface of the pavement about its centre line.

Q: *A horizontal curve of 270 m radius is to be designed for 65 kmph speed. The road is a two-lane road (7 m) and the super elevation is provided by rotating the pavement surface about its crown. The rate of introduction of super elevation is 1 in 150. If the maximum wheel base length is 6 m, calculate the required minimum length of the transition curve.*

A: Design speed, $v = 65$ kmph $= 65 \times 0.278 = 18.07$ m/s

CRITERION 1: By rate of change of acceleration (equations (2.25) and (2.26)),

$$A_R = \frac{80}{75 + 3.6v} = \frac{80}{(75 + 3.6 \times 18.07)} = 0.571$$

Take, $A_R = 0.571$ $\quad (\because A_{R_{\min}} = 0.5$ and $A_{R_{\max}} = 0.8)$

$$L_t = \frac{(18.07)^3}{0.571 \times 270} = 38.27 \text{ m}$$

Therefore, take $L_t = 39$ m.

CRITERION 2: Based on the rate of change of super elevation, by equation (2.5),

$$\text{Super elevation, } e = \frac{(0.75v)^2}{gR_c} = \frac{(0.75 \times 18.07)^2}{9.81 \times 270} = 0.0693 \text{ m} < e_{\max} = 0.07 \text{ m}$$

$\therefore$ Provide full $e = 6.93\%$

Widening of carriageway on curve: From equation (2.18),

$$X_e = \frac{0.5 \times 2 \times 6^2}{270} + \frac{0.36 \times 18.05}{\sqrt{270}} = 0.133 + 0.395 = 0.528 \text{ m}$$

Now, the width of carriageway, $W = W + X_e = 7.0 + 0.528 = 7.528$ m

From equation (2.12),

$$\text{Depth, } Y_A = \frac{W}{2} \times \frac{\text{full } e(\%)}{100} = \frac{7.528}{2} \times \frac{6.93\%}{100} = 0.260 \text{ m}$$

From equation (2.27),

$$L_t \geq \left(\frac{100}{G_{P\&R}\%} \times Y_A\right)$$

$$G_{P\&R}\% = \frac{1}{150} \times 100 = 0.67\% \qquad \text{(given)}$$

$$= \left(\frac{100}{0.67\%} \times 0.260\right) = 38.8 \text{ m}$$

$$L_t \geq 39 \text{ m}$$

Therefore, provide final length of transition curve (L_t) = 40 m

NOTE: Always select the higher value from the above criteria.

2.8.4 Elements of the Transition Curve

Generally, a spiral curve is the ideal transition curve because its radius of curvature changes inversely as the curve length increases from the tangent point. Figure 2.20 presents the basic elements of a combined curve having a circular curve adjoined by transition curves on its either end.

Let,

L_t	=	Length of transition curve
L_c	=	Length of circular curve
P and P'	=	Tangent points of transition curves
C and C'	=	Junction points of transition and circular curves
R_c	=	Radius of the circular curve and radius of the transition curve at points C and C'
X_Q and X_T	=	Distance along tangent from point P
Y_c	=	Perpendicular ordinate from point T to point C
α	=	Spiral angle with the line PI by a tangent drawn at C
θ	=	Angle subtended by circular arc with radius R_c
r	=	Radius of transition curve at a given point
l_t	=	Any curved length of transition curve measured from origin P, having radius r.

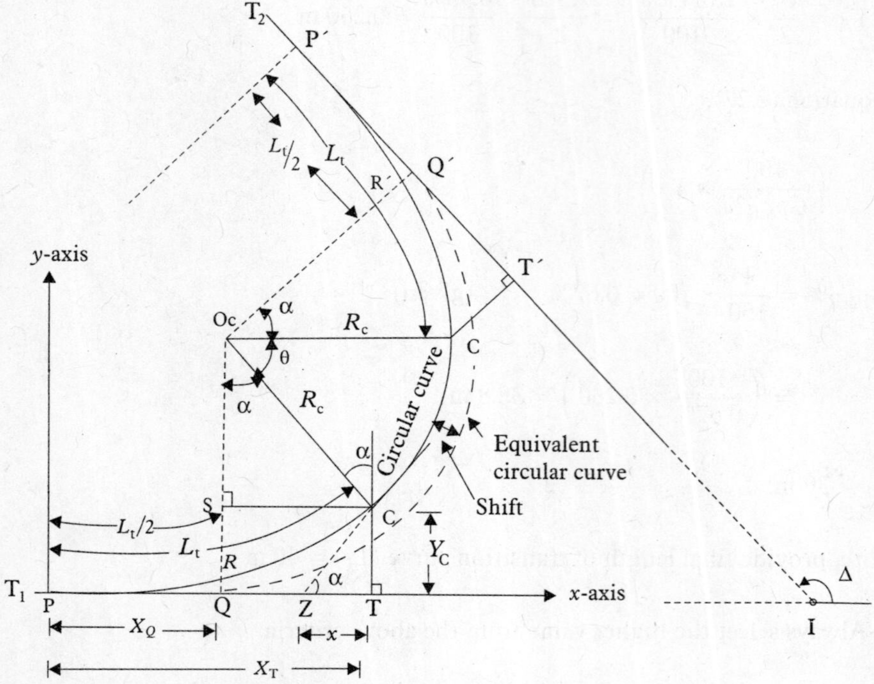

Figure 2.20 *Elements of a horizontal combined curve having transition and circular curves (elaborated based on Roy 1992)*

From the fundamental principle of a clothoid spiral,

$$r \propto \frac{1}{l_t}$$

$$r \times l_t = R_c \times L_t = C, \text{where } C \text{ is a constant.} \tag{2.29}$$

Rectangular coordinates of transition curve at l_t measured from origin P may be written mathematically as (Figure 2.20),

$$X = l_t - \frac{l_t^5}{40C^2} + \frac{l_t^9}{3465C^4} - \frac{l_t^{13}}{599040C^6} + \ldots \tag{2.30}$$

$$Y = \frac{l_t^3}{6C} - \frac{l_t^7}{336C^3} + \frac{l_t^{11}}{42240C^5} - \frac{l_t^{15}}{9676800C^7} + \ldots \tag{2.31}$$

Using the above coordinates, various elements of transition curves as given in Figure 2.20 may be determined approximately from the following relationships.

$$X_T = L_t - \frac{L_t^3}{40R_c^2} \tag{2.32}$$

$$X_Q = \frac{L_t}{2} - \frac{L_t^3}{1280R_c^2} \tag{2.33}$$

$$Y_C = \frac{L_t^2}{6R_c} - \frac{L_t^4}{336R_c^3} \tag{2.34}$$

where, X_T and X_Q are the distances measured along the tangent line from the origin P to points T and Q respectively and Y_c is the perpendicular distance between the tangent lines from points T and point C.

The other parameters of the transition circular curve may be determined based upon the concept of equivalent circular curves as given below (Roy 1992).

From triangle SCO_c: (refer to Figure 2.20),

$$\alpha = \sin^{-1}\left(\frac{SC}{CO_c}\right) = \sin^{-1}\left(\frac{QT}{R_c}\right)$$

$$\alpha = \sin^{-1}\left(\frac{X_T - X_Q}{R_c}\right) \tag{2.35}$$

The distance, $QC_c = QS + SO_c = Y_c + R_c \cos(\alpha)$ (2.36)

$\therefore$ Shift $= QO_c - R_c$ (2.37)

From triangle ZTC,
Distance, $ZT = x = Y_c \cot(\alpha)$ (2.38)
Tangent distance, $ZC = Y_c \operatorname{cosec}(\alpha)$ (2.39)

$$L_c = \frac{\pi R_c \theta}{180^\circ} \tag{2.40}$$

Total length of combined curve $= 2 \times L_t + L_c$ (2.41)
Total length of tangent, PI = PQ + QI

$$PI = X_Q + (QO_c) \times \tan\left(\frac{\Delta}{2}\right) \tag{2.42}$$

where $\Delta = 2\alpha + \theta$ (2.43)

The design of highway transition curves can also be carried out by using different methods based on the unit curve concept (Rao 1995) and by other methods (García and Conesa 1997; Lipičnik 1998).

The design of two and three centred compound curves, with and without transition spirals at points of change of curvature, can be found in literature (AASHTO and Roy 1994).

A generalised solution to determine various elements of hairpin alignments having transition curves is also available (García and Conesa 1992).

Q. *Determine the required length of the transition curve and calculate the salient elements of a combined curve consisting of a circular curve joined with a transition curve to its either end. The required curve design inputs are as follows.*

Road class = National Highway
Design speed = 50 kmph
Terrain and climate = Snow bound mountainous terrain
Road type = Undivided two lanes, 7.0 m wide
Radius of the horizontal curve (R_c) = 160 m
Angle of deflection between two tangents of the proposed combined curve (Δ) = 64°
Chainage at the point of intersection (I) = 500.00 m
Permissible rate of change of super elevation = 1 in 60 ($G_{H\&M} \approx 1.67$ %)

The super elevation is attained by the rotation of the pavement surface about its centre line. Take the maximum permissible super elevation as 7 per cent .

A: This problem is solved in two parts. The first part consists of calculating the length of the transition curve using two criteria. In the second part, elements of the combined curve are determined. The notations used here are with reference to Figure 2.20.

Design speed = 50 kmph = 50 × 0.278 = 13.9 m/s

PART I:

CRITERIA 1: By rate of change of radial acceleration and equatins (2.25) and (2.26),

$$A_R = \frac{80}{75 + 3.6v} = \frac{80}{75 + 3.6 \times 13.9} = 0.639$$

Take $A_R = 0.639$, $\quad (\because A_{R_{\min}} = 0.5 \text{ and } A_{R_{\max}} = 0.8)$

$$L_t = \frac{13.9^3}{0.639 \times 160} = \frac{2685.619}{102.24} = 26.27 \text{ m}$$

Therefore, take $L_t = 27$ m.

CRITERION 2: Based on the rate of change of super elevation by equation (2.5),

$$\text{Super elevation, } e = \frac{(0.75v)^2}{gR_c} = \frac{(0.75 \times 13.9)^2}{9.81 \times 160} = 0.0692 \text{ m} < e_{\max} = 0.07 \text{ m}$$

$\therefore$ Provide full $e = 6.92\%$

Widening of carriageway on curve: From equation (2.18),

$$X_T = \frac{0.5 \times 2 \times 6^2}{160} + \frac{0.36 \times 13.9}{\sqrt{160}} = 0.225 + 0.395 = 0.62 \text{ m}$$

Now, the width of the carriageway, $W = W + X_T = 7.0 + 0.62 = 7.62$ m

From equation (2.12),

$$\text{Depth, } Y_A = \frac{W}{2} \times \frac{\text{full } e(\%)}{100} = \frac{7.62}{2} \times \frac{6.92\%}{100} = 0.263 \text{ m}$$

From equation (2.23), $L_t \geq \left(\dfrac{100}{G_{H\&M\%}} \times Y_A \right)$

$$G_{P\&R}\% = \frac{1}{60} \times 100 = 1.67\% \qquad \text{(given)}$$

$$L_t \geq \left(\frac{100}{1.67\%} \times 0.263 \right) = 15.7 \text{ m}; \qquad \therefore L_t \geq 15.7 \text{ m}$$

NOTE: Select the higher value from the above criteria.
Therefore, provide final length of transition curve $(L_t) = 27$ m

PART II:

Various geometric elements of the combined curve consisting of a circular curve joined with transition curves on either end are determined below. The notations used here are the same as those used in Figure 2.20.

From equation (2.33),

$$X_Q = \frac{L_t}{2} - \frac{L_t^3}{1280\, R_c^2} = X_Q = \frac{27}{2} - \frac{27^3}{1280 \times 27^2} = 13.4994 \text{ m}$$

From equation (2.32),

$$X_T = 27 - \frac{27^3}{40 \times 160^2} = 26.9808 \text{ m}$$

From equation (2.34),

$$Y_c = \frac{L_t^2}{6\, R_c} - \frac{L_t^4}{336\, R_c^3} = \frac{27^2}{6 \times 160} - \frac{27^4}{336 \times 160^3} = 0.75899 \text{ m}$$

From equation (2.35),

$$\alpha = \sin^{-1}\left(\frac{X_T - X_Q}{R_c} \right) = \sin^{-1}\left(\frac{26.9808 - 13.4994}{160} \right) = 4.8334°$$

From equation (2.36),

Distance, $QC_c = QS + SO_c = 0.75899 + 160\cos(4.8334°) = 160.1900$ m

From equation (2.7),

$$\text{Shift} = QC_c - R_c = 160.1900 - 160 = 0.1900 \text{ m}$$

From equation (2.42), tangent length of combined curve (PI),

$$= X_Q + (QO_c) \times \tan\left(\frac{\Delta}{2}\right) = 13.4994 + (160.1900)\tan\left(\frac{64°}{2}\right) = 113.5972 \text{ m}$$

From equation (2.43),

$$\theta = \Delta - 2\alpha = 64° - 2 \times 4.833° = 54.3332°$$

From equation (2.40),

$$\text{Length of circular curve} = L_c = \frac{\pi R_c \theta}{180°} = \frac{\pi \times 160 \times 54.3332°}{180°} = 151.7269 \text{ m}$$

From equation (2.41),

$$\text{Length of combined curve} = 2 \times L_t + L_c = 2 \times 27 + 151.7269 = 205.7269 \text{ m}$$

Chainage at salient points on the combined curve:

Chainage at point I = 500.00 m (given)

Chainage at point P = Chainage at I − PI = 500.00 − 113.5972 = 386.4028 m

Chainage at junction point (C), at the end of the transition curve and beginning of the circular curve = Chainage at P $+L_t$

$$= 386.4028 + 27 = 413.4028 \text{ m}$$

Chainage at junction point (C'), at the end point of the circular curve and beginning of the second transition curve = Chainage at $C' + L_c$

$$= 413.4028 + 151.7269 = 565.1297 \text{ m}$$

Chainage at point, P′ = Chainage at $C' + L_t = 565.1297 + 27 = 592.1297$ m

2.9 Longitudinal Gradient

Generally, the natural ground consists of undulations or uneven surfaces. To make a levelled surface, it becomes necessary to fill or cut the uneven ground surface according to the existing ground profile. Depending on the type of terrain, the magnitude of ground rise or fall is observed. This rate of rise or fall of ground along its length is termed as longitudinal slope or gradient or grade. Profiles of natural ground and desired pavement surfaces are shown in Figure 2.21.

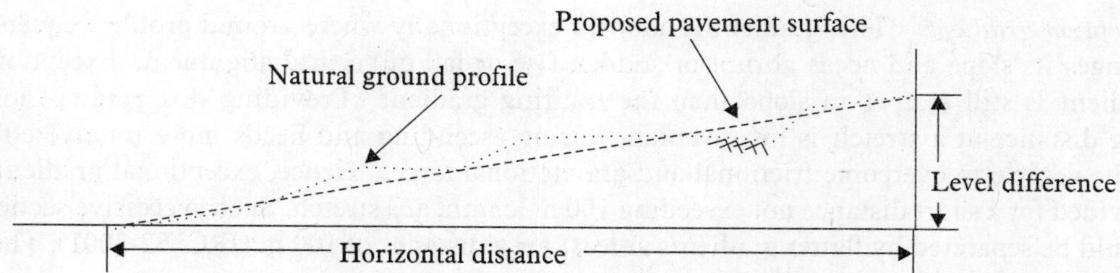

Figure 2.21 *Longitudinal gradient*

The gradient can be expressed to the following forms,

1. In percentage: $\text{Grade (\%)} = \dfrac{\text{Level difference}}{\text{Horizontal distance}} \times 100$
2. 1 in N : 1 vertical to N horizontal distance
3. Vertical: Horizontal

Factors affecting gradient selection:

- Existing ground profile and surrounding floor levels of developed areas especially with reference to surface and sub-surface drainage
- Levels of control, mandatory and obligatory points along the desired alignment
- Type and importance of highway
- Design speed and type of vehicles anticipated, i.e., bullock cart or motor vehicles
- Operating cost of vehicles and energy savings
- Cost of construction and practical problems with surrounding locality
- Excessive excavation and high embankments
- Natural sub-soil, water table and artesian conditions.
- Earth quake conditions

Types of gradients: The different types of gradients are ruling gradient, limiting gradient, exceptional gradient and minimum gradient. Values of the gradients based upon the terrain type are presented in Table 2.11 (according to the recommendation given by IRC).

Ruling gradient It is the maximum allowable grade or longitudinal slope considered during alignment of a highway in the vertical plane. This gradient is also termed as the design gradient. The magnitude of the ruling gradient depends on the type of terrain, design speed, curves and altitude.

Limiting gradient This gradient is slightly steeper than the ruling gradient. Limiting gradient is provided when the natural ground profile is slightly steeper than the ruling gradient. It is necessary to adopt such a steeper gradient, to keep the earth work operation minimum. The limiting gradient is generally adopted to connect plain and rolling terrains or to reach hilly areas.

Exception gradient This gradient is adopted exceptionally where ground profile frequently changes its slope and needs abrupt or sudden rise or fall of vertical alignment. Exceptional gradient is still steeper in slope than the limiting gradient. Providing this gradient for a long distance at a stretch is inconvenient during ascending and needs more tractive effort of the vehicle to overcome frictional and gravitational forces. Hence, exceptional gradient is provided for a short distance not exceeding 100 m length, at a stretch. Such successive sections should be separated by flatter gradients at least for a distance of 100 m (IRC: 52-2001). These gradients are used in steep hilly areas.

Minimum gradient To drain off surface or rain water in side drains it is necessary to provide a certain amount of longitudinal slope. A minimum amount of gradient is provided based on surface characteristics of drains, intensity of rainfall, soil type, type of terrain and existing average floor level of the developed area. A minimum gradient of 0.5% and 1.0% is provided for lined and unlined side drains respectively (IRC: 73-1980).

Table 2.11 *Road gradients (IRC:66-1976)*

Sl. No.	Type of terrain		Longitudinal gradient, G (%)		
			Ruling	Limiting	Exceptional
1	Plain and rolling		3.3	5.0	6.7
2	Mountainous and steep	Up to 3000 m of elevation above MSL	5.0	6.0	7.0
		More than 3000 m of elevation above MSL	6.0	7.0	8.0

2.10 Compensation of Grade on Horizontal Curves

To facilitate easy driving on horizontal curves in hilly areas, a certain amount of grade is deducted from the design gradient value. Gradients steeper than 4% should be eased. The grade compensation value is determined using the following formula (IRC: 73-1980).

$$\text{Grade compensation} = (30 + R_c)/R_c \tag{2.44}$$

$$\text{The maximum allowable value of grade compensation} = 75/R_c \tag{2.45}$$

The method of determination of grade compensation is explained below.

Q: *A ruling gradient of 1 in 18 is to be provided for a hill road having a horizontal curve radius of 70 m. Determine the value of grade compensation.*

A: Design gradient $= (1/18) \times 100 = 5.55\%$ (given)

Radius of horizontal curve, $R_c = 70$ m (given)

From equation (2.44),

$$\text{grade compensation} = (30 + R_c)/R_c = (30 + 70)/70 = 1.428\%$$

From equation (2.45),

$$\text{maximum allowable grade compensation} = 75/R_c = 75/70 = 1.071\%$$

Now, select the least value from the above.

Grade compensation value = 1.07%. Therefore, net grade = 5.55 − 1.071 = 4.479%

2.11 Vertical Curves

Proper design of vertical alignment of highways is important to ensure adequate sight distance and to provide uniform change in grade. This will facilitate safe, smooth and comfortable ride over the road. Circular and parabolic curves are used in vertical alignment of highways. However, parabolic curves are preferred as the rate of change of slope along its length is constant and the sight distance available is more than that available for a circular curve having equal length (Figure 2.22). Calculation of reduced levels along the parabolic curve is simple and easy to set out. Therefore, vertical axis parabolas are generally used for the design of vertical alignment of highways.

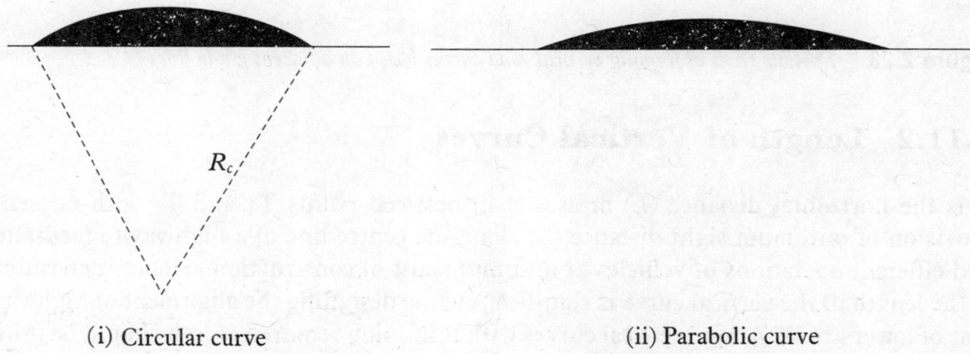

Figure 2.22 *Availability of sight distance on a circular and a parabolic vertical curve*

2.11.1 Types of Vertical Curves

Based on the nature and intensity of steepness of adjacent grade lines, different types of vertical curves are formed (Figure 2.23). They are (i) summit (or crest) curves and (ii) sag (or valley) curves. An intersection point of adjacent grade lines is termed as the vertical point of intersection (I). When the elevation (or reduced level, RL) of the point I is higher than or equal to any point on the vertical curve, such curves are termed as summit curves. When elevation of the point I is lower than or equal to any point on the vertical curve, such curves are termed as sag curves.

The point of curvature (which is at the curve beginning) and the point of tangency (which is at the curve end point) are termed as T_1 and T_2 respectively. The nature of gradient (g%) in terms of positive and negative signs indicate upward and downward slopes of ground respectively. G is the angle of deviation of adjacent grade lines which is equal to the algebraic difference of tangent grades $|g_2 - g_1|$ and its value is expressed in decimal form. The above notations are used in the following paragraphs.

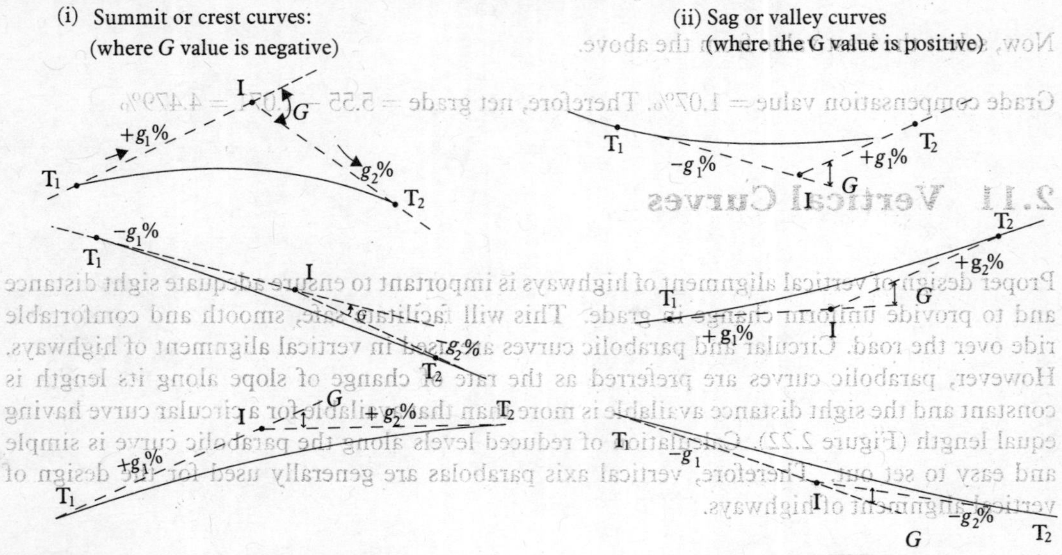

Figure 2.23 *Possible cases of forming vertical road curves based on adjacent grade lines*

2.11.2 Length of Vertical Curves

It is the horizontal distance (L) measured in between points T_1 and T_2 with reference to provision of minimum sight distance (S) along the centre line of a highway to facilitate safe and efficient operations of vehicles at minimum cost of construction. Hence, determination of the length of the vertical curve is significant while designing the alignment of highways. In case of lower grade change, vertical curves with minimum required length should be provided for aesthetic reasons (Table 2.11).

Table 2.11 *Minimum required length of vertical curves (A partial Table 13 of IRC: 52-2001).*

Sl.No.	Design speed (km/h)	Minimum desirable length of vertical curve (m)	Maximum change in grade (G) for which vertical curve is not required
1	≤ 35	15	1.5 %
2	50	20	1.0 %

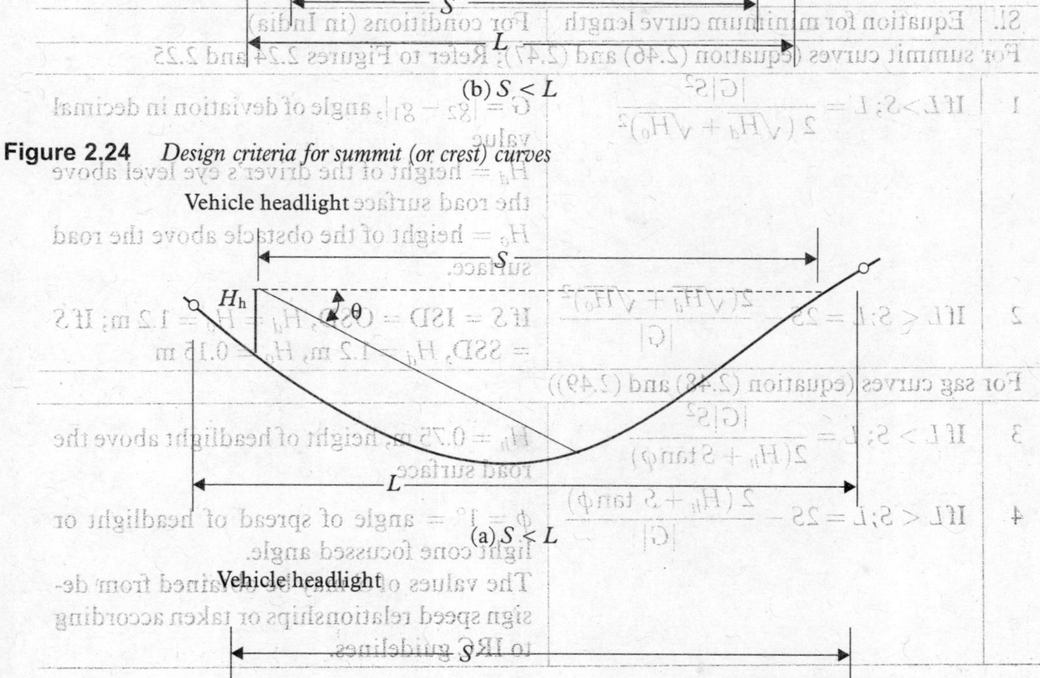

Figure 2.24 *Design criteria for summit (or crest) curves*

Figure 2.25 *Design criteria for sag curves*

Sight distance (S) is a major design parameter used for determining the length of summit (or crest) curves. The main reason is that the driver's visibility (or sight distance) is restricted by the high point of the curve.

For sag curves, during day time there will be no restriction to sight (except during snow fall) but at night, the sight distance is limited and is equal to the length of the spread of light of the vehicle headlights. Therefore, the length of the spread of headlights is considered as a major design parameter for determining the length of sag curves (AASHTO). In other words, length of sight distance depends on the length of the roadway covered by the focussed light from the headlights of a vehicle. The upward angle of the head lamp beam (θ) is taken as 1° and the height of the head lamp above the road surface (H_h) is taken as 0.75 m. These are considered as standard conditions for determining the length of sag curves in India (IRC: SP: 23-1993). The recommended formulae to determine the length of summit and sag curves and the details are given below (IRC: SP: 23-1993).

Sl.	Equation for minimum curve length	For conditions (in India)
For summit curves (equation (2.46) and (2.47); Refer to Figures 2.24 and 2.25		
1	If $L>S$; $L = \dfrac{\lvert G\rvert S^2}{2\,(\sqrt{H_d}+\sqrt{H_o})^2}$	$G = \lvert g_2 - g_1\rvert$, angle of deviation in decimal value H_d = height of the driver's eye level above the road surface H_o = height of the obstacle above the road surface.
2	If $L < S; L = 2S - \dfrac{2(\sqrt{H_d}+\sqrt{H_o})^2}{\lvert G\rvert}$	If S = ISD = OSD, $H_d = H_o = 1.2$ m; If S = SSD, $H_d = 1.2$ m, $H_o = 0.15$ m
For sag curves (equation (2.48) and (2.49))		
3	If $L > S$; $L = \dfrac{\lvert G\rvert S^2}{2(H_h + S\tan\phi)}$	$H_h = 0.75$ m, height of headlight above the road surface
4	If $L < S; L = 2S - \dfrac{2\,(H_h + S\ \tan\phi)}{\lvert G\rvert}$	$\phi = 1° =$ angle of spread of headlight or light cone focussed angle. The values of S may be obtained from design speed relationships or taken according to IRC guidelines.

AASHTO also recommends the above equations for determining the length of vertical curves, but with different input values.

In USA, the values of sealed beam head lamp (H_h) and ϕ respectively are 0.6 m and 1° (AASHTO 2004). The values of the driver's eye-height and the height of the approaching vehicle are taken as 1.08 m. The value of H_h was taken as 0.76 m in the 1954 AASHTO design policy, was reduced to 0.6 m in the 1965 AASHTO design policy and has remained the same since then. This reduction had the effect of lengthening sag curves by about 3 to 10% at different design speeds. In view of the latest developments in head lamp technology, a study in USA (Hawkins 2007) reveals that when $H_h = 0.6$ m, it is more appropriate to take the ϕ value as 0.75° rather than 1°. The effect would lengthen sag curves from 15 to 30% at different design speeds.

Truck and cab-over-engine tractor driver's eye height (H_d) may be taken up to 2.75 m and the object height (H_o) may be taken as 0.15 or 0.46 m in North America (Easa 1992).

2.11.3 Sight Distance on Sag Curve Passing Under an Overhead Structure

If a sag curve is passing under an overhead structure, the structure may restrict the sight distance. The following equations may be used to find the exact solution of the minimum sight distance (S) on a sag curve with centred overpass.

According to Hickerson (1964); when $S < L$: the minimum sight distance (S) is determined based on

$$\frac{S}{L} = \frac{O_o + c - \left(\frac{H_d + H_o}{2}\right)}{2 \times O_o} \tag{2.50}$$

The similar triangles principle is used for the development of the above relationship.

According to Ease (1992), when $S > L$ (Figure 2.26):

$$S = \frac{1}{|G|}\left[\sqrt{(c + O_o - H_d)} + \sqrt{(c + O_o - H_o)}\right]^2 \tag{2.51}$$

where,

c = vertical clearance; O_o = as given by equation (2.59c); the remaining parameters are as given in Figure 2.26.

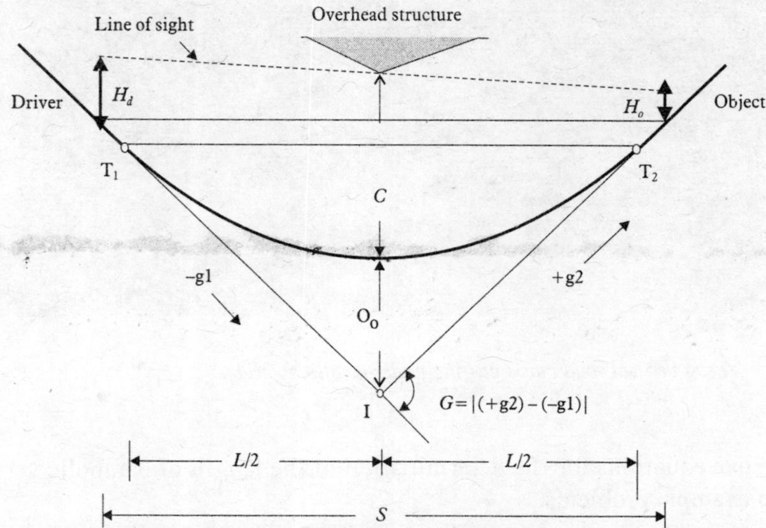

Figure 2.26 *Sight distance on sag curve when passing under an overhead structure; condition: S > L (modified based on Hickerson (1964) and Easa (1992))*

For normal Indian conditions, the minimum value of vertical clearance (*C*) at underpasses is taken as 5 m (Figure. 2.27). To accommodate double-decker buses, this value should be increased to 5.5 m (IRC: 54-1974). According to American practice, the minimum vertical clearance for highways with trucks is taken as 4.42 m (AASHTO).

Normally, sag vertical curves are designed based on the headlight criterion where minimum required sight distance is checked when the sag curve passes under an overhead structure (AASHTO 2004). The determination of minimum sight distance under the overpass is useful for improving existing conditions to facilitate better operational and cost effective measures (Neuman and Glennon 1984).

Till now we have discussed vertical curves which are symmetrical consisting of a constant rate of change of grade. Unsymmetrical vertical curves will be formed when the lengths of tangents are unequal ($T_1I \neq IT_2$) and the curve consists of two arcs having unequal length with two different rates of change of grade connected by a common tangent point. Design of such unsymmetrical vertical curves may be drawn based on sight distance and drainage requirements (Easa and Hassan 1998).

Figure 2.27 *A sag vertical road curve passing under a railway bridge*

Usage of the above equations for the determination of the length of parabolic vertical curves is illustrated in example problems.

Q: *A vertical summit curve is formed when an ascending gradient of 1 in 30 meets a descending gradient of 1 in 40. The curve is to be designed to provide OSD for a design speed of 80 km/h. Calculate the suitable length of the summit curve. Assume suitable data.*

A: Ascending gradient $(+g_1) = 1$ in $30 = (1/30) \times 100 = 3.33\%$

Descending gradient $(-g_2) = 1$ in $40 = (1/40) \times 100 = 2.50\%$

Angle of deviation of adjacent grades,

$$G = (-g_2) - (g_1) = -2.5 - 3.33 = -5.833\% = -0.05833; |G| = 0.05833$$

Assume Indian standard conditions. For the design speed of 80 km/h, assume minimum OSD value as $S = 470$ m (Table 2.9).

Assume $L < S$,

If $S =$OSD, $H_d = H_o = 1.2$ m

From equation (2.47),

$$L = 2S - \frac{2\,(\sqrt{H_d} + \sqrt{H_o})^2}{|G|} = 2(470) - \frac{2(\sqrt{1.2} + \sqrt{1.2})^2}{0.05833} = 940 - \frac{2(4.8)}{0.05833} = 775.42 \text{ m}$$

Therefore, our assumption of $L < S$ is not correct, since $S = 470$ m.

Now, reassume $L > S$ *(or* $S < L$*),*

From equation (2.46),

$$L = \frac{|G|S^2}{2\,(\sqrt{H_d} + \sqrt{H_o})^2} = \frac{0.05833 \times (470)^2}{2(\sqrt{1.2} + \sqrt{1.2})^2} = \frac{12885.097}{2 \times 4.8} = 1342.19 \text{ m} < 470 \text{ m (assumed value)}$$

Therefore, the assumption of $L > S$ is correct. Hence, provide length of the curve $= 1343$ m.

Q: *A summit curve is formed when an ascending gradient of 1 in 20 meets an ascending gradient of 1 in 80. If the value of SSD = 110 m, calculate the total length of the summit curve.*

A: Ascending gradient $(+g_1) = 1$ in $20 = (1/20) \times 100 = 5.00\%$ (given)

Ascending gradient $(+g_2) = 1$ in $80 = (1/80) \times 100 = 1.25\%$ (given)

$$G = g_2 - g_1 = 1.25 - 5.00 = -3.75\% = -0.0375$$

$$|G| = 0.0375$$

Assume, SSD $= S = 110$ m (given)

Length of the curve $= L$; Height of the drivers eye level above the road surface, $H_d = 1.2$ m;

Height of an object above road surface, $H_o = 0.15$ m

Assume L < S,

From equation (2.47),

$$L = 2S - \frac{2\left(\sqrt{H_d} + \sqrt{H_o}\right)^2}{|G|} = 2 \times 110 - \frac{2\left(\sqrt{1.2} + \sqrt{0.15}\right)^2}{0.0375} = 220 - \frac{2(2.1985)}{0.0375} = 102.74 \text{ m}$$

Our assumption of $L < S$ is correct, since $S = 110$ m. Hence, provide $L = 103$ m.

Q: *A valley curve is formed by a descending gradient of 1 in 30 meeting an ascending gradient of 1 in 50. If the design speed is 80 kmph, calculate the total length of the valley curve.*

A: Descending gradient $(-g_1) = -1$ in $30 = -(1/30) \times 100 = -3.33\%$

Ascending gradient $(+g_2) = 1$ in $50 = (1/50) \times 100 = 2.00\%$

$$G = -(g_2) - (-g_1) = 2.00 + 3.33 = 5.833\% = 0.05833; |G| = 0.05833$$

For a design speed of 80 km/h, stopping sight distance (SSD) may be assumed as $S = 120$ m (or may be determined by equation (2.1)).

Assume L>S ,

From equation (2.48),

$$L = \frac{|G|S^2}{2\,(H_h + S\,\tan\phi)} = \frac{0.05833 \times 120^2}{2(0.75 + 120 \times \tan(1°))} = \frac{839.952}{2(0.75 + 120 \times 0.017455)} = 147.64 \text{ m}$$

Therefore, our assumption of $L > S$ is correct, since $S = 120$ m. Hence, provide $L = 148$ m.

2.11.4 Elements of a Vertical Curve

As we know, the equations of the parabola may be written as follows (Macklin 1956),

$$y = ax^2 + bx + c \tag{2.52}$$

$$\text{Slope of the parabola} = \frac{dy}{dx} = 2ax + b \tag{2.53a}$$

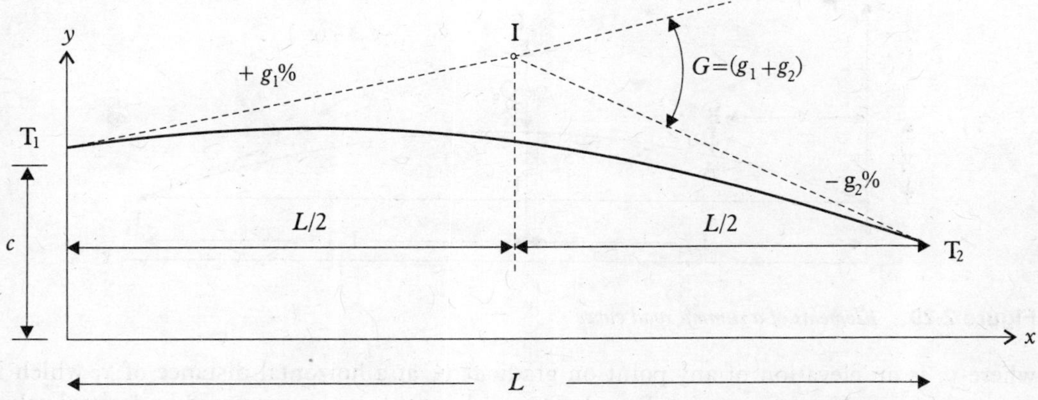

Figure 2.28 *Elements of a parabolic vertical road curve*

With reference to Figure 2.28, at point T_1, if $c = 0$, $b = g_1$, the above equation may be written as,

$$\frac{dy}{dx} = 2ax + g_1 \tag{2.53b}$$

$$\text{Rate of change of slope} = \frac{dy^2}{dx^2} = 2a = \text{constant} \tag{2.53c}$$

The ratio between $|G|$ and L is a constant value. Therefore, $\forall = \dfrac{|G|}{L} = \text{constant}$ (2.54)

Now, equation (2.53c) can be written as,

$$a = \frac{\forall}{2} \tag{2.55}$$

Hence, the equation (2.52) and (2.53a) can be written as, when $c = 0$,

$$y = \frac{\forall}{2}x^2 + g_1 x \tag{2.56}$$

$$\text{slope} = \forall x + g_1 \tag{2.57}$$

(i) Salient features of summit (or crest) curve (refer to Figure 2.29):

Horizontal distance between T_1 and T_2 = Total length of vertical curve = L

Horizontal distance between T_1 and I = $(T_1I) = \dfrac{L}{2}$

Horizontal distance between I and T_2 = $(IT_2) = \dfrac{L}{2}$

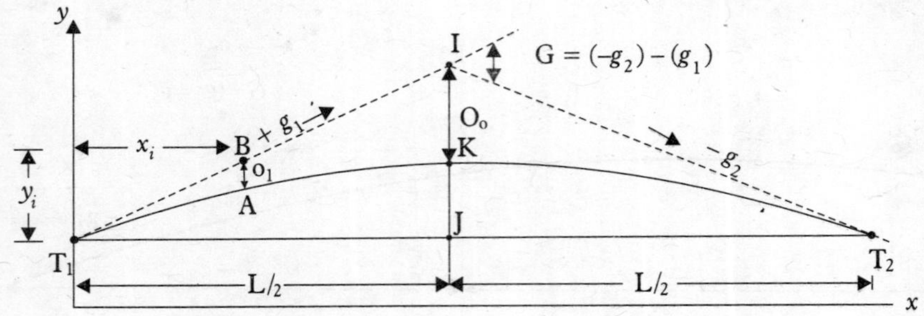

Figure 2.29 *Elements of a summit road curve*

where y_i is an elevation of any point on gradient g_1 at a hoizontal distance of x_i which is measured from the tangent point T_1 to J. The gradient value g_1 is expressed in decimal value. Consider $x_i \leq \frac{L}{2}$. On grade line g_1, reduced level (RL) of point $B_i = \text{RL of } T_1 + y_i$.

Let us take offset below the tangent line (T_1I) = BA = O_i. From the basic principle of parabola, we know that, $O_i \propto (x_i)^2$.

Therefore, we can write, $O_i = \frac{\forall}{2} \times (x_i)^2$ (2.59)

$$\text{where, } \frac{\forall}{2} = \left[\frac{O_o}{\left(\frac{L}{2}\right)^2}\right] \tag{2.59a}$$

$$\text{Apex distance} = O_o = \frac{IK}{2}$$

By equating equation (2.54) to equation (2.59), we get,

$$\frac{|G|}{L} = 2\left[\frac{O_o}{\left(\frac{L}{2}\right)^2}\right] \tag{2.59b}$$

$$O_o = \frac{|G|}{8} \times L \tag{2.59c}$$

$$\text{RL of } A_i = \text{RL of } T_1 + y_i - O_i \tag{2.60}$$

where A_i is a point on the curve at a horizontal distance x_i between T_1 and J.

Similarly, RLs of points on the other half of the curve may be calculated. Slope of the curve becomes zero on its highest point; its location from T_1 can be determined by equating equation (2.57) to zero, we get,

$$\forall x + g_1 = 0$$

$$\text{Therefore, } x = \frac{-g_1}{\forall} \tag{2.61}$$

Q: *Determine the minimum required sight distance when a sag curve is passing under an overhead structure. The conditions given are:*

(i) $S < L$; $|G| = 0.05833$; $L = 148$ m; $H_d = 1.2$ m; $H_o = 0.15$ m; and vertical clearance at midway of the sag curve under an overhead structure, $c = 4.42$ m.

(ii) $S > L$; $|G| = 0.0389$; $L = 74.2$ m; $H_d = 2.75$ m; $H_o = 0.15$ m; and vertical clearance between carriageway and an overhead structure, $c = 4.42$ m.

A: (i) When $S < L$:

From equation (2.59 c), $O_o = \dfrac{|G|}{8} \times L = \dfrac{0.05833}{8} \times 148 = 1.079$ m

From equation (2.50),

$$S = L\left[\frac{O_o + c - \left(\frac{H_d+H_o}{2}\right)}{2 \times O_o}\right] = 148\left[\frac{1.079 + 4.42 - \left(\frac{1.2+0.15}{2}\right)}{2 \times 1.079}\right] = 330.8\,\text{m}$$

(ii) When $S > L$:

$$O_o = \frac{0.0389}{8} \times 74.2 = 0.3608\text{ m}$$

From equation (2.51),

$$S = \frac{1}{|G|}\left[\sqrt{(c + O_o - H_d)} + \sqrt{(c + O_o - H_o)}\right]^2$$

$$= \frac{1}{0.0389}\left[\sqrt{(4.42 + 0.3608 - 2.75)} + \sqrt{(4.42 + 0.3608 - 0.15)}\right]^2 = 328.9\,\text{m}$$

(ii) Salient features of a sag curve (refer to Figure 2.30)

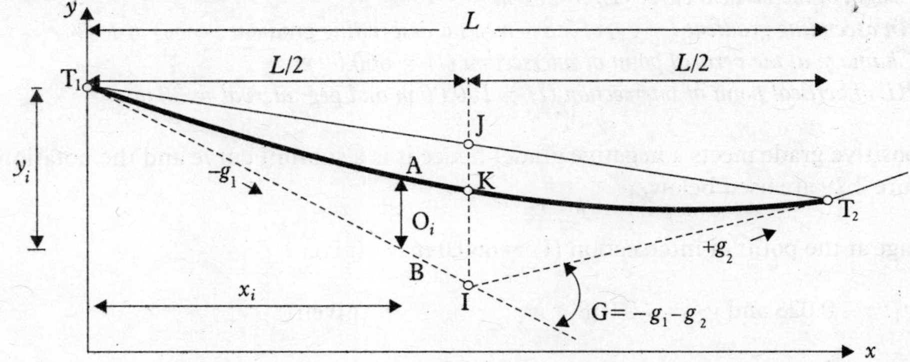

Figure 2.30 *Elements of a sag road curve*

Horizontal distance between T_1 and T_2 = Length of vertical curve = L

Horizontal distance between T_1 and I = $(T_1I) = \frac{L}{2}$

Horizontal distance between I and T_2 = $(IT_2) = \frac{L}{2}$

Let offset above the tangent = BA = O_i and let y_i be the elevation of a point below the grade line g_i. For sag curves also the equations from (2.52) to (2.54) are used for determining the y_i and O_i values,

$$\text{Reduced level (RL) of point B on the descending grade } g_i = \text{RL of } T_1 - y_i \tag{2.62}$$

Let A_i be a point on the sag curve at x_i horizontal distance from T_1. Consider $x_i \leq \frac{L}{2}$.

$$\text{RL of } A_i = \text{RL of } T_1 - y_i + O_i \tag{2.63}$$

RLs of points on the other half of the curve may be calculated using equations (2.53) and (2.54). Lowest point on the curve,

$$x = \frac{-g_1}{A} \tag{2.64}$$

The example problems given below illustrate the method of determining RLs at various locations on the summit (or crest) and sag curves.

Q: *Calculate the setting out data of a vertical curve based on the following data:*

Based on the design speed and standard conditions,

Length of the vertical curve (L) = 300 m
An ascending gradient $(+g_1)$ *of 2.8% meets a descending gradient* $(-g_2)$ *of 1.8%*
Chainage at the vertical point of intersection (I) = 660.00 m
RL of vertical point of intersection (I) = 100.00 m and peg interval = 30 m

A: A positive grade meets a negative grade; hence it is a summit curve and the notations used in Figure 2.29 are used below.

Chainage at the point of intersection (I) = 660.0 m (given)

$g_1 = +0.028$ and $g_2 = -0.018$ (given)

Chainage at the tangent (starting) point of the curve T_1 = Chainage at I $- L/2$

$= 660.0 - 300/2 = 510.0$ m

Chainage at the end of the curve T_2 = Chainage at $T_1 + L$

$= 510.0 + 300 = 810.0$ m

$G = g_2 - (g_1) = -1.8 - (2.8) = -4.6\%$

Therefore, $|G| = 0.046$

From equation (2.54),

$$\forall = \frac{|G|}{L} = \frac{0.046}{300} = 1.533 \times 10^{-4};\ \frac{\forall}{2} = 7.67 \times 10^{-5}$$

From equation (2.61), distance of the highest point on the curve from T_1:

$$x = \frac{g_1}{\forall} = \frac{0.028}{1.533 \times 10^{-4}} = 182.6\,\text{m}$$

Chainage of highest point on the curve $= 660.0 + (182.608 - 300/2) = 692.6$ m

Elevation or RL of $I = RL_I = 100.0$ m (given)

RL of $T_1 = RL_I -$ downward elevation of T_1 due to $(+2.8)\%$ grade for $L/2$ distance

$= 100.0 - ((2.8/100) \times 300/2) = 100.0 - 4.2 = 95.8$ m

RL of $T_2 = RL_I -$ downward elevation of T_2 due to $(-1.8)\%$ grade for $L/2$ distance

$= 100.0 - ((1.8/100) \times 300/2) = 100.0 - 2.7 = 97.3$ m

RL of mid-point of the curve (RL_o) = (RL of T_1 + RL of T_2)/2 = (95.8 + 97.3)/2 = 96.55 m

From equation (2.59 c),

$$O_o = \frac{|G|}{8} \times L = \frac{0.046}{8} \times 300 = 1.725\ \text{m}$$

Calculations from T_1 to mid-point (K):

Chainage	Point on curve	From equation (2.59); Offset height at the point, $O_i = \frac{\forall}{2} \times (x_i)^2$	Grade elevation = (RL of $T_1 + y_i$)	From equation (2.60); Curve elevation at point
510.0	T_1	$7.67 \times 10^{-5} \times (0)^2 =$ 0.000 m	95.8 + (2.8/100) × 0 = 95.8 m	95.8 − 0 = 95.8 m
540.0	A_1	$7.67 \times 10^{-5} \times (30)^2 =$ 0.069 m	95.8 + (2.8/100) × 30 = 96.64 m	96.64 − 0.069 = 96.571 m
570.0	A_2	$7.67 \times 10^{-5} \times (60)^2 =$ 0.276 m	95.8 + (2.8/100) × 60 = 97.48 m	97.48 − 0.276 = 97.204 m

600.0	A_3	$7.67 \times 10^{-5} \times (90)^2 =$ 0.621 m	$95.8 + (2.8/100) \times 90$ = 98.32 m	$98.32 - 0.621$ = 97.699 m
630.0	A_4	$7.67 \times 10^{-5} \times (120)^2 =$ 1.104 m	$95.8 + (2.8/100) \times 120$ = 99.16 m	$99.16 - 1.104$ = 98.056 m
660.0	K (Mid)	$7.67 \times 10^{-5} \times (150)^2 =$ 1.725 m	$95.8 + (2.8/100) \times 150$ = 100.0 m	$100.0 - 1.725$ = 98.275 m

Calculations from mid-point (K) to T_2:

Chainage	Point at	From equation (2.53); Offset height at the point, $O_i = \frac{\forall}{2} \times (x_i)^2$	Grade elevation = (RL of $T_1 - y_i$)	Curve elevation at point
810.0	T_2	$7.67 \times 10^{-5} \times (0)^2 = 0.000$ m	$97.3 - (-1.8/100) \times 0$ = 97.3 m	$97.3 - 0.000$ = 97.3 m
780.0	A_8	$7.67 \times 10^{-5} \times (30)^2 =$ 0.069 m	$97.3 - (-1.8/100) \times 30$ = 97.84 m	$97.84 - 0.069$ = 97.771 m
750.0	A_7	$7.67 \times 10^{-5} \times (60)^2 =$ 0.276 m	$97.3 - (-1.8/100) \times 60$ = 98.38 m	$98.38 - 0.276$ = 98.104 m
720.0	A_6	$7.67 \times 10^{-5} \times (90)^2 =$ 0.621 m	$97.3 - (-1.8/100) \times 90$ = 98.92 m	$98.92 - 0.621$ = 98.299 m
690.0	A_5	$7.67 \times 10^{-5} \times (120)^2 =$ 1.104 m	$97.3 - (-1.8/100) \times 120$ = 99.46 m	$99.46 - 1.104$ = 98.356 m
660	K (Mid)	$7.67 \times 10^{-5} \times (150)^2 =$ 1.725 m	$97.3 - (-1.8/100) \times 150$ = 100.0 m	$100 - 1.725$ = 98.275 m

The above details are illustrated in Figure 2.31.

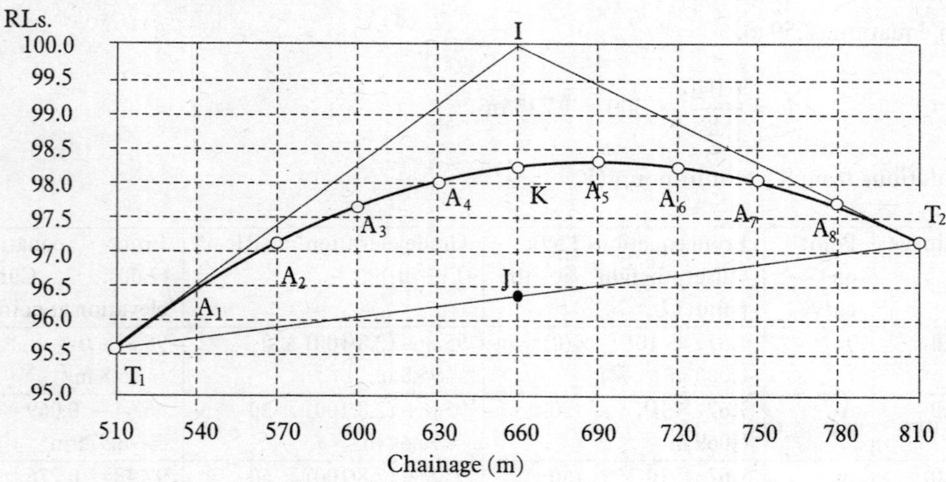

Figure 2.31 *Details of an example problem*

Q: *Calculate the setting out data of a vertical curve based on the following data collected from surveying.*
Proposed length of the vertical curve (L) = 280 m
A descending gradient ($-g1$) of 3.0 per cent meets another ascending gradient ($+g_2$) of 2.0 per cent
Chainage at the vertical point of intersection (I) = 780.00 m
RL of vertical point of intersection (I) = 100.00 m
Peg interval = 30 m

A: A negative grade meets a positive grade; hence it is a sag curve and the notations used in Figure 2.30 are used below.

Chainage at the point of inter section (I) = 780.0 m (given)
Chainage at the beginning of the curve T_1 = Chainage at I $-L/2 = 780.0 - 280/2 = 640.0$ m
Chainage at the end of the curve T_2 = Chainage at I $+L/2 = 780.0 + 280/2 = 920.0$ m
Check length of the curve = Chainage at $(T_2 - T_1) = 920.0 - 640.0 = 280.0$ m (O.K.)

$G = g_2 - (-g_1) = 2.0 - (-3.0) = 5.0\%; \ |G| = 0.05$

From equation (2.54),

$$\forall = \frac{|G|}{L} = \frac{0.05}{280} = 1.785 \times 10^{-4}; \ \frac{\forall}{2} = 8.928 \times 10^{-5}$$

From equation (2.61), distance of lowest point on the curve from T_1

$$x = \frac{g_1}{\forall} = \frac{0.03}{1.785 \times 10^{-4}} = 168 \text{ m}$$

Chainage of lowest point on the curve $= 780.0 + (168 - 280/2) = 808$ m

Elevation or RL at I = RL_I = 100.0 m (given)

RL at T_1 = elevation of T_2 due to -3.0% grade for $L/2$ distance + RL_I

$= ((3.0/100) \times 280/2) + 100.0 = 4.2 + 100.0 = 104.2$ m

RL at T_2 = elevation of T_2 due to 2.0% upward grade for $L/2$ distance + RL_I

$= ((2.0/100) \times 280/2) + 100.0 = 2.8 + 100.0 = 102.8$ m

RL of mid-point of the curve above the point I (RL_o) = (RL at T_1 + RL at T_2)/2

$= (104.2 + 102.8)/2 = 103.5$ m

From equation (2.59 c),

$$O_o = \frac{|G|}{8} \times L = \frac{0.05}{8} \times 280 = 1.75 \text{ m}$$

Calculations from T_1 to mid-point (K):

Chainage	Point on curve	From equation (2.59); Offset height at the point, $O_i = \frac{\forall}{2} \times (x_i)^2$	Grade elevation = (RL of $T_1 + y_i$)	From equation (2.60); Curve elevation at point
640.0	T_1	$8.928\times 10^{-5}\times(0)^2$ = 0.000 m	104.2 − (3.0/100) ×0 = 104.2 m	104.2 + 0.00 = 104.200 m
670.0	A_1	$8.928\times 10^{-5}\times 30^2$ = 0.080 m	104.2 − (3.0/100) × 30 = 103.3 m	103.3 + 0.080 = 103.380 m
700.0	A_2	$8.928\times 10^{-5}\times (60)^2$ = 0.321 m	104.2 −(3.0/100) × 60 = 102.4 m	102.4 + 0.321 = 102.721 m
730.0	A_3	$8.928\times 10^{-5}\times (90)^2$ = 0.723 m	104.2 −(3.0/100) × 90 = 101.5 m	101.5 + 0.723 = 102.223 m
760.0	A_4	$8.928\times 10^{-5}\times (120)^2$ = 1.285 m	104.2−(3.0/100)× 120 = 100.6 m	100.6 + 1.285 = 101.885 m
780.0	K (mid-point)	$8.928\times 10^{-5}\times (140)^2$ = 1.750 m	104.2−(3.0/100) ×140 = 100.0 m	100.0+1.750 = 101.750 m

Calculations from mid-point to T_2:

Chainage	Point at	From equation (2.59); Offset height at the point, $O_i = \frac{\forall}{2} \times (x_i)^2$	Grade elevation = (RL of $T_1 - y_i$)	Curve elevation at point
920.0	T_2	$8.928\times 10^{-5}\times(0)^2$ = 0.000 m	102.8− (2.0/100) × 0 =102.8 m	102.8 +0.000 = 102.800 m
900.0	A_5	$8.928\times 10^{-5}\times (20)^2$ = 0.035 m	102.8− (2.0/100) ×20 = 102.4 m	102.4 + 0.035 = 102.435 m
870.0	A_6	$8.928\times 10^{-5}\times (50)^2$ = 0.223 m	102.8− (2.0/100)×50 = 101.8 m	101.8 + 0.223 = 102.023 m
840.0	A_7	$8.928\times 10^{-5}\times (80)^2$ = 0.571 m	102.8− (2.0/100)× 80 = 101.2 m	101.2+ 0.571 = 101.771 m
810.0	A_8	$8.928\times 10^{-5}\times (110)^2$ = 1.08 m	102.8-(2.0/100) ×110= 100.6 m	100.6+1.08 = 101.680 m
780.0	K (mid-point)	$8.928\times 10^{-5}\times$ 1402=1.75 m	102.8− (2.0/100)×140 = 100.0 m	100.0+1.750 = 101.750 m

The above details are illustrated in Figure 2.32.

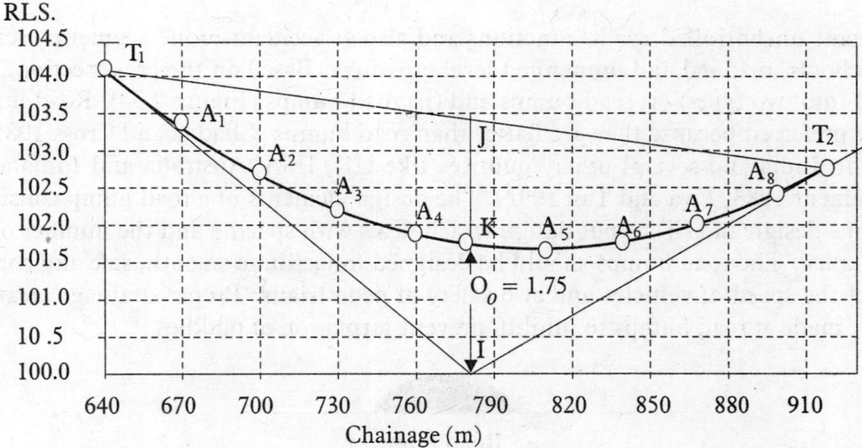

Figure 2.32 *Details of the above example problem*

2.12 Bus Bay

The traffic in India is heterogeneous in character and composition consisting of slow-moving animal-drawn vehicles and fast-moving motor vehicles of different sizes. For smooth flow of vehicles, the slow-moving ones should be segregated suitably and traffic in urban areas regulated. To avoid congestion at bus stops, bus bays of suitable geometry, which will segregate slow and fast moving traffic and facilitate safe passage of pedestrians (Figure 2.33), should be constructed. Standard procedures for segregation and regulation of traffic in urban areas are given in detail in IRC: 70-1977.

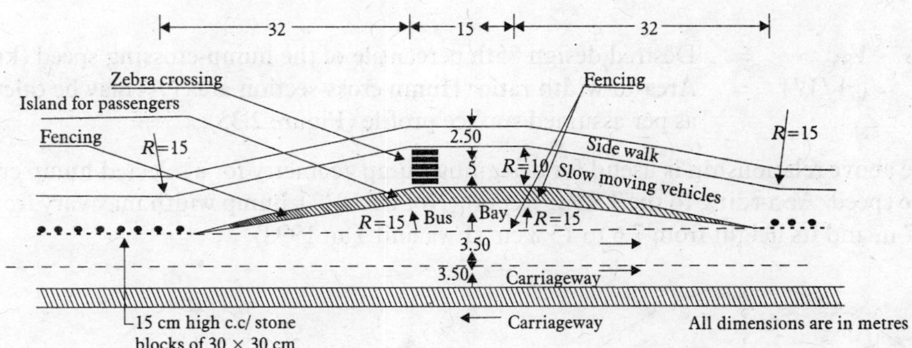

Figure 2.33 *A typical layout of a bus bay (IRC: 70-1977)*

2.13 Road Hump and Bump

These are round-shaped elevated/protruded surfaces formed across roadways as physical devices to reduce/deter/control the speed of vehicles on minor or secondary/tertiary and unimportant uncontrolled roads/ junctions and also at accident-prone segments, residential streets, schools, manned and unmanned level crossings. Based on the cross-section, they are classified into two types: (i) road bumps and (ii) road humps (Figure 2.34). Road humps are generally preferred because they are flatter than road bumps (Chadda and Cross 1985). They are used in India and several other countries like UK, USA, Australia and Finland (Jarvis 1980; Clement 1983; Fwa and Tan 1992). The design elements of a road hump consists of (i) dimensions design and (ii) layout design which deals with spacing and the number of humps to be installed. The road humps should be designed to facilitate smooth, safe and convenient control of the speed of vehicles and also safety of pedestrians. Proper drainage arrangement should be made at road humps to inhibit/ prevent formation of puddles.

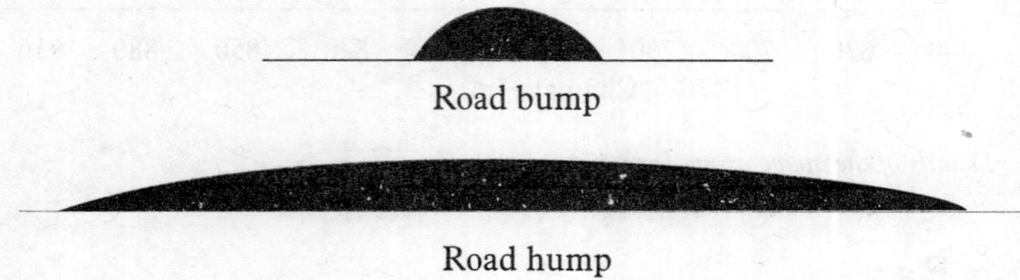

Figure 2.34 *Typical cross-sections of road bump and road hump*

Geometric design of road humps may be carried out based upon the findings of field experiments by Fwa and Tan (1992). They observed that the ratio of the cross-sectional area (A) to width (W) of the road hump is significant for controlling hump cross-speed. The relationship is

$$\frac{1}{V_{85}} = 0.0212 + 0.4072\,(A/W) \tag{2.65}$$

where, V_{85} = Desired design 85th percentile of the hump-crossing speed (km/h)
(A/W) = Area-to-width ratio (Hump cross-section area (A) may be calculated as per assumed surface profile (Figure 2.35).

The above relationship is useful for designing hump geometry for a selected hump crossing vehicle speed. According to the TRRL Report (No. LR1017), hump width may vary from 2.44 to 3.67 m and its height from 7.6 to 15.2 cm (Fwa and Tan 1992).

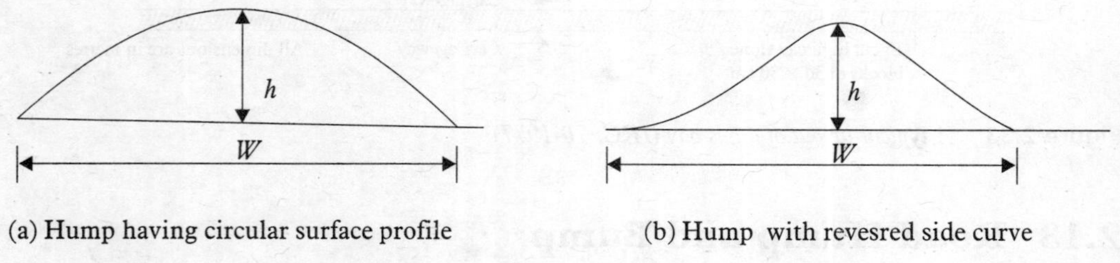

Figure 2.35 *Typical surface profiles of road humps (from Fwa and Tan 1992)*

The geometric design of road humps, according to Indian practice, is given in Figure 2.36. Drivers should be warned of the presence of a speed breaker, at least 40 m in advance. This can be done by installing visual aids according to the prescribed standards (IRC: 67-1977 and IRC: 99-1988).

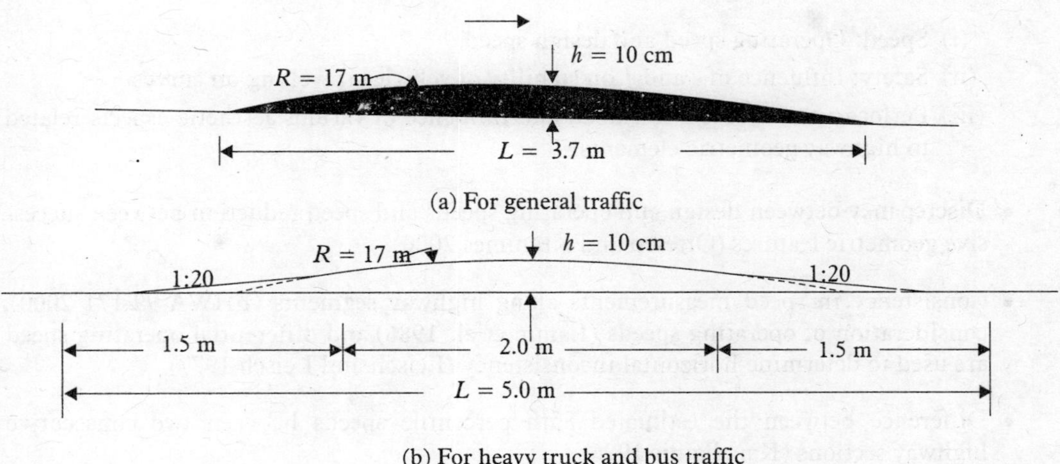

Figure 2.36 *Sectional details of hump type speed breakers for different traffic at a preferred crossing speed of 25 km/h (IRC: 99-1988)*

It is a good engineering practice to impose speed restrictions on traffic by installing mandatory speed limit signs, flash beacons and road markings of various types. It should be noted that speed breakers in the form of road bumps/humps are not intended to control speed of vehicles as a substitute for mandatory, warning or informatory signs. They are merely provided to draw the attention of drivers to possible hazards ahead. However, use of speed breakers on important and major intercity roads outside urban areas is not recommended by the IRC (IRC: 99-1988).

2.14 Geometric Design of Bike Paths

Bike path facilities are useful to bicyclists, non-motorised vehicles and very rarely for certain kinds of motorised vehicles. The guidelines for bike path geometric design are described in the AASHTO guide for the development of bicycle facilities (1999). Existing bike facilities can be evaluated according to the equations and design charts for determination of minimum sight distance, setback distance on horizontal curves and minimum length of crest vertical curves (Jia et al. 2007).

2.15 Consistency in Highway Geometric Design

The design of highways and streets should be sound enough to fulfill the safety requirements by providing consistency of alignment in horizontal and vertical planes, harmonisation between design speed and operating speed and human factors (Kanellaidis 1996). The following factors are considered to detect design inconsistencies and promote highway safety.

- Consistency of geometric design can be evaluated by considering the following three major categories (Gibreel et al. 1999):

    (i) Speed: Operating speed and design speed.
    (ii) Safety: Influence of e and f on stability of vehicles travelling on curves.
    (iii) Performance: Drivers workload and influence of various aesthetic aspects related to highway geometric elements.

- Discrepancy between design and operating speeds and speed reduction between successive geometric features (Ottesen and Krammes 2000).

- Consistency in speed measurements along highway segments (FHWA-99-171 2000), consideration of operating speeds (Lamm et al. 1986) and differential operating speed are used to determine horizontal inconsistency (Leisch and Leisch 1977).

- Difference between the estimated 85th percentile speeds between two consecutive highway sections (Kanellaidis 1996).

- Character of alignment changes between segments of roadway where the terrain passes from level to rolling or mountainous areas; and the average rate of vertical curvature for a roadway section (FHWA-99-173 2000).

- Conditions of acceleration and deceleration (FHWA-99-173 2000).

- The choice of super elevation and side friction when the horizontal curve radius exceeds the minimum (Nicholson 1998).

- Minimum radius and radii of consecutive horizontal curves.

- Lateral placement of vehicles in a study lane which presents traffic conflict and erratic manoeuvres of vehicles (FHWA-99-173 2000).

- Visual demand/driver workload: This may be defined as the required capacity of a driver to process and analyse visual information for decision making—in order to avoid an obstacle or navigate (Kanellaidis 1996 and FHWA-99-173 2000).

Consistency in geometric design of various elements of highway is a measure to assess the quality of alignment in horizontal and vertical planes of new projects as well as existing roads. The following relationships may be used to evaluate design consistency of highways based on vehicle speeds (Lamm et al. 1988):

- Good design: $(V_{85} - V_d) = 10$ km/h
- Fair design: 10 km/h $< (V_{85} - V_d) = 20$ km/h
- Poor design: $(V_{85} - V_d) > 20$ km/h
  where V_{85} and V_d are operating and design speeds respectively.

As a simple check, speed evaluation studies can be carried out on existing highways to provide more harmony with driver behaviour. For more details, readers may refer to the cited references.

Exercises

2.1 State the vehicle parameters useful for geometric design of highways with the relevant design element.

2.2 State the factors to be considered during geometric design of highways.

2.3 Define terrain. What are the different terrains according to IRC: 73?

2.4 What is the significance of design speed in the geometric design of highways?

2.5 What is the significance of operating speed in the geometric design of highways?

2.6 Distinguish between design speed and operating speed.

2.7 Draw a neat sketch showing the salient cross-sectional details of a highway.

2.8 Define: (i) control line; (ii) building line; (iii) road land boundary line; (iv) set-back distance (SBD); (v) right of way and roadway.

2.9 Define camber. Why is camber provided to road surfaces?

2.10 What are the different types of cambers based upon the surface profile?

2.11 State the standard specifications of camber used for construction of different type of roads based upon the materials used.

2.12 State the formula used for the determination of a camber profile provided with a parabolic curved surface.

2.13 Define and state the different type of sight distances provided in geometric design of highways with reference to the height of the driver's eye level and an object on the road.

2.14 Derive the formulae for determination of minimum sight distance in the following cases: (i) on a level road surface; (ii) on a sloped road surface.

2.15 Define overtaking sight distance (OSD or PSD) using a neat sketch with reference to Indian practice.

2.16 Explain the standard procedure of overtaking according to AASHTO using a neat sketch.

2.17 State the conditions assumed for determination of OSD according to IRC: 66.

2.18 State the conditions assumed for determination of OSD according to AASHTO.

2.19 State the factors affecting OSD and their influence on minimum OSD.

2.20 Define intermediate sight distance. How is it determined?

2.21 Define intersection sight distance using a neat sketch and state the design criterion according to IRC: 66.

2.22 State the assumption made by AASHTO for determination of intersection sight distance.

2.23 Distinguish between intermediate sight distance and intersection sight distance using diagrams .

2.24 How is the sight distance determined in medians?

2.25 Define super elevation and derive an expression based on radius of curve, design speed, side friction and acceleration due to gravity.

2.26 What are the factors that affect super elevation?

2.27 State the assumption and formula recommended by IRC: 73 for the determination of the rate of super elevation.

2.28 What are the standard values of super elevation adopted in different countries for different conditions?

2.29 State the maximum allowable values of super elevation considered in different countries.

2.30 Define the significance of side friction factor for various design parameters related to horizontal curves.

2.31 What are the factors affecting side friction factor? State why lower values of e_{max} are suitable in cold and snow falling areas.

2.32 Determine the minimum radius of horizontal curve and restriction of speed recommended by IRC: 73.

2.33 What do you understand by design speed margin of safety (DSMS) and negative super elevation?

2.34 Define equilibrium cant using a neat sketch.

2.35 State and explain different methods of attaining super elevation.

2.36 Describe the suitability of the different methods of attaining super elevation.

2.37 Formulate the relationships used for design of super elevation by revolving the roadway about its centre line.

2.38 State the limiting values of the rate of change of super elevation for (i) plain and rolling terrain; (ii) hilly and mountainous terrain.

2.39 State the reasons for extra-widening the carriageway on horizontal curves.

2.40 Derive an expression for determining the extra width of carriageway on curves. Also write the formula used for determining the total widening of curves.

2.41 Draw typical forms of different horizontal curves used for centre line alignment of highways.

2.42 State the assumption made for design of transition curves for the geometric design of highways.

2.43 State the possible cases of insertion of transition curves in centre line alignment of highways.

2.44 Why are transition curves with spirals preferred in highway alignment?

2.45 How is the length of a transition curve determined?

2.46 Derive the formulae for determinaing salient elements of a typical combined curve which consists of a circular arc connected with a transition curve on either side. Draw a neat sketch showing the salient features.

2.47 Derive expressions with neat sketches for the determination of salient elements of (i) twin centred compound circular curves and (iii) three centred compound circular curves.

2.48 Define and describe the different types of longitudinal gradients according to IRC: SP-23.

2.49 What are the factors affecting the selection of appropriate longitudinal gradients in highways?

2.50 Why is grade compensation necessary for design of highway curves in hilly areas? What is the formula recommended by IRC: 73?

2.51 Define summit (or crest) and sag curves with reference to angle of deviation of adjacent grade lines. Draw figures wherever applicable.

2.52 State when design of vertical curves are not required with reference to the maximum change in grade and design speed.

2.53 State the design criteria, according to (i) IRC: SP-23 and (ii) AASHTO standards, used for determining the minimum length of vertical curves with reference to the height of the driver's eye level, the minimum depth of object and the vehicle's headlight. Draw figures showing the salient details.

2.54 Write the formulae used for determination of the minimum sight distance on the sag curve passing under an overhead structure. Draw figures showing salient details.

2.55 Distinguish between a road hump and a road bump.

2.56 Why is the usage of speed breakers not favoured by the IRC? State a few good engineering practices to control speed on roads.

2.57 What do you understand by inconsistency of highway geometric design? State the factors to be considered to evaluate the consistency of the design geometric elements of a highway.

2.58 State the speed relationships between operating speed and design speed for evaluating design consistency of highways.

2.59 What do you understand by "consistency in geometric design of highways"? State the factors and conditions considered to judge and evaluate the quality of facilities designed under the geometric design of highways.

3

Characterisation of Sub-Grade Soil and Mineral Aggregates

Introduction

Various materials with appropriate engineering properties are used for road construction. They play a vital role in design, construction and maintenance operations. Suitability of different materials according to their availability and their specific application should be thoroughly examined before undertaking a design methodology. Different pavement design methods need different input parameters. Hence, it is important to determine the engineering properties of materials that are used in pavement construction. Figure 3.1 shows the natural and artificial materials generally used for construction of road pavements.

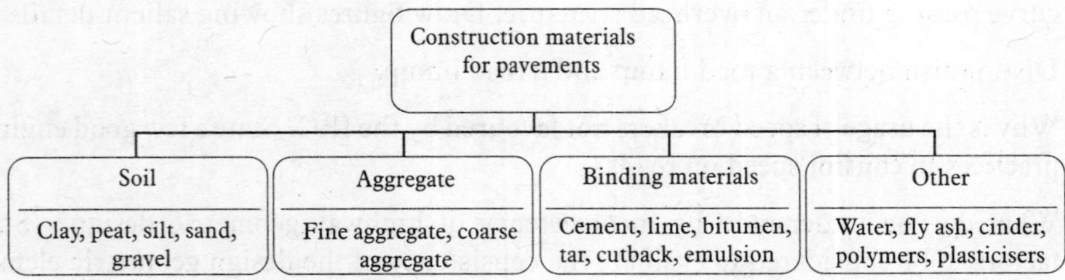

Figure 3.1 *Types of pavement construction materials*

In this chapter, a few important methods that are generally used in India for testing pavement materials are described.

Soil consists of various inorganic–mineral residues of rocks from the earth's crust produced as a result of geological processes like weathering. It is one of the major components of sub-grade, base course, foundations, embankment, soil aggregate mix and mixtures with other materials, viz. cement, bitumen, cutback, emulsion, fly ash, tar etc, used in the construction of road works. To understand the behaviour of soil alone and with other admixtures, it is essential to determine its characteristics under similar climatic and environmental conditions as that prevailing at the proposed construction site. Various organisations have designed different soil test methods to simulate field conditions. Engineering properties of a particular type of soil are found to have correlation with its mineral content and particle size distribution.

3.1 Particle Size Analysis of Soils

The given sub-grade soil particles are separated by sieving through a set of sieves of standard sizes. The soil contents retained on and passed through respective sizes of sieve are weighed and recorded for further analysis to interpret the results in terms of soil character (Burmister 1939; IS: 2386 (Part 1)-1963; 2004). Particle size analysis of soils is classified as

(i) *Dry-mechanical analysis* The limitation of the test is up to 75 microns size of soil particles.

(ii) *Wet-mechanical analysis* The limitation of the test is up to 2 microns size of soil particles.

This method is also suitable for separating washout of finer particles of soil/dust present over the surface of coarse aggregate.

For classification of soils of grain size less than 75 microns, sedimentation analysis is performed using a hydrometer (Figure 3.2) or the pipette method based on Stoke's law. The above test methods are described in detail in IS: 2720 (Part 4)-1985.

(a) Hydrometer (b) Test in progress

Figure 3.2 *Grain size distribution of fine grained soil using hydrometer*

Soil classification charts were developed by various agencies based on the percentage of soil grains passing through different sizes of sieves. Classification based upon grain or particle size is also termed as textural soil classification and is discussed in Section 3.5. Table 3.1 enlists the general methods used to classify soil based on the diameter of the particle size. The terminology used to designate different types of soil particles based on their size slightly differs in different countries (Figure 3.3).

Table 3.1 *Soil texture based on particle size (according to IS: 1498-1970)*

Sl. No.	Soil texture		Particulars	
			Diameter of particle (mm)	IS sieve size (mm)
1	Gravel (G)		75–4.75	Retained on 4.75
2	Sand (S)		4.75–0.075	Passes 4.75 and retained on 0.075
3	Fines	Silt (M)	0.075 to 0.002	Passes 0.075; For detailed investigation, a hydrometer analysis may be carried out.
4		Clay (C)	Less than 0.002	

NOTE:

1. One micron = 1×10^{-3} mm
2. Sands and silts are further classified as coarse, medium and fines based on particle size
3. Clays are further divided as colloids if their particles size is less than 0.001 mm.

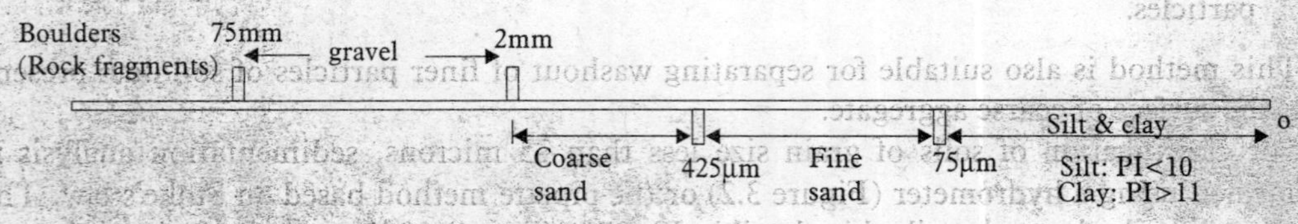

Figure 3.3 *Terminology used by ASTM designation: D3282-93.*

Fine-grained soils consist of grains of equal size. Their behaviour under service conditions depends not only on their grain size composition but also the following factors (Fadum 1948; Feld 1948).

- Different mineralogical composition.
- Variability in shape of soil particles.
- Cohesion effect due to wetness caused by electrostatic charge with different intensities on grain surfaces.

For all these reasons, fine-grained soils are classified not only according to the size of grains (or gradation) but also on the basis of degree of plasticity and dry strength.

3.2 Soil Gradation

The percentage of material passing and retained on respective sieves (or a set of sieves) are noted down in a tabular form and the cumulative percentages finer than each sieve size are calculated. These values are plotted on a semi-log graph, with the grain sizes on logarithmic scale as abscissas and cumulative percentages by weight (passing) on ordinary scale as ordinates. By joining all the points smoothly, a curve similar to an elongated S-shape may be observed. This curve is called a grading curve or a grain size distribution curve and is a method of international expression, or a universal language presenting grain size data graphically (Campbell 1939). The shape, slope and position of the grading curve are useful for determining the following properties of soils.

- Percent passing through 0.075 mm IS sieve size, which is used for soil classification
- Grading characteristics, viz. effective size (D_0).
- Uniformity coefficient, $C_u = \dfrac{D_{60}}{D_{10}}$ (3.1)
- Coefficient of curvature, $C_c = \dfrac{D_{30}^2}{D_{10} \times D_{60}}$ (3.2)
- Geometrical characteristics of gradation curve, viz. poorly graded, open graded, well graded and gap graded (Figure 3.4).

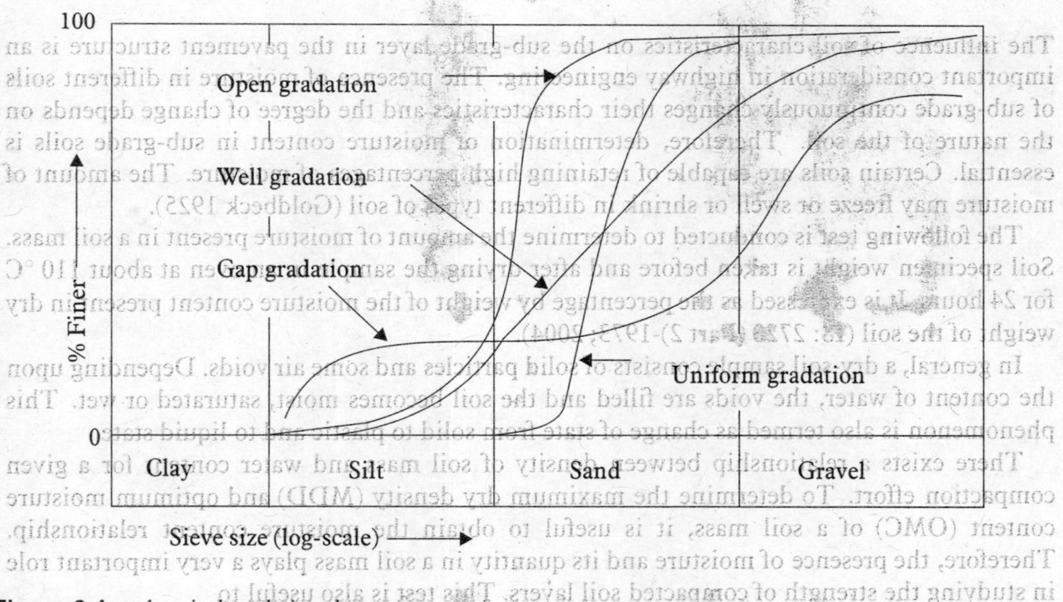

Figure 3.4 *A typical gradation chart*

Well or dense graded This gradation consists of all sizes of soil particles ranging from fine to coarse which gives maximum density. The S-curve spreads almost evenly along the x-axis covering all sizes. This gradation is generally preferred for constructing sub-grades or embankments and other pavement layers where heavy traffic is anticipated. The value of C_u will be greater than 6.

Gap or skip graded Certain sizes of particles in the middle-size range are available only in small quantity (%) compared with the other sizes. Hence, the shape of the S-curve appears to be flat in the middle-size range. To make these soils useful, it is required to blend them with other soils which supplement the missing sizes.

Open graded The finer size of particles are present only in a small quantity. Due to this reason, there are more number of air voids because there are not enough of that particular size of fines which would generally fill the voids between coarser particles. The S-curve appears to be flat at the finer particle size zone.

Poorly or uniformly graded In this type, the soil mass consists of similar size particles which results in more voids due to less percentage of finer particles. The S-curve appears to be steep in a limited size range.

Gradation analysis of the particle sizes of soil mass helps the soil engineer in many ways, such as for blending soils to achieve satisfactory gradation and dense soil mass in compaction, and for attaining desired permeability and shear strength properties.

The above definitions of soil gradation also holds good for gradation of mineral aggregate which is used for mix design of cement and bituminous concrete.

3.3 Moisture Content

The influence of soil characteristics on the sub-grade layer in the pavement structure is an important consideration in highway engineering. The presence of moisture in different soils of sub-grade continuously changes their characteristics and the degree of change depends on the nature of the soil. Therefore, determination of moisture content in sub-grade soils is essential. Certain soils are capable of retaining high percentages of moisture. The amount of moisture may freeze or swell or shrink in different types of soil (Goldbeck 1925).

The following test is conducted to determine the amount of moisture present in a soil mass. Soil specimen weight is taken before and after drying the sample in an oven at about 110 °C for 24 hours. It is expressed as the percentage by weight of the moisture content present in dry weight of the soil (IS: 2720 (Part 2)-1973; 2004).

In general, a dry-soil sample consists of solid particles and some air voids. Depending upon the content of water, the voids are filled and the soil becomes moist, saturated or wet. This phenomenon is also termed as change of state from solid to plastic and to liquid state.

There exists a relationship between density of soil mass and water content for a given compaction effort. To determine the maximum dry density (MDD) and optimum moisture content (OMC) of a soil mass, it is useful to obtain the moisture content relationship. Therefore, the presence of moisture and its quantity in a soil mass plays a very important role in studying the strength of compacted soil layers. This test is also useful to

- Study the water retention capacity of the soil.
- Investigate the quantity of moisture present in a compacted layer during quality control operations.
- Determine the moisture changes in the sub-grade soil in different seasons of a year.
- Study the capillarity characteristics of soils.
- Evaluate the density of compacted pavement layers and embankments.

The oven drying method is a standard approach to determine moisture content in a soil sample. To carry out this test, about 50 to 100 g of soil specimen have to be collected from a soil layer. If the soil sample is collected from the field, it is packed in an air-tight cup and carried to the laboratory without any loss of moisture. The weight of the empty cup with its cap is taken and recorded as W1 g. The collected soil is filled in the cup and weighed along with the cap as W2 g. The cup filled with soil along with its opened cap is kept in an oven at 105 to 110 °C for about 24 hours. After drying, the soil cup is placed in a desiccator to allow the contents to cool down to room temperature without any absorption of atmospheric humidity. The dried sample along with its cup and cap are weighed and recorded as W3 g. The following equation is used to calculate the moisture content present in the soil (IS: 2720 (Part 2)-1973; 2004).

$$\text{Moisture content in the soil } (w\%) = \frac{\text{Weight of moisture present in soil (W2} - \text{W3)} \times 100}{\text{Dry weight of the soil (W3} - \text{W1)}} \tag{3.3}$$

At least 3 samples are tested similarly to get an acceptable average value. The demerit of this test is that because the soil sample has to be kept in the hot air oven for 24 hours to completely evaporate the moisture present in the soil, at least a day is required to obtain the test value.

The following alternative methods are generally employed for rapid determination of the moisture present in a given soil sample.

(i) Sand bath method

(ii) Alcohol method

(iii) Infrared lamp drying method

(iv) Calcium carbide method

(v) Nuclear radiation method

The nuclear radiation method is widely used and prescribed in almost all national and international road organisations. Though these tests may take less time, they do need frequent calibration. Reliability of the test values depends on the precision and accuracy maintained during calibration.

3.4 Consistency Tests of Soil

3.4.1 Liquid Limit Test

The liquid limit (LL) is the minimum water content (expressed in percentage) at which the soil will flow on application of a very small shearing force, i.e., at this limit, the soil possesses very low shear strength and begins to exhibit liquid characteristics. The stress history and other characteristics of a soil can be well predicted by its liquid limit value. Further, the compression index and settlement can also be estimated based on liquid limit values. This test is also used to determine the flow index value and for soil classification. There are two methods of conducting the LL test. They are (i) the mechanical method and (ii) the cone penetration method. The test procedures are explained below.

Mechanical Method (according to IS: 2720 (Part 5)-1985; 2004)

To carry out this test, about 120 g of dry pulverised soil sample passing through a 0.425 mm size IS sieve is to be taken. The soil should be thoroughly mixed with distilled water in the porcelain evaporating dish to make a soil paste of uniform consistency. The apparatus used for this test is given in Figure 3.5(a). The brass cup is set to have a free fall of 10 mm above its base.

A portion of the prepared soil paste is placed in the brass cup so as to almost half fill it. A spatula is used to smooth the paste so that it will have a horizontal surface. The maximum depth at the centre of the brass cup should be 10 mm. A 'V' shaped groove is made along the symmetrical axis of the cup (Figure 3.5(b)) using a grooving tool. To lift and drop the cup on to the base, the handle of the cup is rotated at a rate of 2 revolutions per second. The number of blows is recorded till the two parts of the soil paste come into contact with each other at the bottom for a length of above 10 to 12 mm by flow (Figure 3.5(c) and (d)). To determine the moisture content in the soil, a portion of soil paste is taken from the brass cup.

The above procedure may be repeated for at least another three trials, preferably with different moisture contents of the soil paste, resulting in the number of blows ranging from 15 to 35. The soil paste, prepared for the first trial should be with lower water content. In later trials, the water content can be increased in suitable increments. At lower water content, the soil specimen records more blows and vice versa.

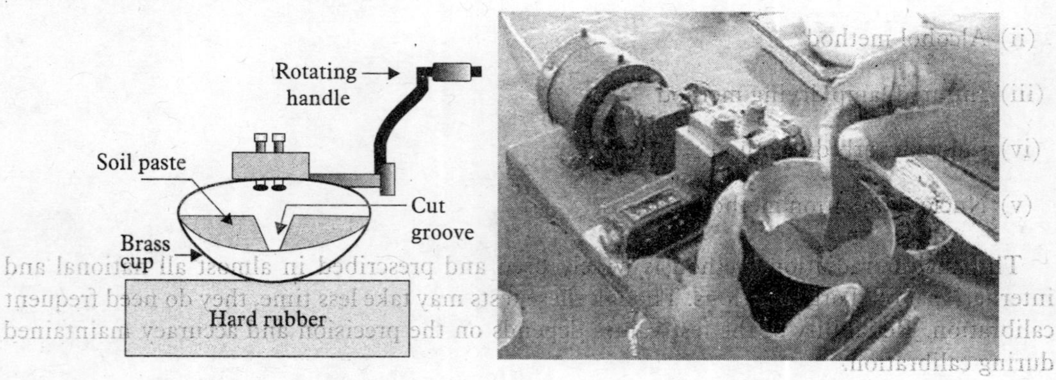

Figure 3.5(a) *Liquid limit test device. (with manual operation)*

Figure 3.5(b) *Cutting a groove in the soil paste (electrically operated device)*

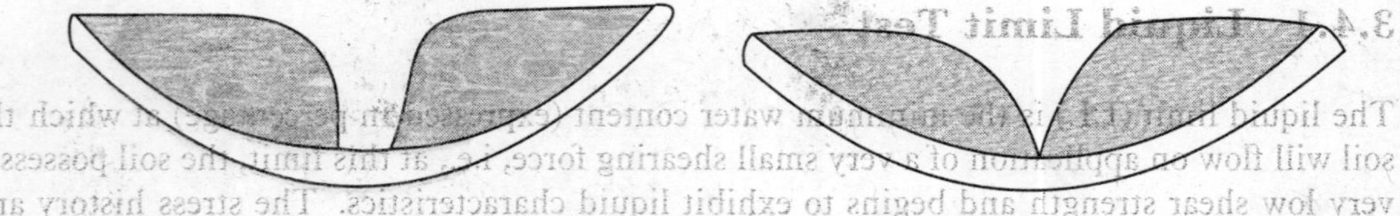

Figure 3.5(c) *Soil paste before the procedure*

Figure 3.5(d) *Soil paste after the procedure*

The test data is plotted on a semi-log graph by taking the number of blows on the log scale (x-axis) and water content in percentage on the ordinary scale (y-axis). A straight line is obtained by joining all the points. The line obtained is called a flow curve. The water content corresponding to 25 blows is taken as the liquid limit of the soil (Figure 3.6).

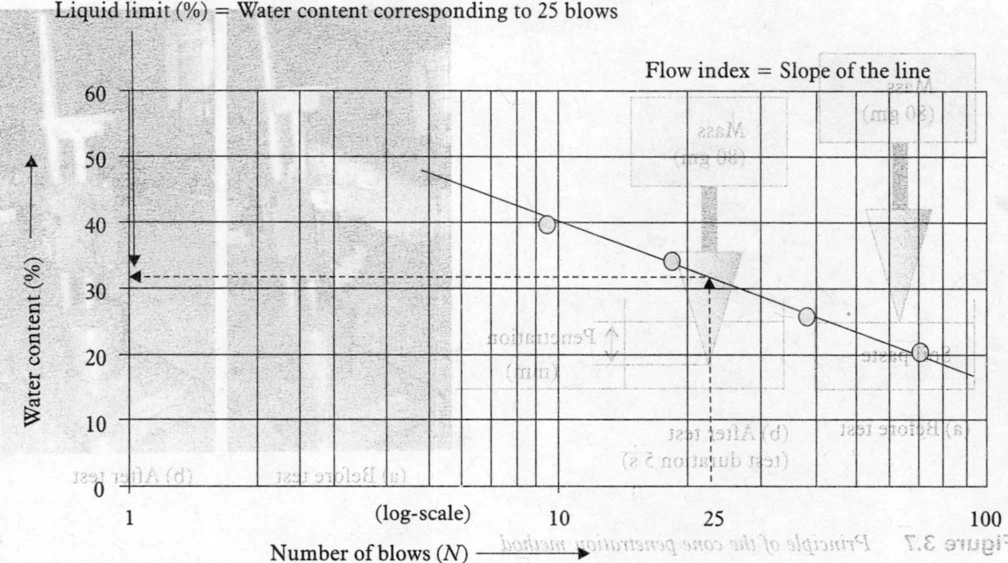

Figure 3.6 *Flow curve*

From the liquid limit test data, soil flow index property can be calculated using the following equation.

$$\text{Flow index} = \text{Slope of flow curve} = FI = \frac{W_2 - W_1}{\log_{10}\frac{N_1}{N_2}} \tag{3.4}$$

where N_1 and N_2 are the number of blow counts corresponding to the water contents of W_1 and W_2.

This test is also called the Casagrande method. It is a slow procedure and requires skill during addition of water.

Cone Penetration Method

In this test, about 150 g of soil sample passing a 0.425 mm size IS sieve is taken. Distilled water is mixed to obtain a uniformly consistent soil paste. A standard cone of 30° angle with 35 mm depth, having an 80 g plunger is allowed to penetrate into the soil paste kept in a standard size cup for a duration of 5 seconds (IS: 2720 (Part 5)-1985 and IS: 11196-1985; 1985). The principle of the cone penetration method is presented in Figure 3.7. At least four tests are conducted on the soil sample by varying the water content in the soil. The measured penetration values of the cone are plotted on the x-axis and the corresponding water contents (%) are plotted on the y-axis. The points are connected by a straight line and the liquid limit value in percentage is determined at 20 mm penetration value (Figure 3.8).

This method is widely used in many parts of the world because the limitations associated with the traditional Casagrande apparatus, such as the difficulty in making grooves and adjustment of drop of the brass cup, the possibility of the sides of the groove edges tearing and the soil slipping, and the ambiguity experienced during stoppage of number of blows may be avoided.

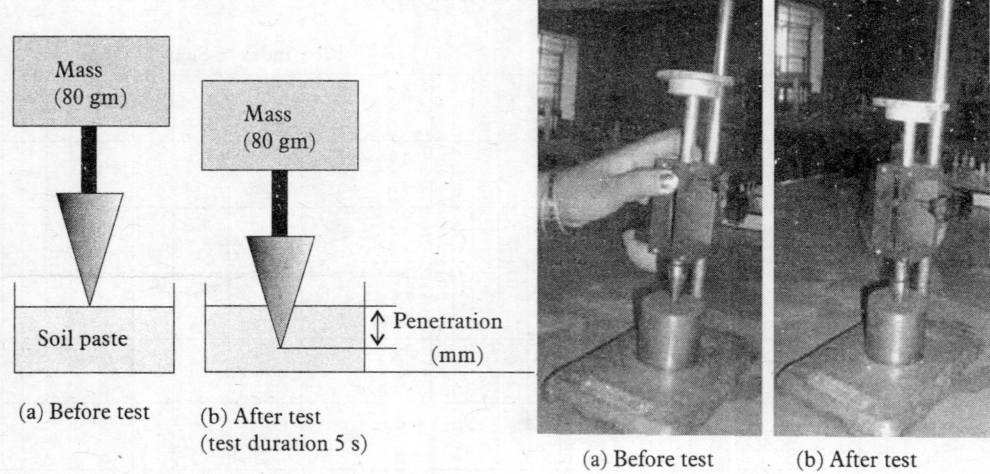

Figure 3.7 *Principle of the cone penetration method*

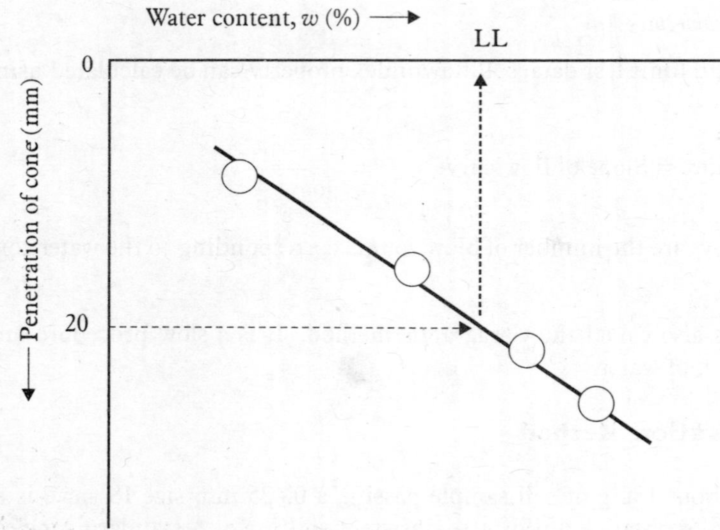

Figure 3.8 *Determination of LL value from test results of cone penetration method*

The characteristics and suitability of soils for pavement construction can be interpreted based upon LL (Figure 3.9).

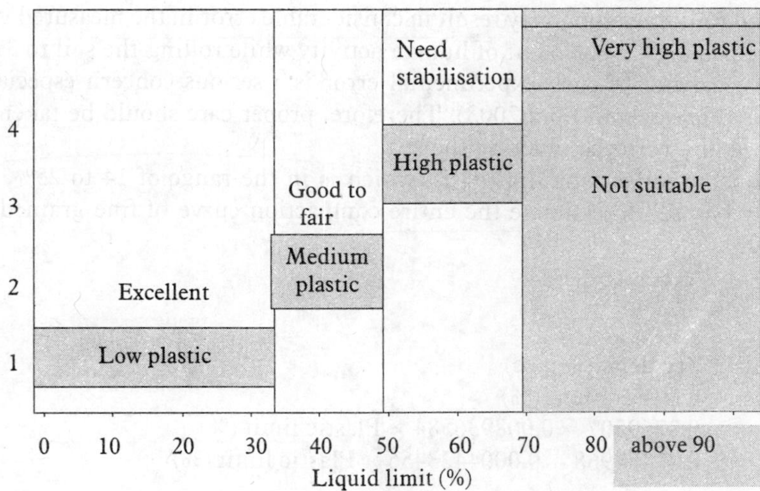

Figure 3.9 *Suitability of soil based on LL*

3.4.2 Plastic Limit Test

The plastic limit (PL) of a soil is the water content at which the soil begins to crumble when rolled into a thread of approximately 3 mm diameter (IS: 2720 (part 5)-1985). It is the water content which indicates the boundary between the plastic and semi-solid states of consistency of the soil. This test is carried out to determine the semi-solid state of soil. The PL value is widely used to classify soil.

About 20 g of dry pulverised soil sample passing through a 0.425 mm size IS sieve is taken and mixed with distilled water in a porcelain evaporating dish till it becomes plastic enough to be easily rolled with the fingers. In case of clayey soils, the soil paste should be kept for 24 hours in order to ensure uniform distribution of moisture throughout the soil mass.

About 8 g of the prepared soil paste is taken to make a small ball with the fingers. The soil ball is rolled on a plane glass plate to form a thread of slightly more than 3 mm diameter. The soil is pressed together and again rolled until the soil thread of 3 mm diameter just starts crumbling (Figure 3.10). The crumbled pieces of soil are taken into a moisture container to determine the water content. The test is repeated at least three times and the average of the results is rounded off to the nearest whole number as a final result.

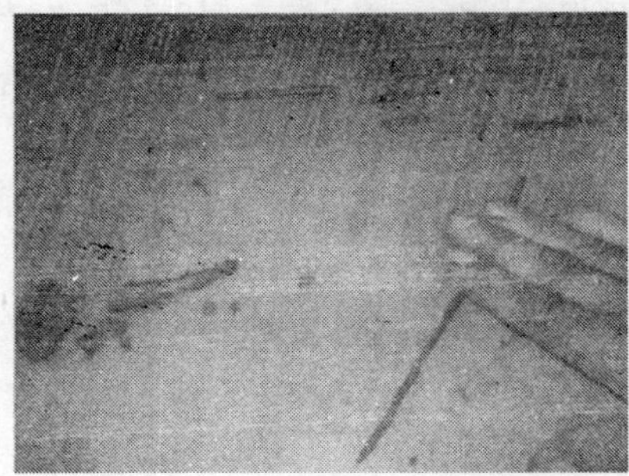

Figure 3.10 *Plastic limit test in progress*

This thread rolling method may result in considerable error in the measured value of plastic limit as there is more involvement of human activity while rolling the soil to 3 mm diameter of thread. Occurrence of such experimental error is a serious concern especially in case of cohesive soils (Sharma and Bora 2003). Therefore, proper care should be taken to follow the standard procedure while conducting the test.

Based upon the soil plastic limit (PL) which is in the range of 14 to 25%, the following equation may be used to estimate the entire compaction curve of fine grained soil (Sharma and Bora 2003).

$$\gamma_d = A \times w - B \times w^2 \tag{3.5}$$

where γ_d = dry density (g/cc)

w = water content (%)

A = 0.3769507 – 0.008936584 × Plastic limit (%)

B = 0.01458968 – 0.0004423456 × Plastic limit (%)

The numerical difference between the values of the liquid limit (LL) and the plastic limit (PL) of soil is known as plasticity index (PI). This index indicates the range of water content through which the soil remains plastic, the upper and lower limits being in the liquid and semi-solid states respectively.

$$\text{Plasticity index (PI)} = \text{LL} - \text{PL} \tag{3.6}$$

Based on plasticity and liquidity indices, soils can also be classified as shown in Figure 3.11 and 3.12.

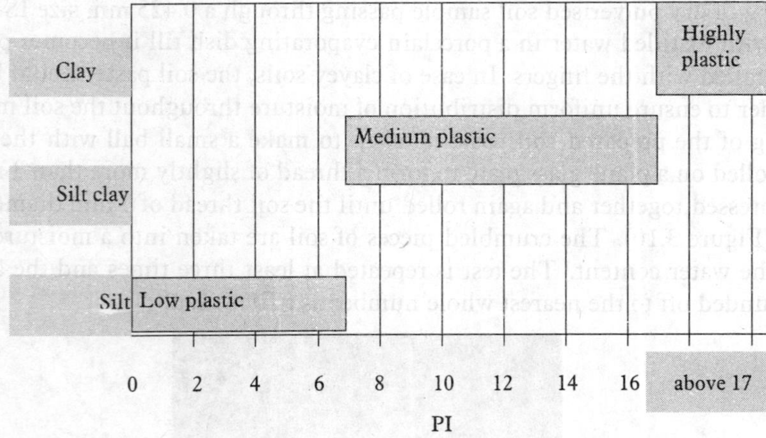

Figure 3.11 *Soil class based on PI*

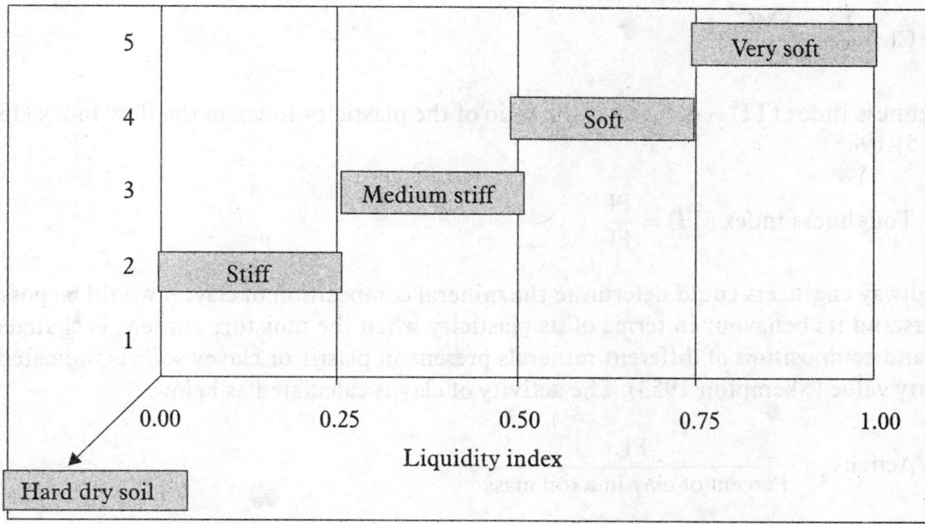

Figure 3.12 *Soil type based on LI*

An investigation on soil compressibility reveals that when soils having the same LL possess approximately equal compressibility, their dry strength increases but permeability decreases as the value of PI increases (Casagrande 1948).

The soil consistency or sensitivity of fine grained soils is determined by relating field or in situ moisture content (FMC) to the plastic and liquid limits. The behaviour of heavy soils such as suspension clay and clay soil with respect to various engineering parameters such as change in state of soil with moisture content, shear strength and compressibility are best studied based on the value of liquidity index (Skemton and Northley 1952). The relationship between liquidity index and different states of soil is presented in Figure 3.13. The equation used to determine liquidity index (LI) is given below (IS:2720 (part 5)-1985).

$$\mathrm{LI} = \frac{\mathrm{FMC} - \mathrm{PL}}{\mathrm{PI}} \tag{3.7}$$

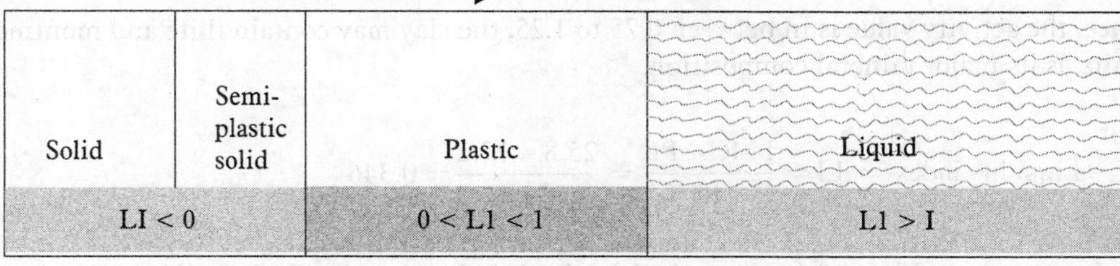

Figure 3.13 *The relationship between liquidity index and different states of soil*

Consistency index (CI), is defined as the ratio of the liquid limit minus FMC to the plasticity index of a soil (IS: 2720 (part 5)-1985).

$$CI = \frac{LL - FMC}{PI} \tag{3.8}$$

Toughness index (TI) is defined as the ratio of the plasticity index to the flow index (IS: 2720 (part 5)-1985).

$$\text{Toughness index (TI)} = \frac{PI}{FI} \tag{3.9}$$

If highway engineers could determine the mineral composition of clay, it would be possible to understand its behavour in terms of its plasticity when the moisture content is changed. The type and composition of different minerals present in plastic or clayey soils is indicated by its activity value (Skempton 1953). The activity of clay is calculated as below.

$$\text{Activity} = \frac{PI}{\text{Percent of clay in a soil mass}} \tag{3.10}$$

The activity of a clay soil in fact signifies its swelling characteristics which are thought to be dependent upon the plasticity index and the quantity of colloidal particles present in the soil. High values of activity (above 1.40) indicate that the soil is more prone to swelling.

Q: *Determine the activity and liquidity index of a soil from the following data:*
Liquid limit = 42%
Plastic limit = 17.2%
In situ moisture content = 25.8%
Clay content = 26.4 % of particles are passed through a 2 μm size sieve.

A: PI = LL − PL = 42 − 17.2 = 24.8%

Activity value indicates the type and composition of different minerals present in clay soils

$$\text{Activity} = \frac{PI}{\text{Percent clay particles}} = \frac{24.8}{26.4} = 0.96$$

Since, the activity value is in between 0.75 to 1.25, the clay may contain illite and montmorillonite as its major mineral composition.

$$\text{Liquidity index} = LI = \frac{FMC - PL}{PI} = \frac{25.8 - 17.2}{24.8} = 0.346$$

With reference to Figure 3.13, since the LI value is in between 0 to 1, the soil is in plastic state.

Q: *A soil sample was tested in a pycnometer to determine its specific gravity. Calculate the specific gravity of the soil using the following data:*
Weight of empty pycnometer, W1=515 g

Weight of pycnometer with soil, W2 = 1025 g
Weight of pycnometer with soil and water, W3 = 1866 g
Weight of pycnometer completely filled with water, W4 = 1548 g

Figure 3.14 *Determination of specific gravity of soil using pycnometer*

A:

$$Gs = \frac{\text{Weight of soil}}{\text{Weight of water equal to the volume of soil displaced}} = \frac{W2 - W1}{W4 - W3 + (W2 - W1)}$$

$$= \frac{1036 - 515}{1548 - 1866 + (1025 - 515)} = 2.71$$

3.5 Methods of Soil Classification

Soils are generally classified for easy understanding of the constituents like gravel, sand, silt, clay. It helps to know which component and its characteristics is predominant as it apparently influences the proportioning of soils in general. The principle of classifying soils purely based upon grain size distribution using sieve analysis data is termed as textural classification of soil. For classification of fine grained soils, the following three textural soil classification methods by trilinear graphs (Figure 3.15) are available in literature (Casagrande 1948 and Morales 1948).

1. U.S. Bureau of Soils classification.
2. Soil classification by Lower Mississippi Valley Division of the U.S. Engineer Department.
3. Soil classification by Swiss engineers.

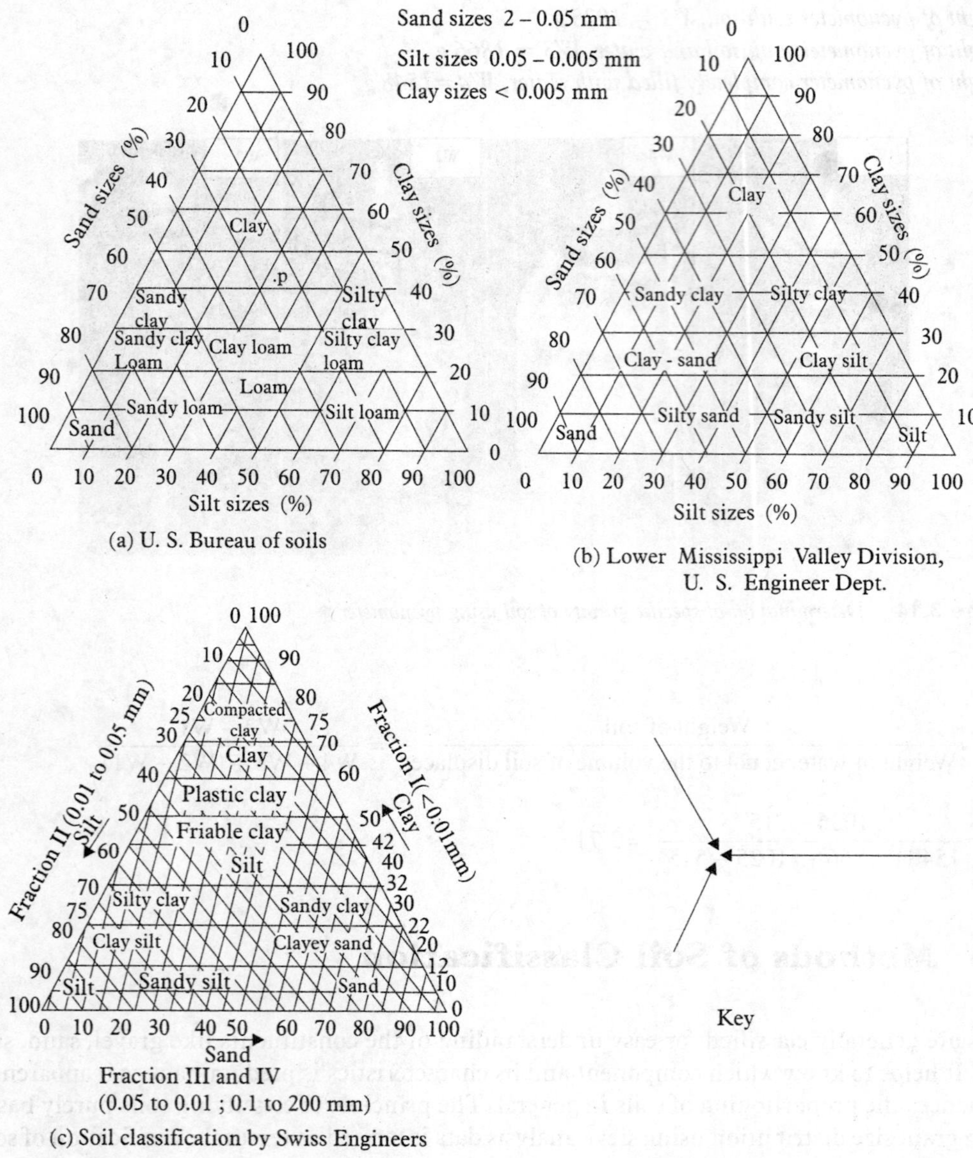

Figure 3.15 *Triangle textural soil classification systems (From Casagrande 1948 and Morales 1948)*

The triangular textural classification of fine grained soil is simple and easy but these methods fail to distinguish soils possessing different physical characteristics which have similar grain size distribution. The limitations of the triangular textural classification for fine grained soils are listed below (Casagrande 1948 and Fadum 1948).

- The three grain size fractions (sand, clay and silt) do not reflect the soil's physical properties, viz. plasticity, cohesiveness, compressibility and strength.
- The discrepancies between grain size distribution and physical characteristics of fine grained soils are not conveyed in these methods.
- A large range of soils is covered for identical grain size distribution curves.

Precise classification of soils can be done by grouping various types of soils based on the characteristics which influence engineering performance. A soil classified under a particular group based upon a standard method is taken as one of the input parameters which dictate (or influence) design of pavements. However, susceptibility of the pavement layer to frost action depends not only on soil characteristics but also on factors related to climate, geophysical and service conditions (Spangler 1948).

Soil classification facilitates soil surveys and correlates empirical knowledge to a specific engineering application (Casagrande 1948). Sieve analysis or grain size distribution data, Atterberg limits and other soil indices like the coefficient curvature and the uniformity coefficient of soil guide highway engineers towards a better understanding of the soils situated at different sites. The above parameters are generally employed during classification of the soil by the group index method to evaluate its suitability for mix composition, stabilisation and pavement design.

The following methods are generally used for classification of soils in highway engineering.

1. Highway Research Board (HRB) classification or American Association of State Highway and Transport Officials (AASHTO) classification or modified Public Roads Administration (PRA) classification.
2. Unified soil classification system (UCSC) or revised Casagrande soil classification.
3. Indian standard method of soil classification (ISMSC).

3.5.1 AASHTO Soil Classification System

In 1928, the Bureau of Public Roads (BPR) introduced a new method of soil classification based on different sub-grade soil parameters and their characteristics. In this method of classification, soils are broadly divided into eight major groups namely, A-1 to A-8.

In 1945, this method was modified and revised by a committee of the Highway Research Board (HRB). It was simplified by using limited parameters, viz. liquid limit, plasticity index, percent passing of soil fraction through 0.075 mm, 0.425 mm and 2.0 mm size sieves and group index value. This revised method of soil classification is also known as the American Association of State Highway and Transport Officials (AASHTO) classification or the modified Public Roads Administration (PRA) soil classification method. In this method, soils are divided into seven major groups namely A-1 to A-7. The groups A-1, A-2 and A-7 were further divided into 2, 4 and 2 sub-groups, respectively. Therefore, the soils were classified into a total of 12 types, viz. A-1-a, A-1-b, A-2-4, A-2-5, A-2-6, A-2-7, A-3, A-4, A-5, A-6, A-7-5 and A-7-6. The AASHTO soil classification system is presented in Figure 3.16.

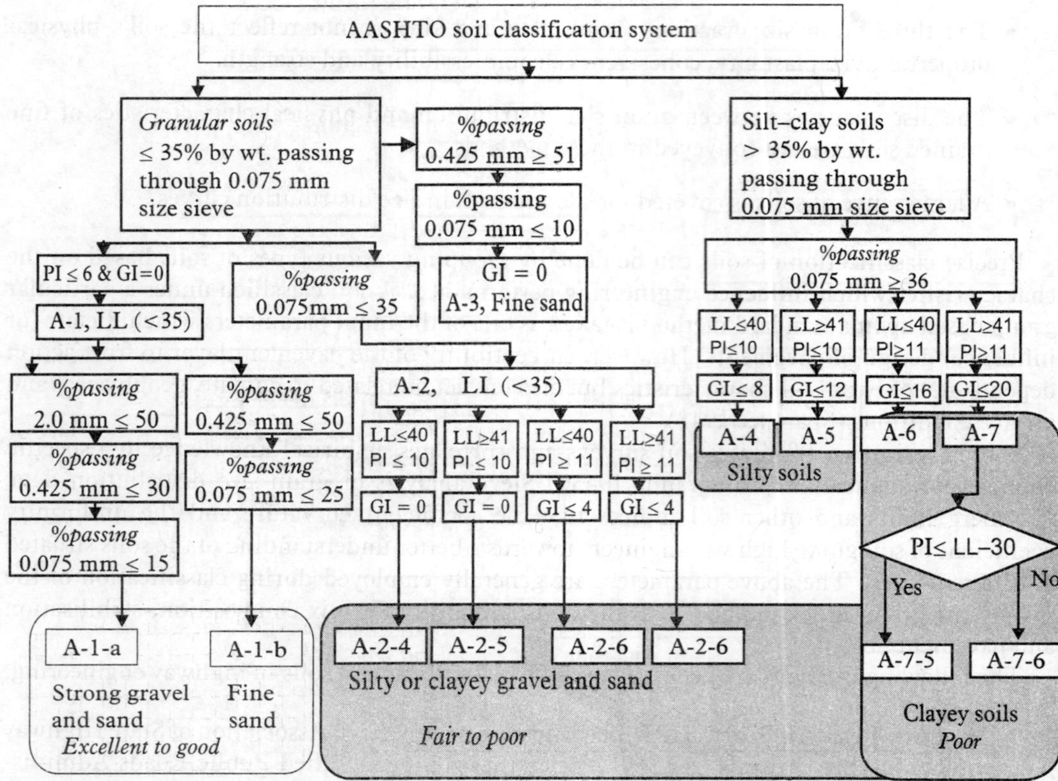

NOTE: The symbol ≤ is read as maximum and ≥ as minimum values.

Figure 3.16 *AASHTO soil classification system*

For further classification of fine grained soils within their sub-groups, an additional input parameter called group index (GI) value was introduced apart from the use of liquid limit, plasticity index and sieve analysis values. GI is an empirical value or number which utilises both gradation and Atterberg limits of soil and indicates sub-grade soil strength. A greater value of GI represents poorer strength of soil and vice versa. The value of GI may be calculated using the following empirical formula which has been derived using the original Public Roads classification (Spangler 1948) and must be expressed as nearest to a whole number.

$$GI = 0.2\,I + 0.005\,IK + 0.01\,JL \tag{3.11}$$

where,

I = $(PP_{75} - 35)$, PP_{75} being the percent of soil passing through a 0.075 mm sieve and expressed as a whole number (the material taken should be smaller than 0.075 mm); the value of I should be between 0 to 40.

K = (LL – 40), LL being the liquid limit; the value of K should be between 0 to 20.

L = (PI – 10), PI being the plasticity index; the value of L should be between 0 to 20.

J = $(PP_{75} - 15)$; the value of J should be between 0 to 40.

Some salient points related to the AASHTO soil classification system are presented below.

- The A-2 group of soil is further divided into sub-groups based on PI, LL and GI.
- As the value of GI increases from 0 to 20, the sub-grade soil rating varies from very strong (excellent) to very weak (poorest). Hence, the required pavement thickness increases as the GI value increases. This relationship also holds good if the soil group varies from A-1 to A-7.
- For highway sub-grade, the soil groups ranging from A-1 to A-3 are generally prescribed but A-1 group is the best. The soil group A-3 is better than A-2 since they are mostly non-plastic and contain slightly coarser particles.
- The rounded value of GI to its whole number should be written in brackets just after the soil group. Example: A-7-6 (19), where GI = 19.

CRRI classification of Indian black cotton soils: The A-7 group of Indian origin soils, specifically black cotton soils having PI $\leq$ (LL $-$ 30) and PI $\geq$ 11, are not exactly classified into the two groups A-7-5 and A-7-6 when the GI value is limited to 20. According to an investigation carried out at the Central Road Research Institute (CRRI), New Delhi (1953), the A-7 group is divided into four sub-groups, A-7, A-7a, A-7b and A-7c, based upon the values of PP_{75}, LL, PI and GI. The maximum permissible GI value is extended from 20 to 50 and the corresponding maximum values of I, J, K and L are recommended as 65, 65, 45 and 34 respectively. For more information, the following brief details are given. The notations are the same as before.

(i) A-7: $PP_{75} \leq 75$; LL<55; PI<25 and GI $\leq$ 20,

(ii) A-7a: PP_{75} = 55 to 95; LL<65; PI<42 and GI = 20 to 30,

(iii) A-7b: PP_{75} = 80 to 95; LL<65; PI<42 and GI = 30 to 40 and

(iv) A-7c: PP_{75} = 85 to 100; LL>65; PI>42 and GI = 40 to 50.

Q: *Classify the soil based on PRA or AASHTO classification system from the following data: Soil passing 0.075 mm size sieve = 85%; liquid limit = 72%; plasticity index = 31%.*

A: Given input values: PP_{75} = percent of soil passing through a 0.075 mm size sieve = 85; LL = liquid limit = 72; PI = plasticity index = 31.

From equation (3.11), GI = 0.2 I + 0.005 I K + 0.01 J L

On substitution,

I = (PP_{75} – 35) = (85 – 35) = 50 ; I value should be between 0 and 40. Hence, take I = 40.

J = (PP_{75} – 15) = (85 – 15) = 70; J value should be between 0 and 40. Hence, take J = 40.

K = (LL – 40) = (72 – 40) = 32; K value should be between 0 and 20. Hence, take K = 20.

L = (PI – 10) = (31 – 10) = 21; L value should be between 0 and 20. Hence, take L = 20.

$$GI = 0.2 \times 50 + 0.005 \times 50 \times 20 + 0.01 \times 40 \times 20 = 20$$

The answer can be obtained from Figure 3.17.

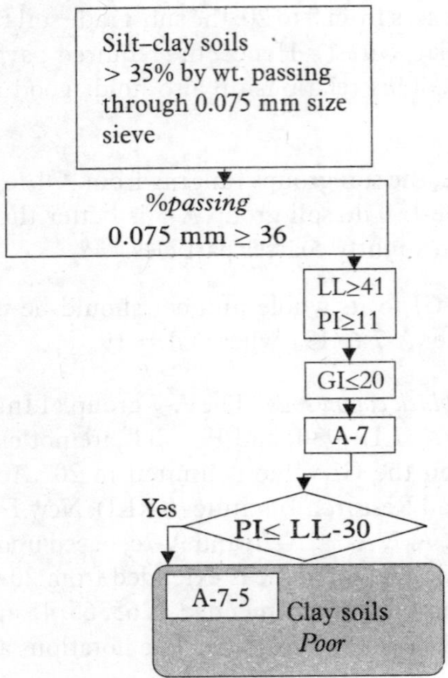

Figure 3.17 *Example problem.*

$$PI \leq LL - 30$$
$$31 \leq 72 - 30$$

Therefore, the soil is classified as A-7-5 (20).

3.5.2 Unified Soil Classification System (USCS)

Professor Casagrande (1942) developed a system of soil classification termed as the airfield classification (AC) system for construction of airfield pavements during Second World War. Later this system was modified and generalised by Professor Casagrande, US Army Corps of Engineers and the US Bureau of Reclamation, for use in various civil engineering construction projects. It was named the Unified Soil Classification System (USCS). The American Society for Testing Materials (ASTM) adopted the USCS in 1969 as the standard method for classifying soil for engineering applications (ASTM D-2487) and highway construction purposes (D 3282-93). This system of soil classification is based on grain size analysis, Atterberg limits of soil, viz. liquid limit (LL) and plastic limit (PL), and a wide range of experience associated with the behaviour of soil as a construction material. Basically, soil is classified into two broad categories namely, coarse and fine grained soils. If the soil fraction retained on sieve no. 200 (0.075 mm) is more than 50 per cent by weight, it is classified as coarse grained soil and if the soil passing through no. 200 (0.075 mm) is more than 50 per cent by weight, it is classified as fine grained soil. These two types of soil are further classified into two types each.

To distinguish different types of fine grained soils among and between the groups of silts and clays and the fine grained part of coarse grained soils, a plasticity chart was first developed by Casagrande (Figure 3.18) and it has been modified and incorporated as part of the USCS. The modified plasticity chart is adopted by the Bureau of Indian Standards as IS: 1498-1970 (Figure 3.19). The given soil classification can be determined by plotting a plasticity chart with plasticity index (PI) as the ordinate and liquid limit (LL) as the abscissa. Location of the plotted point on the plasticity chart yields useful information for classification of fine grained soils.

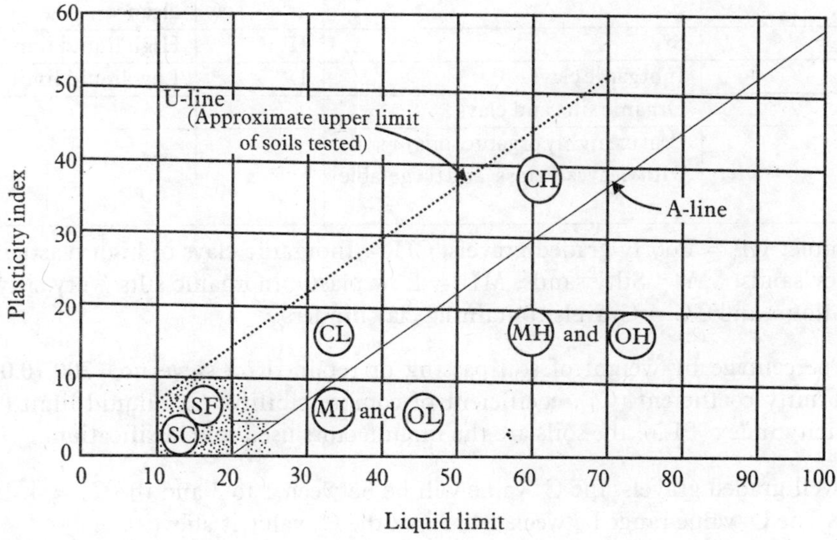

Figure 3.18 *Plasticity chart (After Casagrande 1948).*

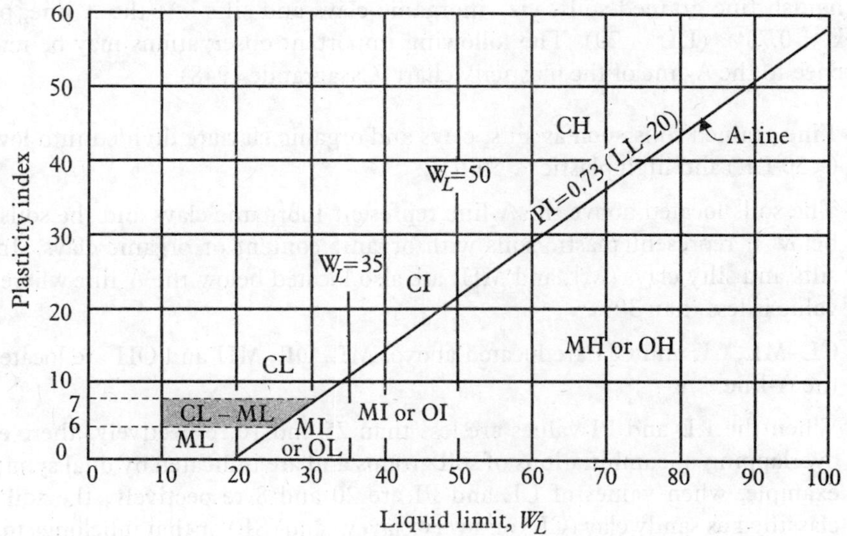

Figure 3.19 *Plasticity chart used in USCS and ISMSC (IS: 1498-1970).*

Details of the USCS and salient points related with the plasticity chart are presented below.

(a) Each soil class is designated with two capital letters. The first letter indicates the soil class or group and the latter indicates its gradation or plasticity or compressibility. The details are given below.

First letter		Second letter	
Symbol	Soil class	Symbol	Soil mix type
G	Gravel	W	Well graded, clean
S	Sand	P	Poorly graded, fairly clean
M	Silt	H	High liquid limit
C	Inorganic clays	L	Low liquid limit
O	Organic silts and clays		
Pt	Peat or highly organic soils or soils with leaves, grass and vegetable matter		

Example: GP = Poorly graded gravels, CH = Inorganic clays of high plasticity, SC = Clayey sands, SM = Silty sands, ML = Low plastic inorganic silts (very silty sand or rock flour) and GC = Gravels containing clay binders.

(b) The percentage by weight of soil passing or retained on sieve no. 200 (0.075 mm), uniformity coefficient (C_u), coefficient of compressibility (C_c), liquid limit (LL) and plasticity index (PI) of the soils are the input factors used for classification.

(c) For well graded gravels, the C_c value will be between 1 to 3 and the C_u = 4. In case of sands, the C_c value range between 1 to 3 and the C_u value is above 6.

(d) An imaginary boundary called the A-line was incorporated in the plasticity chart to distinguish fine grained soils, viz. inorganic clays and silts. At the A-line, plasticity index = 0.73 × (LL − 20). The following important observations may be made with reference to the A-line of the plasticity chart (Casagrande 1948).

- Fine grained soils such as silts, clays and organic clay are divided into low plastic (<50 LL) and high plastic (>50 LL).
- The soils located above the A-line represent inorganic clays and the soils located below it represent plastic soils with organic content or organic clays. Inorganic silts and silty clays (ML and MH) are also located below the A-line where the LL value is less than 30%.
- CL–ML, CL and CH are located above. ML, OL, MH and OH are located below the A-line.
- When the LL and PI values are less than 25 and 10 respectively, there exists an overlapping of combinations of soil groups and are indicated by dual symbols. For example, when values of LL and PI are 20 and 8 respectively, the soil may be classified as sandy clay (CL) or a very clayey sand (SF) or that it belongs to a group of SC. Such soils may be indicated by dual symbols, viz. CL−SC or CL−SF. As another example, a soil having LL = 20 and PI = 5 may be classified as CL−ML.

- Fine grained soils of the Kaolin type of clay derived from feldspar in granite rocks possess some of the characteristics of inorganic silts. Such soils plot below the A-line and may be classified as boundary cases, viz. ML–CL and MH–CH.
- An upper boundary line (U-line) was also introduced in the plasticity chart to indicate the upper boundary limit of different soil groups. At the U-line, plasticity index = 0.9 × (LL − 8).
- The A- and U-lines represent important empirical boundaries used for classifying fine grained soils.
- There is no clear cut separation between border line cases (for soil which have dual characteristics).

3.5.3 Indian Standard Method of Soil Classification (ISMSC)

The Indian standard method of soil classification (IS: 1498-1970, 1st revision) is essentially based on the USCS with minor modifications in the classifications of fine grained soils. The fine grained soils are divided based on compressibility characteristics (Figure 3.20). In USCS, the fine grained soils are classified based on low and high liquid limit values having less than 50 and more than 50 per cent respectively. In the Indian standard method of soil classification (ISMSC), the fine grained soils were classified into three types, viz. low, medium and high liquid limit values having less than 35, 35 to 50 and above 50 per cent respectively (Figure 3.20).

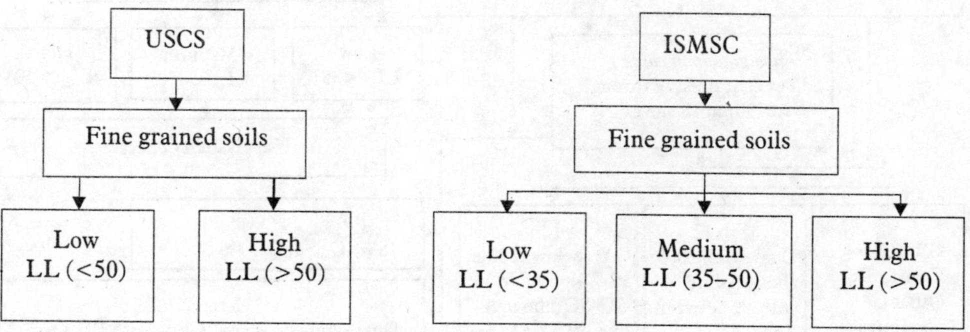

Figure 3.20 *Difference between USCS and ISMSC.*

The flow chart depicted in Figure 3.21 briefly presents the procedure followed by the ISMSC for classifying soil using laboratory results. The plasticity chart given in Figure 3.19 is used for classifying fine grained soils.

In addition to the above given details of the ISMSC (IS: 1498-1970) and USCS, the following salient features may also be considered for classification of soils.

- For identification of organic soils, the following rule of thumb may be used: LL found after oven drying of the soil should be ≤ 3/4th of the LL found before oven drying of the soil.
- Gravel is said to be the fraction size of the soil mass ranging between 75 mm to 4.75 mm. Sand is between 4.75 mm to 0.075 mm size IS sieve.

- Based on the value of LL and with reference to the A-line of the plasticity chart, boundary classification occurs commonly in the following cases,
  - (i) Within gravel or sand group: GW–GP, GM–GC, GW–GM, GW–GC, SW–SP, SM–SC, SW–SM and SW–SC.
  - (ii) Between gravel and sand group: GW–SW, GP–SP, GM–SM and GC–SC.
  - (iii) Between coarse and fine grained soils: SM–ML and SC–CL.
  - (iv) Within fine grained soils which consist of ML–MI, CL–CI, OL–OI, MI–MH, CI–CH, OI–OH, CL–ML, ML–OL, CL–OL, CI–MI, MI–OI, CI–OI, MH–CH, MH–OH and CH–OH.

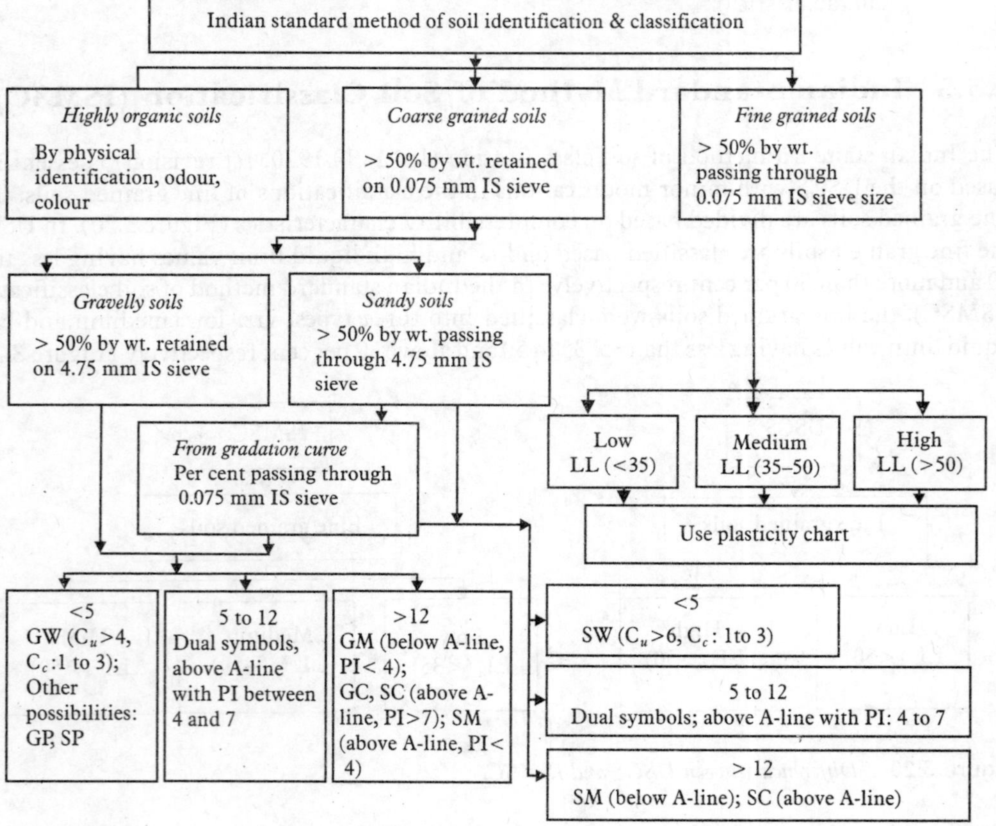

Figure 3.21 *Indian standard method of soil classification (ISMSC)*

A few important points:

- Generally, Atterberg limits are used to correlate various engineering properties of soils.
- Clays having high values of plasticity index (PI>6) are difficult to compact due to their low permeability characteristics.
- For highway embankments or sub-grade, PI value of not more than 6 is preferred to attain the desired degree of compaction under standard compactive effort.

- Shrinkage limit (SL) values may be used to eliminate excessive cracking of highway embankments but the SL value of the soil may be highly sensitive and inconsistent due to slight variation in its texture.

Q: *What is the classification of soil if the percentage passing the 0.075 mm IS sieve is 42, percentage passing the 4.75 mm IS sieve is 76, liquid limit is 41% and plasticity index is 15.*

A: With reference to Figure 3.21, the procedure followed is as given below.

STEP 1: Per cent retained on the 0.075 mm IS sieve = 100 – per cent passing = 100 – 42 = 58.
It is more than 50%.
Hence, the soil belongs to the group of coarse grained soils.

STEP 2: Per cent passing through the 4.75 mm IS sieve = 76.
It is more than 50%. Hence, the soil belongs to the group of sandy soils.

STEP 3: Per cent passing through the 0.075 mm IS sieve = 42 which is more than 12% fine.

STEP 4: A-line = 0.73 (LL – 20) = 0.73(41 – 20) = 15.33.

Therefore, the plotted point having LL = 41 and PI = 15 falls above the A-line.
Hence, the soil is classified as SC.

Q: *What is the gradation of a soil having D_{10} = 0.04 mm, D_{30} = 0.8 mm and D_{60} = 10 mm.*

A: $C_u = \text{Coefficient of uniformity} = \dfrac{D_{60}}{D_{10}} = \dfrac{10}{0.04} = 250$ (more than 4)

$C_c = \text{Coefficient of curvature} = \dfrac{D_{30}^2}{D_{10} \times D_{60}} = \dfrac{0.8^2}{0.04 \times 10} = 1.6$ (between 1 to 3)

The C_u value is more than 4 and the C_c value is between 1 to 3. Hence, the soil is well graded.

Q: *The following data was obtained from a sieve analysis of soil acquired from a proposed borrow area for construction of sub-grade. Plot the grain size distribution curve and classify the soil according to the Indian method of soil classification.*

IS sieve size (mm)	*16*	*10*	*6.3*	*4.75*	*2.8*	*2*	*1.4*	*0.6*	*0.425*	*0.3*	*0.212*	*0.125*	*0.075*	*Pan*
Wt. retained (g)	*0*	*5*	*8*	*10*	*20*	*30*	*30*	*90*	*40*	*30*	*20*	*15*	*10*	*9*

A: The given data may be analysed as shown below.

IS sieve size	Weight retained			% finer (passing)
	(g)	%	Cumulative	
16	0	0.0	0.0	100.0
10	5	1.6	1.6	98.4
6.3	8	2.5	4.1	95.9
4.75	10	3.2	7.3	92.7
2.8	20	6.3	13.6	86.4
2	30	9.5	23.0	77.0
1.4	30	9.5	32.5	67.5
0.6	90	28.4	60.9	39.1
0.425	40	12.6	73.5	26.5
0.3	30	9.5	83.0	17.0
0.212	20	6.3	89.3	10.7
0.125	15	4.7	94.0	6.0
0.075	10	3.2	97.2	2.8
Pan	9	2.8	100.0	0.0
Total	317	100.0		

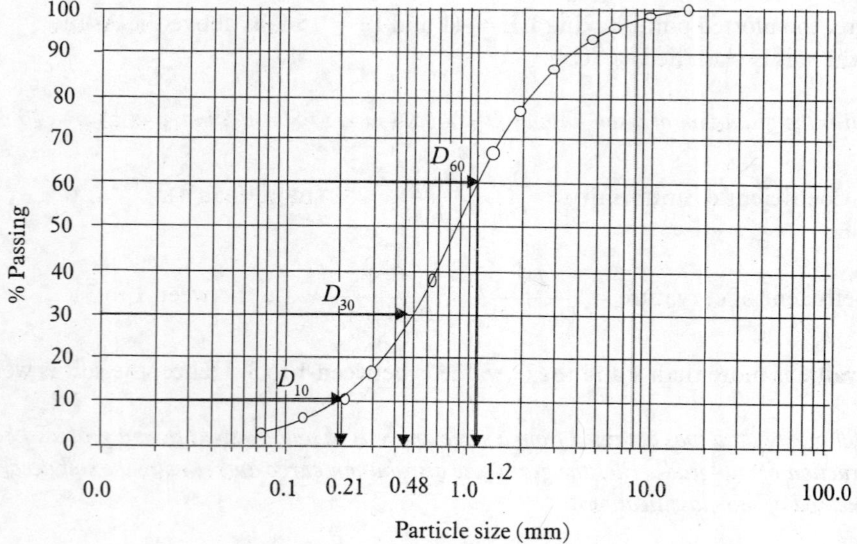

Figure 3.22 *Example problem*

$$C_u = \text{Coefficient of uniformity} = \frac{D_{60}}{D_{10}} = \frac{1.2}{0.21} = 5.71 \text{ (more than 4)}$$

$$C_c = \text{Coefficient of curvature} = \frac{D_{30}^2}{D_{10} \times D_{60}} = \frac{0.48^2}{0.21 \times 1.2} = 1.52 \text{ (between 1 to 3)}$$

The C_u value is more than 4 and the C_c value is between 1 to 3. Hence, the soil is well graded.

With reference to Figure 3.22, a further procedure is adopted as given below,

STEP 1: The soil retained on the 0.075 mm IS sieve is 97.2 % (> 50%). Hence, it is a coarse grained soil.

STEP 2: The soil passing through the 4.75 mm IS sieve is 92.7 % (> 50%). Hence, it is sandy.

STEP 3: From the gradation curve (Figure 3.22), soil passing through the 0.075 mm size IS sieve is 2.8 % ; $C_u = 5.71$ and C_c is between 1 to 3.

Hence, the soil is classified as a well graded sand (SW).

3.6 Composition of Soil Mass

Any soil mass consists of chiefly two elements, viz. solid particles (V_s) and voids (V_v). The voids are again sub-divided into air voids and voids occupied by water. In dry soil masses, there will be no water component. In completely saturated soils, the voids are fully occupied by water. A typical cross-section of soil mass in a partially saturated condition is shown in Figure 3.23. This kind of chart gives clarity during study and analysis of soil properties.

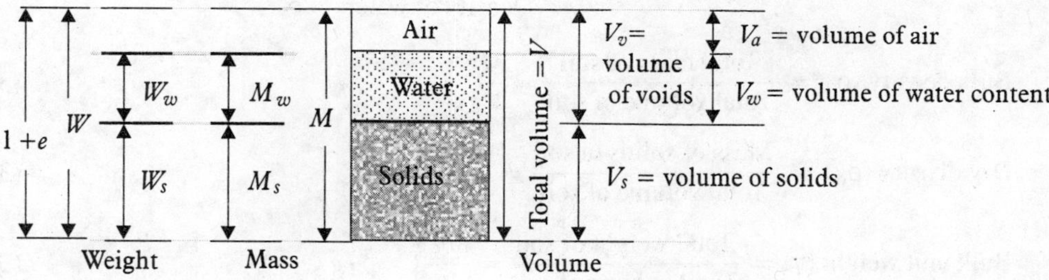

Figure 3.23 *Elements in a partially saturated soil mass*

From the Figure 3.23, the following fundamental relationships may be defined.

$$\text{Moisture content or water content } (W) = \frac{\text{Weight of moisture}}{\text{Weight of solid particles in soil}} = \frac{W_w}{W_s} \quad (3.12)$$

$$\text{Degree of saturation (Sr)} = \frac{\text{Volume of water in soil}}{\text{Volume of voids in soil}} \times 100 = \frac{V_w}{V_v} \times 100 \quad (3.13)$$

(Sr value may range between zero for completely dry soils to 100 % for fully saturated soil)

$$\text{Void ratio } (e) = \frac{\text{Volume of voids in soil}}{\text{Volume of solids in soil}} = \frac{V_v}{V_s} = \frac{V_a + V_w}{V_s} \quad (3.14)$$

$$\text{Porosity}(n) = \frac{\text{Volume of voids in soil}}{\text{Total volume of soil}} = \frac{V_v}{V} = \frac{V_a + V_w}{V_a + V_w + V_s} = \frac{e}{1+e}$$

or $$e = \frac{n}{1-n} \tag{3.15}$$

Volume of air (V_a)= Volume of voids − volume of water

$$V_a = V_v - V_w = e - e \times \text{Sr} = e\,(1-\text{Sr}) \tag{3.16}$$

$$\text{Air voids or air content } (A) = \frac{\text{Volume of air in soil}}{\text{Specific volume of soil}} = \frac{V_a}{1+e} \tag{3.17}$$

$$A = \frac{e\,(1-\text{Sr})}{1+e} = n(1-\text{Sr}) \tag{3.18}$$

Units:

Unit weight of water = γ_w = density of water × acceleration due to gravity = $\rho_w \times g$

$\gamma_w = 1000\ \text{kg/m}^3 \times 9.81\ \text{m/s}^2 = 9810\ \text{kg.m/s}^2/\text{m}^3 = 9810\ \text{N/m}^3 = 9.81\ \text{kN/m}^3$

Density of water $= \rho_w = 1000\ \text{kg/m}^3 = 1\ \text{tonne/m}^3 = 1\ \text{Mg/m}^3 = 1\ \text{g/ml} = 1\ \text{g/cm}^3$

For water : $\gamma_w = \rho_w$; $G_s = 1$.

$$\text{Specific gravity of solid particles} = G_s = \frac{\text{Density of solids}}{\text{Density of water}} = \frac{\rho_d}{\rho_w} \tag{3.19}$$

$$\text{Bulk density } (\rho) = \frac{\text{Total mass of soil}}{\text{Total volume of soil}} = \frac{M}{V} \tag{3.20}$$

$$\text{Dry density } (\rho_d) = \frac{\text{Mass of solids in soil}}{\text{Total volume of soil}} = \frac{M_s}{V} \tag{3.21}$$

$$\text{Bulk unit weight } (\gamma) = \frac{\text{Total weight of soil}}{\text{Total volume of soil}} = \frac{M \cdot g}{V} = \rho \cdot g \tag{3.22}$$

$$\gamma = \frac{W}{V} = \frac{W_s + W_w}{V_s + V_v} = \frac{\gamma_d \cdot V_s + \gamma_w \cdot V_v \cdot \text{Sr}}{V_s + V_v} = \frac{(\rho_d \cdot g) \cdot V_s + \gamma_w \cdot V_v \cdot \text{Sr}}{V_s + V_v}$$

$$= \frac{G_s(\rho_w \cdot g)V_s + \gamma_w \cdot V_v \cdot \text{Sr}}{V_s + V_v} = \frac{G_s \cdot \gamma_w \cdot V_s + \gamma_w \cdot V_v \cdot \text{Sr}}{V_s + V_v}$$

$$\gamma = \frac{(G_s + e \cdot \text{Sr})}{1+e} \times \gamma_w \tag{3.23}$$

$$\text{Degree of saturation (Sr)} = \frac{\text{Volume of water}}{\text{Total volume of voids}} = \frac{V_w}{V_v} = \frac{V_w}{V_a + V_w} \tag{3.24}$$

$$\text{If the soil is partially saturated, } e = \frac{G_s \cdot w}{\text{Sr}} \tag{3.25}$$

If the soil is completely saturated, $V_a = 0$. Hence, Sr = 1.

If Sr = 1, Porosity $(n_{sat}) = \frac{V_w}{V}$; Saturation deficit $= \frac{n - n_{sat}}{n}$ (3.26)

Saturated unit weight soil (when Sr = 1) $= \gamma_{sat} = \frac{\text{Saturated weight}}{\text{Total volume}} = \frac{(G_s + e) \times \gamma_w}{1+e}$ (3.27)

Dry unit weight of soil $= (\gamma_d) = \frac{\text{Weight of solids in soil}}{\text{Total volume of soil}} = \frac{W_s}{V} = \frac{M_s}{V} \times g = \rho_d \times g$ (3.28)

$$\text{If Sr} = 0, \gamma_d = \frac{(G_s \cdot \gamma_w)}{1+e} \quad (3.29)$$

Due to increased water level, the sub-grade soil or embankment will be submerged in water and that portion of the soil is considered for buoyant weight.

This submerged unit weight is equal to the numerical difference between γ_{sat} and γ_w

Relation between dry and bulk unit weight of soil: $\gamma_d = \frac{\gamma}{1+w}$ (3.30)

Relative density of soil (Rd) or density index (DI) $= \frac{e_{max} - e}{e_{max} - e_{min}}$ (3.31)

where, e_{max} = porosity of soil when the soil is compacted to its min. possible density (loosely packed) in case of loosely packed granular soils, $e \approx e_{max}$ and Rd ≈ 0

e_{min} = porosity of soil when the soil is compacted to its max. possible density (densely packed) and in case of densely packed granular soils, $e \approx e_{min}$ and Rd ≈ 1

Q: *Weight of a soil sample with cup was found to be 55.8 g and 51.9 g before and after oven drying respectively. The weight of the empty cup was 21.8 g. The soil mass has 29% of porosity and specific gravity of 2.68. Determine (i) the water content present in the soil sample, (ii) the void ratio, (iii) the dry unit weight of soil, (iv) the bulk unit weight of soil, (v) the degree of saturation, (vi) the unit weight of saturated soil and (vii) the submerged unit weight of soil.*

A:

(i) water content present in the soil sample $(w) = \frac{M_w}{M_s} = \frac{55.8 - 51.9}{51.9 - 21.8} = \frac{3.9}{30.10}$

$= 0.129 = 12.9\%$

(ii) void ratio $(e) = \frac{n}{1-n} = \frac{0.29}{1-0.29} = \frac{0.29}{0.71} = 0.408$

(iii) dry unit weight of soil $(\gamma_d) = \frac{(G_s \cdot \gamma_w)}{1+e} = \frac{(2.68 \times 1\text{g/cm}^3)}{1+0.408} = 1.903\ \text{g/cm}^3$

(iv) bulk unit weight of soil (γ)

We know $\gamma_d = \frac{\gamma}{1+w}$, therefore, $\gamma = \gamma_d(1+w) = 1.903 \times (1 + 0.129) = 2.14\ \text{g/cm}^3$

(v) degree of saturation (Sr) $= \frac{G_s \times w}{e} = \frac{2.68 \times 0.129}{0.408} = 0.847 = 84.7\%$

(vi) unit weight of saturated soil

$$\gamma_{sat} = \frac{(G_s + e) \times \gamma_w}{1 + e} = \frac{(2.68 + 0.408) \times 1}{1 + 0.408} = 2.19 \text{ g/cm}^3$$

(vii) submerged unit weight of soil

$$\gamma_{sub} = \gamma_{sat} - \gamma_w = 2.19 - 1 = 1.19 \text{ g/cm}^3 \text{ or}$$

$$\gamma_{sub} = \frac{(G_s - 1) \times \gamma_w}{1 + e} = \frac{(2.68 - 1) \times 1}{1 + 0.408} = 1.19 \text{ g/cm}^3$$

Q: *A sandy soil sample was tested in a highway engineering laboratory and found to have a water content of 23% with a unit weight of 18.54 kN/m³. From additional lab tests, it was found that the soil's minimum and maximum void ratio values were 0.88 and 0.53 respectively and specific gravity was 2.7. Calculate the degree of saturation and relative density of the soil.*

A: To calculate the required parameters, it is necessary to calculate the value of void's ratio (e) first.

We know, $\gamma_d = \dfrac{\gamma}{1 + w} = \dfrac{18.54}{1 + 0.23} = 15.07 \text{ kN/m}^3$

From the equation of dry unit weight of soil (γ_d) $= \dfrac{(G_s \cdot \gamma_w)}{1 + e}$

On substitution of available values,

$$15.07 = \frac{2.7 \times 9.81 \text{ kN/m}^3}{1 + e}, \therefore \text{ void ratio } (e) = 0.757$$

Degree of saturation (Sr)$= \dfrac{G_s \times w}{e} = \dfrac{2.7 \times 0.23}{0.757} = 0.820 = 82.0\%$

Relative density of soil (Rd) or density index (DI) $= \dfrac{e_{max} - e}{e_{max} - e_{min}}$

On substitution, $\text{Rd} = \text{DI} = \dfrac{0.88 - 0.757}{0.88 - 0.53} = 0.35 = 35\%$

Q: *Calculate the bulk density, dry unit weight, porosity and degree of saturation of a soil sample belonging to A-7-6 group. The soil sample was weighed before and after coating with wax and the weight was 710.2 g and 701.1 g respectively. The soil coated with wax was immersed in water and the total volume was found to be 366.7 cm³. From other tests, it was found that the value of moisture content was 15.7% and the specific gravities of soil and wax were 2.71 and 0.89 respectively.*

A:

$$\text{Volume of wax} = \frac{\text{Mass of wax}}{\text{Specifc gravity of wax}} = \frac{710.2 - 701.1}{0.89} = \frac{9.1 \text{ gm}}{0.89} = 10.22 \text{ cm}^3 = 10.22 \text{ ml}$$

Volume of soil = total volume of sample with wax – volume of wax = 366.7 – 10.22

$$= 356.48 \text{ ml}$$

(i) Bulk density of soil: $\rho = \dfrac{\text{Mass of soil}}{\text{Total volume of soil}} = \dfrac{M}{V} = \dfrac{701.1}{356.48} = 1.966 \text{ Mg/m}^3$

Unit weight of soil: $\gamma = \rho \times \gamma_w = 1.966 \times 9.81 = 19.28 \text{ kN/m}^3$

(ii) Dry density of soil: $\gamma_d = \dfrac{19.28}{1+0.157} = 1.966 \times 9.81 = 16.66 \text{ kN/m}^3$

(iii) Porosity of soil:

We know, $\gamma_d = \dfrac{G_s \cdot \gamma_w}{1+e}$

Given, $16.66 \text{ kN/m}^3 = \dfrac{2.71 \times 9.81}{1+e}, \quad e = 0.595, \quad \therefore n = \dfrac{e}{1+e} = 0.373$

(iv) Degree of saturation:

We know, $e = \dfrac{G_s \cdot w}{\text{Sr}} = 0.595 = \dfrac{2.71 \times 0.157}{\text{Sr}}, \quad \therefore \text{Sr} = 0.715 = 71.5\%$

3.7 Determination of Soil Compaction

In soil compaction test, the relationship between the quantity of moisture or water content present in a soil sample and the maximum density achieved with minimum voids is determined for a given standard compactive effort. Generally, the relationship is parabolic.

By compaction, soil mass attains maximum dry density (MDD) at a particular moisture content only. This moisture content is termed as the optimum moisture content (OMC). Any deviation from the OMC value may result in low dry density of soil either on the wet or dry side of OMC. By compactive effort, at OMC, particles of soil are forced to orient themselves closely in such a fashion that maximum density is obtained with minimum voids. As the compactive effort increases, the value of maximum dry density increases even at lower values of moisture content (Figure 3.24) (Lambe 1960).

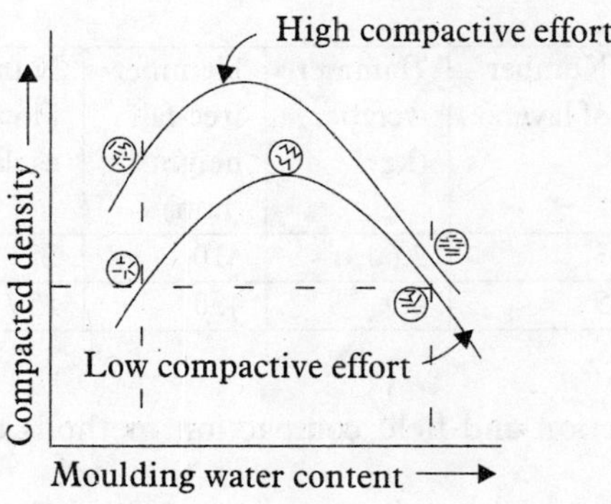

Figure 3.24 *Effects of compaction on soil particles (after Lambe 1960)*

Due to compaction, the following useful changes in soil properties are expected to happen (Mullis 1939; Lambe 1960):

- Increase in density
- Increase in shear strength characteristics
- Decrease in permeability characteristics
- Decrease in swell and shrinkage characteristics
- Decrease in compressibility characteristics

Origin of the test In the year 1933, four articles on soil compaction were published by E. R. Proctor in *Engineering News Record*, Volume III. In the second article, he explained a laboratory compaction test to determine OMC and MDD of a given soil under normal compaction procedure. This test is now termed as the *Standard Proctor Test.*

3.7.1 Principles of Compaction Test Methods

(a) The knowledge of MDD helps to improve in situ ground conditions which otherwise may be unsuitable for construction purposes.

(b) The compaction energy usually employed as

(i) Light weight compaction = 592.77 kJ/m^3
(ii) Heavy weight compaction = 2697.26 kJ/m^3
(Ratio = 4.55)

Magnitude of compaction energy is recommended based on the importance of roads, the intensity of traffic loads anticipated, the number of pavement layers and type of soil. Table 3.2 shows the details of dynamic compaction recommended by the Bureau of Indian Standards.

Table 3.2 *Details of dynamic compaction (IS: 2720 (Part 7)-1980 and IS: 2720 (Part 8)-1983)*

Compaction type	Number of layers	Hammer weight (kg)	Hammer free-fall height (mm)	Number of blows on each layer
Light compaction	3	2.60	310	25
Heavy compaction	5	4.9	450	25

(c) The laboratory compaction and field compaction methods usually conform to similar energy conditions.

3.7.2 Test Procedure

The soil specimen (about 3 kg) should be air dried, thoroughly mixed and passed through 20 mm and 4.75 mm size sieves. The same proportion of soil which passed through the 4.75 mm sieve and that which was retained is taken during the test. The fraction retained on the 20 mm sieve is not used for the test. If soil lumps are present, they should be thoroughly broken, but care should be taken that the natural size of the individual particles is not reduced.

Potable water is added to the soil specimen such that its water content is about 3 to 5% (for gravelly or sandy soils) or 12 to 16% (for clayey soils) less than the plastic limit of the soil. This soil is then placed in an air-tight container for a duration of about 16 hours to achieve homogeneity.

For light compaction Fill the wet soil sample (about 2.5– 3.0 kg which passes through the 20 mm size IS sieve) in the proctor mould in three layers of approximately equal thickness. Compact each layer by giving 25 blows with the 2.6 kg hammer falling through a height of 31 cm of free fall under gravity. The level of the compacted soil should be slightly above the top of the mould and project into the collar after the compaction of the third layer (IS: 2720 (Part 7)-1980; 2004).

For heavy compaction Fill the wet soil sample (about 2.5–3.0 kg which passes through the19 mm size IS sieve) in the proctor mould in five layers of approximately equal thickness. Compact each layer by giving 25 blows with the 4.9 kg hammer falling through a height of 45 cm under gravity. The level of the compacted soil should be slightly above the top of the mould and project into the collar after the compaction of the fifth layer (IS: 2720 (Part 8)-1983; 2004).

Water is added to the soil sample to increase the moisture content by about 2 to 3 per cent and the above procedure is repeated 5 to 6 times. The values of dry densities obtained for each trial test are calculated using following equations.

$$\text{Bulk density, } \rho = \frac{M}{V} \text{ (g/cc)} \tag{3.32}$$

$$\text{Dry density, } \rho_d = \frac{\rho}{1+w} \text{ (g/cc)} \tag{3.33}$$

where, M = weight of compacted soil in g
w = weight of moisture present in g
V = Volume of mould in cm^3

A curve is plotted with the values of the moisture content (w, %) on the x-axis and dry density on the y-axis. A smooth curve is drawn by joining these points. On this curve, the MDD on the y-axis and the corresponding value of the moisture content (w) on the x-axis, which gives the OMC of the soil, are noted. Figure 3.25 shows a typical example of an MDD and OMC determination method using experimental data.

A zero air-void line is also drawn on the same chart. This line suggests the degree of saturation value obtained at the OMC condition. Therefore, it is customary to plot the zero air-void line or 100 per cent saturation curve using the following equations.

$$\text{Dry density, } \rho_d = \frac{G.\rho_\omega}{1+e} \tag{3.34}$$

where, e = void ratio = $w.\ G/$ Sr
G = specific gravity of water
ρ_w = Unit weight of water (9.81 kN/m^3 or 1 g/cc)
Sr = Degree of saturation (for 100 per cent degree of saturation, Sr = 1)

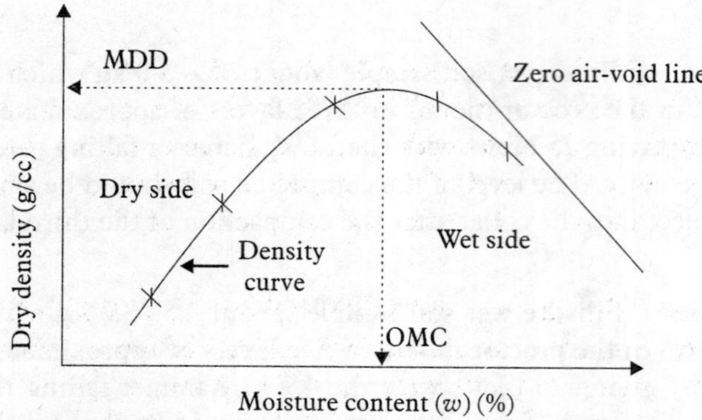

Figure 3.25 *Soil density curve*

The method of determining MDD and OMC of a given soil by the standard proctor density test is illustrated below (Figure 3.30).

OBSERVATIONS AND CALCULATIONS

Diameter of mould, D = 10.0 cm; Height of mould, H = 12.73 cm;
Volume of mould, V = 1000 cm^3.

(a) ***Determination of water content of soil***

Container number	1	2	3	4	5
Weight of empty moisture container (M_1 g)	23.00	25.50	22.22	24.20	25.02
Weight of container + wet soil (M_2 g)	48.00	40.90	41.10	43.32	37.00
Weight of container + dry soil (M_3 g)	47.00	39.90	39.10	40.52	35.00
Weight of dry soil, $M_d = (M_3 - M_1)$ g	25.00	15.40	18.88	19.12	9.98
Weight of water in soil, $M_w = (M_2 - M_3)$ g	1.00	1.00	2.00	2.80	2.00
Water content, $w = \dfrac{M_w}{M_d} = \dfrac{M_2 - M_3}{M_3 - M_1} \times 100(\%)$	4.00	6.48	10.59	14.64	20.04

(b) ***Determination of bulk density and dry density of soil***

Determination number	1	2	3	4	5
Water added by weight (%)	4	8	12	16	20
Weight of soil (g)	3000	3000	3000	3000	3000
Weight of water added (w g)	120	240	360	480	600
Weight of mould (empty) (M_1 g)	2280	2280	2280	2280	2280
Weight of mould + compacted soil (M_2g)	3896	3976	4104	4148	4110
Weight of compacted soil, $M = (M_2 - M_1)$ g	1616	1696	1824	1868	1830
Bulk density, $\rho = \frac{M}{V}$ (g/cc) or kN/ m^3	1.61	1.69	1.82	1.86	1.83
Dry density, $\rho d = \frac{\rho}{1+w}$ (g/cc) or kN/ m^3	1.55	1.59	1.65	1.63	1.52

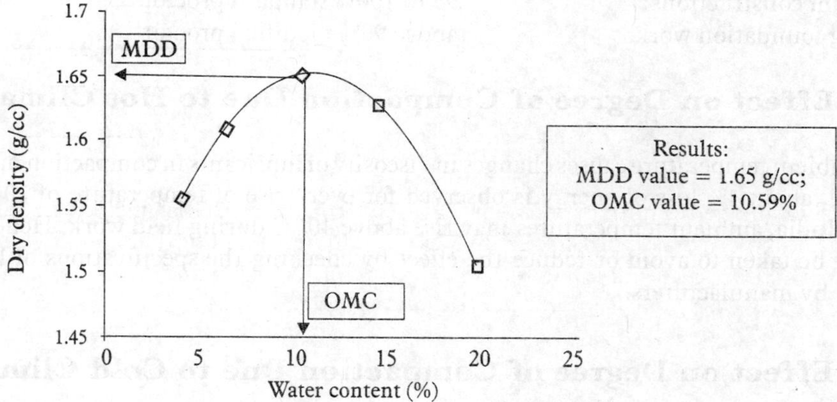

Figure 3.30 *Example problem*

INTERPRETATION OF TEST RESULTS

The lower and higher values of MDD indicate low and high strength of soils respectively. Therefore, it is always preferred to have soils that have higher MDD values at optimum conditions of moisture content.

3.7.3 Degree of Compaction

Degree of compaction is the percentage of the maximum field dry density (FDD) obtained to that of laboratory test conditions. The degree of compaction (DoC) may be expressed as follows.

$$\text{DoC} = \frac{\text{MDD obtained at field}}{\text{MDD obtained at laboratory}} \times 100 \tag{3.35}$$

During construction and quality control operations of highways, embankments and other soil compaction works, DoC is used as a criterion to judge whether the desired quality of compaction work is achieved or not. DoC is the minimum field density to be obtained with reference to the density obtained in the lab. In no case should the field density be less than the specified value. For example, 95 per cent of DoC means all field density values must be equal to or higher than 95 per cent of the MDD value obtained in the laboratory. In all national and international contracts, this specification is invariably prescribed.

The DoC is specified based on the type of construction, anticipated loads, nature of loads, climate and other field conditions. In general, the following are the standard range of DoC specified for different applications.

Base courses of highways and airfields:	98 to 100% modified proctor
Road embankments:	95 to 100% standard proctor
Earth dam constructions:	95 to 100% standard proctor
Building foundation work:	above 90% modified proctor

3.7.4 Effect on Degree of Compaction Due to Hot Climate

Rise in ambient temperature causes changes in viscosity of lubricants in compaction machinery. In general, about 4% loss of energy is observed for every rise of temperature of 10 °C above 20 °C. In India, ambient temperatures may rise above 40 °C during field work. Hence, proper care must be taken to avoid or reduce the effect by checking the specifications of lubricants suggested by manufacturers.

3.7.5 Effect on Degree of Compaction Due to Cold Climate

Viscosity of lubricants used in compaction engines is significantly affected by hot or cold climate. In cold climates, synthetic lubricants are used to avoid freezing and hardening effect. In cold countries, where the ambient temperature falls below 10 °C, the cost of compaction increases drastically because special arrangements have to be made for heating.

Under extreme cold conditions, the soil becomes hard due to the presence of ice crystals in the pores which strongly hold on to the soil particles. In such conditions, the presence of more fines (high void ratio) and more moisture content in the soil makes it very difficult to reach the desired degree of compaction. During the process of thawing frozen soils, the net effective MDD drastically reduces and leads to failure of pavements and embankments.

3.7.6 Quality of Water Needed for Soil Compaction

Generally, potable water is preferred for mixing water during compaction. In some special conditions, sea water is used for soil compaction work in deserts. In such cases, proper laboratory compaction tests are to be conducted and verified with the desired degree of compaction value. Its deleterious effects must be evaluated.

In general, use of saline water for soil compaction causes changes in the values of OMC and MDD based on the percentages of salts present in the water. A thorough investigation is necessary while deciding compaction test parameters such as MDD, OMC and degree of compaction.

3.7.7 Field Compaction Methods

Field compaction can be classified into:

(i) Static compaction
(ii) Kneading compaction
(iii) Pneumatic compaction
(iv) Dynamic compaction
(v) Impact compaction

The type and kind of compaction machinery employed depends upon the prevailing conditions. The type of soil to be compacted, degree of compaction to be achieved and nature of work are the main factors which govern the choice of compacting machinery. Generally, the following points may be considered during selection of suitable equipment for compaction.

A smooth wheel roller is generally used for compacting sub-base and base layers of gravelly soils. They are available in different capacities ranging from 50 kN to 100 kN. Pneumatic and sheep's foot rollers are used for compaction of clayey type of soils. Vibratory rollers produce multiple pressure waves in the soil and soil particles get adjusted closely without any internal friction between the particles. These rollers are generally used for compacting or densification of cohesion-less soils.

In general, the sheep's foot roller is recommended for cohesive soils and the vibratory roller for cohesion-less soil.

3.7.8 Methods for Measuring Field Compaction of Soil Layers

The following are the methods generally adopted to measure field densities.

(i) Core cutter method (IS: 2720 (Part 29)-1975; 2006)
(ii) Sand replacement method (IS: 2720 (Part 28)-1974)
(iii) Ring and water replacement method (IS: 2720 (Part 33)-1971)
(iv) Rubber balloon method (IS: 2720 (Part 34)-1972) (Figure 3.26)
(v) Penetration metre (puncture needle)
(vi) Nuclear density metre (NDM)

The first two methods are generally employed during field compaction control. A brief explanation of these two methods is given below.

The *core cutter method* is suitable for fine grained soil of which not less than 90 per cent passes through a 4.74 mm size IS sieve (IS: 2720 (Part 29)-1975; 2006). In this test, a sharp edged, steel cylindrical hollow mould having internal diameter 100 mm and depth 130 mm with suitable thickness is used. A suitable size steel dolly is placed over the mould during the testing. The mould with the dolly is driven into the soil by hammering on its top. The mould is then dug out from the soil and excess soil from the top and bottom of the mould is trimmed off with a knife. By establishing the weight of the soil in the mould and volume of the empty mould, the bulk density of the soil is determined. A certain amount of soil is taken from the mould and weighed before and after drying in the oven. The moisture content in the soil is expressed as the ratio between the weight of water present in the soil to the initial weight of the soil sample kept in oven.

Sand replacement method is suitable for coarse grained soils. A sand pouring cylinder of suitable capacity is used for this test. A hole of 100 mm diameter having depth less than 150 mm is dug into the soil and the material is carefully collected and weighed. Later, the hole is filled with sand of known density using a sand pouring cylinder. By ascertaining the volume of the sand and weight of the soil collected, the bulk density of the in situ soil is determined. A suitable amount of soil sample is taken for moisture content determination.

The first four methods listed above need some time to determine the value of moisture content but instantaneous results can be obtained using the nuclear density metre (NDM). Therefore, NDM is preferred in almost all quality control of compaction works. NDM consists of a probe or radiation emitting source (shielded suitably) and a detector for receiving the radiation (Figure 3.26 and 3.27). The intensity of transmitted or scattered radiation is correlated with field moisture content (FMC) and in situ dry density of soil. Standard correlation charts are used for determination of in situ dry density and FMC values from the detected intensity of radiation. For reliable results, NMD needs frequent calibration.

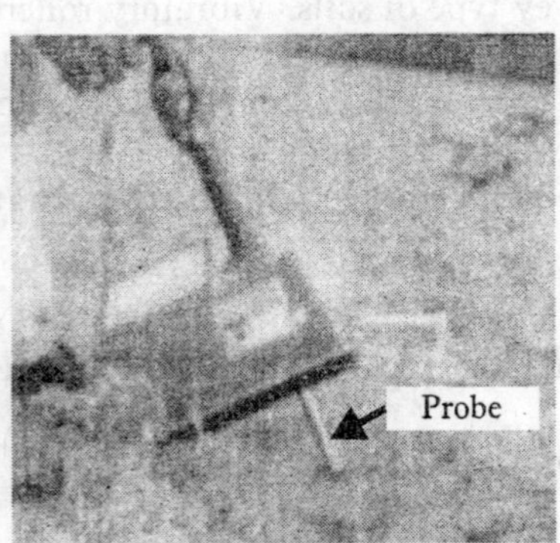

Figure 3.26 *Nuclear density metre*

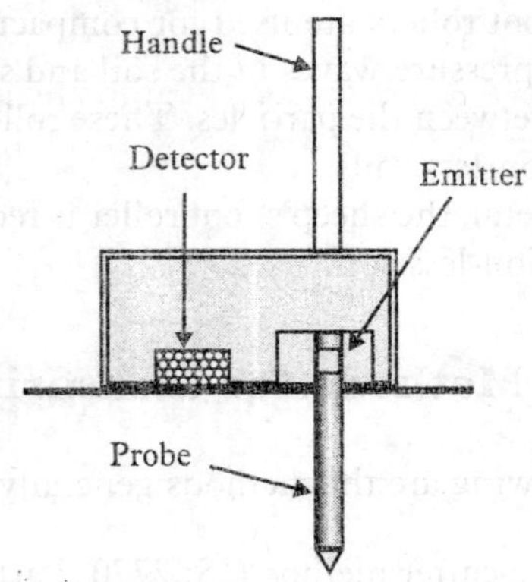

Figure 3.27 *Components of NDM*

3.7.9 Other Applications of Soil Compaction Test Results

Following are some of the important applications of the soil compaction test.

- It is useful for calculating the quantity of soil borrow area required for construction of a soil layer of desired thickness and density.
- The test is useful for designing the sub-grade, sub-base, base and embankment soil layers and for exercising quality control during construction.
- MDD and OMC of soils can be correlated to various other energy properties of soils for better understanding.

- Laboratory soil compaction results are useful for selecting suitable type of compaction machinery to be employed for field compaction works.
- Using the test, one can arrive at a standard deviation value that can be adopted for large-scale embankment compaction works.

A few types of soil compaction methods depending on the water content, climate, energy used and altitude are presented in Figure 3.28.

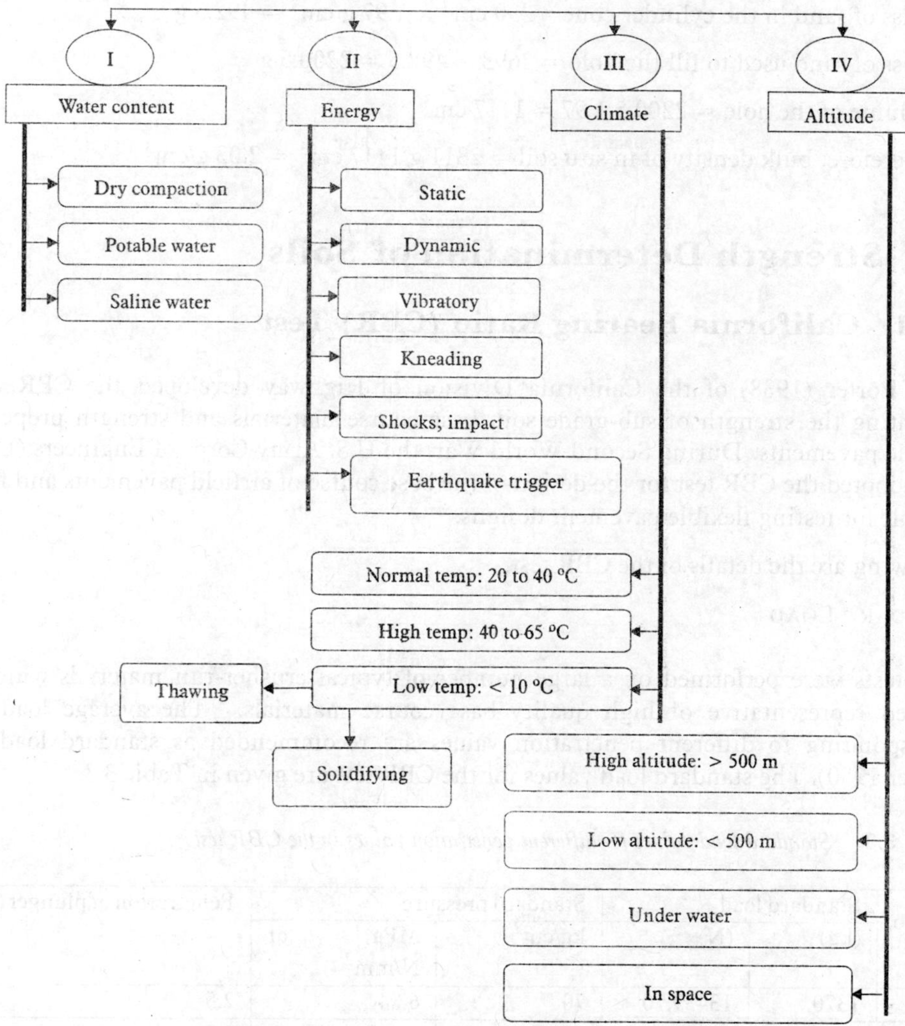

Figure 3.28 *Different types of soil compaction methods*

Q: *A sand replacement test was conducted on a sub-grade soil. Calculate the bulk density of the soil from the following data:*

Mass of soil removed from hole = 2311 g
Mass of sand pouring cylinder completely filled with sand = 5875 g
Mass of sand pouring cylinder after test = 3182 m
Volume of cone in sand pouring cylinder = 250 cc; pouring sand density = 1.97 g/cm^3

A: Mass of sand filled in the hole = (5875 – 3182) = 2693 g

Mass of sand in the cylinder cone= 250 cm^3 × 1.97 g/cm^3 = 492.5 g

Mass of sand used to fill the hole = 2693 – 492.5 = 2200.5 g

Volume of the hole = 2200.5/1.97 = 1117 cm^3

Therefore, bulk density of in situ soil = 2311 g/1117 cm^3 = 2.03 g/cm^3

3.8 Strength Determination of Soils

3.8.1 California Bearing Ratio (CBR) Test

O. J. Porter (1938) of the California Division of Highway developed the CBR test for evaluating the strength of sub-grade soil, base course materials and strength properties of flexible pavements. During Second World War, the U.S. Army Corps of Engineers (USACE) first adopted the CBR test for the design of the base course of airfield pavements and found it suitable for testing flexible pavement designs.

Following are the details of the CBR test.

STANDARD LOAD

CBR tests were performed on a large number of typical crusher-run materials which were deemed representative of high quality base course materials. The average load values corresponding to different penetration values are recommended as standard load values (Porter 1950). The standard load values for the CBR test are given in Table 3.3.

Table 3.3 *Standard load values for different penetration values in the CBR test*

Sl No.	Standard load		Standard pressure		Penetration of plunger (mm)
	(kg)	(N)	kg/cm^2	MPa or N/mm^2	
1	1370	13439.70	70	6.84	2.5
2	2055	20159.55	105	10.27	5.0
3	2630	25800.30	134	13.14	7.5
4	3180	31195.80	162	15.89	10.0
5	3600	35316.00	183	17.99	12.5

PRINCIPLE

A hydraulically loaded cylindrical-plunger of 50 mm diameter is allowed to penetrate vertically into the test soil at the rate of 1.25 mm per minute. The values of load applied are recorded corresponding to the plunger penetration values at 2.5 mm and 5.0 mm. The penetration values are indicative of the combined influence of cohesion and internal friction. The CBR is an index of the shearing strength of soil (Turnbull 1950). These recorded test loads are used to calculate the percent ratios with respect to standard loads at 2.5 mm and 5 mm as 1370 kg and 2055 kg respectively (IS: 2720 (part 16)-1987; 2004).

APPARATUS REQUIRED

Loading system A machine capable of providing constant rate of penetration of 1.25 mm per minute with a capacity of 50 kN (5 tonnes) is used for loading the plunger with a proving ring. If a standard loading system is not available, either a hydraulic or a machine operated loading system with proper calibration can be used. A plunger of 50 mm diameter with a proving ring attachment at the bottom of the loading frame is used for conducting the test.

Mould set To conduct a CBR test, a specimen of compacted soil of 150 mm diameter and 127.3 mm height is prepared. The mould is attached with a collar of about 50 mm length and a detachable perforated base.

Surcharge weights Annular weights of 2.5 kg and 147 mm diameter are placed over the top of the soil specimen to simulate overlying pavement weight in actual field conditions. Suitable surcharge weight is used during soaking and testing the soil samples.

Soaking system The compacted soil specimens are soaked for 4 days under the surcharge weight. Soaking of specimens simulate the worst field condition that a sub-grade soil can be subjected to, similar to monsoon and post-monsoon conditions.

Miscellaneous Dial gauges (least count 0.01 mm), balance (least count 10 g), graduated jar, straight edge, mixing pan, spatula, oven, sieves (sizes: 20 mm and 4.75 mm) and filter paper.

TEST PROCEDURE

Re-moulded as well as undisturbed soil specimens are used for CBR testing. Undisturbed soil specimens are obtained by pushing the CBR mould fitted with a steel cutting edge into the soil. The recommended size of the soil specimen may be obtained by trimming excess portion of the soil at the top and bottom of the mould.

In case of re-moulded soil samples, they should be suitably compacted using light or heavy compaction methods. Tests are performed for both soaked and un-soaked specimens and the CBR values are compared.

The test sample is first prepared. About 20 kg of air-dried soil specimen which has passed through the 20 mm size IS sieve is taken and compacted at OMC with an imparted energy of compaction according to specifications to obtain maximum dry density (MDD). Compaction methods have already been discussed in detail in Section 3.6. After the soil sample is prepared, the sample-filled mould is kept in a soaking bath for four days. Before testing, the specimen is drained for 15 minutes (Jervis and Eustis 1950).

CBR TEST

The base plate along with the mould under the loading system is fixed as shown in Figure 3.31(b) and annular weights (surcharge weights) are placed on the test specimen. The penetration plunger is placed in contact with the top surface of the specimen by applying a seating load of 4 kg. A dial gauge is firmly fitted in position with a proving ring and set to zero before applying the load on the plunger. The plunger is allowed to penetrate into the soil at a uniform rate of 1.25 mm per minute. The values of the load on the proving ring are noted at plunger penetration values of 0.0, 0.5, 1.0, 1.5, 2.0, 2.5, 4.0, 5.0, 7.5, 10.0, and 12.5 mm. The maximum load and the corresponding penetration values are recorded if the plunger penetrates less than 12.5 mm.

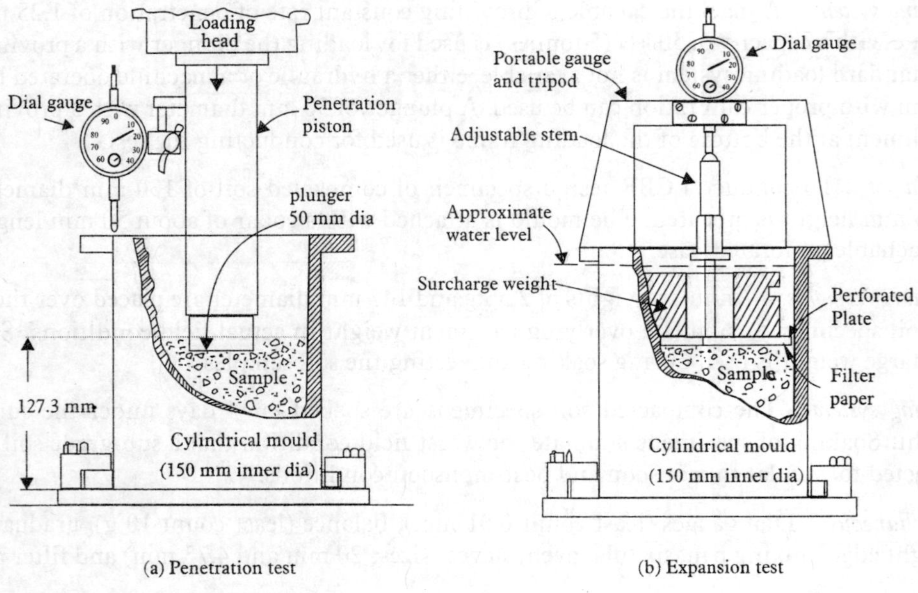

Figure 3.31 (a) *CBR and expansion test set-ups (after Porter 1950)*

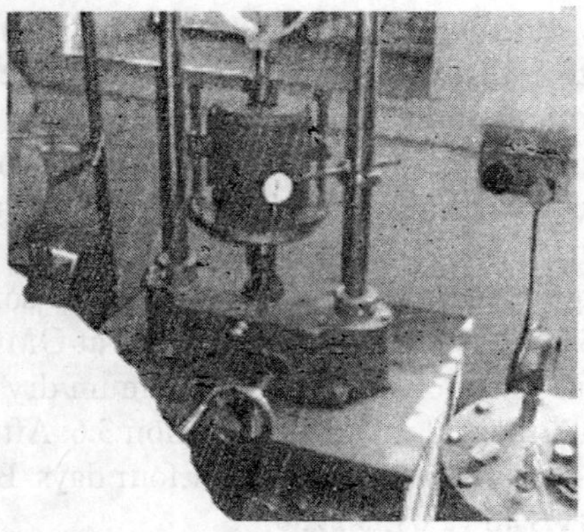

Figure 3.31 (b) *CBR test in progress*

CORRECTION

A typical plot of load vs. penetration is shown in Figure 3.32, including details of the correction required to the plotted CBR curve. If the CBR curve is concave upwards at the initial portion of the curve, it indicates that some irregularities were present on the surface of the compacted specimen. To correct the error in the initial penetration value, draw a tangent from the point of the steepest slope of the curve and extend the line to intersect the x-axis as shown in Figure 3.32. Read the intersection point of tangent on the x-axis as the zero penetration value and establish it as the origin. Read penetration values with reference to the new origin. A typical example is also shown in Figure 3.32.

To calculate the CBR value, the recorded load is expressed as a percentage of the standard load value for the respective penetration value. The CBR values are calculated using the following formulae.

CBR value (%) at 2.5 mm penetration:

$$CBR_{2.5\text{mm}} = \frac{\text{Test load at 2.5 mm penetration (kg)}}{\text{Standard load at 2.5 mm penetration (1370 kg)}} \times 100 \tag{3.36}$$

CBR value (%) at 5.0 mm penetration:

$$CBR_{5.0\text{mm}} = \frac{\text{Test load at 5.0 mm penetration(kg)}}{\text{Standard load at 5.0 mm penetration (2055 kg)}} \times 100 \tag{3.37}$$

Design CBR value = $CBR_{2.5\text{nm}}$%

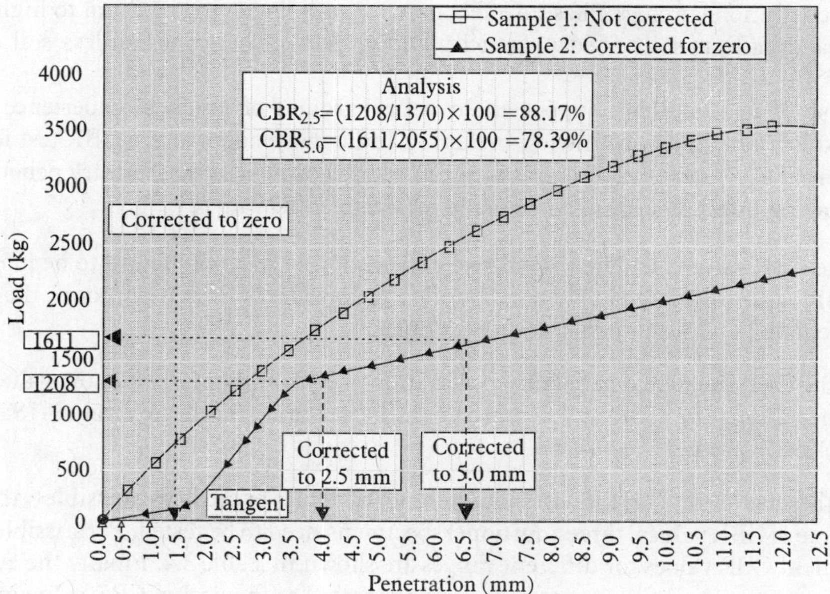

Figure 3.32 *A typical CBR load–penetration curve*

Interpretation of expansion values Expansion of compacted soil samples during soaking indicates the tendency of the soil to swell when exposed to excess water (Figure 3.33). Therefore, uplift of the compacted surface takes place by non-uniform volumetric changes in soil which result in surface irregularities along the road surface. A study of expansion (swell) of soils during the four-days soaking are carried out and the materials are classified as good when they expand less than 1% of the initial height of the specimen, satisfactory when they expand less than 3% and poor when the expansion ranges from 7 to 20% (Porter 1950).

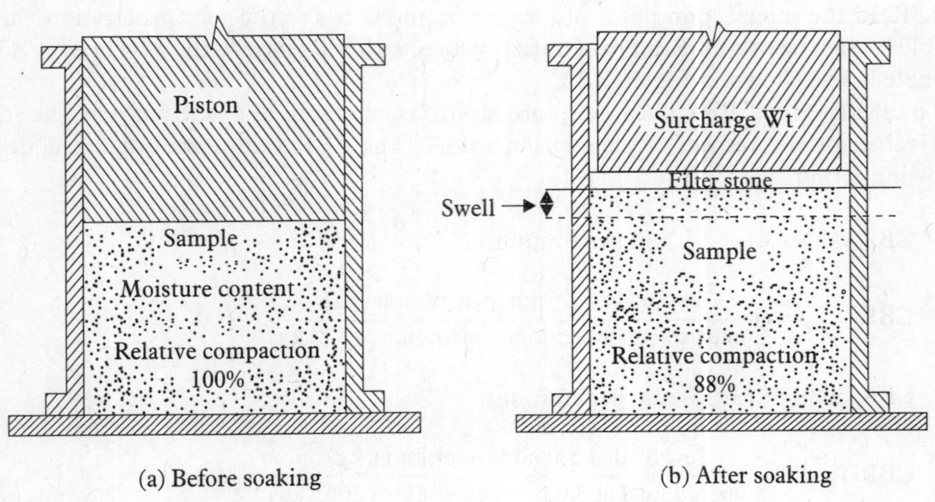

Figure 3.33 *A typical example on expansion of soil when soaked (after Porter 1950)*

The penetration surcharge has no effect on CBR of soils having medium to high plasticity. It moderately affects soils of low plasticity and greatly affects cohesion-less soil (Jervis and Eustis 1950).

Because of its simplicity supported by a background of practical experience (Turnbull 1950) and low cost, many countries, including India, have adopted the CBR test for strength evaluation of sub-grade soil and granular materials though it is an arbitrary penetration test. The following interpretations can be made regarding CBR values.

- The CBR value calculated at 2.5 mm penetration is generally found to be more than the CBR value calculated at 5.0 mm. For flexible pavement design purposes, the CBR value calculated at 2.5 mm penetration is adopted.
- If the CBR calculated at 5.0 mm penetration is constantly more than the value at 2.5 mm penetration, the CBR at 5.0 mm should be taken as the design value (IS: 2720 (part 16)-1987; 2004).
- If the maximum variation in laboratory CBR values exceeds permissible variation for a range of CBR values, three additional specimens need to be tested. Permissible variations in field CBR values for different ranges are shown in Table 3.4. Finally the average CBR value of the six specimens tested is to be reported as the design CBR value in per cent.

Table 3.4 *Maximum allowable variation in field CBR values (IS: 2720 (part 31)-1987)*

Sl. No.	Range of CBR values	Max. allowable variation in CBR value
1	More than 60%	Not significant
2	30 to 60%	10.0
3	10 to 30%	5.0
4	0 to 10%	3.0

According to IRC (*IRC Pocket Book* 2006), the sub-grade soil should conform to the minimum CBR requirement. In general, the CBR value of sub-grade soil should be more than 2%. If not, the soil should be suitably stabilised to improve the CBR value. In case of embankment, after compaction, the soil used as sub-grade should preferably have a CBR value more than 7%. Soil having less than 5% CBR is not suitable for sub-grade.

3.8.2 Plate Load Test

This test is conducted to determine the modulus of sub-grade reaction (k value) of in situ sub-grade soil for analysis of pavements. In this test, sub-grade soil is subjected to different compressive stresses through some standard circular rigid plates. The corresponding vertical surface deflections of the plate are measured. Magnitude of surface deflections due to applied compressive stresses depends mainly on the supporting capacity of the soil below and its stiffness or the load bearing capacity of the soil.

The values of sub-grade reaction are dependent on the type of sub-grade soil, density, frost action, saturation and intensity of stress applied. To analyse pavements, we need to find a representative value of the modulus of sub-grade reaction. From different studies and based on past experience, it has been found that the most representative value of sub-grade reaction can be obtained at a pressure of 0.7 kg/cm^2 (T 222-81 AASHTO; Yoder and Witczak; IS: 9214-1979; 1980).

NEED AND SCOPE

Plate load test results are generally used in the following cases:

1. To design rigid pavements according to IRC: 58 where the value of the modulus of sub-grade reaction (k) is useful in Westergaard's analysis.

2. To determine in situ sub-grade soil support in McLeod's design method for flexible pavements.

3. To determine modulus values of sub-grade and base layers in Burmister's design method for flexible pavements based on the elastic two-layer theory.

4. In modelling and understanding the behaviour of sub-grade soil in the design of flexible or rigid pavements. The behaviour is investigated based on the area of the loading plate, values of static loads vs. deflection, soil type and presence of moisture content in the soil.

Origin of the Test

In 1943, McLeod, a soil engineer, performed a few plate load tests to characterise the strength properties of different layers of airfield pavements in Canada. The test results were used to design the thickness of highway and airfield pavement layers. This test is also used to determine the load bearing capacity, modulus of sub-grade reaction, and elastic and plastic deformation of soil stratum.

Apparatus

1. *Loading plates* A mild steel plate of 75 cm (≈30 inches) diameter with 20 to 40 mm thickness is used as the main loading plate. Three other mild steel plates of the same thickness having diameters of 60.96 cm (≈24"), 45.72 cm (≈18") and 30.48 cm (≈12") are used as stiffeners. The main plate is in contact with the sub-grade soil and the remaining plates are placed over it as shown in Figure 3.34. Stacking of plates is useful to avoid bending of the main plate during loading.

2. *Loading system* A dead load and a hydraulic or reaction loading system of about 15 tonnes capacity is used along with a dial gauge fitted with a proving ring or electronic load measuring system to read up to half per cent of load applied.
3. *Deflection sensors* Three dial gauges or LVDTs (linear variable differential transformers) with suitable electronic devices are used to measure deflections with a least count of 0.002 mm. The plate deflections are measured with reference to a datum or independent support which is not in the deflected area of the soil. The reference datum may be selected at least four and half metres away from the loading plate. The deflection sensors are fixed along the periphery of the main loading plate 120° apart.
4. *Other accessories* Mild steel spacer blocks, spirit level and other tools

Test Setup

The test site is cleaned and levelled so that the main loading plate is in full contact with the ground surface. The top layer may be removed up to a certain depth if the test is being conducted on loose or natural ground.

The main loading plate of 75 cm diameter is placed on the levelled sub-grade soil. If the surface of the sub-grade is rough or not level, a bed is made out of sand and plaster of Paris of a thickness not more than 25 mm. After hardening the bed, the main plate is placed over the bed and stiffener plates are placed over it. A suitable loading system such as a truck or any vehicle suitably connected with a reaction beam and a hydraulic jack with a load measuring device is arranged as shown in Figure 3.34. Three dial gauges are placed along the periphery of the loading plate and they are fixed to a support or datum which is not in the deflected area.

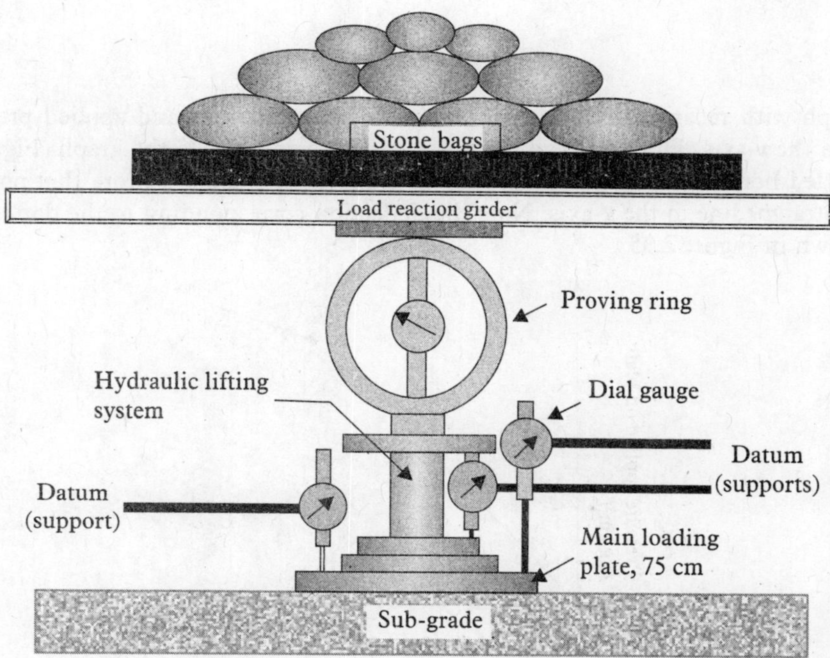

Figure 3.34 *A typical plate load test setup*

TEST PROCEDURE

The steps followed to determine the *k* value useful for design of light to medium loaded pavements are given below.

STEP 1: A seating load of 310 kg (a pressure of 70 g/cm^2) is applied.

STEP 2: Dial gauges of the deflection sensors are set to zero reading.

STEP 3: In addition to the seating load, 3100 kg is applied on the plate and allowed to complete settlement until the rate of settlement of the plate is not more than 0.005 mm per minute.

STEP 4: Deflection measurements are to be taken from the three deflection sensors which are fitted along the periphery of the main loading plate.

STEP 5: The load is increased further in increments of 1550 kg to a maximum value of 9410 kg.

STEP 6: After every load increment, deflection readings are taken. A time gap of about 15 minutes should be maintained in between successive load increments.

For the design of heavily loaded pavements, the *k* value may be determined based on a separate test procedure. For further details, IS: 9214-1979 may be referred.

RESULT

Plot a graph with mean deflection of plate (in cm) on the x-axis and applied pressure (in kg/cm^2) on the y-axis. Draw a smooth curve joining the points. On the graph (Figure 3.35), draw a dotted horizontal straight line from the y-axis at 0.7 kg/cm^2. From that point, draw a vertical straight line to the x-axis. Note the deflection corresponding to the dotted vertical line as shown in Figure 2.35.

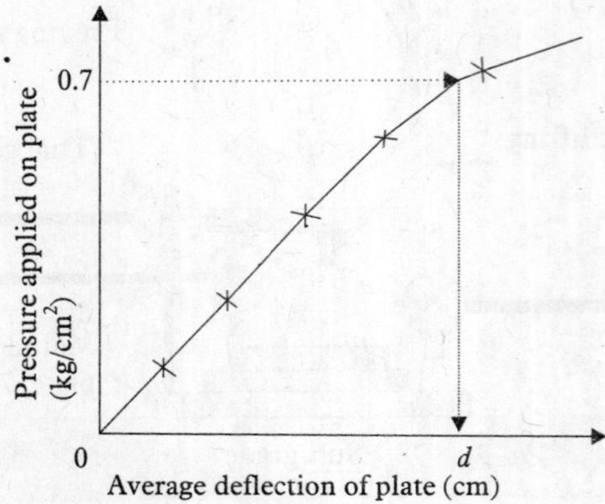

Figure 3.35 *Pressure–deflection curve of plate load test*

CALCULATIONS

Modulus of sub-grade reaction (k value)

$$= \frac{\text{Pressure on 75 cm dia. plate due to 3100 kg load}}{\text{Average plate deflection}}$$

or

$$k \text{ value (kg/cm}^2\text{ /cm)} = \frac{0.7 \text{ kg/cm}^2}{\text{The deflection (in cm) obtained at the pressure of } 0.7 \text{ kg/cm}^2} \quad (3.38)$$

CORRECTIONS

The calculated k value needs to be corrected due to variability in test conditions such as change in diameter of plate, load–deflection pattern, bending of plates and saturation condition of sub-grade soils. The following points need to be considered before incorporating corrections.

- According to IS: 9214-1979, no correction is required to be made if the diameter of the loading plate is 75 cm.
- Due to loading, deformation or deflection of sub-grade soil is different based on soil type and field density. The assumption of a linear relationship between load and deflection is incorrect if the sub-grade soil is non-uniform and granular. For correction, plot a graph with mean deflection of plate (in cm) on the x-axis and applied pressure (in kg/cm^2) on

the y-axis. Draw a line passing through the origin and parallel to the first three points of the curve (AASHTO 1995). Now read the value of deflection corresponding to 0.7 kg/cm^2. Equation (3.38) is used for calculating the k value by using average deflection of the loading plate.

- Mild steel plates may bend under loading. Due to this reason, the k value obtained from the test result is required to be corrected according to IS: 9214-1979. The bending of plates does not require correction if the calculated k value is less than 2.75 kg/cm^2/cm. The corrected value (k_b) may be calculated using equation (3.39) (developed from Figure 5 of IS: 9214-1979; 1980).

$$k_b = 0.9556 \times k - 0.0113 \times k^2 \tag{3.39}$$

- The load–settlement behaviour of a soil depends on different factors such as soil type, area of loading plate, density and quantity of moisture present in the soil. For a loading plate of standard size and a given soil type, the soil behaves differently at different saturation levels and density. The load bearing capacity of a soil drastically reduces under soaked conditions. To obtain the minimum value of k for a soil under saturated conditions, it is necessary to conduct the plate load test on the soil when it is soaked. However, due to practical reasons, it is not always possible to conduct the test on soaked sub-grade soil. Therefore, it is necessary to determine a correction factor by which we can obtain an equivalent k value for soaked soil if the k value of unsoaked soil is available in situ. To determine the correction factor, the following procedure may be adopted.

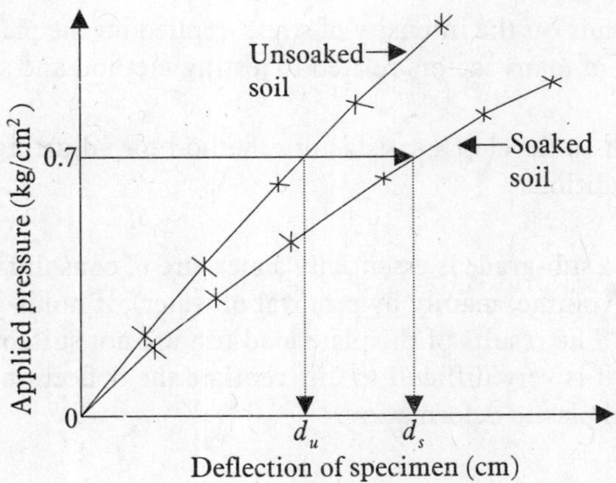

Figure 3.36 *Typical curves resulting from the plate load tests*

Two simple compression tests need to be conducted in the laboratory on two soil samples which are collected from the test site. The first test is conducted at the field moisture content and field density of the soil. The second test is conducted on soaked soil having the same density. Average plate deflections obtained from both the tests are measured at a pressure of 0.7 kg/cm^2.

From the above test results, two curves are plotted with deflection values (in cm) on the x-axis and pressure values (in kg/cm^2) on the y-axis as shown in Figure 3.36. Draw a horizontal dotted line from the y-axis at 0.7 kg/cm^2 pressure and read the corresponding deflection values of the unsoaked (d_u) and soaked (d_s) soil curves. The correction factor required to be multiplied with the calculated k value is obtained as a ratio between d_u and d_s (i.e., d_u/d_s).

The correction factor for k of a soaked specimen is calculated by using the following expression.

$$k_{\text{soaked}} = \text{Correction factor} \times k_{\text{unsoaked}} \tag{3.40}$$

where Correction factor $= d_u/d_s$

k_{unsoaked} = Modulus of sub-grade reaction of unsoaked soil from plate load test

k_{soaked} = Equivalent modulus of sub-grade reaction on soaked soil

- The diameter of the loading plate is not fixed. It is variable depending on the purpose of the test being conducted. Generally, a loading plate having a minimum diameter of 30 cm and a maximum of 75 cm is used for design of highway and runway pavements respectively. It is noted that, in no case, the maximum plate load should be less than the maximum wheel load or design wheel load anticipated. The following relationship is used to determine the equivalent k value.

$$k_{30} = \text{Correction factor} \times k_{75} \tag{3.41}$$

where Correction factor $= d_{75}/d_{30}$ or may be assumed to be equal to 75/30 = 2.5

k_{75} and k_{30} = k values determined using 75 cm and 30 cm diameter of plates respectively

d_{75} and d_{30} = Deflections measured using 75 cm and 30 cm diameter of plates respectively

Limitation of the plate load test (Mcfadden and Pringle 1950):

(a) The k value depends on the intensity of stress applied on the plate and varies according to a combination of many factors related to testing method and soil type.

(b) It is very difficult to develop a satisfactory method for adjusting test results to various soil moisture conditions.

(c) As the k value of a sub-grade is essentially a measure of consolidation (process by which soils decrease in volume, mainly by removal of water), it holds good only for design of rigid pavements. The results of the plate load test are not suitable for design of flexible pavements since it is very difficult to differentiate the deflection under the plate due to consolidation and plastic deformation.

PLT is more time consuming, has a more elaborate calculation procedure and is costly. Therefore, for thickness design of concrete cement slab pavement (IRC: 58-2002), the following relationship (Table 3.5) between the values of CBR and k may be used.

Table 3.5 *Relationship between values of CBR and k of a homogeneous soil sub-grade (IRC: 58-2002)*

k value (kg/cm^3)	2.08	2.77	3.46	4.16	4.84	5.54	6.92	13.85	22.16
CBR value (%)	2	3	4	5	7	10	20	50	100

For design of rigid pavements, the soil may be classified based on the value of the modulus of sub-grade reaction (k value in kg/cm^2/cm) (Moore 1956).

Very good	:		$k > 7.61$
Good	:	7.61 >	$k > 6.22$
Fair	:	6.22 >	$k > 4.84$
Poor	:	4.84 >	$k > 2.76$
Very poor	:		$k < 2.76$

Q. *What is the k value after necessary corrections, if the uncorrected k value is 5.2 kg/cm²/cm when the plate diameter is 75 cm?*

A: In sequential order, the required corrections to be made are given below:

(i) *Correction for bending of plates:*

The correction for bending of plates has been recommended in IS: 9214-1979. An approximate correction may be calculated using equation (3.39).

$$k_b = 0.9556 \times k - 0.0113 \times k^2$$

$$k_b = 0.9556 \times (5.2) - 0.0113 \times (5.2)^2 = 4.66 \text{ kg/cm}^2\text{/cm}$$

(ii) *Correction for saturation:*

The correction value (d_u/d_s) should be determined from results of consolidation tests conducted on the sub-grade soil in the un-saturated and the saturated condition. If the correction value is not available, a suitable value may be assumed based on the soil type.

Now, let us assume, $(d_u/d_s) = 0.78$

$$k_{sat} = (d_u/d_s) \times k_b = 0.78 \times 4.66 = 3.63 \text{ kg/cm}^2\text{/cm}$$

(iii) *Correction for variable size of plate:*

As the plate size = 75 cm diameter, no correction is required. Hence, $k = 3.63$ kg/cm²/cm.

(iv) *Correction for load–deflection curve:*

As the k value is less than 5.55 kg /cm²/cm, no correction due to load-deflection curve is required. Hence, $k = 3.63$ kg/cm²/cm.

Q: *According to the AASHTO guidelines, apply necessary corrections to the k value based on the following plate load test data.*

Diameter of the plate used is 50 cm. Take correction factor for lesser diameter of the plate = 1.5 and correction factor for saturation = 0.82.

Pressure (kg/cm²)	*Settlement (cm)*
0.7	*0.026*
1.4	*0.067*
1.75	*0.085*

A: The required corrections to be made to the k value are given below:

(i) *Correction for load–deflection curve:*

Plot a curve from the given load–settlement data. Join these points. This curve or straight line is called the uncorrected curve. Now draw a straight line passing through the origin and parallel to the uncorrected curve. This line is called the corrected curve. On the corrected curve, read the value of the settlement on the y-axis at 0.7 kg/cm^2 pressure. The details of the plot are shown in Figure 3.37.

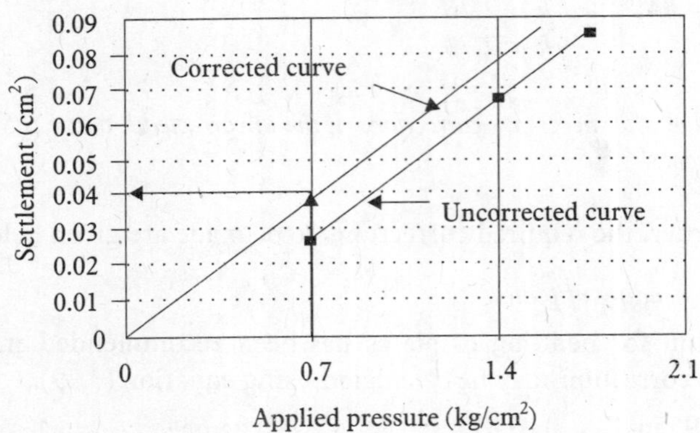

Figure 3.37 *Example problem on load–settlement curve*

$k_{\text{curve}} = 0.7/0.039 = 17.94$ kg/cm^2/cm

(ii) *Correction for bending of plates:*

An approximate correction may be determined by using equation (3.39).

$$k_b = 0.9556 \times k_{\text{curve}} - 0.0113 \times k_{\text{curve}}^2$$

$$k_b = 0.9556 \times (17.94) - 0.0113 \times (17.94)^2 = 13.5 \text{ kg/cm}^2\text{/cm}$$

(iii) *Correction for saturation*:

The given correction value = 0.82.

$$k_{\text{sat}} = 0.82 \times k_b = 0.82 \times 13.5 = 11.07 \text{ kg/cm}^2\text{/cm}$$

(iv) *Correction for variable size of plate:*

Diameter of plate used = 50 cm $\neq$ 75 cm (standard size), hence, correction is required.

$$k_{\text{final}} = k_b \times \text{ correction factor} = 11.07 \times 1.5 = 16.60 \text{ kg/cm}^2\text{/cm}$$

3.8.3 Shear Strength of Soil

To understand the behaviour of sub-grade soil, it is mandatory to know its shear strength properties. The sub-grade undergoes deformation or deflection due to application of wheel loads. The degree of deformation depends on soil texture, class, moisture content and confinement around the pavement layers. The sub-grade should also be strong enough to resist the stresses caused due to shear forces during wheel load applications. To understand the shear strength properties of soils, it is necessary to know Coulomb's law.

In 1776, Coulomb developed a relationship to determine shear resistance of soil based on friction and cohesion of soil particles. This law states that (Figure 3.38) the frictional resistance offered by soil particles varies based on the intensity of the normal stress (σ) applied on the failure plane. But the value of cohesive resistance (C) of the soil is constant and does not depend on the intensity of pressure applied. The following relationship represents Coulomb's law.

Shear stress at failure or shear strength of soil,

$$\tau = C + \sigma \tan \Phi \tag{3.42}$$

where, C = Cohesion of soil
σ = normal stress on failure plane
Φ = angle of shearing resistance
$\tan \Phi$ = coefficient of friction

The above relationship holds good for coarse grained soil such as gravel and sand. But it does not estimate satisfactory shear strength values for fine grained soils such as silts and clays. This may be due to the factors that influence internal friction between soil particles, shape and size of soil particles, degree of interlocking of particles, density, gradation, moisture content and drainage conditions. All these factors effect the strength value of fine grained soils and thus coarse grained soils offer more resistance against shear stresses. It may also be observed that as the interlocking or frictional resistance of soil particles increases due to the presence of coarser particles, the angle of friction also increases. Terzaghi's theory of effective stress (1925) presented a scientific explanation of this phenomenon. Based on his theory, the Coulomb's equation was modified as given below.

Shear stress at failure or shear strength of soil,

$$\tau = C' + \sigma' \tan \Phi' \tag{3.43}$$

where, C' = cohesion of soil corresponding to effective stress.
σ' = effective normal stress on failure plane = ($\sigma -$ neutral stress).
Φ' = angle of shearing resistance corresponding to effective stress.

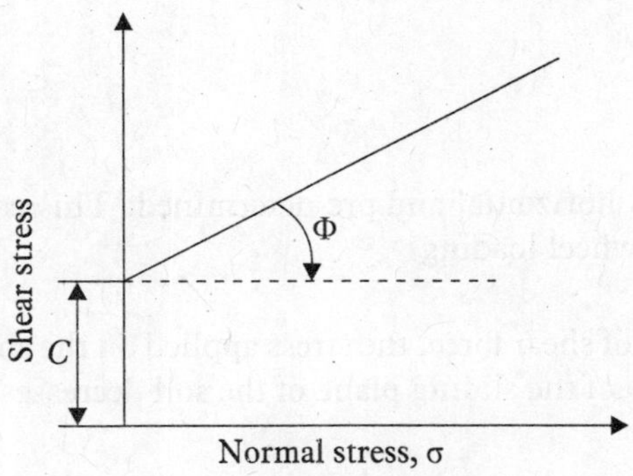

Figure 3.38 *Shear strength parameters of soil*

The above shear strength parameters of soil may be generally determined by laboratory based tests like the direct shear box test, tri-axial test, and unconfined compression test or by conducting the vane shear test on cohesive soils of lower shear strength (IS: 2720 (Part 30)-1980).

Direct Shear Box Test

The direct shear test apparatus consists of a square brass box of suitable dimension which splits horizontally into two equal parts (Figure 3.39). The lower half of the box is fixed and the upper part of the box can move horizontally depending on the shear force exerted on it. The soil is placed in between the porous plates. A normal static force is applied on the soil through the top of the upper half of the box. A horizontal shearing force is exerted on the upper half of the box to produce a constant rate of strain. The rate of shear for clays and sands may be taken as $\leq$ 0.01 and 0.2 mm/min. respectively (IS: 2720 (Part 13)-1986). The values of shear force with respect to the displacement of the upper half of the box are taken at regular intervals. Failure of the sample is observed when there is a sudden drop of the values of the load or when the longitudinal displacement is observed to be 20 per cent (IS: 2720 (Part 13)-1986). The test is conducted a minimum of three times at different normal loads. Care should be taken to maintain the same density of the soil sample for each of the trial tests.

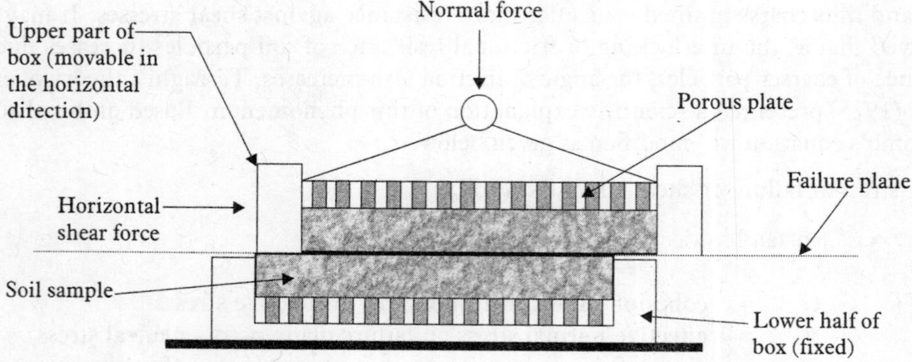

Figure 3.39 *Working principle of shear box apparatus*

Drawbacks of the test:

1. The failure plane is horizontal and pre-determined. This condition may not always be true, during actual wheel loading.

2. During application of shear force, the stress applied on the shearing plane is not uniform and the contact area of the sliding plane of the soil decreases.

Q: *The data obtained from shear box tests conducted on a soil sample are given below.*

Test No.	*1*	*2*	*3*	*4*
Normal stress (kN/m^2)	*100*	*200*	*300*	*400*
Failure shear stress (kN/m^2)	*112*	*150*	*188*	*228*

Determine the values of cohesion and angle of shearing resistance of the soil corresponding to failure shear stress.

A: Plot the values as shown in Figure 3.40. Draw a best fit line connecting the four points and read the C value by extending the line on to the y-axis. From the chart,

$$C = 73 \text{ kN/m}^2$$

$$\text{Value of } \Phi\text{: Slope} = \tan(\Phi) = (228 - 73)/400 = 155/400 = 0.3875$$

$$\Phi = \tan^{-1}(0.3875) = 21.18°$$

Shear strength of soil, $\tau = 73 + 0.3875\,\sigma$ kN/m^2

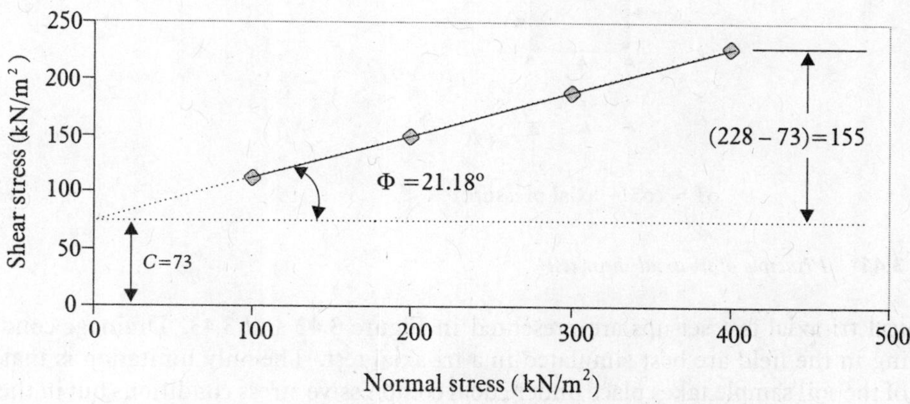

Figure 3.40 *Example problem*

Tri-axial Shear Test

In this test, a cylindrical soil sample with its height equal to twice its diameter is prepared at a pre-determined density. The soil sample is enclosed in a rubber membrane. The confinement pressure around the sample is kept at a constant pre-determined intensity by placing it in a suitable encasement filled with water at a constant pressure. Hence, the soil sample is subjected to compressive stresses as well as an axial compressive stress until the sample fails due to shear (Figure 3.41). Gradually, the axial stress on the soil sample is increased at a constant rate (pre-determined). The values of vertical deformation (change in original depth) of the sample corresponding to the applied axial loads are recorded throughout the period of the test. A suitable arrangement is made to measure the pressure due to pore water of the soil sample. The shear failure of the sample may be observed as slip surface at an angle of ($45° + \Phi/2$) to the vertical axis or a bulge or a combination of these deformations. The detailed test procedure may be found elsewhere (Bishop and Henkel 1962; Head 1982; Vickers 1983; BS: 1377-1990; IS: 2720 (Part 12)-1981).

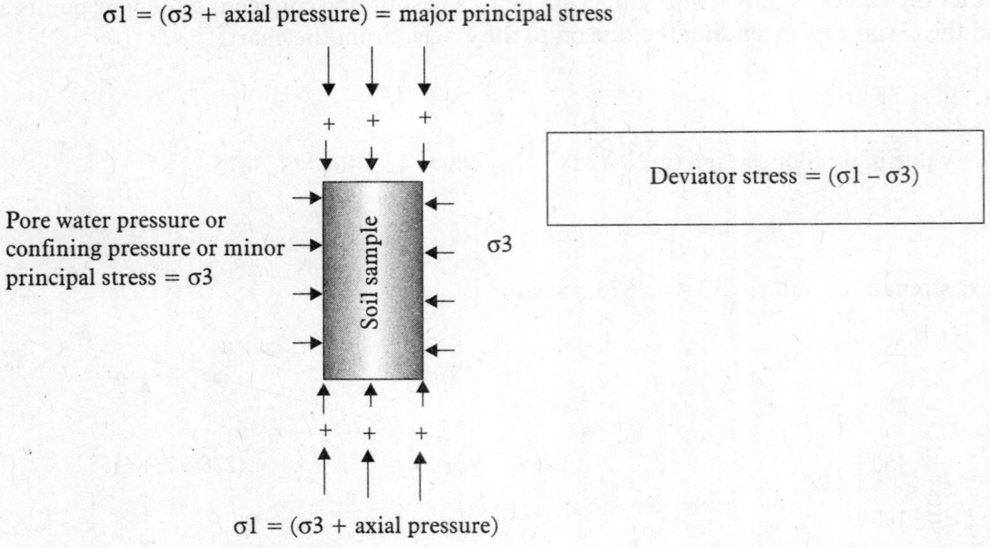

Figure 3.41 *Principle of tri-axial shear test*

Typical tri-axial test set-ups are presented in Figure 3.42 and 3.43. Drainage conditions prevailing in the field are best simulated in a tri-axial test. The only limitation is that shear failure of the soil sample takes place under equal compressive stress conditions but in the field, the soil may be subjected to anisotropic stress conditions.

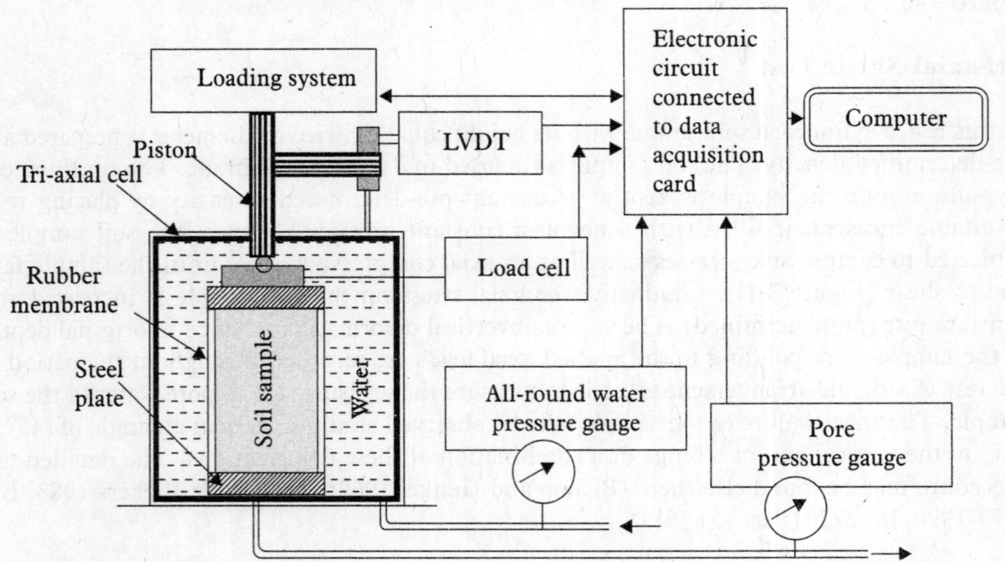

Figure 3.42 *A typical computer based tri-axial shear test set-up (schematic)*

(a) Tri-axial test in progress

(b) Close view of a soil sample encased in a rubber membrane

Figure 3.43 *Tri-axial test set-up (conventional type)*

Q: *Determine the parameters of Coulomb's equation by drawing Mohr's rupture of envelope of a soil sample. A sample, 40 mm in diameter and 80 mm depth, was cut and an un-drained tri-axial test conducted. Shear failure was observed at 5.8 mm of vertical deformation. Following are the details of stresses applied on the sample during testing.*

Pore water pressure (kN/m²)	*220*	*440*	*660*
Additional axial load at shear failure of the soil sample (N)	*519*	*772*	*1017*

A: Volume of the soil sample = $(\pi/4) \times (40 \text{ mm})^2 \times 80 \text{ mm} = 100530.9 \text{ mm}^3$

The cross-sectional area at shear failure $= \dfrac{1000530.9 \text{ mm}^3}{(80 - 5.8)\text{mm}} = 1354.8 \text{ mm}^{\ 2}$

Pore water pressure, σ3 (kN/m²)	200	400	600
Axial load at shear failure (N)	519	772	1017
Deviator stress, (σ1 – σ3) (kN/m²)	(0.519 kN×10⁶÷ 1354.8 mm²) = 383.1	(0.772 kN×10⁶÷ 1354.8) = 569.8	(1.017 kN×10⁶ ÷ 1354.8) = 750.6
Axial stress, σ1 (kN/m²)	200 + 383.1 = 583.1	400 + 569.8 = 969.8	600 + 750.6 = 1350.6

The details of Mohr circles with the strength envelope of the best common tangent are given in Figure 3.44. The value of soil cohesion = 81.0 kN/m^2; Φ = 17°.

Shear strength of soil, $\tau = 81 + \sigma \tan(17^\circ)$ kN/m^2

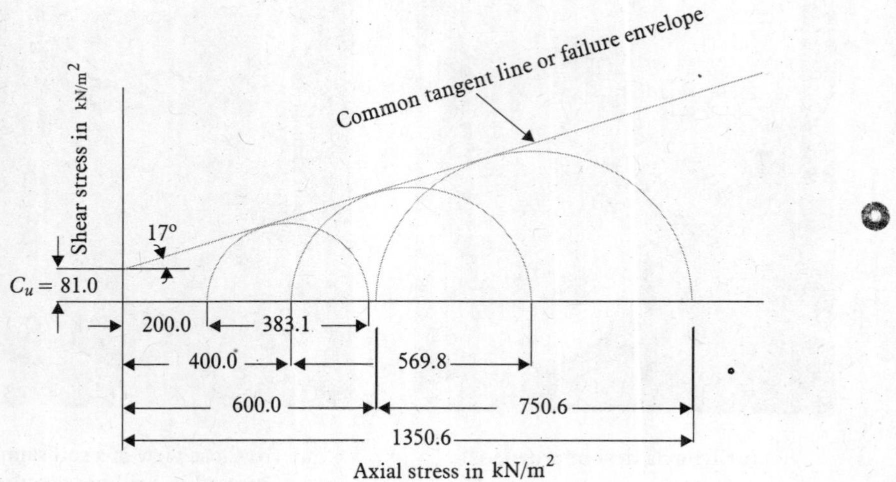

Figure 3.44 *Example problem*

Unconfined Compression Test

In this test, the soil sample is subjected to axial stress only (Figure 3.45), without pore water pressure. The soil sample is not enclosed in a rubber membrane. It is not suitable for granular soils as no confinement is provided. This test is more suitable for cohesive or saturated clays. It is also simple and easy to perform in the field. The soil sample prepared for this test may be re-moulded or undisturbed. The axial stress applied on the soil sample is increased gradually at a constant rate (pre-determined). The values of axial deformation (change in original depth) of the sample corresponding to the applied axial loads are recorded throughout the length of the test. The shear failure of the soil sample may be observed at the point where the value of axial stress drops suddenly. But in case of highly plastic saturated clays, there will be no definite sudden drop of the axial stresses. In such cases, an appropriate value of failure stress may be taken based on the soil type, field conditions and purpose of use or until an axial strain of 20 per cent is reached (IS: 2720 (Part 10)-1991). The cohesion value of the soil is calculated as one-half of the axial stress recorded at sample failure and the angle of shearing resistance is equal to zero ($\Phi = 0$), since the line of failure envelope is assumed to be horizontal.

The unconfined undrained compression tests conducted in the laboratory on samples of in situ saturated clay show quite different shear strength properties based on direction of axial stress experienced by the soil under in situ conditions and unequal pressure prevailing around the soil (Duncan and Seed 1966).

(a) Free body diagram of soil sample

(b) Test in progress

Figure 3.45 *Unconfined compression test*

The details regarding unconfined compressive strength of cohesive soils are given in IS: 2720 (Part 10)-1991.

Soil may be classified based upon its unconfined compressive strength. The normal range is given below (Cooling et al. 1948).

Class	Unconfined compressive strength	
	(kPa)	PSI
Very soft	Less than 34.5	< 5
Soft	34.5 to 68.9	5 to 10
Firm	68.9 to 137.9	10 to 20
Stiff	137.9 to 275.8	20 to 40
Hard	Greater than 275.8	> 40

Q : *An unconfined undrained compression test was conducted on a saturated clay sample. The failure stress of the sample was found to be 204 kN/m^2. Calculate its shear strength properties.*

A: The value of the angle of shearing resistance (Φ) may be assumed to be zero, since the soil sample is a saturated clay. The undrained cohesion value (C_u) of the soil = failure stress (σ) / 2 = 204/2 = 102 kN/m^2.

The above answer may be also obtained using Mohr's circle.

Comparison of Soil Shear Strength Tests

Comparison of the above three soil shear strength tests based on suitability, testing principle, conditions of simulation and failure criteria is presented in Table 3.6.

Table 3.6 *Comparison of different shear tests of soil*

Point of comparison	Direct shear box test	Tri-axial test	Unconfined compression test
Drainage condition simulated	Undrained and drained tests but undrained tests on sandy and silty soils are not possible	Undrained and drained tests	Undrained
Rubber membrane to encase specimen	Not used	Used	Not necessary
Shear plane or failure plane	Pre-determined in horizontal direction	Not pre-determined	Not pre-determined
Load/stress application on soil mass	Vertical load is placed on top o fthe soil and shear force is gradually applied in the horizontal direction	Compressive stresses are applied in three directions at right angles to each other and axial load is applied at a constant rate of strain until the sample fails	No all-round pressure; only axial compressive stress is applied to produce a constant rate of strain until the sample fails
Exertion of shear force	In horizontal direction only	In axial direction	In axial direction
Types of failure	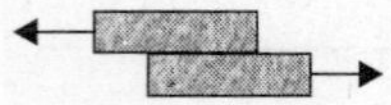	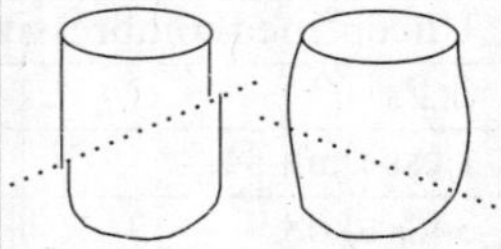	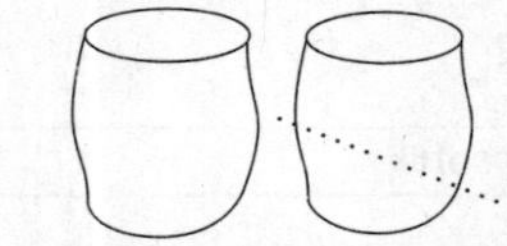
Generally tested on	All types of soil	All types of soil	Cohesive soils or materials having high values of cohesion
Simulation of lateral pressure or confinement	Not possible	Possible by application of all-round pressure	Not possible
Results	Cohesion (C) and angle of soil friction (Φ)	C and Φ	C (saturated clay, $\Phi \approx 0$)

Interpretation of Tri-axial Test Results

In addition to the shear strength properties (C and Φ) of soil, the data obtained from the tri-axial test, viz. stress–strain relationship may be used to determine the elastic modulus (E)

of the soil. In the recent past, mechanistic methods of pavement designs have been adopted to determine individual thickness of pavement layers. In these methods, critical stresses and strain are evaluated based on in situ properties of the various materials which constitute the pavement layers. The critical stress, allowable vertical compressive strain (ε_z) and surface deflection (Δ) of the sub-grade are computed based on its elastic modulus, anticipated wheel loads, overburden pressure (or confinement) and drainage conditions using mathematical equations and statistical correlations. For this purpose, a representative value of the elastic modulus can also be determined in the laboratory or by conducting tests at in situ conditions (Figure 3.46). In both cases, the surface deflection of the pavement is kept within allowable limits. To summarise, determination of the elastic modulus of sub-grade soil is always useful as an input parameter for analysis as well as design of pavements by mechanistic–empirical methods.

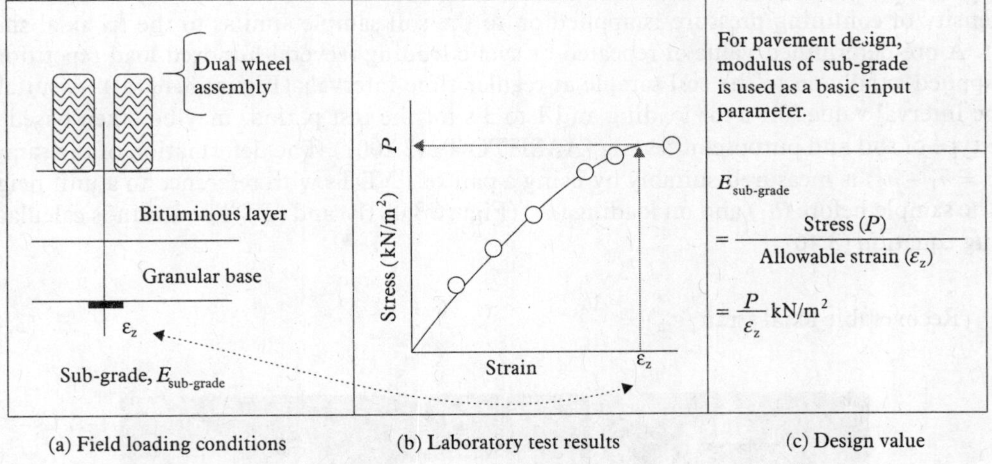

Figure 3.46 *Interpretation of stress–strain relationship of sub-grade soil*

3.8.4 Resilient Modulus

The elastic modulus value of pavement material is also evaluated by dynamic load tests as these tests simulate repeated application of traffic loads on pavements. For sub-grade soils and granular materials, the elastic modulus is evaluated by employing dynamic loads in the laboratory and is referred to as resilient modulus (M_R). It is generally determined from repeated tri-axial tests (Seed et al. 1963).

The difference between the generally expressed elastic modulus and resilient modulus is simply explained by the following relationships.

Elastic modulus or

$$\text{modulus of elasticity } (E) = \frac{\text{Stress}}{\text{Recoverable axial strain under gradually applied load}} \tag{3.44}$$

$$\text{Resilient modulus } (M_R) = \frac{\text{Stress}}{\text{Recoverable axial strain under dynamic load}} \tag{3.45}$$

Basically, the above parameters refer to the slope of the stress–strain curve within the elastic range. Due to change in load application, the values of the above parameters differ greatly. As there is repetitive application of wheel loads, pavement layers are subjected to deformation or experience strain which is equal to cyclic load application in a tri-axial test. This is the reason why resilient modulus is used to characterise pavement materials.

Resilient modulus of sub-grade soil is determined in the laboratory by repeated tri-axial tests (FHWA 1978). Repeated or cyclic load tri-axial tests are generally conducted on a re-moulded soil sample compacted to a pre-determined density of undisturbed state (Figure 3.47). The sample size may be of 100 mm diameter and 200 mm depth (ratio of depth to diameter ≈ 2). Preparation of soil sample will be that required for a tri-axial shear test. A thin rubber membrane is used to enclose the cylindrical soil sample. A pre-determined intensity of confining pressure is applied on to the soil sample similar to the tri-axial shear test. A pre-determined value of repeated or cyclic loading (several hundred load repetitions) is applied axially on to the soil sample at regular time intervals (Figure 3.48 (a)). A suitable time interval value (0.1 s for loading and 1 to 3 s for the rest period) may be taken based on the type of soil and purpose of testing (AASHTO T292 2001). The deformation of the sample ($\Delta h = h_1 - h_2$) is measured suitably by using a pair of LVDTs with reference to a unit height of the sample before (h_1) and on loading (h_2) (Figure 3.48 (b) and (c)). The strain is calculated using equation (3.46).

$$\text{Recoverable axial stran } (\varepsilon_{ra}) = \frac{\Delta h}{h_1} \tag{3.46}$$

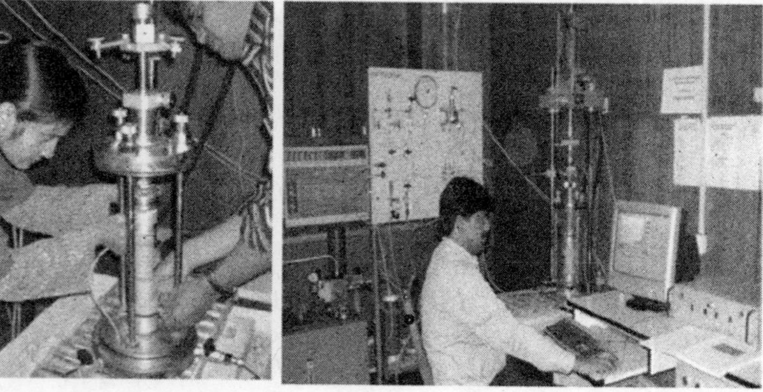

Figure 3.47 *Servo-controlled cyclic loading tri-axial test set-up*

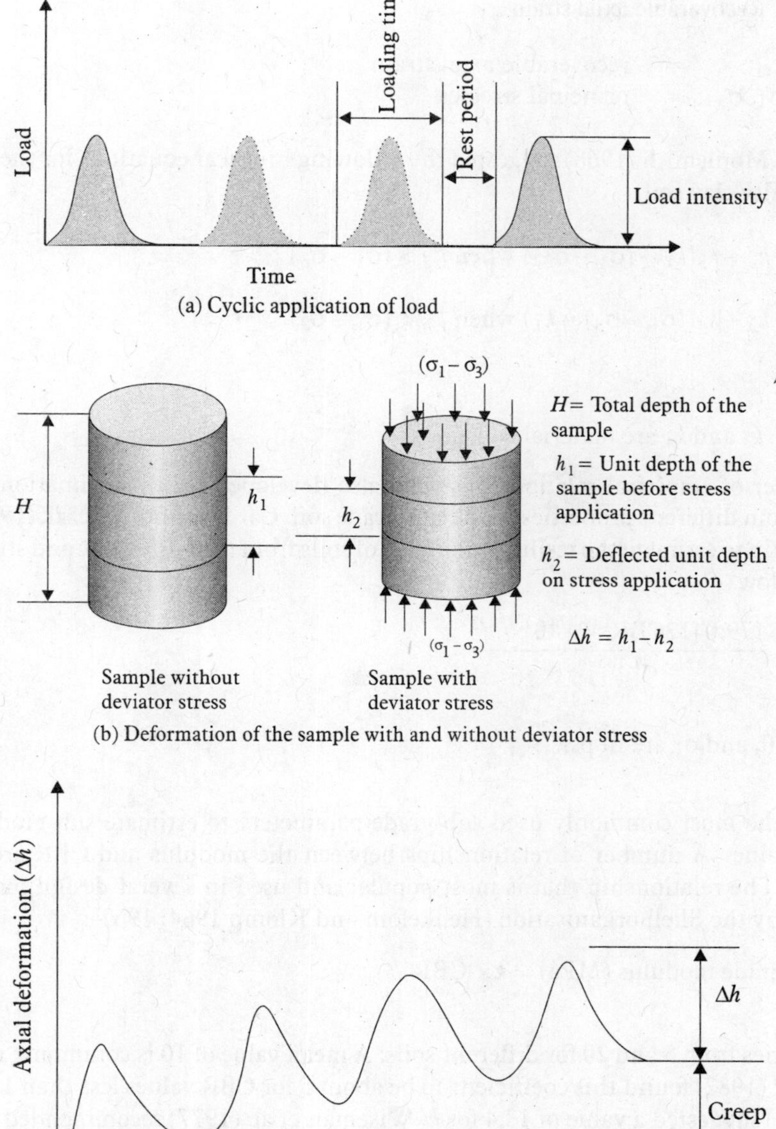

Figure 3.48 *Typical deformation pattern of a sample*

Sub-grade soil The following expression is used to determine the resilient modulus (M_R) of sub-grade soil.

$$M_R = \frac{\text{Deviator stress } (\sigma_d)}{\text{Recoverable axial strain}} = \frac{\sigma_1 - \sigma_3}{\varepsilon_{ra}} \tag{3.47}$$

where, ε_{ra} = recoverable axial strain
σ_1, σ_3 = principal stresses

Shifley and Monismith (1968) suggested the following bi-linear equations for the computation of M_R for silty clay soil.

$$M_R = k_2 + k_3(k_1 - (\sigma_1 - \sigma_3)) \text{ when } k_1 > (\sigma_1 - \sigma_3) \tag{3.48}$$

$$M_R = k_2 + k_4((\sigma_1 - \sigma_3) - k_1) \text{ when } k_1 < (\sigma_1 - \sigma_3) \tag{3.49}$$

where,

k_1, k_2, k_3 and k_4 are material constants

A number of empirical relationships were also developed for the estimation of sub-grade modulus from different properties of the sub-grade soil. Cardoso and Witczak (1991) presented a relationship to estimate the resilient modulus of soils from the CBR value and stress condition as given below.

$$M_R = \frac{179.0412\text{CBR}^{1.08774}\theta^{1.43833}}{\sigma_1^{1.18598}} \tag{3.50}$$

where M_R, θ, and σ_1 are in psi.

One of the most commonly used sub-grade parameters to estimate sub-grade modulus is the CBR value. A number of relationships between the modulus and CBR are available in literature. The relationship that is most popular and used in several design methods is that developed by the Shell organisation (Heukelom and Klomp 1964; 1967):

$$\text{Sub-grade modulus (MPa)} = k \times \text{CBR} \tag{3.51}$$

where k varies from 5 and 20 for different soils. A mean value of 10 is commonly used. Dauzats and Linder (1982) found this coefficient to be about 5 for CBR values less than 15%. Skok and Finn (1962) suggested a value of 13.4 for k. Wiseman et al. (1977) recommended a value of 20. Freeme et al. (1982) recommended a range of 8 to 15 for k when CBR values range from 15 to 30%.

There are also non-linear relationships between sub-grade modulus and CBR. The general form of the non-linear relationship is

$$\text{Sub-grade modulus (MPa)} = k_1\text{CBR}^{k_2} \tag{3.52}$$

where k_1 and k_2 are material constants. The values of k_1 and k_2 obtained in different investigations are 6.5, 0.67 (Jeuffroy and Bachelez 1962), 10.0, 0.73 (Ullidtz 1987; The Danish Road Laboratory adopted this equation), 17.6, 0.64 (Lister and Powell 1987) which is known as the TRL–UK relationship, and 37.3 and 0.711 are suggested by the US Army of Corps Waterway Experiment Station.

Granular materials Selection of a representative modulus value for granular layers has always been a difficult task due to the high degree of stress dependency of the modulus value. For a given stress condition, the resilient modulus value of granular material can be determined from repeated tri-axial tests using equation (3.47).

The M_R value of granular materials varies with variation in stress conditions. Two of the commonly used (Cardoso and Witczak 1991; Kirwan and Snaith 1976) relationships between the resilient modulus value and state of stress are given as equations (3.53) and (3.54).

$$M_R = k_1\theta^{k_2} \tag{3.53}$$

$$M_R = k_3\sigma_3^{k_4} \tag{3.54}$$

where σ_3 = confining pressure or minor principal stress, θ = bulk stress (sum of principal stresses) and k_1, k_2, k_3, k_4 are regression constants.

Equation (3.53), popularly known as the $k-\theta$ model, has been adopted by several researchers and organisations (Brown and Pell 1972; Allen and Thompson 1974; Monismith et al. 1967; Hicks and Monismith 1971; Khedr 1985; Barksdale 1972; Boyce et al. 1976). However, field and laboratory studies (May and Witczak 1985; Uzan 1985) using the $k-\theta$ model implies that for constant confining pressure, M_R should increase with increase in the value of repeated deviator stress. But an opposite trend was observed for deviator stress less than 70 kPa. An additional parameter, octahedral shear stress, was introduced in the $k-\theta$ model to account for the effect of shear on the M_R value of granular materials. The modified equation is given as

$$M_R = k_1\theta^{k_2}\tau_{oct}^{k_3} \tag{3.55}$$

where, τ_{oct} = octahedral shear stress and k_1, k_2 and k_3 = material constants.

Determination of the elastic modulus values of sub-grade and granular soils in the laboratory requires costly equipment and is a time-consuming process. Moreover, the strength value obtained in a laboratory may not represent the true value existing in the field due to variability in compaction level and in situ confinement. Therefore, it is better to determine in situ values of elastic moduli using non-destructive testing (NDT) methods based on the evaluation of sub-grade and granular layers of pavements already in service. Details of various NDT equipment used and standard correlations available for estimation of in situ elastic modulus values are discussed in subsequent chapters.

Q: *Resilient modulus tests were conducted on granular soil. The specimen of granular soil was conditioned and failed after 192 repetitions of the deviator stress. Determine experimental constants of k_1 and k_2 in the equation $M_R = k_1\theta^{k_2}$ from the following resilient modulus test data. Take initial reference depth of the sample as 100 mm.*

Deviator stress (kPa)	*Pore water pressure (kPa)*	*Elastic deformation ($\times 10^{-3}$ mm)*
137.89	*6.89*	*7.6454*
	13.79	*12.9591*
	34.47	*30.5308*
	68.95	*62.3062*
	103.42	*98.8060*
	137.89	*121.4120*
103.42	*6.89*	*8.1788*
	13.79	*15.1384*
	34.47	*35.1028*
	68.95	*75.9460*
	103.42	*106.9340*
	137.89	*127.5080*
68.95	*6.89*	*9.9568*
	13.79	*18.0848*
	34.47	*59.1820*
	68.95	*106.6800*
	103.42	*115.5700*
34.47	*6.89*	*15.4991*
	13.79	*33.8328*
	34.47	*72.6440*
	68.95	*114.5540*
	103.42	*158.2420*
6.89	*6.89*	*17.5006*
	13.79	*25.1714*
	34.47	*86.8680*
	68.95	*101.3460*
	103.42	*133.6040*

A: The values in column 4, 5 and 6 of the table given below are calculated as follows:

Column (4): $\text{Elastic strain} = \dfrac{\text{Elastic deformation}}{\text{Initial reference depth of sample}}$

$$= \frac{7.6454 \times 10^{-3}\ \text{mm}}{100\ \text{mm}} = 0.076454$$

Column (5): $M_R = \dfrac{\text{Deviator stress (2)}}{\text{Elastic strain (4)}} = \dfrac{6.89\ \text{kPa}}{0.076454 \times 10^{-3}} = 90.11 \times 10^3\ \text{kPa}$

Column (6): $\theta = \sigma_1 + 2\sigma_3 = \sigma_d + 3\sigma_3 = 6.89 + 3 \times 137.89 = 420.58\ \text{kPa}$

Pore water pressure (σ_3) (kPa)	Deviator stress (σ_d) (kPa)	Elastic deformation ($\times 10^{-3}$ mm)	Elastic strain ($\times 10^{-3}$ mm)	Resilient modulus (M_R) ($\times 10^3$ kPa)	Bulk stress (θ) (kPa)
(1)	(2)	(3)	(4) = (3)/100 mm	(5) = (1)/(4)	(6) = 3×(1)+ (2)
137.89	6.89	7.6454	0.0765	90.18	420.58
	13.79	12.9591	0.1296	106.41	427.47
	34.47	30.5308	0.3053	112.91	448.16
	68.95	62.3062	0.6231	110.66	482.63
	103.42	98.8060	0.9881	104.67	517.10
	137.89	121.4120	1.2141	113.58	551.58
103.42	6.89	8.1788	0.0818	84.30	317.16
	13.79	15.1384	0.1514	91.09	324.05
	34.47	35.1028	0.3510	98.21	344.74
	68.95	75.9460	0.7595	90.78	379.21
	103.42	106.9340	1.0693	96.71	413.68
	137.89	127.5080	1.2751	108.15	448.16
68.95	6.89	9.9568	0.0996	69.25	213.74
	13.79	18.0848	0.1808	76.25	220.63
	34.47	59.1820	0.5918	58.25	241.32
	68.95	106.6800	1.0668	64.63	275.79
	103.42	115.5700	1.1557	89.49	310.26
34.47	6.89	15.4991	0.1550	44.48	110.32
	13.79	33.8328	0.3383	40.76	117.21
	34.47	72.6440	0.7264	47.46	137.89
	68.95	114.5540	1.1455	60.19	172.37
	103.42	158.2420	1.5824	65.36	206.84
6.89	6.89	17.5006	0.1750	39.40	27.58
	13.79	25.1714	0.2517	54.78	34.47
	34.47	86.8680	0.8687	39.69	55.16
	68.95	101.3460	1.0135	51.02	72.39
	103.42	133.6040	1.3360	51.61	89.63

Draw a plot of the resilient modulus (M_R) vs. bulk stress (θ) as shown in Figure 3.49. Draw a best fit line and measure intercept on the y-axis as $k_1 = 9.4328 \times 10^3 = 9432.8$ kPa, and slope of the line as $k_2 = 0.3796$.

Therefore, the equation of $M_R = k_1 \theta^{k_2}$ can be written as $M_R = 9432.8\ \theta^{0.3796}$.

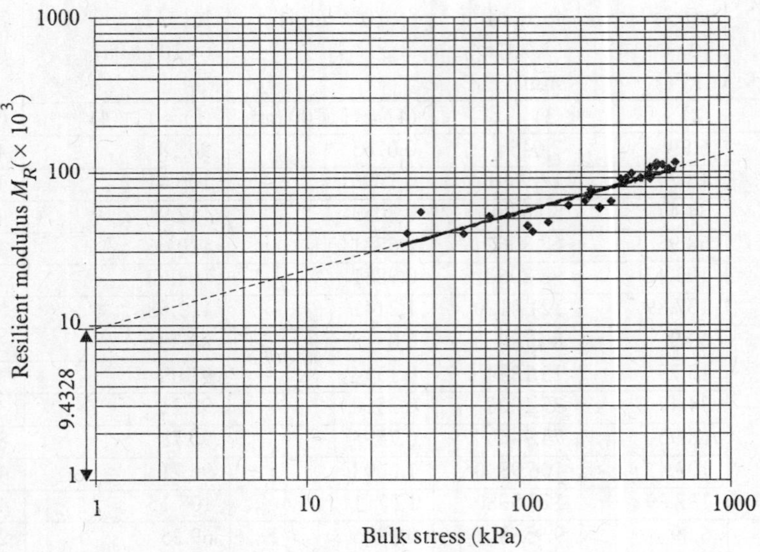

Figure 3.49 *Example problem*

3.8.5 Poisson's Ratio

It is difficult to accurately measure the deformations required to compute Poisson's ratio. For most pavement materials, the influence of Poisson's ratio on various critical parameters is normally small. This allows the use of typical constant values in the analysis rather than resorting to complex laboratory testing (Mitchell and Monismith 1977).

For clayey sub-grades, Poisson's ratio varies from 0.4 to 0.5. A value of 0.5 is normally adopted for wet conditions (Brown and Pell 1972). Mitchell and Monismith (1977) recommended a value of 0.5 for saturated clays and 0.35 for sands. For sub-grade soils, a value of 0.4 was selected. Typical values of Poisson's ratio for unbound granular material vary from 0.2 to 0.5. Allen et al. (1974) recommended a range of 0.35 to 0.4 for Poisson's ratio of granular material. Uzan et al. (1972) discussed the non-linearity of Poisson's ratio value for granular material and reported that it may even assume a value of 0.6 to 0.7. The recommendations of AASHTO (1993) for the selection of Poisson's ratio value for different pavement layers are given in Table 3.7.

Table 3.7 *AASHTO's recommendation for selection of Poisson's ratio*

Material	Range	Typical value	Remarks
Granular	0.30–0.40	0.35	Lower value for crushed material and higher value for uncompressed rounded gravels/sands
Sub-grade	0.30–0.50	–	0.3 for cohesion-less soil and 0.5 for plastic clay

(from *AASHTO Guide for Design of Pavement Structures* 1993, by the American Association of State Highway and Transportation Officials, Washington, DC. Used by permission. Documents may be purchased from the AASHTO bookstore at 1-800-231-3475 or online at http://bookstore.transportation.org.)

3.9 Strength Properties of Mineral Aggregates

3.9.1 Introduction

Mineral aggregates consist of any type of rock (igneous, sedimentary and metamorphic) possessing strong, hard and tough properties. Generally they are crushed stone, gravel, sand, slag, rock dust or rock powder. Aggregates of different sizes are obtained from different sources. The characteristic strength and durable properties of aggregate materials are generally influenced by their origin of occurrence. Knowledge about the origin of the rock is important for understanding the mineral content of the rock and deciding its suitability as road aggregates.

Geologically, rocks are classified into three types. They are

(i) Igneous rocks

(ii) Sedimentary rocks

(iii) Metamorphic rocks

(i) ***Igneous rocks*** Igneous rocks are formed by the cooling, solidification and crystallisation of molten rock at different depths of the earth's crust. The various minerals in different proportions present in the rock, the type of crystallisation or rate of cooling of magma all play an important role in strength characterisation of the rock mass. However, igneous rocks are comparatively stronger than sedimentary and metamorphic rocks. Examples of intrusive rocks which forms at deep layers in the earth's crust are granite, gabbro, diorite etc. Examples of extrusive rocks which forms at the top layers of the earth's crust are basalt, diabase, rhyolite etc.

(ii) ***Sedimentary rocks*** Fine mineral fragments or fine particles of mineral or rock particles are transported by water or wind and deposited to form sedimentary rocks in geological times. Sometimes, animal or plant remains are also deposited, cemented and restructured together with the rock fragments. Because of this, sedimentary rocks consist of a layered structure or stratification of rock beds. This stratification results in the porous nature and low strength of sedimentary rocks. Examples of calcareous rocks are limestone, dolomite etc. Examples of siliceous rocks are sandstone, argillite etc.

(iii) ***Metamorphic rocks*** These rocks are formed due to re-crystallisation or modification of igneous and sedimentary rocks by geological or natural agents such as movements of rock beds, temperature, moisture, humidity and pressure. Major changes in the parent rock takes place due to natural agents and results in re-formation or formation of foliations. Along the foliation, the rock tends to split or crack easily and make it weak against loading. But some types of rocks such as marble and gneiss are used for flooring or face work. Examples of foliated rocks are gneiss, slate, schist etc. Examples of un-foliated rocks include marble, quartzite and serpentine.

The hardness and toughness of these rocks depend upon the following fundamental properties (Hunting 1945).

- Composition of minerals.

- Chemical composition (relates to hardness, toughness and cleavage of individual minerals).
- Texture (relates to size and shape of grains and porosity).
- Freshness of minerals in terms of degree of weathering and hydrothermal alteration of original minerals.
- Fracturing and jointing.

3.9.2 Sources of Mineral Aggregate

Generally, aggregates are obtained along river banks or pits in the form of gravel (75–4.75 mm), sand (4.75 mm–75 micron) and others (less than 75 micron) by using suitable sizes of sieves. If any clay content is present, it is washed before using for construction purposes.

They are also obtained by crushing naturally available rocks and screening them to obtain different sizes of aggregates. For special purposes, like reduction in weight and for skid resistance, aggregates are also obtained from blast furnace slag.

3.9.3 Water Absorption and Specific Gravity Tests

Strength properties of road aggregates are indirectly related to its specific gravity and water absorption characteristics. In general, it is observed that an aggregate sample having high specific gravity and low water absorption is dense, less porous, durable and possesses high strength. This concept is used while judging suitability of aggregates for construction of pavements. Further, specific gravity is an index value which indicates its origin and constituent minerals. Its value is used for computation of densities and amounts of voids while designing the mix of cement and bituminous concrete.

Specific gravity It is the ratio between the dry weight of aggregates in air to the weight of water equivalent to volume of the aggregates tested at a standard temperature.

$$\text{Specific gravity} = \frac{\text{Dry weight of aggregates}}{\text{Weight of water equivalent to the volume of aggregates}} \tag{3.56}$$

Water absorption It is the percentage by weight of water absorbed by the aggregates to the oven dried weight of the aggregates at standard temperature.

$$w\,(\%) = \frac{\text{Weight of water absorbed by aggregates}}{\text{Dry weight of the aggregates}} \times 100 \tag{3.57}$$

Aggregates which possess higher values of density and specific gravity with less porosity are found to be strong, tough and more resistant against the action of abrasive forces. Hence, it is desirable to select aggregates having higher specific gravity values.

A typical relationship between specific gravity, density, porosity, compressive strength and mineral constitution of aggregates tested from different sources are presented in Table 3.8 to 3.10. It is observed that as the specific gravity value of aggregates decreases, its porosity value increases. In other words, as the density of the aggregate decreases, the value of the compressive strength also declines.

Table 3.8 *Strength properties of aggregates (Venkat 1995)*

Sl. No.	Specific gravity	Porosity (%)	Compressive strength (MPa)
1	2.67	1.45	175
2	2.65	1.51	172
3	2.60	1.74	170
4	2.58	1.80	167

Table 3.9 *Strength properties of rocks (Waltham 2002)*

Sl No.	Type of rock	Porosity (%)	Range of compressive strength (MPa)	Remark
1	Granite	50–350	Strong	
2	Basalt	2	100–350	Very strong
3	Sandstone	12–25	5–100	
4	Limestone	3–15	15–150	
5	Shale	15	5–30	Moderately weak
6	Clay	30	1–4	Weak
7	Marble and gneiss	1	50–200	
8	Slate	1	20–250	
9.	Schist	3	20–100	

Table 3.10 *Specific gravity and its constituent minerals or origin*

Specific gravity	Remarks
2.7 to 2.9	The rock originates from gneiss or granite rock.
3.0 to 3.5	A typical example of bauxite.
7.2 to 8.2	The rock originates from an iron compound.
2.0 to 6.5	The rock mostly contains silica, horneblende, bauxite etc.
Less than 1.5	It consists of organic matter or peat.

Determination of specific gravity and water absorption of aggregates can be performed based on the size of the aggregates.

METHOD 1 (IS: 2386 (Part 3)-1963):

The following test procedure is adopted for aggregates of size greater than 10 mm.

About 2 kg of washed aggregates of more than 10 mm size are taken in a wire basket and immersed in a container filled with distilled water. The temperature of the water should be maintained between 22 to 32 °C. The immersed basket with aggregates should be at least 5 cm below the water level. Entrapped air is removed by jolting the basket in water up and down 25 times. The rate of jolting is taken as one drop per second for a total of 25 drops. The basket filled with aggregates is kept immersed in water for a duration of about 24 hours and its submerged weight is recorded as M_1 g. If the weight is taken in another water container, the basket with aggregates is again jolted 25 times and immersed in water for 24 hours before weighing.

The basket with aggregates is removed from water and drained for a few minutes. It is emptied by slowly pouring the aggregates on to a dry cloth. The submerged weight of the empty basket is also noted by jolting it 25 times to remove any entrapped air. The weight is recorded as M_2 g. The surface of the wet aggregates is wiped with a cloth and completely dried by blowing air, if required. During the drying process, the aggregates are not exposed to direct sunlight or any kind of heat. After air-drying, the weight of the aggregates is taken and recorded as N g.

The aggregates are then kept in an oven at a temperature between 100 to 110 °C for 24 hours. The dried aggregates are removed from the oven and allowed to cool in an air-tight container. The weight of the aggregates is recorded as P g. Specific gravity of the aggregate sample is determined by the following equations (IS: 2386 (Part 3)-1963).

$$\text{Specific gravity} = \frac{P}{(N-M)} \tag{3.58}$$

$$\text{Apparent specific gravity} = \frac{P}{(P-M)} \tag{3.59}$$

$$\text{Water absorption by per cent weight of aggregates (\%)} = \frac{(N-P)}{P} \times 100 \tag{3.60}$$

where,

M_1	=	Total weight of the basket filled with saturated aggregates in water
M_2	=	Empty weight of the wire basket in water
$M = (M_1 - M_2)$	=	Net weight of saturated aggregates in water
N	=	Weight of saturated surface-dry aggregates in air
P	=	Weight of oven dried aggregates in air

METHOD 2 (IS: 2386 (Part 3)-1963):

A separate test procedure is adopted in case of aggregates of size less than 10 mm. A pycnometer bottle of suitable capacity with its standard accessories is used for conducting the test.

About 1000 g of aggregate of size in between 10 mm and 4.75 mm or 500 g of aggregates of size less than 4.75 mm is taken in a tray and immersed in distilled water. The entrapped air bubbles in the aggregates are removed by gently stirring with a rod. The water temperature is maintained at standard temperature (22 to 32 °C) for 24 hours. Later, they are dried and the weight of the saturated surface-dry aggregates is recorded as Q_1 g.

The saturated aggregates are placed in a pycnometer and the remaining portion of the pycnometer is filled with distilled water without any air bubbles in it. The outer surface of the pycnometer is allowed to dry and its weight recorded as Q_2 g.

The aggregates in the pycnometer are removed and drained on to a tray. During this process there should not be any loss of aggregate particles. The drained aggregates are kept in an oven to dry further for 24 hours at a temperature between 100 to 110 °C. The weight of the oven dried aggregates is recorded as R g. Finally, the pycnometer is completely filled with distilled water and the weight recorded as S g. Figure 3.50 depicts the details of the weight measurements to be taken to conduct the test.

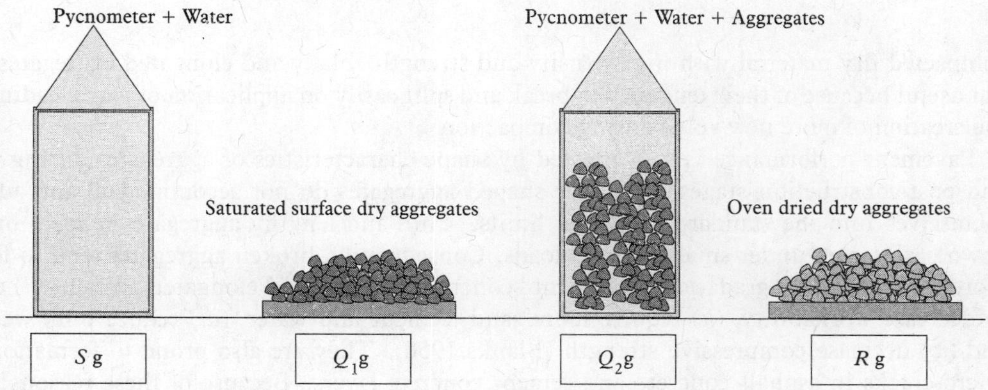

Figure 3.50 *Details of weight measurements*

The specific gravity of the aggregate sample is calculated as given below (IS:2386 (Part 3)-1963):

$$\text{Specific gravity} = \frac{R}{Q_1 - (Q_2 - S)} \tag{3.61}$$

$$\text{Apparent specific gravity} = \frac{R}{R - (Q_2 - S)} \tag{3.62}$$

$$\text{Water absorption by per cent weight of aggregates} = \frac{(Q_1 - R)}{R} \times 100 \tag{3.63}$$

where,

Q_1 = weight of saturated surface-dry aggregates
Q_2 = total weight of pycnometer filled with saturated aggregates and water
S = weight of surface-dry pycnometer filled with water
R = weight of oven dried aggregates

According to the IRC (*IRC Pocket Book 2006*), the maximum allowable limit of water absorption for any aggregate used for highway pavement construction should not be more than 2% the weight of the aggregate. However, the maximum allowable limit of water absorption is relaxed to 5% for aggregates used in CC slab pavements of rural roads (IRC: SP: 62-2004).

3.9.4 Shape Tests

Generally, coarse aggregates may be in various shapes such as granular, spherical, cubical, flaky (thin chips or platy) and elongated (long). The interlocking of aggregates is achieved by using various sizes and shapes like graded cubical, flaky or elongated aggregates having rough fractured surfaces. Use of cubical shaped aggregates is preferred in order to obtain high compacted dry material with high density and strength. Flaky and elongated aggregates are not useful because of their tendency to break and split easily on application of loads leading to the creation of more new voids during compaction.

Pavement performance is also affected by shape characteristics of aggregates during pre- and post-construction stages. Irregular shaped aggregates do not accommodate and adjust themselves into the standard gradation limits. Thin and lengthy aggregates tend to break down easily even under small external loads. Consequently, broken aggregates tend to form more voids and alter gradation. In cement–concrete mix, flat and elongated particles (*i*) tend to decrease workability, (*ii*) require more sand, cement and water, (*iii*) reduce bulk weight and (*iv*) decrease compressive strength (Blanks 1950). They are also prone to formation of micro-cracks in asphalt concrete and cement concrete layers. Because of these reasons, the shape of aggregates is important in construction of pavements.

Further, during quality control of road construction works, proper care should be taken to keep the aggregates within specified limits. Elimination of irregular shaped aggregates may not be completely possible—it depends on the type of crusher used for production of aggregates, type and origin of rocks.

Tests are prescribed in IS: 2386 (Part 1)-1963 to evaluate the percentage of irregular shaped aggregates in a mass of crushed aggregates. Flaky shaped aggregates are measured using a thickness gauge (TG) and by determining the flakiness index (FI). Elongated aggregates are measured using a length gauge (LG) and by determining the elongation index (EI). Details of the aggregate shape tests are given below.

Flakiness Test

Flakiness index (FI) of a given size of aggregate sample is expressed in terms of percentage by weight of aggregates, whose smallest dimension or thickness is less than 3/5 or 0.6 times their average size (IS: 2386 (Part 1)-1963; 2004). In other words, FI is the percentage by weight of flaky aggregate particles whose least thickness is less than 0.6 times the average size of the aggregates.

The thickness gauge consists of a steel plate having 9 slots or openings of suitable dimensions by which an aggregate can be measured (Figure 3.51).

Following is a typical example for calculating the least dimension of the slot of TG for the size of aggregates used.

$$\text{For an aggregate size in between 63 mm to 50 mm} = 0.6 \times \frac{(63+50)}{2} = 33.9 \text{ mm}$$

The given aggregate sample is sieved through standard sieves of nine sets. It is then checked whether each aggregate particle from all the sets passes through the slot designated. The aggregate particles which pass through the respective slots are weighed separately. FI may be calculated using the formulae given below.

$$\text{FI}(\%) = \frac{\sum_i^n w_i}{\sum_i^n G_i} \times 100 \tag{3.64}$$

Figure 3.51 *Flakiness test of aggregates using a thickness gauge*

where, w_i = Weights of various sizes of aggregate particles passed through the respective slots of TG, i.e., 63–50 mm, 50–40 mm, 40–25 mm, 31.5–25 mm, 25–20 mm, 20–16 mm, 16–12.5 mm, 12.5–10 mm and 10–6.3 mm

G_i = Total weight of aggregates considered for the test

Elongation Test

Length evaluation of coarse aggregates is conducted using a length gauge (LG) and expressed in terms of the elongation index (EI) of a given aggregate sample. EI of a given size of aggregate sample is expressed in terms of percentage by weight of aggregates whose longest dimension is more than 1.8 times their average size (IS: 2386 (Part 1)-1963, 2004). In other words, EI is the percentage by weight of long aggregate particles whose length is more than 1.8 times the average size of the aggregates.

The LG is a handy and portable tool (Figure 3.52) which consists of a rectangular steel plate attached to a suitable size of wooden plate. Eight steel rods of suitable diameter are fixed in vertical direction in a row on the steel plate. The method of calculating clear distances (CD) between successive rods according to the size of aggregates used is shown below for aggregate sizes in between 50 mm to 40 mm = $1.8 \times \frac{(50+40)}{2} = 81.00$ mm.

The given aggregate sample is sieved through the standard sieves of 7 sets. For all the sets, it is checked whether each aggregate particle passes in between the spaces of respective rods of designated sizes. The aggregate particles *not passed* in between the respective rods are weighed separately. The EI is expressed in terms of percentage by weight of aggregate particles not passing between the rods of the sets of sieves considered to the total weight of the aggregates used for the test. EI may be calculated as mentioned below.

$$EI(\%) = \frac{\sum_{i}^{n} m_i}{\sum_{i}^{n} G_i} \times 100 \tag{3.65}$$

where, m_i = Weights of various sizes of aggregate particles which are not passed between the respective slots of LG, i.e., 50–40 mm, 40–25 mm, 25–20 mm, 20–16 mm, 16–12.5 mm, 12.5–10 mm and 10–6.3 mm

G_i = Total weight of aggregates taken for the test

Flakiness and elongation tests are not applicable when the aggregate size is smaller than 6.3 mm (IS: 2386 (Part 1)-1963; 2004).

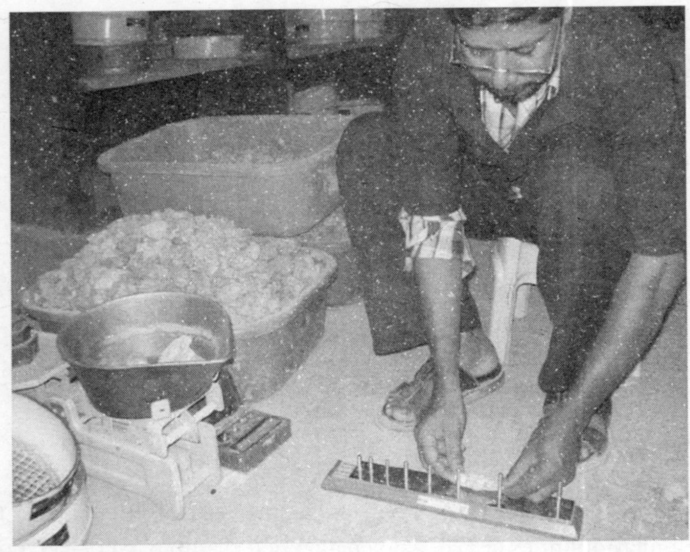

Figure 3.52 *Elongation test of aggregates using length gauge*

IRC has specified maximum allowable limits of combined flakiness and elongation indices (Table 3.11) for non-flaky aggregates in a sample.

Table 3.11 *Maximum allowable combined flakiness and elongation indices*

Sl No.	Description	Max. allowable combined flakiness and elongation indices (%)
N 1	Water bound macadam for sub-base or base	30
2	Wet mix macadam for sub-base or base	30
3	Crushed run macadam	30
4	Bituminous base	30
5	Dense graded bituminous macadam	30
6	Semi-dense graded bituminous macadam	30
7	Bituminous concrete	30

NOTE: For conventional, thin and ultra-thin white topping, the flakiness index of the aggregate should be less than 40% (IRC: SP: 76-2008). For CC rural roads, the value of the flakiness index of aggregate should not exceed 35% (IRC: SP: 62-2004).

Angularity Test

A compacted layer of aggregate mix does not possess the required capacity to retain loads because of their round shape and smooth surface which tends to slide away at interface contact points on loading. But use of more angular aggregates is also not suitable. The workability of concrete will be reduced if angular aggregates are used. Therefore, it is important to determine the angularity of aggregate particles while designing bituminous and cement–concrete mixes.

A compacted aggregate mix is usually made up of equal size spherical material and consists of 67 per cent solid volume and 33 per cent air voids (Shergold 1953). Therefore, angularity of aggregates is calculated with reference to the maximum theoretical density of 67 per cent.

The degree of angularity of coarse dry aggregates is expressed in terms of angularity number (AN). The AN is determined by filling a given sample of aggregates (which are retained and which pass through two standard sizes of IS sieves) in approximately three layers in a cylinder of known volume. To attain maximum density, each layer of aggregate is uniformly tamped 100 times to adjust the aggregate particles closely together in the cylinder. The average weight of aggregates filled in the cylinder is calculated from at least three trial test results. The AN is calculated as (IS: 2386 (Part 1)-1963; 2004):

$$\text{AN} = 67 - 100 \times \frac{\text{Average weight of aggregates (g)}}{\text{Volume of water required to fill the cylinder (ml)} \times \text{Sp. gr. of aggregates}} \tag{3.67}$$

The value of AN is approximated to a nearest whole number. If the aggregates are more angular, the calculated value of AN will be higher and vice versa.

3.9.5 Aggregate Crushing Test

The property of hardness or resistance of aggregates to withstand external pressures is evaluated in the aggregate crushing test. It is an important tests conducted on road aggregates. Under a standard load of 40 tonnes, the given aggregates are allowed to be crushed. The weight of crushed powder which passes through a 2.36 mm size sieve is measured. The aggregate crushing (AC) value is expressed in terms of per cent of weight of stone powder passing through a 2.36 mm sieve to the total weight of the aggregate sample taken for the AC test. The AC value is very sensitive to small changes in quality of aggregates tested (Shipway 1964). The strength of the aggregate in terms of its impact value can be estimated from the test results of aggregate crushing tests (Spence et al. 1974).

In this test, about 3.5 kg of dry aggregates passing through a 12.5 mm size IS sieve and retained on a 10 mm size IS sieve are taken and filled in a standard measuring cylinder in three equal thick layers. Each layer is tamped 25 times by a tamping rod with a rounded end. Excess aggregates on the top of the measuring cylinder are levelled off. The weight of the compacted aggregate filled in the cylindrical is measured (W_1 g) up to 1 g accuracy. The aggregates are transferred to the test mould in three layers of equal thickness, tamped 25 times for each layer (Figure 3.53 (a)). The piston assembly with the mould (Figure 3.53 (b)) is put in position for loading. A vertical compressive load is applied on the plunger to the sample of aggregates placed in the mould at a rate of 4 tonnes per minute gradually up to 40 tonnes (IS: 2386 (Part 4)-1963).

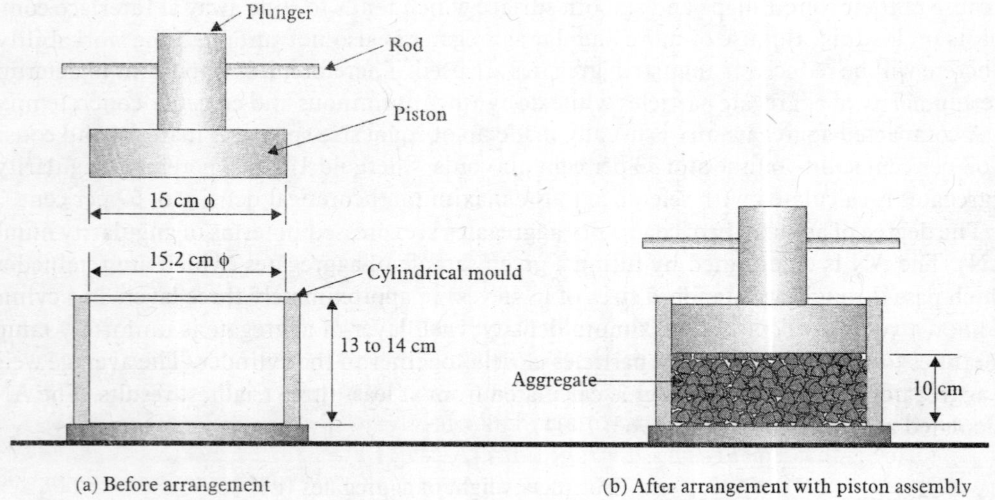

Figure 3.53 *Details of mould and plunger*

After releasing the load, the test mould with the piston assembly is removed from the compression test machine. The tested aggregates are sieved through a 2.36 mm sieve and the weight of the aggregate powder passing the sieve is recorded as W_2 g, to an accuracy of 0.1 gm. The above test procedure is repeated with fresh aggregates. A minimum of two tests are specified for each type of aggregate. The aggregate crushing value is calculated using equation (2.68) (IS: 2386 (Part 4)-1963).

Aggregate crushing (AC) value (%) = $(W_2/W_1) \times 100$ (3.68)

where, W_1 = Weight of the compacted aggregate filled in the test mould in g
W_2 = Weight of aggregate powder passing through a 2.36 mm size sieve in g

If the tested aggregate sample is hard in nature, the numerical AC value will be low and vice versa. Generally, aggregates with lower crushing values are selected for the surface course of pavement layers where direct heavy compressive forces are anticipated. The limits of aggregate crushing values according to the IRC for various types of pavement layers are presented in Figure 3.54.

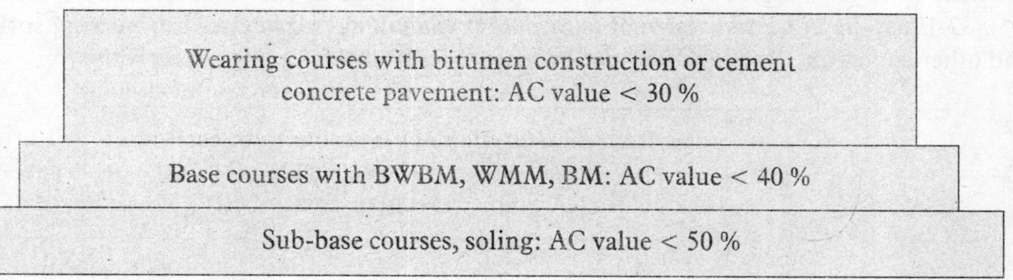

Figure 3.54 *Aggregate crushing values for different pavement layers*

Non-standard size of aggregates The test procedure followed for non-standard sizes of aggregates (i.e., not in between 12.5 mm to 10 mm) is same as for the standard size aggregates (explained before) but the apparatus used like the cylindrical mould, tamping rod and sieve sizes (Table 3.12) (IS: 2386 (Part 4)-1963, 2005) are different in dimensions.

Table 3.12 *Test details of non-standard sized aggregates (IS: 2386 (Part 4)-1963: 2005)*

Size of aggregate (mm)		IS sieve size (mm) to separate fines after test	Test description
Retained	Passing		
3.35	2.36	0.60	Cylindrical mould = 7.5 cm dia; Cylindrical measure = 6 cm dia, with 9 cm height; tamping rod = 8 mm dia, with 30 cm length; after tamping, the depth of the aggregate in the mould = 5 cm; loading rate @ 1 tonne per minute, up to a total of 10 tonnes in ten minutes.
4.75	3.35	0.85	
6.3	4.75	1.18	
10	6.3	1.70	
20	12.5	3.35	Standard test procedure
25	20	4.75	Standard test procedure

Ten Per Cent Fines Test

This test is generally prescribed when the aggregate crushing value slightly exceeds 30 per cent and the trail test results are inconsistent (IS: 2386 (Part 4)-1963; 2005). In this test, the crushing load at which 10 per cent of fines of aggregates are produced is determined. The test procedure is the same as the standard aggregate crushing test explained in Section 3.8.5. The aggregate size used for this test should be in between 12.5 to 10 mm. But different loads are applied to each of the test sample (say 4 or 5 number of trials). The percentage of fines obtained is plotted against the respective load applied (Figure 3.55). The load at which 10 per cent fines are observed (from Figure 3.55) is reported as the test result. According to BS:882-1965, the minimum value of ten per cent fines of aggregates used in wearing surfaces and other concreting works should not be more than 10 and 5 tonnes respectively.

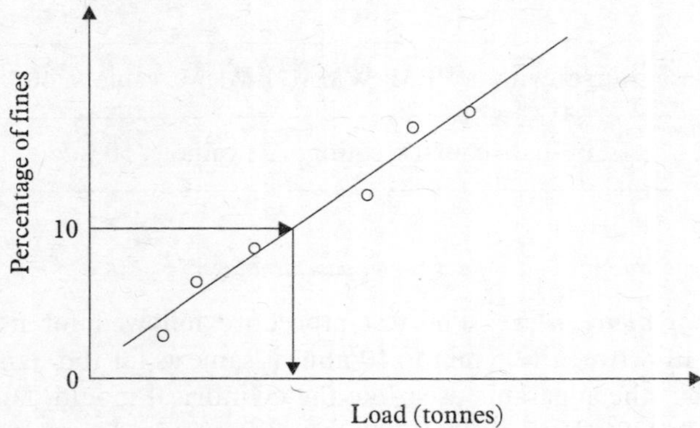

Figure 3.55 *Result of ten percentage fines test*

3.9.6 Aggregate Impact Test

Repetitive traffic wheel loads cause damage to the pavement layers by compression, impact and abrasion. Traffic loads are mainly supported by aggregates. Therefore, the aggregates should be tested for their resistance against impact or shock loads caused due to the movement of vehicles at high speed. The property of toughness of aggregates to sustain these loads is evaluated by the aggregate impact (AI) test. AI value is expressed as the percentage of aggregate powder formed under impact loads in standard test conditions

Based on the source and type of mineral content of the aggregates, some aggregates can resist static or slow compressive loads but fail to resist impact loads caused due to shocks. Hence, it is mandatory to evaluate AI value of aggregates.

Details of the test procedure are presented below (IS: 2386 (Part 4)-1963).

An oven dried aggregate sample which passes a 12.5 mm sieve but is retained on a 10 mm sieve is obtained. The aggregate is filled in a measuring cylinder in three equal layers and each layer is tamped 25 times with the round end of a standard tamping rod. Excess aggregates in the measuring cylinder are struck off by a straight edge. The net weight of the aggregates is recorded (W_1 g) to 1 g accuracy. The measured aggregates are transferred to a cylindrical cup and tamped 25 times with the rounded end of a tamping rod.

The cup having the aggregate sample is placed in the centre of the base plate of the impact test set-up (Figure 3.56) and screwed firmly to it. A hammer of weight 13.5 to 14 kg is arranged to fall on to the top surface of the aggregates in the cup from a height of 38 ± 0.5 cm. The weight should be lifted and allowed to fall freely on to the aggregate sample in the cup 15 times at an interval of 15 s (i.e., 1 blow/ 1 second). Therefore, the total energy of impact = 135 Nf × 0.38 m × 15 times in 15 s = 769.5 N-ms.

The crushed aggregates are sieved through a 2.36 mm sieve and the weight of aggregate passing and retained are weighed separately to the nearest 0.1 g accuracy. If the difference between the weight of aggregate powder passing (W_2 g) and the aggregates retained (W_3 g) on a 2.36 mm size of IS sieve is more than 1 g, the test result is discarded. The AI value is calculated using equation (3.69).

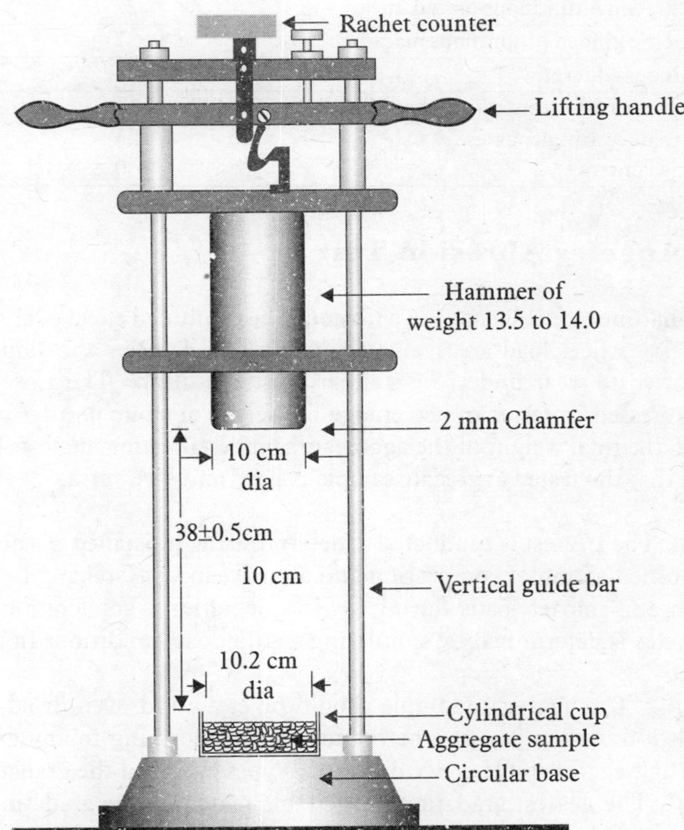

Figure 3.56 *Aggregate impact test apparatus*

$$\text{Aggregate impact value} = 100 \times W_2/W_1 \tag{3.69}$$

where W_1 = weight of aggregate filled in measuring cylinder, in g

W_2 = net weight of aggregate passing through a 2.36 mm size IS sieve in g

The AI values are correlated with field performance of various types of pavement layers. To decide the suitability of aggregates for various types of pavement layers, Indian Roads Congress (*IRC Pocket Book* 2006) recommended the following limiting values (Table 3.13).

Table 3.13 *Maximum allowable aggregate impact value (Pocket Book 2006)*

Sl.No.	Description	Maximum allowable aggregate impact value (%)
1	Wet mix macadam for sub-base or base	30
2	Crushed run macadam base	30
3	Bituminous base	30
4	Dense graded bituminous macadam	27
5	Semi-dense graded bituminous macadam	27
6	Bituminous concrete	24
7	Aggregate used for concreting according to IS:383-1993:	
	Other than wearing courses	45
	Wearing courses	30

3.9.7 Los Angeles Abrasion Test

The property of hardness or resistance to withstand the combined effect of abrasion and impact forces by repetitive wheel load are evaluated in the Los Angeles abrasion test. The given aggregate is allowed to wear under the standard test condition. The Los Angeles abrasion (LA) value is expressed in terms of percentage by weight of stone powder passing through a 1.70 mm sieve to the total weight of the aggregate sample taken for the test. If the LA value is low, it indicates that the tested aggregate sample is hard and vice versa.

TEST PRINCIPLE: The LA test is conducted to determine the resistance of a given dry aggregate against the combined action of compaction and abrasive loads (Orchard 1964). The capacity to bear abrasion and impact loads during vehicle operations, acceleration, deceleration or breaking of vehicles is determined by simulating similar load conditions in the laboratory.

TEST PROCEDURE: The aggregate sample should be clean and oven dried at 105 to 110 °C (allowed to cool to room temperature before testing), conforming to any gradation given in Table 3.14. The aggregate sample is divided into 7 types based on the gradation namely A, B, C, D, E, F and G. The nearest gradation in the table matching the gradation requirement of a pavement layer is selected and the recommended size and weight of the aggregate sample is taken for testing.

The prepared aggregate sample and prescribed number of steel balls are placed in a steel hollow drum of 50 cm length with an internal diameter of 70 cm (Figure 3.57). The cylinder is capable of being rotated along its horizontal axis. A steel plate of size 8.8 cm × 2.5 cm × 70 cm is fixed to close the drum along its length (IS: 2386 (Part 4)-1963; 2005).

Table 3.14 *Gradation of aggregate for conducting the Los Angeles abrasion test (IS: 2386 (Part 4)-1963; 2005)*

Square sieve size (mm)		Weight of aggregate (kg)						
Passing	Retained	A	B	C	D	E	F	G
4.75	2.36				5.0			
6.30	4.75			2.5				
10.00	6.30			2.5				
12.5	10.00	1.25	2.5					
20.00	12.50	1.25	2.5					
25.00	20.00	1.25						5.0*
40.00	25.00	1.25					5.0*	5.0*
50.00	40.00					5.0*	5.0*	
63.00	50.00					2.5*		
80.00	63.00					2.5*		
Total (kg)		5.0	5.0	5.0	5.0	10.0	10.0	10.0
No. of steel spheres used		12	11	8	6	12	12	12
Weight of charge (kg)		5.0 ± 0.025	4.584 ± 0.025	3.330 ± 0.020	2.5 ± 0.015	5.0 ± 0.025		
No. of revolutions		500				1000		

* Tolerance of ± 2 % is permitted.

In the LA test, the aggregates are tested for abrasion by interaction with steel spheres (as abrasive charge) and other aggregates. Impact forces are applied on the aggregates by rotation of the drum. The shelf which is fixed inside the drum along its length facilitates the transfer of the aggregates and steel spheres to the top of the drum and their sudden drop to the bottom of the rotating drum.

The aggregate loaded steel drum is allowed to rotate at the rate of 30 to 33 rpm to the desired total number of rotations as prescribed (Table 3.12). After a prescribed number of rotations, the aggregate, the aggregate powder along with the steel balls are collected. The dust on the steel balls is also carefully collected by using a brush. The fine dust particles from the aggregate sample are separated through a 1.70 mm IS sieve. The aggregates which are coarser than 1.70 mm are washed. The LA value is obtained by using equation (3.70).

$$\text{Aggregate crushing value} = 100 \times (W_1 - W_2)/W_1 \tag{3.70}$$

where,

W_1 = Weight of the selected grade of the aggregate used for the test in g

W_2 = Weight of the aggregate retained on a 1.70 mm size IS sieve in g

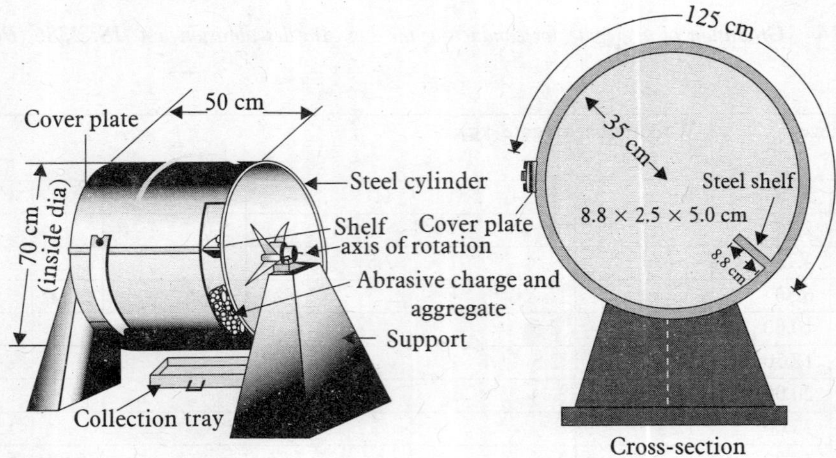

Figure 3.57 *Los Angeles abrasion test apparatus*

Generally, aggregates with lower LA values are selected for surface course or for pavement layers where direct heavy abrasive forces are anticipated. According to IRC (*Pocket Book* 2006), allowable limits of aggregate LA values for various types of pavement layers are presented in Figure 3.58.

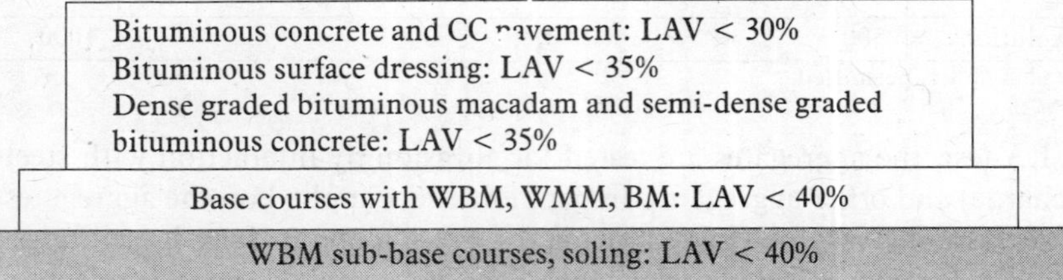

Figure 3.58 *Los Angeles abrasion test limiting values for various pavement layers*

There are two other tests available to evaluate the abrasion resistance of aggregates namely, Deval's and Dorry's abrasion tests.

Deval's abrasion test is similar to the Los Angeles abrasion test with slight deviations in the test procedure. But the desirable limits of percentage wear of aggregate for various types of pavement layer construction is not clearly specified by the IRC or the Bureau of Indian Standards. Hence, the Deval's abrasion test is not widely used in India.

Dorry's abrasion test is used in the UK to determine the percentage loss in weight of aggregate due to abrasion with sand. This test is not prescribed by IRC. Hence, it has very limited use in India. Details of the test procedure may be found in the BS: 812 of the British Standard Institute.

3.9.8 Stripping Value of Aggregates

The adhesion property of bitumen to the surface of freshly crushed aggregates is determined using the stripping value of aggregates. During the construction of bituminous layers, the aggregates are properly mixed with a suitable quantity of bitumen at a standard temperature. But the surfaces of aggregates may not be coated fully with bitumen. Following are the reasons for partial coating of aggregates.

- If the temperature (or viscosity) of bitumen is not maintained at a standard value during mixing, the surface of aggregate particles may not be fully coated with bitumen.
- If the aggregates used for bituminous road construction are wet or are obtained from a snow fall area, the aggregate particles may be partially coated with bitumen even though the standard temperature of bitumen is maintained during mixing. This is due to a thin film of water present on the aggregate surface leading to improper adhesion or coating.
- The aggregates might have also been contaminated by dust or mud or clay during crushing, transportation and storage of operations.

In the above cases, the compacted pavement surface may not have good adhesion or interlocking bond between bitumen coated aggregate particles. Hence, under traffic loading, the pavement surface fails due to ravelling of aggregate and subsequently results in the formation of potholes.

In bituminous surface layers where open graded aggregates have been used, there is a possibility of ingress of rain water into surface voids. This subsequently affects the adhesion capacity of bitumen and leads to displacement or stripping of the coated bituminous film from the surface of aggregates.

The stripping of bitumen from aggregates is due to the high silica content (acidic) of some aggregates which have more affinity for water with dipole characteristics since its surface has a tendency to become negatively charged. If both the aggregate and bitumen have the same electrical charge (i.e., positive or negative), then they have a tendency to repel. In this situation, the surface of the aggregates tries to attract water or moisture instead of bitumen and remain electrically stable. Therefore, bitumen strips out from the surface of aggregates. It is noted that the problem of stripping is not only related to the percentage of silica content in aggregates. The problem is with both aggregates and bitumen having the tendency to become electrically stable although their electrical charges are the same.

The adhesion property of bitumen acquired using different aggregates from various sources is evaluated with the aggregate stripping test. The static immersion test was formulated by CRRI to determine the stripping value (%) of bitumen and tar from aggregates. In 1971, this method was standardised by the Bureau of Indian Standards (IS: 6241-1971; 2006).

In the static immersion test, about 200 g of aggregates passing a 20 mm sieve and retained on a 12.5 mm size IS sieve, and about 5 per cent by weight (10 g) of bitumen is taken. The bitumen and aggregates are preheated separately at 160 and 150 °C respectively (IS: 6241-1971; 2006). Then they are mixed thoroughly in order to coat the aggregate surfaces completely with bitumen. This mixture is transferred to a beaker and allowed to cool at room temperature for 2 hours. The beaker is filled with distilled water just sufficient to immerse the aggregate–bitumen mix. It is then covered and kept in a water bath at a temperature of 40 °C for about 24 hours. Afterwards, the beaker is taken out of the water bath and allowed to cool at room temperature. The extent of stripping of bitumen from the aggregates surface is estimated by visual examination when the mixture is immersed in water. The following equation is used for calculating the stripping value of bitumen from the aggregates surface.

$$\text{Stripping value} = \frac{\text{Uncovered surface area of aggregates by visual examination}}{\text{Total surface area of aggregates}} \times 100 \qquad (3.71)$$

The above test procedure is also followed for tar. Except that instead of 160 and 150 °C, the tar and aggregates are preheated to a temperature of 110 and 100 °C respectively (IS: 6241-1971; 2006).

According to IRC, the minimum allowable retained coating and stripping of bitumen–aggregate mixtures for different bituminous layers are presented in Table 3.15.

Table 3.15 *Coating and stripping of bitumen–aggregate mixtures (Pocket Book 2006)*

Sl. No.	Type of bituminous layer	Minimum retained coating (%)
1	Bituminous base	95
2	Dense graded bituminous macadam	95
3	Semi-dense bituminous concrete	95
4	Bituminous concrete	95

This test may not provide accurate results because it depends on visual examination of the aggregates. But it is simple, easy to perform in the field and gives an approximate estimation of the stripping value during selection of suitable aggregates acquired from various sources.

Exercises

3.1. What are the uses of soil classification and state how the knowledge of the soil characteristics is useful for design of pavements? Give an example stating what other factors must be considered in addition to the soil classification data.

3.2. Define particle size analysis of soil and distinguish between IS and ASTM methods of designation of particles based on their size?

3.3. What are the factors affecting the behaviour of fine grained uniformly graded soil under service conditions?

3.4. Define gradation of soil. What are the different types of grades of soil or mineral aggregate?

3.5. Draw a typical gradation chart showing different types of soils and their grades

3.6. State the uses of moisture content present in a given soil.

3.7. What are the different methods used for determining the moisture present in the soil and state the limitations of each method?

3.8. Distinguish between field moisture content (FMC) and optimum moisture content (OMC).

3.9. Define (i) liquid limit, (ii) plastic limit, (iii) liquidity index, (iv) consistency index, (v) toughness index and (vi) activity of soil.

3.10. How is the degree of plasticity of soil measured?

3.11. Briefly explain the test standards and procedure adopted for determination of (i) liquid limit of soil by (a) mechanical method and (b) cone penetrometer method, and determination of (ii) plastic limit of a given soil.

3.12. What are the limitations and suitability of mechanical and cone penetrometer methods for determination of liquid limit of soil?

3.13. What are the generally accepted interpretations with reference to liquid limit, plasticity and liquidity index?

3.14. State the significance of LL and PI values in characterisation of soil properties that are used for road construction.

3.15. Cone penetrometer tests conducted on a soil sample gave the following test data:

Moisture content (%)	32.0	33.4	34.4	36.1	37.3
Cone penetration (mm)	16.5	18.0	19.5	20.9	22.8

Draw the plot and determine the liquid limit of the soil.

3.16. Liquid limit tests were conducted on a clay sample and the following observations were obtained.

Test No.	1	2	3	4
Water content (%)	69	63	48	43
No. of blows (*N*)	5	8	9	44

Draw the flow curve on a semi-log paper and determine the LL value.

3.17. The following observations were recorded from an LL test.

Test No.	1	2	3	4
Wt. of container (g)	13.3	13.1	13.4	12.9
Wt. of container + wet soil (g)	26.3	21.8	21.4	22.7
Wt. of container + dry soil (g)	22.5	18.1	18.3	19.7
No. of blows (*N*)	12	18	21	29

Determine the LL value by drawing the density curve. What is the value of PI if the plastic limit value is 22%?

3.18. Define specific gravity of soil and state where this value is useful.

3.19. State the need for soil classification. What is the significance of soil classification in construction and performance of roads?

3.20. Define textural soil classification. What are the different types of textural classification methods available for classifying fine grained soils.

3.21. What are the limitations of textural classifications?

3.22. Describe the salient features of (i) the unified soil classification system, (ii) the AASHTO method of soil classification and (iii) the Indian method of soil classification. Distinguish between the different systems.

3.23. Classify the soil for the given data: A coarse grained soil containing fines (0.075 mm) less than 9%; C_u=20; C_c=2.0 and PI = 6. (ANS: GW-GM)

3.24. Following are the results obtained from sieve analysis:

IS sieve size (mm)	50.0	37.5	19.0	9.5	4.75	0.6	0.3	0.075
Weight retained (g)	0	150.1	170.3	210.2	1100.5	75.6	120	10.2

Plot the gradation curve and determine the effective size, coefficient of uniformity, coefficient of curvature and soil classification based on the Indian soil classification method.

3.25. What observations can be made from the plasticity chart first developed by Prof. Casagrande and the chart used in IS: 1498-1970.

3.26. What do you understand by borderline cases of soil classification and write a few possible cases for (i) coarse grained soil, (ii) fine grained soil and (iii) a combination of both fine and coarse grained soils.

3.27. What do you understand by group index and describe its significance in the classification of fine grained soils?

3.28. Write the empirical formula of group index and state the limiting values of each parameter involved with it.

3.29. Write a short note on classification of Indian black cotton soils by CRRI.

3.30. Draw a figure that represents a typical partially saturated soil mass and write the related formulas with their definition.

3.31. Determine the values of dry density and void ratio if a sand sample has a porosity of 34.5 % and the specific gravity is given as 2.70.

3.32. What happens when soil is compacted (i) at different moisture levels and (ii) at different compactive efforts? Explain with a neat sketch.

3.33. What are the useful changes that occur in a compacted soil mass?

3.34. What is the test principle of (i) a standard soil compaction method and (ii) the modified soil compaction method?

3.35. Define degree of compaction of soil. What is its relevance to field compaction levels?

3.36. State the effect of hot climate and cold climate on the degree of compaction.

3.37. What is the effect of the quality of water used for compaction of soil?

3.38. State different methods of compaction of soil and explain core cutter and sand replacement methods.

3.39. What is the working principle of the nuclear density metre and state its limitations? What are the applications of soil compaction values?

3.40. A laboratory compaction test was performed to determine the density of a clay soil. Following are the results:

Volume of the mould = 1000 cc

Weight of mould (empty) = 2295 gm

Weight of mould + compacted soil = 4122 gm

Weight of mould + compacted soil after drying = 3470 gm

Specific gravity of soil particle = 2.69

Calculate the water content, bulk and dry densities of soil, void ratio and its degree of saturation.

3.41. A compacted soil sample has a bulk density of 21 kN/m^3 at a water content of 14%. Determine its dry density and degree of saturation. Assume G = 2.65. If the soil sample is fully saturated, what will be its bulk density value?

3.42. State the test principle of CBR test. Write the standard specifications followed for preparation of soil sample and for testing?

3.43. Why is the CBR value determined at 2.5 mm penetration generally greater than the CBR determined at 5.0 mm penetration? Why is surcharge weight used for testing of soil sample by the CBR method?

3.44. Comment on CBR as an empirical value of soil strength.

3.45. State what characteristics of soil are indicative of CBR value.

3.46. Draw sketches showing standard details of CBR penetration test and expansion test.

3.47. How can the values obtained from the expansion test of soil be interpreted with reference to soil cohesion and swell?

3.48. State the allowable values of CBR of soil that can be used for road construction and embankment.

3.49. With the help of a figure explain the plate load test procedure.

3.50. State the uses of the plate load test. What are the standard specifications of the test?

3.51. What is the drawback of PLT? State how the k value does not represent the stress distribution due to load on flexible pavements, base and sub-grade.

3.52. Why are corrections made to the k value determined by the plate load test? Describe the different corrections made.

3.53. State the general classification of the soil based on the k value?

3.54. State how shear strength parameters are useful for pavement and road embankment design in general.

3.55. State the drawbacks of the shear box test that does not allow it to simulate in situ pavement service conditions.

3.56. Explain how the tri-axial test best simulates field loading conditions. Describe with a neat sketch the test principle, set-up and procedure.

3.57. What are the factors affecting unconfined compressive strength of a given soil?

3.58. Compare the different shear strength tests carried out on sub-grade soil.

3.59. Interpret the tri-axial test results with relevance to pavement design.

3.60. Determine the shear strength properties of soil (*C* and Φ) from the following results obtained from an undrained tri-axial test conducted on a soil.

All-round pressure (kN/m²)	18.5	32.3
Deviator stress at failure (kN/m²)	55.3	85.7

3.61. Note down the Poisson's ratio values that are generally used for design and analysis of pavements.

3.62. What is the difference between modulus of elasticity and resilient modulus of pavement material?

3.63. Write the different formulas used for determination of resilient modulus of sub-grade soil.

3.64. Briefly explain how geological concepts are useful for selection and identification of mineral aggregate used for road construction.

3.65. Discuss the geological classification of rocks and state the fundamental properties of rocks that cause them to be hard and tough.

3.66. State the sources of mineral aggregate used for road construction.

3.67. Explain how specific gravity and water absorption values of aggregate are used by the pavement engineer.

3.68. Briefly describe the test procedure adopted for determining the specific gravity of aggregates when the aggregate size is greater than 10 mm and less than 10 mm.

3.69. Explain the significance of shape test of aggregates used for (i) cement concrete and (ii) bituminous concrete.

3.70. Write a short note on (i) flakiness test and (ii) elongation test of road aggregates.

3.71. What is the significance of the angularity test of road aggregates? Describe the test principle.

3.72. What is the significance of the (i) aggregate crushing test, (ii) Los Angeles abrasion test, (iii) aggregate crushing test, (iv) ten per cent fines test and (v) aggregate impact test? Describe the principle behind the tests.

3.73. State the reasons for partial coating of bitumen on aggregate surfaces.

3.74. What is the significance of the stripping value test? Describe the principle behind the test.

4

Bituminous Materials

Introduction

Bituminous materials are used for constructing wearing courses. They are also used as stabilising agents for other layers of flexible pavements. The properties of bituminous materials, viz. adhesion, cementation, ductility, strength and imperviousness are useful for constructing pavements. Basically, bituminous materials are thermoplastic hydrocarbons which possess high molecular weight. They become soft on heating and harden on cooling. They are obtained from natural sources or are prepared artificially. Based on the origin, type of mineral composition and method of processing in refineries, bituminous materials are classified into different types. A few of the different types used for highway construction are given below (IS: 334-2002).

Bitumen Bitumen is obtained from natural sources or vacuum distillation of crude petroleum products at a temperature of about +400 °C. It is a black or brown to black, non-crystalline material in solid or semi-solid state having good adhesive property. Bitumen is completely soluble in carbon disulphide but largely non-volatile and resistant to most acids, alkalis and salts (Dickinson 1984).

Asphalt Based on the origin of occurrence (by nature or artificial preparation), the bitumen may contain a certain amount of mineral matter. The bitumen associated with inert mineral matter is known as asphalt.

NOTE: In some parts of Europe and North America, bitumen is referred to as asphalt.

Straight-run bitumen The bitumen extracted as a residue from crude oil refinery without any diluents is called straight-run bitumen. It is generally found to have higher viscosity. Bitumen cutbacks are prepared by adding soluble volatiles to straight-run bitumen to obtain bitumen which has lower viscosity and is more workable.

Mastic asphalt Coarser filler material (stone grit) is mixed with bitumen to remove any internal voids. This mixture, called mastic asphalt, can be used to construct impervious layers for surfacing, bridge decks and roofs.

Bitumen blends of different types and grades will be discussed in subsequent sections of this chapter.

4.1 Desirable Properties of Bitumen

Following are the important desirable properties of bitumen which makes it suitable for constructing pavements.

- Low cost
- Workability
- Strength
- Durability
- Imperviousness
- Minimal sensitivity to aging
- Cohesion
- Adhesion

Till today, bitumen is the most cost-effective binding material which can effectively bind aggregate particles of different sizes together into a strong, stable and impervious compact layer. However, the bitumen may be subjected to an ageing process in two situations, viz. due to longer duration of storage and by oxidation. Bitumen gets hard due to long-term storage, although it can be made soft by heating. But when bitumen oxidises, i.e., the hydrogen present in the bitumen reacts with the oxygen in atmosphere, it becomes permanently brittle due to change in chemical properties (Shen et al. 2006) and cracks. Bitumen oxidises due to sunlight raising the temperature of the pavement. The hydrogen ions are lost via water molecules. It is noted that the phenomenon of oxidation of bitumen only takes place in the presence of oxygen (Dickinson 1982). The oxidised bitumen may be physically identified by its change in colour from black to grey.

For pavement construction purposes, the following criteria should be considered for selection of a suitable binder of bituminous material.

1. The bitumen binder should satisfy the criteria of strength and durability for the prescribed loading and temperature variations.
2. The workability of the bitumen should be studied carefully at temperatures similar to climatic conditions of the in service pavement. The viscosity of bitumen is largely dependent on its working temperatures during mixing, laying and compaction. Hence, the equipment used for mixing of bitumen with aggregate, the method of storage, transportation, laying and compaction of a bituminous layer should be decided in advance.
3. Susceptibility and durability of bitumen under prevailing environmental conditions should be evaluated throughout its period of serviceable life. To prevent the bitumen from cracking and undergoing undue deformations, it should neither be brittle or too soft during cold and hot climates respectively. The bitumen should allow elastic deformations in the range of temperature changes that may occur in different seasons of a year.
4. Partial coating and stripping off of bitumen film from the surfaces of aggregates due to poor adhesion should also be studied under prevailing climatic and drainage conditions.

The above requirements were set and standardised by various institutions in different countries based on the intensity of traffic loads, temperature, climatic conditions, materials availability, design criteria and methods of construction. The suitability of bitumen for road construction according to design criteria should be evaluated by various tests.

4.2 Tests on Bituminous Materials

Materials which are to be used as binders in constructing pavements should have desirable properties such as high strength, stability and durability to withstand the desired number of repeated wheel loads even under adverse environment and climatic conditions. To characterise bitumen before using it in the field, it is necessary to evaluate its strength under different test conditions in the laboratory. Temperatures maintained for conducting the different tests in the laboratory and the relevant working range of the temperature of pavements is given in Figure 4.1.

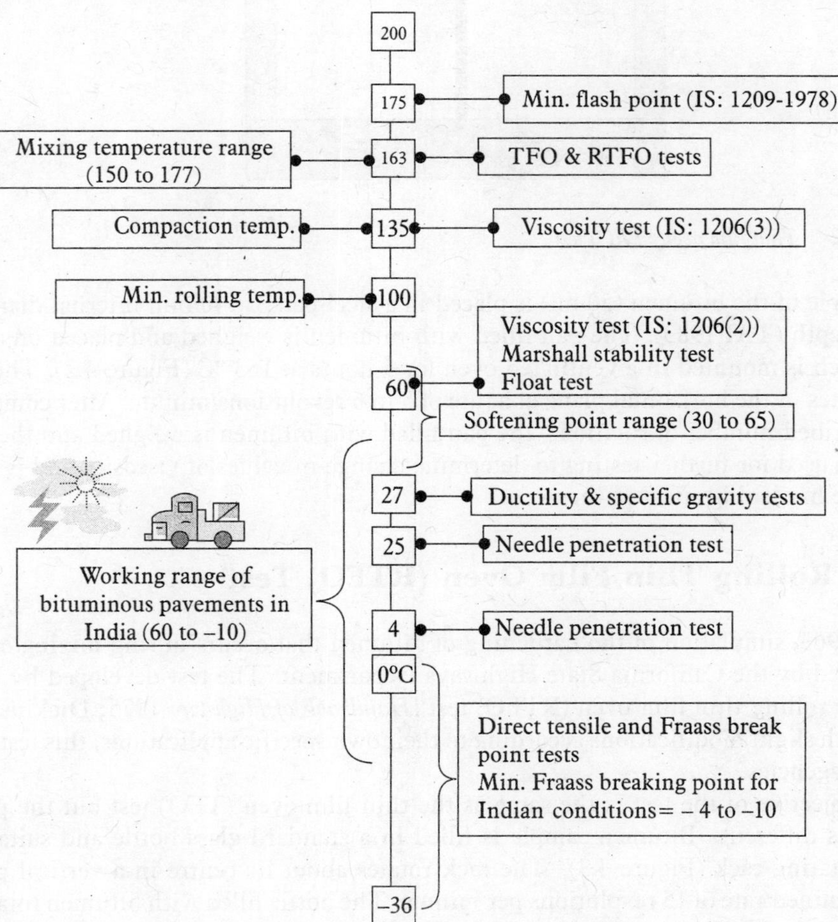

Figure 4.1 *Working temperatures (°C) with bitumen and bituminous pavement*

4.2.1 Thin Film Oven (TFO) Test

This test is intended to evaluate the changes in behaviour characteristics of bitumen, viz. loss in value of weight, penetration and viscosity, when a sample is subjected to hardening (by evaporation of volatile content) in the presence of hot air. Basically, the susceptibility of bitumen to heating is evaluated when it is exposed to adverse hot conditions that are present during mixing operations.

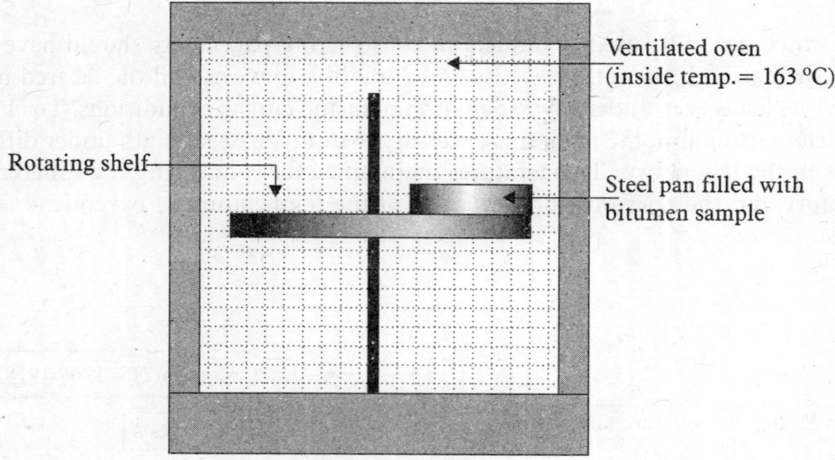

Figure 4.2 *Thin film oven (TFO) test*

A sample of the bitumen (50 ml) is placed in a steel pan of 140 mm internal diameter and 10 mm depth (TAI 1983). The pan filled with bitumen is weighed and placed on a rotating shelf which is mounted in a ventilated oven for 5 hours at 163 °C (Figure 4.2). The rotating shelf rotates in the horizontal plane at a rate of 5 to 6 revolutions/minute. After completion of the prescribed number of rotations, the pan filled with bitumen is weighed and the bitumen residue is used for further testing to determine change in values of viscosity and penetration due to the hardening effect in the oven.

4.2.2 Rolling Thin Film Oven (RTFO) Test

During 1963, simulation of the hardening of bitumen that occurs during mixing operations was studied by the California State Highways Department. The test developed by them was called the rolling thin film oven (RTFO) test (*Handbook of Highway* 1975; Dickinson 1984). Later, with slight modifications according to their own specific applications, this test was used by many agencies.

The objective of the test is the same as the thin film oven (TFO) test but the procedure adopted is different. Bitumen sample is filled in a standard glass bottle and suitably fixed onto a rotating rack (Figure 4.3). The rack rotates about its centre in a vertical plane at a pre-determined rate of 15 revolutions per minute. The bottle filled with bitumen rotates about its horizontal axis. The rotating rack system is assembled in an oven which is maintained at a temperature of 163 °C (TAI 1983). While the bottle is rotating, the liquid bitumen also rolls inside the bottle and is exposed to heat. To accelerate the hardening, hot air is blown into the bottle by means of an air jet (400 ml/minute) after each rotation of the rack.

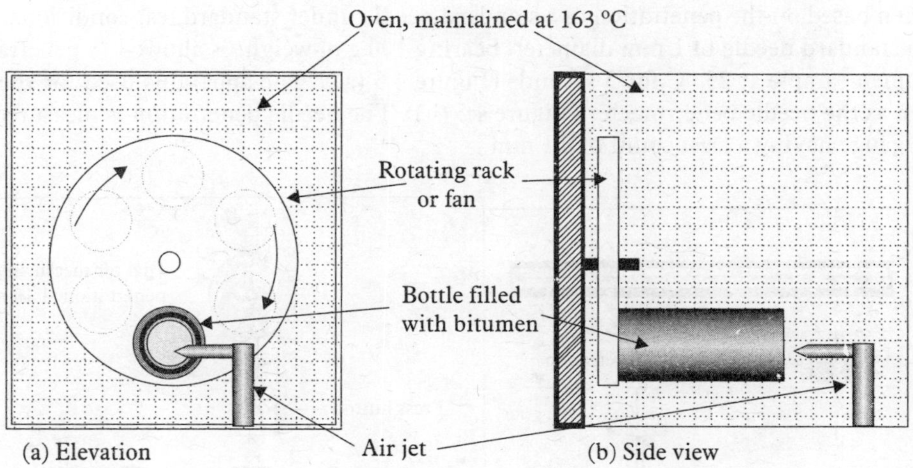

Figure 4.3 *Rolling thin film oven test*

The rack can accommodate many bottles so that more than one sample can be tested at a time in the oven.

After the test, the percentage loss in weight of the bitumen is determined and the residual bitumen is used to conduct further tests for determination of change in the values of viscosity, needle penetration and softening point. In this test, the paving binder is subjected to high temperatures and exposed to blasts of hot air thus simulating an accelerated aging process.

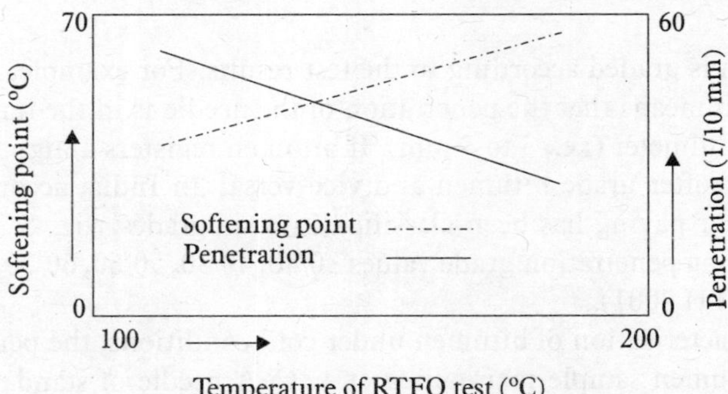

Figure 4.4 *Typical effect of RTFO test temperature on softening point and penetration*

The test temperature is the prime influencing parameter that dictates post-test properties of a binder. After conducting the test, the penetration value of an aged binder linearly decreases with the increase of test temperature whereas the softening point increases with increased temperature (Figure 4.4). This indicates that the RTFO test temperature simulates the accelerated effect of aging of bituminous mixes which happens in service conditions (Shen et al. 2006).

4.2.3 Needle Penetration Test (IS:1203-1978 and AASHTO T 49)

Bowen (1889) designed a bitumen test for determining the consistency range or grade of bitumen based on the penetration of a standard needle under standard test conditions. In this test, a standard needle of 1 mm diameter, bearing 100 g of weight is allowed to penetrate into a bitumen sample at 25 °C for 5 seconds (Figure 4.5 (a)). The apparatus used for the test is known as the needle penetrometer (Figure 4.5 (b)). The needle penetration is measured using a dial gauge having a least count of 0.1 mm.

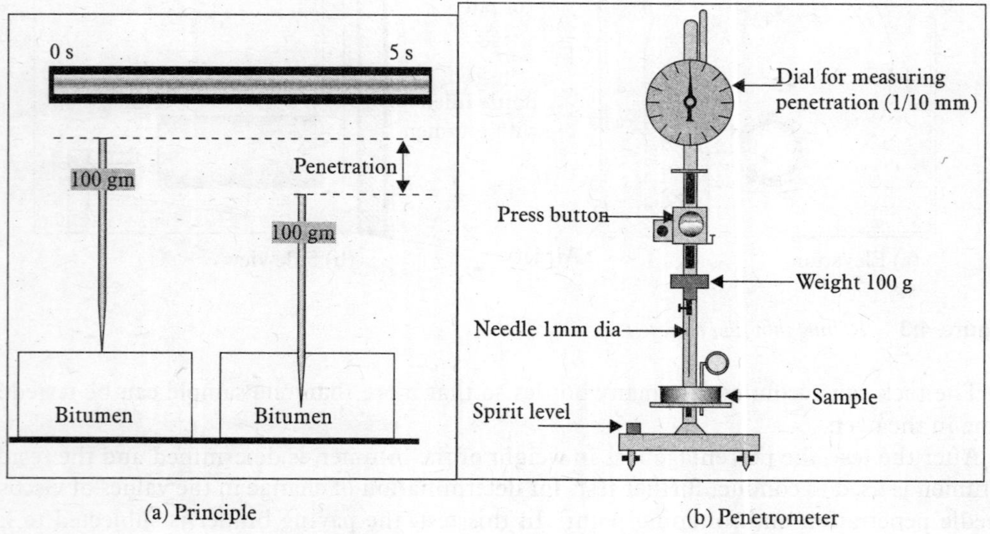

Figure 4.5 *Bitumen penetration test*

The tested bitumen is graded according to the test results. For example, if a bitumen sample is graded as 30/40, it means that the penetration of the needle is in the range of 30 to 40 times of one-tenth of a millimeter (i.e., 3 to 4 mm). If bitumen registers a higher penetration value, it is classified as a softer grade bitumen and vice versa. In India, according to IS:73-1992, the bitumen used for paving has been classified into six grades, viz. S-35, S-45, S-55, S-65, S-90 and S-200 having penetration grade values 30/40, 40/50, 50/60, 60/70, 80/100 and 175/225 respectively (MORTH 2001).

For further characterisation of bitumen under cold conditions, the penetration test can be conducted on a bitumen sample maintained at 4 °C. A needle of standard size with a 200 g weight is applied on the sample for 60 seconds. To study the behaviour of bitumen with respect to temperature, an index parameter termed as the penetration ratio (PR) is determined (IS:1203-1978; 2002). The equation used for calculation of PR is given below.

$$PR = \frac{\text{Penetration value found at 4 °C, under 200 g of weight, loaded for 1 minute}}{\text{Penetration value found at 25 °C, under 100 g of weight, loaded for 5 seconds}} \times 100 \tag{4.1}$$

According to IS: 73-1992 (MORTH 2001), the minimum required value of PR for most grades of bitumen is 35.

The consistency or grade of bitumen largely depends on its viscosity. Viscosity of bitumen is susceptible to minor changes in temperature. This property of bitumen (viscosity) is used as one of the basic input parameters for the design of bituminous mixes

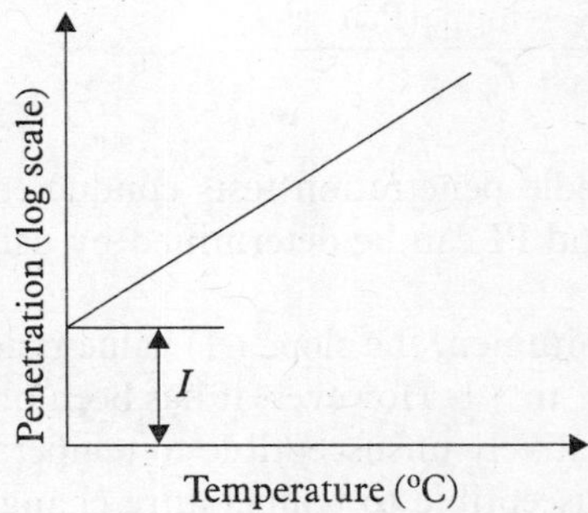

Figure 4.6 *Relationship between temperature and log (Pen) of bitumen*

A linear relationship was found between temperature and logarithm of the penetration value (Figure 4.5) (Pfeiffer and Doormaal 1936). This was used to determine the temperature susceptibility of bitumen. The relationship may be written in the following form.

$$\log(\text{Pen}) = A\,T + I \tag{4.2}$$

where, $\log(\text{Pen})$ = logarithmic value of penetration of bitumen
T = temperature
A = slope of the line or temperature susceptibility of bitumen
I = intercept

Pfeiffer and Doormaal (1936) initiated a concept called the penetration index (PI) based on the following relationship between logarithmic value of penetration and softening point value of bitumen.

$$\text{PI} = \frac{500\log(\text{Pen}_{25}) + 20\,T_{\text{R\&B}} - 1951.55}{T_{\text{R\&B}} - 50\log(\text{Pen}_{25}) + 120.15} \tag{4.3}$$

where, Pen_{25} = Bitumen penetration in 1/10 mm at 25 °C and

$T_{\text{R\&B}}$ = Bitumen softening point (°C) by ring and ball test

This concept was further developed by Heukelom (1973). The relationship used for determining temperature susceptibility of bitumen is as follows.

$$A = \frac{1}{50}\left[\frac{20-\text{PI}}{10+\text{PI}}\right] \tag{4.4a}$$

where, PI = Penetration index

$$A = \frac{\log_{10}(\text{Pen}) \text{ at } T_1 - \log_{10}(\text{Pen}) \text{ at } T_2}{T_1 - T_2} \tag{4.4b}$$

Based on the results of needle penetration tests conducted at two different temperatures (T_1 and T_2), the values of A and PI can be determined by using equations (4.2), (4.4(a)) and (4.4(b)).

For many types of paving bitumen, the slope (A) value ranges between 0.015 and 0.06 and the value of PI ranges from -1 to $+1$. However, it has been observed that bitumen having PI value greater than zero are relatively unsusceptible to temperature changes and those having PI values less than zero are susceptible to temperature changes. The PI values for the most commonly used bitumen range from -0.5 to $+0.5$ (Ullidtz and Peattie 1980).

The needle penetration test is an empirical test and suffers from many drawbacks (The Asphalt Institute 1983; MORTH 2001). Bitumen obtained from different sources and manufacturing processes and having the same penetration grade at 25 °C may have a wide range of viscosity from 500 to 3000 poises at a standard temperature of 60 °C (Discussions, IRC 1994). Bitumen obtained from different sources may also contain significant quantity of wax. Thus, the test results may vary. Only 2 to 3% wax can be tolerated in paving bitumen (Nair 1977). Therefore, to determine the true consistency of bitumen, in addition to the needle penetration test, viscosity and other relevant tests should be conducted.

Due to the above reason, different agencies such as HRB, FHWA, Asphalt Institute, AASHTO and ASTM insist on using the value of viscosity to grade bituminous binders rather than grading them by the needle penetration value. In the third revision of IS:73-2006, paving bitumen is classified into four types of grades based on viscosity, viz. VG 10, VG 20, VG 30 and VG 40 having standard needle penetration test values of 80/100, 60/70, 50/70, and 40/60 respectively.

4.2.4 Softening Point by the Ring and Ball Method

In this test, the temperature of the bitumen is measured at the point when it becomes soft. As a standard test procedure (IS: 1205-1978; 2002), bitumen sample is heated until it become completely fluid. This fluid is filled into two brass rings of standard dimensions. Steel spears of weight 3.5 g and diameter 9.5 mm are placed over the bitumen filled brass rings. The brass rings, each with a spear, are placed on the top plate of a frame (Figure 4.7). The frame is immersed in a distilled water bath which is maintained initially at 5 °C for 15 minutes. The height of water above the steel spears should be 50 mm and the vertical distance between the two plates of the frame should be 25 mm. The water is heated at a uniform rate of 5 °C per minute throughout the length of the test. When the steel spears sink through the rings along certain portions of melted bitumen and just touch the bottom plate of the frame, the water temperatures are recorded. The softening point of the bitumen tested is reported as the average of both the temperatures (i.e., spear 1 and 2). If the expected softening point of bitumen is above 80 °C, glycerin is used instead of a water bath at an initial temperature of 35 °C.

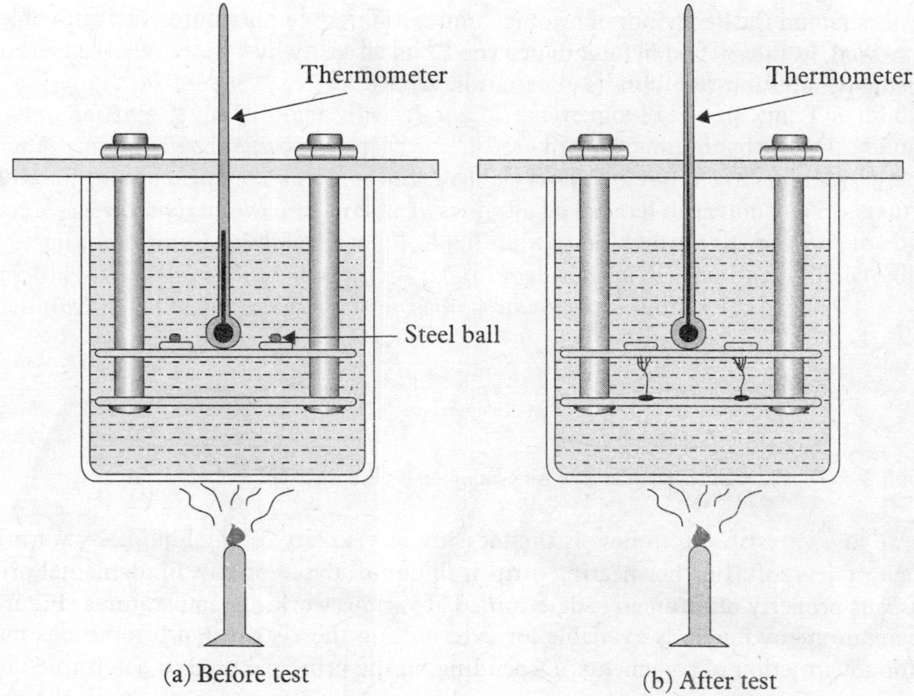

Figure 4.7 *Bitumen softening point test*

If the softening point (temperature) of bitumen is high, it indicates a harder grade of bitumen and if it is low, it indicates softer grades of bitumen. The value of the softening point of bitumen is very useful for determining the penetration index, temperature susceptibility, temperature shear resistance and other visco-elastic properties of bitumen.

According to IS:73-2006, the minimum temperature of the softening point for paving bitumen of grades VG 10, VG 20, VG 30 and VG 40 should be 40, 45, 47 and 50 °C respectively.

The softening point of different types of bitumen may vary from 25 to 120 °C. From literature, it is found that most bitumen types have a needle penetration value of 800 at the softening point.

4.2.5 Viscosity Test

Viscosity is defined as the internal resistance offered by the molecules of a substance against flow with time. To understand the viscous nature of a substance, it is essential to study its rheological properties. Rheologically, substances are classified as Newtonian, Bingham and power law fluids (S.S Chary).

To understand the behaviour of bitumen under different temperatures and rates of loading, it is essential, as mentioned before, to determine its viscosity by a more reliable method than the needle penetration test with its penetration values.

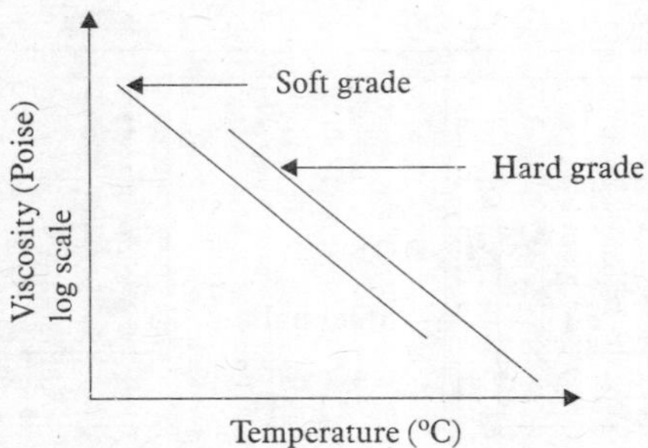

Figure 4.8 *Typical relationships between temperature and viscosity of bitumen*

As we know, resistance to flow is the measure of viscosity of any liquid. By warming the bitumen, it gets soft. Further heating turns it to liquid. Based on this fundamental principle, the viscous property of bitumen is determined at various working temperatures (Figure 4. 8).

There are many methods available for determining the viscosity of bituminous materials used for construction of pavements. Depending on the principle used to determine viscosity, different apparatus are used, namely, (i) the glass tube capillary viscometer, (ii) the orifice or efflux viscometer, (iii) the rotational viscometer and (iv) the sliding plate viscometer.

Glass Tube Capillary Viscometers

Liquid bitumen is filled in one limb of a U-shaped glass tube to a pre-determined level and allowed to flow further into its other limb (Figure 4.9). The time (in seconds) required for the liquid bitumen to flow between two given markings on the limb of the U-tube is recorded. The viscosity is calculated by multiplying the calibration factor of the U-tube to the recorded time duration in seconds. This viscosity is called the dynamic or absolute viscosity of bitumen. The units of dynamic viscosity are poise (1dyne. s/cm^2) or Pascal second (N. s/m^2). The unit is determined by a standard test recommended by AASHTO, designated as T202 (AASHTO 2001). The unit poise was named after Jean Louis Marie Poiseuille.

These tests evaluate the consistency of the bitumen at 135 °C and 60 °C which represent the temperature of bitumen during construction and service life of pavement respectively (TAI 1983). Based upon geometrical differences, there are different types of capillary glass tube viscometers. They are described below.

Vacuum tube capillary viscometers Pre-heated bitumen (in fluid state) is allowed to flow through a limb of a calibrated capillary glass U-tube which is kept in a water bath at 60 °C. A certain amount of vacuum is created at the other end of the tube and the time duration (in seconds) is recorded when the bitumen flows between the timing marks of the tube (Figure 4.9). During the test, the bitumen should be maintained at a constant temperature of 60 °C. Absolute viscosity of the bitumen is calculated by using the following equation.

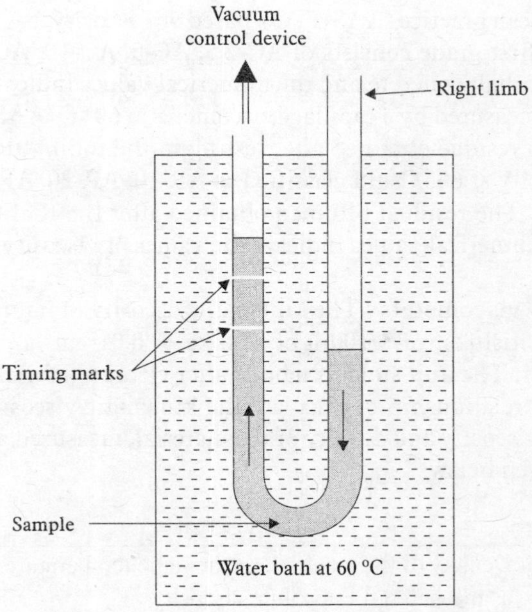

Figure 4.9 *The Asphalt Institute vacuum viscometer (schematic) (Courtesy: The Asphalt Institute)*

$$\text{Absolute viscosity (in poise)} = \text{CF} \times t \tag{4.5}$$

where, CF = calibration factor of the capillary glass tube
t = duration of time in seconds, required for the bitumen to flow in between the timing markings of the capillary glass tube

From the following relationship, the viscosity in poises can be converted to Pascal seconds.

$$1 \text{ Pascal second} = 10 \text{ poises} \tag{4.6}$$

As a matter of interest, at 20 °C, the viscosity of water is 10^{-2} (in poise) whereas for different types of bituminous materials it ranges between 10 and 10^{12}.

To determine the absolute viscosity of tar and bituminous materials, the Bureau of Indian Standards has recommended the following types of capillary viscometers. These viscometers can test fluids having viscosity in the range of 42 to 200 000 poises (IS: 1206 (Part 2)-1978; 2002).

- Cannon–Manning vacuum capillary viscometer
- Asphalt Institute vacuum capillary viscometer
- Modified Koppers vacuum capillary viscometer

Details of the above capillary type viscometers are given in IS: 1206 (Part 2)-1978; 2002.

According to Indian practice (IS:73-2006), at 60 °C, the paving bitumen should have a minimum absolute viscosity of 800, 1600, 2400 and 3200 poises for grades VG 10, VG 20, VG 30 and VG 40 respectively.

According to American practice (AASHTO), based on viscosity, paving bitumen is classified into two grades. The first grade consists of AC-2.5, AC-5, AC-10, AC-20, AC-30 and AC-40, where AC stands for asphalt concrete and the numerical values indicate the values of viscosity in hundreds of poises measured by a capillary viscometer at 60 °C (AASHTO test T202). In the second grade, bitumen residue obtained after testing in the rolling thin film oven (RTFO) is used to measure viscosity at 60 °C and classified as AR-10, AR-20, AR-40, AR-80 and AR-160 (AASHTO test T240). The residual bitumen obtained after the RTFO test is termed as aged residue (AR) and the numerical values indicate the values of viscosity in hundreds of poises.

Gravity flow capillary viscometers The kinematic viscosity of liquid bituminous materials, in stoke (cm^2/s) or centistoke (or 1/100th of a stoke = 0.01 cm^2/s), is measured by using a gravity flow viscometer. The unit stoke is named after George Gabriel Stokes.

There is a standard relationship to calculate the kinematic viscosity of any liquid. It uses the values of absolute viscosity and density of the material, measured at the same temperature. The relationship is given below.

$$\text{Kinematic viscosity} = \frac{\text{Absolute viscosity}}{\text{Density of the material, at the same temperature as measured for absolute viscosity}} \tag{4.7}$$

To determine the kinematic viscosity of liquid bitumen there is no need to apply vacuum. This is because at 135 °C, the bitumen is less viscous and free to flow by gravity. Hence, there is no need to apply vacuum at the other end of the capillary tube.

According to the AASHTO test procedure (T201), liquid bitumen at a pre-determined height is allowed to flow by gravity through a calibrated capillary tube, of standard size and shape, kept in an oil bath maintained at 135 °C. The time taken for the liquid to flow in between the two timing marks of the capillary tube is recorded. The kinematic viscosity of the bitumen in stokes is calculated by multiplying the calibration factor of the capillary tube with the duration of time (in seconds) taken for the liquid bitumen to flow in between the pre-determined timing marks.

To determine the kinematic viscosity of paving grade cutbacks of bituminous materials and distillation residues of cutbacks, the Bureau of Indian Standards recommends the following capillary type viscometers. These viscometers can be used to test materials having viscosity in the range of 30 to 100 000 centistokes (IS: 1206 (Part 3)-1978; 2002).

- Cannon–Fenske viscometer for opaque liquids
- BS U-tube modified reverse flow viscometer

Details of the above capillary type viscometers are given in IS: 1206 (Part 3)-1978 2002; According to Indian practice (IS: 73-2006; 2006), at 135 °C, paving bituminous materials should have a minimum kinematic viscosity of 250, 300, 350 and 400 centistokes for grades VG 10, VG 20, VG 30 and VG 40 respectively.

Orifice or Efflux Viscometers

A specified volume of liquid bitumen maintained at standard temperature is allowed to flow by gravity through an orifice of standard diameter. The time in seconds is recorded. Based on this principle, different types of equipments are available for determination of viscosity of bitumen. Following are some of the apparatus widely used to measure the viscosity of bitumen, tar and bitumen cutback.

- Tar viscometer [10 mm Φ of orifice; 50 ml of volume; at 35, 40, 45 or 50 °C (IS:9026-1985) and for cutbacks: 4 mm Φ of orifice; 50 ml of volume (IS:1206 (Part I)-1978)].
- Saybolt Furol viscometer [3 mm Φ of orifice; 60 ml of volume; at 25 or 50 °C (ASTM D88 & E102)] (Figure 4.10).

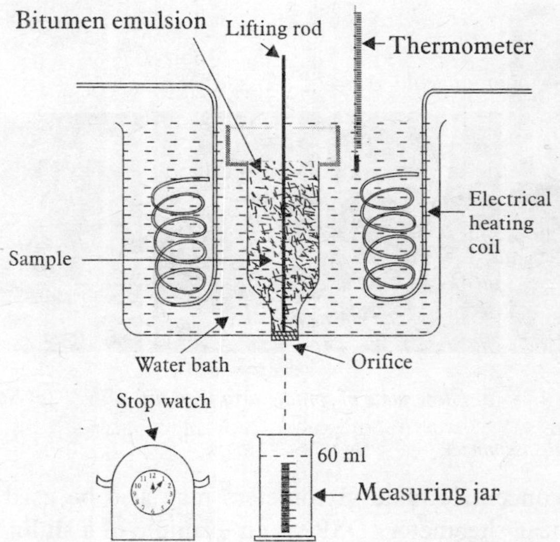

Figure 4.10(a) *Schematic set-up diagram of a Saybolt Furol viscometer*

Figure 4.10(b) *Saybolt Furol viscometer set-up*

Using orifice viscometers, the duration of time measured does not provide any scientific relationship to understand the visco-elastic behaviour of bituminous materials. However, the tests are very simple and the values (in seconds) obtained by the orifice or efflux viscometers can be correlated to test values obtained using other standard viscometers.

Rotational Viscometers

A spindle is vertically inserted into a chamber filled with bitumen liquid and allowed to rotate at a given rate. The torque required to maintain the specified rate of rotations of the spindle per minute at a standard test temperature gives the viscosity. This kind of viscometer is gaining importance because it is simple to use and the test can also be carried out on modified binders at a wide range of temperature. The Brookfield viscometer (Figure 4.11) and the portable Haake rotational viscometer (Kandhal 2006) are good examples of this kind of viscometer.

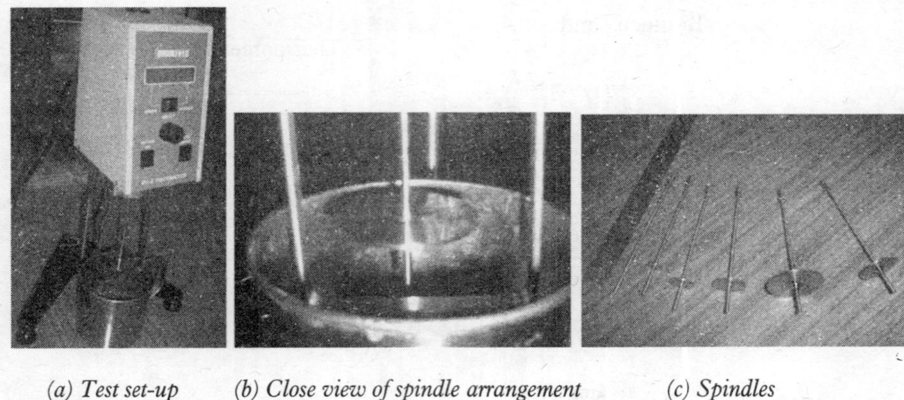

(a) Test set-up *(b) Close view of spindle arrangement* *(c) Spindles*

Figure 4.11 *Rotational viscometer*

Sliding plate and concentric plate viscometers may also be used to determine dynamic viscosity. Dynamic shear rheometer (DSR) is an example of a sliding plate viscometer. It is explained in more detail in Section 4.3.9.

4.2.6 Ductility Test (IS: 1208-1978)

A thin film of bitumen coated over and in between aggregates undergoes elastic deformation under repetitive axle loads. The elastic homogeneity of the bituminous mix must be maintained at all working temperatures and stresses. Ductility is an essential property of the bitumen in view of the following requirements.

- During mixing of bitumen with aggregates at a given standard temperature, the molten bitumen should have enough consistency or viscosity to evenly spread over and coat the surface of aggregates.
- During service life, the bituminous layer should become neither too soft nor brittle during summer and winter seasons, respectively.
- During application of traffic loads, the bituminous pavement undergoes repeated deformations. To keep the deformation within elastic limits or allowable limits in its design life, the bitumen film coated around the surface of the aggregates should have enough ductility.

If the bitumen is obtained from different sources or refineries, it may satisfy the minimum criteria of penetration value but may fail to have the required ductile property. Hence, the property of stretchability (or ductility) of bituminous materials must be ascertained during selection of suitable binder.

In the ductility test, bitumen is heated to become completely fluid and poured into a briquette mould of standard size. It is allowed to cool to room temperature. The minimum cross-sectional area of the bitumen filled in the briquette mould is 1 sq. cm. The mould with bitumen is suitably fixed to two jaws in a water bath which is maintained at 27 °C (Figure 4.12 (a)). One side of the briquette mould is attached to a fixed jaw and the other end is attached to a movable jaw which is allowed to stretch away in the horizontal direction at a constant rate of 5 cm per minute using a suitable mechanical pulling system. During the process, the bitumen become like a thin thread and at a certain point breaks on further pulling. The length of the bitumen thread just before breaking is measured on a scale (Figure 4.12 (b)).

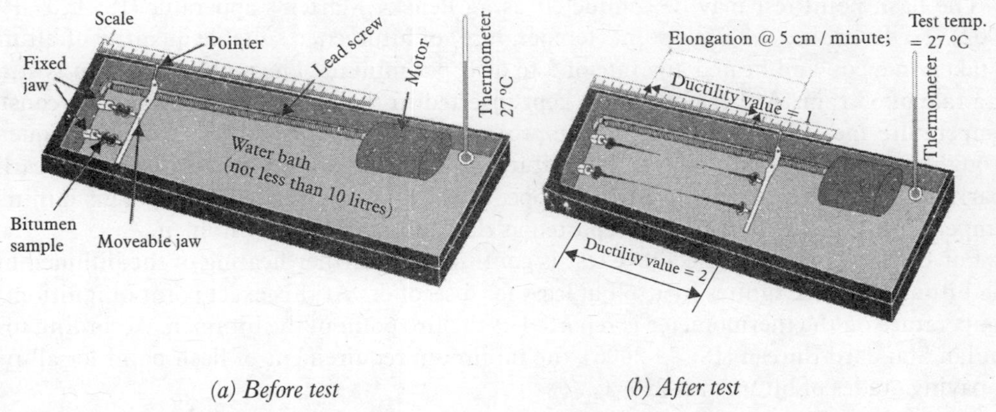

(a) Before test *(b) After test*

Figure 4.12 *Bitumen ductility test*

Briquette mould filled with bitumen

Figure 4.13 *Ductility test in progress*

According to Indian practice (IS: 73-2006), the ductility test (Figure 4.13) should be conducted at 25 °C on a residual bitumen obtained after an RTFO test. The minimum ductility value for the bitumen grades of VG 10, VG 20, VG 30 and VG 40 are 75, 50, 40 and 25 cm length respectively. A pavement constructed with bitumen having a higher ductility value will serve longer. However, the ductility property of bitumen may reduce with age and under different service conditions.

The bitumen ductility test is also conducted at a lower temperature. A temperature of 4 °C should be maintained (this is done using a water bath) and the rate of pulling is 10 mm/minute (IS: 1208-1978; 2002).

4.2.7 Flash and Fire Point Tests (IS:1209-1978; 2002)

Flash and fire point tests are conducted on bitumen to determine at what temperatures the surface of heated bitumen can flash and be ignited. The test results are useful to prevent fire hazards during heating, mixing and compaction of bituminous layers.

The flash point test may be conducted using Pensky Marten's apparatus (IS: 1209-1978; 2002). To determine the flash point (temperature) of bitumen, a suitable quantity of bitumen is taken in a cup and heated at a rate of 5 to 6 °C per minute. The molten bitumen is stirred at a rate of 60 rpm. A thermometer is kept inserted in the molten bitumen to take constant temperature measurements. During the process of heating, a small test flame is frequently brought over the surface of the molten bitumen. The temperature is recorded at the earliest spark or flash. Stirring is temporarily stopped while applying the test flame. This minimum temperature of the earliest flash is reported as the flash point of the bitumen.

For the fire point test, the above test is continued by further heating of the bitumen until the bitumen surface ignites by itself at least for 5 seconds. At this exact point of ignition, the temperature on the thermometer is reported as the fire point of the bitumen. According to the Indian Standard Bureau (IS: 73-2006), the minimum requirement of flash point for all types of paving grades of bitumen is 220 °C.

4.2.8 Loss on Heating Test

Loss of volatile matter of bitumen (in percentage by weight) is determined in this test. About 50 g of bitumen is weighed into a container and the container is placed in an oven for 5 hours with the temperature maintained at 163 °C (IS: 1212-1978). After the test, the weight of bitumen is recorded and the loss is reported as a percentage of the original weight of the sample. According to IS: 73, the maximum allowable value of matter loss by heating for bitumen should not exceed 1 per cent. But, in case of 180/200 grade of bitumen, the loss by heating should be less than 2 per cent.

4.2.9 Solubility Test

This test is conducted to determine the purity of bitumen. As we know, bitumen is completely soluble in carbon disulphide (CS_2). As a safety measure, instead of carbon disulphide, trichloroethylene is used as solvent for the solubility test. If any insoluble matter, viz. minerals, salts and inorganic matter are present in the bitumen, the bitumen is said to be contaminated or impure. In this test, about 2 g of bitumen is dissolved in 100 ml of trichloroethylene and filtered through an asbestos fibre mat. The amount of contaminants retained on the mat is weighed and expressed as the percentage of the weight of the bitumen sample taken for the test. The minimum solubility of bitumen in trichloroethylene should be 99 per cent (AASHTO 2001 and IS: 73-2006).

4.2.10 Presence of Water Test

This test is also used to evaluate the purity of bitumen. During storage or transportation, the bitumen may be contaminated due to the presence of water. Water in bitumen produces a foam if the bitumen is heated to above 100 °C. The foam of bitumen may pose fire accidents (TAI 1983). Hence, the bitumen is heated to 175 °C and observed. If there is any foam formation, the bitumen is reported as impure and hazardous due to the presence of water (AASHTO 2001). A similar test is prescribed by the Bureau of Indian Standard to check paving bitumen homogeneity (IS: 73-2006; 2006).

4.2.11 Specific Gravity Test

The specific gravity of bituminous material may be determined by using a pycnometer, otherwise known as the balance method (IS: 1202; 1978). The knowledge of the specific gravity of bitumen is useful for calculating the volume of bitumen required $\left(\text{Volume} = \frac{\text{weight}}{\text{specific gravity}}\right)$ in the density–void relationship of the bitumen–aggregate mixture. Normally, the specific gravity of paving bitumen and tar are in the range of 0.97 to 1.02 and 1.10 to 1.25 respectively.

4.2.12 Fraass Breaking Point Test

The Fraass breaking point is the temperature at which a bitumen film (0.5 mm thick) breaks due to brittleness at standard test conditions. In the test, bitumen is coated on a thin flat flexible steel plaque and undergoes, under standard test conditions, a descending series of change in temperature. When the earliest crack appears on the surface of the bitumen film on being flexed under standard test conditions, the temperature is recorded. The bending force versus temperature curve is drawn and the curve shape is related to characteristics of bitumen at lower temperatures (down to −30 °C).

4.2.13 Value of Poisson's Ratio

The Poisson's ratio of bitumen is highly sensitive to change in temperature. It varies from 0.15 to 0.45 at low (< -1 °C) and high temperatures ($\sim$48 °C) respectively (AASHTO 1986). A typical value of 0.4 may be taken for analysis purposes (Brown and Brunton 1992).

4.3 Other Binders

Bitumen is available as a solid or semi-solid material. But to make it workable, it is necessary to make it less viscous by heating, adding cutbacks and blending with petroleum solvents or making emulsions by mixing with water. Ordinary bituminous binders fail to perform satisfactorily under increased over-loaded truck traffic, in extreme temperature conditions and intensive abrasive conditions (viz. roundabouts, junctions and at signal intersections). To further improve the performance of these traditional bituminous materials, some compounds are added to improve the strength and durability of the mix constituents. Various types of bituminous materials and their modifications obtained by adding different type of additives are presented in the following sections. Here the word 'bituminous binder' is used for both modified and unmodified bituminous materials.

4.3.1 Bitumen Cutbacks

The viscosity of bitumen is reduced suitably by mixing or blending with a volatile diluent or petroleum distillate. Thus, they have to be used even though they do not play a vital role in making bitumen stronger. Based upon the rate of volatility, the bitumen cutbacks are divided into three types, viz.

(i) Rapid curing (RC70, RC250, RC 800 and RC3000),

(ii) Medium curing (MC30, MC70, MC250, MC800 and MC3000) and

(iii) Slow curing (SC70, SC250, SC800 and SC3000) cutbacks.

The above designated numerical values indicate initial kinematic viscosity (IS: 217-1988;1993). The diluent used to prepare RC (highly volatile; low viscosity) is gasoline, for MC (medium viscosity) is kerosene and for SC (lower volatility; highly viscous) is gas oil. Cutbacks are found to be more costly than ordinary bitumen because extra cost is involved in the use of petroleum solvents. Moreover, use of cutbacks with a little extra amount of petroleum solvents may pose problems related to safety and environmental pollution.

For further details regarding specification for cutback bitumen, please refer to IS: 217-1988; 1993.

4.3.2 Bitumen Emulsions

A bitumen emulsion is a liquid blend of water and emulsifier (an additive) containing a suspension of dispersed minute particles of bitumen (i.e., oil in water). A colloidal mill may be used to prepare the bitumen emulsion. Based on why and where the emulsion is used, the amount of bitumen to be mixed with water may range between 40 to 70 per cent. A suitable emulsifier (depending on the ionic nature of the mix) may be added to the bitumen–water mix to keep the minute particles of bitumen in the water away from each other and in a dispersed form. Emulsified bitumen is used in cold mix preparations for paving bituminous layers in difficult and inaccessible conditions.

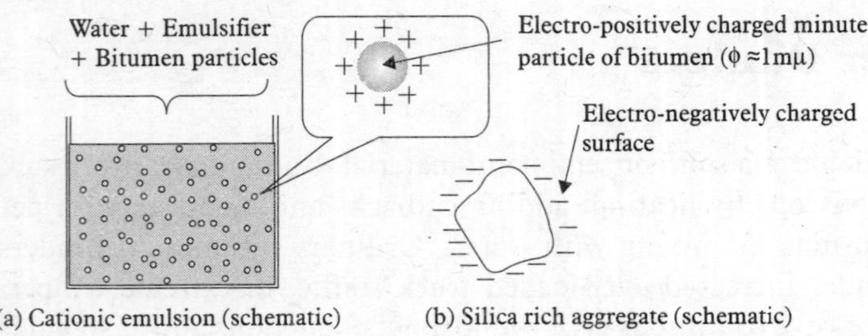

Figure 4.14 *Surface charges on particles of bitumen in cationic emulsion and silica rich aggregate*

Based upon the type of surface charge, bitumen emulsions are classified into two types. They are (i) anionic bitumen emulsions (particles of bitumen are electro-negatively charged) and (ii) cationic bituminous emulsions (particles of bitumen are electro-positively charged) (Figure 4.14 (a)). Cationic emulsions are widely used in today's construction works. The type of emulsion should be selected based on the mineral composition of aggregates used for construction. For example, if the aggregate used for construction is rich in silica (SiO_2), then the surface of the aggregate possesses strong electro-negative charge (Figure 4.14 (b)). In this case, cationic mulsions are found to be more suitable since the minute particles of bitumen in the cationic emulsion possess electro-positive charge. To become electrostatically stable, the positively charged particles of bitumen are strongly attracted to the negatively charged aggregates surface. Hence, the compacted layer becomes strong and stable.

Similar to bitumen cutbacks, bitumen emulsions are also classified into three types based on setting time and purpose of use. They are (i) rapid setting (RS), (ii) medium setting (MS) and (iii) slow setting (SS) emulsions. The word 'setting' here means separation of the emulsion. In other words, when the water present in the emulsion evaporates, the minute bitumen present in the emulsion coats the surface of aggregates. Later, curing of the emulsion takes place, by which the compacted layer of the emulsion–aggregate mixture hardens and attains strength. In this context, rapid setting emulsion, for example, means that the emulsion sets and cures rapidly. Following are the factors affecting setting and curing of emulsion mixes.

- Percentage of water absorption of aggregates (depends on the surface texture).
- Dampness of the aggregates.
- Amount of dust on aggregates.
- Gradation of aggregates.
- Mineral composition and intensity of charge on the surface of aggregates.
- Ingredients of emulsion and quantity used.
- Meteorological conditions, viz. weather, climate, temperature, humidity, wind velocity and altitude.
- Drainage conditions prevailing around the construction site.

The uses and advantages of emulsions for the construction of pavements (Discussions, IRC 1994) are enumerated below.

- The strength properties of bitumen are preserved in emulsion mixes since emulsions do not need hot mixing. Generally, cold mixing or just slightly warming the ingredients of the emulsion mix are done for construction of pavements.
- In cold and damp conditions, emulsions are also used as slurry seal, pre-mix carpet, seal coat, for repair, soil stabilisation and other works.
- Emulsions possess anti-stripping properties.
- Emulsions with lower viscosity or thinner consistency improve spreadability and allows better coating of the bitumen on to the aggregate surfaces.
- There is no wastage during laying and storage.

- Since emulsions are water based, there is less effect on the environment.
- It is the least energy intensive of all construction material; there is no need to heat.

Limitations of emulsions:

- A suitable type of emulsion has to be selected based on the acidic or basic nature of the aggregates used for road construction.
- The setting time may vary depending on the air temperature, wind velocity and type of emulsion.
- There is a wide range of curing time; a suitable emulsion mix needs to be designed for a particular need, i.e., we need to determine for each case, the optimum quantity of emulsion based on the zone, type of emulsion, mix grade and desired mechanical properties.
- It has a restricted storage time (ranging from a few days to six months).

For fine grained aggregates, the surface area is large and the time required to mix an emulsion for them is more. Hence, slow setting emulsions are preferred. It gives ample time for blending the mix uniformly before it sets.

In general, bituminous pavements laid using emulsions are considered inferior compared to hot mix bituminous pavements that cater to heavy traffic loads.

4.3.3 Tar

Tar is a black or brown to black, non-crystalline material in the viscous state having binding properties. It is obtained from the destructive distillation of organic materials (viz. coal, petroleum, oil, wood, shale, peat etc.) in the absence of air at about 1000 °C. Tar is completely soluble in carbon tetrachloride. It is more susceptible to change in temperature than bitumen because it consists of more volatile oils than bitumen (McGovern and Alderton 1972). Therefore, tar quickly hardens during the summer and become brittle during winter. Generally, tar is used for surface dressing on the wearing course since it possesses a comparatively good adhesive property in damp conditions.

Paving tar is classified into two types based on the ratio of the pitch/anthracene (the materials obtained as a result of the distillation process of tar) viz. type A and B. Again these two types of tars are further classified into five grades (viz. RT1, RT2, RT3, RT4 and RT5) which are intended to be used for specific paving purposes. The details of the requirements of these paving tars are given in IS: 215-1995; 2000.

4.3.4 Tar–bitumen Mixture

Blending tar with a suitable quantity of bitumen may result in a mixture which has good binding properties and lower susceptibility to temperature changes, but the blend of tar–bitumen may pose problems of incompatibility since tar and bitumen have different chemical compositions. Thus, the blend of tar–bitumen may be used for pavement construction but with proper care and suitable specifications.

4.3.5 Sulphur Modified Bitumen

About 15 to 18 per cent of sulphur is added as a chemical modifier to bitumen (MORTH 2001). This modified bitumen provides better workability, higher elastic modulus of bituminous mixes and reduces the demand for bitumen (Deme 1974; Fromm and Kennepohl 1979). A few useful properties of sulphur are given below (Love 1979).

- The specific gravity of solid sulfur is about 2.0.
- Three forms of sulphur are generally used for paving works. They are orthorhombic, polymeric and monoclinic sulphur. However, polymeric sulphur mixed with suitable plasticisers, termed as Sulfex, has the most desirable characteristics for use as pavement binders.
- For best workability and strength, the mixing temperature of sulphur should be in the range of 120 to 150 °C. In this range, the sulphur reacts slowly and forms polysulphide resins that dissolve with unreacted sulphur and impart highly desirable mechanical properties to the final mix.
- Sulphur becomes viscous at higher temperatures and maintains lowest viscosity at 150 °C.
- When a bitumen–sulphur mix is heated to higher temperatures, a dehydrogenation reaction occurs and sulphur forms hydrogen sulphide (H_2S) and sulphur dioxide (SO_2) which pose health hazards.
- However, emission of hydrogen sulphide can be avoided if the mixing temperature is controlled.

4.3.6 Lime Modified Bitumen

Hydrated lime is also used as a modifier in hot mix bituminous concrete. The advantages of using lime in hot mix bituminous concrete are enumerated below (Witczak and Bari 2004).

- It is n excellent anti-stripping agent.
- It reduces bitumen's susceptibility to change in temperature and moisture.
- It enhances binder viscosity and adhesion.
- It increases stiffness of the mix thus making it resistant to shear and the formation of ruts.
- It retards the oxidation process.
- It improves durability of the compacted bituminous layer.

4.3.7 Polymer Modified Bitumen (IRC: SP: 53-2002; Taylor 1991; Kumar et al. 2006; www.bpitumen.com 2006)

Polymers are mixed with bitumen to improve the strength of bitumen so that the service life of bituminous pavements can be extended.

Generally, there are two types of synthetic thermoplastic polymers which are widely used for pavement construction—plastomers and elastomers. The word 'thermoplastic' means polymers which melt by heating and set to harden by cooling. Plastomers induce plasticity or viscosity or stiffness to bitumen. They consist of polyethylene, ethylene vinyl acetate, ethylene butyl acrylate, linear low-density polyethylene (LLDPE) (Kumar et al. 2006) etc. Elastomers induce elasticity as well as stiffness properties to bitumen. They consist of styrene – isoprene–styrene, styrene–butadiene–styrene, ethylene/propylene, styrene– butadiene, poly-butadiene,some types of rubber, etc. In India, three types of polymers are commonly available, viz. polyethylene, vinyl acetate, and styrene–butadiene–styrene. These three types of polymers are used to prepare modified bitumen as well as emulsions (Discussions, IRC 1994). Different grades may be obtained by changing their composition and grade of bitumen. The CRRI has developed high performance polymer modified binders by using suitable additives for use in high temperature regions and construction of heavy duty pavements.

Following are a few advantages of using polymer modified binders for construction of pavements (IRC: SP: 53-2002; Vasudevan et al. 2003; Gopal Raju and Rengaraju 2003).

- Reduces permanent deformation
- Increases viscosity and shear resistance
- Increases softening point
- Retards oxidation process
- Improves adhesive and cohesive properties
- Bitumen content can be reduced by around 10% (Vasudevan et al. 2006)
- The ill effects of waxy bitumen such as susceptibility to temperature changes, bleeding at hot climates and brittleness during cold climates can be reduced by using bitumen blended with EVA, aromatic resin and SBS (Shukla and Jain 1984)
- The Marshall stability value, indirect tensile strength and durability of asphalt mixes can be considerably increased (Bose and Jain 1984)
- The resistance of bituminous concrete against fatigue cracking, temperature cracking and stripping increases (Brule et al. 1998)
- Elastomer binders improve resistance against rutting but affect fatigue life while plastomer binders improve resistance against rutting without compromising the fatigue properties (Maccarrone et al. 1995)
- In surfacings, use of modified bitumen extends the service period by 50 per cent as compared to unmodified bitumen (IRC: SP: 53-2002)

However, polymers are costly; hence cost-effective economic conditions have to be evaluated while considering their use.

4.3.8 Rubber Modified Bitumen

Compounds of rubber materials are obtained either from natural sources or manufactured by using different types of polymers which undergo different processes. The inherent predominant properties of polymers are imparted to rubber materials. The rubbers are also called elastomers since their strain capabilities are very high—even more than hundred per cent in some cases. Following are the uses of rubber modified bitumen.

- Rubber introduces more elastic property to the bitumen
- It improves ductility under low temperature and high rate of loading
- Rubberised roads offer very less skid resistance; therefore, it provides more safety
- It is useful for sealing cracks on roads
- It improves the fatigue property of bitumen
- It reduces permanent deformations to a great extent

A certain quantity of rubber compounds is mixed with bitumen to impart elastic property to bitumen. About 2 to 5 per cent of these compounds of rubber is suitably mixed with bitumen at a given temperature and laid using usual construction machinery. While mixing, the rubber swells initially and later spreads into the bitumen (Discussion, IRC 1994).

Based upon the source of rubber, it may be classified as synthetic or belonging to other types (IRC: SP: 53-2002). Synthetic rubber include styrene butadiene rubber (SBR) latex and in case of other types, latex, unvulcanised rubber powder, vulcanised rubber, ground rubber mix and ground tire rubber or powder of rubber crumbs obtained from scrap tyres are a few commonly used ones. Use of natural rubber is preferred to synthetic rubber for pavement construction, as increased quantity of natural rubber in bitumen provides proportional improvement of elastic strain recovery (Oliver 1981).

For preparation of rubber modified bitumen, the following factors have to be considered.

- Type and grade of rubber
- Quantity of rubber to be added to the bitumen
- Method of blending rubber with bitumen at hot or cold temperatures

For detailed specifications of binder properties and mix design of rubber and polymer modified bitumen, please refer to IRC: SP: 53-2002.

4.3.9 Performance Graded (PG) Binders (TAI 2001; CITGO 2003; TAI 1997)

Traditional binders fail to perform to the desired level of service when exposed to huge traffic loads and extreme temperature variation conditions. In most traditional laboratory methods of testing, binders are tested at a particular standard point of temperature and loading only. But the conditions of moisture and temperature changes that service pavements experience are different. To solve this problem, in 1987, the Strategic Highway Research Programme (SHRP) initiated a package of research activities to develop a new pavement building technology called Superpave. Superpave stands for *su*perior *per*forming asphalt *pave*ments. As part of the Superpave technology, modified and unmodified bituminous binding materials are graded according to the prevailing climatic temperatures and traffic demands. This new binder grading technology is termed as the performance grade (PG) system. Since 1993, performance graded binder specifications have been used in the USA for pavement construction (MORTH 2001).

Critical performance characteristics of binders considered in PG binder specifications are as follows.

- Thermal cracking
- Fatigue cracking
- Moisture sensitivity
- Deformations
- Accelerated ageing process

The existing test methods for binders were revised to evaluate strength properties throughout the working temperature range by simulating conditions that were close to conditions prevailing during the performance period, viz. loading, hardening, pressure, deformation, ageing etc. The important feature of this specification is that the criteria or allowable value of the strength parameter to be evaluated is kept unchanged with variations in temperature. The temperature at which the criteria must be satisfied is changed according to the grade of binder and in situ conditions. Therefore, a suitable grade of binder is selected based upon the temperature range as well as strength criteria.

A suitable grade of binder is selected based upon maximum and minimum pavement design temperatures, such that, the binder provides enough resistance against permanent deformations and thermal cracking. The maximum value of the pavement design temperature should be taken as the average of the highest pavement temperatures observed in seven consecutive days ever recorded and the minimum value of pavement design temperature is taken as the lowest pavement temperature observed in that locality. For both the cases, past history and present trend of temperatures observed each year at a given locality are considered for calculation of mean and standard deviation values.

The final selection of the grade of the binder is made by considering the location of the construction site, design temperatures, design speed of vehicles and number of equivalent standard axle load (ESAL) repetitions. Different PG binder grades are developed based on anticipated temperatures in different seasons. The typical designation of the PG binder is given below.

$$\text{PG } T_{max} - T_{min} \tag{4.8}$$

where,

PG	=	Performance grade
T_{max}	=	Average of the highest pavement temperatures observed (in °C) in seven consecutive days for which the binder properties are evaluated
T_{min}	=	Minimum pavement temperature (in °C), for which the binder is resistant against thermal cracking

For example, PG 58 – 22 means that up to a maximum temperature of +58 °C (a positive value) and a minimum of −22 °C (a negative value), the binder will be able to resist deformations during its service life. The range of temperatures is calculated as 58 + 22 = 80 °C. If the value of maximum temperature is higher, the binder is more resistant to rutting. If the value of the minimum temperature is lower, the binder is more resistant to cracking at lower temperature.

In the PG specification, to evaluate the binder properties, different test conditions are simulated that are close to field conditions during storage, mixing, construction and ageing of bitumen for a period ranging from 7 to 10 years. The test temperatures are prescribed according to the climate of a given locality and the binders are graded according to a range of temperatures that are to be experienced by a pavement in a given locality. As part of the PG graded specification, the following tests are conducted in sequence on paving binders.

Dynamic shear rheometer (DSR) test In this test, the binder is tested to evaluate its tendency to become too soft or deform due to fatigue cracking and rut at given maximum and minimum values of temperatures. At a given test temperature, a small binder sample is placed in between two circular plates which are kept horizontally one above the other. The lower circular plate is fixed and the upper circular plate is allowed to rotate on the bitumen sample in to and fro directions. The stiffness modulus of the binder is determined by obtaining the relationship between the applied stress and the observed strain. The results obtained from this test are used for fatigue and rutting characterisation.

Rolling thin film oven (RTFO) test RTFO simulates ageing and hardening of the binder which are similar to what happens to it during hot mixing and construction. The principles behind the test procedure have already been explained in Section 4.2.1. After ageing in the oven, the residual binder is further tested and its strength properties are evaluated based on its characteristics before and after testing in the RTFO.

Pressure ageing vessel (PAV) test This test simulates the ageing that happens to a binder due to the detrimental effect of weather during the service life of the pavement. The binder residue obtained after testing in the RTFO is placed in a container called the pressure ageing vessel (PAV). To simulate an ageing effect that is equivalent to 7 to 10 years of service period, the binder is subjected to higher temperatures (90, 100 or 110 °C) and pressure (2070 kPa) for a duration of 20 hours. In the PAV test, the process of oxidation as well as significant changes in the binder properties can be observed by increasing the temperature. Appropriate test temperature should be selected based upon prevailing practical conditions (Peterson and Harnsberger 1998; Shen et al. 2006)..

After this test, the residual binder obtained from the PAV is again tested in the dynamic shear rheometer at medium temperature to evaluate susceptibility of the binder to low temperature cracking or fatigue cracking.

Bending beam rheometer (BBR) test It is a flexural creep test used to study the creepcharacteristics of a bitumen beam subjected to static load at lower temperatures.

The residual binder obtained after the PAV test is moulded to a small beam of size 6.35 × 12.7 × 125 mm. At lower test temperatures, the binder–beam is simply supported and statically loaded at its centre. The deflection of the beam at its centre with respect to time is measured. In the BBR test, the susceptibility of the binder to crack at lower temperatures is evaluated.

Direct tension (DT) test In this test, at lower test temperatures (0 to – 36 °C), a small beam of bitumen is subjected to a constant rate of pulling and the length of elongation is measured at its failure. Failure is defined as the load at which the stress in the bitumen beam reaches its maximum value. The ratio between changes in length at failure to the original length of the binder–beam is termed as failure strain and it should not exceed 1%. DT test can also be used to evaluate the susceptibility of bitumen failure at lower temperatures.

Rotational viscometer (RV) test The ability of bitumen as well as modified binders to be easily pumped and handled is evaluated by measuring its viscosity at different higher temperatures similar to mixing and compaction temperatures. This characteristic of bitumen is useful during pumping and mixing bitumen with aggregates. In this test, a spindle is allowed to rotate in the vertical direction at a constant rate in a chamber filled with the binder. The resistance offered by the binder to the rotation of the spindle is measured to determine the viscosity of the binder. A Brookfield viscometer is a best example of this kind of viscometer and it has already been explained in Section 4.2.5 under rotational viscometers.

A comparison of ordinary and performance graded binders is given in Table 4.1.

Table 4.1 *Comparison between ordinary and performance graded binders*

Sl.No.	Ordinary grading of binders	Performance graded binders
1	Binders are graded either based upon penetration or viscosity.	Binders are graded based upon pavement temperatures, which are close to in service conditions of pavements.
2	Binders are graded based on tests conducted at a particular critical test temperature only.	Binders are graded based on different ranges of pavement temperatures similar to field conditions.
3	Past experience, empirical and semi-empirical test results are used.	Purely scientific and performance-based studies are considered.
4	Hardening and ageing due to storage, mixing, spraying, exposure and oxidation are not considered.	Hardening and ageing during storage, mixing, spraying, exposure and oxidation is simulated by conducting RTFO and PAV tests (Button et al. 1993; Chiu et al. 1994; Domke et al. 1997, Shen et al. 2006).
5	The properties of the binder at minimum pavement temperatures are not considered.	Susceptibility of the binder to lower temperatures is carefully evaluated by conducting BBR and DT tests.
6	The characteristics of flow and workability during mixing of the binder are not considered.	Flow, workability and viscosity properties of the binder are determined at higher temperature by using the RV test.
7	Visco-elastic properties are not much considered.	Visco-elastic properties are determined by using DSR.
8	There is no concept of ageing of bitumen.	Accelerated ageing of the binder up to 7–10 years is simulated using the PAV test.
9	A suitable binder is selected using values of penetration, viscosity, softening point and based upon location.	Final selection of a suitable grade of binder is made after considering the location of the construction site, maximum and minimum design temperatures, design speed of vehicles and number of equivalent standard axle load (ESAL) repetitions.

4.4 Engineering Properties of Bituminous Materials

How bitumen behaves in pavement should be determined with reference to anticipated climatic conditions and intensity of traffic loads. These input parameters play a vital role during selection of suitable binders for construction of pavements. Thus, engineering properties of bitumen should be determined considering the following factors.

- Temperature (maximum, minimum and average values)
- Loading time
- Intensity of load

Bitumen behaves differently in different combinations of the above values. For example, bitumen behaves elastic under short duration of loading at normal temperature. But, in case of prolonged loading and as the temperature increases, it loses elasticity and flows like a fluid. This is the reason why bituminous pavements at higher temperature tend to deform without cracking.

4.4.1 Stiffness Modulus of Bitumen

In 1954, van der Poel developed the concept of a stiffness modulus for thermoplastic polymers which was useful for determining of the engineering properties of bitumen. The concept was modified by Heukelom and Klomp (1964) and Heukelom (1973). In this method, the bitumen is characterised by its stiffness modulus, (E_{bit}), the ratio between applied stress to the observed strain at a given time of loading (t in s) and temperature (T in °C). The value of the stiffness modulus of bitumen may be expressed as follows.

$$E_{\text{bit}}(t, T) = \text{stress/strain at } (t, T) \tag{4.9}$$

The above equation holds good and is suitable for in service pavements if the assumed strain is not more than 1 per cent. If the loading time changes, preferably under variable temperatures similar to seasonal variations, the value of stiffness of bitumen also changes. To account for this variability of the stiffness modulus of bitumen, a stiffness nomograph was developed by van der Poel and modified by Heukelom based on three parameters, viz. time of loading (t), temperature difference (T-T800 pen) and penetration index (PI).

The equation developed by Heukelom and Klomp (1964) or a method prescribed by Bonnaure et al. (1977) may be used to determine the stiffness values of bituminous mixes. Measured stiffness values greatly agree with the values predicted by Bonnaure's method and it is adopted by the Shell method (1977) of the asphalt pavement design (Ullidtz and Peattie 1980).

To understand the implication of the true engineering properties of bitumen at different ranges of temperatures from cold to hot under cyclic loading similar to field conditions, it is necessary to know its visco-elastic properties.

4.4.2 Visco-elastic Properties of Bituminous Materials

Bitumen becomes hard and soft by cooling and heating respectively. These states of bitumen may be reversed as and when required. This property of bitumen is known as *thermo-plasticity*. Based on temperature and rate of loading, the bitumen may behave like a dual characteristic material.

Elastic material At a given temperature, the material undergoes immediate deformation or strain under loading and immediately recovers upon unloading. In other words, if the material is linear elastic, the stress is proportional to the strain according to Hooke's law, i.e., stress =

Young's modulus value × strain (Wilhelm Flugge 1975).

Viscous material At a given temperature, the material undergoes delayed deformation or strain under loading but it may or may not recover its initial conditions. A Newtonian material will recover completely. But in Bingham materials, power law fluids and pseudo-plastic materials, complete recovery of strain will not take place due to plastic straining during loading. In other words, if the material is viscous, the stress is proportional to the strain rate (Wilhelm Flugge 1975).

Bitumen exhibits intermediate characteristics ranging from elastic to viscous and vice versa due to change in temperature and rate of application of load. Because of this, bituminous mixes are known as visco-elastic materials. The behaviour of visco-elastic material depends on temperature, time and frequency of loading.

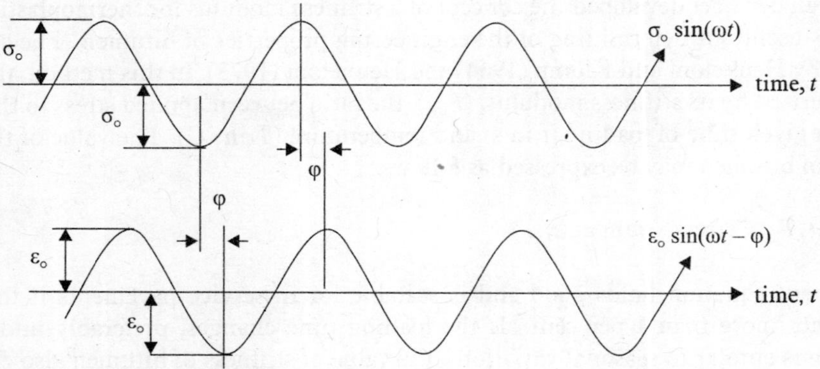

Figure 4.15 *Phase difference between stress and strain (Yang 2004; Relem 2001)*

When a visco-elastic material is subjected to sinusoidal loading (Figure 4.15), the occurrence of strain (ε_0) is delayed due to the phase difference of the applied stress (σ_0) at a given time (t). This difference of response is known as phase angle (φ). As the material transforms from being elastic to visco-elastic during change of temperature, the value of the phase angle (φ) changes from 0 °C to 90 °C. The energy dissipated by the material is determined by using the phase angle value. The values of complex modulus and dynamic complex modulus of bitumen are determined from the following popularly known relationships (Huang 2004; Di Benedetto et al. 2001 and Kallas 1970).

Complex modulus ($E^\star$) = Real part of modulus value + Imaginary part of modulus value

$$E^*(f,T) = (\sigma_o/\varepsilon_o)\sin(\omega t) + i.\ (\sigma_o/\varepsilon_o)\sin(\omega t - \varphi) \tag{4.10}$$

where,
f = frequency
T = temperature
σ_0 = maximum stress
ε_0 = maximum strain
ω = angular velocity or pulsation = $2\pi f$
φ = phase angle
t = a point of time with reference to stress application

$$\text{Dynamic modulus} = \text{Absolute value of complex modulus} = |E|^* \quad (4.11)$$

If the viscous effect is ignored, the ratio between the maximum values of stress to strain is termed as the elastic modulus.

The values of complex bulk modulus (K^*) and shear modulus (G^*) may be determined from the following popularly known relationships.

$$K^* = E^*/(3-6\mu) \quad (4.12)$$

$$G^* = E^*/[2(1+\mu)] \quad (4.13)$$

where, μ = Poisson's ratio

To characterise visco-elastic properties of binders at lower temperatures, another parameter called the creep compliance is used. The creep compliance may be calculated using the following relationship.

$$D(t,T) = 1/E_{\text{bit}}(t,T) \quad (4.14)$$

Shear compliance is also used to characterise the visco-elasticity of bituminous materials. The following relationship is used to calculate shear compliance ($J\,(t,T)$).

$$J(t,T) = 3/E_{\text{bit}}(t,T) \quad (4.15)$$

The above equations holds good if the material is assumed to be linear visco-elastic and isotropic. The values of dynamic modulus, bulk modulus, shear modulus, creep compliance and shear compliance provide important information to explain the visco-elastic behaviour of the bituminous mix over a range of temperature and frequency of loading.

The visco-elastic properties of bituminous materials are characterised using the following mathematical models.

- Elastic model
- Viscous model
- Maxwell model
- Kelvin model
- Power law model
- Huet model
- Huet–Sayegh model
- Burger model
- 2S2P1D model
- Combined model consisting of all the above models

The above mathematical simulation models are not discussed here since the topic is beyond the scope of this book. Detailed description of these topics may be obtained elsewhere (Huang 2004; Chary; Flugge 1975; Wistuba et al. 2006).

4.5 Mix Design

The mix design consists of proportioning bitumen, coarse aggregate, fine aggregate, filler, air–voids and admixtures (if any) suitably to provide a strong, durable and stable pavement that serves for a design period without premature failure. The main aim of mix design is to determine the optimum quantity of bitumen binder that will hold the mineral aggregates (of suitable gradation) together as a compact layer providing maximum strength to resist deformations and durability. The mix should have minimum air–voids to allow volumetric changes during the working range of temperatures. In addition to this, site-specific requirements should also be satisfied by the designed mix.

4.5.1 Factors Affecting Mix Design

The following factors should be considered while designing bituminous mixes for use in pavement construction.

- Stability
- Durability
- Workability
- Stress–strain relationship
- Permanent deformations
- Fatigue and low-temperature racking
- Imperviousness
- Susceptibility to moisture
- Cost-effectiveness

In addition to the above factors, in-service conditions of pavement, viz. seasonal temperature changes, traffic intensity, humidity, drainage, rainfall and soil class are also to be taken into account while designing bituminous mixes.

4.5.2 Desirable Properties of Bituminous Mixes

Physical Requirements

The binding material and mineral aggregate (i.e., coarse aggregate, sand and filler) should be qualified with reference to their engineering properties (discussed in Chapter 3) according to the given standard specifications. The standard specifications should be that in the IS and IRC (in India) or BIS or AASHTO or any other standard specification in force.

Maximum Size of Aggregate

The maximum size of the aggregate should depend on the design thickness of the layer. As a rule of thumb, the maximum size of the aggregate should not exceed one-half of the compacted layer thickness.

Gradation

A mixture of different sizes, ranging from coarse to very fine mineral particles, should attain the desired density after compaction. Different types of aggregate gradations and the typical shape of gradation curves were discussed in Section 3.2.

Maximum Density

Maximum density of the mix is determined based on the particle size distribution of the mineral aggregate. To examine the geometry of the curve with reference to a maximum mix density curve, a gradation curve is drawn for the proposed mixture of mineral aggregate. Based on theoretical considerations, the maximum density may be determined by using Fuller's equation.

$$P = \left(\frac{d}{D}\right)^n \times 100 \tag{4.16}$$

where, P = Per cent passing through the sieve (%)
d = Size of the sieve considered in mm
D = Maximum sieve size used in a given sieve set in mm
n = Adjustment parameter of the density curve (for maximum density, n is taken as ≈ 0.5 (Fuller and Thompson 1907)

FHWA 0.45 power gradation curve After extensive research conducted by the Federal Highway Administration (FHWA), a dense gradation curve was developed for comparing and evaluating aggregate gradations used for bituminous paving mixtures (*Handbook Highway Eng.* 1975; WSDOT 2006). The maximum density curve (or line) is represented by a diagonal straight line connecting points between per cent passing of maximum size of aggregates to theoretical zero per cent passing of a zero size of sieve opening. In this chart, the units on the x-axis consist of values of openings of sieve sizes raised to the 0.45th power.

For design of gradation of hot bituminous mixtures, exact matching of the gradation curve with the 0.45 power line is undesirable. This is because the 0.45 power gradation curve provides fewer voids in the mixture leaving insufficient space in between aggregate particles to accommodate the desired film thickness of bitumen around the surfaces of aggregates and insufficient space to accommodate volumetric changes during different seasons. Hence, the 0.45 power gradation curve is used only for comparison and evaluation of aggregate gradations. The following example problem explains the method of drawing FHWA 0.45 power gradation curves.

Q: *Draw the FHWA 0.45 power gradation curve from the following set of sieve sizes (mm).*

26.5	*19.0*	*13.2*	*9.5*	*4.75*	*2.36*	*1.18*	*0.6*	*0.3*	*0.15*	*0.075*

A: By examination of the above sieve size openings, the maximum value is 26.5 mm. Substituting the above values suitably in equation (4.1), we get the value of P for d = 0.075 mm sieve size,

$$P = \left(\frac{d}{D}\right)^n \times 100 = \left(\frac{0.075}{26.5}\right)^{0.45} \times 100 = 7.31\,\%$$

Similarly, the remaining values can be calculated as given below.

Sieve size opening in mm (d)	(Sieve size opening)$^{0.45}$ (value on the x-axis)	$P = 100 \times \left(\frac{\text{sieve size opening}}{26.5}\right)^{0.45}$ (value on the y-axis)
0.000	0.00	0.00
0.075	0.31	7.13
0.150	0.43	9.74
0.300	0.58	13.31
0.600	0.79	18.18
1.180	1.08	24.65
2.360	1.47	33.68
4.750	2.02	46.14
9.500	2.75	63.03
13.200	3.19	73.08
19.000	3.76	86.10
26.500	4.37	100.00

By plotting the above values, we get the chart shown in Figure 4.16.

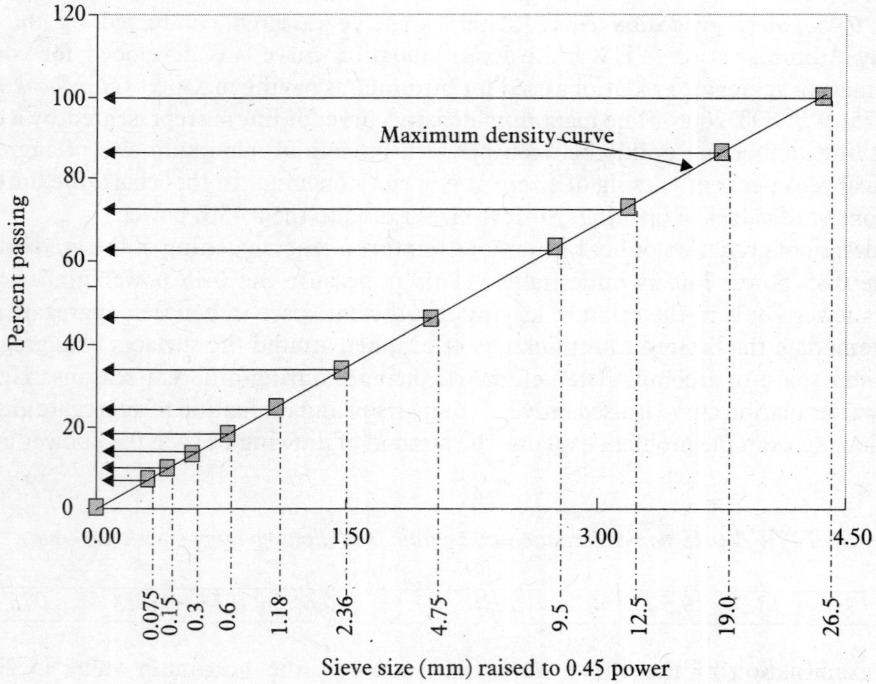

Figure 4.16 *Example (FHWA 0.45 power gradation curve)*

Proportioning of Mineral Aggregate

To get the desired density of mix, optimum utilisation of available materials by blending in suitable proportions is necessary. Once the specifications or target gradation is finalised, the process of proportioning the available different sizes of aggregates is evaluated. There are many methods available for suitable proportioning of mineral aggregates (i.e., coarse aggregates, fine aggregates and mineral dust) obtained from different sources. The final proportion of different materials should satisfy and approach the mean values of the standard grading specification in force, viz. IRC, AASHTO, BS, Superpave etc. In no case should the percentage of mineral aggregates passing fall off the given standard gradation limits (it must be within the upper and lower limits). Different methods of proportioning mineral aggregates are presented in Figure 4.17.

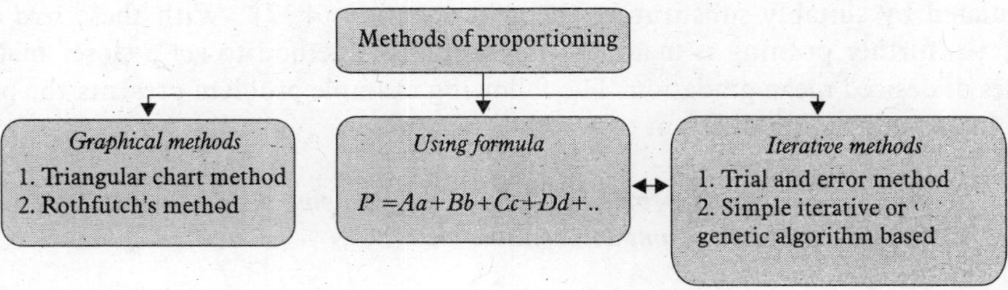

Figure 4.17 *Proportioning methods of mineral aggregates*

Graphical methods By triangular chart method, exactly three material types should be blended. This method is not useful if two or four types of materials are to be blended. In Rothfutch's method, an approximation is required in order to draw straight lines representing enclosures of equal area on either side of different given curves of particle size distribution. Graphical methods are not used very often as they need more time and become complicated as the number of blending materials increases (TAI 1983).

Using formulae and trial and error methods (TAI 1983) According to the Asphalt Institute, the following formula is used to determine the appropriate proportions of the given types of materials.

$$P = Aa + Bb + Cc + Dd + \dots \quad (4.17)$$

where, P = per cent passing of combined different type of aggregates $(A + B + C + D + \dots)$

$A, B, C, D, \dots$ = per cent of different type of aggregates passing through a given set of sieves

$a, b, c, d, \dots$ = contribution or proportion of the different type of aggregates in decimals, i.e., $a + b + c + d + \dots = 1.0$

For example, if two types of aggregates are to be blended, equation (4.17) can be re-written as

$$P = Aa + Bb \tag{4.18}$$

$b = (1.0 - a)$ since $a + b = 1.0$. By substituting the value of b in equation (4.18), we get,

$$a = (P - B)/(A - B) \tag{4.19}$$

In this method of proportioning, an aggregate type is examined from the given types of aggregates $(A, B, C, D\ldots)$ that will contribute the major portion of the proposed mix and a size of sieve in the given types of aggregate is identified such that a distinguishable value of per cent passing is observed. This means that a value of sieve size identified from the above types of aggregate may be labelled as a *separation sieve* which reasonably separates the given set of values of per cent passing of aggregates. By using equation (4.19), values of $a, b, c, d\ldots$ are calculated by suitably substituting them in equation (4.17). With these *seed values* of $a, b, c, d, \ldots$, further pruning is made by trial and error method to get a closer matching to the values of desired mean gradation. The following example problem presents the procedure adopted for proportioning different types of aggregates.

Q: *Determine proportion values and final gradation of the following per cent passing of three types of mineral aggregates for a proposed bituminous concrete mix.*

Size of sieve (mm)	19	13.2	9.5	4.75	2.36	1.18	0.6	0.3	0.15	0.075
Desired gradation	100	79—100	70—88	53—71	42—58	34—48	26—38	18—28	12—20	4—8
Material A	100	80	65.2	39.2	9	2.1				
Material B	100	100	90	81.2	71.6	52.3	38.2	25	17.8	1.1
Material C	100	100	100	100	100	100	99	98	90	84

A: From examination of the per cent passing values, the separation sieve may be taken as 2.36 mm. Now let us calculate seed values of *a, b, c*.

$P = (42 + 58)/2 = 50; A = 9; B = 71.6$

We know that $a = (P - B)/(A - B)$ from equation (4.19). On substitution, we get

$a = (50 - 71.6)/(9 - 71.6)$

$a = 0.34$

With reference to 0.075 mm sieve size,

$P = Aa + Bb + Cc$

$((4 + 8)/2) = 9 \times 0.34 + 1.1b + 84c$

$6 = 3.06 + 1.1b + 84c, (a + b + c = 1, b + c = 1 - 0.34, b + c = 0.66, \text{ or } c = 0.66 - b)$

$6 = 3.06 + 1.1b + 84(0.66 - b)$, therefore we get, $b = 0.63$ and $c = 0.03$

Excel spread sheet or a simple calculator may be used to carry out the trials.

TRIAL 1: Take seed values of $a = 0.34, b = 0.63$ and $c = 0.03$.

Size of sieve (mm)	19	13.2	9.5	4.75	2.36	1.18	0.6	0.3	0.15	0.075
Desired gradation	100	79–100	70–88	53–71	42–58	34–48	26–38	18–28	12–20	4–8
Mid values	100	89.5	79	62	50	41	32	23	16	6
0.34× Material A	34	27.2	22.168	13.33	3.06	0.714				
0.63× Material B	63	63	56.7	51.15	45.10	32.95	24.06	15.75	11.21	0.69
0.03× Material C	3	3	3	3	3	3	2.97	2.94	2.7	2.52
Total	100	93.2	81.87	67.48	51.17	36.66	27.03	18.69	13.91	3.21

TRIAL 2: Take $a = 0.32, b = 0.62$ and $c = 0.06$.

Size of sieve (mm)	19	13.2	9.5	4.75	2.36	1.18	0.6	0.3	0.15	0.075
Desired gradation	100	79–100	70–88	53–71	42–58	34–48	26–38	18–28	12–20	4–8
Mid values	100	89.5	79	62	50	41	32	23	16	6
0.32 × Material A	32	25.6	20.864	12.544	2.88	0.672	0	0	0	0
0.62 × Material B	62	62	55.8	50.344	44.392	32.426	23.684	15.5	11.036	0.682
0.06 × Material C	6	6	6	6	6	6	5.94	5.88	5.4	5.04
Total	100	93.6	82.664	68.888	53.272	39.098	29.624	21.38	16.436	5.722

Similar trials may be made for more accurate results. The comparison between calculated gradation and desired gradation (mid-values) is presented in Figure 4.18.

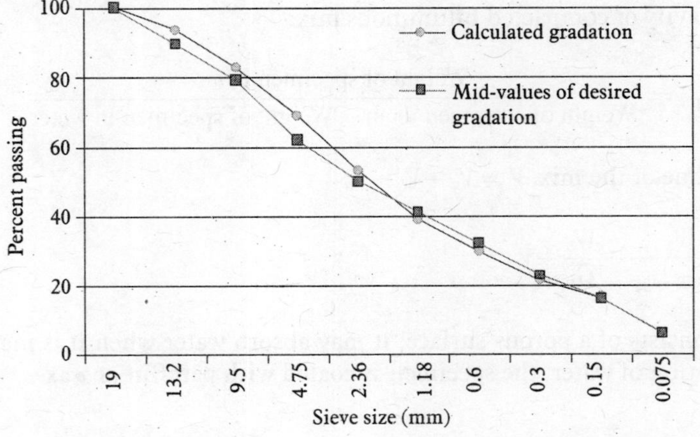

Figure 4.18 *Comparison betwen calculated gradation and mid-values of desired gradation*

4.5.3 Volumetric Analysis of Bituminous Mix (TAI 1983; MORTH 2001)

Density and voids present in the mineral aggregate and compacted bituminous mix are important volumetric parameters that decide the performance of bituminous pavements. Bituminous mixes of high density are undesirable because there will be no room for expansion or internal adjustment of constituents during temperature changes. Therefore, the presence of a sufficient amount of air voids in a compacted bituminous mix is important for better performance of in-service pavements. In this connection, volumetric analysis of the material used is desirable before preparing a bituminous mix. For volumetric analysis of bituminous mixes, Figure 4.19 and the formulae given below are used.

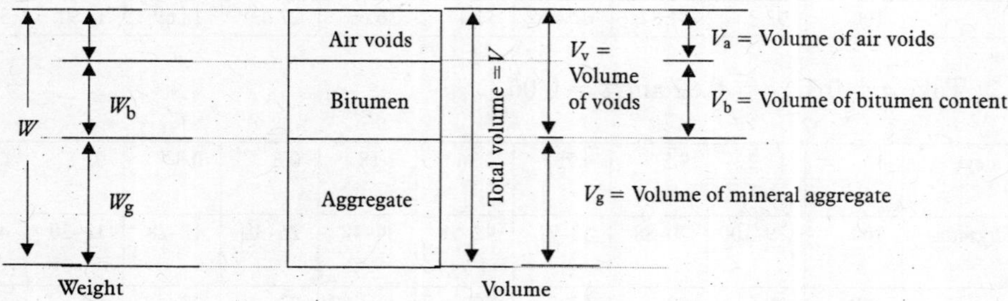

Figure 4.19 *Elements in a bituminous concrete mix*

Weight = Volume × Specific gravity.

$$\text{Bulk specific gravity of combined aggregates } (G_{\text{bulk-agg}}) = \frac{p_1 + p_2 + p_3}{\dfrac{p_1}{G_1} + \dfrac{p_2}{G_2} + \dfrac{p_3}{G_3}} \tag{4.20}$$

where, p_1, p_2, p_3 = per cent by weight of coarse, fine aggregate and filler respectively
G_1, G_2, G_3 = bulk specific gravity of coarse, fine aggregate and filler respectively

Bulk specific gravity of compacted bituminous mix:

$$(G_{\text{bulk-comp}}) = \frac{\text{Weight of specimen in air}}{\text{Weight of specimen in air} - \text{Weight of specimen in water}} \tag{4.21}$$

$$\text{Total volume of the mix, } V = V_g + V_b + V_a \tag{4.22}$$

$$\text{or } V = \frac{W_g}{G_{\text{bulk-agg}}} + \frac{W_b}{G_b} + V_a \tag{4.23}$$

If a specimen consists of a porous surface, it may absorb water when it is measured in water. To avoid absorption of water, the specimen is coated with paraffin or wax.

Then, the bulk density of the wax coated specimen $G_{\text{bulk-wax}} = \dfrac{W_{\text{spec.}}}{W_{\text{wax-air}} - W_{\text{wax-water}} - \left(\dfrac{W_{\text{wax}}}{G_{\text{wax}}}\right)}$ (4.24)

where,
$W_{\text{spec.}}$ = weight of specimen in air
$W_{\text{wax-air}}$ = weight of wax coated speciman in air
$W_{\text{wax-water}}$ = weight of wax coated specimen in water
W_{wax} = weight of coated wax in air = $W_{\text{wax-air}} - W_{\text{spec}}$
G_{wax} = specific gravity of the wax

Voids present in the mix in percentage $= 100 \times \dfrac{V_a}{V}$ (4.25)

where,
$V_a = V - V_g - V_b$
V = Total volume of the specimen
V_g = Volume of the three mineral aggregates
V_b = Volume of bitumen

Voids in mineral aggregate, VMA (%) $= 100\% - V_g\%$ (4.26)

where, $V_g\%$ = per cent volume occupied by total mineral aggregates

$$V_g\% = (p_1 + p_2 + p_3) \times \frac{G_{\text{bulk-comp}}}{G_{\text{bulk-agg}}}$$

Voids filled with bitumen, VFB (%) $= 100 \times \dfrac{V_b\%}{\text{VMA}}$ (4.27)

$V_b\%$ = volume of bitumen in percentage = (per cent of bitumen) $\times \dfrac{G_{\text{bulk-comp}}}{G_b}$ (4.28)

Volume of bitumen absorbed by aggregates due to the presence of pores on aggregates surface (ASTM D 2041)

$$V_{\text{ab}} = 100 \times \left(\frac{1}{G_{\text{bulk-agg}}} - \frac{1}{G_{\text{se}}}\right) \times G_b \quad (4.29)$$

where, G_{se} = effective specific gravity of mineral aggregates (ASTM D 2041)

$$G_{\text{se}} = \left(\frac{100 - \text{per cent of bitumen}}{\dfrac{100}{G_{\text{mm}}} - \dfrac{\text{per cent of bitumen}}{G_b}}\right) \quad (4.30)$$

where, G_{mm} = Max. specific gravity of mix without air voids according to ASTM D 2041

Q: *Calculate the bulk specific gravity of the combined aggregates from the following data.*

Aggregate type	*Bulk specific gravity*	*Proportion in mix (%)*
Coarse aggregate	*2.61*	*54.5*
Fine aggregate	*2.71*	*38.0*
Mineral filler	*2.69*	*7.5*

A: From equation (4.20),

$$\text{Bulk specific gravity of combined aggregates } (G_{\text{bulk-agg}}) = \frac{p_1 + p_2 + p_3}{\dfrac{p_1}{G_1} + \dfrac{p_2}{G_2} + \dfrac{p_3}{G_3}}$$

$$\text{On substitution, } G_{\text{bulk-agg}} = \frac{54.5 + 38.0 + 7.5}{\dfrac{54.5}{2.61} + \dfrac{38.0}{2.71} + \dfrac{7.5}{2.69}} = \frac{100}{20.88 + 14.02 + 2.78} = 2.65$$

Q: *Calculate the bulk specific gravity of a compacted bituminous concrete mix from the following data.*

Specimen weight in air = 3055.1 g
Specimen weight in water = 1725.7 g

A: From equation (4.21), Bulk specific gravity of compacted bituminous mix:

$$G_{\text{bulk-comp}} = \frac{\text{weight of specimen in air}}{\text{weight of specimen in air} - \text{weight of specimen in water}}$$

$$G_{\text{bulk-comp}} = \frac{3055.1}{3055.1 - 1725.7} = 2.298$$

$\therefore$ Unit weight of compacted bituminous mix = 2.298 × 1 g/cc = 2.298 g/cc

Q: *A few laboratory tests were conducted to design a bituminous concrete mix. Using the following data, calculate the (i) bulk density of the compacted mix, (ii) bulk density of the compacted mix specimen coated with paraffin, (iii) combined specific gravity of aggregates, (iv) percentage of voids present in the compacted mix, (v) voids in mineral aggregates and (vi) voids filled with bitumen.*

Weight of compacted uncoated specimen in air = 1195.4 g
Weight of compacted uncoated specimen in water = 684.4 g
Weight of compacted specimen (coated with paraffin) in air = 1240.9 g
Weight of compacted specimen (coated with paraffin) in water = 678.3 g
Take specific gravity of paraffin as 0.91 and maximum specific gravity of mix as 2.539 according to ASTM2041.

Material	*Specific gravity*	*Composition of mineral aggregate (% by weight)*	*Proportion in mix (% by weight)*
Coarse aggregate	*2.61*	*54.5*	*51.5*
Fine aggregate	*2.71*	*38.0*	*35.9*
Mineral filler	*2.69*	*7.5*	*7.1*
Bitumen	*1.02*		*5.5*

A: (i) *Bulk density of compacted mix (without paraffin coating):*

$$G_{\text{bulk-comp}} = \frac{1195.4}{1195.4 - 684.4} = 2.339$$

$\therefore$ Unit weight of compacted bituminous mix = 2.339 × 1 g/cc = 2.339 g/cc

(ii) *Bulk density of compacted mix specimen coated with paraffin:*

The bulk density of paraffin or wax coated specimen $G_{\text{bulk-wax}} = \dfrac{W_{\text{spec}}}{W_{\text{wax-air}} - W_{\text{wax-water}} - \left(\dfrac{W_{\text{wax}}}{G_{\text{wax}}}\right)}$

$$= \frac{1195.4}{1240.9 - 678.3 - \left(\dfrac{45.5}{0.9}\right)} = 2.33 \qquad (\because W_{\text{wax}} = 1240.9 - 1195.4 = 45.5 \text{ g})$$

(iii) *Combined specific gravity of aggregates:*

Bulk specific gravity of combined aggregates $(G_{\text{bulk-agg}}) = \dfrac{p_1 + p_2 + p_3}{\dfrac{p_1}{G_1} + \dfrac{p_2}{G_2} + \dfrac{p_3}{G_3}}$

On substitution, $G_{\text{bulk-agg}} = \dfrac{54.5 + 38.0 + 7.5}{\dfrac{54.5}{2.61} + \dfrac{38.0}{2.71} + \dfrac{7.5}{2.69}} = \dfrac{100}{20.88 + 14.02 + 2.78} = 2.653$

Based on individual specific gravities

$$= \frac{51.5 + 35.9 + 7.1}{\dfrac{51.5}{2.61} + \dfrac{35.9}{2.71} + \dfrac{7.1}{2.69}} = \frac{94.5}{19.73 + 13.24 + 2.63} = 2.654$$

(vi) *Percentage of voids present in the compacted mix:* $= 100 \times \dfrac{V_a}{V}$

$V_a = V - V_g - V_b$

V = Total volume of the specimen $= 1195.4 \times \dfrac{1.0}{2.339} = 511.07$ cc

V_g = Volume of the three mineral aggregates

$$V_g = 1195.4 \times \left[\left(\frac{0.515}{2.61}\right) + \left(\frac{0.359}{2.71}\right) + \left(\frac{0.071}{2.69}\right)\right] = 425.78 \text{ cc}$$

V_b = volume of bitumen $= 1195.4 \times \dfrac{0.055}{1.02} = 64.45$ cc

$V_a = 511.07 - 425.78 - 64.45 = 20.84$ cc

% voids $= 100 \times \dfrac{20.84}{511.07} = 4.07\%$

(vii) *Voids in mineral aggregates:*

Voids in mineral aggregate, VMA (%)=100% $-V_g$%

V_g % = per cent volume occupied by total mineral aggregates

$$V_g\% = (p_1 + p_2 + p_3) \times \frac{G_{\text{bulk-comp}}}{G_{\text{bulk-agg}}} = (94.5) \times \frac{2.339}{2.65} = 83.31\%$$

VMA (%) = 100 – 83.31 = 16.69 %

(viii) *Voids filled with bitumen:*

Voids filled with bitumen, VFB (%) $= 100 \times \dfrac{V_b\%}{\text{VMA}}$

$$V_b\% = (\text{per cent of bitumen}) \times \frac{G_{\text{bulk-comp}}}{G_\text{b}} = 5.5 \times \frac{2.339}{1.02} = 12.61\%$$

$$\text{VFB } (\%) = 100 \times \frac{12.61}{16.69} = 75.56\%$$

(ix) *Volume of bitumen absorbed by aggregates:*

$$G_{\text{se}} = \left(\frac{100 - \text{per cent of bitumen}}{\dfrac{100}{G_{\text{mm}}} - \dfrac{\text{per cent of bitumen}}{G_b}} \right) = \left(\frac{100 - 5.5}{\dfrac{100}{2.539} - \dfrac{5.5}{1.02}} \right) = 2.779$$

$$V_{\text{ab}} = 100 \times \left(\frac{1}{G_{\text{bulk-agg}}} - \frac{1}{G_{\text{se}}} \right) \times Gb = 100 \times \left(\frac{1}{2.654} - \frac{1}{2.779} \right) \times 1.02 = 1.728\%$$

4.5.4 Marshall Mix Method

The Marshall mix method is widely used in India as well as in many countries to design hot bituminous paving mixtures. This method was developed by Bruce Marshall of the Mississippi State Highway Department in 1940. Later, it was modified and improved by the U.S. Army Corps of Engineers and formulated as the mix design criteria ASTM D 1559 and AASHTO T 245 (TAI 2001).

The Marshall method is used to determine the optimum bitumen content which satisfies a given design criteria of stability, deformation or flow, density, minimum air void, V_{MA} and V_{FB} of hot mixed mineral aggregates and bitumen under standard test conditions.

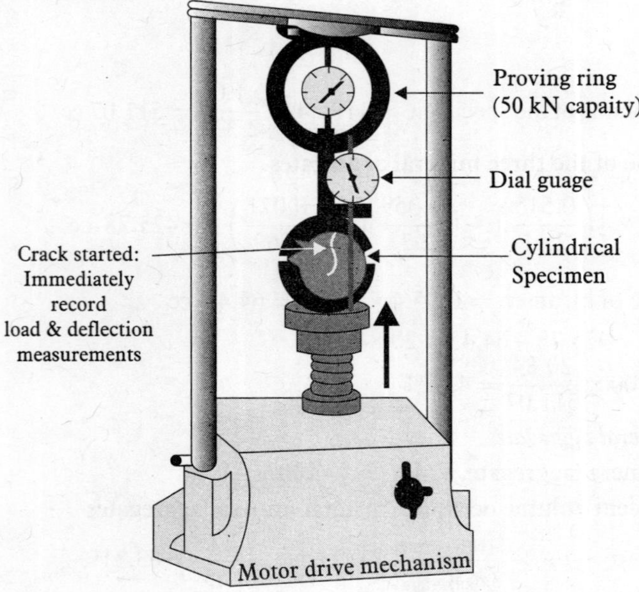

Figure 4.20 *Marshall stability test set-up*

(i) Preparation of specimens A number of specimens are prepared by changing the mix proportions of bitumen (at increments of 0.5% by weight) with a selected grade of aggregate samples whose maximum size is restricted to 25 mm. About 1200 g of mineral aggregates consisting of coarse aggregates, fine aggregates and mineral fillers is taken according to a given standard grade. The mineral aggregates and bitumen are separately heated to a temperature of up to 154–160 °C and 175–190 °C respectively. The quantity of bitumen is measured by the weight of the mix and poured into the heated mineral aggregate. The mix is blended until all the aggregate surfaces are evenly coated with bitumen. During mixing, the bitumen viscosity should be maintained at 170±20 centistokes. The hot mixture is placed in a standard cylindrical mould (of diameter size 102 mm and depth 64 mm) which is heated to 93–149 °C. It is compacted by applying 75 blows with a standard weight of hammer on each of its face. During compaction, the bitumen viscosity should be maintained at 280±30 centistokes. The prepared specimen is allowed to cool at room temperature for 12 hours and later kept in a water bath at 60 °C for about 30 minutes before being tested.

(ii) Tests on the prepared specimens The sample is taken out from the water bath and diametrically placed in position as shown in Figure 4.20. Load is vertically applied on to the specimen at a constant rate of 5 cm per minute. The maximum load at failure (on the proving ring) is taken as the stability value (kN) and the corresponding deformation value obtained from the dial gauge is taken as the flow value (mm). The flow value is expressed in units of 0.25 mm.

(iii) Presentation of the test data The data obtained from the Marshall tests should be analysed with reference to the voids–density relationship of the bituminous mixes as discussed in Section 4.5.3. From the results of the volumetric analysis, six curves are plotted. The details of the curves are shown in Figure 4.21.

(iii) Interpretation of the curves

Curve (a): Unit weight vs. bitumen content and curve (e): Marshall stability vs. bitumen content.

The above curves show similar trends. Initially, at lower content of bitumen, the values of unit weight and stability of mix is less but as the bitumen content increases, these values attain a peak. Afterwards, they show a decreasing trend. At lower content of bitumen, the specimen fails at smaller loads since the quantity of bitumen mixed with aggregates is not enough to develop sufficient bond between aggregates to withstand the applied load. Specimens with excess quantity of bitumen (above a certain level) also fail at smaller loads due to the thickness of the bituminous film at the interface of aggregates which do not effectively transmit the applied load on to the aggregates. Therefore, it is only at a particular quantity of bitumen that maximum values of density and Marshall stability are observed.

Curve (b): Air voids vs. bitumen content

As the quantity of bitumen increases, the air voids present in the mix decreases to a low value. Thereafter, it increases as the quantity of bitumen further increases. At a given temperature, though, stiffness of bituminous concrete decreases as air void content increases (Mackenzie and Fletcher 1980).

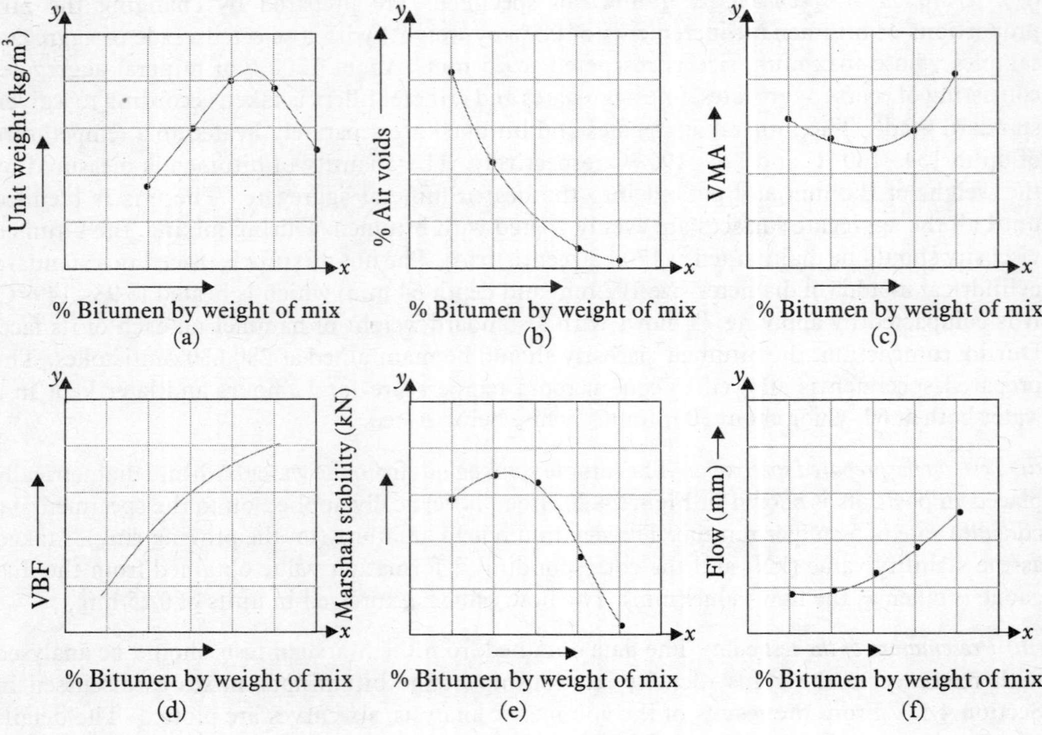

Figure 4.21 *Typical curves of the Marshall test data (courtesy: The Asphalt Institute)*

Curve (c): V_{MA} vs. bitumen content

As the bitumen content increases, slight variation may be observed in the shape of the curve. This may be due to adjustment of mineral aggregates with increased bitumen content.

Curve (d): V_{FB} vs. bitumen content

V_{FB} increases with increase of bitumen content since the bitumen fills all the available voids in the mix.

Curve (f): Flow vs. bitumen content

Flow (in mm) is a measure of the deformation due to applied load. The value of flow increases (the compacted specimen fails even at lower load) with increase of bitumen content because the presence of thick bitumen film around mineral aggregates prevents strong aggregate interlocking.

For mix design of various bituminous mixes, viz. bituminous macadam, bituminous concrete and semi-dense bituminous concrete, polymer modified binders can also be used according to the usual (or regular) procedure of the Marshall method of mix design (ASTM D 1559 1979). According to IRC: SP: 53-2002, the hot mix design of the above bituminous mixes should meet the requirements listed in Table 4.2.

Table 4.2 *Design requirements of hot mix prepared with modified bitumen* (From Table 7 of IRC: SP: 53-2002)

Sl.No	Properties	Requirement			Test method to be followed
		Hot climate	Cold climate	High rainfall	
1	Marshall stability at 60 °C, (kg), minimum	1200	1000	1200	ASTM D 1559 (1979)
2	Marshall flow at 60 °C (mm)	2.5 to 4.0	3.5 to 5.0	3.0 to 4.5	
3	Marshall quotient (kg/mm)		250 to 500		(Stability/ Flow)
4	Voids in compacted mix (%)		3.0 to 5.0		
5	Requirement of re-tained stability after 24 hours in water at 60 °C (%), minimum	90	95	100	ASTM D 1075 (1979)
6	Coating with aggregate (%)	95	95	100	AASHTO T 182

The procedure followed for the determination of optimum bitumen content by the Marshall mix method is explained in the following example problem.

Q: *Marshall tests were conducted on different specimens with varying bitumen content. Following are the curves prepared from the Marshall test data. Determine the optimum bitumen content from the curves based on the following specifications for the bituminous concrete layer. Take the normal size of the aggregate to be 25 mm.*

Requirements for the bituminous concrete pavement layer (Table 500-19. MSRTH 2006):
Minimum stability (kN) = 9.0; Minimum flow = 2 mm; Maximum flow = 4 mm;
Per cent voids = 3 to 6%; Minimum V_{MA} *= 12 to 14%;* V_{FB} *= 65 to 75%.*

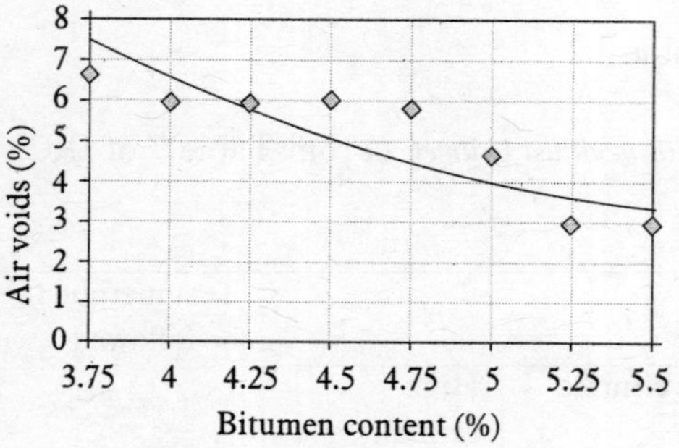

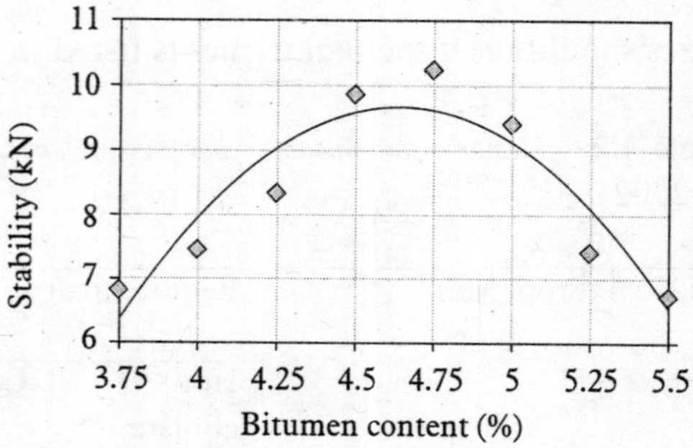

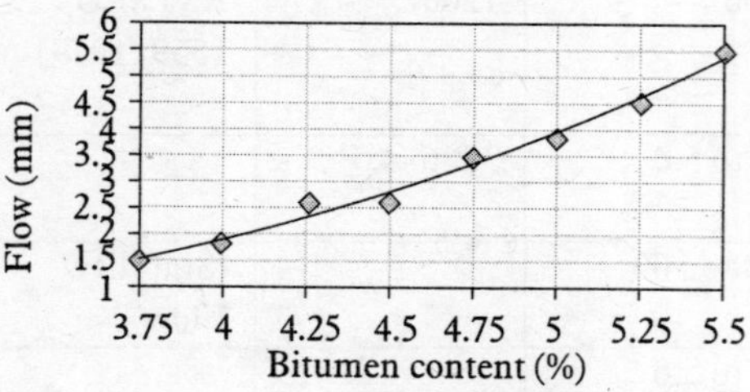

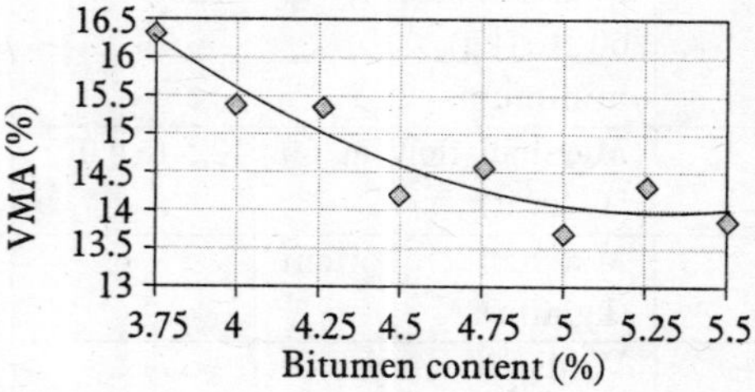

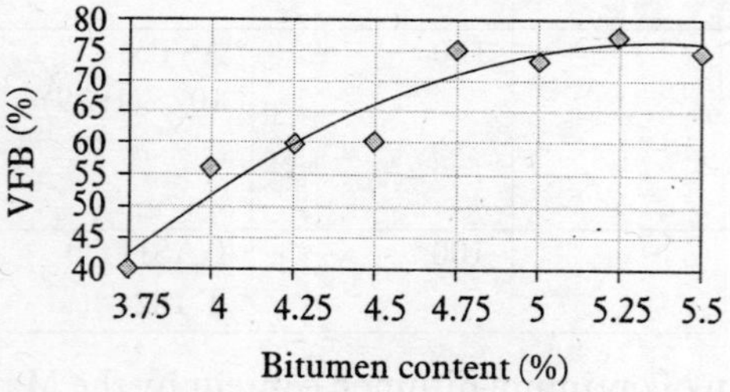

Air voids (%)
Bitumen content (%)

Stability (kN)
Bitumen content (%)

Flow (mm)
Bitumen content (%)

VMA (%)
Bitumen content (%)

VFB (%)
Bitumen content (%)

A: From the above curves and according to the given specifications, let us select a bitumen content at which the value of air voids = 4.5% (which is in between 3 to 6%). Then the corresponding value of bitumen from the given curve is 4.75%. Now, check the other requirements of the specifications with respect to a bitumen content of 4.75 %.

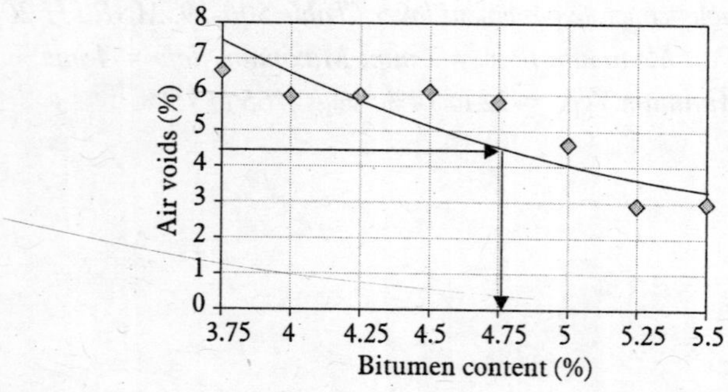

The value of stability from the curve (given below again for easy reference) = 9.6 kN (which is more than 9.0 kN).

11
10
9
8
7
6
Stability (kN)
3.75 4 4.25 4.5 4.75 5 5.25 5.5
Bitumen content (%)

The value of flow from the curve = 3.4 mm (which is in between 2 to 4 mm).

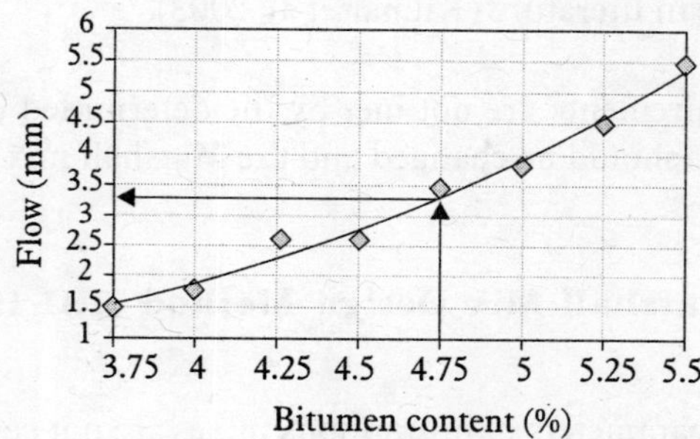

The value of VMA from the curve = 14.4% (which is more than 14%).

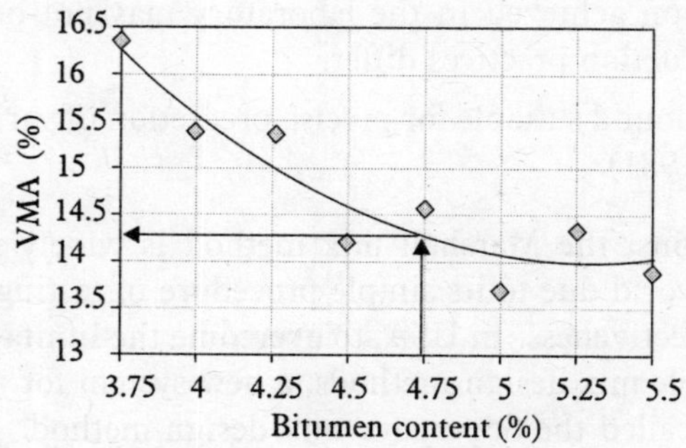

The value of VFB from the curve = 71% (which is in between 65 to 75%).

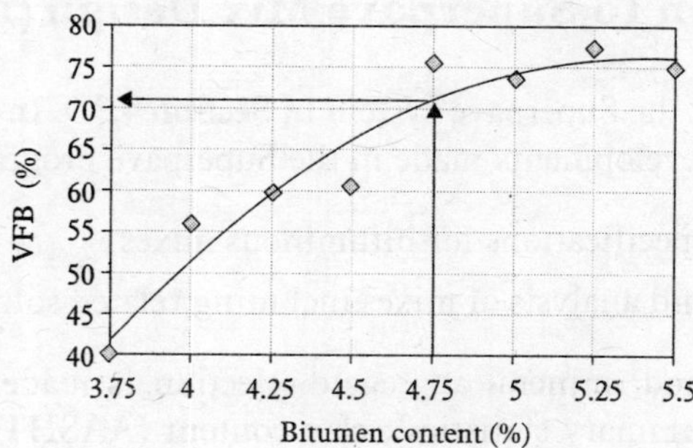

Hence, the design criteria are met. Therefore, optimum bitumen content (OBC) may be taken as 4.75%. However, further trials may be made to determine a more appropriate content of bitumen that satisfies the design criteria according to the given conditions of a project requirement better.

Alternatively, the optimum binder can also be calculated as follows.

The binder contents corresponding to the (i) maximum stability value, (ii) maximum unit weight and (iii) permissible air void content are determined from the curves prepared with the help of the Marshall test results and their average value is reported as the optimum binder content. The optimum binder content should meet the required design criteria; otherwise, an appropriate value may be determined from the curve which satisfies the design criteria and mix economics. A computer programme to determine the optimum binder content by using this procedure is available in literature (Kumar et al. 2003).

NOTE: If the desired requirements are not met by the determined optimum binder content, gradation of the aggregates should be changed and the Marshall mix design method should be followed again.

Limitations of the Marshall Mix Design Method (TAI 1997; TAI 2001; Pandey 2003)

- The shear strength parameters of bituminous mixes are not considered.
- This is an empirical mix design method. There is no scientific analysis behind it to explain pavement failures due to fatigue, rutting, durability etc.
- Degree of compaction achieved in the laboratory may not be comparable to real life conditions as construction practices differ.
- This method is not found suitable for precise prediction of various permanent deformations (Brown et al. 1981).

Despite these limitations, the Marshall mix method is widely used in India as well as many other parts of the world due to its simple procedure of testing, analysis of results, past experience and its cost effectiveness. In USA, to overcome the limitations of the Marshall mix method and other available mix design methods, a new system for the design of bituminous mix has been developed called the Superpave mix design method. In the following section, the salient features of the Superpave method are briefly presented.

4.5.5 Introduction to Superpave Mix Design (TAI 2001 and TAI 1997)

We have already discussed the Superpave system in Section 4.3.9. In addition to those details, following are the salient developments made in the Superpave programme.

- Performance based specifications for bituminous mixes
- A system of design and analysis of mixes including related software development

In the Superpave method, mineral aggregate selection is made based on design ESAL (cumulative traffic load summary statistics), clay content (AASHTO T 176), shape characteristics (ASTM D 4791, ASTM D 5821 and AASHTO T 304) and gradation of aggregates which provides sufficient voids in the mixture to accommodate desired thickness of binder film around the surface of aggregates and to allow elastic volumetric adjustments during different seasonal changes. According to the recommendation of SHRP (Strategic Highway Research Programme) researchers, the 0.45 power gradation curve is used for comparison and evaluation of desired gradation. To obtain the maximum density at the desired volume of voids in the aggregate mixture (Section 4.5.4), the following new concepts are introduced in the Superpave to guide the selection of the final gradation curve shape with respect to the 0.45 power gradation curve.

- Control points
- Restricted zone

Control points are introduced on nominal maximum size (NMS), intermediate and finer sieve sizes of aggregates and the desired gradation curve is forced to pass through these points. The NMS of an aggregate is a sieve size opening which is larger than the first sieve to retain more than 10 per cent of the total aggregates. The maximum size of an aggregate is the size of sieve opening which is larger than the NMS. Superpave developed five types of gradations based on the NMS of the aggregate, viz. 37.5, 25, 19, 12.5 and 9.5 mm.

A restricted zone is introduced along the 0.45 power gradation curve at intermediate sizes of aggregates which is adjacent to the finer sizes of aggregate. By extensive research, Superpave recommended that the desired gradation of the curve should not pass through this zone. Because, if a curve passes through this zone, the blend of aggregate mixture consists of excess quantity (or proportion) of finer sand particles which leads to poor aggregate interlocking, inadequate voids in mineral aggregates and lowers shear strength. It makes the mix susceptible to permanent deformations.

The compaction effect of rollers as applied in the field during construction of a bituminous layer is simulated by using a new compactor called the Superpave gyratory compactor (SGC). The SGC can be used to compact aggregates of larger size (up to 50 mm) too. To obtain the desired level of compaction, kneading action of compactive energy (similar to the field conditions) is applied on to the bituminous mix which is placed in a rotating mould with its base tilted at 1.25°. The required number of rotations is adjusted based on the desired density to be accomplished. The aggregate characteristics (viz. angularity, flakiness and elongation) and shear resistance of the mixture are related to slope of curve obtained from SGC test results.

Performance of bituminous mixes is evaluated by testing the mixes with the Superpave shear tester and the Superpave indirect tensile tester. These testers are used to evaluate susceptibility of bituminous mixes to deformations such as rutting, fatigue cracking, thermal cracking, shear failure etc. The above designed mix is also evaluated using the moisture sensitivity test according to AASHTO T 283.

A brief discussion of the Superpave mix design has been discussed above. The detailed procedure can be obtained from standard literature (TAI 2001; Harman et al. 2002). Table 4.3 compares the Indian method of designing hot bituminous mixes with the Superpave system.

Table 4.3 *Comparison between Indian method and Superpave system of design of hot bituminous mixes.*

Sl.No.	Indian method	Superpave method
1	There is no scientific analysis behind this method to explain pavement failures due to fatigue, rutting, durability etc. It is a performance related method.	Design criteria of mixes is fixed scientifically based upon analysis failures due to fatigue, rutting, durability, traffic loads etc. It is purely a performance based method.
2	Mix design is based upon the Marshall mix method which uses Marshall stability, density, minimum voids content, VFB and VMA.	The Superpave shear tester and the Superpave indirect tensile tester are used to evaluate susceptibility to various deformations such as rutting, fatigue cracking, thermal cracking, shear failure etc.
3	Degree of compaction achieved in the laboratory may not be comparable to field conditions if the construction practices differ.	Superpave gyratory compactor is used which simulates compaction similar to that obtained in the field by a roller compactor.
4	Mix design criteria are in accordance to the MOSRT&H specifications.	Mix design criteria are based upon the Superpave system.
5	The shear strength parameters of bituminous mixes are not considered.	The shear strength parameters of bituminous mixes are considered.
6	Large size aggregates cannot be compacted. The maximum size of aggregate is restricted to 25 mm.	Large size aggregates are also used for compaction. The maximum size of aggregate can be taken up to 50 mm.
7	This method is simple, inexpensive and easy to adopt for mix designs.	This method is complex, costly; it needs sophisticated equipment and very skilled personal.
8	There is no concept of different gradation lines. Only upper and lower limits of gradation are recommended.	0.45 power gradation line is taken as the reference maximum density line.
9	There is no concept of Superpave control points and restricted zones.	The concept of control points and restricted zone is incorporated along the 0.45 power gradation line.

4.5.6 Resilient Modulus of Bituminous Mix

The behaviour of bituminous material is complex. Its properties are visco-elastic and susceptible to temperature changes. The elastic modulus of a bituminous mix is normally determined in the laboratory by an appropriate test at representative temperatures similar to field conditions. The test is usually conducted under repeated constant load conditions or constant strain mode. The modulus of the bituminous mix is influenced greatly by test conditions, temperature and parameters related to the mix.

Resilient modulus (MR) or the elastic modulus value of a bituminous mixture is the ratio between repetitive vertical compressive stresses to the corresponding recoverable strain. A cylindrical bituminous mix specimen (similar to the size and shape of the specimen prepared for the Marshall stability test) is subjected to a vertical compressive stress by the application of a repetitive compressive load in the form of a Haversine wave which is similar to traffic wheel load repetitions. The load is applied on the specimen diametrically in opposite direction by loading strips (Figure 4.22). To determine the resilient modulus of the bituminous mix, elastic deformation of the specimen ($D_d - D_0$) is measured. The values of repetitive load, duration of loading, rest period and test temperature should be taken in accordance with filed conditions.

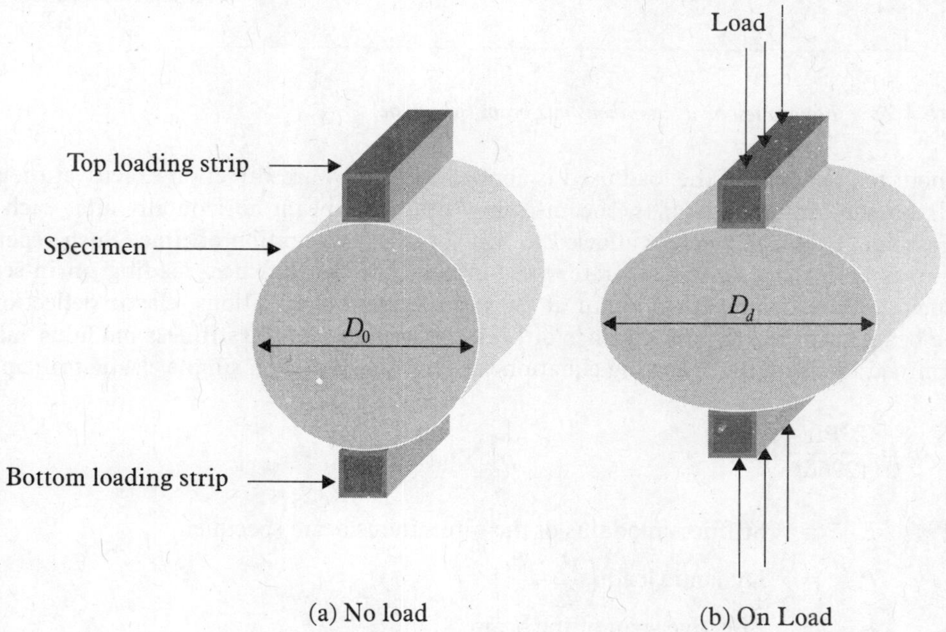

Figure 4.22 *Principle of repeated load indirect tensile test (schematic)*

The above test method is given in detail in ASTM D4123-82, titled 'Standard test method for indirect tensile test for resilient modulus of bituminous mixtures'.

4.5.7 Stiffness Modulus and Fatigue Life of Bituminous Mix (Kallas and Puzinauskas 1972; Yoder and Witczak 1975; Monismith and Deacon 1969)

The stiffness or elastic modulus of a bituminous mix can be determined by fatigue testing of a beam specimen. In this test, a beam of standard size made up of bituminous mix is subjected to repetitive dynamic loading in the form of a Haversine wave (1/10 s loading and 4/10 s rest period), at 1/3rd distance from both of its ends (Figure 4.23).

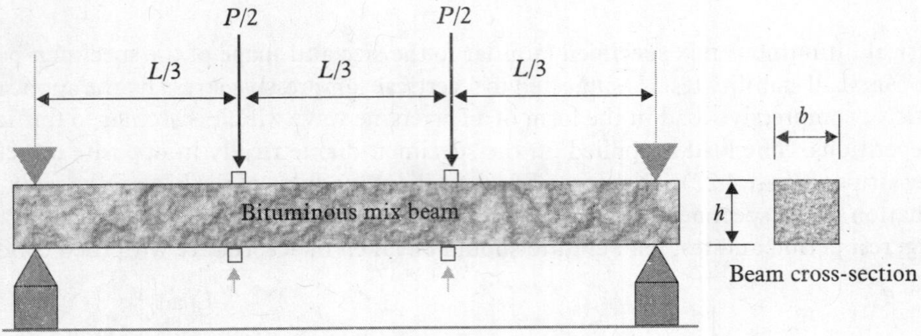

Figure 4.23 *Fatigue test on a bituminous mix beam (schematic)*

About ten per cent of the load used is applied in the upward direction exactly at the same points on the bottom side of the beam to reposition the beam horizontally after each load application. Then the beam is allowed to rest for a given duration of time. Such repetitive loading is performed in the laboratory to simulate the traffic wheel loading on in-service pavements. After initial straining or at a given number of repetitions, elastic deflection (δ) of the beam at its centre (at a distance of $L/2$) is measured and the stiffness modulus value is determined by using the following equation which is derived from simple elastic principles.

$$E_s = \frac{23PL^3}{1296\delta I} \tag{4.31}$$

where,

E_s	=	Stiffness modulus of the bituminous beam specimen
P	=	Dynamic load $\left(\frac{P}{2}+\frac{P}{2}\right)$
L	=	Effective span of the beam
I	=	$\frac{bh^3}{12}$
δ	=	Elastic deflection of the beam at its mid-span
b	=	Average breadth of the beam
h	=	Average depth of the beam

The above test set-up (Figure 4.23) is also used for fatigue testing of bituminous mixes. In this test, the number of dynamic load repetitions is measured until the beam fails at a known range of stress. It is conducted at different temperatures similar to the temperatures experienced by in-service pavements. The fatigue test is conducted under controlled stress and strain conditions which are suitable to evaluate thick (>150 mm) and thin (< 50 mm) bituminous pavement layers respectively (Yoder and Witczak 1975; Monismith, Secor and Blackmer 1961). Fatigue performance of a bituminous mix is generally expressed using the following relationship between fatigue life, the initial tensile strain at the bottom fibre of the beam and its elastic modulus (IRC:37-2001).

$$N_{\text{fail}} = C_1\left(\frac{1}{\varepsilon t}\right)^{C_2}\left(\frac{1}{Es}\right)^{C_3} \tag{4.32}$$

where, N_{fail} = No. of dynamic load repetitions to fail the beam
εt = Initial tensile strain at the bottom fibre of the beam
E_s = Stiffness modulus of bituminous mix
C_1, C_2 and C_3 = Constant values obtained from regression analysis of the fatigue test results

Q: *The following test results were obtained from a fatigue testing of a bituminous beam. Calculate the stiffness modulus of the bituminous mix.*

Beam dimensions: Breadth = 75 mm; Depth = 75 mm; Span length = 380 mm
Loading details: 0.1 s of loading and 0.4 s of rest period
Magnitude of loads at 1/3rd distance from both ends of the beam = 1.5 kN
Deflection at centre of the beam = 0.02 mm.

A: On substituting in equation (4.31), $E_s = \dfrac{23\,P\,L^3}{1296\,I\,\delta}$

P = total load = 1.5 + 1.5 = 3.0 kN
L = 380 mm
δ = 0.02 mm

$$I = \frac{bh^3}{12} = \frac{75 \times (75)^3}{12} = 2636718.75 \text{ mm}^4$$

$$E_s = \frac{23 \times 3.0 \times (380)^3}{1296 \times 2636718.75 \times 0.02} = 55.4 \text{ kN/mm}^2$$

Exercises

4.1 Define the following
(i) Bitumen, (ii) asphalt, (iii) straight-run bitumen, and (iv) mastic asphalt.

4.2 State the desirable properties of bitumen and explain their significance of pavement design.

4.3 What is meant by the ageing process of bitumen? Define oxidation of bitumen.

4.4 What criteria should be considered for selection of a suitable binding material for construction of pavements?

4.5 Enumerate the various types of tests conducted on bitumen and explain the principle of each test?

4.6 What are the standard test temperatures at which bitumen is tested, temperatures relevant to the service condition and construction of pavements?

4.7 State the significance of the RTFO test for characterising bitumen.

4.8 How does an RTFO test simulate adverse temperature conditions?

4.9 Explain the relationship between temperature and needle penetration of bitumen with standard equations.

4.10 State the limitations of the needle penetration test. Why is the viscosity test mandatory?

4.11 What is the difference between AASHTO and IRC methods of classification of bitumen? List the different types with their viscosity values?

4.12 Discuss different types of viscometers with their working principles.

4.13 State the limitations of the orifice or efflux type of viscometers.

4.14 With a neat sketch, explain the working principle of the Saybolt Furol viscometer.

4.15 State the difference between dynamic and kinematic viscosity.

4.16 Explain the working principle of a rotational viscometer with a neat sketch.

4.17 For different grades of bitumen, write limiting values of (i) the softening point, (ii) ductility values, (iii) loss on heating value, (iv) solubility value in CS_2 and (v) normal range of specific gravity according to IRC specifications

4.18 What is the significance of the Fraass breaking point in characterising paving bitumen? Write the limiting values of the Fraass breaking point for bitumen used in India.

4.19 What is meant by bitumen emulsions? State their merits and demerits in pavement construction.

4.20 Distinguish between cutback and emulsion. Explain the basic properties and uses of each.

4.21 What are the different types of bitumen emulsions used for road construction?

4.22 What are the factors affecting selection of suitable emulsion for pavement construction?

4.23 State the factors affecting setting and curing of emulsion mixes.

4.24 Explain with a figure the bonding phenomenon of emulsion with aggregates.

4.25 Differentiate between tar and bitumen. How are their predominant properties useful for pavement construction?

4.26 Note down the different types of road tars according to IS: 215.

4.27 How is sulphur used as a bitumen modifier? Note down the useful properties of sulphur modified bitumen for road construction.

4.28 State the advantages of lime modified bitumen for road construction.

4.29 Write a short note on polymer modified binders for road construction.

4.30 What is meant by thermosetting polymers? How they are useful in pavement construction?

4.31 What are the main differences between elastomers and plastomers?

4.32 Enumerate the different type of plastomers and elastomers.

4.33 What are the different types of thermoplastics used for pavement construction?

4.34 What are the uses of rubber modified bitumen?

4.35 What is meant by performance grade binders? Explain how it is superior to that of ordinary grade bitumen.

4.36 What are the salient features of performance graded binders?

4.37 What is mean by Superpave technology? Enumerate its main features.

4.38 What tests are conducted for performance graded binders and how are they relevant to conditions of in-service pavements?

4.39 How are the design temperatures determined in performance graded binders? What other factors are considered before selecting a suitable grade of binder?

4.40 Write a short note on stiffness modulus of bitumen.

4.41 Define dynamic modulus, creep compliance and shear compliance of a bituminous material.

4.42 What are the factors affecting bituminous mix design?

4.43 State the desirable properties of bituminous mixes.

4.44 What is the FHWA 0.45 power gradation curve? Explain its significance for gradation of aggregates for bituminous paving mixes.

4.45 Explain different methods of proportioning mineral aggregates.

4.46 Write the salient features of the Marshall method for designing bituminous mix.

4.47 Using charts, interpret the results obtained from a Marshall test.

4.48 Explain the Superpave method of mix design with a typical gradation chart.

4.49 What is the significance of control points and restricted zones in the Superpave system of bituminous mix design?

5

Design of Cement Concrete Mixes for Pavements

Introduction

Cement concrete is a versatile and commonly used product for civil engineering constructional works of the 20th and 21st century (A cement factory is shown in Figure 5.1). A fresh cement concrete mix consists of ingredients like cement, mineral aggregates, water and admixtures, if required. A good proportion design of these ingredients will provide good workability during placing and compaction. After hardening, the concrete provides a strong, stable and durable compacted pavement layer which can resist repetitive impact wheel loads as well as withstand effects of environmental variations.

Figure 5.1 *Different views of a cement manufacturing factory (Courtesy: Suvarna Cement Factory)*

Therefore, it is imperative that the ingredients of a mix should be properly selected based on their geological origin, physical, chemical and engineering properties. In the following sections of this chapter, various properties of these ingredients and methods of proportioning the mixes for cement concrete pavement construction will be briefly discussed.

5.1 Cement

Cement is the most important constituent of the mix. In the presence of water, it binds together all other ingredients, viz. mineral aggregates in a compacted form. Cement mixed with water becomes a plastic paste and spreads all over the surface area of aggregates forming a thin film. It subsequently sets with time due to a chemical reaction in which the compounds of cement form aluminum silicates. The process which results in the hardening of cement concrete with time, in the presence of water, is known as the hydration process.

The first artificial cement was patented by Joseph Aspdin, in England in the year 1824. This early cement had similar chemical composition of what is now known as ordinary Portland cement (OPC). Details about proportions of different chemical compounds in cement and its manufacturing processes with different mineral ingredients can be found in literature (Nawy 1997; Neville 2005).

Calcarious and silicate mineral compounds are blended and heated to high temperatures of the order of 1500 °C to form clinkers of cement. During this process, new chemical compounds are formed. These clinkers are ground to fine particles. The resulting fine powder is called cement. The new compounds in the form of oxides are generally determined by Bogue's method (Taylor 1991). Different types of chemical compounds in OPC with their approximate proportion are given below.

- Tricalcium silicate ($3CaO\ SiO_2$) $\approx$ 50%
- Dicalcium silicate ($2CaO\ SiO_2$) $\approx$ 22%
- Tricalcium aluminate ($3CaO\ Al_2O_3$) $\approx$ 9%
- Tetracalcium aluminoferrite ($4CaO\ Al_2O_3\ Fe_2O_3$) $\approx$ 9%
- Other compounds $\approx$ 10%

Tricalcium and dicalcium silicates contribute to the gain (rapid or slow) of strength in cement. The other compounds do not contribute to immediate strength gain but they do have an effect on long-term strength gain. Any slight change in proportioning of raw materials during the process of manufacturing the clinker form of cement may result in large variations in formation of the above-mentioned compounds. Thus, the chemical composition has a significant effect on cement properties and also on the performance of the concrete.

Cements are classified into different types based on their chemical composition and their utility. The properties of cement can be modified by blending in different types of admixtures at different stages of the manufacturing process. Following are some of the different types of cements widely used in India.

- Ordinary Portland cement (OPC)
- Rapid hardening Portland cement, RHPC (IS: 8041)

- Sulphate resisting cement (IS: 12330)
- Hydrophobic cement (IS: 8043)
- High alumina cement (IS: 6452)
- Low heat cement (IS: 12600)
- White cement (IS: 8042)
- Portland Pozzolana cement (IS: 1489) (It reduces the heat generated in concrete by hydration and helps to gain early strength)
- Portland blast furnace slag cement (IS: 455) (It reduces the heat due to the hydration process and helps to gain strength. Setting time can also be altered)

According to the Bureau of Indian Standards (BIS), ordinary Portland cement (OPC) is classified based on its grade.

- OPC grade 33 (IS: 269)
- OPC grade 43 (IS: 8112)
- OPC grade 53 (IS: 12269)

The grade number indicates the compressive strength of cement mortar in MPa at 28 days. Generally, OPC grade 43 is widely used for construction of highway pavements since its rate of heat of hydration and shrinkage cracks are found to be considerably less compared to OPC grade 53. It also meets other basic requirements (NAC 2001).

Rapid hardening Portland cement (RHPC) (IS: 8041) is preferred for remedial and rehabilitation works of concrete pavements where gain of strength in a short duration is desired to restore traffic corridors. The rapid strength gain of RHPC is due to the high specific surface area of the cement which is more than 325 m^2 per kg. In terms of chemical composition, the proportion of dicalcium silicate compound is kept lower than tricalcium aluminate.

According to the American Society for Testing Materials (ASTM), cements are classified into five major types (viz. type I, type II, type III, type IV and type V) and five minor types (viz. type IS, type IP, type IA, type IIA and type IIIA). Type I is similar to OPC and the remaining types are classified based upon different chemical compositions for specific uses.

As technology has advanced to meet the increased demand for specific construction purposes, many improved types of cements have become available. Their suitability must be determined thoroughly before using them for pavement constructional works.

5.2 Properties of Cement

As already mentioned, properties of cement are very sensitive to even a slight change in their chemical composition. The desirable properties of cement should be first ascertained in a laboratory before manufacturing it. During construction, if a particular brand of cement is changed, its properties should be checked with reference to design specifications (Hall 1932). The various tests conducted to determine the properties of cement and their limitations are briefly discussed below.

5.2.1 Fineness

The cement clinkers formed in kilns are pounded and ground to fine particles of the order of 90 micron and less. Fineness of cement particles is related to its grain size and specific area. The smaller the size of particles, the higher will be the specific surface area of cement. These are the indicative parameters of the fineness of cement.

Fineness is a desirable feature in cement—it helps cement concrete or cement paste to attain high strength within a required time interval. It is, thus, related directly to the cement's intensity of hydration and gain of strength. But, excessive fineness of cement also poses problems related to cost of grinding and more water requirement for hydration which may result in reduced strength and durability. Hence, an optimum value of fineness is a desirable feature to be considered at the time of manufacturing.

The following tests are performed to determine the fineness of the cement.

- Sieve analysis
- Wagner turbidimeter test
- Blain air permeability test

In the sieve analysis method, dry cement is sieved through a sieve of 90 micron size and the weight of cement retained on the sieve is reported in percentages. According to IS: 269-1967, the retained weight of OPC and RHPC should not be more than 10% and 5% respectively. This test is not generally preferred since the percentage of cement retained on a standard size of sieve does not provide information regarding proportions of other sizes of finer particles in the cement.

In the Wagner turbidimeter (ASTM C 115-93) and Blain air permeability tests (ASTM C 204-92), the surface area of cement particles per unit weight is determined. In the Blain air permeability test, the surface area of a sample of OPC and RHPC should not be less than 225 m^2/kg and 325 m^2/kg respectively (IS: 269-1993 and IS: 8041-1998).

5.2.2 Setting Time

The term *setting time* is related to the preparation of a workable cement mortar paste with water using a desired cement–water ratio and the time taken to harden the paste (calculated from the point of mixing water to the cement). Thus, it is indirectly related to the initial chemical reaction of cement with water to form aluminum-silicate compounds.

The setting time of cement depends upon environmental factors such as temperature, climatic conditions, humidity. There should also be no physical disturbances such as vibrations. As a standard, setting times are determined at a temperature of 20 ± 2 °C and at a relative humidity of 65%.

The degree of consistency of the cement–water paste is determined based upon the percentage of water needed to be mixed to obtain a standard consistency (IS: 4031, Part 4). The setting time of cement is basically classified into two types, viz. initial and final setting times. Vicat test apparatus is used to determine both the setting times.

Initial setting time The duration of time required to transform a wet cement paste to an initial solid state is termed as *initial setting time* of the cement. The reckoning of setting time starts immediately after adding water to the cement. This time duration is essentially required to delay the process of hydration or hardening. Determination of initial setting time is important for transportation, placing and compaction of cement concrete. The minimum initial setting time for OPC and RHPC should not be less than 30 minutes (IS: 269-1993 and IS: 8041-1998).

Final setting time The final setting time is the time taken for the cement mortar paste or cement concrete to harden sufficiently and attain the shape of the mould in which it is cast. During this period of time, the primary chemical reaction of cement with water is almost completed and the secondary chemical reaction commences to permanently form aluminum silicate bonds. The determination of setting time period also facilitates safe removal of scaffolding or forms. The maximum duration of time for final setting is generally about 10 hours for OPC and RHPC (IS: 269-1993 and IS: 8041).

5.2.3 Soundness

The term *soundness* of cement is used to describe its ability to resist volume expansion as a result of physical and chemical changes when water is added.

The change in volume in cement is caused by unburnt free lime (CaO), dead burnt MgO and also $CaSO_4$ which form calcium sulphonates. The presence of these materials is due to defective proportioning of raw materials and malfunctioning of the heating process in kilns during manufacture of cements.

There are two types of tests to evaluate the expansion characteristics of cement, viz. the Le Chatelier test and the autoclave test. In the Le Chatelier test, volume expansion of cement due to free lime is evaluated under increased temperature of steam for 3 hours. It is then immersed for 24 hours in water at 27 °C and after aeration for 7 days (BS: 4550 (Part 3)- 1978; IS: 269-1993; IS:4031 (Part 3)). Under standard test conditions, the expansion after the first and second stages of testing should not be more than 10 mm and 5 mm respectively (IS: 269-1993 and IS: 8041). If the tested cement does not satisfy any one of the above specified limits, it is not recommended for use.

In the autoclave test (IS: 269 and ASTM C 151-89), under standard test conditions of humidity, at a room temperature of 27 °C, cement cube samples are tested for 60 to 75 minutes at a steam pressure of 2.1 MPa. Longitudinal expansion due to the presence of free lime and magnesia are evaluated. The linear expansion in the autoclave test during the first and second stages should not be more than 0.8 and 0.6% respectively (IS: 269 and IS: 8041).

To determine the soundness of cement due to the presence of sulphates and other compounds, it might be necessary to resort to chemical analysis.

Strength

The strength of cement is generally evaluated by testing the cement–sand mortar or cement concrete cubes for compression, tension and flexural strength. In some cases, torsion tests are also prescribed.

The structural adequacy of a cement concrete pavement to withstand the pounding action of traffic wheel loads and resist environmental conditions will primarily depend upon the strength of the cement paste which binds the aggregates. Therefore, conducting strength tests on cement mortar or cement concrete is an important parameter to decide suitability of the cement.

Conducting strength tests on pure cement paste is not recommended since it will undergo considerable shrinkage on drying and micro cracks will develop in its mass. Therefore, the strength tests are carried out either on hardened cement mortar cubes made of cement and standard sand or on cement concrete cubes. In case of cement mortar cubes, the standard sand comprises three equal proportions (33.33%) of sizes 2 to 1 mm, 1 mm to 500 microns and 500 to 90 microns (IS: 650-1991). In south India, Ennore sand is recommended for all testing laboratories.

The compression test is conducted on a cube of cement–sand mortar prepared by mixing cement with standard sand (IS: 650-1991) in 1:3 proportion by weight and mixed with a quantity of water (($P/4 + 3$) per cent of the combined weight of cement and sand, where P is the water content at standard consistency limit for OPC and RHPC (IS: 269-1993; IS: 4031 (Part 6)-1988)). Generally, water–cement ratios of 0.4, 0.5 and 0.6 are also considered to ascertain the strength of cement mortar cubes. The compressive strength of OPC should be tested after curing under water for 3, 7 and 28 days. The strength should not be less than 16, 22 and 33 MPa respectively (IS: 269-1993). In case of RHPC, the compressive strength of cubes which are tested after curing for 1 and 3 days should not be less than 16 and 27 MPa respectively (IS:8041).

If cement concrete cubes are used, the relationship of strengths of either cement mortar or cement concrete with different proportions is evaluated and correlated to 3, 7 and 28 day compressive strengths.

According to the American practice, the strength of cement can also be determined by conducting flexural tests on cement–sand mortar beams. The test details are given in ASTM C 348-93. The other important tests required by the IS standards to be conducted on cement are given in Table 5.1.

Table 5.1 *Important tests on cement*

Sl. no.	Test name	Relevant IS code
1	Fineness tests:	
	Dry sieve analysis	IS: 4031 (Part 1)
	Blain air permeability test	IS: 4031 (Part 2)
	Wet sieve analysis	IS: 4031 (Part 15)
2	Setting time tests:	
	Initial and final setting times by the Vicat apparatus test	IS: 4031 (Part 15)
3	Soundness test by the Le Chatelier apparatus or autoclave test	IS: 4031, Part 3, 1988
4	Strength test by compressive strength test	IS: 650 and IS: 4031 (Part 6)
5	Specific gravity test	
6	Heat of hydration by calorimeter	IS: 4031 (Part 9)
7	Chemical composition by chemical analysis	ASTM C 348-93
8	Density using the Le Chatelier flask	IS: 4031 (Part 11)
9	False set using the Vicat apparatus	IS: 4031 (Part 14)

Nowadays, standard deviations of the strength of the cement mortar for various proportions and for each month of storage are also demanded by the users.

5.2.5 Chemical Composition Test of Cement

Another very important factor to consider while recommending a particular brand of cement for a bulk work of cement concrete pavement construction is the chemical composition of cements. For this the saturation of lime factor in the composition has to be determined (IS: 269-1989 (4th Revision)). It is expressed as follows.

$$\text{Lime saturation factor (LSF)} = \left(\frac{\text{CaO} - 0.7\,\text{SO}_3}{2.8\text{SiO}_2 + 1.2\text{Al}_2\text{O}_3 + 0.65\,\text{Fe}_2\text{O}_3}\right) \tag{5.1}$$

In general, LSF should be in the range of 0.66 to 1.02. Typical allowable range of LSF values are given below (IS: 269-1989 (4th Revision)).

OPC, 33 and 43 grades	:	0.66–1.02
OPC, 43 grade	:	0.66–1.02
OPC, 53 grade	:	0.80–1.02
Sulphate resisting cement	:	0.66–1.02
RHPC	:	0.66–1.02

If cement contains alkalis (Na_2O and K_2O), they react with aggregates containing higher content of silica. This reaction causes expansion of the resulting hardened concrete and fails by cracking. The integrity of the aggregate particles in the concrete matrix will be disturbed. The extent of expansion, of course, depends on the quantity of silica in aggregates and alkalis in cement. To prevent this failure, the aggregates used for concrete should possess less quantity of reactive silica and the cement should contain low alkali content; or a suitable mineral admixture like fly ash or pozzolana should be used to offset the effect of the alkali–silica reaction to a certain extent (Stanton 1940).

The concrete may also fail due to expansion if the alkalis in cement react with carbonates ($CaCO_3$ or $MgCO_3$) in certain types of limestone (Poole 1981). In such cases, a low alkali cement must be used.

5.2.6 Hydration of Cement

When water is mixed with cement, heat is liberated due to hydration—the reaction is an exothermic chemical reaction. The heat of hydration may be of the order of 60 calories per gramme in low heat cements to 120 calories per gramme in normal cements. The liberation of heat is greatest in the first 72 hours. A temperature rise of the order of 40–50 °C has been reported in technical literature while building massive foundations and concrete dam works. This heat causes cracking and shrinkage of cement concrete on curing. The rate of liberation of heat due to the hydration process increases if the following quantities are increased.

- Fineness of cement
- Tricalcium silicate
- Tricalcium aluminate

The heat of hydration can be determined by the vacuum flask method or by using an adiabatic calorimeter. In case of low heat cement, the quantity of heat generated is reported to be of the order of 65 calories per gramme at 7 days and 75 calories per gramme at 28 days.

In hot weather concreting, the following measures may be taken to control the excess liberation of heat due to hydration.

- The mixing water should be cooled—if required, crushed ice pieces may used.
- Minimum cement quantity should be used.
- Use of mineral admixtures such as fly ash, pozzolana or slag; or chemical admixtures such as retarders or water reducers will considerably reduce the heat of hydration.

5.3 Mineral Aggregates

Mineral aggregates consist of coarse aggregates (above 4.75 mm), fine aggregates (between 4.75 to 0.075 mm) and stone dust (below 0.075 mm). The major portion by volume (about 75%) of the cement concrete mix comprises of mineral aggregate only. Most of the impact and abrasive forces generated by the movement of traffic are borne and resisted by coarse aggregates along with cement paste as a binder. The fine aggregates and stone dust as a mass assist to attain a dense and durable mix. Therefore, the strength properties of the hardened cement concrete, viz. toughness, strength, stability, resistance to abrasion and durability against external harmful agents, are influenced largely by the properties of mineral aggregates. Hence, mineral aggregates for construction of cement concrete pavements should be carefully selected based on tests (Table 5.2). The tests have been described in detail in Chapter 3.

Table 5.2 *Important tests to be carried out on mineral aggregate for cement concrete pavements*

Sl.no.	Test name	Property to be determined	Relevant IS code
1	Sieve analysis	Size distribution and gradation	2386 (Part 1) and 383
2	Aggregate crushing test	Aggregate crushing value	2386 (Part 4)
3	Aggregate impact test	Aggregate impact value	2386 (Part 4)
4	Los Angeles abrasion test	Aggregate abrasive value	2386 (Part 4)
5	Water absorption test	Quantity of water absorbed	2386 (Part 4)
6	Shape test	Angularity, flakiness and elongation indices	383 and 2386 (Part 1)
7	Soundness test	Durability	2386 (Part 5)
8	Specific gravity test	Specific gravities	2386 (Part 3)
9	Bulk density	Bulk density or bulkage of sand	2386 (Part 3)
10	Deleterious substance test	Impurities	2386 (Part 2) and 383

The specific gravity of natural mineral aggregates generally varies from 2.55 to 2.75. Therefore, density of concrete will be in the range 22.5 to 24.5 kN/m^3.

5.3.1 Gradation or Particle Size Distribution

The strength of a compacted and hardened cement concrete mix depends upon its density or air void content. Suitable proportioning of different sizes of aggregates has to be made to get a dense mix. If the mineral aggregates are not properly proportioned, the resulting mix may contain more air voids or the cement paste content may not be sufficient to bind all the aggregates. This results in low strength of concrete. To avoid this unwanted mix proportion, a suitable standard gradation curve should be adopted for a specified mix and flexural strength. The basic definitions and details of gradation have already been discussed in Section 3.2.

Standard guidelines have been specified by the Bureau of Indian Standards, MORTH and IRC for construction of concrete pavements (IS: 383-1970; MOSRTH 2002; *Pocketbook 2002*) According to IS: 383-1970, the following types of gradation have been prescribed for different sizes of aggregates.

1. Coarse aggregates (Table 5.3)
2. Fine aggregates (Table 5.4)
3. All-in-one aggregates (Table 5.5)

The coarse aggregates are graded according to the nominal size of aggregates.

Table 5.3 *Coarse (graded) aggregates gradation (a part of Table 2 from IS:383)*

IS sieve size (mm)	Percent passing of graded aggregates of nominal size (mm)			
	40	20	16	12.5
40	95–100	100	—	—
20	30–70	95–100	100	100
16	—	—	90–100	—
12.5	—	—	—	90–100
10	10–35	25–55	30–70	40–85
4.75	0–5	0–10	0–10	0–10
2.36	—	—	—	—

Table 5.4 *Fine aggregates gradation (from IS:383)*

IS sieve size (mm)	Percent passing for grading			
	Zone I	Zone II	Zone III	Zone IV
10	100	100	100	100
4.75	90–100	90–100	90–100	95–100
2.36	60–95	75–100	85–100	
1.18	30–70	55–90	75–100	90–100
0.6	15–34	35–39	60–79	80–100
0.3	5–20	8–30	12–40	15–50
0.15	0–10	0–10	0–10	0–15

Table 5.5 *All-in aggregates gradation (from IS:383)*

IS sieve size (mm)	Percent passing of all-in aggregates of nominal size (mm)	
	40	20
80	100	
40	95–100	100
20	45–75	95–100
4.75	25–45	30–50
0.6	8–30	10–35
0.15	0–6	0–6

For fine aggregates, the gradation is classified into four types, viz. Zone I (coarse), Zone II (medium), Zone III (medium) and Zone IV (fine) (IS: 383-1970). The distribution of aggregate particle sizes in all the four zones is in between 10 to 0.15 mm. From Zone I to Zone IV, variation of gradation ranges from coarser to finer sizes. A tolerance of ±5% is allowed for all the sieves mentioned except for the 0.6 mm size sieve. This allowance may be taken to account for the variation in sizes of crushed aggregates. But the upper and lower limiting gradation for the 0.6 mm size sieve should be strictly followed to keep the fine-to-coarse aggregate ratio within the standard limit. The ratio of fine-to-coarse aggregate should be proportionately increased as the gradation changes from Zone I to Zone IV. For high strength concreting, especially for construction of pavements, the fine aggregate gradations may range from Zone I to Zone IV. But care should be taken while designing the concrete mix to provide for suitable workability in order to achieve the desired durability and strength.

In gradation of *all-in-aggregates*, suitable blending of different locally available aggregates may be carried out according to the limits of gradation given in IS: 383. They are also classified into two types based on the nominal size of aggregates, viz. 40 and 20 mm, for which the sieve sizes range between 80 to 0.15 mm and 40 to 0.15 mm, respectively.

Mineral aggregates of different sizes obtained from different sources may be blended with reference to the above specifications of gradation to achieve the desired density and number of air voids. For this purpose, any suitable method of proportioning mineral aggregate may be followed as discussed in Section 4.5.2.

To preserve scarce natural river sands (quartzite), use of artificial sands obtained during crushing of stones is preferred. In such cases, blending of these materials to the required gradation assumes prominence.

For mix design of cement concrete, especially for gradation of fine aggregates, a design parameter called fineness modulus (FM) is used. FM is a dimensionless number which indicates particle size distribution of fine aggregates. It is obtained from the cumulative percentage of all constituent sizes divided by 100. If the value of FM is lower, it indicates that the material is finer and vice versa. Table 5.6 illustrates the method of calculation of FM from sieve analysis of fine aggregate.

5.4 Water

Generally, potable water is used for concrete works. However, in extreme situations or at inaccessible sites, deserts or sea shores, the quality of water may be checked against tolerable level of impurities, viz. turbidity, algae, salts, fluorides, sulphates, chloride etc. The pH value of the water should be preferably in between 6 to 8. The properties of water and permissible limits of contaminants are mentioned in IS: 456.

Table 5.6 *Example calculation of fineness modulus*

Sl.no.	Sieve size (mm)	Weight retained (gm)	Percentage of retained weight		Cumulative retained weight of particles in per cent
			Individual fractions	Cumulative	
1	10.0	0	0	0	0
2	4.75	60	3	3	3
3	2.36	240	12	15	15
4	1.18	460	23	38	38
5	0.06	420	21	59	59
6	0.03	440	22	81	81
7	0.015	340	17	98	98
8	Pan	40	2	100	–
Total		2000	100		294
Fineness modulus = 294/100 = 2.94					

If soil or water consists of sulphates (SO_3), the sulphate ions penetrate into the concrete. A chemical reaction takes place between the sulphate ions and cement in the presence of water to form gypsum and ettringite. Thereby, the volume of the concrete increases and results in the formation of surface cracks. This effect is considered significant if the sulphate content in water is in excess of 150 ppm. It can be prevented by reducing the permeability of concrete using high content of slag as mineral admixture (Bakker 1983) or lowering the water–cement ratio (<0.4) (Nawy 1997). It can also be prevented by using sulphate resistant cement.

According to the Indian practice, if sub-grade soils are contaminated with soluble salts like sulphates (SO_3) by more than 0.5 per cent, it is preferable to use sulphate resistant cement (IS:6909; MOSRTH 2001; IRC: SP:62-2004).

5.5 Admixtures

Different types of fibres and additives, viz. chemical compounds, resins and synthetic polymers, are blend with the cement concrete mix during the process of batching to modify its properties. Setting time, strength, workability and durability can be modified by reducing the water and cement quantities and introducing admixtures. A cement concrete mixed with an admixture should be evaluated according to the guidelines in codes of practices (IS: 9103 and IS: 6925) before it is used for construction works. In the following sections, the different additives or admixtures generally used in cement concrete works are described. The economics of the use of these have to be ascertained before using them.

5.5.1 Retarders

Retarders increase the setting time of cement concrete by retarding the process of hydration with minimal loss of the final strength. They are useful in construction works during the hot summer season (IS: 9103). Retarders include lignin, borax, sugars, molasses etc and slow down the setting time by hours. For example, about half per cent of sugar by weight of cement retards the setting time of cement by 4 hours (Ghosh et al. 1973).

5.5.2 Acceleratorss (IS: 9103)

This type of admixture is blend with cement concrete mix to accelerate the process of hydration which is useful during construction in winter seasons or where rapid strength gain is required for early removal of forms or for road repair works. Calcium salts or triethanol-amine may be used as accelerators (Tucker 1936). Calcium chloride ($CaCl_2$) of not more than 1.5 per cent by weight of cement is mixed in concrete for reinforced and un-reinforced concreting works (IS: 7861 (Part 2)).

5.5.3 Plasticisers and Super-plasticisers

Plasticisers increase the workability of cement concrete even at lower water content (water–cement ratio of less than 0.3). It is also used to reduce the heat of hydration. Plasticisers are also called *workability aids*. The reduction of mixing water content varies from 5 to 15 per cent depending upon the type and quality of the concrete ingredients (Bagui 2004). These admixtures are extensively used when cement concrete has to be pumped to great heights for constructing high storied structures.

Super-plasticisers are also used to improve plasticity of fresh concrete. They are often high range water-reducing admixtures which are used in manufacturing high strength concrete (above 60 MPa). They reduce the requirement of water by 15 to 30 per cent with no loss of viscosity and strength; they improve flowability characteristics. This admixture is also used to prevent loss of slump when ready mix concrete is to be transported for long distances. Superplasticiser is generally limited to 1 to 2% by weight of cement as the compressive strength of concrete may be reduced if higher quantity of super-plasticiser is used.

There are mainly three types of super-plasticisers (Jagadish et al. 1997; Ramachandran et al. 1998; Chaubal and Hans 2000) that are commonly used.

- Modified ligno-sulphonates
- Melamine formaldehyde sulphonates
- Naphthalene formaldehyde sulphonates

Water soluble polymers referred to as polyacrylate esters (PAE) or polycarboxylates are also used as super-plasticisers at lower dosages to yield very high strength concrete (40–100 MPa) at low water–cement ratio (<0.3). Proper care should be taken while fixing dosages, otherwise it may entrain air and cause problems related to set-retarding (Nelu and Carmel 2006). Plasticisers are also very costly and only specific commercial firms deal with these chemicals.

5.5.4 Air-entraining Agents

Minute air bubbles (<0.1mm Φ) at uniform inter-bubble spacing are introduced in the concrete mix to improve workability and increase resistance to frost action. Frost action causes the water molecules in cement concrete to expand and during the process of thawing they decrease in volume. This phenomena increases alternative stresses in the mass of concrete due to frost expansion. The stress can be relieved by the presence of very small pores or cavities which bring into play a stress diffusion mechanism. They act as barriers which prevent propagation of micro cracks (Jackson et al. 1944). Care should be taken not to use air-entraining agents in excess quantity as it may result in highly porous concrete (IS: 9103). Animal or vegetable oils, surfactants (soaps or synthetic analogs of tall oil fatty acids), wood resins etc may be used as air-entraining agents in concrete mix. Generally, in cold countries like the Antarctic region, the use of air-entraining agents is fairly common.

5.5.5 Water Reducers

Pozzolana (IS: 3812 (Part 2), burnt clay (IS: 1344), polycarboxylic acids and their salts improve workability at low water content and improve flow properties of fresh concrete by dispersing the flocculated cement particles. Pozzolans or blast furnace slags are used as replacements for cement up to a certain extent to prevent alkali–aggregate expansion. Use of super-plasticisers also reduces the required quantity of water by improving workability and reducing porosity. Extracts from pulp and paper industry in the form of derivatives of lignins acts as retarders and dispersants (Mark 1938). Polynapthalene sulphonate is also used as a water reducing as well as a pigment dispersion agent in concrete (Nelu and Carmel 2006). The economics of these admixtures are to be worked out before using them.

5.5.6 Pigments

Mineral oxide pigments are also used as admixtures to impart colour to the cement concrete mix for aesthetic and beautification purposes. Generally, pigmentation is added for crosswalks, pedestrian ways, footpaths and any specific purpose of paved surfaces. The quantity of mineral oxide is limited to not more than 10% by weight of cement since it may considerably reduce the strength of the concrete (PCA 1995). Natural or synthetic iron oxides of different colours, chromium oxide and cobalt oxide are some widely used pavement pigments, to name a few. Some more details and standard specifications of pavement pigments can be found in ASTM C 979 or the manufacturer's recommendations.

5.5.7 Others

Silica fumes, fly ash, blast furnace slag, rice husk ash, calcined clay (metakaolin), diatomaceous earth are other mineral additives used in cement concrete. They are called supplementing cementitious materials. They modify the mix chemistry and thereby influence its strength, durability and workability properties (Nelu and Carmel 2006). Use of silica fumes and blast furnace slag makes the cement concrete mix dense.

High strength and low permeability concrete is produced by using silica fumes (having a diameter $\approx 0.1\ \mu$) since it has a high specific surface area (13,000 to 30,000 m^2/kg) and brings forth high pozzolanic activity (Nawy 1997; Arora 2003). Silica fumes are obtained from the blast furnaces of iron and steel manufacturing units. The workability of the concrete mix can be considerably increased as silica fumes act as powerful dispersants and water reducers at an acceptable water content (Spiratos et al. 2003). Depending upon the required strength and workability, silica fume in the order of 5 to 30% by weight of cement is used (Nawy 1997). Silica fumes were used in Srisailam dam to achieve high strength cement concrete.

Fly ash is used as a partial substitute for cement. It improves workability, reduces water content and thermal cracking of concrete. Fly ash concrete pavements are less susceptible to thermal cracking since the fly ash enables the hydration process to occur with the liberation of less heat. This lower hydraulic activity of fly ash may result in concrete bleeding and segregation (Khayat 1998). A study reveals that the static flexural and flexural fatigue strength of concrete decreases when the cement replaced with fly ash increases from 15 to 50% (Naik and Singh 1994). In addition to this, excess quantity of carbon (1 to 10%) in fly ash behaves like activated carbon which strongly affects the performance of air-entraining admixtures by erratic generation of air voids (Hill et al. 1997). The severity of this erratic formation of air voids depends on the fly ash constitution, viz. amount of residual carbon, surface area and chemical composition. These problems should be carefully addressed and investigated in the laboratory before selecting fly ash from different sources. Suitable admixtures should be used to balance the ill-effects of residual carbon in fly ash and to improve water retention, stability and rate of strength gain.

Fly ash should be selected according to the following standard specifications (IS: 3812-1981; IRC: SP: 62-2004)

- Minimum surface area: 320 m^2/kg
- Minimum lime reactivity: 4.5 MPa
- Compressive strength at 28 days: above 80% of the standard cement mortar cubes
- Maximum drying shrinkage: 0.15%
- Maximum expansion by autoclave test: 0.8
- Maximum loss on ignition: 5%

Any one of the above admixtures or admixtures in multiple combinations may be used in a cement concrete mix to serve the desired purpose based upon scientific analysis. A proper analysis is needed as these admixtures may become problematic in the hardening or hydration stage. They may cause mix disproportions and ill or non-performance due to their adverse reactions with the ingredients of the mix.

Uniformly dispersed alkali-resistant glass fibres in homogeneous concrete make the concrete mass resistant to a high degree of stress distribution. They improve the modulus of rupture and impact strength which acts as a crack arrestor. The following commercially available glass fibres are used for concrete works (Grimer and Ali 1969).

- Strands (200 or 400 single filaments of 10 μm Φ each)
- Rovings (20 or 60 single filaments of 10 μm Φ each)
- Woven or chopped strand mat

For more details on different types of admixtures and their usability in cement concrete, please refer to the *Concrete Admixtures Handbook* (Ramachandran 1995).

5.6 Properties of Fresh Concrete

For any kind of concreting work, mixing, placing and compaction of concrete are the important operations to be performed until the final setting time is reached. The engineer desires to perform these tasks smoothly and in a cost-effective manner without compromising on the strength. The ease with which the above-mentioned operations can be performed is called workability. The workability of concrete is one of the most important factors to consider while handling fresh concrete (Venable 1930). It decides the overall cost of the project as well as the performance in the post-construction period.

A few more details on workability of concrete are given below.

5.6.1 Workability

It is an important consideration while economically deciding the various design parameters related to their proportion in the mix. A concrete mix may be said to have good workability if we are able to perform the following operations with ease.

- mixing
- transportation and placing without segregation of coarse aggregate particles
- adjustment of mix in the desired shape of form or placing
- compacting
- achieving desired surface finish, strength and durability

The following important factors affect the workability of cement concrete mix.

- maximum size of coarse mineral aggregates and their gradation
- flakiness and elongation indices of aggregates
- water–cement ratio (WCR)
- aggregate–cement (a/c) ratio
- fine aggregate–coarse aggregate (f/c) ratio
- type and quantity of admixtures used
- type of concreting work—mixing, placing, compaction and finishing

- temperature control
- quality of work

Strength of the fully compacted concrete is related to the water–cement ratio (WCR). According to Abrams' law (Abrams 1918), the relation can be stated as

$$\text{Strength of concrete} = P/Q^{WCR} \tag{5.2}$$

where P and Q are empirical constants which depend on cement type, aggregates type, curing method, age and test method. WCR is the ratio between water and cement by weight. Abrams' law indicates that reduction of WCR beyond the minimum requirement does not improve concrete strength and results in poor workability.

The workability of cement concrete mix is generally determined by

(i) slump test
(ii) compacting factor test
(iii) veebee (VB) time test
(iv) flow test

Depending on the field conditions of the placement of cement concrete, an appropriate test may be followed. Standard guidelines for selecting a suitable type of test for determining the workability of cement concrete are discussed below.

For construction of highway pavements with a desired target strength of cement concrete, a very low degree of workability, less than or equal to 25 mm of slump, is desirable. However, for paving works, a slump value of 35 ± 15 mm may be suitable, depending on the site requirement (MOSRTH 2001). To achieve lower degree of workability, greater care should be taken to control the proportioning of ingredients during mixing. For low workability cement, the compacting factor test is preferred and found to be more relevant than the slump. The values of the compaction factor prescribed are of the order 0.75 to 0.80 (IS: 456-2000). If the value of the compacting factor is lower than 0.7, it indicates an extremely stiff mix. In such cases, the veebee time test is more suitable (SP: 23-1985).

Although the slump test is suitable for determining low to high workability when the slump value is between 25 to 125 mm (SP: 23-1982), it is more useful and simple for controlling the manufacturing of concrete in field at all field temperatures. In case of very high workability of concrete, when the slump value is expected to be more than 150 mm, the flow test method is more suitable.

The detailed standard procedures for testing the workability of cement concrete by the above methods are given in IS: 1199-1959.

5.7 Tests on Hardened Concrete

A brief discussion on the important tests conducted on hardened concrete is given below.

5.7.1 Compressive Strength Test

The value of the compressive strength of hardened concrete is an important property used while designing cement concrete mixes. Determination of compressive strength is very simple. Due to this reason, many other strength parameters of concrete, viz. tensile strength, shear strength, elastic modulus value, bond strength etc., are correlated with the values of compressive strength to determine its overall structural strength.

The compression test may be performed by any one of the following standards adopted in different countries, viz. the Indian practice (IS: 516-1959; 1999), the British practice (BS: 1881 (Part 108)-1983) and the American practice (ASTM C 39-86). The compression test procedure according to the Indian practice is described below.

The compressive strength of hardened cement concrete is determined by preparing a specimen of standard size (a cube of 150 mm size or a cylinder having a diameter of 150 mm and a height of 300 mm). It is cured by submerging in water for 28 days or steam curing for 7 days. After the given period of curing, the specimen is tested in a compression machine (Figure 5.2)—a compressive load is applied at a uniform rate of approximately 14 N/mm^2/minute on to the specimen (IS: 516-1959; 1999). The specimen is loading gradually until it fails by cracking or breakdown. The failure stress is calculated from the maximum failure load (or peak value) and is recorded as the compressive strength of the concrete. An average value of three such test results is reported as the final compressive strength of the concrete. For approximate calculation of the equivalent compressive strength of a cylinder, about 80 per cent of the cube strength may be taken.

Figure 5.2 *Cube compression test in progress*

Strength tests are also performed on cement concrete cubes cured under water for 3 days and 7 days—this is only to determine the trend of strength gain during short periods. These test values are projected and compared to the probable strength gain at 28 days. Generally, the ratio of strength gain for 7 to 28 days is calculated to be 2/3rd value approximately.

Long-term strength evaluation tests of 90 and 365 days are also conducted for important works like concrete for dams and hydraulic structures.

The characteristic compressive strength of concrete is defined as the value below which not more than 5 per cent of the test results are expected to fail (IS: 456). It is also called as the 95 percentile characteristic value. The target mean strength for a mix design takes into account the characteristic strength of concrete plus the standard deviation times the desired tolerance limit. The tolerance limit is expressed in terms of *Molesworth* risk factors (such as *1* in *n*).

5.7.2 Elastic Modulus Test

The elastic modulus (E) value of concrete is an indicative property for predicting many aspects of its strength and durability. It also helps in evaluating various mathematical models in engineering practices. It describes the stress and strain relationship. It is also used as an important input parameter along with Poisson's ratio (μ) for evaluation of the strergth of a structural member.

The modulus of elasticity of cement concrete may be defined as a linear relationship (i.e., slope) between applied stresses to the corresponding recoverable or elastic strains. The value is determined by many methods. A conventional static load method for determination of modulus of elasticity is described below.

A cylindrical cement concrete specimen having standard size (150 mm diameter and 300 mm height) is suitably placed in an extensometer–compressometer and tested in a compression testing machine. The extensometer–compressometer consists of two dial gauges—one dial gauge is used to measure change in original length of specimen and the other is used to measure the diametrical expansion of the specimen under loading. A loading machine similar to the compression testing machine is used for loading the specimen in three cycles. About 30 per cent of the ultimate compressive strength of the stress is gradually applied on to the specimen in the axial direction (IS: 516-1959). About 25 and 40 per cent of the ultimate compressive stress may also be taken (ASTM C 469). Changes in lateral and diametric dimensions are recorded under loading and unloading processes. If the test results are consistent, the average values of Poisson's ratio and different types of modulus values based on the slope of the stress–strain curve (Figure 5.1) will be calculated. For Indian conditions, the Poisson's ratio value for normal weight of concrete may be taken as 0.15.

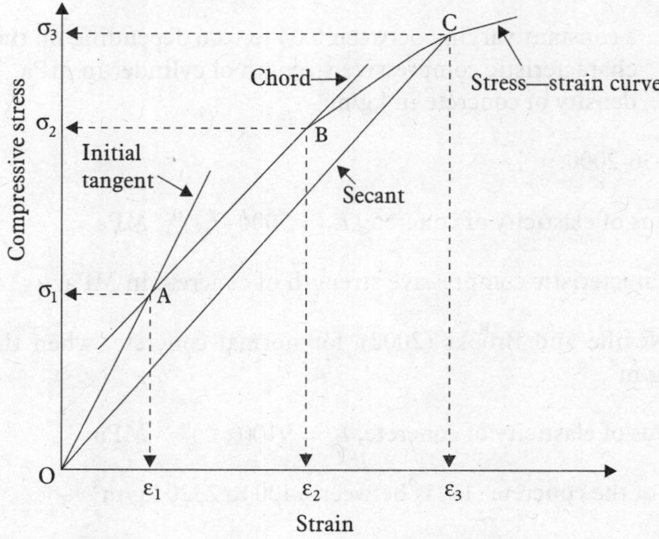

Figure 5.3 *Types of elastic moduli*

The details of the calculation of different types of static modulus values are as follows. With reference to Figure 5.3:

By considering OA,

$$\text{Initial tangent modulus} = \frac{\sigma_1}{\varepsilon_1} \tag{5.3}$$

By considering AB,

$$\text{Chord modulus} = \frac{\sigma_2 - \sigma_1}{\varepsilon_2 - \varepsilon_1} \tag{5.4}$$

By considering OC,

$$\text{Secant modulus} = \frac{\sigma_3}{\varepsilon_3} \tag{5.5}$$

Dynamic modulus of concrete is also determined by a non-destructive testing (NDT) method called electro-dynamic or ultrasonic pulse velocity method. In general, the dynamic modulus values are more than the static modulus of elasticity values. The ratio between static and dynamic modulus may be taken as 0.8 (IRC: 58-2002). Details of the above test procedure may be obtained from IS: 516-1959 and ASTM C 469.

The following relationships may be suitably used to estimate the elastic modulus value of cement concrete for a typical value of normal weight and compressive strength.

According to Carse and Behan (Carse and Beehan 1980),

$$\text{Elastic modulus of concrete} = C \times W^{1.5}(f_c)^{0.5}\ \text{MPa} \tag{5.6}$$

where C = a constant varying between 0.04 to 0.06 depending on the type of concrete
f_c = characteristic compressive strength of cylinder in MPa
W = density of concrete in kg/m^3.

According to IS: 456-2000,

$$\text{Static modulus of elasticity of concrete, } E_s = 5000\,(f_{ck})^{0.5}\ \text{MPa} \tag{5.7}$$

where f_{ck} is the characteristic compressive strength of concrete in MPa.

According to Neville and Brooks (2002), for normal concrete, when the density of the concrete is 2320 kg/m^3,

$$\text{Static modulus of elasticity of concrete, } E_s = 9100\,(f_c)^{0.33}\ \text{MPa} \tag{5.8}$$

When the density of the concrete (W) is between 1400 to 2320 kg/m^3

$$\text{Static modulus of elasticity of concrete, } E_s = 1700\,W^2(f_c)^{0.33}\ \text{MPa} \tag{5.9}$$

where f_c is the cube compressive strength of concrete in MPa.

According to the ACI Building Code 318-89 (Neville and Brooks 2002),

$$\text{Static modulus of elasticity of concrete, } E_s = 4700(f_c)^{0.5} \text{ MPa} \tag{5.10}$$

where f_c is the cylinder compressive strength of concrete in MPa.

According to the ACI 318 Code (ACI Committee 318-1996; Nawy 1997),

$$\text{Concrete modulus} = 0.043\, W^{1.5}\, (f_c)^{0.5} \text{ MPa} \tag{5.11}$$

where compressive strength (f_c) up to 42 MPa and density of concrete (W) for normal and light weight concrete is 2400 and 1765 kg/m^3 respectively.

According to the ACI 435 Code (ACI Committee 435-1995; Nawy 1997),

$$\text{Concrete modulus} = (6895 + 3.32(f_c)^{0.5}) \times (W)/2320)^{1.5} \text{ MPa} \tag{5.12}$$

where compressive strength (f_c) ranges from 42 to 83 MPa and density of concrete (W) for normal and light weight concrete is 2400 and 1765 kg/cm^3 respectively.

According to the UK practice of BS: 8110 (Part 2)-1985 (Neville and Brooks 2002),

$$\text{Modulus of elasticity at 28 days} = 20000 + 0.2 \times f_c \tag{5.13}$$

where f_c is the cube strength at 28 days. Equation (5.13) is valid for normal weight aggregate concrete.

For the thickness design and prediction of deformations of concrete pavements, the average value of the static modulus of elasticity of concrete is required. It depends upon the cement type, the ingredients of the concrete, the proportion, the prevailing construction practices and the testing procedures adopted. Different organisations prescribe different values (Table 5.7). When actual test results are not available, an appropriate selection of a suitable static elastic value may be made.

Table 5.7 *Values of static modulus of elasticity of concrete (IRC: 58-2002; Neville and Brooks 2002)*

Sl.No.	Static modulus of elasticity of concrete (MPa)	Concrete grade	According to
1	Mean values: 28,000	M40	BS: 8110 (Part 2)-1985
2	Mean values: 32,000	M40	The ACI Building Code 318-89
3	Mean values: 28,000		PCA, USA
4	21,000; 28,000; 35,000; 42,000; 49,000		AASHTO
5	Between 35,000 to 40,000		Croney and Croney
6	Mean values: 29,430 (3×10^5 kg/cm^2)	M40	IRC: 58-2002

5.7.3 Flexural Strength Test

This test is conducted to determine the extreme fibre tensile strength of concrete in pure bending by indirect means. In this test, a concrete beam (150 × 150 × 450 mm) simply supported at its ends is loaded at two points. When concentrated loads are applied, the bottom fibres of the beam experience maximum tensile stresses up to failure. The maximum tensile stress developed may be termed as modulus of rupture. If an unequal settlement of the base course occurs, it causes loss of support by creating voids underneath the pavement. Therefore, the flexural strength or tensile strength in bending of concrete pavement slabs play an important role in resisting traffic wheel loads. This is true even when there is loss of support for distributing the load over a wider area. Hence, the flexural strength property of concrete is a very relevant property to evaluate critical stresses and strains in thickness design of rigid pavements.

In the flexural strength test, a cement concrete beam having standard cross-sectional area (150 ×150 mm) is moulded and compacted according to a given standard specification. The prepared beam is cured for 28 days and tested by applying equal loads at one-third points of the beam (whose effective length of span ranges from 450 or 600 mm) (Figure 5.4). The beam is uniformly loaded at a constant rate (4 to 4.5 kN/minute) until it fails due to fracture. Tensile stresses are induced along the bottom fibre of the beam due to loading. The beam fails by fracture when the bending moment in the beam is unable to withstand the induced tensile stresses. The failure load at fracture and the distance from a nearest support of the fracture is recorded to calculate the flexural strength of the concrete beam.

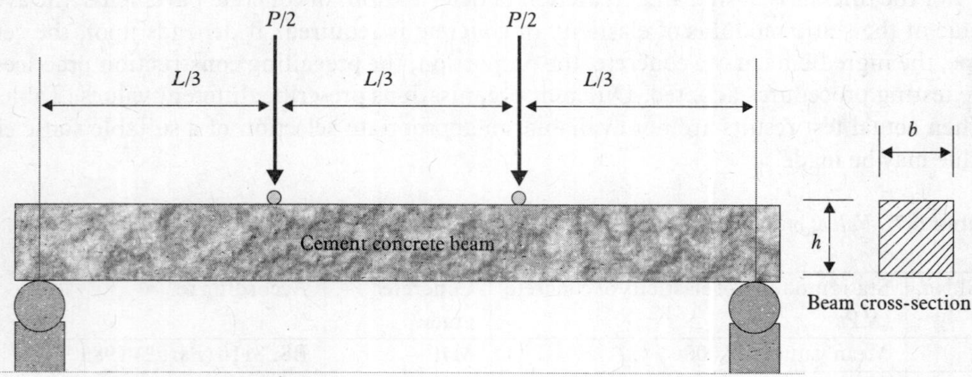

Figure 5.4 *Flexural strength test on cement concrete beam (schematic)*

The following equations are used to calculate the flexural strength of modulus of rupture (MR) of the concrete.

(i) If the fracture occurs in the middle third of the beam (i.e., the horizontal distance in between the application of loads)

$$\mathrm{MR} = PL/(bh^2) \tag{5.14}$$

(ii) If the fracture occurs at one-third distance from any support (i.e., along one end of the beam, one-third distance from a support)

$$\mathrm{MR} = P \times 3a/(bh^2) \tag{5.15}$$

where, P = total load $(P/2+P/2)$
L = span of the beam
b = average breadth of the beam
h = average depth of the beam
a = occurrence of fracture at a minimum distance from the nearest support (the value should not be closer than 5 per cent of the span) or $a=(L/3)-(0.05\times L)$

For more details of the flexural strength test procedure, readers may refer to Codes ASTM C 78-84, IS: 516-1959 and BS: 1881 (Part 118)-1983.

The tensile strength of the concrete may also be estimated by using following equations.

According to IS:456: 2000 and IRC:SP:62-2004,

Flexural strength or modulus of rupture, $f_{cr}=0.7(f_{ck})^{0.5}$ MPa (5.16)

According to PCA (SP: 23-1985, 2001),

Flexural strength of crushed quartzite aggregates, $f_{cr}=0.73(f_c)^{0.5}$ MPa (5.17)

Flexural strength of rounded river pebbles, $f_{cr}=0.48(f_c)^{0.5}$ MPa (5.18)

According to ACI 318-77 (SP: 23-1985, 2001),

Flexural strength of crushed quartzite aggregates, $f_{cr}=0.63(f_c)^{0.5}$ MPa (5.19)

where, f_c is cube compressive strength of concrete in MPa.

According to Croney and Croney (IRC: 58-2002),

Flexural strength or modulus of rupture of gravel aggregates, $f_{cr}=0.49(f_{ck})^{0.55}$ MPa (5.20)

Flexural strength or modulus of rupture of crushed aggregates, $f_{cr}=0.36\,(f_{ck})^{0.7}$ MPa (5.21)

where, f_{ck} is the characteristic compressive strength of concrete in MPa.

According to IRC:76-1979, for design of airfield pavements,

Flexural strength at 28 days, $f_{cr}=(f_c-2.58)/7.63$ MPa (5.22)

where, f_c is the compressive strength of concrete in MPa after 28 days.

Flexural strength of concrete is required for design of concrete pavements. It is more appropriate to determine the flexural strength by experimental methods. The bove- mentioned statistical relationships may result in slight deviations from the values actually measured based on many parameters, viz. cement–type, water–cement ratio, cement–aggregate ratio, compaction method, density, type of admixtures used in concrete, aggregate size, shape and type. However, if such experimental data is not available, a suitable approximate estimation may be made using the above equations. For Indian conditions, based on the type of aggregate, a flexural strength value of 45 kg/cm^2 should be taken for M40 grade of concrete (IRC: 58-2002).

Q: *A few samples of cement concrete mix beams are prepared to determine its flexural strength. The beams are tested at one-third loadings. Calculate the modulus of rupture of concrete beams from the following results of the flexural strength test?*

Specimen 1:

Span of the beam = 450.5 mm
Average breadth of beam = 150.2 mm
Average depth of beam = 150.2 mm
Total failure load = 35,126 N
Location of fracture = 200 mm from a nearest support
Curing period = 7 days

Specimen 2:

Span of the beam = 450 mm
Average breadth of beam = 150.0 mm
Average depth of beam = 149.99 mm
Total failure load = 46,709 N
Location of fracture = 135 mm from a nearest support
Curing period = 28 days

Specimen 3:

Span of the beam = 450 mm
Average breadth of beam = 150.0 mm
Average depth of beam = 150.0 mm
Total failure load = 36,947N
Location of fracture = 90 mm from a nearest support
Curing period = 14 days

Specimen 1:

On substituting the given values in equation (5.14), we get

$$MR = 35{,}126 \times 450/(150.1 \times 150.2^2) = 4.67 \text{ MPa}$$

Specimen 2:

On substituting the given values in equation (5.15), we get

$$MR = 46{,}709 \times 3 \times 135/(150.0 \times 149.99^2) = 5.60 \text{ MPa}$$

Specimen 3:

The minimum distance should be calculated as follows.

$$a = (450/3) - [(5/100) \times 450] = 150 - 22.5 = 127.5 \text{ mm}$$

The value of a is within 5% of the span from a nearest support or 90 mm < 127.5 mm. Hence, the test value may be discarded.

Generally, the ratio of flexural and compressive strengths is determined for correlation purposes. As an example, concrete of grade M25 has a flexural strength of 8 to 13% of compressive strength.

5.7.4 Split Tensile Strength Test

This test is also conducted to determine the tensile strength of concrete by indirect means. A concrete test specimen is made into a cylindrical shape of diameter 150 mm and length 300 mm (or a cubical shape whose size is $\geq$ 150 mm). It is loaded diametrically (Figure 5.5) at a uniform rate of 1.2–2.4 N/mm^2/minute (IS: 5816-1999). On loading, the specimen fails by splitting across the diameter due to the development of tensile stresses on its diametrical plane. The maximum failure load is recorded and the following equation is used to calculate the splitting tensile strength of concrete (IS: 5816-1999).

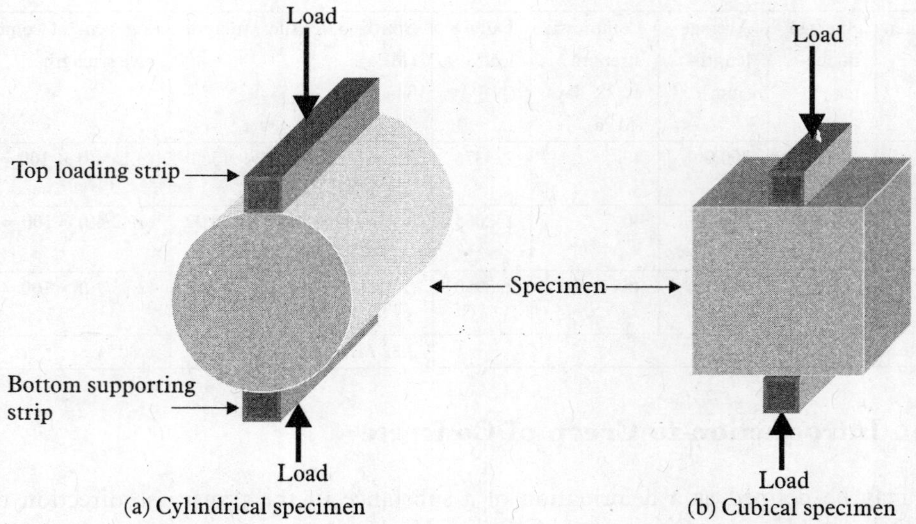

Figure 5.5 *Principle of indirect tensile strength test (schematic)*

$$\text{Splitting tensile strength } (f_{st}) = \frac{2 \times P}{\pi \times D \times L} \tag{5.23}$$

where, P = Maximum failure load (N)
D = Diameter or depth of the specimen (mm)
L = Length or depth of the specimen (mm)

The relevant codes may be referred to for detailed test procedures (IS: 5816-1999; BS: 1881 (Part 117)-1983 and ASTM C 496-90). This test may also be performed on extracted cores from the field. Suitable care should be taken during testing of these cores. The standard test specifications should be strictly followed to obtain consistent and reliable results.

The ratio of the split tensile and compressive strengths of cement concrete is also evaluated to correlate its strength properties. To determine the tensile splitting strength for normal weight concrete, the following equation is recommended by the ACI Committee 363, 1992 and ACI 1997 (Nawy 1997).

$$f_{st} = 0.59 \times (f_c)^{0.5} \tag{5.24}$$

where, f_{st} = Tensile splitting strength of concrete in MPa
f_c = Cylinder compressive strength in MPa

Q: *Calculate the splitting tensile strength of cement concrete from the following test results:*

Specimen	*Average diameter (mm)*	*Average length (mm)*	*Compressive strength at 28 days (MPa)*	*Failure load (N)*
1	*150.0*	*300.0*	*40*	*223376*
2	*149.99*	*300.0*	*40*	*242065*
3	*150.0*	*300.0*	*40*	*238950*

A:

Specimen	Average diameter (mm)	Average length (mm)	Compressive strength at 28 days (MPa)	Failure load (N)	Splitting tensile strength (MPa)	Per cent of compressive strength
1	150.0	300.0	40	223376	$(2 \times 223376)/(\pi \times 150.0 \times 300.0) = 3.16$	$(3.16/40) \times 100 = 7.90$
2	149.99	300.0	40	242065	$(2 \times 242065)/(\pi \times 149.99 \times 300.0) = 3.42$	$(3.42/40) \times 100 = 8.55$
3	150.0	300.0	40	238950	$(2 \times 238950)/(\pi \times 150.0 \times 300.0) = 3.38$	$(3.38/40) \times 100 = 8.45$
Average					3.32 MPa	8.30 %

5.7.5 Introduction to Creep of Concrete

Creep may be defined as a deformation of a substance in the transverse direction due to prolonged static loading. Over a period of time, hardened cement concrete undergoes creep. We can see this kind of deformation in pavements used for parking heavy vehicles or concrete paved layers used for stacking loads at transport terminals, ports and harbours where the concretes are loaded for longer durations of time.

As a function of time, the total deflection due to creep can be calculated by using the following equation (ACI Committee 435, 1995; ACI Committee 318, 1996; Nawy 1997).

$$\Delta_{LT} = \Delta_i + \Delta_i \times C_f \times (t^{0.6} \div (10 + t^{0.6})) \tag{5.25}$$

where, Δ_{LT} = long-term deflection
Δ_i = instantaneous deflection
t = time in days
C_f = ultimate creep factor is 2.35

The creep increases linearly as the temperature increases up to 80 °C. The increase may be about 3 folds at this temperature as compared to ambient temperature (Nawy 1997). This may be one of the reasons why concrete pavements fail to perform satisfactorily during hot summer seasons. In addition, there are other reasons, such as overloading, higher water–cement ratio of mix, change in volume of coarse aggregate, age of concrete and time of loading.

5.8 Design of Cement Concrete Mix

Basically, design of cement concrete mix consists of proportioning its ingredients in order to attain the desired workability, strength, durability and economy. A few of the methods are enumerated below. .

- Arbitrary method
- Minimum void method
- Fineness modulus method
- Talbot–Richart method
- American Concrete Institute (ACI) method
- US Bureau of Reclamation method
- Road note no. 4 method
- British method
- Indian method according to the
    i. Bureau of Indian Standards (IS:10262)
    ii. Indian Roads Congress (IRC:44)

The first four methods are purely empirical and need many trial tests to attain the desired degree of workability and strength even though there is not much change in the quality of the ingredients. The economy as well as the durability of the hardened concrete are also not given due consideration.

The rest of the mix design methods were developed in different countries and are based on standard formulae, correlations, charts and tables which were developed from experience, extensive research and practical considerations on its ingredients, proportioning, compaction methods, density, curing, content of air voids, admixtures, temperature, climatic conditions, quality of materials, durability, strength and finally, cost effectiveness. The inherent basic principles of the different mix design philosophies are similar when the proportions, strength, durability, performance and cost effectiveness are considered. But they slightly differ with respect to variations in mix ingredients, compaction methods, air void content, temperature, corrections due to change in material properties, target strength and purpose of construction by employing standard mathematical and probabilistic methods. In this chapter, the Bureau of Indian Standard method of concrete mix design (IS: 10262) and Indian Roads Congress (IRC: 44) methods are described.

5.9 Factors Considered for Durable Concrete

Besides the quality of materials, compaction methods etc, the following factors also should be considered for the design of durable concrete mix.

- The effect of freezing and thawing on concrete
- Salt and chemical actions

- Differential thermal stresses
- Structurally weak and alkali reactive aggregates
- Water quality
- Leaching and efflorescence
- The action of abrasive and impact loads of traffic
- Shrinkage of concrete

5.10 The Bureau of Indian Standards Method of Cement Concrete Mix Design

The method of cement concrete mix proportioning as recommended by IS: 10262-1982 (MOSRTH 2001) along with the details and factors affecting it are briefly described below.

5.10.1 Methods of Mix Design

According to the Indian Standards, depending on the grade of concrete, the mix is designed on the basis of the absolute volume method (IS: 10262; IS: 456;and IRC:44). The concrete mix design methods are classified into two types, viz. (i) design mix (DM) and (ii) nominal mix design (NMD). The NMD method is adopted when the grade of concrete is lower than or equal to M 20. It is also used for small-scale lean concrete works (IS: 456-2000).

In case of DM, the design strength of concrete is based on the target strength using desired standard deviation and tolerance limits. It is precisely proportioned mostly by weight of ingredients per one cubic metre of cement concrete. Frequent standard quality control tests are usually performed under strict supervision using standard statistical acceptance criteria for calculating its strength requirement. The DM method is suitable and economical for large-scale concreting works using cement concrete mixing plants. For construction of pavements, where the work involves open and expansive land with long track lengths of alignment extending to several kilometers, DM is preferred since a higher grade of concrete is generally prescribed for achieving the desired quality of work. The Indian Standard method of concrete mix design is briefly explained in the following section.

5.10.2 Grade of Concrete

The grade of concrete is designated according to the characteristic compressive strength of a 150 mm size cube of concrete mix which has been cured for 28 days. The grade of any cement concrete is indicated by a letter M followed by its compressive strength value in N/mm^2 or MPa. According to Indian standards, grades of cement concrete are classified into three types—(i) ordinary concrete, (ii) standard concrete and (iii) high strength concrete. The range of compressive strength of ordinary concrete is 10 to 20 N/mm^2, for standard concrete it is 25 to 55 N/mm^2 and for high strength concrete 60 to 80 N/mm^2 (IS: 456-2000). Generally, for construction of highway pavements, standard grade of concrete not lower than M 35 is used. Its flexural strength should not be less than 3.924 N/mm^2 (40 kg/cm^2) (IRC: 101-1988). For sub-base course construction, M10 grade may be used.

No standard method has yet been evolved by the Bureau of Indian Standards for the design of high strength cement concrete.

5.10.3 Type and Quality of Ingredients

The strength and workability of concrete mix is largely dependant on the type of ingredients such as the type of cement, the strength and physical characteristics of mineral aggregates, the quality of water and the type of admixtures used in the concrete. Climatic conditions and temperature are also governing factors (Hall 1932). We have already discussed how these factors affect the mix in Sections 5.1–5.4. To achieve economy in construction, the mix should consist of larger nominal size of aggregates so that the quantity of cement paste required is minimum (the surface area of the larger aggregate particles are comparatively less than finer aggregate particles). But the maximum size of aggregates used for concrete pavement should be based on its compacted thickness. Standard gradations of aggregates are given in IS: 383.

5.10.4 Selection of Water–Cement Ratio (WCR)

For better workability, a suitable and appropriate water–cement ratio (WCR) is selected from standard correlation charts formulated based on research work. It may also be assumed based on experience. Generally, WCR is selected based on the desired compressive strength of cement and concrete. The Bureau of Indian Standards (IS: 10262-2000) has furnished charts for the estimation of WCR based on the desired compressive strength of concrete and cement. Simple regression equations are also developed based on the curves prescribed by BIS (Table 5.8).

Table 5.8 *Water–cement ratios for design of concrete mixes using 28 day compressive strength of cement and concrete. (Useful range of WCR: 0.3 to 0.65)*

Curve type	Equations: WCR = free water–cement ratio by mass; f_{ck} = 28 day compressive strength of concrete in N/mm^2	28 day compressive strength of cement tested (N/mm^2)	Range of f_{ck}	Reference
1	$WCR = 1.5683 - 0.3224 \log_e (f_{ck})$	–	17 to 51	Figure 1 of IS: 10262-2000
A	$WCR = 1.4571 - 0.3195 \log_e (f_c k)$	31.9 to 36.8	13 to 34	Figure 2 of IS: 10262-2000; Tested according to IS: 4031-1968
B	$WCR = 1.5009 - 0.3204 \log_e (f_{ck})$	36.8 to 41.7	14 to 38	
C	$WCR = 1.5076 - 0.3113 \log_e (f_{ck})$	41.7 to 46.6	16 to 43	
D	$WCR = 1.5687 - 0.3191 \log_e (f_{ck})$	46.6 to 51.5	18 to 48	
E	$WCR = 1.5736 - 0.3114 \log_e (f_{ck})$	51.5 to 56.4	19.5 to 53	
F	$WCR = 1.6225 - 0.3178 \log_e (f_{ck})$	56.4 to 61.3	21.5 to 57	

5.10.5 Target Strength

The strength of concrete in terms of compressive strength is a highly sensitive value due to the variation of the quality of ingredients used and their proportioning, mixing, placing, compaction and curing. Therefore, to account for such variation, it is necessary to design the concrete mix for additional strength. This additional strength is known as the target mean strength. According to the IS: 456 and IS: 10262, the target mean strength (F_t) is defined as

$$F_t = f_{ck} + K \times \sigma \tag{5.26}$$

where, f_{ck} = Characteristic compressive strength of concrete in N/mm^2. It may be defined as the average value of compressive strength of standard cubes below which not more than five per cent of the test results are found to fail.

K = A statistical constant representing the tolerance limits desired. From statistical consideration, for a tolerance limit of 1:20, the value is 1.65.

σ = Standard deviation of test values which depends upon the degree of quality control during concrete production and construction. A suitable value may be taken from Table 5.9.

Table 5.9 *Suggested values of standard deviation (Table 1 of IS: 10262-1982)*

Concrete grade	Standard deviation for different degrees of quality control		
	Very good	Good	Fair
M 10	2.0	2.3	3.3
M 15	2.5	3.5	4.5
M 20	3.6	4.6	5.6
M 25	4.3	5.3	6.3
M 30	5.0	6.0	7.0
M 35	5.3	6.3	7.3
M 40	5.6	6.6	7.6
M 45	6.0	7.0	8.0
M 50	6.4	7.4	8.4
M 55	6.7	7.7	8.7
M 60	6.8	7.8	8.8

5.10.6 Selection of Entrapped Air Content

For calculating the quantity of fine and coarse aggregate by volume, it is necessary to determine the quantity of entrapped air in a concrete mix. The entrapped air in the concrete largely depends on the nominal maximum size of aggregate in the concrete. Approximate values of entrapped air content in concrete with nominal maximum sizes of aggregate of 10, 20 and 40 mm may be taken as 3, 2 and 1% respectively (Table 3 of IS: 10262-1982). The maximum size of coarse aggregate used for paving concrete is restricted to 25 mm (MOSRTH 2001).

5.10.7 Selection of Water and Fine Aggregates (FA) or Sand Content

Appropriate quantities of water and FA may be taken according to Table 5.10 for standard conditions.

Table 5.10 *Approximate quantities of water and sand per m^3 of concrete of different grades*

a. Cement grade up to M35 when the water–cement ratio = 0.6 by mass

Aggregate nominal maximum size (mm)	Water content for saturated surface dry aggregate (kg)	Per cent sand of total aggregate by absolute volume
10	208	40
20	186	35
40	165	30

b. Cement grade above M35 when the water–cement ratio = 0.35 by mass

Aggregate nominal maximum size (mm)	Water content for saturated surface dry aggregate (kg)	Per cent sand of total aggregate by absolute volume
10	200	28
20	180	25

Source: Table 4 and 5 of IS: 10262.

The standard conditions taken for mix design are given below.

- Sand or FA should conform to Zone II of IS: 383
- Compacting factor is equal to 0.80
- Rounded aggregates are used
- WCR is equal to 0.35 for M35 grade concrete.

If any deviations are observed with respect to the above standard conditions, suitable adjustments must be made to the quantities of water and sand in the total aggregate of the mix according to Table 5.11.

Table 5.11 *Adjustment of quantities of water and sand for other conditions*

Change in condition stipulated above		Water content adjustment	Adjustment of sand in total aggregate (%)
For sand grades of Table 4 in IS:383	Zone I	0	+ 1.5
	Zone II	0	0.0
	Zone III	0	– 1.5
	Zone IV	0	– 3.0
Increase or decrease in the value of compacting factor by 0.1		± 3 %	0.0
Each 0.05 increase or decrease in free water–cement ratio		0	± 1.0
For rounded aggregates		– 15 kg /cm^2	– 7.0

Source: Table 6 of IS: 10262

5.10.8 Determination of Cement Content

The required cement quantity can be calculated from the values of WCR and the final quantity of water. But in view of durability consideration, the minimum cement quantity should not be less than 250 kg/m^3 and the value of water–cement ratio should not be greater than 0.6 (Fenwick 1982). According to the durability consideration, in any case, the quantity of cement mixed should not be less than the minimum quantity of cement for different exposures given in Table 5.12. Use of higher quantity of cement (more than 550 kg/m^3) does not contribute any additional strength to concrete. It may result in shrinkage, cracking, and creep and becomes uneconomical (SP: 23-1982). According to IS: 456-2000, the maximum quantity of cement, without any fly ash or slag contents, should not be more than 450 kg/m^3. This amount may be increased for special conditions. According to the IRC, the minimum and maximum quantities of cement per cubic metre of paving concrete are prescribed as 350 and 425 kg respectively (MOSRTH 2001). For rural roads, the minimum and maximum quantities of cement should be 310 and 425 kg per cubic metre of concrete respectively (MORD 2004).

Table 5.12 *Appropriate values of minimum cement content, maximum water–cement ratio and minimum grade of concrete for different exposures at maximum nominal aggregate size of 20 mm conditions*

Sl No.	Exposure	Plain concrete			Reinforced Concrete		
		Min. cement content kg/m^3	Max. water–cement ratio	Min. grade of concrete	Min. cement content kg/m^3	Max water–cement ratio	Min. grade of concrete
1	Mild	220	0.60	Not specified	300	0.55	M 20
2	Moderate	240	0.60	M 15	300	0.50	M 25
3	Severe	250	0.50	M 20	320	0.45	M 30
4	Very severe	260	0.45	M 20	340	0.45	M 35
5	Extreme	280	0.40	M 25	360	0.40	M 40

Source: Table 5 of IS: 456: 2000

If the nominal maximum size of aggregate is 20 mm, no adjustment is required for the minimum content of cement. For other nominal maximum sizes of aggregates, viz. 10 and 40 mm, the adjustment for the minimum and maximum cement content should be 40 kg/m^3 extra and 30 kg/m^3 less respectively (IS:456-2000).

5.10.9 Determination of CA and FA Contents

The values of CA and FA or sand quantities per m^3 of concrete may be calculated using the following equations (IS 10262).

$$FA = [10(100 - A_e) - (W_w + C/S_c)] \times \text{FTR} \times S_{fa} \qquad (5.27)$$

$$CA = [10(100 - A_e) - (W_w + C/S_c)] \times (1 - \text{FTR}) \times S_{ca} \qquad (5.28)$$

where, FA = Weight of fine aggregate (kg)
A_e = Entrapped air content (%) based on the nominal max. size of aggregate
W_w = Weight of water (kg)
C = Weight of cement (kg)
FTR = Ratio of fine aggregate to total aggregate by absolute volume
CA = Weight of coarse aggregate (kg)
S_c, S_{fa} and S_{ca} = Specific gravity of cement, fine aggregate and coarse aggregate respectively

5.10.10 Corrections for Water Absorption and Free Surface Moisture Content

Necessary corrections towards water content in coarse and fine aggregates should be made based on water absorption by aggregates and free surface moisture on aggregates. If free moisture is present on the surface of aggregates, the moisture content should be deducted from the total computed water content and the same quantity of aggregates should be added to the aggregates content. But if aggregates tend to absorb water, the quantity of water likely to be lost by absorption should be added to the total water content and the same quantity of aggregate should be deducted from the aggregates content.

Generally, for convenience, mix designs are carried out under oven-dry conditions. Suitable allowance has to be made towards the hygroscopic moisture content of ingredients at room temperature. In wet samples, differentiation of free moisture content should be made from the moisture content obtained at room temperature. During mix design, room temperature and climatic conditions of the day should be mentioned. These details should be quoted to make adjustments for field conditions.

The procedure for determining the proportion of different ingredients of concrete according to the Indian Standard method is given in Figure 5.4. The following problem illustrates the details of the calculations involved in mix design.

Q: *Design cement concrete mix proportions for the following requirements:*

Design requisites:

Characteristic compressive strength of cube at 28 days = 30 N/mm²
Maximum size of aggregate = 20 mm
Shape of aggregate = crushed stone having angular shape
Degree of workability = 0.78 of compacting factor
Quality control = very good
Exposure type = mild
Materials test data:
Cement type = OPC
Cement strength at 28 days = 52 N/mm²
Specific gravity of cement = 3.15
Specific gravity of coarse aggregate (CA) = 2.60
Specific gravity of fine aggregate (FA) = 2.58
Water absorbed in coarse aggregate (CA) = 0.48 %

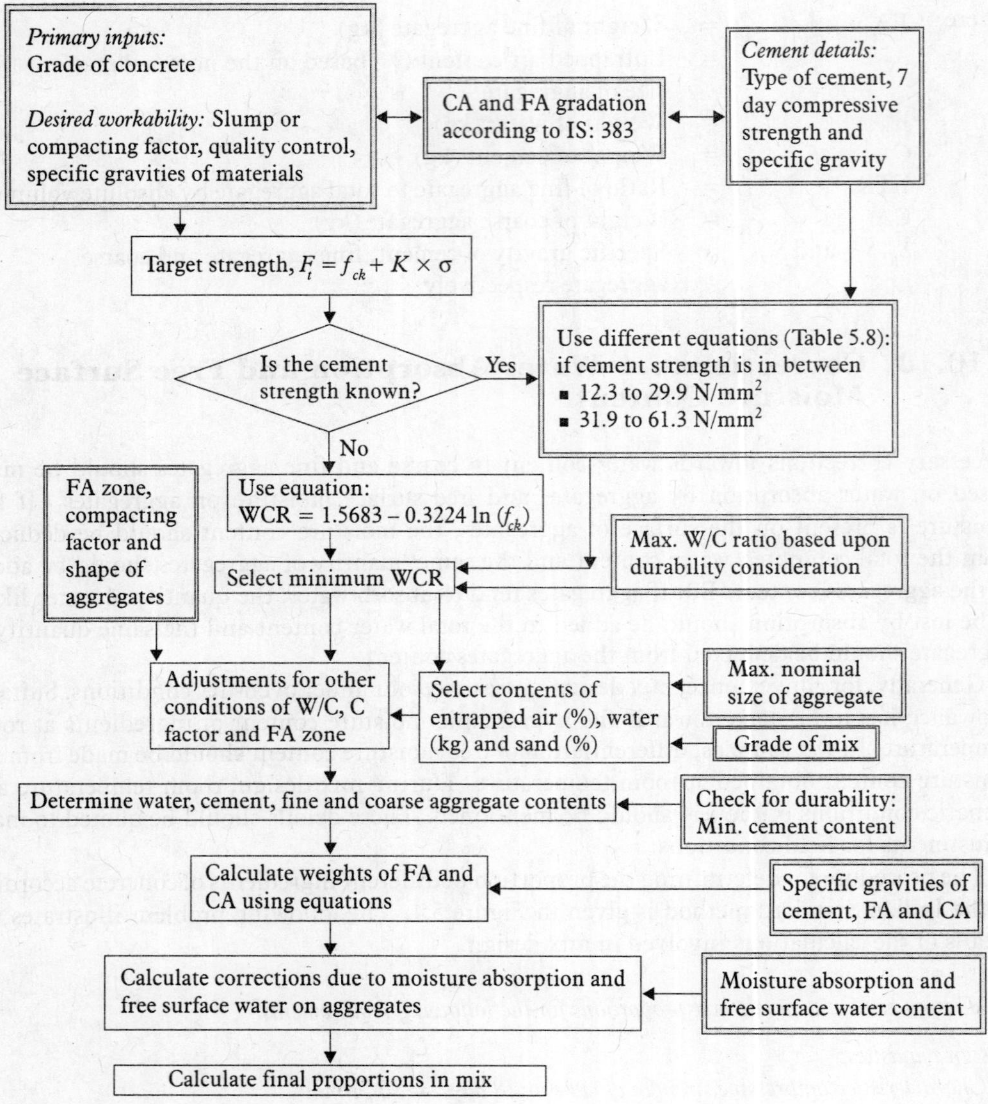

Figure 5.4 *Flow chart for design of cement concrete mix according to Indian standards*

Water absorbed in fine aggregate (FA) = 0.98 %
Free surface moisture present in coarse aggregate (CA) = 0 %
Free surface moisture present in fine aggregate (FA) = 1.8 %
Gradation of coarse and fine aggregates conform to Table 2 of IS:383 and Zone III of Table 4 of IS: 383 respectively.

A: (i) *Target mean compressive strength:*

$$F_t = f_{ck} + K \times \sigma$$

where $f_{ck} = 30$ N/mm^2, $K = 1.65$, $\sigma = 5.0$ (since, the quality control is very good).

$F_t = 30 + 1.65 \times 5.0 = 38.25$ N/mm^2

(ii) *Select minimum water–cement ratio (WCR)*:

The cement strength = 52 MPa, from curve E of Table 5.8:

WCR = 1.5736 – 0.3114 $\log_e (f_{ck})$

On substitution, we get, WCR = WCR = 1.5736 – 0.3114 $\log_e$ (38.25) = 0.438

For durability consideration, from Table 5.10, WCR = 0.6. Therefore, take WCR = 0.438 as minimum value.

(iii) *Quantities of water and fine aggregate (FA)*:

Select the above quantities from IS: 10262 of Table 5.10 (a).

Water quantity = 186 kg and FA quantity = 35% of the total aggregate by absolute volume, when compacting factor is 0.8, WCR is 0.60 and FA conforms to Zone II.

(iv) *Adjustments in water and FA quantities since the above selected quantities belong to standard conditions:*

The above quantities should be adjusted to the present requirements.

Change in values	Adjustment in	
Proposed WCR = 0.438	Water (%)	FA (%)
Standard WCR = 0.60 Change in WCR= (0.438 – 0.60)= – **0.162** Adjust @ of 1.0 % for each 0.05 change	0	(–0.162/0.05)×1 = – 3.24
Proposed compacting factor = 0.78 Standard compacting factor = 0.8 Change in compacting = 0.78 – 0.8= **–0.02** Adjust @ of 3.0 % for each 0.1 change	(–0.02/0.1)×3 = – 0.6	0
For FA conforming to Zone III, adjust @ of –1.5 % of FA quantity	0	–1.5
Total =	–0.6	–4.74

Therefore,

Water quantity = 186 + (–0.6/100) ×186 = 184.88 kg

FA quantity = 35 + (–4.74) = 30.26 %

Ratio of FA to total aggregate by absolute volume (FTR) = 30.26/100 = 0.3026

(v) *Cement:*

If WCR = 0.438 and water quantity (W_w) = 184.88 kg,

Cement quantity (C) = 184.88 /0.438 = 422.1 kg < 425 kg, O.K.

(which is less than the maximum recommended by IRC)

(vi) *Determination of CA & FA quantities per m^3 of concrete*:

According to Table 3, IS 10262, entrapped air (A_e) = 2% for 20 mm max. nominal size of aggregate. On substituting in the following equations, we get,

$$\text{FA} = [10(100 - A_e) - (W_w + C/S_c)] \times \text{FTR} \times S_{fa}$$

$$\text{FA} = [10(100 - 2) - (184.88 + 422.1/3.15)] \times 0.3026 \times 2.58 = 516.13 \text{ kg}$$

$$CA = [10(100 - A_e) - (W_w + C/S_c)] \times (1 - FTR) \times S_{ca}$$
$$CA = [10(100 - 2) - (184.88 + 422.1/3.15)] \times (1 - 0.302) \times 2.60 = 1198.75 \text{ kg}$$

(vii) *Mix proportions in kg per m³ of concrete*:

Water (W_w)	Cement (C)	FA	CA
184.88	422.1	516.13	1198.75

Mix proportions in kg per one bag of cement:

Water (W_w)	Cement (C)	FA	CA
21.9	50	61.13	142.0

Mix proportions (per m³) by ratio:

W/C	C/C	FA/C	CA/C
0.438	1	1.222	2.839

(viii) *Corrections due to moisture absorption and free surface water on aggregates per m³ of concrete:*
Additional quantity of water to be added to CA due to absorption of moisture = 0.48 % by mass of CA = (0.48/100) × 1198.75 = + 5.75 kg

Note: There is no need to consider the water absorbed by FA (i.e. 0.98%) in this problem because the FA has free (surface) moisture so that there is no possibility of further absorption of water.

Reduction in the water content due to the presence of free moisture in FA = 1.8 % of FA = (1.8/100) × 516.13 = −9.29 kg

The final corrections in the ingredients in kg per one cubic metre of concrete are as follows:

	Water (W_w)	Cement (C)	FA	CA
	184.88	422.1	516.13	1198.75
For CA	+ 5.75	–	–	– 5.75
For FA	– 9.29	–	+ 9.29	
Total (kg)	**181.34**	**422.1**	**525.42**	**1193.0**

Three more trial mixes should be prepared by varying the quantity of WCR by ± 10 %. These trial mixes should be tested for compacting factor and 28-day compressive strength. To get the desired compacting factor or workability and strength, suitable adjustments—by adding or deducting the quantity of water, cement and fine aggregate—may be made. The mix proportion after these adjustments is called job mix formula. If the concrete is produced by mechanised plants, the proportions of the mix ingredients should be verified and adjusted, if required, according to the site conditions.

In case of higher grades of concrete, when WRC is less than 0.35, the concrete mix will become stiff and harsh. In such cases, to improve its workability, a suitable super-plasticiser of stipulated quantity as prescribed by its manufacturer should be mixed as admixture to the concrete mixture.

5.11 Indian Roads Congress Method of Cement Concrete Mix Design (IRC: 44-2008)

In the IRC method (IRC: 44-2008), the mix proportions are determined based on the absolute volume of the ingredients, similar to the mix design of IS: 10262, except with a few changes. The following are the major modifications made in the second revision of IRC: 44-2008

(a) Normal concrete pavements should be constructed with minimum M40 grade concrete having flexural strength of 4.5 MPa. In case of rural roads, minimum M30 grade concrete having flexural strength of 3.8 MPa is used. For whitetopping works, high performance concrete of grade M50 is prescribed.

(b) The absolute volume of air in the mix is considered as nil. However, to counter freezing and thawing effect, air-entraining agents are used to allow the air volume in the mix to be 5±1.5 per cent for nominal aggregate size of 20 mm. To control bleeding and segregation of concrete, up to 2 per cent of air volume may be used.

(c) Tentative guidelines are recommended for the (initial) selection of standard deviation of compressive cube strength, water–cement ratio, water content and volume of coarse aggregate. Necessary adjustments should be made to proportions of mix ingredients according to test results of trial mixes/ batches.

(d) To enhance the properties of concrete mix such as ductility, resistance to abrasion and fatigue life, use of steel, granulated blast furnace slag, metakaoline, silica fume (5 to 10 per cent by mass of cementitious material in mix), fly ash (up to 20 per cent by mass of cementitious materials) and polymeric fibres (0.2 to 0.4 per cent by mass of cement) are recommended.

(e) According to IS: 9103, the fresh concrete mix workability can be improved by using super-plasticisers, plasticisers and retarders up to 2, 1 and 0.5 per cent respectively.

(f) Temperature of the concrete at the time of placement should be preferably in between 5 to 30 °C.

There are further details.

(g) Design strength of the concrete in terms of flexural strength and target mean strength should be determined using equations (5.17) and (5.26) respectively.

(h) Standard deviation of the test strength should be determined from not less than 30 samples of concrete mix obtained from the site after the first batch. However, a suitable value may be assumed at the preliminary stage of trials as 5.0 and 6.0 N/mm^2 for proper site control and poor site control conditions respectively when the concrete grade is M30 and above.

(i) Preliminary selection of water–cement ratio (WCR) should be made from established relationships based on cube compressive strength after 28 days, aggregate gradation, maximum size, texture and other relevant data. If such data is not available, the values in Table 5.13 may be used for preliminary selection of WCR.

(j) The approximate quantity of water used for concrete, for 20 ± 5 mm slump, at WCR 0.5, has been presented in the first two columns (shaded part) of Table 5.10(a). These values are applicable when the concrete mix is made without using super-plasticiser/ plasticiser. The prescribed quantity of water (in Table 5.10(a), first two columns) should be *reduced* for the following conditions.

Table 5.13 *Water–cement ratios*

Concrete grade	Water–cement ratio (WCR) ⋆
M25	0.50
M30	0.45
M35	0.42
M40	0.38
M50	0.34
M60	0.28

Source: IRC: 44-2008

⋆ If mineral admixtures are used in the mix, they should be considered in the WCR calculation and the ratio is to be referred to as water–cementitious material ratio (WCMR).

(i) 10 kg when sub-angular aggregate is used; 20 kg when gravel with some crushed particles is used; and 25 kg when rounded gravel is used, to produce similar workability.

(ii) 5 to 10 per cent by mass of cementitious material when plasticiser is used; and, 20 to 30 per cent by mass of cementitious material when super-plasticisers are used. However, reduced water quantity may be adjusted according to the actual quantity and type of plasticiser/ super-plasticiser used during preparation of trial batches.

(k) The minimum quantity of cement should not be less than 325 kg/m^3 and the maximum quantity should not exceed 425 kg/m^3, exclusive of cementitious materials used as mineral admixtures.

(l) The CA gradation should conform to Table 5.3 (Table 2 of IS: 383). Estimation of the approximate volume of coarse aggregates (CA) per 1 m^3 of concrete is determined from Table 5.14.

Table 5.14 *Volume of angular coarse aggregates (in SSD condition) per 1 m^3 of total aggregate when WCR = 0.5*

Nominal max. size of aggregate (mm)	For zones of fine aggregate according to IS:383 ⋆			
	Zone I	Zone II	Zone III	Zone IV
40	0.69	0.71	0.73	0.75
20	0.60	0.62	0.64	0.66
10	0.44	0.46	0.48	0.50

Source: IRC: 44-2008

⋆ For every decrease of 0.05 in WCR, the above values should be increased by 0.01.

(m) The volume of fine aggregates (FA) per 1 m^3 of concrete should be obtained by deducting the volume of CA from unit volume of concrete (i.e., FA = 1.00 – CA). The FA gradation should conform to Table 5.4 (Table 4 of IS: 383) and the details furnished in Para 4.3.2 of IS: 383 are applicable.

A few worked out examples of concrete mix design and proportioning according to IRC: 44 (2008) are presented below.

Q. *Determine the minimum specified concrete strength at 28 days, for the following data:*
Grade of concrete = M60 @ flexural strength = 5.42 N/mm²
For quality control: (a) proper site control and (b) poor site control.
Assume the required data to be according to IS/ IRC standards.

A: By equation (5.26), target (or design) mean strength, $F_t = f_{ck} + K \times \sigma$

Assume K value as 1.65 at tolerance limit of 1:20; and σ value as 5.0 N/mm² for proper site control and 6.0 N/mm² for poor site control (Refer to Section 5.11(h)).

For quality control: (a) Proper site control

$$F_t = 60 + 1.65 \times 5.0 = 60 + 8.25 = 68.25 \text{ N/mm}^2$$

(b) Poor site control

$$F_t = 60 + 1.65 \times 6.0 = 60 + 9.90 = 69.90 \text{ N/mm}^2$$

By equation (5.16), flexural strength or modulus of rupture of concrete, $f_{cr} = 0.7 \times (f_{ck})^{0.5}$

For quality control: (a) Proper site control

Design flexural strength $= f_{cr} = 0.7 \times (68.25)^{0.5} = 5.78$ N/mm²

(b) Poor site control

Design flexural strength $= f_{cr} = 0.7 \times (69.90)^{0.5} = 5.85$ N/mm²

Similarly, the procedure may be adopted for other grades of concrete.

The following examples illustrate proportioning of concrete mix.

Q: *Design cement concrete mix proportions, according to IRC: 44 (2008), for the data given below:*

Design requisites:

Grade of concrete = M40
Maximum nominal size of aggregate = 20 mm
Shape of aggregate = crushed stone having angular shape
Workability in terms of slump = 20 ± 5 mm
Quality control = Poor site control
Minimum cement content=325 kg per 1m³
Maximum cement content=425 kg per 1m³

Materials test data:

Cement type = OPC grade 43
Chemical admixture type = Super-plasticiser
Specific gravity of cement, $S_c = 3.15$
Specific gravity of coarse aggregate, $S_{ca} = 2.60$
Specific gravity of fine aggregate, $S_{fa} = 2.58$
Water absorbed in coarse aggregate = 0.48 %
Water absorbed in fine aggregate = 0.98 %

Free surface moisture present in coarse aggregate (CA) = 0 %
Free surface moisture present in fine aggregate (FA) = 1.8 %
Gradation of coarse and fine aggregates conform to Table 2 of IS: 383 and Zone III of Table 4 of IS: 383 respectively.
Sieve analysis:

IS sieve size (mm)	*Desired final gradation after blending aggregates (From Table 5.3, for maximum nominal size of aggregate 20 mm)*	*Sieve analysis, % passing*		*% passing of individual type of aggregates (mm)*		*Combined Gradation, 100 % (with reference to column 2) (5+6=7)*
		Material Type 1 (20 to 10 mm)	*Material Type 2 (10 mm down)*	*Material Type 1 59% (0.59 × 3=5)*	*Material Type 2 41% (0.41 × 4 = 6*	
1	**2**	**3**	**4**	**5**	**6**	**7**
20	*95–100*	*100.00*	*100.00*	*59.00*	*41.00*	*100.00 (OK)*
10	*25–55*	*3.10*	*81.21*	*1.83*	*33.27*	*35.10 (OK)*
4.75	*0–10*	*Nil*	*9.40*	*0.00*	*3.85*	*3.85 (OK)*

A: (*i*) *Target mean compressive strength:*

$$F_t = f_{ck} + K \times \sigma$$

where $f_{ck} = 40$ N/mm^2, $K = 1.65, \sigma = 6.0$ (since the quality control at site is poor).

$$F_t = 40 + 1.65 \times 6.0 = 49.9 \text{ N/mm}^2$$

Design flexural strength = $f_{cr} = 0.7 \times (49.90)^{0.5} = 4.94$ N/mm^2

(*ii*) *Minimum water–cement ratio (WCR)*:

From Table 5.13, for M40 grade, WCR = 0.38.

(*iii*) *Quantity of water*:

Select the water quantity from Table 5.10 (a) of shaded columns. For 20 mm aggregate, mix without super-plasticiser @ WCR = 0.5, for 20 ± 5 mm slump,

Water quantity = 186 kg

According to Section 5.11 j(ii), reduce water content by 18% to account for the use of super-plasticiser in the mix.

$$\text{Reduced water quantity } (W_w) = 186 \times \frac{(100 - 18)}{100} = 152.52 \text{ kg}$$

(*iv*) *Cement content*:

WCR = 0.38

Water quantity (W_w) = 152.52 kg per 1 m^3

Therefore, cement quantity (C) = 152.52 /0.38 = 401.1 kg per m^3 < 425 kg, O.K. (which is more than the minimum (325 kg per m^3) recommended according to IRC:15) (*v*) *CA and FA quantities per m³ of concrete:*

From Table 5.14, for aggregates of 20 mm nominal max. size and FA grading zone III, volume of CA = 0.64 per m³ of total aggregates @ WCR = 0.5.

The present WCR = 0.38. Therefore, the CA content has to be increased by 0.01, for every decrease of 0.05 in WCR.

$$\text{Increased volume of coarse aggregate (VCA)} = 0.64 + \left(\frac{0.5 - 0.38}{0.05}\right) \times 0.01 = 0.664$$

Volume of fine aggregate (VFA) = 1−VCA = 1 − 0.664 = 0.336 per m³

(*vi*) *Volumetric analysis of mix ingredients per m³ of concrete:*

Volume of cement concrete (VCM) = 1 m³

Volume of cement $(V_c) = (C/S_c) \times (1/1000) = (401.1/3.15) \times (1/1000) = 0.1273$

Volume of water $(V_w) = (W_w/S_w) \times (1/1000) = (152.52/1.00) \times (1/1000) = 0.1525$

Volume of chemical admixture (V_{CADM}) = (Weight of chemical admixture/Specific gravity of chemical admixture) × (1/1000) = (2.81/1.21) × (1/1000) = 0.00232 m³

(Content of super-plasticiser taken as 0.7% by mass of cementitious material

$$= \left(\frac{0.7}{100}\right) \times 401.1 = 2.81 \text{ kg}).$$

$$\text{Volume of all aggregates in mix } (V_{AAM}) = V_{CM} - (V_c + V_w + V_{CADM})$$
$$= 1 - (0.1273 + 0.1525 + 0.00232) = \mathbf{0.7178} \text{ m}^3$$

$$\text{Mass of CA (CA)} = V_{AAM} \times V_{CA} \times S_{CA} \times 1000 = \mathbf{0.7178} \times 0.664 \times 2.60 \times 1000$$
$$= 1239.2 \text{ kg/m}^3$$

$$\text{Mass of FA (FA)} = V_{AAM} \times V_{FA} \times S_{FA} \times 1000 = \mathbf{0.7178} \times 0.336 \times 2.58 \times 1000$$
$$= 622.2 \text{ kg/m}^3$$

(*vii*) *At Trial 1: Mix proportions in kg per m³ of concrete based on aggregates in SSD condition*:

WCR	Water (W_w)	Cement (C)	FA	CA	CADM
0.38	152.52	401.1	622.2	1239.2	2.81

Mix proportions (per m³) by ratio:

W/C	C/C	FA/C	CA/C	CADM/C
0.38	1	1.3019	3.0895	0.0562

Mix proportions in kg per one bag of cement:

Water (W_w)	Cement (C)	FA	CA	CADM
19	50	77.561	154.475	0.226

(*viii*) *Corrections due to moisture absorption and free surface water on aggregates per m³ of concrete:*

Additional quantity of water to be added to account for absorption of moisture by CA = 0.48 % by mass of CA = (0.48/100) × 1239.2 = + 5.948 kg

Reduction in water content due to presence of free moisture in FA = 1.8 % of FA = (1.8/100) × 622.2 = − 11.2 kg

The final corrections in the ingredients in kg per one cubic metre of concrete are as follows:

@ WCR = 0.38	Water (W_w)	Cement (C)	FA	CA	CADM
	152.52	401.1	622.2	1239.2	—
For CA	+ 5.948	—	—	– 5.948	—
For FA	– 11.2	—	+ 11.2	—	—
Total (kg)	**147.268**	**401.1**	**633.4**	**1233.252**	**2.81**

(*ix*) With the above calculated proportions, a trial mix should be prepared and the proportions of water, cement and chemical admixture should be adjusted to achieve required workability in terms of slump value and durability requirements.

(*x*) With the above adjusted proportions, two other trial mixes should be prepared by varying the quantity of WCR by ± 10%. These trial mixes should be tested again for slump or compacting factor and compressive strength. To get the desired slump or workability and strength, suitable adjustments should be made by adding or deducting the quantity of water, cement and chemical admixture. The final content of the cement should be checked to see if it satisfies the criteria of minimum and maximum allowable values according to IRC: 15. The mix proportions after these adjustments are called job mix formula.

(*xi*) In ready mix concrete (RMC), the contents of water, chemical admixtures and other ingredients are suitably adjusted to achieve desired workability or slump value at initial point (i.e., before transit) and at the time of placement.

Q: *Calculate proportions of concrete mix ingredients if fly ash is intended to be used in the mix which was proportioned in the above problem, according to IRC:44-2008. The data given is:*
Assume (a) *content of fly ash to be used = 16 per cent of the total cementitious material content.*
(*b*) *the cementitious material content should be increased by 12 per cent of the total cementitious material content to account for reactivity of fly ash.*

A: Let us take the necessary values (as inputs) from the above solved problem.

(*i*) *Contents of cement and fly ash*:
WCR = 0.38
Cement content = 152.52/0.38 = 401.36 kg/m^3
Cementitious material content (CM) = 401.36 × 1.12 = 449.53 kg/m^3
Water content = 152.52 kg/m^3
Therefore, water–cementitious material ratio (WCMR) = 152.52/ 449.53 = 0.339
Fly ash @ 16 per cent of total cementitious material content (FLY) = 449.53 × 16/100 ≈ 71.92 kg/m^3
Therefore, cement content = 449.53 – 71.92 = 377.61 kg/m^3 > 325 and < 425 kg/m^3; OK.

(*ii*) *Volume proportion of CA and FA contents*: From Table 5.14, for aggregates of 20 mm nominal max. size and FA grading zone III, volume of CA = 0.64 per m^3 of total aggregates @ WCR = 0.5.

The present revised WCR = WCMR = 0.339. Therefore, increase the CA content by about 0.01, for every decrease of 0.05 in WCR.

Increased volume of coarse aggregate (VCA)= $0.64 + \left(\frac{0.5 - 0.339}{0.05}\right) \times 0.01 = 0.6722$

Volume of fine aggregate (VFA) = 1 – VCA = 1 – 0.6722 = 0.3278 per m^3

(*iii*) *Volumetric analysis of mix ingredients per m^3 of concrete:*

Volume of cement concrete (VCM) = 1 m^3.

Volume of cement (V_c) = (C/S_c) × (1/1000) = (377.61 /3.15) × (1/1000)

= 0.1198 m^3

Volume of fly ash (V_{FLY}) = (FLY/S_{fly}) × (1/1000) = (71.92/2.3) × (1/1000)

= 0.0312 m^3

Volume of water (V_w) = (W_w/S_w) × (1/1000) = (152.52/1.00) × (1/1000) = 0.1525 m^3

Volume of chemical admixture (V_{CADM}) = (weight of chemical admixture/specific gravity of chemical admixture) × (1/1000) = (4.04/1.21) × (1/1000) = 0.0033 m^3

(Content of super-plasticiser taken as 0.9% by mass of cementitious material

$= \left(\frac{0.9}{100}\right) \times 449.53 = 4.04$ kg).

Volume of fly ash in all in aggregates (V_{FAA}) = V_{CM} – (V_C + V_{FLY} + V_W + V_{CADM})

$= 1 - (0.1198 + 0.0312 + 0.1525 + 0.0033)$

$= 0.6932$ m^3

Mass of CA (CA) = $V_{FAA} \times V_{CA} \times S_{CA} \times 1000$ = **0.6932** × 0.6722 × 2.60 × 1000

= 1211.51 kg/m^3

Mass of FA (FA) = $V_{FAA} \times V_{FA} \times S_{FA} \times 1000$ = **0.6932** × 0.3278 × 2.58 × 1000

= 586.25 kg/m^3

(*iv*) *At Trial 1: Mix proportions in kg per m^3 of concrete based on aggregates in SSD condition*:

WCMR	Water (W_w)	Cement (C)	Fly ash (FLY)	FA	CA	CADM
0.339	152.52	377.61	71.92	586.25	1211.51	4.04

(*v*) *Corrections due to moisture absorption and free surface water on aggregates per m^3 of concrete:*

Additional quantity of water to be added to account for absorption of moisture by CA

= 0.48 % by mass of CA = (0.48/100) × 1211.51 = + 5.815 kg

Reduce the water content due to the presence of free moisture in FA = 1.8% of FA

= (1.8/100) × 586.25 = – 10.552 kg

The final corrections in the ingredients in kg per one cubic metre of concrete are as follows:

These values are @ WCMR = 0.339	Water (W_w)	Cement (C)	FA	CA	Fly ash (FLY)	CADM
	152.52	377.61	586.25	1211.51	–	–
For CA	+ 5.815	–	–	– 5.815	–	–
For FA	– 10.552	–	+ 10.552	–	–	–
Total (kg) =	**147.783**	**377.61**	**596.802**	**1205.695**	**71.92**	**4.04**

(*vi*) The procedure explained in (ix) to (xi) of the previous solved problem remain the same with the fly ash cement concrete mix also.

Q: *Design cement concrete mix proportions* according *to IRC: 44 (2008) for the data given below:*

Design requisites:

Grade of concrete = M50

Maximum nominal size of aggregate = 20 mm

Shape of aggregate = crushed and angular shape

Workability in terms of slump= 20 ± 5 mm

Minimum water–cement ratio = 0.40

Quality control = Good site control

Minimum cement content=325 kg per 1m^3

Maximum cement content=425 kg per 1m^3

Materials test data:

Cement type = OPC grade 43

Chemical admixture type = Super-plasticiser

Specific gravity of cement, $S_c = 3.15$

Specific gravity of silica fume, $S_{sf} = 2.20$

Specific gravity of coarse aggregate, $S_{ca} = 2.60$

Specific gravity of fine aggregate, $S_{fa} = 2.58$

Water absorbed in coarse aggregate = 0.48 %

Water absorbed in fine aggregate = 0.98 %

Free surface moisture present in coarse aggregate (CA) = 0 %

Free surface moisture present in fine aggregate (FA) = 1.8 %

Gradation of coarse and fine aggregates conform to Table 2 of IS: 383 and Zone III of Table 4 of IS: 383 respectively.

Sieve analysis:

IS sieve size (mm)	*Desired final gradation after blending aggregates (From Table 5.3, for maximum nominal size of aggregate 20 mm)*	*Sieve analysis, % passing*		*% passing of individual type of aggregates (mm)*		*Combined Gradation, 100 %*
		Material Type 1 (20 to 10 mm)	*Material Type 2 (10 mm down)*	*Material Type 1 61% (0.61 × 3=5)*	*Material Type 2 39% (0.39 × 4 = 6*	*(with reference to column 2) (5+6=7)*
1	2	3	4	5	6	7
20	*95–100*	*100.00*	*100.00*	*61.00*	*39.00*	*100.00 (OK)*
10	*25–55*	*2.91*	*80.71*	*1.77*	*31.47*	*33.24 (OK)*
4.75	*0–10*	*Nil*	*9.35*	*0.00*	*3.64*	*3.64 (OK)*

A:(*i*) *Target mean compressive strength*:

$F_t = f_{ck} + K \times \sigma$

where $f_{ck} = 50$ N/mm^2, $K = 1.65$, $\sigma = 5.0$ (since the quality control at site is good).

$F_t = 50 + 1.65 \times 5.0 = 58.25$ N/mm^2

Design flexural strength $= f_{cr} = 0.7 \times (58.25)^{0.5} = 5.34$ N/mm^2

(*ii*) *Minimum water–cement ratio (WCR)*:

From Table 5.13, for M50 grade, WCR = 0.34, which is less than max. of 0.4, OK.

(*iii*) *Quantity of water*:

Select the water quantity from Table 5.10 (a) of shaded columns. For 20 mm aggregate, mix without super-plasticiser @ WCR = 0.5, for 20 ± 5 mm slump,

Water quantity = 186 kg

As mentioned in Section 5.11 (j (ii)), reduce water content by 25% to account for the use of super-plasticiser in the mix.

$$\text{Reduced water quantity } (W_w) = 186 \times \frac{100-25}{100} = 139.5 \text{ kg}$$

(*iv*) *Cement content:*

WCR = 0.34

Water quantity (W_w) = 139.5 kg per 1 m^3

Therefore, quantity of cementitious material (CM) = 139.5 /0.34 = 410.3 kg per m^3 < 425 kg, O.K. (which is more than the minimum (325 kg per m^3) recommended according to IRC: 15).

Silica fume @ 8 per cent of total cementitious material content (SiFu) = 410.3 × 8/100 = 32.82 kg/m^3

Therefore, cement content (C) = 410.3 –32.82 = 377.48 kg/m^3 > 325 and < 425 kg/m^3; OK.

(*v*) *Determination of CA and FA quantities per m^3 of concrete*:

From Table 5.14, for aggregates of 20 mm nominal max. size and FA grading zone III, volume of CA = 0.64 per m^3 of total aggregates @ WCR = 0.5.

The present WCR = 0.34. Therefore, increase the CA content by about 0.01, for every decrease of 0.05 in WCR.

Increased volume of coarse aggregate $(V_{CA}) = 0.64 + \left(\frac{0.5-0.34}{0.05}\right) \times 0.01 = 0.672$

Volume of fine aggregate $(V_{FA}) = 1 -$ VCA = 1 – 0.672 = 0.328 per m^3

(*vi*) Volumetric analysis of mix ingredients per m^3 of concrete:

Volume of cement concrete $(V_{CM}) = 1$ m^3

Volume of cement $(V_C) = (C/S_c) \times (1/1000) = (377.48/3.15) \times (1/1000) = 0.1198$

Volume of silica fume $(V_{SiFu}) = (\text{SiFu}/S_{sf}) \times (1/1000) = (32.82/2.2) \times (1/1000)$

$= 0.0149$

Volume of water $(V_w) = (W_w/S_w) \times (1/1000) = (139.5/1.00) \times (1/1000) = 0.1395$

Volume of chemical admixture (V_{CADM}) = (Weight of chemical admixture/Specific gravity of chemical admixture) × (1/1000) = (8.2/1.2) × (1/1000) = 0.00683 m^3

(Content of super-plasticiser taken as 2% by mass of cementitious material

$= \left(\frac{2}{100}\right) \times 410.3 = 8.2$ kg

Volume of all aggregates in mix $(V_{AAM}) = V_{CM} - (V_c + V_{SiFu} + V_w + V_{CADM})$

$= 1 - (0.1198 + 0.0149 + 0.1395 + 0.00683) = 0.71897$ m^3

Mass of CA (CA) $= V_{AAM} \times V_{CA} \times S_{CA} \times 1000 = 0.71897 \times 0.672 \times 2.60 \times 1000$

$= 1256.18$ kg/m^3

Mass of FA (FA) $= V_{AAM} \times V_{FA} \times S_{FA} \times 1000 = 0.71897 \times 0.328 \times 2.58 \times 1000$

$= 608.42$ kg/m^3

(*vii*) *At Trial 1: Mix proportions in kg per m^3 of concrete based on aggregates in SSD condition:*

WCMR	Water (W_w)	Cement (C)	Silica Fume (SiFu)	FA	CA	CADM
0.34	139.5	377.48	32.82	608.42	1256.18	8.2

(*viii*) *Corrections due to moisture absorption and free surface water on aggregates per m^3 of concrete:*

Additional quantity of water to be added to account for absorption of moisture by CA = 0.48 % by mass of CA = (0.48/100) × 1256.18 = + 6.03 kg

Reduce the water content due to the presence of free moisture in FA = 1.8% of FA

= (1.8/100) × 608.42 = –10.95 kg

The final corrections in the ingredients in kg per one cubic metre of concrete are as follows:

@ WCMR = 0.34	Water (W_w)	Cement (C)	FA	CA	SiFu	CADM
	139.5	377.48	608.42	1256.18	—	—
For CA	+ 6.03	—	—	− 6.03	—	—
For FA	− 10.95	—	+ 10.95	—	—	—
Total (kg)	**134.58**	**377.48**	**619.37**	**1250.15**	**32.82**	**8.2**

(*ix*) The procedure explained in (ix) to (xi) of the previous solved problem remain the same here too.

5.12 Dry Lean Cement Concrete (MOSRTH 2001)

The concrete mix used for construction of dry lean cement concrete sub-base should be proportioned with a maximum cement aggregate ratio of 1:15 in which the maximum size of coarse aggregate should not be more than 25 mm. The aggregate should be blended according to the standard gradation prescribed by IRC (MOSRTH 2001). The minimum content of cement should not be less than 150 kg per cubic metre of concrete. At least five trial mixes should be made by varying the water content—ranging from 5.0 to 7.0 per cent in increments of 0.5 per cent. They should be checked for compactability and strength. The compressive strength of these cubes of standard dimension should not be less than 10 N/mm^2 at 7 days. A similar procedure may be adopted for proportioning concrete mix for construction of rolled cement concrete base.

5.13 Concrete Mix Design for Rural Roads (IRC:SP: 62-2004)

For rural roads or low volume roads, the characteristic compressive and flexural strengths at 28 days should not be less than 30 MPa and 3.8 MPa respectively. Flexural strength of cement concrete based on characteristic compressive strength is determined using equation (5.16). The target strength to be achieved should be taken as the minimum required flexural strength in the field. Similar to the conventional concrete mix design, the following equation is used to determine the target average flexural strength of cement concrete (IRC: SP: 62-2004; MORD, 2004).

$$F_{TF} = f_{cf} + K \times \sigma \tag{5.29}$$

where,

F_{TF} = Average target flexural strength at 28 days in N/mm^2.

f_{cf} = Characteristic flexural strength of concrete in N/mm^2; it may be defined as the average value of flexural strength of standard beams below which not more than five per cent of the test results are found to fail.

K = A statistical constant representing the tolerance limits desired. From statistical consideration, for a tolerance limit of 1:20, the value is 1.65.

σ = Standard deviation of field test values which depend upon degree of quality control during concrete production and construction. A suitable value may be taken from Table 5.9.

Mix design for cement concrete rural roads is made based upon the type of equipment used for compaction. There are two methods for compaction, viz. roller compaction and compacting using other tools. Roller compacted concrete is a zero slump concrete which is transported, placed, spread and compacted using vibratory rollers with a 10 tonne capacity low-amplitude high frequency vibration (Schrader 1997; Seehra 2001 and Ashraf 2004). Roller compacted concrete does not relate to the Abram's rule of water–cement ratio since it is a no-slump concrete (Seehra 2001 and IRC: SP: 62-2004). To minimise segregation, the maximum size of aggregates in roller compacted concrete is restricted to 25 mm (Seehra 2001 and IRC: SP: 62-2004). Roller compacted pavements are used for low volume village, mandal or sub-arterial roads. The concrete is designed by weight of all ingredients to satisfy equation (5.29). Concrete trail mixes should be made with water content ranging from 5 to 7 per cent at an interval of 1 or 0.5 per cent. Optimum moisture content (OMC) should be determined from the above trial samples which give maximum dry density (AASHTO T-180). Veebee consistometer apparatus may be used with some modifications for evaluation of consistency of the concrete (Seehra 2001). Suitable final minor adjustments in the OMC are to be made to achieve the desired dry density. At this optimum moisture content, samples are prepared and flexural strength tests are conducted at 7 and 28 days. Necessary final adjustments in the proportions of water–cement ratio or cement or fly ash (if used) are made to achieve the desired consolidation and to meet the target flexural strength.

The other compaction tools are vibratory screed, needle vibrator, hand temper and plate compactor. Trial mixes should be prepared on a conventional basis according to IRC: 44-1976 or IS: 10262-1982. Suitable adjustments to the proportion of ingredients should be made to meet the target strength requirement. Table 5.15 shows the gradation applicable for the design of concrete mix in the above two cases.

Table 5.15 *Aggregate gradation for cement concrete rural roads*

Sl. No.	IS sieve size (mm)	Per cent passing by weight
1	26.5	100
2	19.00	80–100
3	9.50	55–75
4	4.75	35–60
5	0.60	10–35
6	0.075	0–8

Source: IRC: SP: 62-2004 and Table 1500.3 of MORD 2004

The maximum and minimum quantity of cement or cement with fly ash or cement with slag or cementitious materials per cubic metre of concrete should be 425 and 310 kg respectively. If fly ash is replaced with cement content, the cement content should not be less than 250 kg per cubic metr eof concrete (MORD 2004).

Exercises

5.1 What is the chemical composition of cement? Explain the significance of each component element useful to gain strength.

5.2 What are the different types of cements available and state how they are different from OPC?

5.3 State the classification of cement according to ASTM.

5.4 Discuss the various properties of cement and briefly explain the related test methods.

5.5 Distinguish between initial and final setting times of cement. Explain the methods of determining these setting times according to the Bureau of Indian Standards.

5.6 State the significance of initial and final setting times of cement used for pavement construction.

5.7 State the importance of the soundness test of cement and write its basic principle.

5.8 Explain the significance and principle of testing cement strength by the cube compressive test method.

5.9 What is the chemical composition test of cement? Explain how such test results are useful to understand alkali–silica reactions.

5.10 Define hydration of cement. State the factors affecting rate of liberation of heat of hydration process.

5.11 State the measures to be taken to control excess liberation of heat due to hydration in hot weather concreting.

5.12 Write a brief note on particle size distribution according to IS: 383.

5.13 Write a short note on fine aggregate gradation according to IS: 383.

5.14 What are the different types of admixtures useful in cement concreting? Explain their effect on strength gain and workability of cement concrete mix.

5.15 What is workability of cement concrete mix? State the factors affecting workability of the concrete mix.

5.16 Briefly explain the following tests which are conducted on hardened concrete: (i) Compressive strength test, (ii) elastic modulus test, (iii) flexural strength test and (iv) split tensile strength test.

5.17 Enumerate the different methods available for design of cement concrete mix.

5.18 State the factors affecting durability of hardened cement concrete.

5.19 In detail, explain the method of design of cement concrete mix according to IS: 10262.

5.20 State the significance of air voids in hardened cement concrete.

5.21 How is the water--cement ratio selected according to IS: 10262?

5.22 Draw a typical flow chart illustrating the design procedure for cement concrete mix according to IS:10262.

5.23 What are the salient features of the design method of cement concrete mix according to IRC: 44-2008?

5.24 In detail, explain the design method of cement concrete mix according to IRC: 44-2008.

5.25 Define dry lean cement concrete. State where it is useful.

5.26 Write a short note on cement concrete mix design for rural roads according to IRC: SP: 62-2004.

6

Factors Affecting Pavement Design

Introduction

Pavement design consists of determining pavement thickness or the thickness of individual layers of the pavement in order to serve traffic for an anticipated design period based upon various factors, viz. intensity of traffic wheel loads, repetitions, temperature, rainfall, humidity, frost, drainage conditions, sub-grade soil strength, properties of materials used, criteria of mix design and economic considerations. The factors affecting pavement design are discussed in this chapter.

6.1 Functions of Pavements

The following are the main functions of pavements

- They provide a firm, strong, smooth and adequately skid-resistant riding surface with low noise generation in all seasons.
- They receive and distribute traffic wheel loads safely over a larger area of the sub-grade so that stresses and strains are kept within allowable limits.

The basic structure of a pavement comprises of a bound surface or wearing course which transmits wheel loads onto subsequent layers safely. Under a wheel load, the surface course experiences compressive and tensile stresses at the top and bottom fibres respectively (Figure 6.1). The wheel load is distributed further onto the subsequent bottom layers in the form of a cone having an angle of about 45 degrees.

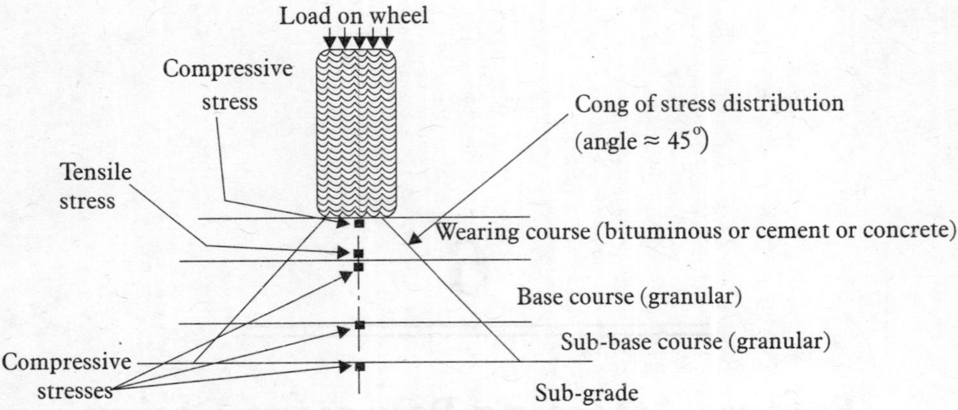

Figure 6.1 *Structural function of pavement*

The sub-grade will experience compressive stresses over the conical spread area with lower intensity of stress as compared to the stress on the surface course. The over-all crust thickness of a pavement should be sufficient to keep the stresses or strains occurring due to wheel loads within allowable limits so that the sub-grade can withstand traffic loads without any plastic deformation. Therefore, each layer of pavement structure should be strong enough to resist wheel loads for a given design period under prevailing seasonal climatic conditions.

Structural behaviour, stress distribution patterns, service performance, resistance to deformation due to repetitive action of wheel loads under the influence of variable environmental conditions, all depend on the type of material used for construction, the method of compaction, quality control during construction, failure criteria, and the mix and thickness design methodology adopted.

6.2 Types of Pavements

Based on the type of materials used for construction, pavements may be classified into three types, viz. flexible pavements, rigid pavements and composite pavements. Salient features of these pavements are discussed below.

6.2.1 Flexible Pavements

Flexible pavement consists of multiple layers constructed using granular materials. To serve in all weather conditions, its top layer is constructed to be impervious by using different types of binders, viz. bitumen, tar and modified bituminous materials. Such layers are termed as bound layers and resist loads by developing tensile stresses at its bottom fibres. The particles that make up the granular layers are not bound together by any binder. Such layers are termed as unbound layers. The unbound layers are stabilised either by mechanical action or treated with additives by which the unbound layers possess very low tensile strength. Unbound layers are constructed as sub-base and base courses since they lie under the impervious surface course. Cross-sectional details of typical flexible pavement structures are shown in Figure 6.2 (a)–(c).

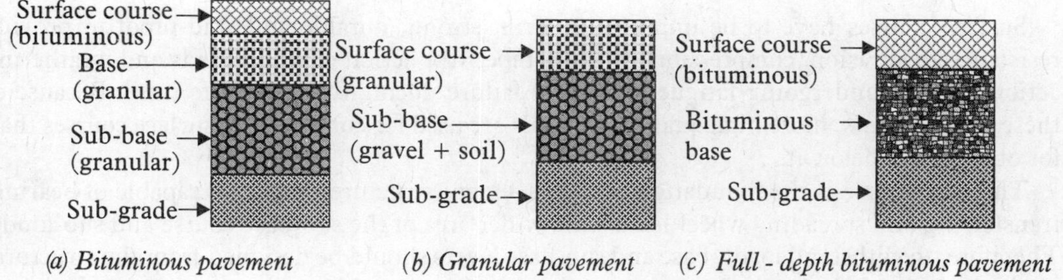

Figure 6.2 *Cross-sectional details of typical flexible pavement structures*

The surface course of flexible pavements acts as a flexible layer. On wheel loading, the surface layer bends with elasticity into a concave shape. This bowl-like surface moves in the longitudinal direction under the moving wheel (on the load path). Every application of wheel load on the pavement surface causes elastic deflection (or elastic strain). Repetitive application of wheel loads in different climatic conditions causes unrecoverable deformations in pavement structure which are termed as plastic deformations (or uneven surface). Plastic deformations will occur in the vertical and horizontal directions due to vertical compressive stresses and horizontal tensile stresses respectively. Occurrence of such plastic deformations in the vertical direction, viz. rutting, consolidation, shear failure, upheaval or any kind of undulation in any one of the layers, causes a similar *trend* of deformation in the rest of the layers. These deformations may propagate in any vertical direction ranging from the sub-grade to the surface course and vice versa (Figure 6.3 and 6.4). The plastic deformations caused by horizontal tensile stresses are generally observed as cracking in bound layers and displacement of materials in case of unbound layers.

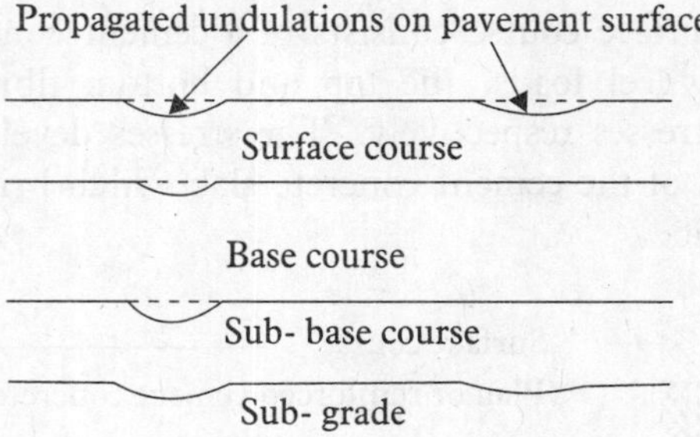

Figure 6.3 *Pavement surface undulations caused due to plastic deformation of the sub-grade*

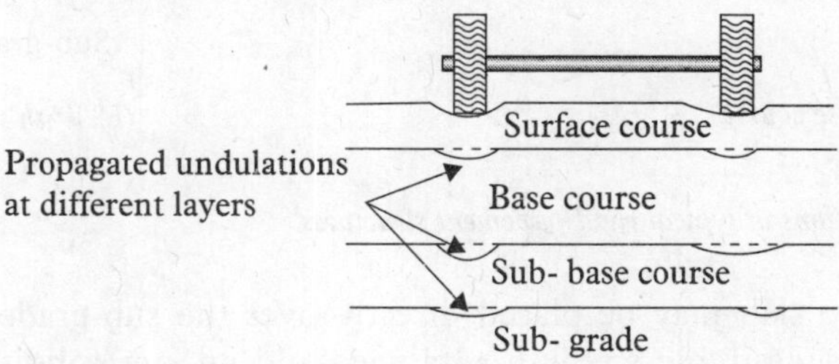

Figure 6.4 *Undulations caused due to rutting of surface course*

Surface courses have to be impervious, firm, strong, durable and skid-proof to provide resistance to abrasion, compression, tension, repetitive action of wheel loads and weathering action without undergoing fatigue (cracking) failure during its design life time. Because of these requirements, more high quality materials are used for constructing surface courses than for other layers below it.

The base course is the foundation of the pavement structure making it capable of bearing, transferring and spreading wheel loads onto wider area of the sub-base course and sub-grade. Therefore, to withstand loads, base and sub-base layers should be designed from the structural strength point of view. The base and sub-base courses should be adequately thick to reduce the intensity of stresses caused by wheel loads on to the sub-grade. Further, the sub-base layer should be designed to improve the sub-grade soil strength, control capillary rise of ground water and act as a drainage layer too.

The sub-grade may be natural ground or a treated soil layer having a thickness of 500 mm or more. Requirement of overall crust thickness will depend on the strength of the sub-grade. If the sub-grade soil is weak (clay soil), the required pavement crust thickness is more and vice versa. A satisfactory sub-grade should posses the following requirements (Mullis 1939).

- Adequate compressive strength to withstand maximum wheel load applied.
- Limited volume of effective pore space so that entry of water, which causes plasticity, is restricted.
- Be able to withstand abrasive and impact forces of traffic and weathering action.

6.2.2 Rigid Pavements

In rigid pavements, the surface course consists of a cement concrete slab with or without reinforcements. Under wheel loads, the top and bottom fibres of the slab experience compressive and tensile stresses respectively. The stresses developed are resisted by beam action or flexural strength of the cement concrete slab which bridges over soft spots in the supporting layers of the slab.

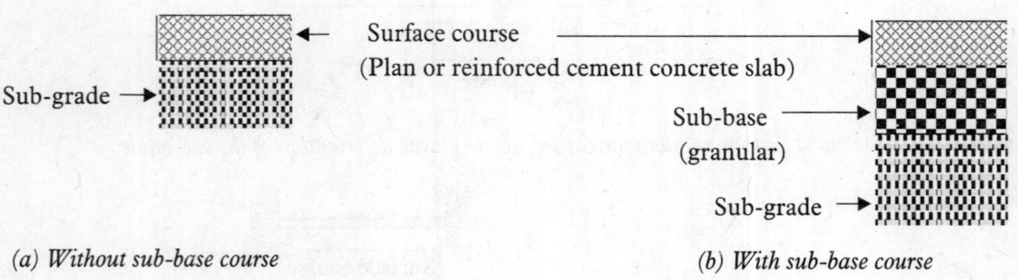

Figure 6.5 *Cross-sections of typical rigid pavement structures*

The cement concrete slab may be placed directly over the sub-grade if the sub-grade has favourable minimum desirable strength, drainage and on site conditions (Figure 6.5 (a)). Sub-base layer is provided for the following reasons/conditions (Figure 6.5 (b)) (Collins and Sharp 1958; Childs et al. 1559).

- To decrease deflections of slab with an accompanying reduced tendency for pumping mud.
- Sub-base layer is required if the plastic sub-grade soil is susceptible to pumping and has a tendency to weaken severely in the presence of melting frost.
- Sub-base layer should be provided if the sub-grade tends to change its volume significantly with varying moisture content.

Use of sub-base which is thicker than normal to prevent pumping of mud does not greatly enhance the load-carrying capacity of the pavement. Moreover, thicker sub-bases may not be structurally economical.

The structural functions of the remaining layers below the surface course are similar to the layers of a flexible pavement.

6.2.3 Composite Pavements

In this category, the wearing course of the pavement is constructed by spreading bricks or pre-cast rectangular cement concrete blocks, or interlocking concrete blocks (Figure 6.6 (a)). The joints between them are filled with fine sand of standard gradation. These pieces of blocks act as small rigid plates. Hence, the wearing course constructed of these blocks is neither truly flexible nor is it a truly rigid layer. It possesses dual properties and is suitable for low volume village roads or foot paths.

A composite pavement consists of cement concrete or cement-treated granular and bituminous layers. These kinds of pavements are observed when an old concrete pavement is overlaid with a bituminous layer or any granular layer below a bituminous wearing course is treated with cement or lime (Figure 6.6 (c) and (d)). While designing composite pavement structures, the flexural strength of the base slab or treated granular material should be taken into consideration for resisting tensile stresses.

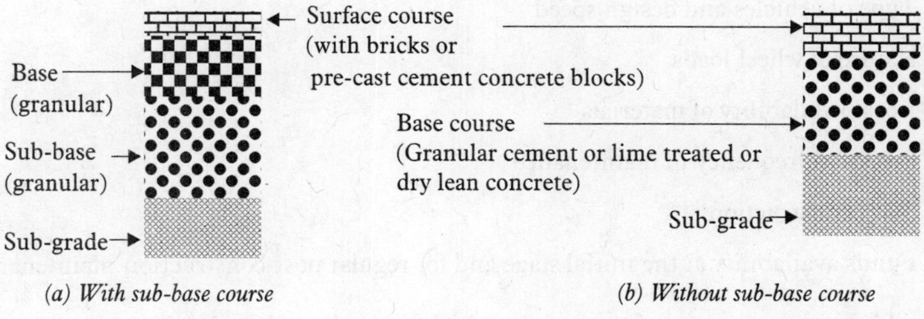

Figure 6.6 *Cross-sections of typical composite or semi-flexible or semi-rigid pavement structures*

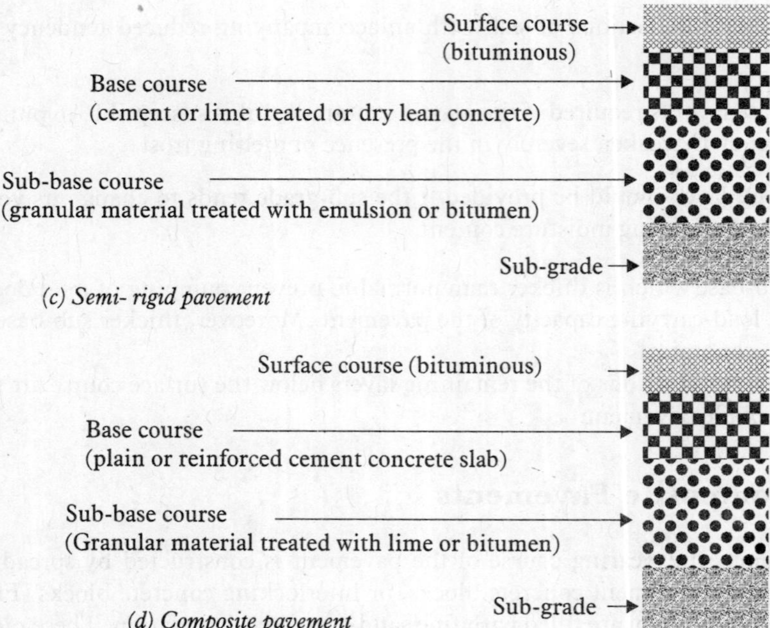

(c) Semi- rigid pavement

(d) Composite pavement

Figure 6.6 *Continued*

The following factors should be considered at the planning stage of constructing a pavement.

- Importance and purpose of the road
- Location, climate and natural ground conditions
- Traffic intensity and growth rate
- Type of vehicles and design speed
- Nature of wheel loads
- Local availability of materials
- Proposed frequency of maintenance
- Stage construction
- Funds availability at the initial stage and for regular post-construction maintenance

Flexible pavements are preferred when initial funds allotted are less or stage construction is proposed. Regular maintenance is necessary for flexible pavements which involves more maintenance costs. Whereas, the initial cost of full depth bituminous pavements is higher than the traditional flexible pavements since the base course is also constructed with good quality bituminous layer. Full depth bituminous pavements are very strong and cost-effective when considering their life cycle cost. They are also preferred when total pavement crust thickness is restricted to avoid drainage related problems, especially in well-developed urban localities with higher volume of traffic.

For rigid pavements, the initial cost is more compared to the cost of flexible pavements. But the maintenance cost of rigid pavements is low and the life cycle cost is economical and justified with reference to its performance during its serviceable period of life.

Brick or concrete block pavements may be used for low volume roads (like cycle tracks) or village roads or roads of least importance where the funds allotted are less. New construction of composite pavements involves higher cost. To improve the structural capacity of an old concrete pavement, a bituminous layer may be overlaid as a maintenance measure.

Base and sub-base courses may be stabilised with suitable admixtures or binders to improve their structural capacity. A cost-effective suitable treatment may be made to these layers to meet minimum strength requirement.

6.3 Factors Affecting Design of Pavement

Pavement design comprises thickness determination of different layers for projected volume of traffic, in situ and climatic conditions. The designed pavement should serve traffic to the presumed level of service for the design period. During the service period of the pavement, there are many factors related to traffic, nature and engineering considerations which should be taken into account for cost-economy and durable service. The factors affecting pavement design are given below.

6.3.1 Material Characteristics

Pavement materials consist of different types of sub-grade soil, fine aggregates, granular materials, binders, viz. bitumen, tar, cement, emulsions, lime etc. Physical and engineering properties of different materials used for constructing any kind of pavement plays an important role in thickness design of pavements. These have been discussed in detail in Chapters 3 to 5.

6.3.2 Traffic Volume

Traffic volume is one of the main factors which decide pavement thickness. Traffic count surveys are conducted at road junctions or imaginary sections of roads to determine passage of a number of vehicles per unit time period. According to Indian practice (IRC: 9-1972), an average traffic volume per day is calculated from a 7 day 24-hours traffic count. If it is not possible to conduct a count survey for 7 days, a 3 day (Saturday, Sunday and Monday) count survey may be conducted. The final traffic volume estimate should also incorporate the additional traffic volume that may be expected in the near future during the design life by considering local economic developmental activities.

Estimation of future traffic volume for a design period is calculated in terms of cumulative standard axles per year (csa/year). The following equations are used to estimate the traffic volume for a given period (say n years) and design value of traffic (IRC: 37-2001 and IRC: 58-2002).

$$A = P(1+r)^{nc} \tag{6.1}$$

$$N_{\text{flexible}} = 365 \times \text{TGF} \times A \times \text{VDF} \times \text{LDF} \times 10^{-6} \tag{6.2}$$

$$N_{\text{rigid}} = 365 \times \text{TGF} \times A \times 10^{-6} \tag{6.3}$$

where,

A	=	Estimated traffic volume during the road construction period (commercial vehicles/day)
P	=	Present traffic volume from traffic count survey (commercial vehicles/day)
r	=	Growth rate of traffic (decimal value)
nc	=	No. of years from the date of traffic count to the date of opening of road to traffic
N_{flexible} and N_{rigid}	=	Cumulative number of standard axles in million standard axles (msa) which is used for design of flexible and rigid pavements respectively
$\text{TGF} = \left(\dfrac{(1+r)^{nd}-1}{r}\right)$	=	Cumulative traffic growth factor based on geometric growth
nd	=	Design period (no. of years); 30 to 20 years for rigid pavements; above 5 years for flexible pavements.
VDF	=	Vehicle damage factor
LDF	=	Lane distribution factor

Traffic growth rate This value is used to estimate future traffic (A) after n number of years based on present traffic volume (P). The rate of growth of traffic is generally calculated from the growth rate of vehicle registrations, fuel consumption and socio-economic developments in a locality for the past few (10 or 20) years. In the absence of such a data bank, an average traffic growth rate of 7.5 % may be assumed (IRC: 37-2001 and IRC: 58-2002).

Design life Scientifically, the term 'design life' indicates the cumulative number of standard axle load repetitions for which a pavement is supposed to provide the desired level of service before needing strengthening operations. The design life in terms of cumulative standard axles (csa) is calculated based on the desirable service period (in number of years).

For flexible pavements, the design service period (nd), may be taken as 10 to 20 years (IRC: 37-2001). A higher service period is taken in case of expressways and national highways and any economically important roads. A value between 5 to 10 years may also be taken if stage construction of a road is envisaged.

For rigid pavements, design service period varies—in the case of low and high traffic volume roads, it may be taken as 20 to 30 years respectively (IRC: 58-2002). However, any suitable number of years of design service period may be taken according to its purpose and economic point of view.

Lane distribution factor (LDF) Lane distribution factor is a decimal value which indicates the concentration of placement of wheel load repetitions along a road stretch. As a general tendency, on a multi-lane undivided one-way pavement, a driver places his vehicle towards the centre or away from the edge. Therefore, lower concentration of wheel load repetitions is observed near the edges. Due to this reason, as an economic consideration, based on the number of lanes, only a part of the commercial traffic volume is taken as the design traffic volume. The lane distribution factor (LDF) should be determined from realistic and appropriate field surveys based on special repeatability of wheel paths of different vehicles in the transverse direction of a pavement surface. In the absence of such data, the following LDF may be used to design flexible pavements (IRC: 37-2001).

Table 6.1 *Lane distribution factors (IRC: 37-2001)*

Sl No.	Type of carriageway	LDF	Total number of commercial vehicles considered in
1	Single-lane	1.00	Both directions
2	Two-lane single	0.75	
3	Four-lane single	0.40	
4	Dual two-lane	0.75	Each direction
5	Dual three-lane	0.60	
6	Dual four-lane	0.45	

Q: *Determine the traffic volume just after construction of a road project using the following data:*
Present traffic volume = 1090 commercial vehicles per day
Growth rate of traffic = 7.1 %
Duration of road construction = four and half years

A: Using equation (6.3),

$A = P(1 + r)^{nc} = 1090\,(1 + 0.071)^{4.5} = 1484$ commercial vehicles per day (CVPD).

6.3.3 Factors Related to Axle and Wheel Loads

Axle Load, Wheel Load and Configuration of Wheels

The total weight of a vehicle is carried by its axles. The load on the axles is transferred to the wheels and this load is ultimately transferred on to the surface of the pavement in contact with the tyres.

To keep wheel load induced stresses on pavements within allowable limits, the total vehicle load is distributed onto wider areas of pavement by using more axles and wheels. This is the reason why more number of axles and wheels are fitted to heavy load-carrying trucks. Figure 6.7 shows the different types of configurations of axles and wheels used in the manufacture of road vehicles.

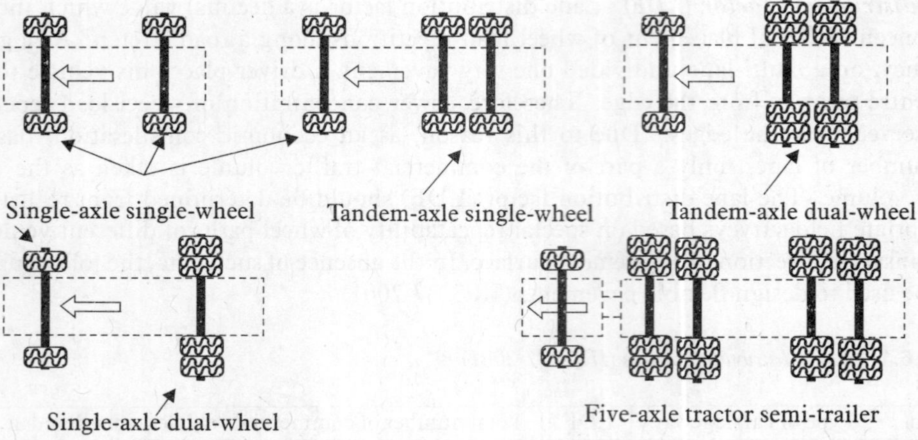

Figure 6.7 *Different axle and wheel configurations*

Different types of configurations can be tried to carry heavier loads (Figure 6.8).

Figure 6.8 *A heavy vehicle having 10 tyres under the engine and 10 × 8 = 80 tyres in the rear side, seen on the Chennai to Bhadrachalam (A.P.) highway (Courtesy: Eenadu, Telugu Daily, on 22-05-2007)*

Measurement of Axle Load and Truck Weight

There are two methods to weigh trucks or axle loads, viz. (i) static weighing (ii) weight in motion (WIM). In the static weighing method, vehicles are stopped and weighed. But in the weight in motion method, vehicles are weighed dynamically, while in motion. A comparison of the two methods is given below.

Sl.No.	Static weighing method	Weight in motion (WIM)
1	Vehicles are stopped and weighed	Vehicles are weighed automatically, while in motion, without disturbing the driver.
2	Accurate weight measurement	Weight measurements may be influenced by parameters related to vehicle speed, suspension system of the vehicle, tyre pressure, acceleration and deceleration of the vehicle and dynamic forces produced due to pavement roughness, wind velocity etc.
3	Takes more time and interrupts free flow of traffic; may pose problems related to safety.	There is no such interruption to flow of traffic; can weigh high volumes of traffic.
4	Other information such as body type of vehicles, loading type etc can be physically ascertained.	Collection of other information is not possible by automated WIM equipment.
5	Less number of vehicles can be measured; selected vehicles are weighed; need more personnel, time and space to weigh all vehicles.	More number of vehicles can be measured; better coverage of all vehicles since it is automatic.
6	Less installation and maintenance cost.	High installation and maintenance cost.
7	The weigh pads can be installed at any location.	The WIM equipment can be installed at fixed locations only.

In the static method, the axle load of a vehicle is weighed using portable weights or load-pads (Figure 6.6) or a weighing platform. Only axle loads having more than or equal to 3 tonnes are taken into account for analysis since the damage caused by axles weighing less than 3 tonnes is negligible. For traffic analysis, vehicles having axle weight = 3 tonnes are referred to as commercial vehicles.

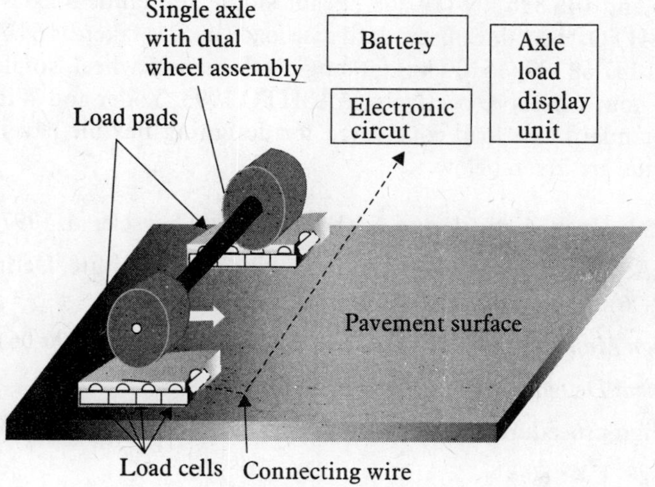

Figure 6.9 *Axle load measurement*

Standard Axle Load

Generally, the load carried by any one truck is not the same as that carried by an axle. Each axle load will impart a certain amount of damage or distress on the pavement. The degree of distress caused by different loads of axle will increase as the magnitude of load and repetitions increase. Under mixed traffic conditions, repetitions of different axles having different loads, plying on a road will not indicate any meaningful value related to how much damage has been caused to the pavement due to their combined action. Different axle loads will cause different degrees of damage. Therefore, it is customary to convert repetitions of axles having different loads to an equivalent standard axle load. Configuration of the Indian standard single axle with dual wheel assembly is presented in Figure 6.10.

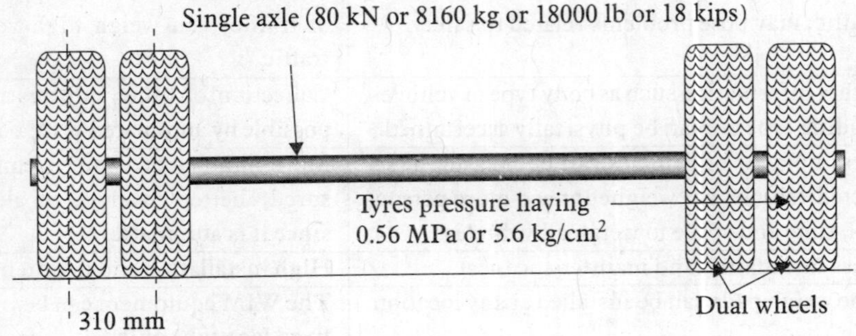

Figure 6.10 *Details of the Indian standard axle*

Charts have been prepared for a specified number of repetitions of standard axle load on the pavement layers. The remaining life of in-service pavements is also incorporated in the charts and specified in terms of number of repetitions of the standard axle.

According to the Indian practice (IRC: 37-2001), standard axle load (W_{std}) is prescribed as 80 kN (8,160 kg) and 146.836 kN (14,968 kg) for single and tandem axles respectively. But according to AASHTO, the value of standard axle load (W_{std}) is taken as 64.7 kN (6600 kg), 80 kN (8160 kg) and 147.68 kN (15100 kg) for single axle–single wheel, single axle–dual wheel and tandem axle–four wheels respectively (AASHTO 1993; Yoder and Witczak 1975).

Value of the standard axle load considered for designing flexible pavements by different agencies world-wide are given below.

- South African Mechanistic design method: 80 kN (Theyse et al. 1997)
- CARE and ASCON (Road and Hydraulic Engineering Institute, Delft): 100 kN (CROW report D06-06)
- *French Design Manual* (LCPC, Paris): 130 kN (CROW report D06-06)
- *Shell Pavement Design Manual*: 80 kN (Shell 1978)
- CROW design procedure for thin asphalt pavements: 100 kN (CROW report D06-06)
- Road Note 29, UK: 80 kN

Load Equivalency Factor (LEF)

Load equivalency factor (LEF) is a number which relates the amount of equivalent damage caused by a given load of axle to the standard axle load. Based on field test data, AASHTO has recommended specific load equivalency factors for single and tandem axles (Table 6.1). These LEFs were developed based on the affect of wheel load on serviceability of pavements.

Equivalent standard axle loads (ESALs) may be calculated from the following relationship.

Repetitions of equivalent standard axle loads (ESALs)

$$= \text{Load equivalency factor (LEF)} \times \text{No. of axles observed} \tag{6.4}$$

Table 6.1 *Partial list of AASHTO axle load equivalency factors (from AASHTO Guide for Design of Pavement Structures, 1993, by the American Association of State Highway and Transportation Officials, Washington, Statedc (Used by permission. Documents may be purchased from the AASHTO bookstore at 1-800-231-3475 or online at http://bookstore.transportation.org.)*

Sl No.	Gross axle weight in		Load equivalency factor (LEF) for	
	kN	kg	Single axle	Tandem axle
1	35.610	3630	0.031	0.003
2	44.537	4540	0.080	0.006
3	53.366	5440	0.176	0.013
4	62.294	6350	0.350	0.024
5	71.221	7260	0.610	0.043
6	80.050	8160	1.000	0.070
7	88.977	9070	1.550	0.110
8	97.904	9980	2.300	0.166
9	106.831	10890	3.270	0.242
10	115.660	11790	4.480	0.342
11	124.587	12700	5.980	0.470
12	133.514	13610	7.800	0.633
13	142.441	14520	10.00	0.834
14	151.270	15420	12.50	1.080
15	160.099	16320	15.50	1.380

If the AASHTO factors are not available, the load equivalency factors are also calculated based on standard axle load by using the fourth power damage rule.

Fourth Power Damage Rule

The following relationships (equation 6.5(a) and (b)) developed from the AASHO road test data (AASHTO 1962) are widely used to determine equivalent standard axle load (ESAL) repetitions when axle load data of different axles is available. This relationship is popularly known as the fourth power damage rule.

$$\frac{N_1}{n_2} = \left(\frac{w_2}{W_1}\right)^4 \tag{6.5a}$$

$$\text{Load equivalency factor (LEF)} = \left(\frac{W_m}{W_{std}}\right)^4 \tag{6.5b}$$

where, N_1 is a number representing repetitions of axle loads each having a weight equal to W_1
n_2 is a number representing repetitions of axle loads each having a weight equal to w_2
W_m = Measured axle load obtained from axle load (survey data)
W_{std} = Standard axle load

Equation (6.5a) may also be explained as the damage caused by N_1 number of repetitions of axle having weight W_1 is equal to the damage caused by n_2 number of repetitions of axle having weight w_2.

The exponent value in equations (6.5a) and (6.5b) is not a constant value of 4 because these are empirical relationships which were developed based on traffic characteristics, strength of pavement layers, in situ and environmental conditions. As the thickness of the pavement decreases and temperature increases, the exponent value varies from 2.5 to 4.6. Higher exponent values are observed when the strength of the pavement is not enough to resist wheel loads.

The following equation was used by Caltrans of California (USA) to estimate the equivalent single axle loads (ESALs) of transit bus data (from Gibby et al. 1996).

$$\text{ESAL} = \sum N\left(\frac{W_m}{80.12}\right)^{4.2} \tag{6.5c}$$

where, W_m = axle load (kN); and N = axle repetitions of a given load or axle number

The ESAL factors are also determined by comparing stress caused by a given vehicle to the stress caused by a standard vehicle. This relationship is referred to as the *Vesic model* and is given below (from Lin et al. 1996).

$$F_j = \left(\frac{\sigma_j}{\sigma_s}\right)^4 \tag{6.5d}$$

The ESAL factor may also be determined by (Yoder and Witczak 1975),

$$F_j = \frac{d_j}{d_s} = \frac{N_s}{N_j} \tag{6.5e}$$

where, F_j = ESAL factor
σ_j = stress caused by vehicle j
σ_j = stress caused by standard vehicle s
d_j = damage per pass of vehicle j
d_s = damage per pass of vehicle s
N_j = number of passes until failure of pavement due to load of vehicle j
N_s = number of passes until failure of pavement due to load of standard vehicles

Q. *For design of a flexible pavement, calculate the ESALs of a vehicle with the following axle and wheel configuration.*

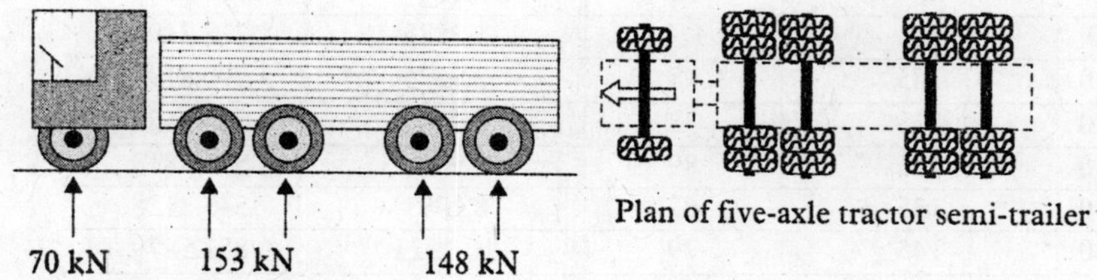

Plan of five-axle tractor semi-trailer

A: ESALs of the vehicle $= \left(\frac{70}{80}\right)^4 + \left(\frac{153}{147.68}\right)^4 + \left(\frac{148}{147.68}\right)^4 = 0.586 + 1.152 + 1.008 = 2.746$

Q. *For the above vehicle, calculate the ESALs for the design of a rigid pavement according to AASHTO guidelines.*

A: Take 129 kN as the standard axle load for rigid pavements.

$$\text{ESALs of the vehicle} = \left(\frac{70}{80}\right)^4 + \left(\frac{153}{129}\right)^4 + \left(\frac{148}{129}\right)^4 = 0.586 + 1.978 + 1.732 = 4.296$$

Q. *The following data is obtained from the axle load survey conducted for 3 days. Determine the equivalent number of standard axle loads of 80 kN repetitions per year.*

Axle load (kN)	*30–40*	*40–50*	*50-60*	*60–70*	*70–80*	*80–90*
No. of axles	*54*	*65*	*64*	*78*	*103*	*98*
Axle load (kN)	*90–100*	*100–110*	*110–120*	*120--130*	*130–140*	*140–150*
No. of axles	*110*	*98*	*78*	*89*	*67*	*79*

A: LEFs are calculated using equation (6.1b). The details are given below.

Average axle class (1)	Average axle load (W_m) in kN (2)	No. of axles (3)	LEF = $(W_m/80)^4$ (4)	$ESAL_{80kN}$ (5) = (3) × (4)
30–40	35	54	0.0366	1.9784
40–50	45	65	0.1001	6.5073
50–60	55	64	0.2234	14.2979
60–70	65	78	0.4358	33.9929
70–80	75	103	0.7725	79.5650
80–90	85	98	1.2744	124.8941
90–100	95	110	1.9885	218.7395
100–110	105	98	2.9675	290.8194
110–120	115	78	4.2700	333.0627
120–130	125	89	5.9605	530.4813
130–140	135	67	8.1091	543.3128
140–150	145	79	10.7923	852.5879
Total=		983		3030.239

80 kN ESAL repetitions for 3 days = 3030.239

80 kN ESAL repetitions per year $\approx (365/3) \times 3030.239 = 368679$

$= 0.368679$ million standard axles or

$= 0.368679$ msa

Q. *Determine the 98th percentile axle load from the data given below.*

Load on single axle		*Load on tandem axle*	
Range of axle load (tonnes)	*Distribution, %*	*Range of axle load (tonnes)*	*Distribution, %*
19–21	*0.2*	*34–38*	*0.1*
17–19	*0.6*	*30–34*	*0.2*
15–17	*0.9*	*26–30*	*2.1*
13–15	*30.5*	*22–26*	*4.3*
11–13	*20.1*	*18–22*	*1.5*
9-11	*19.2*	*14–18*	*0.5*
Less than 9	*18.1*	*Less than 14*	*1.7*
Total	*89.6*	—	*10.4*

A:

Single axle load		Tandem axle load					
Average value of axle load(tonnes)	Distr. %	Average value of axle load(tonnes)	Equivalent single axle load (ESAL)	Distr. %	All single axle	Distr. %	Percentile value
(1)	(2)	(3)	(4)	(5)	(6)	(7)=(2)+(5)	(8)
20	0.2	36	18	0.1	20	0.2 + 0.0 = 0.2	100
18	0.6	32	16	0.2	18	0.6 + 0.1 = 0.7	99.8
16	0.9	28	14	2.1	16	0.9 + 0.2 = 1.1	99.1
14	30.5	24	12	4.3	14	30.5 + 2.1 = 32.6	98.0
12	20.1	20	10	1.5	12	20.1 + 4.3 = 24.4	65.4
10	19.2	16	8	0.5	10	19.2 + 1.5 = 20.7	41.0
8	18.1	14	6	1.7	8	18.1 + 0.5 = 18.6	20.3
Total	89.6	Total	–	10.4	6	0.0 + 1.7 = 1.7	1.7

After plotting the values in Column (6) and (8), we get the 98th percentile axle load = 14 tonnes.

Legal Axle Load Limit

To safeguard pavements against overloading, different agencies (government or any competent authority) in different countries have prescribed maximum allowable limits of axle load depending on their method of compaction, materials used, considerations related to mix design as well as pavement crust thickness. The maximum allowable axle load limit is referred to as the legal axle load limit. This means that no axle of a vehicle should carry more than the legal axle load. The details of the legal axle load limits adopted in different countries are given in Table 6.2. Maximum permissible loads for different type of vehicles in India are given Table 6.3.

Table 6.2 *Legal axle load limits followed in different countries (Kanchan et al. 2006; CSIR Report 2001)*

Sl. No.	Country	Single axle load (tonnes)	Tandem axle load (tonnes)	Tridem axle load (tonnes)	Maximum permissible gross load (tonnes)
1	India	10.2	19.0	24.0	45.0
2	UK	10.5	20.3	22.5	38.0
3	South Africa	9.0	18.0	24.0	56.0
4	USA*	9.0	18.0	20.0	36.0
5	Canada*	9.1	17.1	24.0	53.5
6	Germany	10.0	11.5	21.0	40.0
7	Australia	9.0	16.5	20.0	44.0

NOTE: * May vary in different states/provinces.

Table 6.3 *Maximum permissible loads of different types of vehicles in India (Kanchan et al. 2006)*

Sl. No.	Type of vehicle	Legal limit of load (tonnes)
1	Truck: 2 axles	16.20
2	Truck: Semi-trailer	25.0
3	Truck: Trailer	35.0
4	Truck: 3 axles (rear tandem)	25.0
5	Truck: Multi-axle (rear tandem)	35.0
6	Truck: Multi-axle (both rear tandem)	45.0

Vehicle Damage Factor

Every passage of a vehicle on a pavement will cause a certain amount of damage or distress in different forms. The degree of damage caused by a vehicle depends on its gross weight, number of axles as well as configuration of wheels. For example, if two vehicles have equal gross load, one with a single axle–single wheel and the other with a tandem axle–dual wheel assembly, the damage caused by the former vehicle will be greater. This is because the gross load is transferred onto the pavement surface over a wider area by more number of axles and wheels. The damage caused by different vehicles is calculated using the vehicle damage factor which is used for performance modelling, design and maintenance of pavements.

The vehicle damage factor (VDF) is a numerical value which represents the equivalent number of standard axles per truck (IRC: 37-2001). It is a multiplication factor used to convert different commercial vehicles with varying axle load repetitions to standard axle load repetitions. From axle load survey data, VDF is calculated using the following equation.

$$\text{VDF} = \frac{\sum_{i=1}^{N} [V_i \times \text{LEF}_i]}{N} \tag{6.6}$$

where, V_i = Traffic volume of the ith vehicle load-class
LEF_i = Load equivalency factor of ith vehicle load-class
N = Total number of vehicles weighed

Factors affecting VDF Numerous factors which are related to damage or distress caused to pavement affect VDF. The factors may be related to traffic composition at the time of survey, load on axles, possible occasional (or seasonal) overloading, number of axles, wheels configuration, terrain, type of pavement, region, pavement condition, temperature, rainfall etc.

In pavement design, VDF obtained from axle load survey data should be used rather than an assumed value because the VDF value obtained from survey data represent a realistic value by considering actual traffic loading and other factors related to the region (or pavement) considered.

Q. *The following data were obtained from an axle load survey. Determine VDF based on a standard axle load of 80 kN.*

Axle load (kN)	*30–40*	*40–50*	*50–60*	*60–70*	*70–80*	*80–90*
Frequency (%)	*5.76*	*6.45*	*7.22*	*6.96*	*9.63*	*12.04*
Axle load (kN)	*90–100*	*100–110*	*110–120*	*120–130*	*130–140*	*140–150*
Frequency (%)	*14.02*	*10.49*	*8.43*	*7.82*	*5.25*	*5.93*

A: LEF are calculated using equation (6.1 b). The calculation details are given below.

Average axle class **(1)**	Average axle load (W_m) in kN **(2)**	Frequency (%) **(3)**	LEF = $(W_m/80)^4$ **(4)**	$ESAL_{80kN}$ **(5) = (3)×(4)**
30–40	35	5.76	0.0366	0.21
40–50	45	6.45	0.1001	0.65
50–60	55	7.22	0.2234	1.61
60–70	65	6.96	0.4358	3.04
70–80	75	9.63	0.7725	7.44
80–90	85	12.04	1.2744	15.34
90–100	95	14.02	1.9885	27.87
100–110	105	10.49	2.9675	31.13
110–120	115	8.43	4.2700	35.98
120–130	125	7.82	5.9605	46.64
130–140	135	5.25	8.1091	42.53
140–150	145	5.93	10.7923	64.03
Total=		100.00		276.46

VDF = 276.46 ÷ 100 = 2.76

Q. *The following data was obtained from an axle load survey:*
Total number of vehicles observed (N) = 98
Assume standard axle load (W_{std}) for

(i) single axle–single wheel = 6.6 tonnes

(ii) single axle–dual wheel = 8.16 tonnes

(iii) tandem axle– four wheel = 15.1 tonnes

Axle load class in tonnes (1)	*Number of passes of axles with*		
	Single axle–single wheel (2)	*Single axle–dual wheel (3)*	*Tandem axle–four wheel (4)*
5–6	*47*	*1*	–
6–7	*33*	*3*	–
7–8	*18*	*3*	–
8–9	–	*14*	–

continues . . .

continued . . .

9–10	–	*13*	*6*
10–11	–	*3*	*6*
11–12	–	*3*	*9*
12–13	–	–	*10*
13–14	–	–	*10*
14–15	–	–	*7*
15–16	–	–	*5*
16–17	–	–	*5*
Total	*98*	*40*	*58*

Calculate the value of VDF based on the fourth power damage rule.

A: The fourth power damage rule is used for calculating load equivalency factors (LEF). The calculation procedure is given below.

Average axle load (W_m)	Repetitions of single axle–single wheel	LEF for single axle–single wheel $= (W_m/6.6)^4$	Repetitions of single-axle–dual wheel	LEF for single axle–dual wheel $= (W_m/8.16)^4$	Repetitions of tandem axle four wheel	LEF for tandem axle four wheel $= (W_m/15.1)^4$
5.5	47	0.48	1	0.21	–	–
6.5	33	0.94	3	0.40	–	–
7.5	18	1.67	3	0.71	–	–
8.5	–	–	14	1.18		
9.5	–	–	13	1.83	6	0.02
10.5	–	–	3	2.74	6	0.02
11.5	–	–	3	3.94	9	0.13
12.5	–	–	–		10	0.19
13.5	–	–	–	–	10	0.19
14.5	–	–	–	–	7	0.05
15.5	–	–	–	–	5	0.01
16.5	–	–	–	–	5	0.01
Total	98	3.09	40	11.00	58	0.63

$$\text{VDF} = \left[\frac{\begin{array}{l}(47\times0.48)+(33\times0.94)+(18\times1.67)+(1\times0.21)+(3\times0.4)\\+(3\times0.71)+(14\times1.18)+(13\times1.83)+(3\times2.74)+(3\times3.94)\\+(6\times0.02)+(6\times0.02)+(9\times0.13)+(10\times0.19)+(10\times0.19)+\\(7\times0.05)+(5\times0.01)+(5\times0.01)\end{array}}{98} \right]$$

$$VDF = \left[\frac{(83.64) + (63.89) + (5.66)}{98}\right] = \left[\frac{153.19}{98}\right] = 1.563$$

Miner's Rule

Damage caused by repeated application of axle loads on a pavement structure is referred to as fatigue damage of pavement. Miner's rule is used to calculate cumulative fatigue and linear damage caused due to repetitions of different axle load groups (Figure 6.11).

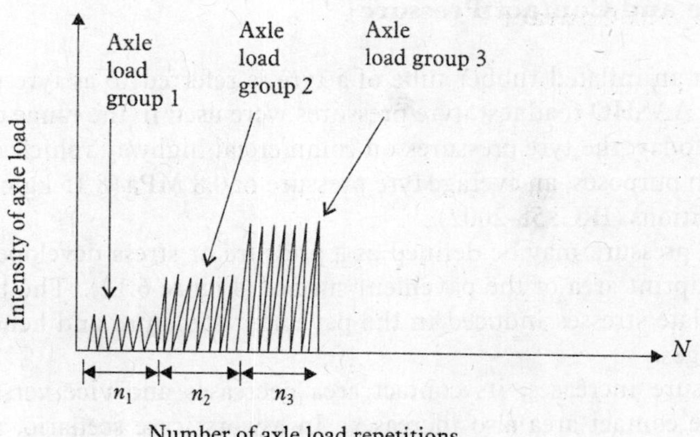

Figure 6.11 *Different axle load groups*

The concept of Miner's rule is given below (Miner 1945).

Consider a pavement subjected to n_j number of repeated uniform loads having load level j. At each level of load application, its theoretical fatigue life is N_j number of repetitions. Then the intensity of damage at one repetition is assumed to be

$$D_j = \frac{1}{N_j} \tag{6.7}$$

The damage after n_j number of repetitions $= n_j\, D_j$

If one hundred per cent damage (as indicative of strain level) occurs after total number of repetitions, the cumulated damage will be

$$\sum(n_j\, D_j) = \left[\frac{n_1}{N_1} + \frac{n_2}{N_2} + \frac{n_3}{N_3} + \frac{n_4}{N_4} + \ldots.. + \frac{n_j}{N_j}\right] = 1.0 \tag{6.8}$$

Miner's fatigue damage rule is used when the fatigue damage caused by individual load groups are considered for design of pavements. Thickness design of flexible and rigid pavements are carried out using this rule (PCA 1984). The basic concept of Miner's distress rule is also used to develop fatigue distress models at different traffic loadings, climatic and in situ conditions.

Load Safety Factor

It is a factor of safety. To take into account unexpected loads or possible occasional overloading or variations in the volume of commercial traffic loading especially on expressways or important roads, the load safety factor is used as a multiplication factor for increasing measured axle loads. Stresses induced by these increased magnitude of axle loads are used for thickness design of pavements. According to IRC: 58-2002, the following load safety factors (LSF) may suitably be assumed for calculation of stresses in cement concrete pavements.

Expressways, national highways and other roads proposed to cater for heavy truck traffic = 1.2
For roads having medium to low truck traffic = 1.1
For village roads and other roads having very low truck traffic = 1.0

Tyre Pressure and Contact Pressure

The pressure in an inflated rubber tube of a tyre is referred to as tyre pressure or inflation pressure. In the AASHO road test, tyre pressures were used in the range of 0.515 to 0.55 MPa. However, as of today, the tyre pressures on commercial highway vehicles vary from 0.7 to 1.0 MPa. For design purposes, an average tyre pressure of 0.8 MPa (8.15 kg/cm^2) may be assumed for Indian conditions (IRC: 58-2002).

Tyre contact pressure may be defined as a pressure or stress developed due to wheel load over the tyre imprint area of the pavement surface (Figure 6.12). The tyre contact pressure is used to calculate stresses induced in the pavement structure and hence, can be related to pavement damages.

As tyre pressure increases, its contact area decreases and vice versa. But the load on the tyre and the contact area also increases. In a worst case scenario, as tyre pressure and axle load increases, the contact pressure also increases. The phenomenon is described in Figure 6.13. This kind of situation is generally observed on a summer day, when trucks are overloaded, since elevated inflation pressures are observed due to higher temperatures of air and pavement. However, for design purposes, tyre contact pressure may be assumed to be equal to tyre pressure.

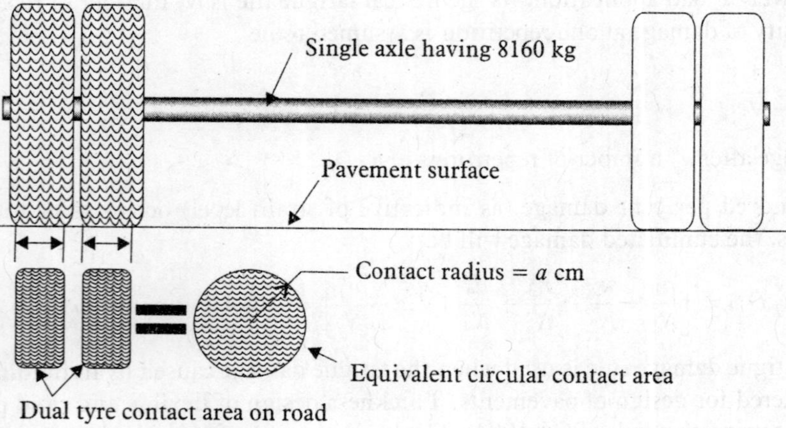

Figure 6.12 *Contact area of a dual tyre*

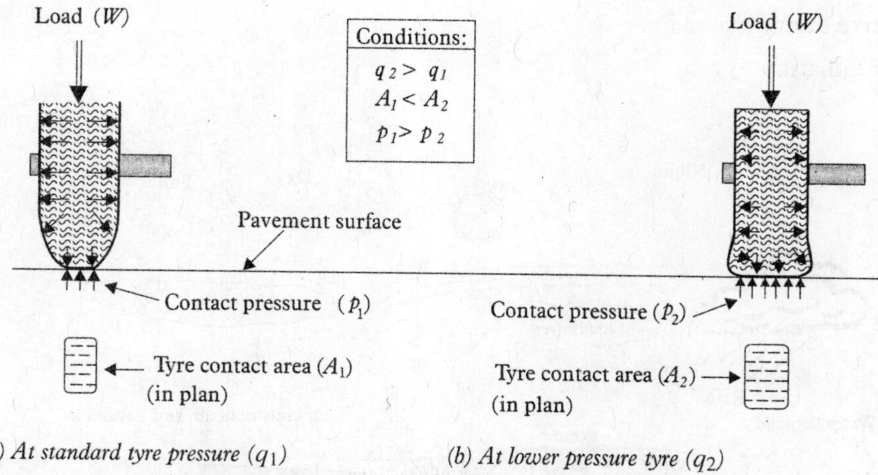

Figure 6.13 *Interactions between tyre and pavement surface*

Q: *Calculate the radius of tyre contact area if tyre pressure is 0.56 MPa and wheel load is 40 kN?*

A: Let tyre contact radius = a

$$\text{Tyre pressure} = \frac{\text{Wheel load}}{\text{Contact pressure}} = \frac{\text{Wheel load}}{\pi a^2}$$

$$\text{Tyre contact radius} = a = \sqrt{\frac{\text{Wheel load}}{\pi \times \text{Tyre pressure}}} = \sqrt{\frac{40 \times 10^3\ \text{N}}{\pi \times 0.56 \times 10^6 \text{N/m}^2}}$$

$$= 0.1507\ \text{m} = 15.07\text{cm}$$

6.3.3 Factors Related to Climatic and Surrounding Environment

In pavement design, climatic and environmental factors (Figure 6.14) must be given as much importance as factors related to traffic because the designed pavement will undergo numerous physical (volumetric) changes in different climatic and environmental conditions during different seasons at various locations.

The following factors should be considered for design of durable and weather-resistant pavements

- Intensity and duration of rainfall, fog or snowfall
- Temperatures of air and pavement
- Surface and sub-surface drainage conditions
- Type of landscape and soil type
- Water bodies nearby
- Ground water level
- Intensity of wind

- Cloud coverage
- Relative humidity
- Solar radiation

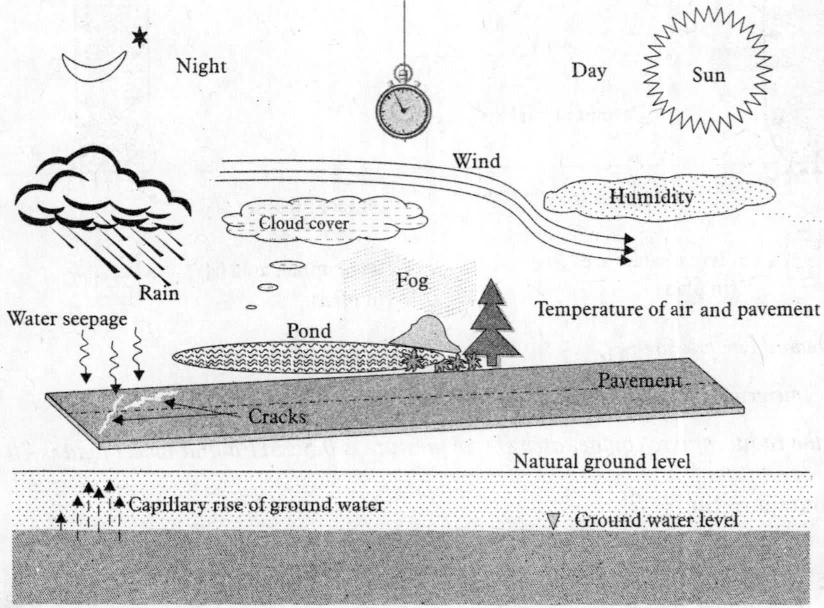

Figure 6.14 *Climatic and surrounding environmental factors*

Moisture

The presence of moisture (other than OMC) from any source in the pavement structure is an undesirable condition which causes volumetric changes in compacted layers at different locations and thereby results in failures in different modes. In particular, parameters related to strength of sub-grade and granular layers are highly sensitive to any little change in OMC. The strength of sub-grades or sub-bases in terms of CBR or modulus or any such strength value decreases as moisture content alters.

The surface water due to rainfall and snowfall should be suitably drained off to side or underground drains and further on to a safe disposable location. Intensity and duration of rainfall data is more helpful than total annual rainfall data to analyse pavement performance. High intensity rainfall of short durations will not cause as much damage as low intensity rainfall over a longer period of time since in the latter case, the pavement will be continuously wet for a long duration and absorb more moisture. Data related to precipitation, viz. rainfall intensity, duration, wind, humidity and air temperature should be collected from the closest meteorological department and used as inputs for design of pavements.

Change in moisture content in the pavement structure is possible under the following two conditions.

(a) Seepage/ infiltration of surface water into the pavement structure takes place from the following locations.

(i) Unpaved shoulders
(ii) Cracked pavement surfaces
(iii) Unsealed pavement joints

If the pavement surface is not completely impermeable due to the presence of cracks, hotspots, potholes, depressions and open joints of cement concrete slabs, the rate of infiltration will increase.

(b) Capillary rise of ground water due to a higher water table and movement of moisture through side drains and nearby water bodies

The severity of distress to the pavement is more if ground water level is raised by surrounding water bodies such as ponds, lakes, rivers and canals. Certain type of soils especially clay-rich soils having particles of size less than 75 microns are more prone to become water-logged. Such soils generally absorb and retain moisture for longer periods. This condition is termed as *poor drainage conditions*. To avoid this undesirable condition, granular materials are used to form a water-filtering layer which is placed over the sub-grade.

Mud pumping is a widely known distress condition in cement concrete pavements. It is a phenomenon in which, water seeps through cracks or enters into joints of concrete slabs and decreases the stiffness of the layers below the slab. Due to weak support, on wheel loading, the slab deflects downward and causes the expulsion of seeped water with small particles of fine-grained sands onto the surface of the slab through the cracks. Under such repetitive application of wheel loads, bigger size voids or cavities will be formed beneath of the slab. Ultimately, the slab breaks into small pieces and settles down forming depressions.

Frost Action

Frost action is a phenomenon of distress which is observed in pavements where the sub-grade and granular layers, consisting of fine-grained soil, freeze over (Bergen and Fredlund 1973). At freezing temperatures, the moisture present in the base, sub-base and sub-grade layers of the pavement become ice crystals (or ice lenses). These ice crystals increase in volume (or swell) and thereby, occupy more space in soil particles. Further, growth of such ice lenses is maintained in a zone of freezing if there is a continuous supply of moisture either by the capillary rise of moisture or raised water table in the vicinity (Taber 1918). An uneven surface formation is observed on the top surface of the pavement and is termed as frost heave (Figure 6.15) (Johnson et al.1982). Frost action is possible when poor drainage conditions and favourable soil characteristics exist (Sourwine 1930).

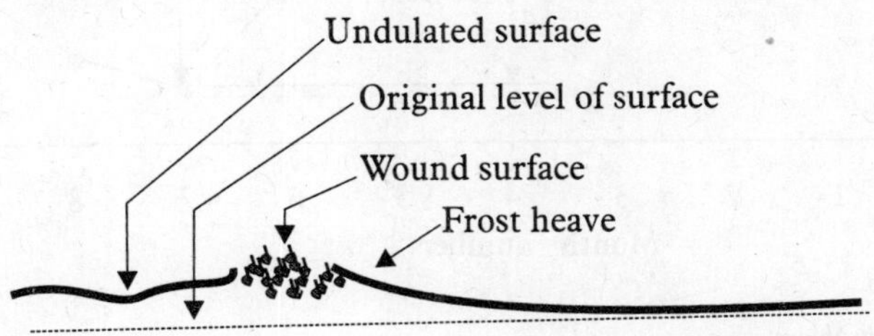

Figure 6.15 *Frost heave*

As the degree of saturation increases, soil expansion takes place thus significantly affecting the resilient modulus of granular soils (Rada and Witczak 1981). This crystallised water (ice lenses) melts when the pavement temperature rises (during thawing) and migrate either in the upward direction or infiltrate into the layers below. Voids will, thus, develop in the pavement due to movement of water in different directions. Under traffic loading, displacement of material particles takes place to fill these voids. Ultimately, compactness of the pavement structure will be disturbed leading to premature failure. The above phenomenon is termed as *frost action* or thaw weakening in pavements. Frost action is related to the *freezing index*—the numerical difference between maximum and minimum values of cumulative degree days (a measure of heating or cooling computed as an integral of a function of time which varies with temperature). The freezing index indicates how many number of degree days a pavement is above (+) or below (–) freezing conditions during a year. The following example problem illustrates the method of calculating the freezing index.

Method of determining the freezing index from the following monthly degree day data:

Month No.	*Month*	*Degree days*	Cumulative value of degree days	Remark
1	*August*	*+98*	*+98*	
2	*September*	*+42*	*+140*	
3	*October*	*+35*	*+175*	
4	*November*	*+15*	*+190*	Maximum
5	*December*	*–98*	*+92*	
6	*January*	*–213*	*–121*	
7	*February*	*–121*	*–242*	Minimum
8	*March*	*+33*	*–09*	
9	*April*	*+74*	*–135*	

Calculation of freezing index is illustrated in Figure 6.16.

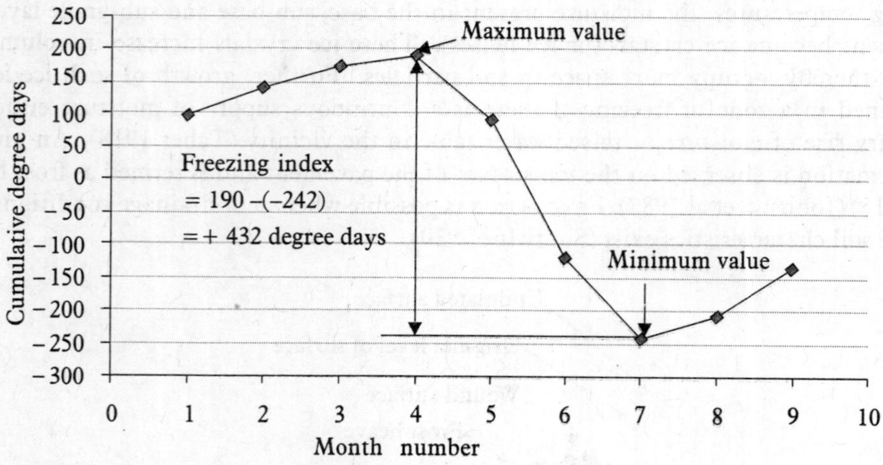

Figure 6.16 *Example problem*

Temperature of Air and Pavement

Short-term and long-term temperature changes are observed between day–night and winter–summer seasons. Due to this repeated or cyclic nature of temperature changes during the service period of a pavement, the durability of the pavement is affected, leading to thermal cracking. At higher temperatures, bituminous surfaces get soft and their stiffness will be lost. The annual average pavement temperature (AAPT) value is used as a standard reference temperature to make corrections to surface deflections and in situ layer moduli measured (or back-calculated) at different temperatures. The correction factors may be in the form of equation (6.5) and (6.6) which are used to correct the deflection and bituminous layer modulus respectively (Park and Kim, TRR No.1570; Ali and Lopez 1996).

$$\Delta_{T_0} = C_{\text{deflection}} \times \Delta_T \tag{6.9}$$

The above equation can be written as $C_{\text{deflection}} = \dfrac{\Delta_{T_0}}{\Delta_T}$

$$E_{T_0} = C_{\text{modulus}} \times E_T \tag{6.10}$$

The above equation can be written as $C_{\text{modulus}} = \dfrac{E_{T_0}}{E_T}$

where, $C_{\text{deflection}}$ and C_{modulus} = Correction factors of deflection and modulus values respectively

Δ_{T_0} = Deflection and modulus value corrected to temperature, T_0

Δ_T = Deflection and back-calculated modulus value measured at temperature, T

E_T = Back-calculated modulus value determined at temperature T

E_{T_0} = Modulus value corrected to temperature T_0

T_0 = Reference temperaure

For correction of deflection and modulus of bituminous layer, different models were developed by many researchers (Park and Kim TRR No.1570; Baltzer and Jansen 1994; Kim et al. 1995; Bosscher et al. 1998; Lukanen et al. 1998) and considered the following factors.

- AAPT, maximum and minimum temperatures at different depths
- Average annual air temperature (AAAT), maximum and minimum air temperatures
- Solar radiation measured with silicon pyranometer
- Latitude of the location
- Properties of bituminous mix
- Thickness of bituminous layer
- Temperature measured at different depths of bituminous layer
- FWD loading amplitude and time

- Visco-elastic parametric study

For visco-elastic design of bituminous layers, it is essential to know the pavement temperature. Pavement temperature depends on air temperature. The velocity of the wind also influences the temperature of the pavement. In addition to these factors, wind coverage, humidity and the time of day are also taken into consideration while estimating temperature gradient in the bituminous layer. Temperature gradient or thermal gradient is also observed in the cement concrete slab due to change in temperature between the top and bottom surfaces. Temperature gradient data is useful to normalise the measured surface deflections to a standard temperature value and to study visco-elastic properties of flexible pavements, contraction and expansion (or curling) of concrete slabs.

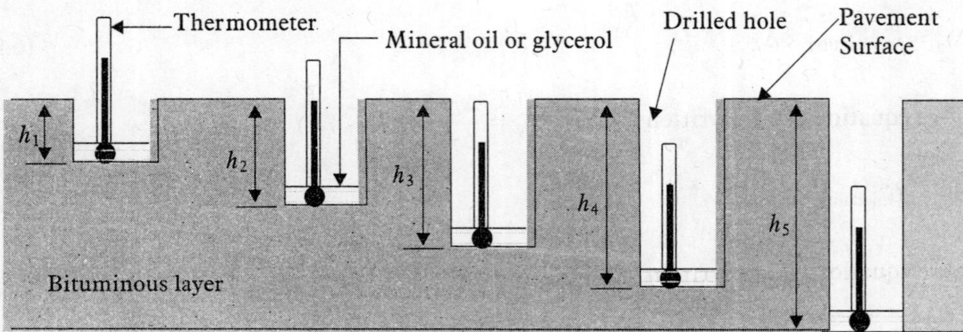

Figure 6.17 *Measurement of bituminous layer temperature at different depths*

The temperature gradient in the bituminous layer is obtained by measuring temperatures at different depths from its surface (Figure 6.17). From the temperature gradient data, a representative temperature is calculated with reference to its depth. To determine the effective or representative temperature of the bituminous layer, the temperature is measured at 1/3rd depth (from top) of the total thickness of the bituminous layer (Baltzer and Jansen 1994). This depth is also termed as the *third-point* in the bituminous layer.

In 1968, Herb Southgate developed relationships for measuring the temperatures in the bituminous bound layers as a function of bituminous layer thickness, time of day and the 5-day mean air temperature. Later many relationships were developed (Baltzer and Jansen 1994; Stubstad et al. 1994; AASHTO 1986) to determine pavement temperature at 1/3rd depth of the bituminous layer.

According to Indian practice, a standard value of annual average pavement temperature (AAPT) is taken as 35 °C for the design of bituminous overlays and new pavements (IRC: 37-2001 and IRC: 81-1997). For design of bituminous overlays, surface deflections are measured using a Benkelman beam (BB) and the deflections are corrected to the standard value of AAPT at the rate of 0.01 mm per each degree centigrade change from the 35 °C. It may be written as

$$\text{Corrected deflection} = \text{measured deflection} + C_{\text{deflection}} \tag{6.11}$$

where, $C_{\text{deflection}}$ = Correction factors of deflection

$C_{\text{deflection}}$ = 0.01 mm/°C × (35 − Temperature of pavement during BB testing (°C))

Correction for temperature is not necessary for thin, cracked and stripped bituminous surface layers, viz. PC or surface dressing, paved layer over granular base. However, temperature correction is compulsory for bituminous layers whose thickness is 40 mm and above (Reddy et al.).

The standard temperature considered for the design of bituminous pavements by different methods is given below (CROW Report D06-06).

- CARE/ASCON (Road and Hydraulic Engineering Institute, Delft): 20 °C.
- CROW design procedure for thin asphalt pavements: 20 °C.
- *French Design Manual* (LCPC, Paris): 15 °C.

In the case of cement concrete pavements, the slabs curl up and down during night and day time. Warping and frictional stresses will develop in the concrete pavement due to expansion and contraction of slabs. Due to this reason, design of joints should be carefully carried out to allow for volumetric changes of slabs at different temperatures as well as to safely transfer a certain amount of the wheel load to an adjacent slab. For design of cement concrete pavements in India (IRC: 58-2002), temperature differential (TD) values (i.e., difference between top and bottom surfaces temperatures in °C) are recommended for different slab thicknesses by dividing the Indian continent into six geographic zones based on the seasonal prevailing temperatures.

6.3.4 Drainage Considerations

In any pavement crust, the presence of uncontrolled and excessive amount of frequent or sustained surface and sub-surface water cause failures in different forms and a few can be listed below.

(a) Erosion of pavement surface layer, shoulders and side drains.
(b) Loss of serviceability of pavement due to premature failures manifested as cracking, rutting, roughness and other distresses.
(c) Inability to transmit dynamic loading on to base, sub-base and sub-grade layers due to loss of structural integrity/ support/ stiffness of pavement layers, mud pumping and other structural failures.
(d) Instability of embankment fills and cut slopes.

Therefore, it is important that, surface and sub-surface water from the pavement should be drained off as early as possible and diverted to a safe place. For this purpose, the designer has to consider the source of water needed to be controlled, suitable changes in the geometric design of the highway, water control across the thickness of pavement and design of a suitable outlet facility. To address these problems, drainage facilities can be provided and classified as (i) surface drainage system and (ii) sub-surface drainage system (Figure 6.18).

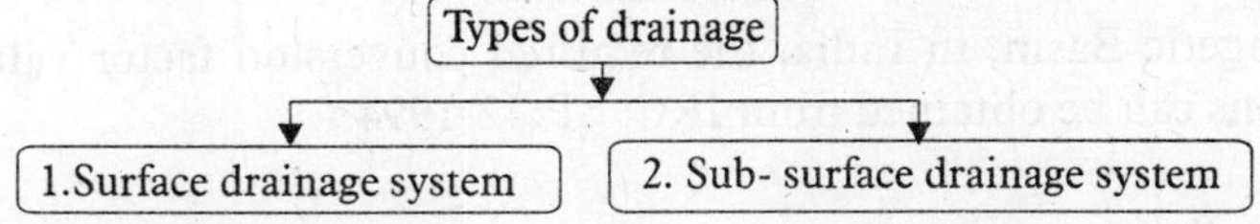

Figure 6.18 *Pavement drainage systems*

6.3.5 Surface Drainage System

Pavement surface drainage problems occur more commonly and are serious in areas of high rainfall. Generally, very high intensity rain falling for a short duration cause heavy outflows and need to be considered while designing surface drainage systems. Surface water is collected in two ways, viz (i) drainage inlets such as grilled manholes, curbs and gutters and (ii) side drains. Side drains are more safe and suitable for conveying large quantities of water in rural areas where the right of way width is sufficient to accommodate them. They can be constructed as open channels or by using huge RCC pipes. Underground pipes are generally preferred in urban localities where there is insufficient right of way.

Estimation of design runoff The storm drain size depends on the quantity of surface water to be drained off and can be determined by using the following formula, called the rational equation.

$$Q = 0.028 \times C \times i \times A \tag{6.12}$$

where, Q = rate of peak runoff, in m^3/s

C = Coefficient of runoff which depends on the surface type (C values range soils from 0.9 for city pavement (like impervious surfaces) to 0.1 for clayey covered with heavy brush and woods)

i = mean intensity of rainfall (in cm/hr) during the *time of concentration* (t_c) and for the frequency interval (say 10 years). (This value can be obtained from rainfall charts of that region prepared by the Meteorological Department)

A = area of drainage, in hectares

NOTE: 1 hectare = 10000 m^2 = 2.47105 acre

An approximate estimation of the design discharge rate of surface rainwater can be obtained by different methods, as given below.

(a) By multiplying a suitable empirical conversion factor to a value of 1 hour rainfall for a frequency period considered in a given locality on the map or intensity–duration–frequency (I–D–F) curves. Such maps are available from the India Meteorological Department and the Directorate of Hydrology, CWC, New Delhi. They show contours of 1 hour rainfall intensity for design frequency periods of 2, 5, 10, 25 and 50 years. Longer frequency periods of 25 years and above may be considered for primary roads and suitable shorter frequency periods may be considered for secondary and tertiary road classes. However, a return period of 10 years and above is considered suitable for designing highway drainage facilities (James and Everitt 1997).

For the Gangetic Basin, in India, the required conversion factor values for typical shorter durations can be obtained from IRC: SP:42-1994.

(b) For shorter duration (up to 120 minutes) of rainfall, IRC:SP: 42-1994 recommends the following equation for estimating the intensity of rainfall.

$$i = \frac{R}{T}\left(\frac{T+1}{t+1}\right) \quad (6.13)$$

where, i = intensity of rainfall (in cm) occurring in a short period (t hours), within a storm.

R = total intensity of rainfall (in cm) occurring in a storm of total duration (T hours)

t = Shorter duration of time interval (in hours) within the storm of total duration T hours

The t value may be assumed to be equal to the *time of concentration* (t_c) which is defined as the minimum duration of time required to flow surface water (as runoff) from a most distant point of the road surface under consideration to a point of reference downstream which is considered as entry into a gutter. As a guideline, the minimum value of t_c may be considered as 5 minutes representing any least value obtained.

The time of concentration (t_c) can be determined from the following.

Kinematic wave equation (Ragan 1971; FHWA-TS-84-202 1984),

$$t_c = \frac{26.285 \times L^{0.6} \times n^{0.6}}{i^{0.4} \times S^{0.3}} \quad (6.14)$$

where, t_c = the time of concentration, in seconds

L_f = length of flow of surface water (min. length on watershed, Figure 6.19), in m

n = Manning's roughness coefficient

S = mean slope of the catchment's area, decimal value

i = intensity of rain fall, in m/hr

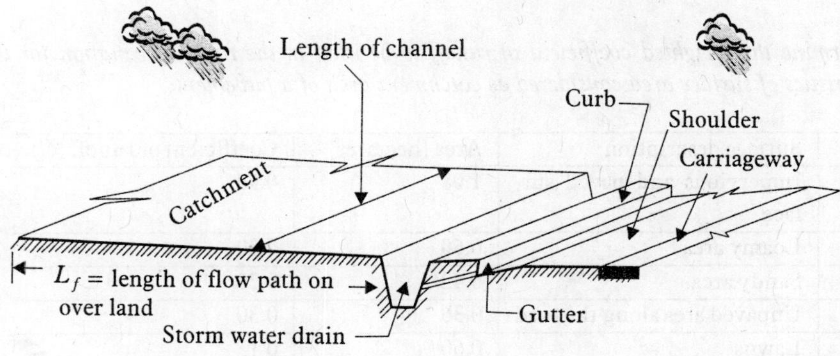

Figure 6.19 *A schematic view of a storm water drain and gutter channel*

The IRC:SP:50-1999 and IRC:SP:13-2004 recommends the following empirical equation of the California Culvert Practice (1944):

$$t_c = \left(0.87 \times \frac{L^3}{H}\right)^{0.385} \quad (6.15)$$

where,

t_c = time of concentration, in hr
L = distance from critical point to entry into an inlet, in km
H = drop or level difference between critical point to the inlet, in m

Q: *Determine the time of concentration based on kinematic wave equation for the following data: Length of flow on overland = 50 m; Average slope of the overland area = 2.5%; Intensity of rainfall in the locality = 60 mm/hr; Manning's surface roughness coefficient for paved surface = 0.8; Design frequency = 10 years.*

A: By substituting the given values in equation (6.14), as $L_f = 50$ m, $S = 2.5/100 = 0.025$, $i = 60/1000 = 0.06$ m/hr, $n = 0.8$; we get,

$$t_c = \frac{26.285 \times L_f^{0.6} \times n^{0.6}}{i^{0.4} \times S^{0.3}} = \frac{26.285 \times 50^{0.6} \times 0.8^{0.6}}{0.06^{0.4} \times 0.025^{0.3}} = 2240.27 \text{ seconds} = 37.33 \text{ minutes}$$

Q: *Determine the time of concentration when the distance between a critical point near the pavement surface to an entry point of inlet is 400 m and the level difference between the critical point to the point of entry of inlet is 10 m.*

A: By substituting the given values in equation (6.15), as $L = 400/1000 = 0.4$ km and $H = 10$ m, we get,

$$t_c = \left(0.87 \times \frac{0.4^3}{10}\right)^{0.385} = 0.1355\,\text{hr} = 8.13 \text{ minutes}$$

Q: *Determine the weighted coefficient of runoff to be used in the rational equation for the following characteristics of surface area considered as catchment area of a pavement.*

Sl. no.	Surface description	Area (hectares)	Coefficient of runoff (C)
1	Impervious and paved surface	1.08	0.90
2	Loamy area	0.60	0.30
3	Sandy area	0.42	0.20
4	Unpaved area along the road	0.36	0.30
5	Lawns	0.60	0.15
6	Built up area having 65 per cent of impervious area	4.34	0.52
Total=		**7.40**	

A: Weighted coefficient of runoff

$$C = \frac{0.90 \times 1.08 + 0.30 \times 0.6 + 0.20 \times 0.42 + 0.30 \times 0.36 + 0.15 \times 0.6 + 0.52 \times 4.34}{7.40} = 0.50$$

Q: *In an area, an intense rainfall of 4 cm is observed in 25 minutes. The average intensity worked out to be 9.6 cm/hr. Estimate the intensity of rainfall which occurred in a short period of 5 minutes within* *the duration of the storm. Also determine runoff from the same locality, intended to be drained through gutters (as surface drainage system) provided at every 150 m length of a pavement having width 50 m. Take Manning's surface roughness coefficient as 0.9.*

A: By substituting the given values in equation (6.13), as R = 4 cm, T = 25/60 = 0.4166 hr and t = 5/60 = 0.0833 hr, we get,

$$i = \frac{R}{T}\left(\frac{T+1}{t+1}\right) = \frac{4}{0.4166}\left(\frac{0.4166+1}{0.0833+1}\right) = 12.55 \text{ cm/hr}$$

By substituting the given values in equation (6.12), as C = 0.9, A = (50×150)/10000 = 0.75 hectares, we get,

$$\text{Runoff} = Q = 0.028 \times 0.9 \times 12.55 \times 0.75 = 0.237 \text{ m}^3/\text{s}$$

Hydraulic design The size and slope of a storm water drain can be determined based on runoff discharge, allowable velocity and flow surface characteristics. Storm water drains can be constructed with any one of the standard cross-sections (Table 6.4)

Table 6.4 *Geometric details of drain sections*

Cross-section (Shape)	Wetted area (A_w)	Wetted perimeter (P_w)	Hydraulic radius ($R_H = A_w/P_w$)	Top width (T_w)	Hydraulic depth (D_H)
Rectangular (h, B)	Bh	$B+2h$	$Bh/(B+2h)$	B	h
Trapezoidal (T_w, h, 1, z, B)	$(B+zh)h$	$B+2h\sqrt{(z^2+1)}$	$(B+zh)h/(B+2h\sqrt{(z^2+1)})$	$B+2zh$	$(B+zh)h/(B+2zh)$
Triangular (T_w, h, 1, z)	zh^2	$2h\sqrt{(z^2+1)}$	$zh/(2\sqrt{(z^2+1)})$	$2zh$	$h/2$
Circular (T_w, D, h, θ)	$(\theta-\sin\theta)D^2/8$	$\theta D/2$	$(1-(\sin\theta/\theta))D/4$	$2\sqrt{h(D-h)}$	$((\theta-\sin\theta)/(\sin\theta/2)D/8$

Design of any drain section (i.e., open channel type from Table 6.4) can be carried out based on Manning's equation of velocity which is substituted in the continuity equation and given as

$$Q = A_w \times V \tag{6.16}$$

where,

$$V = \left(\frac{1}{n}\right) \times R_H^{2/3} \times S_g^{1/2} \tag{6.17}$$

Q = Discharge, m^3/s

V = Manning's equation for determining mean velocity of flow, m/s

n = Manning's roughness coefficient, depends on surface characteristics of channel

R_H = Hydraulic radius (in m); or $R_H = A_w/P_w$; this parameter is used because the flow depth changes across its length

A_w = Wetted area or area of the flow cross-section, m^2

P_w = Wetted perimeter, m

S_g = Longitudinal slope of drain bed

The open channels of drains are designed with reference to *critical conditions* which is defined as the state at which the discharge takes place through the section at minimum *specific energy*. This concept was first introduced by Bakhmeteff in 1912 (1932). The depth of flow in an open channel at the point (P in Figure 6.20) of minimum specific energy is termed as the *critical depth of flow* (d_c) and the depth of flow corresponding to any mild slope, which is *greater than* the critical depth, is termed as the *normal depth of flow* (d_n) (Figure 6.20). The critical depth (d_c) provides boundary conditions for upstream as supercritical flow and downstream as sub-critical flow (Prabhata and Pushpa 2005). To allow greater flow area (i.e., more Q), the depth of flow (as d_n) in the channel should be greater than the critical depth of flow (d_c). At this condition, the flow of water will be sub-critical since the value of velocity is set to be smaller than the critical velocity. Due to this reason, the slope and cross-sectional dimensions of a channel should be designed/or re-designed to satisfy the criterion of $d_n > d_c$. The basic governing relationship used for determining the critical depth is

$$\frac{Q^2}{g} = \frac{A_w^3}{T_w} \tag{6.18}$$

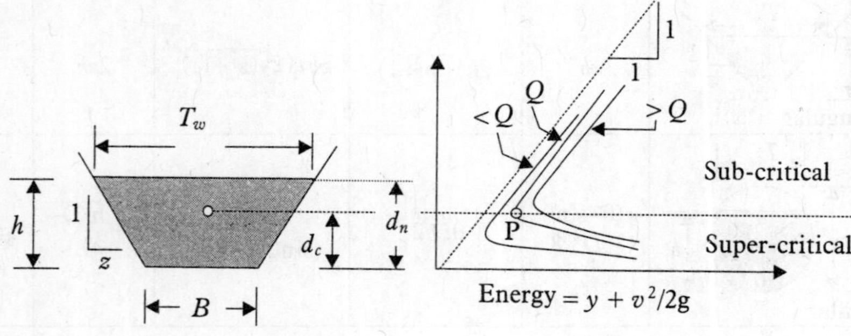

Figure 6.20 *Typical details of minimum specific energy at P on the curve showing critical depth of flow.*

From the above basic relationship, the critical depth (d_c) for a typical rectangular cross-section having B as bottom width and d_c as its critical depth, can be written as

$$\frac{Q^2}{g} = \frac{(B \times d_c)^3}{B}$$

The above expression can be written as $d_c = \left(\dfrac{Q^2}{B^2 \times g}\right)^{1/3}$ (6.19)

The approximate solution for a trapezoidal channel section (Swamee 1993):

$$d_c = \left[\left(\frac{gB^2}{Q^2}\right)^{0.7} + \left(\frac{gz^2}{2Q^2}\right)^{0.42}\right]^{-0.476} \tag{6.20}$$

where, Q = discharge, m^3/s
B = bottom width of the channel (as shown in Table 6.4)
g = gravitational acceleration
z = side slope representing 1(Vertical) : z (Horizontal)

For other geometrical cross-sections of channel, the d_c value can be determined by the trial and error method using the basic equation (equation (6.18)).

Based on the above criterion (equation (6.18)), maximum allowable velocity (V_c) can be deduced from the expression $V_c = (g \times d_c)^{0.5}$, where g = gravitational acceleration and d_c = critical depth of flow.

Sub-critical flow condition (i.e., more flow area) in a channel section can also be evaluated with reference to the Froude number. The criterion can be expressed as

$$\text{Fr} = \left(\frac{V_n}{\sqrt{g \times D_H}}\right) < 1.0 \tag{6.21}$$

Adopt standard guidelines for assuming/selecting minimum and maximum allowable values of velocity, free board, diameter of drain and bottom width of channel.

Q: *Design a side open channel section from the following data:*
Runoff = Q = 0.237 m^3/s
Natural ground slope 1 in 150
Surface characteristics of proposed channel = Average turf with vegetation and easily erodible soil.
Take Manning's coefficient = 0.04, minimum permissible velocity = 0.45 m/s and maximum permissible velocity = 0.9 to 1.2 m/s

A: Let us take a trapezoidal channel section having its bottom width (B) as 0.6, side slopes as 1: 2 and the flow depth as d_n metres.

With reference to Table 6.4 and related equations, the given input values can be written as

Wetted area of the channel $= A_w = (B + zh)h = (0.6 + 2d_n) \times d_n$

Wetted perimeter of the channel $= P_w = B + 2h\sqrt{(z^2+1)} = 0.6 + 2d_n\sqrt{(2^2+1)} = 0.6 + 4.472d_n$

$$\text{Hydraulic radius} = R_H = \frac{A_w}{P_w} = \frac{(0.6+2d_n)\times d_n}{0.6+4.472\,d_n}$$

From Manning's relationship (equation (6.17)),

$Q = A_w \times \left(\frac{1}{n}\right) \times R_H^{2/3} \times S_g^{1/2}$, we get,

$$0.237 = ((0.6+2d_n)\times d_n)\times\left(\frac{1}{0.04}\right)\times\left(\frac{(0.6+2d_n)\times d_n}{0.6+4.472\,d_n}\right)^{2/3}\times\left(\frac{1}{150}\right)^{1/2}$$

Solving the above equation by trial and error, we get $d_n = 0.299$ m

Normal velocity corresponding to the d_n value can be determined using the Manning's equation. We get,

$$V = \left(\frac{1}{0.04}\right)\times\left(\frac{(0.6+2\times 0.264)\times 0.299}{0.6+4.472\times 0.299}\right)^{2/3}\times\left(\frac{1}{150}\right)^{1/2} = 0.662 \text{ m/s}$$

Normal velocity, $V = 0.662$ m/s, which is smaller than the maximum permissible value of 0.9 m/s and greater than the minimum permissible velocity of 0.45 m/s.

Check for the criterion $d_n > d_c$:

Approximate value of the critical depth of a trapezoidal channel can be determined using Swamee's (1993) equation (6.20) as:

$$d_c = \left[\left(\frac{9.81\times 0.6^2}{0.237^2}\right)^{0.7} + \left(\frac{9.81\times 2^2}{2\times 0.237^2}\right)^{0.42}\right]^{-0.476} = 0.240 \text{ m}$$

Check for Froude number (equation (6.21)), $F_n < 1.0$:

$$\text{Hydraulic depth} = D_H = \frac{(B+zh)\,h}{B+2zh} = \frac{(0.6+2\times 0.299)\times 0.299}{0.6+2\times 2\times 0.299} \approx 0.2\,\text{m}$$

$\text{Fr} = \frac{0.622}{\sqrt{9.81\times 0.2}} = 0.44$ which is smaller than 1.0 and indicates that sub-critical flow conditions exist in the trepezoidal channel section. Hence it is OK.

Therefore, d_n value of 0.299 m is greater than the d_c value of 0.240 m. Hence it is OK. Provide minimum free board of 150 mm.

Types of curb channel or gutter channel

indexcurb channel or gutter channel Runoff obtained from the surfaces of carriageway and shoulders is collected into a curb channel having a width about 300 mm and minimum transverse slope of 1 in 6 (16.6 per cent) (IRC:SP:50-1999). Where sufficient space is not available, a V-shaped cross-section is also provided for the curb channel. The longitudinal slope of the curb channel is the same as the road gradient. However, to drain off the surface water effectively, the minimum required slope in the longitudinal direction should be taken as 1 in 333 (0.3 per cent). The curb channel is allowed to intercept the collected runoff discharge by inlets of different types (Figure 6.21), viz. (i) curb inlet, (ii) gutter inlet, (iii) combination of the curb and gutter inlets, (iv) slotted drain inlet and (v) bell mouth drain. These inlets are connected with the collecting chamber and then onto the side channel by drain pipes installed at regular intervals which depends on design discharge.

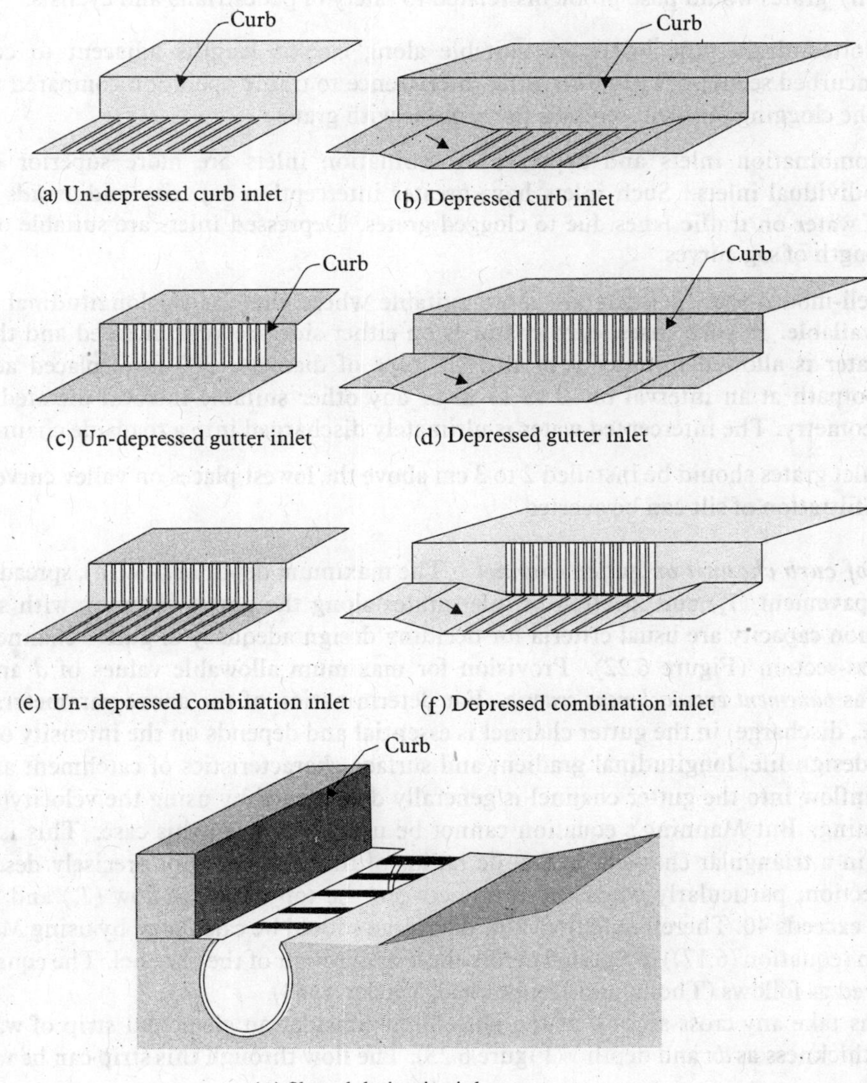

Figure 6.21 *Typical inlet grates*

Suitability of different types of inlets

(a) Grate inlets effectively intercept water flowing in the gutter channel but there is a chance of clogging due to debris.

(b) Curb inlets are relatively free from clogging due to debris. They are preferred where

  (i) grates placed in traffic lanes would cause reduction in the effective width of the lane and

  (ii) grates would pose problems related to safety of pedestrians and cyclists.

(c) Slotted drain pipe inlets are suitable along curved lengths adjacent to curbed or uncurbed sections. They offer little interference to traffic operation compared to grates. The clogging problem remains the same as with grates.

(d) Combination inlets and depressed combination inlets are more superior than the individual inlets. Such inlets have greater interception capacity and avoids ponding of water on traffic lanes due to clogged grates. Depressed inlets are suitable on sloped length of sag curves.

(e) Bell-mouth-shaped inlets are more suitable where there is no longitudinal gradient available. In such cases, curb channels on either side are kept inclined and the runoff water is allowed to enter into an RCC pipe of diameter 300 mm, placed across the footpath at an interval of 10 to 15 m or any other suitable interval dictated by road geometry. The intercepted water is ultimately discharged into a roadside channel drain.

(f) Inlet grates should be installed 2 to 3 cm above the lowest places on valley curves so that infiltration of silt can be averted.

Design of curb channel or gutter channel The maximum depth of flow (d), spread of water on the pavement (T_s) and location of inlet grates along the gutter channel, with sufficient infiltration capacity are usual criteria for deciding design adequacy of gutter channel having any cross-section (Figure 6.22). Provision for maximum allowable values of d and T_s are termed as *pavement encroachment criteria*. For determination of the above parameters, rate of flow (i.e., discharge) in the gutter channel is essential and depends on the intensity of rainfall during design life, longitudinal gradient and surface characteristics of catchment area. The design inflow into the gutter channel is generally determined by using the velocity equation of Manning. But Manning's equation cannot be used as such in this case. This is because usually in a triangular channel, hydraulic radius of the flow does not precisely describe the drain section, particularly when the ratio between the top width of flow (T_s) and depth of flow (d) exceeds 40. Therefore, gutter flow discharge should be calculated by using Manning's equation (equation (6.17)) integrated across the cross-section of the channel. The equation can be derived as follows (Tholin and Keifer 1960; Wasley 1963).

Let us take any cross-section of the gutter and consider an elemental strip of water flow having thickness as dx and depth y (Figure 6.23). The flow through this strip can be written as

$$dQ = v \times y \times dx \tag{6.22}$$

where, dQ is the discharge through the elemental strip in m^3/s, and v is the velocity of flow, in m/s.

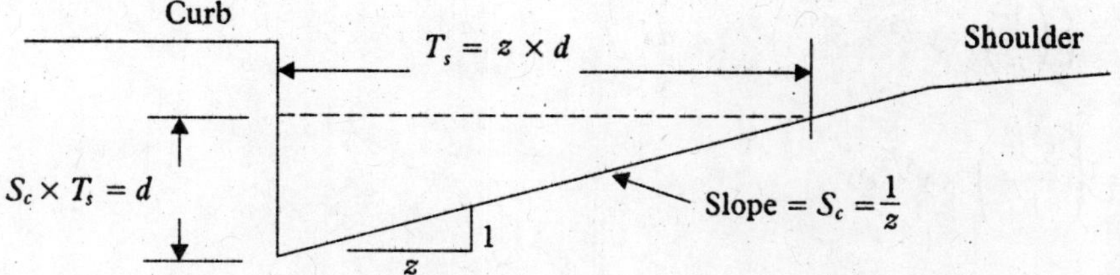

(i) Triangular gutter channel section having a straight curb

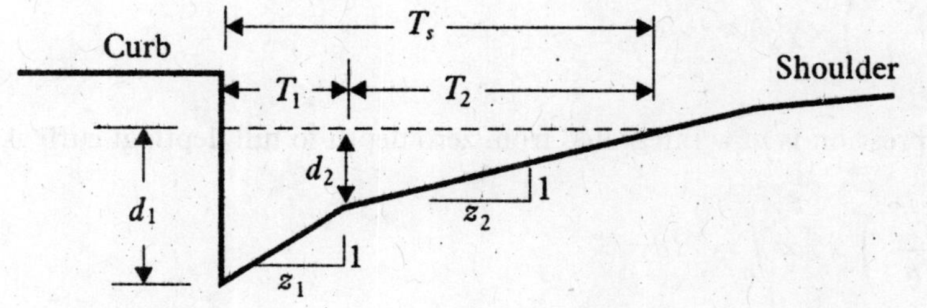

(b) Triangular gutter channel with a compound section

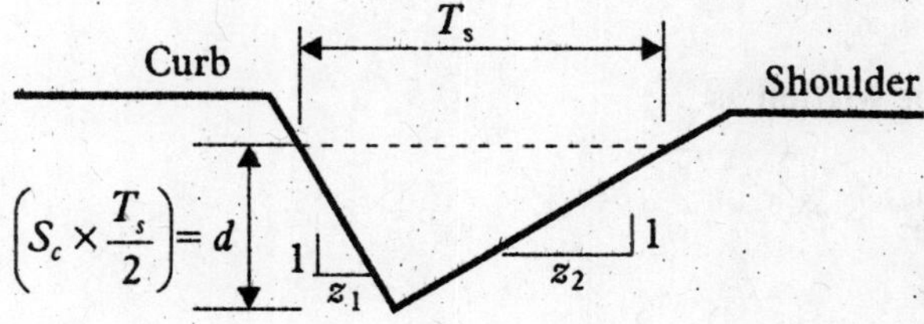

(c) V-shaped triangular gutter channel section

Figure 6.22 *Typical cross-sections of triangular gutter channel*

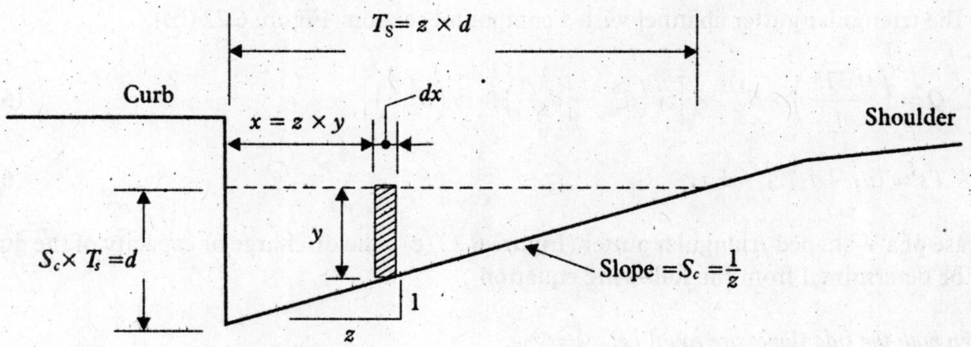

Figure 6.23 *Any cross-section of a gutter and an elemental strip of water*

Now, by substituting Manning's equation of velocity (equation (6.17)) in equation (6.22) and assuming the hydraulic radius as its depth y; we get

$$dQ = \left(\left(\frac{1}{n}\right) \times y^{2/3} \times S_g^{1/2}\right) \times y \times dx$$

$$= \left(\frac{S_g^{1/2}}{n}\right) \times y^{5/3} dx$$

As x is equal to $z \times y$, as shown in Figure 6.23, substituting $dx = z \times dy$, the above equation can be written as

$$dQ = \left(\frac{S_g^{1/2}}{n}\right) \times y^{5/3} \times z \times dy$$

The above expression is now integrated from zero depth to full depth at curb as equal to d.

$$Q = \left(\frac{S_g^{1/2}}{n}\right) \times z \times \int_0^d y^{5/3} dy$$

$$Q = \frac{3}{8} \times \left(\frac{S_g^{1/2}}{n}\right) \times z \times d^{8/3}$$

The above expression can be written as

$$Q = \left(\frac{0.375}{n}\right) \times z \times S_g^{1/2} \times d^{8/3} \tag{6.23}$$

or

$$Q = \left(\frac{0.375}{n}\right) \times S_c^{5/3} \times S_g^{1/2} \times T_s^{8/3} \tag{6.24}$$

For the triangular gutter channel with a compound section (Figure 6.22 (b)):

$$Q = \left(\frac{0.375}{n}\right) \times S_g^{1/2} \times \left[z_1\left(d_1^{8/3} - d_2^{8/3}\right) + z_2\left(d_2^{8/3}\right)\right] \tag{6.25}$$

$$Ts = (d_1 - d_2)\, z_1 + d_2 z_2 \tag{6.26}$$

In case of a V-shaped triangular gutter (Figure 6.22 (c)), the discharge or capacity of the gutter can be determined from the following equation

When both the side slopes are equal i.e., $z_1 = z_2$.

$$Q = \left(\frac{0.75}{n}\right) \times S_c^{5/3} \times S_g^{1/2} \times \left(\frac{T_s}{2}\right)^{8/3} \tag{6.27}$$

$$Ts = 2 \times d \times z_1 \tag{6.28}$$

When both the side slopes are not equal. i.e., $z_1 \neq z_2$.

$$Q = \left(\frac{0.375}{n}\right) \times S_g^{1/2} \times (z_1 + z_2) \times d^{8/3} \tag{6.29}$$

$$Ts = d(z_1 + z_2) \tag{6.30}$$

Inlet capacity The drainage area of an inlet capacity can be calculated by substituting the discharge obtained from any one of the above (gutter cross-section) into Darcy's rational formula (equation (6.12)), which is written as $A = Q/(0.028 \times C \times i)$.

Spacing of inlets By trial and error, match the catchment area (on the contour map) of the street contributing discharge into the inlet to the drainage area obtained from Darcy's rational formula (equation 6.12).

Location of inlet Inlet location should be suitably adjusted along the street based on (i) approximate matching of the catchment and drainage areas, (ii) time of concentration and (iii) street geometry obtained from the contour map.

The following example problems illustrate the above aspects of the design of gutter flow and inlet spacing.

Q: *Determine the discharge in a straight curbed triangular gutter channel. Take the following values with reference to the notations given in Figure 6.22(a).*

Maximum allowable spread of water, $T_s = 1.5$ *m*
Cross slope of the bed, $S_c = 0.03$
Longitudinal slope of the bed, $S_g = 0.01$
Manning's roughness factor, $n = 0.014$
Depth of flow in the gutter $= T_s \times S_c = 1.5 \times 0.03 = 0.0675$ m.

A: Discharge in the straight curbed triangular gutter channel can be determined by equation (6.24).

$$Q = \left(\frac{0.377}{0.014}\right) \times 0.03^{5/3} \times 0.01^{1/2} \times 1.5^{8/3} = 0.023\,\text{m}^3/\text{s}$$

Q: *Determine the depth and spread of water in a V-shaped triangular gutter channel. Take the following values with reference to the notations given in Figure 6.22 (c).*

Cross slopes, $S_c = 0.1667$
Longitudinal slope of the bed, $S_g = 0.01$
Manning's roughness factor, $n = 0.014$
Discharge in the gutter $= 0.03$ m^3/s

A: Let us take depth of flow as d, then cross slope is given as $S_c = 0.1667 = 1$ in 6. Therefore, take $z = 6$.

$$\frac{T_s}{2} = z \times d = 6 \times d$$

Depth of flow (d) in the V-shaped channel can be determined by equation (6.27). Substituting the given values, we get

$$0.03 = \left(\frac{0.75}{0.014}\right) \times 0.1667^{5/3} \times 0.01^{1/2} \times (6 \times d)^{8/3}$$

By solving this equation we get, d = 0.073 m = 7.3 cm and $T_s = 2 \times d \times z = 2 \times 0.073 \times 6 =$ 0.876 m.

Suitable free board is recommended to account for unpredicted excess discharge.

Q: *It is proposed to design triangular gutter inlets which will serve an area consisting of stiff clayey impervious soils with vegetation cover (C = 0.45). A contour map of the catchment area, roadway and proposed cross-sectional details of gutter according to the municipality's pavement encroachment criteria are shown in Figure 6.24. The bituminous roadway (n = 0.015) has a longitudinal slope of 2.7 per cent. Determine the approximate spacing of inlets placed from the east side of the given boundary in the map. The 2-yr average intensity of rainfall observed in the locality is 60 mm/hr.*

Following are the values of the intensity–duration–frequency (IDF) curve for a 10-yr average frequency of rainfall intensity.

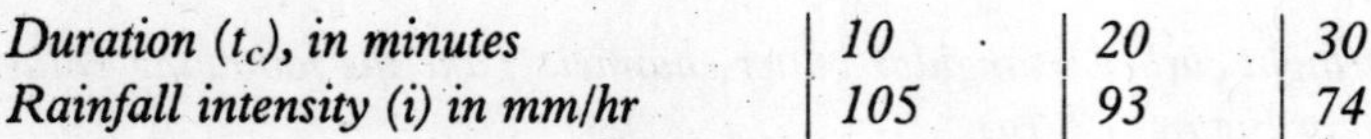

Duration (t_c), in minutes	*10*	*20*	*30*
Rainfall intensity (i) in mm/hr	*105*	*93*	*74*

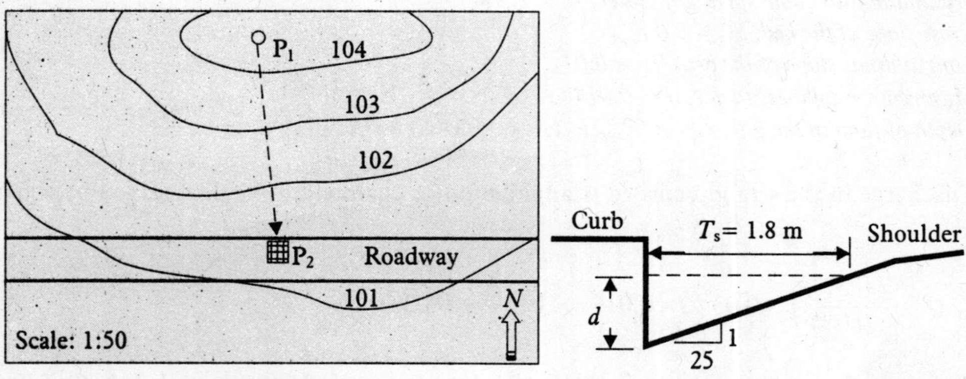

Contour map of catchment area

Cross-section of triangular gutter

Figure 6.24 *Example problem*

A: The given input values can be written as,

Cross slope: $z = 25$

$S_c = 1/25 = 0.04$

Longitudinal slope: $S_g = 2.7/100 = 0.027$

Spread or top width of the flow in gutter: $T_s = 1.8$ m

Depth of flow at the curb: $d = S_c \times T_s = 0.04 \times 1.8 = 0.072$ m

By using equation (6.24), the triangular gutter capacity can be determined as,

$$Q = \left(\frac{0.375}{0.015}\right) \times 0.04^{5/3} \times 0.027^{1/2} \times 1.8^{8/3} = 0.092\,\text{m}^3/\text{s}$$

The drainage area that could be served by a gutter with its full capacity can be determined from the parameters by using Darcy's rational rainfall formula. The design intensity of rainfall is obtained from the IDF curve based on the value of the time of concentration.

Referring to the contour map (Figure 6.24),
Horizontal distance between points, P_1 to P_2 (on the contour map) $\approx$ 125 m
Vertical drop from P_1 to P_2 = 104 − 101= 3 m per 125 m horizontal distance
Gradient across the points P_1 or P_2 = S = 3/125 = 0.024

Time of concentration can be calculated by using FWHA (equation 6.14) and substituting as, overland flow length on a sloped surface, $L_f = 125.0$ m, $S = 0.024, i = 60/1000 = 0.06$ m/hr. Assuming that for short grass conditions, Manning's value for sheet flow $n = 0.15$, we get

$$t_c = \frac{26.285 \times L_f^{0.6} \times n^{0.6}}{i^{0.4} \times S^{0.3}} = \frac{26.285 \times 125^{0.6} \times 0.15^{0.6}}{0.06^{0.4} \times 0.024^{0.3}} = 1440 \text{ seconds} \approx 24 \text{ minutes.}$$

By interpolation of IFD values for $t_c = 24$ minutes, the design rainfall intensity, $i = 93 - 7.6 =$ 85.4 mm/hr = 8.54 cm/hr.

Therefore, drainage area could be served by a gutter with its full capacity = $A = Q/(0.028Ci)$. By substitution we get,

$$A = 0.092/(0.028 \times 0.45 \times 8.54) = 0.85498 \text{ hectares} = 8549.8 \text{ m}^2 \approx 8550 \text{ m}^2.$$

Assuming the given plan area is rectangular with an approximate width of 125 m, the inlet spacing is calculated as,

Approximate spacing of inlet = 8550/125

$\approx$ 68.5 m from east to west side, along the length of the gutter

A suitable capacity of the inlet (as shown in Figure 6.21) should be selected with reference to its interception capacity (i.e., Q) of grate or curb opening or combination inlet as provided by the manufacturer.

A similar design procedure is adopted for locating the second inlet. Due to unfavourable geometry and conditions (such as the C value, time of concentration, encroachment criteria and inlet clogged due to debris) of the road, all the design discharge of the first inlet may not get completely infiltrated. In such cases, that part of the leftover (water) discharge is added to the design discharge of the second inlet.

If the site conditions remain approximately the same along the length of the roadway, the above calculated spacing between the first inlet and the second inlet can be repeated further down along the gutter until an intersection is reached.

6.3.6 Sub-surface Drainage System

In addition to infiltration of the surface water, fluctuations in the level of GWT (ground water table) is one of the important causes of sub-surface drainage failures. Therefore, the quantity of sub-surface water to be removed should be estimated for a given pavement section.

Sources of sub-surface water Interception, cutting off seepage, collection and removal of sub-surface water and thereby drawing down or lowering of GWT are the main functions of the sub-surface water system. Estimation of *net quantity* (Q_N) of accumulated sub-surface water which has migrated from different sources (Figure 6.28) are considered under categories of (i) downward flow (Q_i) (Figure 6.14), (ii) upward flow (Q_g or Q_a or Q_m (Figures 6.29) and (iii) outward flow (Q_o) from the pavement crust by gravity or lost due to evaporation.

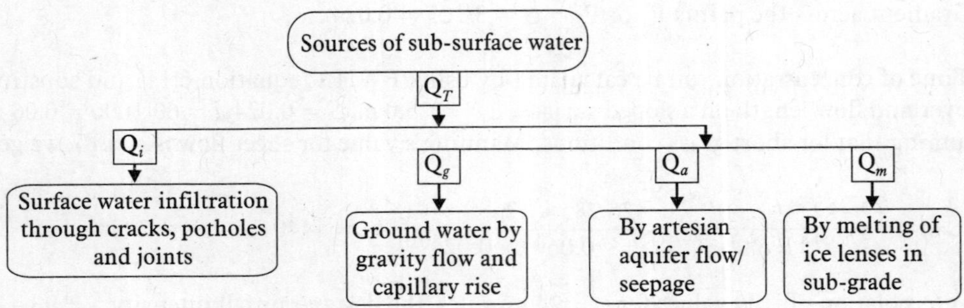

Figure 6.28 *Sources of sub-surface water*

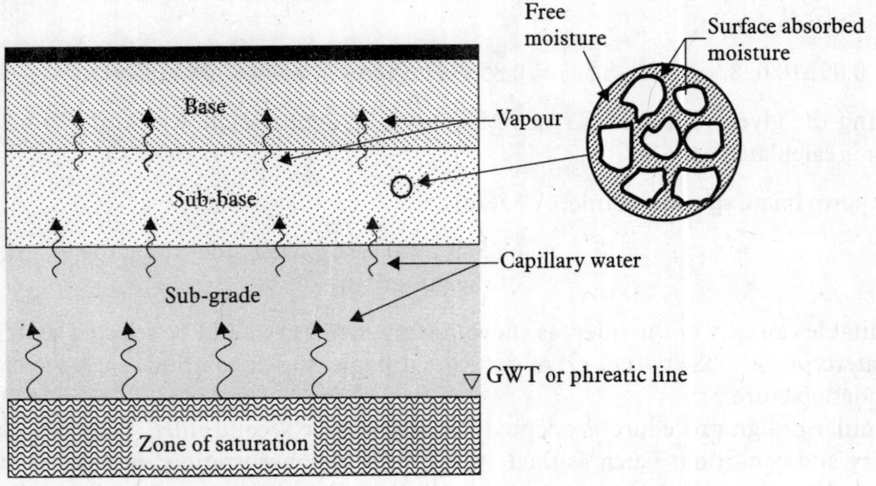

Figure 6.29 *Upward movement of sub-surface water*

Estimation of quantity of sub-surface water to be drained-off Net quantity of sub-surface water to be removed through the drainage layer can be determined from the following expression (FHWA-TS-80-224 1980).

$$Q_N = Q_T - Q_o \tag{6.31}$$

where, $Q_T = Q_i + (Q_g \text{ or } Q_a \text{ or } Q_m)$ (6.32)

The amount of sub-surface water collected by infiltration (Q_i) is generally considered significant and a procedure to estimate it, recommended by FHWA, is presented below. The quantity of water from the remaining sources (Q_g or Q_a or Q_m) and the value of Q_o are most often less compared to the value of Q_i. In such cases, an approximate estimation may be made by assuming a suitable amount compared with the Q_i value and field conditions. However, the net quantity of the water should be determined precisely for the design of a suitable and efficient sub-surface drainage system. A few methods were developed for estimation of sub-surface water quantity from these different sources and can be obtained from relevant literature (Moulton 1979; FHWA-TS-80-224 1980).

Estimation of quantity of sub-surface water due to infiltration (Q_i) Generally, sub-surface drainage problems occur and are serious when the GWT raises due to high rainfall. The reason for such fluctuations in the level of GWT may be correlated to the amount of precipitation in the area. Rain water infiltration intensity depends more on the *duration* of rainfall than its frequency or intensity (Ridgeway 1976). However, in typical sandy soils, a very high intensity of rainfall in a shorter duration also causes infiltration. Therefore, both need to be considered in designing the sub-surface drainage system. Approximate estimation of the design infiltration rate of rainwater can be obtained by different methods, as given below.

(a) A suitable empirical conversion factor is multiplied with a value of 1 hour rainfall for a frequency period considered in a given locality on the map. Values of the conversion factors should be based on pavement type (rigid or flexible), existing surface characteristics (such as cracking, potholes and joints condition) and geometric conditions. According to the guidelines of IRC:SP:50-1999, the coefficient of infiltration for earthen shoulders can be assumed to be 0.4 to 0.6, for bituminous pavements 0.2 to 0.4 and for concrete pavements 0.3 to 0.4.

(b) Based on cracking and joint spacing, the design infiltration rate through pavement sections can be determined using the following equation developed by the Federal Highway Administration (FHWA-TS-80-224), which is based on Ridgeway's work (1976).

$$Q_i = I_c \times \left[\frac{N_c}{W} + \frac{W_c}{(W \times C_s)}\right] + k_p \tag{6.33}$$

where,

Q_i	=	Design infiltration rate, m^3/ day/ m^2 area of drainage layer
I_c	=	Crack infiltration rate, m^3/ day/ m length of crack
N_c	=	Number of longitudinal joints or cracks contributing to infiltration (For new pavements, N_c value may be assumed as number of lanes plus one)

W_c	=	Length of transverse joints or cracks contributing infiltration, in m
W	=	Width of drainage (or granular) layer subjected to infiltration, in m
C_s	=	Spacing of transverse joints or cracks contributing to infiltration, in m
k_p	=	Coefficient of permeability of pavement surface when considered as uncracked, m^3/ day/ m^2 area of the surface of the pavement. The k_p value may be assumed to be zero for new pavement surfaces

A study conducted in Connecticut, USA (Ridgeway 1976), recommended a value for design infiltration rate (I_c) as 2.4 cubic foot/day/feet (0.22 m^3/day/m) of crack.

Q: *Determine the infiltration rate into a new cement concrete pavement section for the following given conditions: width of drainage layer under dual lane carriageway = 7.5 m; width of roadway = 14.0 m; spacing of transverse joints = 4.5 m; design infiltration rate = 0.223 m^3/ day/ m length of crack. Assume the coefficient of permeability of the new pavement surface to be zero.*

A: By substituting the given values in the FHWA equation (6.33) as, W = 7.5 m; W_c = 14.0 m; C_s = 4.5 m; k_p = 0; N_c = (number of lanes +1) = (2 + 1) = 3; and I_c = 0.223 m^3/ day/ m length of crack.

$$Q_i = 0.223 \times \left[\frac{3}{7.5} + \frac{14}{(7.5 \times 4.5)}\right] + 0 = 0.1817 \text{ m}^3/\text{ day}/\text{ m}^2 \text{ area of drainage layer.}$$

Determination of coefficient of permeability The design of drainage and filter layers should be carried out based on the permeability of the layer material. The capacity of a drainage layer to allow/remove the collected water is determined based on its cross-sectional area and coefficient of permeability (k_d, in m/day). Therefore, the designer has to carefully select suitable materials for the drainage layer and its coefficient of permeability should be realistically estimated. The coefficient of permeability of a drainage/filter layer of a pavement can be determined/estimated by different methods. The methods recommended preferably are (i) in situ testing (Milligan 1975; Moulton and Seals 1979), (ii) laboratory testing (Barber and Sawyer 1952; ASTM 1978), (iii) analytical analysis (Jackson and Ragan 1974) and (iv) empirical estimation methods (Loudon 1953), in that order.

Reliable estimation of coefficient of permeability (k_d) can be made by in situ testing and to a certain extent by laboratory investigations. It can also be determined by using statistically developed correlations available between the coefficient of permeability and the drainage layer material properties such as porosity, dry density, effective grain sizes, per cent fines passing through a sieve size of 0.075 mm and specific surface. As an example under this category, the coefficient of permeability of the drainage layer of granular and filter material can be estimated by using the following Federal Highway Administration's relationship (FHWA-TS-80-224, 1980).

$$k_d = \left[\frac{(n)^{6.654} \times (D_{10})^{1.478}}{(\text{PP}_{75})^{0.597}}\right] \times 189.40272 \times 10^3 \tag{6.34}$$

where, n = porosity $= 1 - \left(\dfrac{\gamma_d}{9.733 \times G}\right)$

k_d = Coefficient of permeability of drainage layer, m/day

γ_d = Dry density of the material, kN/m^3

G = Specific gravity of the material

D_{10} = Effective grain size, mm

PP_{75} = Per cent passing through sieve size of 0.075 mm, in percentage. Small increase in the value of PP_{75} will result in a large decrease in the value of the coefficient of permeability of the material (Barber and Sawyer 1952)

It is noted that the k_d value will be indeterminate by equation (6.34) if the PP_{75} value is equal to zero. In such cases, the k_d value can be determined using the nomograph of the Federal Highway Administration (FHWA-TS-80-224 1980).

The value of the coefficient of permeability for clean sand can be estimated from Hazen's equation, written as, $k_d = (D_{10})^2$, where D_{10} is the diameter of particles finer than 10% by mass, in mm and k_d will be in cm/s.

Q: *Determine the coefficient of permeability of a granular layer having dry density as 18.5 kN/m^3, specific gravity as 2.69, per cent passing sieve size of 0.075 mm as 3.0% and effective grain size (D_{10}) as 0.5 mm.*

A: By substituting the given value in equation (6.34), we get,

$$n = \text{porosity} = 1 - \left(\frac{18.5}{9.733 \times 2.69}\right) = 0.29339$$

$$k_d = \text{coefficient of permeability} = \left[\frac{(0.29339)^{6.654} \times (0.5)^{1.478}}{(3.0)^{0.597}}\right] \times 189.40272 \times 10^3$$

$$= 10.09 \text{ m/day}$$

Determination of the length of path flow of water in the drainage layer Geometrically, the pavement surface is inclined in the transverse and longitudinal directions (Figure 6.25) and the details are given below.

Cross slope: 1 Horizontal (H) : S_c Vertical (V)

Longitudinal slope: $1\,H : S_g\,V$

Therefore, for $W\,H$, the cross slope $= W \times S_c$ and the longitudinal slope $= W \times S_g$ (in the vertical plane).

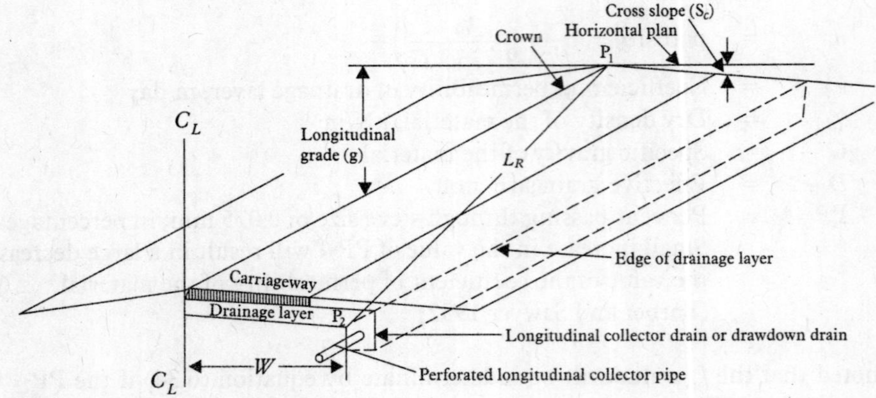

Figure 6.25 *Path of sub-surface water flow in drainage layer (modified and elaborated based on FHWA-TS-80-224, 1980)*

Inclin. l diagonal slope (S_d) due to the longitudinal and cross slopes will be

$$S_d = \sqrt{(W \times S_c)^2 + (W \times S_g)^2}$$

$$S_d = W\sqrt{(S_c)^2 + (S_g)^2}$$

$$\text{or } S_d = (W \times S_c)\sqrt{1 + \left(\frac{S_g}{S_c}\right)^2}$$

$$\text{The resultant slope per unit width of pavement} = S_d = \sqrt{S_c^2 + S_g^2} \tag{6.35}$$

The above value of the slope will be visualised in the vertical plane.

If, $S_c\,V : 1\,H$, for $(W \times S_c)\sqrt{1 + \left(\frac{S_g}{S_c}\right)^2}\ V : ?\,H$

Hence, the inclined horizontal length (L_R) from the point P_1 to P_2, considered as the path of the sub-surface water flow in the drainage layer (Figure 6.21) can be determined as (FHWA-TS-80-224 1980),

$$L_R = \frac{(W \times S_c)\sqrt{1 + \left(\frac{S_g}{S_c}\right)^2}}{S_c}$$

$$\text{Therefore, } L_R = W\sqrt{1 + \left(\frac{S_g}{S_c}\right)^2} \tag{6.36}$$

Conditions:

(a) when the value of $S_g = 0$, minimum length of flow path (L_R) will occur.
(b) when the value of $S_c = 0$, L_R value becomes infinite which does not exist.

General design criteria The following aspects should be considered for design of drainage/ filter layer.

The drainage layer material grain size should be selected such that when the sub-surface water flow in the upward direction, (i) the sub-grade's finer particles should not intrude into the voids of the filter layer which comprises of coarser particles compared to the sub-grade soil and similarly, (ii) the granular drainage layer should not be clogged by the intrusion of finer particles of filter layer or sub-grade soil, which reduces the permeability of the drainage layer due to the pumping action caused by repetitive loading of traffic (Barber and Sawyer 1952). Therefore, for the design of drainage and filter layers, a suitable grade of granular material should be selected based on the following standard criteria recommended by IRC: 37-2001.

D_{15} of drainage layer $\geq (5 \times D_{15}$ of sub-grade), D_{50} of drainage layer $\leq (25 \times D_{50}$ of sub-grade) and D_{15} of drainage layer $\leq 5 \times D_{85}$ of sub-grade.

It is noted that the provision of a filter layer in between coarser and fine grain soils is essential when the standard filter criteria (IRC: 37-2001) is not satisfied. As a common sub-surface drainage practice, the sub-base layer is designed as a drainage layer and checked to see if it satisfies the standard filter criteria (IRC:37-2001) for possible intrusion of sub-grade soil into it. If the sub-base material does not satisfy the standard filter criteria, a filter layer should be designed for the stated conditions and placed in between the sub-grade and sub-base layer (Figure 6.26). The above criteria also holds good between materials of embankment and filter or drainage layer.

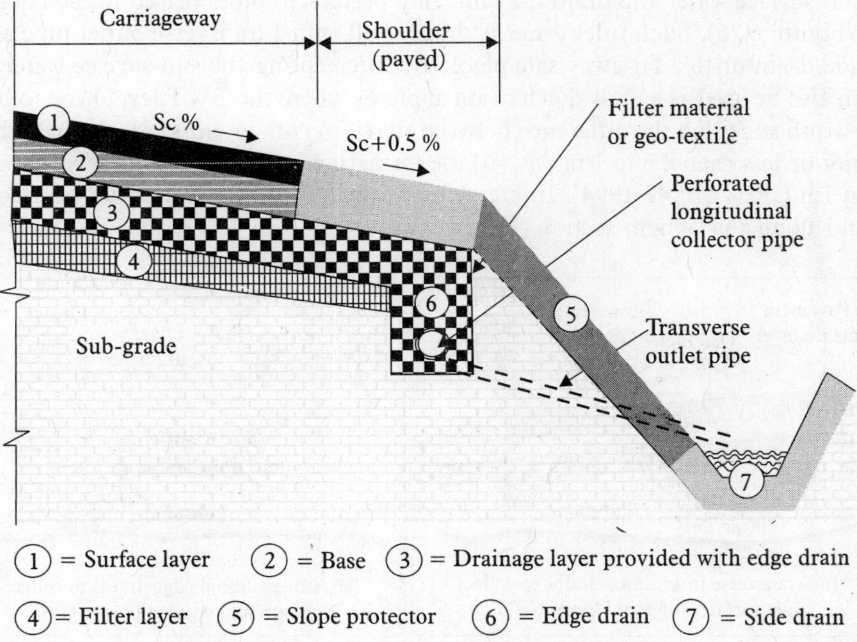

Figure 6.26 *Pavement cross-sectional details of sub-surface drainage system.*

Material selected for base/sub-base layer designed as drainage/filter layer should be permeable enough to drain off the sub-surface water without stagnation and erosion. This means that the required (or design) value of k_d should be greater than the estimated (or available) k_d value of any material selected for the drainage layer. As general guidelines, soil classified according to the unified soil classification system as GW, GP, SW and GM classes of soils are pervious and suitable for drainage layer but CH, MH, OL, CL, ML and SC classes of soils are generally impervious and their possible use by blending with other coarser soils may be explored.

Sufficient cross-sectional area in terms of width and depth of the drainage/filter layer should be provided. As an ideal condition, (i) width of the drainage layer should cover the entire width of the roadway and earthen berms with side slope (if provided) and (ii) its thickness should be more than the maximum theoretical depth of flow of the sub-surface water, such that the value of coefficient of transmissibility ($H_d \times k_d$) will be increased. The depth of the drainage layer (H_d) can be determined using Darcy's law (1856) of laminar flow of water through a porous medium and it can be written as

$$H_d = \left(\frac{Q_N}{k_d \times i} \right) \tag{6.37}$$

where,
H_d = Thickness of drainage layer per unit width, m
Q_N = Quantity of sub-surface water to be removed, m^3/day/m^2
K_d = Coefficient permeability of the drainage layer, m/day
i = slope in the direction of flow of water, decimal value

Edge drain or longitudinal collector drain or draw down drain Edge drains are used to collect sub-surface water and drain the same into perforated pipes placed in each of its bottom surface (Figure 6.26). Such inlet water is drained off into a transverse outlet pipe and finally into a side drain or to a far away safe place. By intercepting the sub-surface water, the edge drain can also be used as a draw down drain at places where the GWT level need to be lowered to a safe depth such that the difference between the (i) top of the sub-grade to the highest GWT should not be less than 0.6 to 1 m and (ii) the formation level and ground level should not be less than 1m (IRC: SP: 42-1994). Interception of the sub-surface water can be accomplished across and along a pavement section (Figure 6.27).

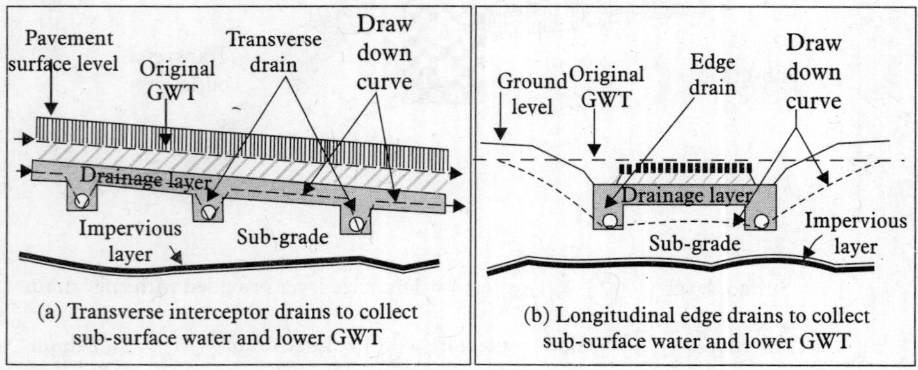

Figure 6.27 *Provision of sub-surface interceptors to lower GWT*

Size of the edge drain trench can be determined by rewriting Darcy's equation in the following form.

$$Q_D = k_t \times S_g \times A_t \tag{6.38}$$

where, Q_D = Quantity of water entering the pipe per running metre = $Q_N \times L_o$
L_o = Maximum distance between successive outlets placed across the longitudinal direction, m
k_t = Permeability of the trench backfill material, m/day
S_g = Gradient or slope of the drain or slope of the ground on which drain is installed, decimal value
A_t = Cross-sectional area of the coarse drainage material of the trench, m^2

Perforation criteria of a longitudinal drain pipe To avoid washed fines of trench material from entering into the perforated pipe, the following criteria are useful for selecting high permeable material surrounding the pipes (FHWA-TS-80-224 1980).

For slotted pipe: D_{85} value of filter material > 1/2 slot width and
For circular hole: D_{85} value of filter material > Hole diameter

There are several factors which affect the selection of the diameter and type of collector pipe. The designer should rationally select its diameter and type based on (i) flow rate in the drain (Q_d), (ii) longitudinal distance (L_o) between outlet pipes placed in transverse direction, (iii) its longitudinal gradient (g) and (iv) economic considerations. The diameter of the pipe can be determined by using the nomograph developed by Cedergren (FHWA-TS-80-224 1980). As a general guideline, the minimum diameter of the PVC and other types of perforated pipes should not be less than 75 mm and 100 mm respectively.

Q: *For the following conditions of pavement cross-section (Figure 6.28), determine the thickness of the drainage layer.*

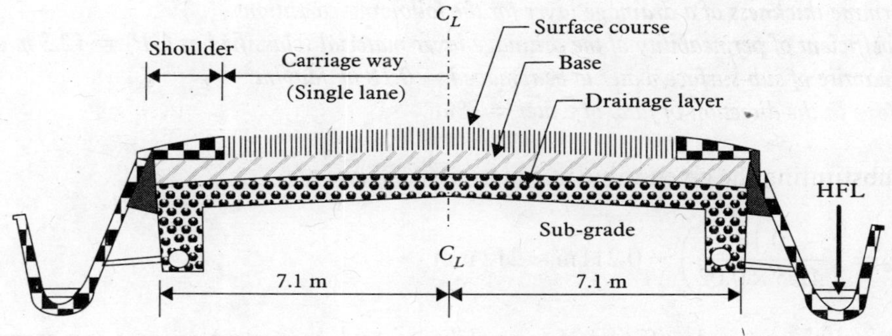

Figure 6.28 *Details of a double-lane pavement cross-section: Example problem*

Longitudinal grade = 3.5 %
Cross slope or camber = 2.5 %
Permeability of drainage layer per unit area = 300 m /day

At location of the pavement, the value of a 25 year 1 hour maximum rainfall = 45 mm
Assume the net quantity of the sub-surface water to be drained as 20% of the rainfall water.

A: (*i*) *Thickness design of drainage layer:*

With reference to Figure 6.25 and 6.28, the given input values can be designated as,

$W = 7.1$ m, $S_g = 3.5$ %, $S_c = 2.5$ %, $k_d = 300$ m/day

The resultant slope $= S_d = \sqrt{S_c^2 + S_g^2} = \sqrt{0.025^2 + 0.035^2} = 0.043$

Sub-surface water flow path length, (by equation (6.36)),

$$L_R = W\sqrt{1+\left(\frac{S_g}{S_c}\right)^2} = 7.1 \times \sqrt{1+\left(\frac{0.035}{0.025}\right)^2} = 12.21 \text{ m}$$

Quantity of sub-surface water to be drained

$$= \frac{20}{100} \times \left(\frac{45}{10^3} \times 24\right) \times (12.21 \times 1\,\text{m}) = 2.6374\ \text{m}^3/\text{day}/\text{m}^2$$

From Darcy's equation (similar to equation(6.38)), the drainage layer thickness (h_d) can be determined as,

$Q_n = k_d \times S_d \times A$
$2.6374 = 300 \times 0.043 \times (h_d \times 1\text{m})$
$h_d = 0.204$ m

Therefore, provide drainage layer thickness not less than 210 mm.

Q: *Determine thickness of a drainage layer for the following conditions.*
Coefficient of permeability of the drainage layer material (classified as GP) = 42.5 m/day
Quantity of sub-surface water to be removed = 0.18 m³/day/m²
Slope in the direction of flow of water = 2%

A: By substituting the given value in equation (6.37), we get,

$$H_d = \left(\frac{0.18}{42.5 \times 0.02}\right) = 0.211\,\text{m} \approx 212\text{ mm}$$

Q: *Determine the required coefficient of permeability of a sub-base course designed as a drainage layer, for the following conditions.*
Thickness of sub-base coarse = 250 mm
Quantity of sub-surface water to be removed = 0.18 m³/day/m²
Slope in the direction of flow of water = 2%

A: By substituting the given value in equation (6.37), we get,

$$k_d = \left(\frac{0.18}{0.250 \times 0.02}\right) = 36 \text{ m/day}$$

The above k_d value can be obtained by testing the soil selected from GW, GP and SW classification of the unified soil classification system. In case of other soils, required changes may be made in their gradation curve by blending with other coarser borrowed material.

6.3.7 Reliability Considerations

The reliability factor should be considered in pavement design to account for the variability in various design input values related to soil conditions, traffic volume, axle loads, load distribution, climatic zones, drainage conditions, material properties, construction quality, compaction, layer thickness, reinforcement, allowable distress level or design criteria etc. Therefore, every input used for the design of pavements should represent an appropriate value that will have to exist during the service period. This means that there should be a close match between measured response and predicted values that are used as design inputs. Otherwise, the pavement will not be compatible to in situ conditions and will finally indicate variability in pavement performance which are measured in terms of rebound surface deflections (Figure 6.29) or rutting or any other parameter related to its strength.

The degree of reliability in the design of pavements will depend on the anticipated variability in the values of inputs and their influence on design outcome. The reliability is indicated by per cent value. For example, a value of 95 per cent reliability means 95 per cent of such pavements perform satisfactorily and above expectation. The rest of the 5 per cent will fail prematurely. According to the *AASHTO Design Guide* (AASHTO 1986), different levels of reliability values are recommended for different class of roads (Table 6.6).

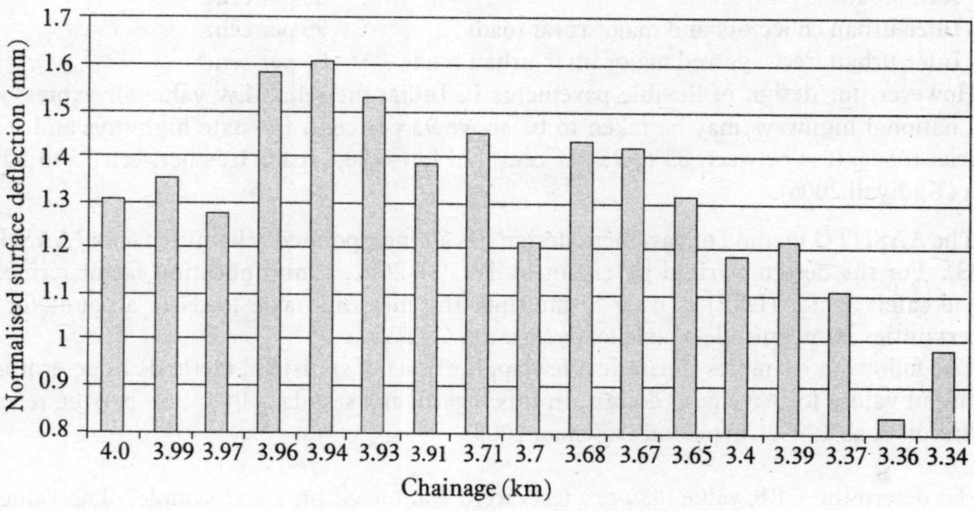

Figure 6.29 *Variations in maximum surface deflections along IIT Kharagpur perimeter road (tested with FWD at 40 kN load)*

Table 6.6 *AASHTO recommended levels of reliability*

Class of road	Ref. *AASHTO, 1993*		Ref. *NCHRP, 2003*	
	for urban roads	for rural roads	for urban roads	for rural roads
Interstate & other freeways	85 to 99.9	80 to 99.9	85 to 97	80 to 95
Principal arterial	80 to 99	75 to 95	80 to 95	75 to 90
Collectors	80 to 95	75 to 95	75 to 85	70 to 80
Local	50 to 80	50 to 80	50 to 75	50 to 75

In case of stage construction, according to AASHTO, the reliability to be adopted in each stage of construction may be calculated using the following relationship.

$$R_i = (R_T)^{(1/N)} \tag{6.39}$$

where, R_i = Reliability to be adopted in each stage of construction
R_T = Combined reliability of all stages of construction
N = Number of stages of construction

The values recommended by AASHTO for overall standard deviation is 0.3 to 0.4 for rigid pavements and 0.4 to 0.5 for flexible pavements. The upper values are more appropriate when the traffic predictions are less reliable.

The reliability values taken according to the South African Mechanistic Design method of flexible pavement are given below (Theyse et al. 1997).

Lightly trafficked rural roads	:	50 per cent
Rural roads	:	80 per cent
Inter-urban collectors and major rural roads	:	90 per cent
Inter-urban freeways and major inter-urban roads	:	95 per cent

However, for design of flexible pavements in India, the reliability value for expressways and national highways may be taken to be above 95 per cent, for state highways and major district roads, it is between 85 to 95 per cent and for village roads it is between 75 to 50 per cent (Kadiyali 2006).

The AASHTO method of pavement design has an incorporated reliability factor (AASHTO 1993). For the design of rigid pavement by IRC:58-2002, a multiplication factor termed as a load safety factor (LSF) is used to multiply the measured axle loads to account for the uncertainties in magnitude of axle loads (Section 6.3.3.9).

The following examples illustrate a few applications of statistical methods in determining the input values for pavement design. In this regard, any standard literature may be referred to (Ireson et al. 1998; Currel and Dowman 2005).

Q: To determine CBR value (%), ten tests were conducted on a soil sample. The values of mean CBR and standard deviation are calculated as 10.2% and 0.71% respectively. Calculate

(i) Standard uncertainty in the measurement of CBR

(ii) Coefficient of variance

(iii) Confidence limits for 50, 70, 85, 90, 95 and 99%, within which the true value of mean CBR lies.

A: Let n = sample size = 10

m = mean value = 10.2

s = standard deviation = 0.71

(*i*) Standard uncertainty in measurement of CBR or standard error of mean (i.e, uncertainty in the mean of measured values of CBR) $= \frac{s}{\sqrt{n}} = \frac{0.71}{\sqrt{10}} = 0.224$

(*ii*) Coefficient of variance (CV) $= \frac{s}{m} \times 100 = \frac{0.71}{10.2} \times 100 = 6.96$

(*iii*) Confidence limits for 50, 60, 80, 90, 95 and 98% reliability, within which the true value of mean CBR lies

As the sample size is small (less than 40), assume Student's t distribution (two-tailed). The confidence interval ranges between upper and lower limits may be determined by using the following equations.

Lower limit $= m - \left(t_r \times \frac{s}{\sqrt{n}}\right)$ and upper limit $= m + \left(t_r \times \frac{s}{\sqrt{n}}\right)$

where, DF = degree of freedom $= (n-1)$

t_r = t distribution value corresponding to the values of DF and percentile

For 90 % $r = 1.0 - \frac{(1.0-0.9)}{2} = 0.95$

∴ The t_r value corresponding to $t_{0.95}$ should be taken.

For DF = 9, the area covered by the distribution curve for different t_r values are given below

	$t_{0.75}$	$t_{0.80}$	$t_{0.90}$	$t_{0.95}$	$t_{0.975}$	$t_{0.99}$
Confidence value (%)	50	60	80	90	95	98
t_r value	0.703	0.883	1.38	1.83	2.26	2.82

CALCULATIONS:

Reliability (%)	Risk (%)	Confidence interval	
		Upper limit $= m + \left(t_r \times \frac{s}{\sqrt{n}}\right)$	Lower limit $= m - \left(t_r \times \frac{s}{\sqrt{n}}\right)$
(1)	(2)	(3)	(4)
50	50	$10.2 + (0.703 \times 0.71 \div \sqrt{10}) = 10.36$	$10.2 - (0.703 \times 0.71 \div \sqrt{10}) = 10.04$
60	40	$10.2 + (0.883 \times 0.71 \div \sqrt{10}) = 10.40$	$10.2 - (0.883 \times 0.71 \div \sqrt{10}) = 10.00$

continues

continued

Reliability (%)	Risk (%)	Confidence interval	
		Upper limit $= m + \left(t_r \times \frac{s}{\sqrt{n}}\right)$	Lower limit $= m - \left(t_r \times \frac{s}{\sqrt{n}}\right)$
80	20	$10.2 + (1.38 \times 0.71 \div \sqrt{10}) = 10.51$	$10.2 - (1.38 \times 0.71 \div \sqrt{10}) = 9.89$
90	10	$10.2 + (1.83 \times 0.71 \div \sqrt{10}) = 10.61$	$10.2 - (1.83 \times 0.71 \div \sqrt{10}) = 9.79$
95	5	$10.2 + (2.26 \times 0.71 \div \sqrt{10}) = 10.71$	$10.2 - (2.26 \times 0.71 \div \sqrt{10}) = 9.69$
98	2	$10.2 + (2.82 \times 0.71 \div \sqrt{10}) = 10.83$	$10.2 - (2.82 \times 0.71 \div \sqrt{10}) = 9.57$

From the above analysis it is understood that,

- As the reliability value increases, the difference between the upper and lower limits increases.
- At any particular value of reliability, if the difference between the upper and lower limits is more, it indicates a large variability in measured CBR values.

Based on the required reliability factor (from Column No. 1), the input design value of CBR may be taken from the lower limit (from Column No. 4), which represents a lower strength of soil than its mean value.

Q: *It was decided to construct the surface layer of an MDR of length 50 km with bituminous concrete. The mix design was carried out according to the Marshall mix design procedure. During construction of the road, the bituminous concrete was tested for Marshal stability value (N) at regular intervals. The grouped data of the Marshall stability value (N) is given below.*

1055–1067	*1067–1079*	*1079–1091*	*1091–1103*	*1103–1115*	*1115–1127*	*1127–1139*
2	*7*	*9*	*12*	*10*	*8*	*2*

Draw the histogram and the cumulative frequency curve. Determine (i) probability of the Marshall stability value in between 1091 and 1103 N and (ii) the chance of getting a value of Marshall stability value less than 1103?

A: The following table describes the calculation of relative frequency and cumulative frequency.

Sl. No	Class of Marshall stability value(*N*)	Mean values (*N*)	Frenquency	Relative frequency	Cumulative frequency
1	1055–1067	1061	2	(2/50)=0.04	0.04
2	1067–1079	1073	7	0.14	0.18
3	1079–1091	1085	9	0.18	0.36
4	1091–1103	1097	12	0.24	0.60
5	1103–1115	1109	10	0.20	0.80
6	1115–1127	1121	8	0.16	0.96
7	1127–1139	1133	2	0.04	1.00
	Total number of tests conducted = 50				

From the above table, the following figures can be drawn.

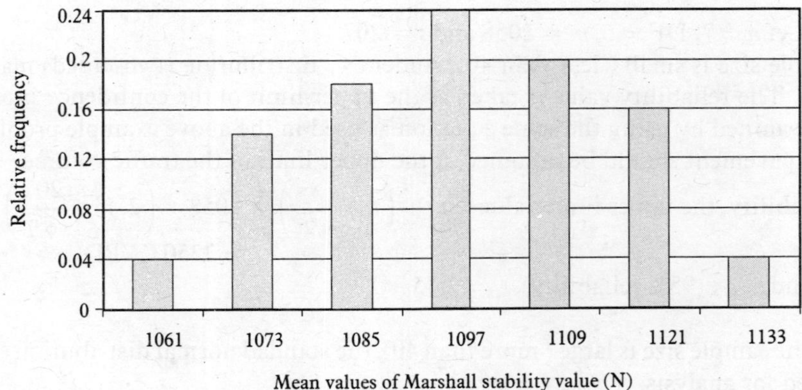

Figure 6.30 *Histogram of example*

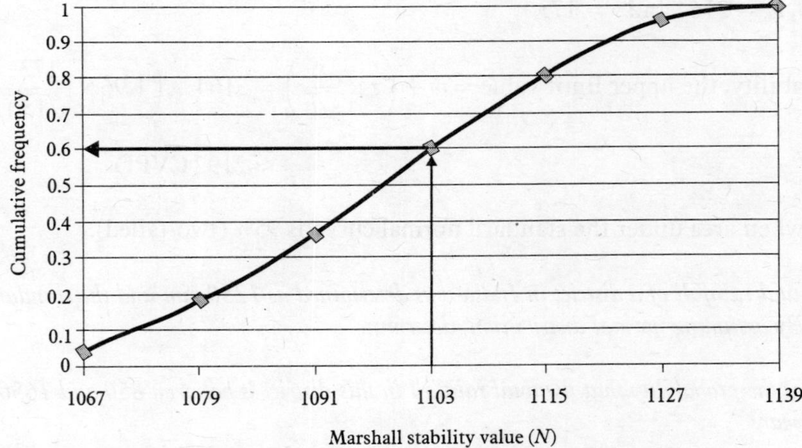

Figure 6.31 *Cumulative frequency curve*

From the above table and figures, the results are given below.

(*i*) Probability of the Marshall stability value in between 1091 and 1103 N
P(1091 Marshall stability value <1103) = 0.24

(*ii*) The chance of getting a value of Marshall stability value less than 1103?
P(Marshall stability value <1103) = 0.60

Q: *The following data is obtained from traffic count surveys which were conducted at a road section.*

Number of days	*Average no. of commercial vehicles per day (CVPD)*	*Standard deviation*
7	*2058*	*207*
150	*2164*	*173*

Determine traffic volume with 95% reliability.

A: *Case 1*: Let $n = 7$, DF $= 6$, $m = 2058$ and $s = 207$

As the sample size is small (less than 40), student's t distribution (two-tailed) may .be taken for analysis. The reliability value is taken as the upper limit of the confidence interval and it may be determined by using the same equation as used in the above example problem.

NOTE: The pavement should be designed at the upper limit of the traffic volume.

$$\text{At 95\% reliability, the upper limit value} = m + \left(t_r \times \frac{s}{\sqrt{n}}\right) = 2058 + \left(2.45 \times \frac{207}{\sqrt{7}}\right)$$

$$\approx 2250 \text{ CVPD}$$

$\because$ DF $= 6$ and $t_{0.975}$ (95% reliability), $t_r = 2.45$

Case 2: As the sample size is large (more than 40), the standad normal distribution (two-tailed) is considered for analysis.

NOTE: The pavement should be designed for the upper limit value of the traffic volume.

Let $n = 150$, $m = 2164$ and $s = 173$

$$\text{At 95\% reliability, the upper limit value} = m + \left(z \times \frac{s}{\sqrt{n}}\right) = 2164 + \left(1.96 \times \frac{173}{\sqrt{150}}\right)$$

$$\approx 2192 \text{ CVPD}$$

$\because z = 1.96$, when area under the standard normal curve is 95% (two-tailed).

Q: *Total annual rainfall of a district in India was determined as 1250 mm and the standard deviation as 250 mm. By assuming normal distribution, determine*

(i) *What is the probability that the total rainfall in this district is between 850 and 1650 mm in any given year?*

(ii) *What is the probability that the total annual rainfall is at least 1000 mm in this district?*

(iii) *95% rainfall value (i.e., 5% of rainfall exceeds).*

A: (i) The probability in any given year that the total rainfall in the given district is between 850 and 1650 mm $= P[850 < \text{Value} \le 1650] = \Phi((1650 - 1250)/250) - \Phi((850 - 1250)/250)$

$$= \Phi(1.6) - \Phi(-1.6) = \Phi(1.6) - [1 - \Phi(1.6)]$$

$$= 0.9452 - [1 - 0.9452] = 0.8904 = 89.04\%$$

(ii) The probability of the total annual rainfall is at least 350 mm in this district

$$= 1 - \Phi((1000 - 1250)/250) = 1 - \Phi((1000 - 1250)/250) = 1 - \Phi(-1)$$

$$= 1 - [1 - 0.8413] = 84.13\ \%$$

(iii) 95th percentile rainfall value (i.e., 5% of rainfall exceeds).

$$\Phi((P_{0.95} - 1250)/250) = 0.95$$

$$P_{0.95} = [250 \times \Phi^{-1}(0.95)] + 1250 = [250 \times 1.64] + 1250 = 1660 \text{ mm}$$

Similar concepts of reliability may be considered during calculation of various design input parameters such as fatigue damage, maximum allowable surface deflection, strength parameters of materials, traffic characteristics, limiting stresses and allowable strains.

Q: *In a pavement design procedure, it was decided to assign reliability requirements to individual components of design inputs. The following values of reliability are assumed to be adopted for each design factor. Determine the system reliability.*

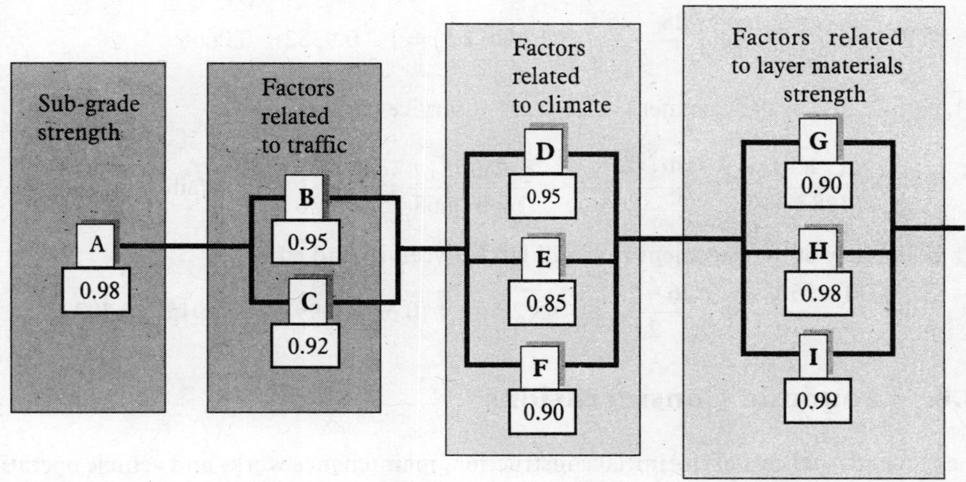

A: System reliability $= 0.98 \times \{1-(1-0.95)\times(1-0.92)\} \times \{1-(1-0.95)\times(1-0.85)\times(1-0.90)\} \times \{1-(1-0.90)\times(1-0.98)\times(1-0.99)\}$

$$= 0.98 \times 0.996 \times 0.99925 \times 0.99998$$

$$= 0.9753$$

Q: *It was decided to test beams of cement concrete to determine its strength. The stress and strength of a beam are represented by the following normal distribution:*
Mean value of strength is 4.5 MPa and its standard deviation value is determined as 0.25 MPa. Mean value of stress is 4.0 MPa and its standard deviation value = 0.35 MPa. Determine the reliability of the beam.

A: Factor of safety $= \dfrac{4.5}{4.0} = 1.125$

Safety margin $= \dfrac{4.5-4.0}{\sqrt{(0.25^2+0.35^2)}} = 1.16$

With $z = 1.16$;

Reliability $= \Phi(1.16) = 0.8770 = 87.7\%$

Q: *A pavement research institute was interested in developing a theoretical model of pavement* *performance based on distress data generated by simulation techniques. Fatigue failure of a pavement is normally distributed with an estimated value of 120 million standard axle (msa) load repetitions. Based on the average value of axle load repetitions per year, the given total axle load repetitions was calculated in terms of time duration as 25 years with a standard deviation of 2 years. Determine (i) the reliability of the pavement at 28 years of service period, (ii) the failure rate of the pavement at 28 years of service period and (iii) reliability of the pavement that will fail between 26 and 30 years of service.*

A:(*i*) Reliability of the pavement at 28 years:

$$R(28\text{ years}) = 1-\Phi\left(\frac{28-25}{2}\right) = 1-\Phi(1.5) = 1-0.9332 = 0.0668$$

(*ii*) Failure rate of the pavement at 28 years of service period:

$$= \frac{\Phi\left(\frac{28-\mu}{\sigma}\right)}{\sigma \times R(28\text{ years})} = \frac{\Phi\left(\frac{28-25}{2}\right)}{2\times 0.0668} = \frac{\Phi(1.5)}{2\times 0.0668} = \frac{0.9332}{0.1336} = 6.98\text{ failures/year}$$

(*iii*) Reliability of the pavement that will fail between 26 and 30 years:

$$= \Phi\left(\frac{30-25}{2}\right) - \Phi\left(\frac{26-25}{2}\right) = \Phi(2.5) - \Phi(0.5) = 0.9938 - 0.6915 = 0.3023$$

6.3.6 Economic Considerations

The estimated total cost of the initial construction, maintenance works and vehicle operations on a highway during its service life is termed as the *life cycle cost*. In the planning stage of any highway development scheme, economic evaluation is carried out to obtain the minimum life cycle cost during design life. Techniques of construction, in situ conditions, climatic and environmental factors are used for the selection of the best possible choice of pavement type based on funds availability, importance of road, traffic factors and use of locally available materials.

Stage construction technique is generally adopted when the funds available for the complete (or full-fledged) construction of a pavement in all respects is not sufficient. In the stage construction procedure, the sub-grade with granular layers are constructed in the first stage and allowed for traffic for a short period (say 2 to 3 years). Later on, with the availability of additional funds, a suitable impervious surface course, viz. bituminous or cement concrete layer is constructed over the existing surface of the granular layer. This construction procedure is advantageous since the existing sub-grade with granular layers which were constructed in the first stage are freely allowed to undergo consolidation under traffic loads and the resulting surface irregularities are corrected in the second stage of construction. Similarly, settlement or plastic deformations of the lower layers of pavement are allowed safely and corrected there of.

Exercises

6.1 What are the functions of road pavement? Draw a neat sketch showing the structural functions of a pavement.

6.2 Explain the behaviour of a pavement under a wheel load with a neat sketch.

6.3 How are road pavements classified based on the materials used? Draw typical sketches for each case.

6.4 How do flexible pavement layers undergo plastic deformation due to wheel loading?

6.5 What are the functions of the individual layers of flexible and rigid pavements?

6.6 Draw typical cross-sections of flexible and rigid pavements.

6.7 What are the basic qualities that are required for a sub-grade layer?

6.8 Why are sub-base layers provided in rigid pavements?

6.9 What are the important factors to be considered for stage construction of pavements?

6.10 Briefly explain the factors affecting pavement design and give some examples.

6.11 Explain how design traffic is calculated from the data obtained from traffic surveys.

6.12 Define and explain the significance of the following: (i) traffic growth rate, (ii) design life and (iii) lane distribution factors.

6.13 Draw a few typical configurations of axle and wheels of vehicles. Explain why tandem axles are preferred to single axles for truck load transfer on to the pavement surface.

6.14 Distinguish between static weighing and weigh in motion methods.

6.15 Explain how axle load is weighed using weigh pads with a neat sketch.

6.16 What do you understand by standard axle load? Draw a sketch showing the salient features of a standard axle according to IRC.

6.17 What is the standard axle load value of a single axle–single wheel, single axle–dual wheel and tandem axle–four wheels according to IRC and AASHTO recommendations?

6.18 What is the value of the standard axle load considered by other agencies for pavement design?

6.19 Define load equivalency factor. Explain its significance for design of pavements.

6.20 Define fourth power rule. Explain its significance for design of pavements.

6.21 What are the different models available for the determination of equivalent single axle loads (ESAL)?

6.22 Define legal axle load. What is its significance for design of pavements? Note down the maximum permissible loads for different types of vehicles in India.

6.23 Define vehicle damage factor (VDF). What are the factors affecting VDF and explain its significance in the design of pavements.

6.24 Explain miner's rule. How is it used to determine the fatigue damage of pavements?

6.25 Define load safety factor (LSF) and state the standard values of LSF according to IRC.

6.26 Define tyre pressure and contact pressure.

6.27 Enumerate the factors that should be considered for the design of durable and weather resistant pavements.

6.28 What is the influence of moisture other than OMC value on the pavement structure? Explain how moisture content changes in the lower layers of the pavement.

6.29 Define poor drainage conditions and mud pumping in rigid pavements.

6.30 Explain how pavements are damaged due to frost action.

6.31 Write model equations for correction of pavement response values in terms of surface deflection and modulus values measured at different temperatures.

6.32 What are the factors considered for the development of different models for correction of deflections and modulus values measured at different temperatures?

6.33 Define temperature gradient in rigid pavements and third point in bituminous layers.

6.34 What is the AAPT value considered for the design of pavements in India? Write the deflection correction equation.

6.35 What are the ill effects of poor drainage of pavements?

6.36 State how surface water is collected and drained off by suitable arrangements.

6.37 Explain the methods of estimating design runoff while designing the surface drainage system.

6.38 What is meant by time of concentration? Explain any two widely used formulae for the determination of time of concentration with the usual notations.

6.39 State the significance of time of concentration while determining the design runoff intensity. How is it related to pavement surface drainage design?

6.40 State the significance of minimum specific energy used for the design of the cross-section of open channel drains.

6.41 Explain why sub-critical conditions is established in the design of the cross-section of the open channel drain.

6.42 Derive an expression for the determination of normal depth of flow in a rectangular cross-section of an open channel drain.

6.43 State the design criteria considered for the design of the cross-section of open channel drains.

6.44 State and draw the different types of gutter channels. Note down their formulae with the usual notations.

6.45 Explain the suitability of different types of gutter inlets.

6.46 What do you understand by the pavement encroachment criteria considered for the design of a gutter?

6.47 Derive an expression with usual notations for the determination of discharge in the gutter having the following cross-sections: (i) Triangular gutter channel section having a straight curb,

(ii) Triangular gutter channel with compound section and

(iii) V-shaped triangular gutter channel section having different side slopes

6.48 Explain the process of determining suitable spacing of inlets along a gutter.

6.49 Determine the depth of flow (i.e., values of d_1 and d_2) in the gutter for the given details. Discharge in the gutter is determined as 0.09 m^3/s. Assume suitable values of T_1 and T_2.

6.50 State the sources of sub-surface water considered for the design of the sub-surface of the pavement.

6.51 Explain the methods of estimating the quantity of sub-surface water due to infiltration through cracks and joints in the pavement.

6.52 With usual notations, note down the FHWA's equation used for determining the quantity of sub-surface water due to infiltration through cracks and joints in pavement.

6.53 State the different methods of estimating the coefficient of permeability of a filter layer. With usual notations, write the FHWA's equation used for determining the coefficient of permeability of the drainage layer of granular and filter material.

6.54 Explain the design criteria for design of drainage/ filter layers of pavement.

6.55 Draw typical pavement cross-sectional details showing various components of the sub-surface drainage system.

6.56 Explain how transverse filter drains and edge or trench drains control the lowering of GWT and intercept sub-surface water. Draw sketches wherever necessary.

6.57 State the FHWA's perforation criteria for longitudinal drain pipes in sub-surface drainage systems.

6.58 How are reliability concepts useful for design pavements? Give examples.

6.59 Define the life cycle cost of a pavement. State the significance of economic considerations of pavement design.

7

Analysis and Design of Flexible Pavements

Introduction

Pavement layers are made of different kinds of materials. To withstand traffic loading under prevailing environmental and in situ conditions, the pavement should be designed based on allowable deflections or stresses or strains. For these reasons all pavement structures should be analysed for different conditions of loading, material characteristics and boundary conditions.

7.1 Stress Analysis of Flexible Pavements

The following sections present a brief review of the equations used to calculate the stresses and surface deflections of an elastic half-space based on linear elastic principles (Boussinesq 1885; Fadum 1948; Foster and Ahlvin 1954; Ahlvin and Ulery 1962).

7.1.1 Boussinesq's Theory (Single Layer Theory)

In 1885, Boussinesq presented a theory for calculating the stresses in soil mass based on the following assumptions.

- The soil is homogenous (without any stratification) and isotropically linear elastic which means that it abides by Hook's law.
- The soil mass boundary is a semi-infinite elastic half-space.
- The load is applied on to a level surface.

- The soil mass is weightless.

The following equations are based on Boussinesq's theory and are widely used to calculate stresses in soil mass.

CASE 1: Point load

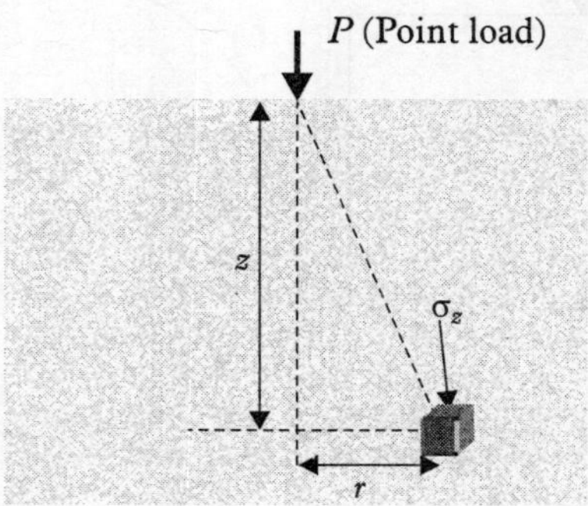

Figure 7.1 *Stress due to point load*

Consider a point load on the soil mass as depicted in Figure 7.1.

$$\text{Vertical stress due to a point load } (\sigma_z) = \frac{3P}{2\pi z^2} \frac{1}{\left[1+\left(\frac{r}{z}\right)^2\right]^{5/2}} \tag{7.1}$$

where, P = point load
z = depth from surface
r = radial distance from the axis of loading
σ_z = vertical stress

The above equation is also used to calculate stresses in a soil mass where the contact pressure is not uniform. Such non-uniform pressures are calculated as equivalent point loads at their centre and total stress under the soil mass can be calculated by super-positioning of the stresses.

Q. *Calculate the intensity of vertical pressure due to a point load of 4200 kg at a depth of 4 m from the surface and a distance of 2 m from the axis of loading.*

A. At 4 m depth and distance 2 m from the axis of loading: $z = 4$ m and $r = 2$ m. From equation (7.1),

$$\text{Vertical stress due to a point load } (\sigma_z) = \frac{3 \times 4200}{2\pi \times 4^2} \frac{1}{\left[1+\left(\frac{2}{4}\right)^2\right]^{5/2}} = 71.74 \text{ kg/m}^2$$

CASE 2: Uniformly distributed load over a circular area

Generally, for pavement analysis, the equivalent circular contact area of a tyre on pavement surface is taken. For this purpose, a uniformly loaded circular area is considered for calculating the stresses in the soil mass. To calculate stresses under a uniformly loaded area using flexible plates (similar to a rubber tyre), equation (7.1) may be integrated over the circular area (Figure 7.2).

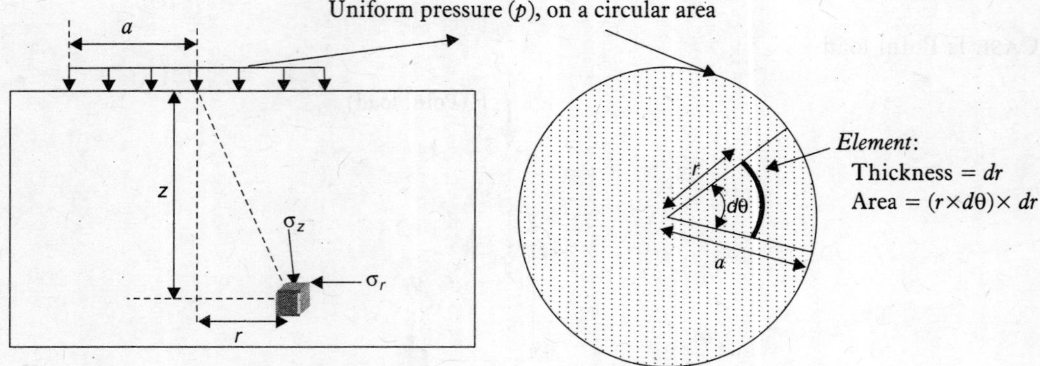

Figure 7.2 *Stress under a uniformly loaded circular area*

Vertical stress due to the uniformly distributed circular area (σ_z)

$$= \int_0^{2\pi} \int_0^a \left(\frac{3p\,((rd\theta)dr)}{2\pi z^2} \left[\frac{1}{1 + \left(\frac{r}{z}\right)^2} \right]^{5/2} \right) \tag{7.2}$$

The above equation can be simplified as (Burmister 1938)

$$\text{Vertical stress under the centre of the circular area } (\sigma_z) = p \left(1 - \left[\frac{1}{1 + \left(\frac{a}{z}\right)^2} \right]^{3/2} \right) \tag{7.3}$$

Horizontal or radial stress beneath the centre of circular area (σ_r),

$$\sigma_r = 0.5p \left[(1 + 2\mu) - \left(\frac{2z(1+\mu)}{\sqrt{(a^2 + z^2)}} \right) + \left(\frac{z^3}{(a^2 + z^2)^{3/2}} \right) \right] \tag{7.4}$$

Elastic vertical displacement at $z = 0$, under a circular flexible plate

$$(\Delta s) = \frac{2pa\,(1 - \mu^2)}{E} \tag{7.5}$$

If $\mu = 0.5$, he above equation can be written as

$$\Delta s = \frac{1.5pa}{E} \tag{7.6}$$

where, p = uniformly distributed pressure
a = radius of the circularly loaded area
μ = Poisson's ratio of soil
E = Elastic modulus of soil (assumed as single layer)

The stress distribution under the flexible plate is uniform since the flexible plate bends (or flexes) under loading, similar to a rubber sheet. Therefore, the elastic surface deflection under the flexible plate is non-uniform.

If a circular rigid plate (or steel plate) is used to apply load on to the soil, the elastic surface displacement is uniform but the stress distribution is non- uniform (Ullidtz 1987). Analysis of plate load test data is one of the best examples of an application of Boussinesq's theory. The following formula may be used to calculate the elastic surface deflection under a rigid plate.

$$\text{Vertical displacement at } z=0\text{, under a circular rigid plate } (\Delta s) = \frac{\pi p a\,(1-\mu^2)}{2E} \quad (7.7)$$

If $\mu = 0.5$, the above equation can be written as

$$\Delta s = \frac{1.18pa}{E} \quad (7.8)$$

Q. *A semi-infinite soil mass is subjected to stress under a circular plate having a 15 cm radius. The load intensity over the plate is 4000 kg. Calculate the vertical stress in the soil under the axis of the circular plate at 2 m depth.*

A. Intensity of pressure over plate $= 4000/(\pi \times 15^2) = 5.66$ kg/cm²
Vertical stress under the centre of the circular area

$$(\sigma_z) = 5.66\left(1-\left(\frac{1}{1+\left(\frac{15}{2}\right)^2}\right)^{3/2}\right) = 5.64 \text{ kg/cm}^2$$

Q. *Calculate the rebound surface deflection on a single layer pavement under a wheel load of 40 kN with a tyre pressure of 0.8 MPa. The effective elastic modulus of sub-grade may be taken as 40 MPa and Poisson's ratio of the soil as 0.5.*

A. Tyre pressure $= \dfrac{\text{Wheel load}}{\text{Tyre contact area}} = \dfrac{\text{Wheel load}}{\pi a^2}$

Radius of tyre contact area =

$$a = \sqrt{\left(\frac{\text{Wheel load}}{\pi \times \text{Tyre pressure}}\right)}\sqrt{\left(\frac{40\times 10^3}{\pi \times 0.8 \times 10^6}\right)} = 0.126 \text{ m} = 12.6 \text{ cm}$$

$$\text{Intensity of pressure} = p = \frac{\text{load}}{\text{area}} = \frac{40\times 10^3}{\pi \times 0.126^2} = 801990.14 \text{ N/m}^2$$

If a flexible plate considered, re-bound surface deflection $= \Delta s$

$$\Delta s = \frac{1.5pa}{E} = \frac{1.5 \times 801990.14 \times 0.126}{40 \times 10^6} = 0.00378 \text{ m} = 3.78 \text{ mm}$$

The theory presented by Boussinesq has resulted in basic fundamental concepts related to the calculation of stresses and deflections of an elastic half-space. But the equations based on Boussinesq's theory does not provide realistic values since

- The soil mass is never ideally elastic and isotropic.
- The pressure distribution may be non-uniform depending on the loading conditions.
- The soil mass is never weightless and homogenous.
- The pavement consists of multiple layers having different thicknesses and material characteristics.

Therefore, layered theories which consider multiple layers of pavement with different material characteristics have more significance for the design and analysis of pavement structures.

7.1.2 Burmister's Theory

In 1943, Donald M. Burmister developed a method of analysing a two-layered soil system which resembled a flexible pavement having its top layer stiffer than its bottom layer. Later, in 1945, he extended the method to include three-layered system. As an important outcome of Burmister's numerical solutions, the flexible pavement thickness design method was developed for airfield pavements (*ASCE* vol.115, 1950). In 1962, Ahlvin and Ulery of the US Army Corps of Engineers (USACE) reported solutions for calculating the stresses, strains and deflections on a homogenous half-space withstanding a uniform circular load (Ahlvin and Ulery 1962). Since then, the Burmister's theory with required modifications is being used for various pavement engineering applications. Many researchers have developed different methods for analysing multi-layered systems based on elastic, non-linear, viscoelastic and finite element methods. The solution of various problems related to a multi-layered system is made easy by the use of computers.

Burmister's two-layered system of analysis is briefly explained below.

ASSUMPTIONS

- Every layer material is homogenous, isotropic and ideally elastic. They are characterised by a unique elastic modulus and Poisson's ratio.
- A pavement consists of two layers. The elastic modulus value of the top layer is more than the bottom layer (i.e., $E1 > E2$).
- The layers are weightless and infinite in the horizontal direction.
- The top layer has finite thickness (h) but the bottom layer is infinitely thick.
- The top layer is in full contact with the bottom layer.

- The interface between these layers is rough and there is no loss of transfer of applied stress from the top layer to the bottom layer.
- There will be no shear and normal stresses outside the loaded area.
- The applied stress is uniform over a circular area.

The displacement equations given by Burmister for a two-layered system are as follows (Figure 7.3).

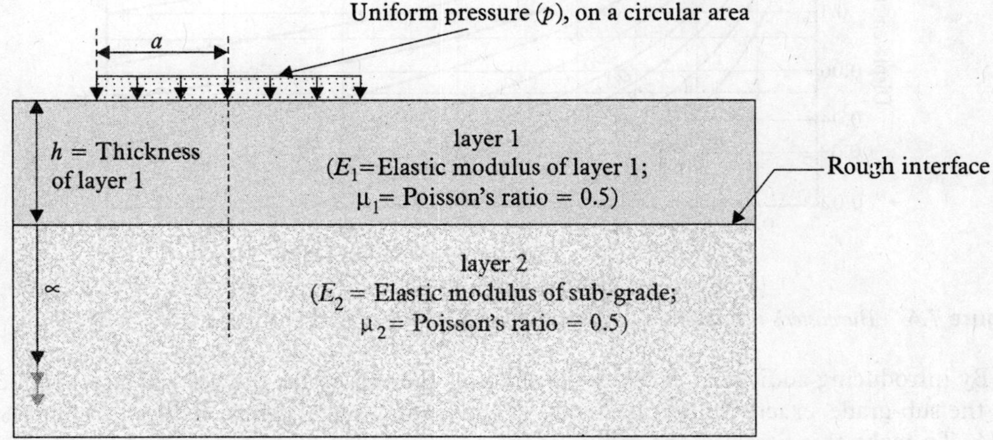

Figure 7.3 *Burmister's two-layered system*

Surface deflection under the centre of the flexible plate:

$$\Delta = \frac{1.5\,pa}{E_2} \times F_d \tag{7.9}$$

Surface deflection under the rigid plate: $\Delta = \dfrac{1.18\,pa}{E_2} \times F_d$ (7.10)

where,

Δ	=	Vertical deflection at surface (when $z = 0$)
p	=	Uniform pressure on circular plate
a	=	Radius of the circular plate
E_2	=	Elastic modulus of sub-grade
F_d	=	Displacement factor, depends on ratios of $\left(\dfrac{E_1}{E_2}\right)$ and $\left(\dfrac{h}{a}\right)$; Refer to Figure 7.4
E_1	=	Elastic modulus of the top layer
h	=	Thickness of the top layer

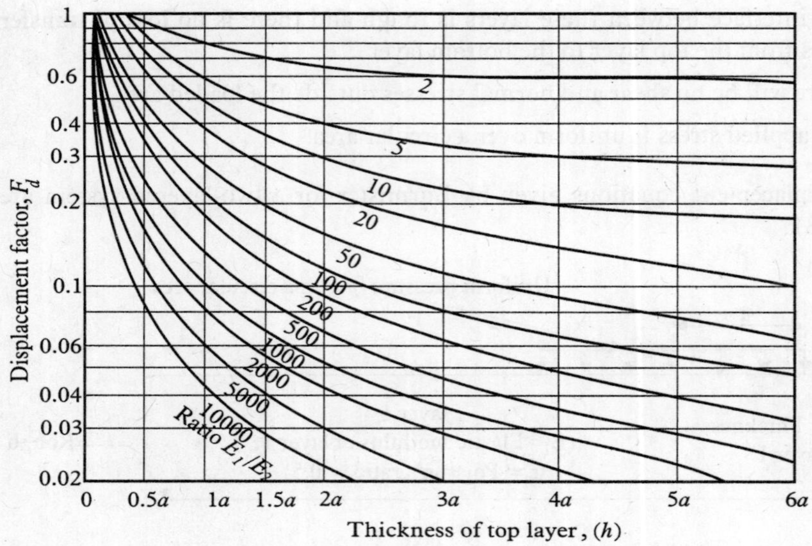

Figure 7.4 *Burmister's two-layered system (after Burmister 1943)*

By introducing additional pavement layers over the sub-grade, the vertical stress induced on the sub-grade, exactly under the centre of the loading plate, can be reduced from 68% to 30%. To make this possible, the radius of the additional layer has to be equal to the radius of the loading plate, the elastic modulus value of the additional layer has to be approximately equal to ten times the elastic modulus value of the sub-grade ($E_1 \approx 10E_2$) and Poisson's ratio of both the layers has to be equal to 0.5. Due to this reason, construction of pavements is carried out in multiple layers instead of a single thicker layer.

Q. *Determine the required thickness of an airfield flexible pavement based on Burmister's theory using the following plate load test (PLT) data and other input parameters:*

Diameter of plate used = 75 cm
Pressure observed at 1.25 mm deflection when the plate load test is conducted on the sub-grade
= 0.82 kg/cm²
Pressure observed at 1.25 mm deflection when the plate load test is conducted on a base course of 16 cm thickness = 2.1 kg/cm²
Design wheel load = 23000 kg; Tire pressure = 15 kg/cm²;
(a) If allowable deflection = 0.125 cm and (b) If allowable deflection = 0.50 cm

A. (i) *Determination of the elastic modulus of the sub-grade from a plate load test conducted on the sub-grade*

From the standard relationship, Deflection $(\Delta) = 1.18\dfrac{p.a}{E_2}$

where, E_2 is the elastic modulus of the sub-grade

On substitution,

$$0.125\text{ cm} = 1.18\frac{0.82\,\text{kg/cm}^2 \times 37.5\text{ cm}}{E_2}$$

$E_2 = 290.28$ kg/cm^2

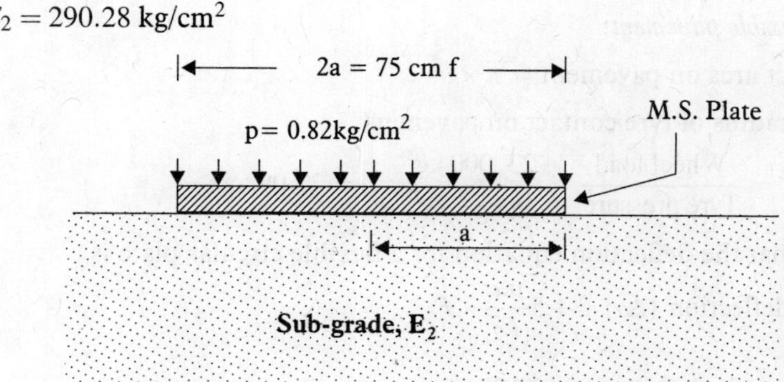

Figure 7.5 *Example*

(ii) *Determination of the elastic modulus of the granular layer from the results of a plate load test conducted on a granular layer*

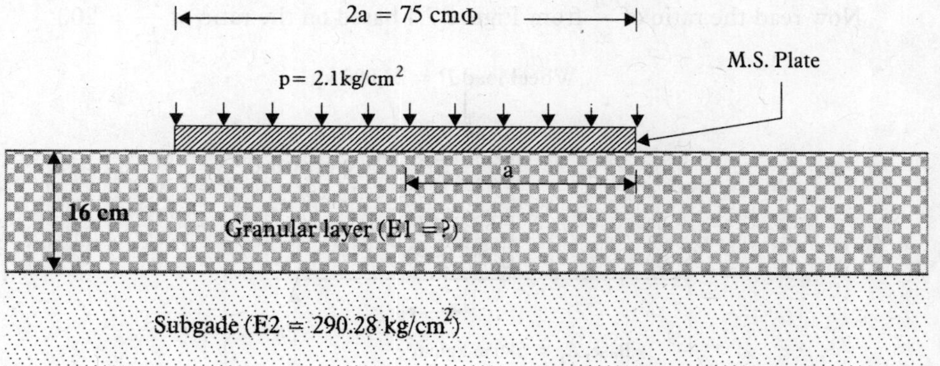

Figure 7.6 *Example*

Deflection; $\Delta = 1.18 \dfrac{p.a}{E_2} \times F_d$

where, E_2 = elastic modulus of the sub-grade

F_d = shape factor, based on the ratios of $\dfrac{h}{a}$ and $\dfrac{E_1}{E_2}$

On substitution,

$$0.125 \text{ cm} = 1.18 \times \frac{2.1 \text{ kg/cm}^2 \times 37.5 \text{ cm}}{290.28 \text{ kg/cm}^2} \times F_d$$

$$F_d = 0.39; \text{ ratio of } \frac{h}{a} = \frac{16 \text{ cm}}{37.5 \text{ cm}} = 0.426$$

Now read the value of $\dfrac{E_1}{E_2}$ ratio from Figure 7.4.

$$\therefore \quad \frac{E_1}{E_2} = 200, \; E_1 = 200E_2; E_1 = 200 \times 290.28 = 58056 \text{ kg/cm}^2$$

(iii) *Design of flexible pavement*:

Tyre contact area on pavement $= \pi \times a^2$

where $a =$ radius of tyre contact on pavement

$$\pi \times a^2 = \frac{\text{Wheel load}}{\text{Tyre pressure}} = \frac{23,000 \text{ kg}}{15 \text{ kg/cm}^2} \therefore a = 22.09 \text{ cm}$$

We know that the deflection equation for a flexible circular plate is

Allowable deflection $(\Delta a) = 1.5 \frac{p.a}{E_2} \times F_d$

(a) If allowable deflection = 0.125 mm

On substitution,

$$0.125 \text{ cm} = 1.5 \times \frac{15 \text{ kg/cm}^2 \times 22.09 \text{ cm}}{290.28 \text{ kg/cm}^2} \times F_d$$

$F_d = 0.073$

Now read the ratio of $\frac{h}{a}$ from Figure 7.4 based on the ratio of $\frac{E_1}{E_2} = 200$

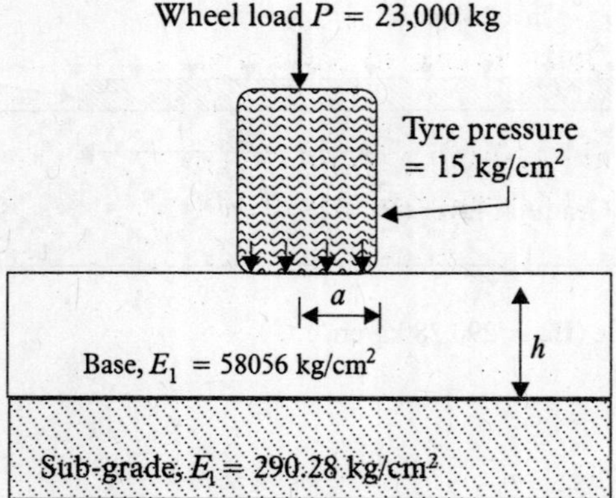

Figure 7.7 *Example*

$$\frac{h}{a} = 2.79,\ h = 2.79 \times a = 2.79 \times 22.09 = 61.63 \text{ cm}$$

$\therefore$ For the base course, provide a thickness of 62 cm.

(b) If allowable deflection = 0.50 cm

$$0.5 \text{ cm} = 1.5 \times \frac{15 \text{ kg/cm}^2 \times 22.09 \text{ cm}}{290.28 \text{ kg/cm}^2} \times F_d$$

$F_d = 0.438$

Now read the ratio of $\frac{h}{a}$ from the ratio of $\frac{E_2}{E_1} = \frac{1}{200}$,

$$\frac{h}{a} = 0.36, h = 0.36 \times a = 0.36 \times 22.09 = 7.95 \text{ cm}$$

$\therefore$ For the base course, provide a thickness of 8 cm.

In the above design example, the thickness of the base course is calculated only based on the allowable elastic surface deflection. This method does not consider traffic loads and non-linear behaviour of pavement materials. These factors are major influencing parameters for thickness design of pavements. Therefore, the basic philosophy of Burmister's method for the analysis of stresses and strains is used in conjunction with the factors affecting pavement design which are discussed in Chapter 6.

7.1.3 Linear Elastic Multi-Layered Pavement System

In reality, a flexible pavement is a multi-layered structure in which each layer is constructed with different thickness (h), each having a respective material characteristics such as the elastic modulus (E) and Poisson's ratio (μ). A typical configuration of a circular plate subjected to a uniform pressure (p) placed on a multi-layered pavement system is depicted in Figure 7.8.

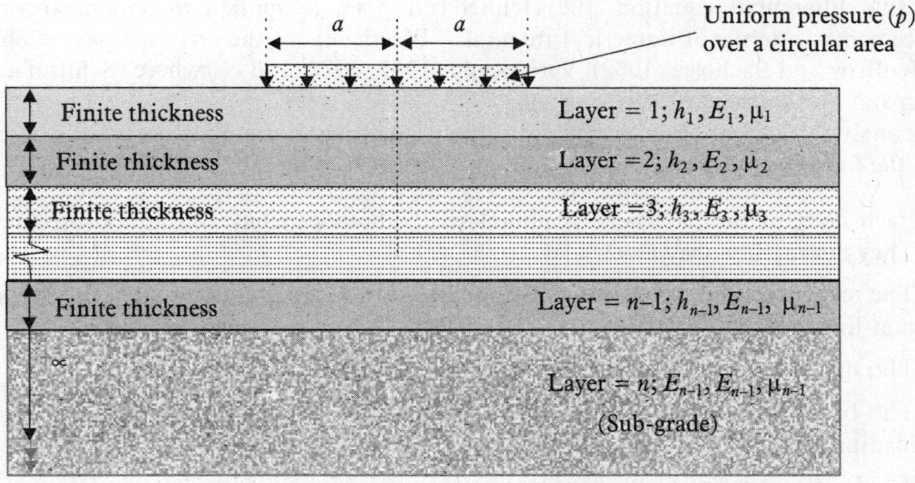

Figure 7.8 *Multi-layered pavement system*

The following considerations/assumptions are generally made for analysis of stresses, strains and deflections in a multi-layered flexible pavement system.

- The bottom (nth) layer is the sub-grade and has an infinite thickness.
- Above the sub-grade, each layer has a finite thickness and infinite dimension in the horizontal direction.
- The self-weight of the sub-grade and other layers are considered as weightless.
- There is no loss of stress at each layer interface. The layers are perfectly in contact at the top and bottom surfaces. But for some methods, a smooth layer interface may also be considered.
- Each layer in the pavement system is linearly-elastic, homogenous and isotropic.
- There will be no stresses, strains and deflections at infinite depth of the sub-grade.
- Only static loads are considered.

- There is no shear stress or radial displacement of the top layer.
- The surface of the top layer is perfectly horizontal and has no undulations.

The stress function adopted by Burmister for analysis of the three-layered flexible pavement is

$$\Phi(r,z) = \left[(A+Bz)\,e^{-mz} + (C+Dz)\,e^{mz}\right] J_o\,(mr) \tag{7.11}$$

where, r = radial distance
z = depth
A, B, C and D = (each layer) constants of integration
J_o = Bessel function of the first kind of order zero

With the above stress function and assumptions (boundary conditions) that satisfy the governing differential equation, the Henkel transform is applied to obtain stresses and displacements in terms of numerical integrals. The details of the analysis may be obtained from Jeuffroy and Bachelez (1962), Verstraeten (1967; 1972) and elsewhere (Schiffman 1962; Ashton and Moavenzadeh 1967).

The analysis methods based on the above-mentioned assumptions are unrealistic in practice due to the following reasons.

- Each layer of the pavement is non-elastic, inhomogeneous and an anisotropic solid. They never truly obey Hook's law.
- The materials used for the sub-base and base layers are granular materials which show non-linear behaviour on loading.
- The sub-grade may consist of non-linear stiffness with depth.
- The bituminous surface layer shows visco-elastic behaviour which varies based on loading time and temperature.
- The Poisson's ratio of pavement materials is variable and depends on in situ conditions and different loading pressures.
- The wheel loading is generally dynamic and transient in nature.
- The boundary condition of being infinite in the horizontal direction is never a true condition.
- Shear and radial stresses will be developed on the surface layer during rolling wheel loads.
- Cracked bound layers cause discontinued distribution of pressure.

To account for the realistic behaviour of pavements under traffic loading during in situ conditions, the multi-layered flexible pavement system has being suitably modified by different researchers. Many software programs (Table 7.1) have also been developed. It can be observed from Table 7.1 that most programs use linear elastic theory since it provides a reasonably good estimate of surface deflections and strains in the bound layers. The linear elastic programs which are simple and easy to perform may be used for an approximate analysis of pavement structures. However, for accurate and realistic modelling of the non-linear behaviour of unbound layers, visco-elastic and plastic behaviour of bituminous pavements by finite element methods are more appropriate. But these methods involve quite complex mathematical concepts which are difficult and require huge capacity computer.

Table 7.1 *A few programs for analytical solution of multi-layered flexible pavements*

Name of the program	Theory used	Program source	Reference
CHEVRON	LEMLT	Chevron Research Corporation	Warren and Diekmann 1963; COST 336, Task Group 1
FEPAVE	FEM (axi-symmetric)	–	Duncan et al. 1968
SLAB30 & SLAB49	FDM	–	Deacon 1969
ELSYM	LEMLT	FHWA (UCB)	Ahlborn 1972
BISAR	LEMLT	Shell International	De Jong et al. 1973
JULEA	LEMLT	USACE WES	Uzan 1976
VEROAD	MLV	Delft University of Technology	Nilsson et al. 1996
CIRCLE	LEMLT	MINCAD, Australia	Wardle 1977; Wardle and Rodway 1998
VESYS	LEMLT or MLV	FHWA	Kenis et al. 1982
ABAQUS	FEM	–	Lee et al, 1998
ILLI-PAVE	FEM	University of Illinois	Thompson and Elliott, 1988
FENLAP	FEM	University of Nottingham	Brunton and d'Almedia, 1992
SAPSI-M	MLV with moving loads	Michigan University	Chatti and Yun (1996)
DAMA	LEMLT	The Asphalt Institute	The Asphalt Institute, 1983
KENLAYER	LEMLT or non-linear elastic or MLV	University of Kentucky	Yang H. Huang, 2004
ELAYER	LEMLT	IIT Kharagpur	Sudhakar, 1993
FPAVE	LEMLT	IIT Kharagpur	Animesh, 1998
NCPA (Non-linear cross-anisotropic pavement analysis)	FEM	–	Jeongho Oh et al. 2007

LEMLT: Linear elastic multi-layer theory; MLV: Multi-layered visco-elastic; FEM: Finite element method; FDM: Finite difference method

7.2 Flexible Pavement Design Methods

Designs of flexible pavement have undergone tremendous changes during the past few decades ranging from empirical procedures to analytical methods. Reaching for perfection, many modifications have been made in different design methods to obtain the desired reliable level of service and structural adequacy of pavement structures using locally available as well as modified materials at a reasonable cost. Different design methods of flexible pavements have been developed by different researchers and organisations around the world. They may be broadly classified as follows.

7.2.1 Empirical Methods

Pavement design factors related to traffic loading, material strength, climatic and environmental conditions are inevitably variable in nature. Therefore, to analyse pavement performance, the mean effect of these factors in terms of distress is measured and related to pavement crust thickness by using empirical relationships. Many empirical relationships have been developed by relating (or correlating) pavement performance in terms of different modes of failures to traffic loading, characteristics of sub-grade soil, climate etc. The following groups explain methods of pavement design based on different empirical relationships.

Group 1: A selection of suitable crust thickness of flexible pavement is made based on soil classification, grain size distribution, moisture content, plastic limit, liquid limit, truck traffic volume and experience record of in situ pavements. Group index (GI) (945) and FAA methods may be considered under this group. These methods have not been found successful because parameters regarding material strength, climatic, environmental and in situ conditions are not considered.

Group 2: Thickness design charts were developed by correlating performance of pavements to various design inputs related to material strength parameters, density, truck traffic volume, climate, environment, frost, ground water level and parameters related to in situ conditions. The anticipated occurrences of uncertainties of these parameters are accounted and analysed based on different methods in different countries. The strength parameters of pavement materials were obtained based on laboratory as well as in situ tests. Different types of empirical design methods for flexible pavements and the required tests on soil for the determination of its strength are given in Table 7.2.

Table 7.2 *List of a few empirical design methods*

Name of the test conducted on the sub-grade soil	Test result (used as a design input)	Design method
California bearing ratio (CBR)	CBR value	California State Highway Dept. (1928), US Corps of Engineers (1958), British Revised CBR, Wyoming CBR, National Asphalt Pavement Association, NAPA (Foster 1965), National Crushed Stone Association, (NCSA 1972), TAI (1970), IRC:37-1970 method and NAASRA (1979).

continues. . .

Table 7.1 *continud*

Name of the test conducted on the sub-grade soil	Test result (used as a design input)	Design method
Cone penetration	Penetration value	North Dakota cone method
Plate load	Deflection of plate or modulus of sub-grade reaction (k)	US Navy method based on Burmister's elastic theory for airfield pavements and Canadian Dept. of Transport or McLeod method
Stabilometer and cohesiometer	R-and C-values respectively	California resistance value method (1948)
Tri-axial compression	Elastic modulus value	Tri-axial method (1910), which was modified by the Kansas State Highway Dept. (A semi-arbitrary method which partly comprises theoretical considerations)

Group 3: Design methods based on the performance serviceability concept may be included in this group. The first of this kind, the AASHO Interim Guide (AASHO 1972) was developed using AASHO test data. In this method, a minimum structural number (SN) (1 to 6) is determined using a nomograph based on sub-grade support value (1 to 10), regional factor (0.2 to 5.0) and equivalent 18-kip (kilo pounds) single-axle load repetitions. The individual layer thicknesses are derived from the SN value using pavement layer equivalent thickness factors. Many modifications were made in later editions (1981; 1986; 1993). However, the design philosophy of all the editions is based on empirical (regression) equations derived from the AASHO road test data related to various characteristics of materials, traffic and different modes of performance. Applicability of the AASHTO design method in different countries should be verified before using since the empirical relationships incorporated in the design are developed from the AASHO road test data obtained from test tracks constructed in Illinois and other places in USA.

7.2.2 Theoretical or Analytical or Pure Mechanistic Methods

In this group of methods the stresses, strains and deflections in a pavement system are calculated based on principles of engineering mechanics which are related to elastic, visco-elastic and non-linear or finite element methods. Thickness design charts were developed based on correlations between pavement performances to theoretically-calculated performance characteristics of layer materials subjected to loading. The correlations include stress–strain relationships or surface deflection strength parameters. The methods described by Burmister based on elastic theory (in 1943 and 1945) are the foremost examples of this kind of analytical pavement design methods.

So far there is no accurate direct solution available to analyse a multi-layered pavement system as it exists in the field under repetitive transient load passes, prevailing climatic and in situ conditions. Research is in progress towards development of models to precisely calculate the realistic behaviour of pavements under differential distribution of stresses and strains which are produced due to variability in material characteristics, loading pattern, in situ conditions and environment conditions. Due to this associated complexity to incorporate realistic conditions in mathematical analysis or modelling, analytical design methods are used for limited applications. Taking the best of both, empirical pavement design methods supported by mechanistic principles are gaining significance.

7.2.3 Mechanistic–Empirical (M–E) or Analytical–Empirical or Rational Design Methods

The M–E design procedure is be carried out in two steps. In the first step, principles related to engineering mechanics are used to calculate the response of pavement layers at critical locations in terms of stresses, strains and deflections for a given loading configuration of wheels–axles, material characteristics of each layer (E_i, μ_i and h_i) and environmental conditions. The theoretically calculated pavement response is compared to the allowable maximum values of stresses or strains in the second step. Distress or damage caused by these critical values of pavement response is determined from empirical relationships in terms of rutting, cracking or other forms of distress (or any defined failure). These relationships are often termed as failure criteria. In these approaches, the major modes of pavement failures are identified and the corresponding terminal (or failure) conditions are defined. Some of the failure modes commonly considered are fatigue cracking of bound layers (top-down or bottom-up cracking), rutting (undulations as permanent deformations) along wheel paths and low temperature (or thermal) cracking. To control the load associated failures of pavements, critical mechanistic parameters (as responses of pavement to applied load), considered to be causative of the failures, are kept within allowable limits during the design process. A similar procedure may be adopted for modelling of pavement performance.

In the design of flexible pavements, the following failure criteria (strain limits) were first used and reported by Dormon (in 1962). This work was based upon the parallel work carried out by Saal and Pell at the University of Nottingham in conjunction with Shell Laboratories in 1960 and by Monismith et al. at the University of California in 1961. These criteria are widely used in many M–E methods of design of flexible pavement including the Indian design method of IRC:37-2001 (Figure 7.9).

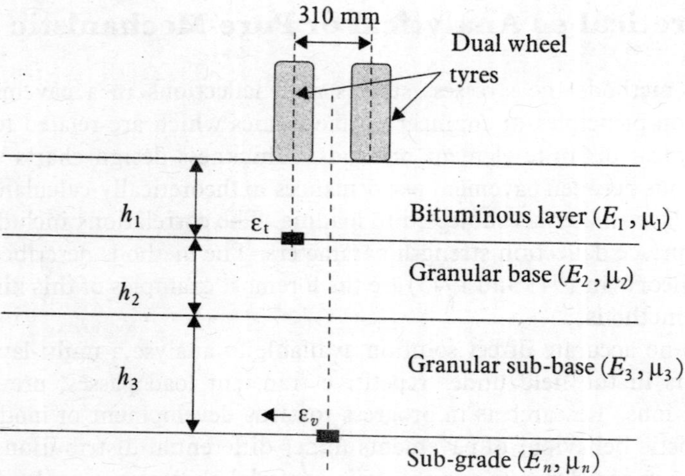

Figure 7.9 *Critical strains in a layered flexible pavement structure*

1. Vertical compressive strain (ε_v) on top of the sub-grade layer under the centre of dual wheels is correlated with rutting (vertical permanent strain) of pavement.
2. Horizontal tensile strain (ε_t) at the bottom fibre of the bituminous bound surface layer under the centre of a wheel of dual wheels is correlated with the fatigue failure (or cracking) of the bituminous surface layer.
3. In addition to the above design criteria, vertical compressive stresses and strains within the bituminous layer, granular base and sub-base courses are also considered (NCHRP 2003).

Relationships correlating the limiting values of the mechanistic parameters with the service life of the pavements are known as performance criteria. The performance criteria developed for the design of new pavements are often used for the design of overlays also. While the performance criteria form the core of the pavement design and evaluation methodology, other important issues involved are (i) the selection of an appropriate theory for analysis of pavements and (ii) the selection of inputs, especially the material properties, for the analytical model. In the case of overlays, the methodology adopted for the evaluation of in-service pavements in terms of structural index or layer properties is important for the design process. A number of empirical and mechanistic methods are available for the design of new pavements and overlays. These methods vary in terms of the failure modes considered, the terminal condition used to define failure, the theory used for the analysis of pavements, the procedure adopted for the selection of material properties (for new or in-service pavements) and performance criteria used. There are also differences in the estimation of traffic loading, reliability concepts used and methods followed for the evaluation of in-service pavements.

A few methods of flexible pavement design based on M–E principles are given below.

- Comparing Mix and Pavement StructureS (COMPASS) by the CROW working group.
- South African mechanistic design method (SAMDM) (Theyse et el. 1996 and 1997).
- CARE (Road and Hydraulic Engineering Institute, Deft) (CROW Report D06-06).
- French Design Manual, LCPC, Paris (CROW Report D06-06).
- Shell Pavement Design Manual (Shell 1985).
- CROW Design Procedure for Thin Asphalt Pavements: (CROW Report D06-06).
- The Asphalt Institute Method, MS-1, USA (TAI 1991). AUSTROADS Pavement Design Guide, Australia (AUSTROADS 1992).
- Washington State Department of Transportation (WSDOT) Pavement Guide (WSDOT 1995; Mahoney and Pierce 1996).
- Minnesota Department of Transportation (MnDOT) mechanistic–empirical flexible pavement design (1998).
- The proposed AASHTO M–E Design Guide for New and Rehabilitated Pavement Structures (NCHRP, 2003).

  Key features: Finite element analysis, load spectra, roughness evaluation in terms of IRI and reliability in life-cycle cost assessment.

- Analytical design methods developed at IIT Kharagpur, India. (Sudhakar 1993 and Animesh 1998).
- Guidelines for the design of flexible pavements according to IRC:37-2001.

7.3 Benefits of Pavement Design Based on M–E Method

The following benefits can be obtained using M–E pavement design methods.

- Structural analysis can be made which will help to calculate critical stresses, strains and deflections at any point in a pavement structure at any period of service life.
- Precise structural strength assessment of individual pavement layers is possible using suitable software.
- Better alternative designs can be attained based on variability in locally available material or alternative materials.
- Cost-effective design with strategic rehabilitation philosophy.
- Uncertainties can be accounted for during the design process as an integrated approach related to traffic loading, climatic factors, moisture, seasonal changes etc.
- Different distress models belonging to specific locations can be effectively incorporated in design.
- Increased precision in analysing locality-specific performance failure modes which provide a realistic behaviour of the pavement during calibration of deterministic or empirical models or transfer functions[‡]. So that the degree of uncertainty in performance prediction can be considerably reduced to a permissible limit.
- Theoretical modelling can be made to verify and validate new techniques related to design, performance, maintenance and rehabilitation strategies.

From literature it can be noticed that there is no clear-cut separation between empirical and arbitrary methods as well as semi-mechanistic and empirical methods of flexible pavement design (Waterhouse 1962; Skok and Finn 1962).

As our understanding of pavement failure mechanisms improved, many developments took place to modify the design concepts—ranging from empirical to mechanistic–empirical methods. In this process, characterisation of pavement materials has taken a significant role for design as well as performance evaluation of pavements. In this regard, many carefully planned and hugely funded road (flexible, rigid and composite pavement) test facilities were developed by different organisations around the globe to determine solutions for unsolved problems of pavement design. A few of them are listed below.

[‡]Transfer functions are the relationships used to relate the state of stress or surface deflection or strain in a pavement structure to its overall performance measured in different forms such as rutting, cracking, roughness and so forth (Thompson 1996). These relationships are useful for developing distress prediction models subjected to extensive field calibration and verification.

7.4 Test Roads

- Bates Test Road, Illinois, in 1921 (Older 1922, 1924; Goldbeck 1922).
- Pittsburg, Calif., Test Road in 1922 (Goldbeck 1925).
- The Arlington Road Tests, USA in 1923 (Goldbeck 1925, Teller and Sutherland 1935).
- Lockbourne No.1 Test Track and Lockbourne No.2, 300,000 lb. Experimental Mat, Corps of Engr., U.S. Dept. of Army, Ohio, 1946 and 1945 (Childs et al. 1959).
- Road Test One-Md (1952).
- Western Association of State Highway Officials (WASHO) Road Test in Malad, Idaho, USA in 1951 (WASHO Special Reports 18 & 22, 1954 and 1955).
- American Association of State Highway Officials (AASHO) Road Test in Ottawa and Illinois, USA during the period 1958–60 (AASHO Special Report 61-G, 1962). This program was carried out and documented under the leadership of W. N. Carey Jr.
- Road Test Sections of Road Research Laboratory (RRL), UK (Now the Transportation Research Laboratory, TRL): Example, (i) Alconbury Hill Motorway, reported by Lee and Croney, 1962 and (ii) TRL loading Facility (Metcalf 1996).
- South African Heavy Vehicle Simulator (HVS) (1992).
- Australian Accelerated Loading Facility (Jameson et al. 1992).
- The Nottingham Asphalt Tester (NAT) for design of bituminous mixes (Brown and Gibb 1996).
- FHWA/LTTP Accelerated Load Facility (ALF).
- The California Department of Transportation Heavy Vehicle Simulator (CDOT-HVS).
- The Texas Department of Transportation Mobile Load Simulator (TDOT-MLS).
- Full Scale Pavement Testing Facilities: CEDEX in Spain; DTU in Denmark; LAVOC in Switzerland; CAPTIF, New Zealand; MnRoad in Minnesota, Nevada Automotive Test Center's WesTrack and the National Centre for Asphalt Technology (NCAT), Alabama, USA (Metcalf 1996).

7.5 Design Methods of Flexible Pavements

The AASHTO method of 1993 and IRC design methods (IRC: 37 and IRC:SP:72) of flexible pavement are discussed below. The 1993 design method of AASHTO is now currently revised as the mechanistic–empirical method. However, the 1993 method may also be used until the proposed AASHTO mechanistic–empirical design method comes into force for complete implementation by all organisations.

7.5.1 The AASHTO Design Method of Flexible Pavements (1993)

The AASHTO design method is basically developed from the results obtained from AASHO test roads constructed at Ottawa and Illinois in 1958–60 and later revised in 1981, 1986 and 1993. The AASHTO design concepts influenced many pavement design methods which were developed all over the world.

The Serviceability Concept

According to the AASHTO design method, the present pavement performance and its condition is subjectively rated by a panel of experienced drivers riding over the pavement, on a scale of 0 to 5 with 0 and 5 representing very poor and very good conditions respectively (Carey and Irick 1962). This numerical expression is termed as the present serviceability rating (PSR).

Using regression analysis, the PSR is converted to equivalent factors called the present serviceability using measured pavement performance on the same pavement sections in terms of objective measurements, viz. slope variance, rutting, cracking and patching. This concept of quantifying the present condition of pavement serviceability is known as the *serviceability concept*. For flexible pavement, the regression equation developed by AASHTO from AASHO road test data is given below.

$$\text{PSI} = 5.03 - 1.91\log_{10}(1+S_V) - 0.01(C+P)^{0.5} - 1.38R_D^2 \tag{7.12}$$

where,

PSI	=	Present serviceability index
S_V	=	Mean slope variance measured along both wheel paths (using profilometer of AASHO)
C	=	sq. ft of cracked area per 1000 sq. ft of pavement surface
P	=	sq. ft of patched area per 1000 sq. ft of pavement surface
R_D	=	Mean rut depth in inches measured on both wheel paths using a 4 ft straight edge

The initial or newly constructed AASHO test section's average value of PSI (p_i) was determined as 4.2. These test sections were then opened for traffic till failure and the mean terminal PSI (p_t) was determined as 1.5. The numerical difference between initial and terminal PSI is termed as loss of PSI (Δ PSI $= p_i - p_t$). For the design of flexible pavements, according to AASHTO, at failure conditions or terminal PSI value, (p_t) may be taken as 2.5 and 2.0 for high and low volume roads respectively.

Traffic Loads

The observed traffic is converted to ESAL of a given design life using axle load equivalency factors as recommended by AASHTO. To determine design ESALs (W_{18}), the calculated cumulative ESALs are multiplied with a suitable lane distribution factor (Table 7.3) and directional distribution factor. The directional distribution factor is a ratio between different directions, viz. west–east, south–north etc.

Table 7.3 *Lane distribution factors*

Number of lanes in each direction	Percent of 18000 lb or 18kip ESAL in the design lane
1	100
2	80 to 100
3	60 to 80
≥ 4	50 to 70

(*From AASHTO Guide for Design of Pavement Structures, 1993, by the American Association of State Highway and Transportation Officials, Washington,* DC. *Used by permission. Documents may be purchased from the AASHTO bookstore at 1-800-231-3475 or online at http://bookstore.transportation.org*)

The Concept of Structural Number (SN)

Based on the AASHO test data, thickness design equations were developed by using structural number (SN) of pavement. The SN is an index number (ranges from 1 to 6) which represents overall strength of the pavement structure and is derived from the stiffness of individual pavement layers. The SN value depends on the

(i) wheel–axle configuration and number of load applications,

(ii) ΔPSI,

(iii) strength of the sub-grade,

(iv) drainage conditions and

(v) the reliability factor.

The SN value is determined by using the following equation (AASHTO 1993).

$$\log(W_{18}) = Z_R S_o + 9.36\log_{10}(1+\text{SN}) - 0.2 + \frac{\log_{10}\left[\dfrac{\Delta\text{PSI}}{(4.2-1.5)}\right]}{0.4+\left(\dfrac{1094}{(1+\text{SN})^{5.19}}\right)} + 2.32\log_{10}(M_R) - 8.07 \qquad (7.13)$$

where,

W_{18} = estimated cumulative 18 kip ESAL during the design life

Z_R = overall standard deviation for a given reliability (refer to Table 7.4)

S_o = combined standard error of the predictions of the performance and traffic (0.45 may be taken for the flexible pavement)

Δ PSI = design loss of PSI = initial PSI (p_i)– terminal PSI (p_t)

M_R = effective resilient modulus of sub-grade in psi (based on monthly variations over a year)

The SN value may be determined by trial-and-error method (using equation (7.13)) or a nomograph. The determined SN value is used to obtain the individual layer thicknesses with the following equation.

$$\text{SN} = a_1 D_1 + a_2 D_2 m_2 + a_3 D_3 m_3 \qquad (7.14)$$

where,

D_1, D_2 and D_3	=	layer thickness (in inches) of asphalt concrete, base and sub-base courses respectively (minimum thickness values may be assumed from Table 7.5)
a_1, a_2 and a_3	=	structural layer coefficient of asphalt concrete (Table 7.6), base (Table 7.7) and sub-base (Table 7.8) courses respectively

If resilient modulus values of base and sub-base are known, the following equations may be used for determining a_2 and a_3 (AASHTO 1993).

$$a_2 = 0.249 \times \log_{10}(\mathrm{MR_{base}}) - 0.977 \tag{7.15}$$

$$a_2 = 0.249 \times \log_{10}(E_{\mathrm{base}} \times 144.7) - 0.977 \tag{7.15a}$$

$$a_3 = 0.227 \times \log_{10}(\mathrm{MR_{sub-base}}) - 0.839 \tag{7.16}$$

$$a_3 = 0.227 \times \log_{10}(E_{\mathrm{sub-base}} \times 144.7) - 0.839 \tag{7.16a}$$

where,

$\mathrm{MR_{base}}$	=	Resilient modulus of base course in psi
E_{base}	=	Resilient modulus of base course in MPa
$\mathrm{MR_{sub-base}}$	=	Resilient modulus of sub-base course in psi
$E_{\mathrm{sub-base}}$	=	Resilient modulus of sub-base course in MPa
m_2 and m_3	=	Drainage coefficients of unbound base and sub-base courses respectively (Table 7.9)

The above relationships (equation (7.15) and (7.16)) are empirical and treated as typical.

Table 7.4 *AASHTO recommended values of standard normal deviate* (Z_R)

Reliability, R (%)	Standard normal deviate (Z_R)
70	−0.524
80	−0.841
90	−1.282
95	−1.645
99	−2.327

(From AASHTO Guide for Design of Pavement Structures, 1993, by the American Association of State Highway and Transportation Officials, Washington, DC. Used by permission. Documents may be purchased from the AASHTO bookstore at 1-800-231-3475 or online at http://bookstore.transportation.org)

Table 7.5 *Minimum thickness of pavement layer*

ESALs	Asphalt concrete (inches)	Granular base (inches)
≤ 50000	1.0	4
50001 to 150000	2.0	4
150001 to 500000	2.5	4
500001 to 2 million	3.0	6
2 million to 7 million	3.5	6
>7 million	4.0	6

1 million = 10^6

(From AASHTO Guide for Design of Pavement Structures, 1993, by the American Association of Highway and Transportation Officials, Washington, DC. Used by permission. Documents may be purchased from the AASHTO bookstore at 1-800-231-3475 or online at http://bookstore.transportation.org)

Table 7.6 *Approximate values of layer coefficient for asphalt surface course*

Asphalt concrete resilient modulus at 70° F (Psi)	a_1
500000	0.466
450000	0.444
400000	0.420
350000	0.390
300000	0.363
250000	0.333
200000	0.298
150000	0.252
100000	0.200

(from Van Til et al. 1972;. Documents may be purchased from the AASHTO bookstore at 1-800-231-3475 or online at http://bookstore.transportation.org)

Table 7.7 *Approximate values of layer co-efficient for untreated granular base course*

Unbound granular base course CBR (%)	a_2
100	0.141
70	0.131
60	0.125
50	0.119
40	0.115
30	0.090
20	0.067

(from Van Til et al. 1972)

Table 7.8 *Approximate values of layer coefficient for untreated granular sub-base course*

Unbound granular sub-base course CBR (%)	a_3
100	0.148
70	0.130
50	0.125
40	0.120
30	0.109
20	0.094
10	0.080
5	0.049

(from Van Til et al. 1972)

Table 7.9 *Drainage coefficients (m_2 and m_3) of untreated granular layers of flexible pavement*

Drainage quality		Percent time of pavement structure is exposed to moisture levels approaching saturation			
Time required to drain-off the water in	Subjective rating	< 1%	1 to 5 %	5 to 25 %	> 25 %
2 hours	Excellent	1.40 to 1.35	1.35 to 1.30	1.30 to 1.20	1.20
1 day	Good	1.35 to 1.25	1.25 to 1.15	1.15 to 1.00	1.00
1 week	Fair	1.25 to 1.15	1.15 to 1.05	1.00 to 0.80	0.80
1 month	Poor	1.15 to 1.05	1.05 to 0.80	0.80 to 0.60	0.60
Never drain	Very poor	1.05 to 0.95	0.95 to 0.75	0.75 to 0.40	0.40

(From AASHTO Guide for Design of Pavement Structures, 1993, by the American Association of State Highway and Transportation Officials, Washington, DC. *Used by permission. Documents may be purchased from the AASHTO bookstore at 1-800-231-3475 or online at http://bookstore.transportation.org)*

The following example problem explains the design procedure.

Q. *Design a flexible pavement according to the AASHTO 1993 Guidelines from the following data:*

Reliability, R = 90 %

Standard deviation, $S_o = 0.40$

Estimated number of 18-kip ESAL repetitions over a design life of 20 years = 10 million

The loss of serviceability = 2.0

Resilient modulus of

asphalt concrete = 400000 psi (400 ksi)

base course = 20000 psi (20 ksi)

sub-base course = 10000 psi (10 ksi)

sub-grade (mean value) = 3.3 % of CBR (1500×3.33 = 5000 psi = 5 ksi)

It will take a duration of one day and a week respectively to drain-off the water from the base and sub-base courses. Time the pavement structure is exposed to moisture levels approaching saturation = 15 %.

A. From the nomograph (Figure 7.10) adapted from AASHTO 1993, the following results can be obtained.

$SN_3 = 5.2$, using Figure 7.10 and sub-grade MR = 5 ksi (given)
$SN_2 = 4.1$, using Figure 7.10 and sub-base MR= 10 ksi (given)
$SN_1 = 3.35$, using Figure 7.10 and base MR= 20 ksi (given)
Structural layer-coefficient of
Asphalt concrete (AC), $a_1 = 0.420$ (from Table 7.6)
Base course, $a_2 = 0.249 \times \log_{10}(20000) - 0.977$ (from equation 7.15)

$$a_2 = 0.094$$

Sub-base course $a_3 = 0.227 \times \log_{10}(10000) - 0.839$ (from equation 7.16)

$$a_3 = 0.07$$

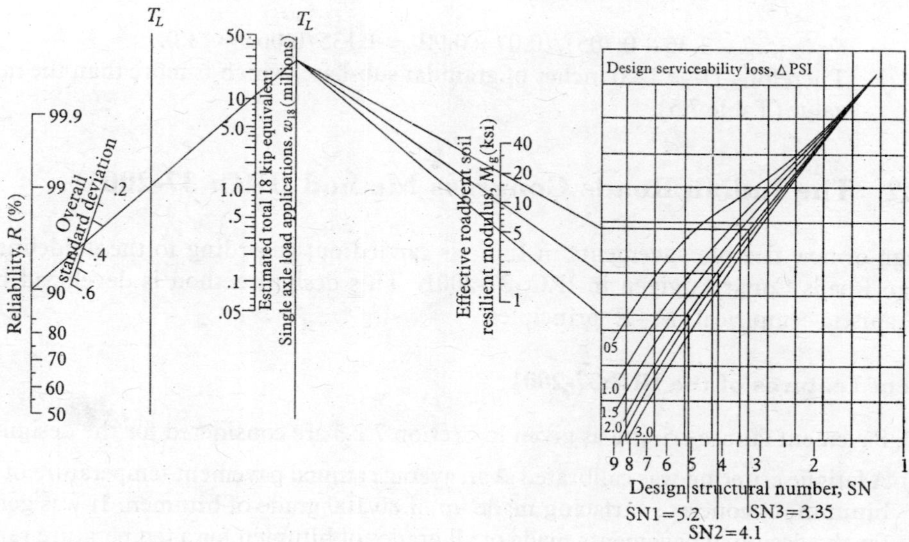

Figure 7.10 *Example*

(Source of the nomograph: *AASHTO Guide for Design of Pavement Structures*, by the American Association of the State Highway and transportation Officials, Washington, DC. Used by permission. Documents may be purchased from the AASHTO bookstore at 1-800-231-3475 or online at http://bookstore.transportation.org).

Drainage coefficients: For the given conditions, take drainage coefficients from Table 7.9.
Time pavement structure is exposed to moisture leading to saturation = 15% (given)
Good; 1 day required to drain-off the water
Base: $\rightarrow m_2 = 1.08$
Fair; 1 week required to drain-off the water
Sub-base: $m_3 = 0.90$

Procedure to be followed to determine individual thicknesses of pavement layers:

$$\text{SN} = a_1 D_1 + a_2 D_2 m_2 + a_3 D_3 m_3$$

STEP 1: $\text{SN}_1 \leq a_1 D_1$

$3.35 \leq 0.420 \times D_1$, therefore, $D_1 \geq 3.6/0.420 = 7.9$, after rounding-off, D_1 = thickness of AC = 8.0 inches, which is more than the minimum value (Table 7.5)

STEP 2: $\text{SN}_2 \leq (a_1 D_1 + a_2 D_2 m_2)$

$4.1 \leq (0.42 \times 8.0 + 0.094 \times D_2 \times 1.08)$

$D_2 \geq (4.1 - 3.36)/(0.094 \times 1.08) = 0.72/0.101 = 7.2$, after rounding-off,

D_2 = thickness of granular base = 7.5 inches, which is more than minimum value (Table 7.5)

STEP 3: $\text{SN}_3 \leq (a_1 D_1 + a_2 D_2 m_2 + a_3 D_3 m_3)$

$5.2 \leq (0.42 \times 8.0 + 0.094 \times 7.5 \times 1.08 + 0.07 \times D_3 \times 1.08)$

$D_3 \geq (5.2 - 3.36 - 0.705)/(0.07 \times 0.90) = 1.135/0.063 = 18.0,$
Therefore, $D_3 = 18.0$ inches of granular sub-base, which is more than the minimum value (Table 7.5).

7.5.2 The Indian Roads Congress Method (IRC: 37-2001)

Design of new flexible pavements in India is carried out according to the guidelines of the Indian Roads Congress given in IRC: 37-2001. This design method is developed based on mechanistic–empirical (M–E) principles.

Salient Features of the IRC:37-2001

(a) Pavement failure criteria as given in Section 7.2.3 are considered for the design.

(b) A fatigue criterion was calibrated at an average annual pavement temperature of 35°C for bituminous concrete surfacing made up of 80/100 grade of bitumen. It was generalised for the design of pavements made of all grades of bitumen for a temperature range of 20 to 40 °C as given below.

$$N_f = 2.21 \times 10^{-4} \times (1/\varepsilon_t)^{3.89} \times (1/E_{\text{bit}})^{0.854} \tag{7.17}$$

where, N_f = Number of cumulative standard axles to cause 20 per cent cracked surface area

ε_t = Tensile strain at bottom fibre of the bituminous concrete layer ($\times 10^{-6}$) and

E_{bit} = Elastic modulus of the bituminous surfacing (MPa). Standard values of E_{bit} at different temperatures may be referred to in IRC:37-2001.

(c) The following rutting criterion used with an allowable rut depth of 20 mm.

$$N_R = 4.1656 \times 10^{-8} \times (1/\varepsilon_v)^{4.5337} \tag{7.18}$$

where, N_R = Number of cumulative standard axles to produce rut depth of 20 mm

ε_v = Vertical compressive sub-grade strain ($\times 10^{-6}$)

(d) For calculating the tensile strains at the bottom fibre of the bituminous layer, dense bituminous macadam with bitumen grade of 60/70 was used.

(e) The following empirical relationships were used to estimate the elastic modulus of subgrade:

$$E_{\text{sub-grade}}(\text{MPa}) = 10 \times \text{CBR for CBR} \leq 5\,\% \tag{7.19}$$
$$E_{\text{sub-grade}}(\text{MPa}) = 17.6 \times (\text{CBR})^{0.64} \text{ for CBR} > 5\,\% \tag{7.20}$$

(f) Elastic modulus of granular sub-base and base courses

$$E_{\text{granular layer}}(\text{MPa}) = E_{\text{sub-grade}} \times 0.2 \times (\text{thickness of granular layer in mm})^{0.45} \tag{7.21}$$

(g) Equivalent thickness calculation of dense bituminous macadam (DBM) to bituminous macadam (BM) is recommended and the following equation provides an accurate estimation of thin bituminous layers (Marchionna et al. 1987).

$$\frac{E_{DBM} \times h_{DBM}^3}{(1-\mu_{DBM}^2)} = \frac{E_{BM} \times h_{BM}^3}{(1-\mu_{BM}^2)} \tag{7.22}$$

where, E_{DBM} and E_{DBM} = Elastic modulus of DBM and BM layers respectively
h_{DBM} and h_{BM} = Thickness of the layers
μ_{DBM} and μ_{BM} = Poisson's ratio's of the layers

(h) Pavement thickness is determined based on mechanistic principles for given values of design (or estimated) traffic volume in terms of cumulative standard axle load repetitions (by equation 6.2) and CBR value (paragraph 3.7.1).

(i) In case of arid regions where the annual rain fall is less than or equal to 500 mm, instead of a 4-day soaked CBR value, the design sub-grade CBR value may be determined at the field moisture content that is prevailing immediately after the monsoon season.

(j) Minimum design sub-grade CBR value should not be less than 2%. If the sub-grade CBR value is less than 2%, the sub-grade should be strengthened with a capping layer of at least 150 mm thickness having a 10% CBR value.

(k) The minimum thickness of granular base, for traffic up to 2 msa is 225 mm and for traffic exceeding 2 msa is 250 mm.

(l) If the WBM layer is constructed as a base course, where traffic is more than 10 msa, the base thickness should be increased from 250 to 300 mm by reducing the thickness of the sub-base course and keeping the overall pavement thickness unchanged.

(m) The granular sub-base layer CBR value should not be less than 20% for traffic up to 2 msa and 30% for traffic more than 2 msa.

(n) Granular sub-base layer thickness should not be less than 150 for traffic up to 10 msa and 200 mm for traffic more than 10 msa respectively.

(o) If the road is to be built by stage construction, the thickness of the sub-base should be provided as required for the total design period by considering all the stages together.

(p) If a pre-mix carpet of thickness upto 25 mm is used as wearing course, its thickness should not be counted as a structural layer.

Drainage Considerations

(a) To drain off the seepage/ percolated/ sub-surface water from the pavement structure, the sub-base layer should be constructed by using a permeable granular material. The granular material should satisfy the following criteria which are adopted in Indian and several other countries.

D_{15} of drainage layer $\geq$ (5 $\times$ D_{15} of sub-grade)

where, D_{15} is the size of the sieve that allows 15% weight of the material to pass through. Similar definition holds good for D_{85}, D_{50} and D_2. These values can be obtained by plotting the particle size distribution curve as explained in Section 3.2. With reference to the curve of the sub-grade soil, the gradation of the granular material used for the drainage layer can be marked on the plot.

The granular material used for construction of drainage layer is treated as very good when (i) $D_{85} < 4 \times D_{15}$ and (ii) $D_2 > 2.5$ mm.

(b) The drainage layer material is designed as open graded. To avoid intrusion of the sub-grade soil fines into the open graded granular layer of the sub-base layer, the following criteria should be considered.

D_{15} of drainage layer $\geq$ ($5 \times D_{15}$ of sub-grade) and D_{50} of drainage layer $\leq$ ($5 \times D_{50}$ of sub-grade).

The above procedure was also suggested by Terzaghi for selection of suitable filter material gradings.

(c) To prevent intrusion of the sub-grade soil fines into the open graded drainage layer, a filter layer made up of non-oven geosynthetic fabric may be placed in between the sub-grade and the drainage layer.

(d) In case of large inflows of sub-surface water, an open graded drainage layer connected with longitudinal porous pipes and connected pipe system should be constructed.

(e) If the granular sub-base is impermeable, its top 100 to 150 mm thickness should be constructed with open graded granular material meeting the above criteria.

(f) Shoulders should be constructed and maintained properly to standard specifications of cross fall and level difference between carriageway and shoulder.

(g) Shoulders should be impervious. Compacted thickness of lime stabilised shoulders shall be in the range of 150 to 200 mm.

General Features

(a) Design charts to determine the total crust thickness of a flexible pavement are separately available for traffic 1–10 msa and 10–150 msa with design sub-grade CBR values of 2, 3, 4, 5, 6, 7, 8, 9 and 10% (Figures 7.11 and 7.12).

(b) Individual layer thicknesses can be deduced from Tables 7.10(a)–(d) and 7.11 (a)–(d). Wherever suitable, interpolation may be made to obtain the total crust thickness of pavement from the charts (Figures 7.11 and 7.12).

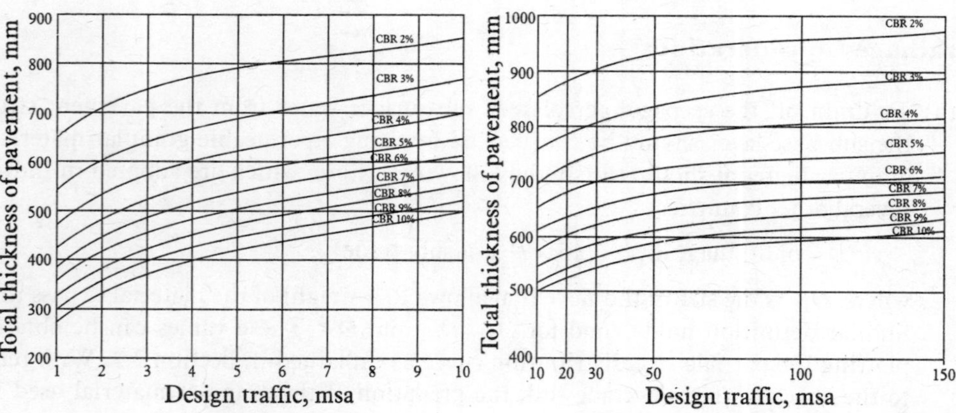

Figure 7.11 *Thickness design chart of flexible pavement for traffic 1 to 10 msa (from IRC:37-2001)*

Figure 7.12 *Thickness design chart of flexible pavement for traffic 10-150 msa (Partial table from IRC:37-2001)*

Table 7.10 *Flexible pavement thickness design catalogue for traffic range 1 to 10 msa (Partial table from IRC: 37-2001)*

(a) For sub-grade CBR = 2%

Cumulative traffic (msa)	Total pavement thickness (mm)	Pavement composition			
		Bituminous surfacing		Granular base (mm)	Granular sub-base (mm)
		Wearing course (mm)	Binder course (mm)		
1	660	20 PC	—	225	435
2	715	20 PC	50 BM		440
3	750	20 PC	60 BM	250	440
5	795	25 SDBC	70 BM		450
10	850	40 BC	100 BM		460

(b) For sub-grade CBR = 3%

Cumulative traffic (msa)	Total pavement thickness (mm)	Pavement composition			
		Bituminous surfacing		Granular base (mm)	Granular sub-base (mm)
		Wearing course (mm)	Binder course (mm)		
1	550	20 PC	—	225	435
2	610	20 PC	50 BM		335
3	645	20 PC	60 BM	250	335
5	690	25 SDBC	60 DBM		335
10	760	40 BC	90 DBM		380

(c) For sub-grade CBR = 4%

Cumulative traffic (msa)	Total pavement thickness (mm)	Pavement composition			
		Bituminous surfacing		Granular base (mm)	Granular sub-base (mm)
		Wearing course (mm)	Binder course (mm)		
1	480	20 PC	—	225	255
2	540	20 PC	50 BM		265
3	580	20 PC	50 BM	250	280
5	620	25 SDBC	60 DBM		285
10	700	40 BC	80 DBM		330

(d) For sub-grade CBR = 5%

Cumulative traffic (msa)	Total pavement thickness (mm)	Pavement composition			
		Bituminous surfacing		Granular base (mm)	Granular sub-base (mm)
		Wearing course (mm)	Binder course (mm)		
1	430	20 PC	–	225	205
2	490	20 PC	50 BM		215
3	530	20 PC	50 BM	250	230
5	580	25 SDBC	55 DBM		250
10	660	40 BC	70 DBM		300

Table 7.11 *Flexible pavement thickness design catalogue for traffic range 10 to 150 msa (from IRC:37-2001).*

(a) For sub-grade CBR = 2%

Cumulative traffic (msa)	Total pavement thickness (mm)	Pavement composition			
		Bituminous surfacing		Granular base (mm)	Granular sub-base (mm)
		Wearing course (mm)	Binder course (mm)		
10	850	40	100	250	460
20	880		130		
30	900		150		
50	925		175		
100	955	50	195		
150	975		215		

(b) For sub-grade CBR = 3%

Cumulative traffic (msa)	Total pavement thickness (mm)	Pavement composition			
		Bituminous surfacing		Granular base (mm)	Granular sub-base (mm)
		Wearing course (mm)	Binder course (mm)		
10	760	40	90	250	380
20	790		120		
30	810		140		
50	830		160		
100	860	50	180		
150	890		210		

(c) For sub-grade CBR = 4%

Cumulative traffic (msa)	Total pavement thickness (mm)	Pavement composition			
		Bituminous surfacing		Granular base (mm)	Granular sub-base (mm)
		Wearing course (mm)	Binder course (mm)		
10	700	40	80	250	330
e 20	730		110		
30	750		130		
50	780		160		
100	800	50	170		
150	820		190		

(d) For sub-grade CBR = 5%

Cumulative traffic (msa)	Total pavement thickness (mm)	Pavement composition			
		Bituminous surfacing		Granular base (mm)	Granular sub-base (mm)
		Wearing course (mm)	Binder course (mm)		
10	660	40	70	250	300
20	690		100		
30	710		120		
50	730		140		
100	750	50	150		
150	770		170		

Q. *Design the thickness of a flexible pavement for a dual lane single carriageway with the following data.*
Traffic expected = 440 commercial vehicles/day (in both directions)
Design life = 15 years
Design CBR value of sub-grade = 5%
Vehicle damage factor = 3.1 (from axle load data)
Assume traffic growth rate = 7.3% (from records)

A: Lane distribution factor (LDF) for a two-lane single carriageway = 0.75 (from Table 6.1)

Using equation (6.2),

$$N_{\text{flexible}} = 365 \times \text{TGF} \times A \times \text{VDF} \times \text{LDF} \times 10^{-6}$$

$$\text{TGF} = \left\{ \left(\frac{(1+r)^{nd} - 1}{r} \right) = \left(\frac{(1+0.073)^{15} - 1}{0.073} \right) \right\} = 25.71$$

$$N_{\text{flexible}} = 365 \times 25.71 \times 440 \times 3.1 \times 0.75 \times 10^{-6} = 9.599 \text{ msa}$$

say, $N_{\text{flexible}} = 10$ msa

Total thickness required for sub-grade CBR = 5% and traffic ≈ 10 msa is 660 mm (from Figure 7.11).

Individual layer thicknesses are as follows (from Table 7.10 d): Provide 40 mm of bituminous concrete, 70 mm of dense bituminous macadam, 250 mm of granular base and 300 mm of granular sub-base having minimum CBR value of 30%.

Q: *It was proposed to design a rural road and use locally available granular material as sub-base course. Sub-grade soil particle size gradation curve and the locally available granular material gradation band are represented in Figure 7.13. Verify the usability of the locally available material for construction of sub-base as drainage layer in order to protect it from intrusion of fines from the sub-grade.*

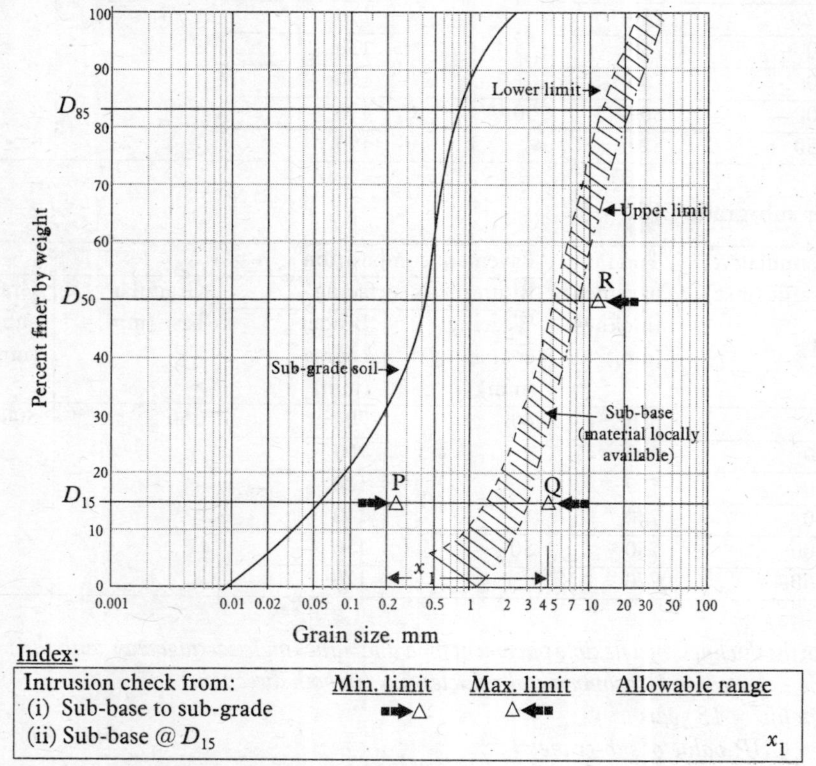

Figure 7.13 *Gradation criteria for sub-base, filter layer and sub-grade soil: Example problem*

A: Clogging of sub-base granular drainage layer due to intrusion of soil particles of sub-grade can be verified based on the drainage layer design criteria recommended by IRC: 37-2001. The details are given below.

From Figure 7.13, the sub-grade soil parameters are found to be $D_{15} = 0.05$ mm, $D_{50} = 0.42$ mm and $D_{85} = 0.90$ mm.

Check for intrusion of sub-base into sub-grade soil:

D_{15} of sub-base $\leq 5 \times D_{85}$ of sub-grade	=	5×0.90	=	4.5 mm	(satisfied)
D_{15} of sub-base $\geq 5 \times D_{15}$ of sub-grade	=	5×0.05	=	0.25 mm	(satisfied)
D_{50} of sub-base $\leq 25 \times D_{50}$ of sub-grade	=	25×0.42	=	10.5 mm	(satisfied)

It can be observed that the sub-base material is satisfied with the desired criteria of minimum and maximum limits of grains finer by weight, at P, Q and R, as indicated in

Figure 7.13. Hence, there is no need to provide a filter layer in between the sub-grade and the sub-base. Therefore, the locally available granular material can be selected without hesitation and used for constructing the sub-base course which is intended to perform as a drainage layer.

Q: *It was proposed to design a pavement's sub-base course as a drainage layer. Gradation curves of the sub-base material and sub-grade soil are represented in Figure 7.14. According to the sub-surface guidelines of IRC:37-2001, verify the clogging of the sub-base layer due to intrusion of the sub-grade soil. If such clogging exists, also verify the possibility of using locally available sand as material for the filter layer.*

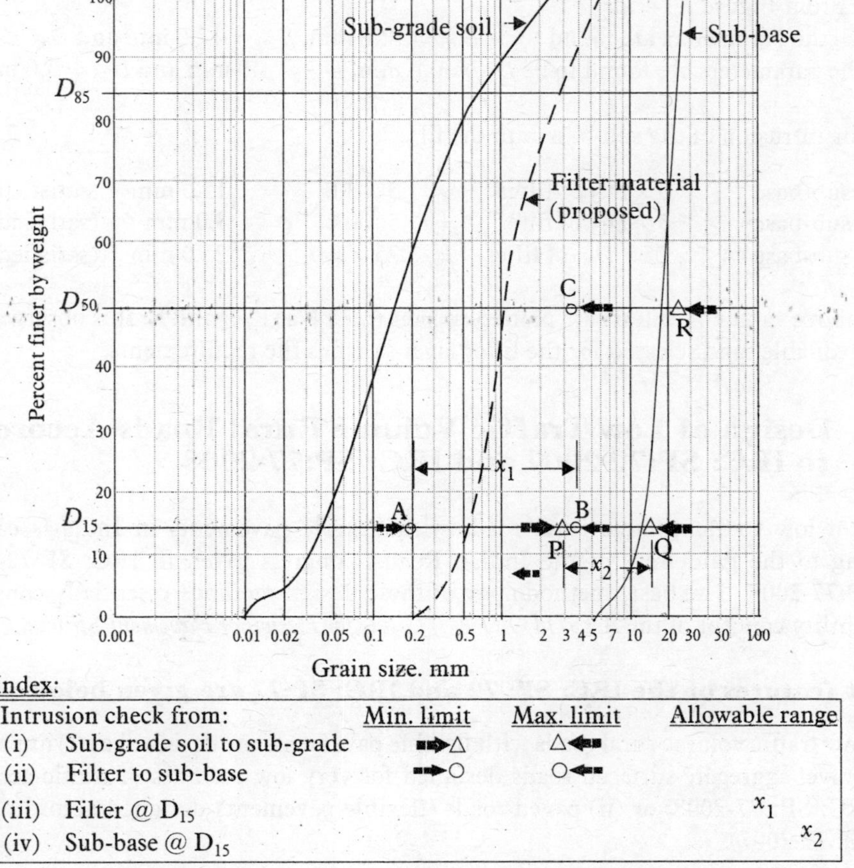

Figure 7.14 *Gradation criteria for sub-base, filter layer and sub-grade soil: Example*

STEP 1: From Figure 7.14, for Sub-base, the parameters are found to be $D_{15} = 12.0$ mm, $D_{50} = 17.0$ mm and $D_{85} = 22.5$ mm.

Sub-grade, the parameters are found to be $D_{15} = 0.04$ mm, $D_{50} = 0.15$ mm and $D_{85} = 0.7$ mm.

Check for intrusion of the sub-base into the sub-grade soil:

D_{15} of sub-base	$\leq 5 \times D_{85}$ of sub-grade	$= 5 \times 0.7$	$=$	3.5 mm	(not satisfied)
D_{15} of sub-base	$\geq 5 \times D_{15}$ of sub-grade	$= 5 \times 0.04$	$=$	0.2 mm	(satisfied)
D_{50} of sub-base	$\leq 25 \times D_{50}$ of sub-grade	$= 25 \times 0.15$	$=$	3.75 mm	(not satisfied)

Therefore, it can be observed that the sub-base material does not satisfy the desired criteria. Hence, a filter layer must be provided between the sub-grade and the sub-base. Locally available sand has been selected for the filter layer and its gradation curve is represented in Figure 7.14. The filter layer material satisfies the criteria of minimum and maximum limits of grains finer by weight, at A, B and C as indicated in Figure 7.14.

The next step is to check for intrusion of the sub-base soil particles into the filter.

STEP 2: From Figure 7.14, for
Sub-base, the parameters are found to be $D_{15} = 12.0$ mm, $D_{50} = 17.0$ mm and $D_{85} = 22.5$ mm.
Filter, the parameters are found to be $D_{15} = 0.6$ mm, $D_{50} = 1.0$ mm and $D_{85} = 3.0$ mm.

Check for intrusion of the sub-base into the filter:

D_{15} of sub-base	$\leq$	$5 \times D_{85}$ of filter	$=$	5×3.0	$=$	15.0 mm	(satisfied)
D_{15} of sub-base	$\geq$	$5 \times D_{15}$ of filter	$=$	5×0.6	$=$	3.0 mm	(satisfied)
D_{50} of sub-base	$\leq$	$25 \times D_{50}$ of filter	$=$	25×1.0	$=$	25.0 mm	(satisfied)

The above values of criteria are plotted in Figure 7.14, at P, Q and R. It is observed that the locally available sand selected for the filter layer satisfies the requirements.

7.5.3 Design of Low Traffic Volume Rural Roads According to IRC: SP:72-2007 and IRC: SP:77-2008

Design of low traffic volume rural roads with flexible pavements in India is carried out according to the guidelines of the Indian Roads Congress given in IRC: SP:72-2007 and IRC: SP:77-2008. The basic methodology of these design methods essentially consist of the serviceability concept of the *AASHTO (1993) Guide for Design of Pavement Structures*.

Salient features of the IRC: SP: 72 and IRC: SP:77 are given below

(a) Low traffic volume rural roads with flexible pavements are designed as (i) unpaved roads (gravel/aggregate surfaced roads designed for very low volumes of traffic according to IRC: SP: 77-2008) or (ii) paved roads (flexible pavements designed according to IRC: SP: 72-2007).

(b) For the design of roads which have very low volumes of traffic, the initial serviceability index (p_i) and terminal serviceability index (p_t) is considered as 4.0 and 2.0 respectively. Therefore, loss of PSI, Δ PSI $= p_i - p_t = 2.0$. The rut depth should not exceed 50 mm under a 3 m straight edge.

(c) For the design of low traffic volume flexible pavements (paved roads) (IRC: SP:72-2007), the structural number (SN) design concept of AASHTO (1993), at 50% reliability level pertaining to Indian climate zones is used.

(d) For both the cases, sub-grade strength in terms of CBR value (in per cent) is classified into 5 groups which consists of S1: very poor (CBR = 2), S2: poor (CBR = 3 to 4), S3: fair (CBR = 5 to 6), S4: good (CBR = 7 to 9) and S5: very good (CBR = 10 to 15).

(e) Traffic volume, in terms ESAL applications, is categorised into 7 groups which consists of T1: 10,000 to 30,000, T2: 30,000 to 60,000, T3: 60,000 to 1,00,000, T4: 1,00,000 to 2,00,000, T5: 2,00,000 to 3,00,000, T6: 3,00,000 to 6,00,000, T7: 6,00,000 to 10,00,000 (maximum up to 10 lakh = 1 million). The traffic groups from T1 to T3 are considered for design of very low traffic volume roads (IRC: SP:77-2008) and the traffic groups from T4 to T7 are considered for design of flexible pavements (IRC: SP: 72-2007).

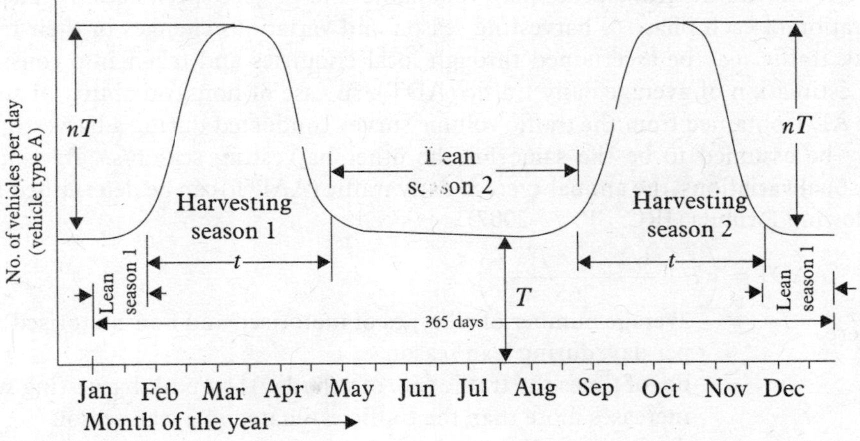

Figure 7.15 *Typical seasonal variations in traffic volume on rural roads (from IRC: SP: 72-2008)*

(f) Seasonal variations in traffic flow on rural roads are considered during peak harvesting and lean seasons (Figure 7.15). Generally, in India, the peak harvesting season may be considered as being of two phases in a year—the first phase during the months of February, March and April (≈90 days) and the second phase during the months of September, October and November (≈90 days). Similarly, the period during the months of May, June, July and August is considered as the first phase of the lean period (≈120 days) and the months, December and January are considered the second phase of the lean period (≈60 days). It should be noted that the above seasons with their durations may differ with location of the road site in India. Single phase harvesting season may also be considered for estimating traffic for the design of low volume rural roads since one harvesting season does exist in a few arid parts in India, viz. a few places in Rajasthan and the Telangana region of Andhra Pradesh.

(g) *Traffic volume estimation* Traffic estimation is necessary for designing the thickness of roads either for upgradation of existing roads or for building new roads. While upgrading existing roads, the traffic volume count survey should be conducted for at least 3 days, during both peak harvesting and lean seasons, for all types of vehicles separately with details of unladen, laden and overloaded commercial vehicles (whose laden weight exceeds 3 tonnes) with their axle load configuration.

Commercial vehicles are classified as heavy commercial vehicles (HCV) and medium commercial vehicles (MCV). HCV comprises full-sized trucks, lorries and buses and

MCV consists of medium-heavy trucks, mini-buses, agricultural tractor trailers and Jugads.

For design of new roads, traffic estimation should be made by considering traffic plying on a similar road in that vicinity of village clusters, agriculture/industrial production, and should also account for the possibility of generated and diverted traffic.

Design traffic is expressed in terms of the cumulative equivalent standard axle load (ESAL) of 80 kN repetitions carried during the design period. The design period is generally taken as 10 years with an annual traffic growth rate of 6%. However, the design period and traffic growth rate may vary subject to project specification. The average duration of each phase of harvesting season and variations/changes in their respective peak traffic may be ascertained through local enquiries and taken into consideration for estimation of average daily traffic (ADT). In case of non-availability of such data, the ADT obtained from the traffic volume survey conducted during a harvesting season may be assumed to be the same for the other harvesting season/s. By considering seasonal variations, the annual average daily traffic (AADT) can be determined from the following formula (IRC: SP: 72-2007).

$$\text{AADT} = \left(T + \frac{1.2 \times n \times T \times t}{365}\right) \tag{7.23}$$

where, T = average number of all types of motorised and non-motorised vehicles per day, during lean season

n = no. of times the traffic (no. of veh./day) at a peak harvesting season increases more than the traffic estimated in a lean season

t = duration of a harvesting season in days

NOTE: In case of steel wheeled carts, the determined AADT should be increased by multiplying with a suitable correction factor as recommended by IRC:SP:72-2007.

The AADT before opening the road to traffic (A) can be determined from the following formula.

$$A = \text{AADT} \times (1+r)^{nc} \tag{7.24}$$

where, A = estimated traffic volume considering the duration between the traffic volume survey conducted and the construction period

r = growth rate of traffic (decimal value)

nc = no. of years from the date of traffic count to the date of opening of the road to traffic

The cumulative ESAL of 80 kN applications ($N_{80\text{kN}}$) during the design period (nd), at traffic growth rate (r), can be determined from the formula (IRC:SP:72-2007).

$$N_{80\text{kN}} = 365 \times \text{TGF} \times A \times \text{VDF} \times \text{LDF} \tag{7.25}$$

where

$\text{TGF} = \left(\dfrac{(1+r)^{nd}-1}{r}\right)$ = Cumulative traffic growth factor based on geometric growth

LDF = Lane distribution factor taken as 1.0 for single/intermediate lanes or 0.75 for dual lanes

VDF = Vehicle damage factor, can be determined from the axle load surveys as discussed in paragraph 6.3.3. In absence of such data, the following guidelines of IRC may be assumed/adopted to determine the VDF for different categories of loaded commercial vehicles.

For laden HCV Comprising a rear single axle and a front axle load of 100.062 kN (10.2 tonnes) and 49.05 kN (5 tonnes) respectively.

$$\text{VDF}_{\text{laden HCV}} = \left(\frac{100.062}{80}\right)^4 + \left(\frac{49.05}{80}\right)^4 = 2.44 + 0.14 = 2.58$$

For unladen/partially loaded HCV Comprising a rear single axle and a front axle load of 58.86 kN (6 tonnes) and 29.43 kN (3 tonnes) respectively.

$$\text{VDF}_{\text{unladen HCV}} = \left(\frac{58.86}{80}\right)^4 + \left(\frac{29.43}{80}\right)^4 = 0.293 + 0.018 = 0.311$$

For over-loaded HCV: (*i*) If 20% over-loading of the rear single axle is assumed with a normal front axle load of 1.2 ×100.062 = 120.074 kN (12.24 tonnes) and 1.2 × 49.05 = 58.86 kN (6 tonnes) respectively.

$$\text{VDF}_{\text{overloaded HCV}} = \left(\frac{120.074}{80}\right)^4 + \left(\frac{58.86}{80}\right)^4 = 5.074 + 0.287 = 5.361$$

(ii) If over-loading is assumed to be 15% of the total laden HCV

$$\text{VDF}_{\text{overloaded HCV}} = \left(\frac{15}{100}\right) \times 5.361 + \left(\frac{85}{100}\right) \times 2.58 = 2.997$$

Similarly, VDF can be calculated for a laden MCV, an unladen/partially loaded MCV and an overloaded MCV. A fully loaded tractor trailer may be taken as a laden MCV having axle loads same as assumed above for the unladen/partially loaded HCV.

(h) *Assessment of sub-grade strength* After estimation of traffic, determination of the sub-grade strength in terms of the CBR value is the second crucial input parameter which should represent the soil support considering the prevailing seasonal variations in environmental, climatic and in situ conditions that exist during the wettest period.

Sub-grade soil surveys should be conducted along the proposed road to obtain soil data such as soil classification, field density, field moisture content, level of ground water table (GWT), annual rain fall and other environment factors influencing sub-grade strength. At least 3 samples per kilometre of the length must be tested for soil classification even though the soil type is the same. On each type of soil, compaction and CBR tests should be conducted. The CBR test should be conducted in the laboratory on representative re-moulded (minimum 3) samples of sub-grade soil compacted to standard Proctor dry density and tested at field representative moisture content that exists during the wettest season. As a worst case scenario, a soaked CBR test may be considered where rainfall exceeds 1400 mm/year and for sub-grade soil having clays, silts and silty sand. However, a representative CBR value may be estimated or checked by using (*i*) equations (NCHRP 2003) based on soil properties and sieve analysis data, (*ii*) nomographs (CRRI 1990) by inputting sieve analysis data and (*iii*) from related soil records of the Geographic Society of India.

(i) The estimated sub-grade strength (i.e., the design CBR value) should be based on any of the following prevailing in situ wettest moisture content likely to occur during the design period (IRC: SP:72 and IRC: SP:77).

For design of new roads Where the GWT is at a shallow depth and likely to influence the sub-grade moisture content, the following possible categories may be considered.

- In non-plastic sub-grade soil where the GWT rises to within 1 metre of the pavement surface.
- In clays having plasticity index (PI) < 20 and where the GWT rises to within 3 metres of the pavement surface; in heavy clays having PI < 40 and where the GWT rises to within 7 metres of the pavement surface.
- Places where GWT is maintained by rainfall and river, lake and sea.

For the above categories, the wettest moisture content in sub-grade soil can be determined by (1) measuring in situ moisture content when the GWT is closer to the pavement surface and (2) using the ratio between sub-grade moisture content and the plastic limit of the soil. In absence of such data, the 4-day soaked CBR value may be taken as the design CBR value of the sub-grade soil.

Even though the GWT may be deep enough under a road, it may fluctuate (Figure 7.16) due to ingress of rain/surface water and migration of sub-soil water (Figure 7.17), therefore moisture content changes across the width of the sub-grade. The accumulated/ absorbed moisture in the sub-grade soil differs based on the location under a pavement crust. In general, surface water accumulates more in the sub-grade than in the layers above and also, more at and near the edges of the carriageway (which is termed as the moisture seasonal variation zone) than in the middle portion (which is termed as the moisture equilibrium zone) of the sub-grade (Figure 7.17). This phenomenon of moisture ingress happens more often where shoulders are not sealed. However, the moisture content in sub-grade soil depends on the balance between the amount of moisture entering through the edges of the pavement during the rainy season and the amount of moisture leaving the sub-grade during the dry season. Such balanced in situ moisture content is termed as equilibrium moisture content (EMC). In the sub-grade seasonal moisture variation zone, moisture content fluctuates with intensity of rainfall. This zone is wetter than the equilibrium zone and becomes drier during the summer season (Emery 1992).

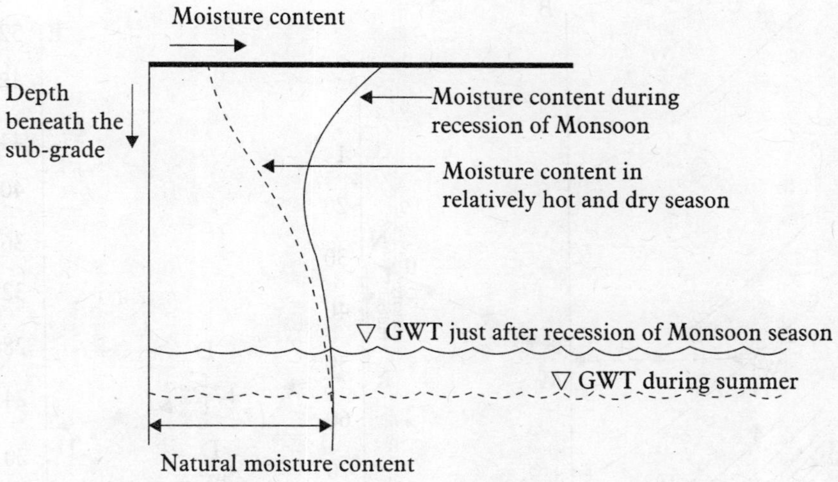

Figure 7.16 *Seasonal variations in sub-grade moisture content (modified and elaborated based on Molenaar 2009)*

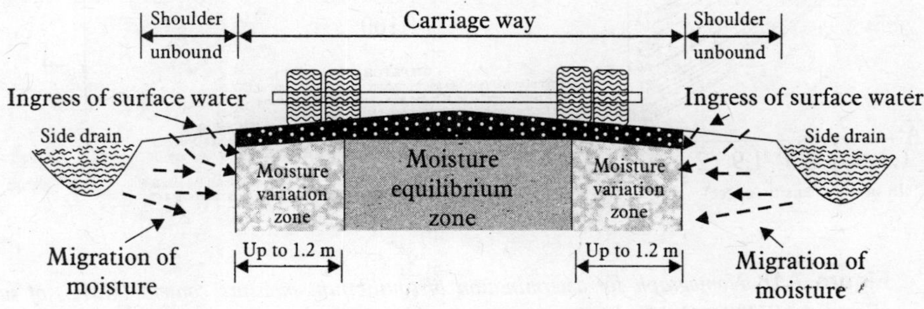

Figure 7.17 *Sub-grade zones based on moisture variation*

As a general observation, when moisture content decreases in a fully saturated soil, the state of moisture content is termed in order as soaked, OMC and EMC respectively. However, based on the fluctuations in GWT and ingress of rainwater, the EMC can be more than OMC. The influence of climatic factors on EMC is predominant in sub-grade rather than sub-base and base courses respectively—in fact, EMC is found to be nearly independent of climate influence on base course (Gourley and Greening 1999).

The EMC can be determined by using a nomograph (Figure 7.18) developed by AASHTO (1993). In the absence of the required data of soil, the OMC value can be taken from the dry density data of the standard Proctor test. The 4-day soaked CBR test value (as default) may also be considered where seasonal flooding influences the GWT.

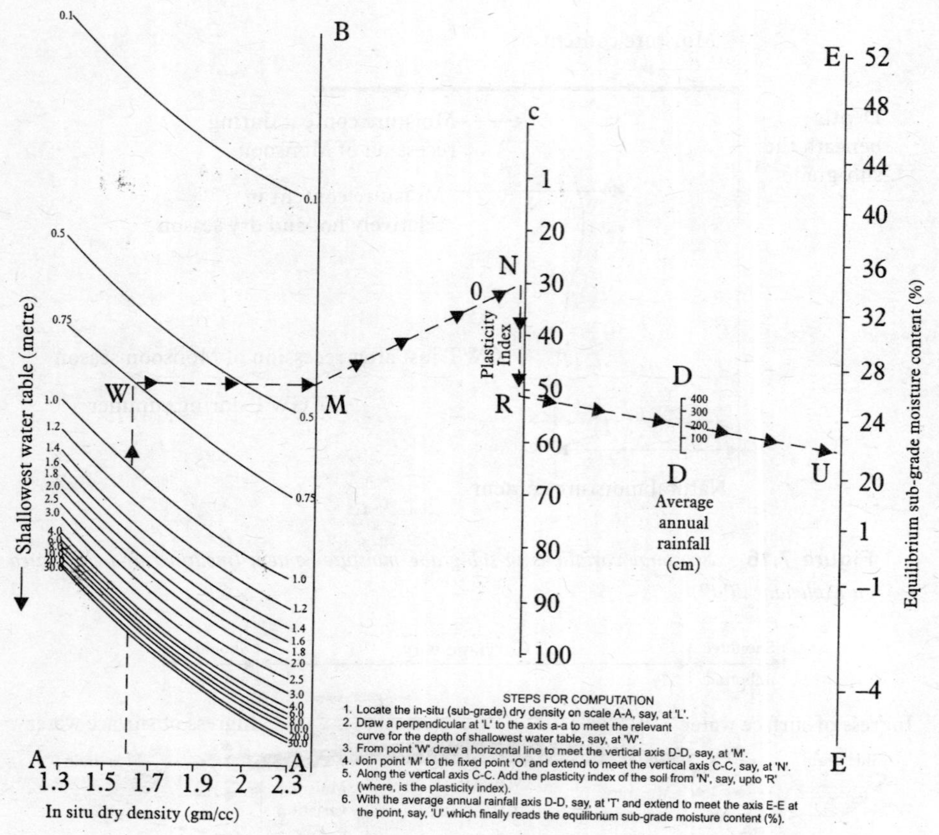

Figure 7.18 *Nomograph for determination of equilibrium moisture content (EMC) of subgrade (From AASHTO Guide for Design of Pavement Structures, 1993, by the American Association of State Highway and Transportation Officials, Wahington,* DC. *Used by permission. Documents may be purchased from the AASHTO bookstore at 1-800-231-3475 or online at htpp//bookstore.transportation.org)*

NOTE: Design of pavements based on soaked CBR may not be appropriate in all cases. It might lead to over-design and undesirable features. Therefore, unsoaked CBR value should be used suitably based on variations of the moisture content in the sub-grade with reference to its OMC and EMC. The following information related to EMC and OMC are useful in estimating sub-grade soil strength.

- The sub-grade's EMC can be estimated using several empirical equations which were developed based on Atterberg's limits, sieve analysis data, Weinert's *N*-value, Thornthwaite's moisture index and OMC determined by the modified AASHTO compaction method (Emery 1988 and Molenaar 2009). The following simple relationship developed for pavements in South African arid climatic conditions with deep GWT may be used for determination of EMC (in per cent) from OMC (in per cent) obtained from the modified AASHTO compaction test (Emery 1988).

$$EMC = 1.3 \times OMC - 1.2 \times c - 3.5 \tag{7.26}$$

Take $c = 0$ for sub-grade and sub-base; $c = 1$ for base course.

- Unsoaked CBR value may be taken as the design CBR of the sub-grade when the ratio of (EMC/OMC@ modified AASHTO compaction) < 1.7 (Molenaar 2009).

For rehabilitation/ upgradation of existing roads In situ strength of existing road sub-grade can be determined by conducting the CBR test on re-moulded soil samples compacted to in situ density at EMC as observed immediately after recession of the rainy season which represent the wettest and weakest soil condition. The sub-grade in situ strength in terms of CBR can also be obtained (as discussed in Chapter 10) by conducting dynamic cone penetrometer (DCP) tests on the sub-grade on either edges of the pavement from 600 to 1000 mm. In the absence of such data, the design CBR value may be obtained by conducting the 4-days soaked CBR test on re-moulded sub-grade soil compacted to field density.

(j) *Thickness design of pavements*:

For very low volume roads or unpaved roads according to IRC:SP:77-2008 According to the design guidelines (Figure 7.19), unpaved roads are designed for the first three categories (T1 to T3) of traffic and for all five (S1 to S5) classes of sub-grade strength. To utilise qualified locally available materials (according to Clause 401 of MORD), the gravel/soil aggregate base layer thickness can be converted to an equivalent thickness of the sub-base with an intermediate CBR value between them (Figure 7.20). The gravel base layer must be provided with a minimum thickness of 100 mm which has 80 per cent of the minimum soaked CBR.

Guidelines for material selection The gravel base and base of the gravel material quality should conform to Clause 402 of MORD specification. Based on the traffic volume/composition and quality of materials used, these gravel layers may be surfaced with a suitable surface gravel layer (having a thickness of 40 to 50 mm), conforming to Table 400.3, Clause 402 of MORD specification.

In frost susceptible areas, the gravel base thickness obtained according to the design chart (Figure 7.19) should be suitably increased according to the category of traffic and class of sub-grade strength (IRC: SP: 72-2007).

For flexible pavements or paved roads according to IRC: SP: 72-2007 According to the design chart of IRC: 72 (Figure 7.19), flexible pavement layers are designed for the remaining categories (T4 to T7) of traffic and for all five (S1 to S5) classes of sub-grade strength. The recommended bituminous surfacing should be constructed according to standard specifications (Clause 507 of MORD 2004 and MoRT&H 2001).

Black-topped roads should be designed where minimum ADT is 200 (or 1,00,000 ESAL applications) and provided base course with a minimum thickness of 150 mm, for a design period of 10 years.

All black-topped flexible pavements in frost susceptible areas are also designed according to the design chart (Figure 7.19) but a minimum crust thickness of 450 mm (comprising 300 mm thick sub-base + 150 mm thick base) should be provided irrespective of design CBR's minimum crust thickness requirement.

Suitable drainage arrangements should be made for all types of pavements (Figure 7.21).

Subgrade strength (CBR)	T1 10,000 TO 30,000	T2 30,000 TO 50,000	T3 50,000 TO 1,00,000	T4 1,00,000 TO 2,00,000	T5 2,00,000 TO 3,00,000	T6 3,00,000 TO 6,00,000	T7 6,00,000 TO 1,000,000
	Cumulative ESAL applications						
Very poor (CBR - 2) S1	200 100	75 150 100	75 100 100 100	75 100 100 150	75 100 150 150	75 100 225 250	75 150 200 225
Poor (CBR - 3 TO 4) S2	200	275	75 100 150	75 100 100 100	75 100 100 150	75 150 100 150	75 150 150 150
Fair (CBR - 5 TO 6) S3	175	250	275	75 100 125	75 100 150	75 100 100 100	75 150 100 100
Good (CBR - 7 TO 9) S4	150	175	225	75 100 100	75 100 125	75 100 150	75 150 150
Very good (CBR - 10 TO 15) S5	125	150	175	75 160	75 100 100	75 100 125	75 150 125

NOTE:
- In situations where locally available suitably processed gravel base material fulfills all requirements and the engineer is satisfied that the gravel base material is well compacted, the top 75 mm WBML layer may be dispensed with for cumulative traffic upto 100000 ESAL applications.
- For aggregate-surfaced gravel roads, the thickness requirement of base gravel should conform to MORD specifications Table 400.3; the thickness of surface gravel layer will generally vary from 40 to 50 m depending on traffic and quality of material.

LEGEND
- Bituminous surface treated CRMB/WBM
- Base of gravel/CRMB/WBM (CBR not less than 100 (where 100 mm thickness recommended it may be modified to 74 mm thickness for WbH construction with corresponding in crease of 25 mm in sub-base thickness)
- Gravel base (CBR not less than 100; in exceptional cases may be relaxed suitably)
- Granular sub-base (CBR not less than 20; in exceptional cases may be relaxed to 15)
- Modified soil/improved sub-grade (CBR not les than 10)

Figure 7.19 *Pavement design chart (from IRC: SP:72-2007)*

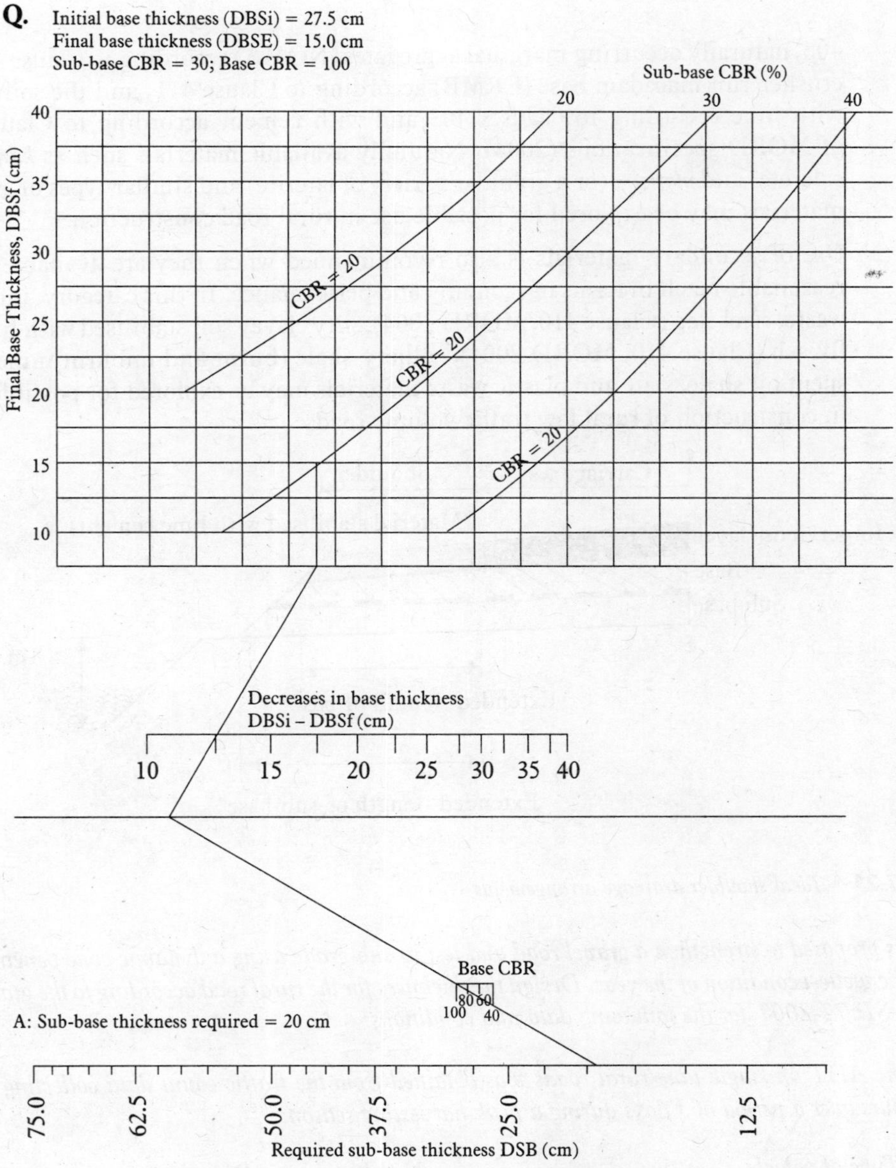

Q. Initial base thickness (DBSi) = 27.5 cm
Final base thickness (DBSE) = 15.0 cm
Sub-base CBR = 30; Base CBR = 100

Sub-base CBR (%)
20 30 40
Final Base Thickness, DBSf (cm)
40 35 30 25 20 15 10
CBR = 20
CBR = 20
CBR = 20
Decreases in base thickness
DBSi – DBSf (cm)
10 15 20 25 30 35 40
Base CBR
100 80 60 40
A: Sub-base thickness required = 20 cm
75.0 62.5 50.0 37.5 25.0 12.5
Required sub-base thickness DSB (cm)

Figure 7.20 *Chart to convert thickness of gravel/soil aggregate base layer to an equivalent thickness of the sub-base layer (From AASHTO Guide for Design of Pavement Structures, 1993, by the American Association of State Highway and Transportation Officials, Washington,* DC. *Used by permission. Documents may be purchased from the AASHTO bookstore at 1-800-231-3475 or online at http://bookstore.transportation.org)*

Guidelines for material selection The design of rural roads should be such that there is maximum utilisation of locally available materials which qualify without using admixtures as according to Clauses 401 and 402; water-bound macadam (WBM) according to Clause 405, wet mix macadam (WMM) according to Clause

406, naturally occurring marginal aggregates (NOMA) according to Clause 408 and crusher run macadam base (CRMB) according to Clause 411; and the soil treated with lime according to Clauses 403 and with cement according to Clauses 404 of MORD specifications (2004). Naturally available materials such as *kankar* (or calcrete) and *morrum* (or a granular variety of laterite) and similar types of granular materials may be explored for possible use in rural road construction.

(k) Use of secondary materials is also recommended when they are available within reasonable reach in terms of economy and performance. In this category, industrial waste, steel slag (Clause 410, MORD 2004), silty clayey soil stabilised with lime and fly ash (Clause 410, MORD 2004), colliery shale (burnt and unburnt minestone), spent oil shale, slate and plastic waste materials may be explored for possible usage in construction of rural low traffic volume roads.

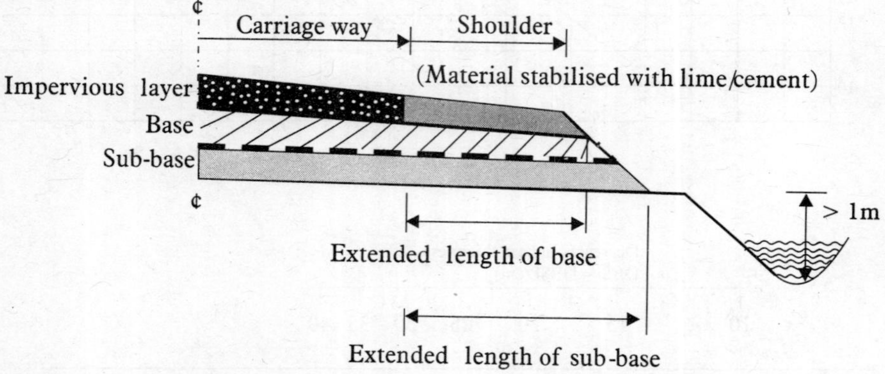

Figure 7.21 *Ideal shoulder drainage arrangements*

Q:*It was proposed to strengthen a gravel road and test its sub-grade using a dynamic cone penetrometer during the wettest condition of the year. Design the thickness for the rural road according to the guidelines of IRC: SP:72-2007, for the following data and conditions:*

(i) *The ADT on single lane rural roads was obtained from the traffic count data collecting for 24 hours over a period of 3 days during a peak harvesting season:*

Type of vehicle		*Number*		*Per cent*
Animal drawn carts:				
Pneumatic tyred	=	*34*	=	*3.6*
Solid wheeled	=	*3*	=	*0.3*
Bicycles	=	*512*	=	*53.7*
Trucks, lorries & buses	=	*16*	=	*1.7*
Mini-trucks, tractor-trailers & Jugads	=	*62*	=	*6.5*
Jeeps, cars & autos	=	*47*	=	*4.9*
Motor cycles	=	*279*	=	*29.3*
Total	=	*953*	=	*100.0*

Approximate proportion of commercial vehicles may be considered under categories, laden, partially laden and over-loaded vehicles as 70, 20 and 10%.

Take no. of lanes = 1, growth rate of traffic = 6.5 % and design life = 10 years.

(ii) *No. of harvesting seasons in the locality = 2*
Duration of each harvesting season ≈ 70 days

(iii) *Road construction period (after traffic count) = 1 year and 6 months*

(iv) *Existing pavement layers, sub-grade and other details:*

Laterite soil + Gravel sub-base CBR value	*= 12.7 %*
Laterite soil + Gravel sub-base thickness = 100 mm	
Granular base CBR value	*= 22.8 %*
Granular base CBR thickness	*= 100 mm*
Mean penetration value of $DCP_{60°}$	*= 59 mm/blow*
Sub-grade soil class	*= CL*
Depth of GWT below the ground surface	*= 8.7 metres*
Average annual rain fall in the locality	*= 850 mm*

A: Computation of AADT:

As the traffic volume data during lean seasons and in other peak harvesting seasons is not available, the following conditions may be assumed.

- Mean traffic volume during lean season is equal to half the traffic volume observed during the peak harvesting season.
- With reference to Figure 7.15 and equation (7.23), take $n = 1$; and $t = 70$ days (given)

Mean ADT during lean season = 953/2 = 477

$$\text{From equation (7.23), AADT} = 477 + \frac{1.2 \times 1 \times 477 \times 70}{365} = 477 + 109.7 \approx 587$$

From equation (7.24), AADT on road at the time of opening to the traffic,

$$A = 587 \times (1 + 0.065)^{1.5} \approx 645$$

$$\text{Proportion of HCV in } A = \frac{16}{953} \times 645 \approx 11$$

$$\text{Similarly, proportion of MCV} = \frac{62}{953} \times 645 \approx 42$$

Animal drawn vehicles are not considered for design because they are pneumatic tyred. Solid wheeled carts are negligible in number (0.3%) and there is no need for applying a correction to AADT since the computed AADT > 500 (IRC: SP:72-2007).

Computation of ESAL of 80 kN aplications:

For HCV:

According to IRC, assume that for a laden HCV, the axle load on the rear single axle = 10.2 tonnes and the front axle load = 5 tonnes; $VDF_{\text{laden HCV}} = 2.58$

For an unladen HCV, the axle load on the rear single axle = 6 tonnes and the front axle load = 3 tonnes; $VDF_{\text{unladen HCV}} = 0.311$

Assume that for an over-loaded HCV, with 20% over-loading, the rear single axle load and normal front axle load is 1.2 × 10.2 = 12.24 tonnes and 1.2 × 5 = 6 tonnes respectively; $VDF_{\text{overloaded HCV}} = 5.361$

ESAL applications of all categories of HCV =

$$= \left[\left(\frac{70}{100}\right) \times 11 \times 2.58\right] + \left[\left(\frac{20}{100}\right) \times 11 \times 0.311\right] + \left[\left(\frac{10}{100}\right) \times 11 \times 5.361\right] = 26.45$$

Similarly, for MCV:

According to IRC, assume that for a laden MCV, the axle loads on the rear single axle = 6 tonnes and the front axle load = 3 tonnes; $VDF_{\text{Laden MCV}} = 0.311$

For an unladen MCV, the axle loads on the rear single axle =3 tonnes and the front axle load = 1.5 tonnes; $VDF_{\text{unladen MCV}} \approx 0.02$

Assume that for an over-loaded MCV, with 20% over loading, the rear single axle load and normal front axle load is 1.2 × 6 = 7.2 tonnes and 1.2 × 3 = 3.6 tonnes respectively; $VDF_{\text{overloaded MCV}} = 0.645$

ESAL applications of all categories of MCV

$$= \left[\left(\frac{70}{100}\right) \times 42 \times 0.311\right] + \left[\left(\frac{20}{100}\right) \times 42 \times 0.02\right] + \left[\left(\frac{10}{100}\right) \times 42 \times 0.645\right] = 12.02$$

Therefore, ESAL applications of HCV+MCV = 26.45 + 12.02 = 38.47

Computation of cumulative ESAL applications:

From equation (7.25),

$$\text{TGF} = \left(\frac{(1+r)^{nd} - 1}{r}\right) = \left(\frac{(1+0.065)^{10} - 1}{0.065}\right) = 13.494$$

$$N_{80\text{kN}} = 365 \times \text{TGF} \times (A \times \text{VDF}) \times \text{LDF} = 365 \times 13.494 \times (38.47) \times 1.0 \approx 189477$$

Evaluation of sub-grade CBR:

The IRC:SP:72-2007 recommends estimating sub-grade strength in terms of the CBR value by using an equation (10.10) developed in UK (TRL, Road Note 8, 1990). By substituting the mean DCP penetration value in the equation, we get,

$$\log_{10}(\text{CBR}) = 2.48 - 1.057 \times \log_{10}(59)$$

Sub-grade CBR value = 4.05 %,
Therefore, take the sub-grade design CBR value as 4%.

Details of pavement layer thickness:

For the obtained values of ESAL ($N_{80_{kN}}$) load applications of 1,89,477 and with the sub-grade CBR value as 4%, the following design details can be obtained from Figure 7.19.

Referring to the category of traffic as T4 and sub-grade class as S2, we get thicknesses of different layers from the bottom to the top of the pavement crust as,

Layer1: Thickness of modified soil sub-grade (having CBR $\geq$ 10 %) = 100 mm
Layer2: Thickness of granular sub-base (having CBR $\geq$ 20 %) = 100 mm
Layer3: Thickness of gravel/ CRMB/ WBM layer (having CBR $\geq$ 100%) = 100 mm
Layer4: Thickness of bituminous surface treated CRMB/ WBM layer = 75 mm

As the existing layers, laterite soil + gravel sub-base and granular base layers can be considered as layer 1 and layer 2, since both the existing layers qualify with respect to the minimum required values of CBR and thickness. Therefore, the remaining layers, layer 3 and layer 4 should be constructed over the existing pavement, in compliance with the respective standards and specifications of MORD for rural roads. It is noted that before constructing layer 3, the existing surface of the granular layer should be corrected suitably where undulations and pot holes exist. Arrangements for shoulder drainage should be provided with due consideration.

Exercises

7.1 What is the significance of deflection and stress analysis of pavements?

7.2 State and write the assumptions used in Boussinesq's theory of analysis of single layer pavement.

7.3 What is the limitations of Boussinesq theory of stress analysis?

7.4 Derive an expression for determination of vertical stress under a uniformly loaded circular area with a neat sketch.

7.5 Explain why the pressure distribution is different under flexible and rigid plates.

7.6 Write the salient features and assumptions used in Burmister's theory of analysis of flexible pavements with a neat sketch showing details of a two-layer pavement system.

7.7 What is the significance of multi-layered flexible pavement analysis? Explain the considerations/assumptions made for analysis of stresses, strains and deflections in a multi-layered flexible pavement system.

7.8 Define how the assumptions made in a multi-layered flexible pavement system are unrealistic in practice or in service conditions of pavement.

7.9 List out a few programs with salient details of the analytical solution/programs of multi-layered flexible pavements.

7.10 In detail, explain the different methods for design of flexible pavements.

7.11 Write the broad classification of design methods for flexible pavements. Explain each method with suitable examples.

7.12 What are the limitations of empirical methods of pavement design? Explain the M–E methods widely used for design of pavements.

7.13 Distinguish between empirical and M–E methods of pavement designs.

7.14 Write the design criteria used in many M–E methods of design of flexible pavement. Draw a neat sketch showing details of critical strains in a layered flexible pavement structure.

7.15 What are the critical strains considered in design of M–E methods of flexible pavement design? Write how performance evaluation criteria is decided based on the relationships correlating the limiting values of the mechanistic parameters.

7.16 List out a few methods of flexible pavement design based on M–E principles.

7.17 Explain the benefits of pavement design based on M–E method.

7.18 Explain how pavement failure mechanism is related with critical strains in different layers of flexible pavement.

7.19 List out a few historical and important test road facilities developed in different countries.

7.20 Define the serviceability concept of the AASHTO design method of flexible pavement.

7.21 Distinguish between PSR and PSI.

7.22 Define and explain (i) PSR (ii) PSI and (iii) TSI.

7.23 Describe the concept of structural number (SN) of AASHTO flexible pavement design. Write the factors affecting the SN value.

7.24 Explain the AASHTO subjective rating of drainage of granular layers based on the percent of time pavement structure is exposed to moisture levels approaching saturation.

7.25 Write the failure criteria adopted in flexible pavement design according to IRC:37-2001. Draw a neat sketch showing the salient details.

7.26 Write the relationship used for determining equivalent thickness of dense bituminous macadam (DBM) to bituminous macadam (BM) layer according to the guidelines of IRC:37-2001.

7.27 State why the sub-base layer is constructed as a drainage layer. Why are open graded granular material used for construction of drainage layer?

7.28 Write the significance of providing a filter layer in between the drainage layer and sub-grade.

7.29 What is the IRC:37-2001 design criteria of drainage layer material and sub-grade soil?

7.30 Write a short note on the drainage layer design criteria and related recommendations of IRC:37-2001.

7.31 Write the salient design features of flexible pavements according to IRC:37-2001.

7.32 Write the salient features of the AASHTO method of flexible pavement design.

7.33 Compare flexible pavement design methods according to AASHTO and IRC:37-2001.

7.34 Write the salient design features of low volume rural roads according to IRC: SP-72 and IRC: SP-77.

7.35 Write a short note on traffic volume estimation method adopted for design of low volume rural roads according to IRC: SP-72 &77.

7.36 Write a short note on seasonal variations in traffic flow on rural roads considered during peak harvesting and lean season.

7.37 Determine the value of VDF of a laden HCV comprising a rear single axle and a front axle of 120 KN and 67 KN respectively.

7.38 How is sub-grade strength determined for design of low volume roads? State the generally adopted methods for estimating the representative CBR value.

7.39 Sketch a typical cross-section of a flexible pavement showing sub-grade zones based on moisture variations.

7.40 Write a short note on seasonal variations in sub-grade moisture content. Draw a typical sketch.

7.41 State the possible categories of influence of sub-grade moisture content when the GWT is at shallow depth.

7.42 Define equilibrium zone and state the influence of GWT and EMC on sub-grade moisture seasonal variation zone.

7.43 Write the factors affecting variations in sub-grade moisture content.

7.44 What are the different methods of estimating EMC of sub-grade?

7.45 Draw a typical sketch of a flexible pavement cross-section showing ideal shoulder drainage arrangements.

7.46 Determine the value of equivalent CBR value by the UK-TRL equation when the DCP mean penetration value is 63 mm/blow.

8

Analysis and Design of Rigid Pavements

Introduction

The design phase of rigid pavement should incorporate numerous factors like subgrade support, material properties, traffic loads, drainage and prevailing climatic/environmental conditions, for which the pavement should withst and during its design life. Due to this reason, for any given boundary condition, the rigid pavement structure should be analyzed to determine allowable deflections or stresses or strains.

8.1 Analysis of Rigid Pavements

Stresses in concrete pavement slabs are induced by wheel loads and by variations in temperature. The intensity and nature of stresses developed at different locations of the slab are dependent upon various factors, viz. magnitude of load, lateral placement of wheel loads, flexural strength of the slab, temperature changes, moisture, humidity and location of joints. Excessive stresses at the bottom of the concrete slab pavement produce cracks. The major types of significant stresses in a concrete pavement may be classified as (Moore 1956)

- Direct tensile stresses which are produced due to slab contractions
- Flexural tensile stresses which are developed by wheel loads
- Flexural tensile stresses caused by restraint due to warping of slab

In this analysis, preparation of sub-grade and base course layers are assumed to be carried out according to the specifications of relevant standard codes. The minimum and maximum requirements of k-values (or equivalent CBR values) are assumed to be taken care of. It is also assumed that the necessary stabilisation methods are followed.

Further, it is worth mentioning that, however satisfactory a rigid pavement design is developed, it becomes an ineffective exercise if proper drainage facilities are not provided for the sub-surface and surface layers.

Hence, before designing and constructing the rigid pavement, the above two aspects must be assured by the client and the contractor.

The basic concepts of stress analysis in concrete slabs are given below.

8.1.1 Stresses Produced by Wheel Load

Unlike flexible pavement design, for rigid pavements, mechanistic principles have to be used in the primitive stages of design development itself. The stress analysis of cement concrete slabs developed by Westergaard has evolved into a scientifically based procedure to address problems related to rigid pavement design. His work was published in several research papers (1926; 1927; 1933 and 1948). Certain considerations were taken into account while performing the stress analysis developed by Westergaard. They are presented below.

(a) Three critical locations of wheel loadings were considered, viz. interior, along the longitudinal edge and the corner of the slab (Figure 8.1).

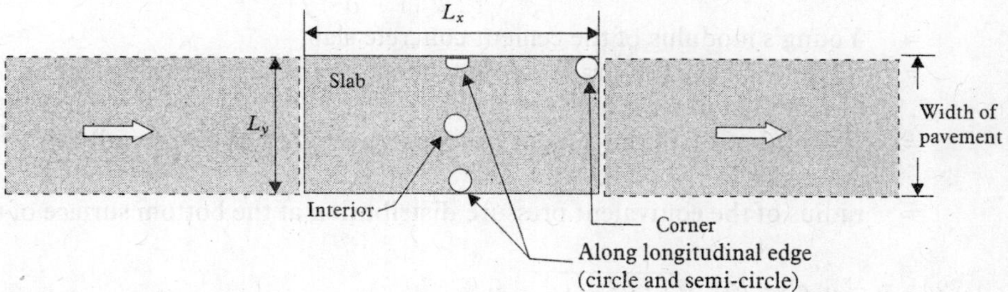

Figure 8.1 *Plan view of critical locations of wheel loads on a rigid pavement*

(b) Elliptical, semi-elliptical and circular areas of loadings were considered. In this book, we will consider calculation of stresses due to circular loading in the interior and at the corner; circular and semi-circular loading at the edge.

(c) The cement concrete slab is assumed to be homogenous, isotropic, ideally elastic, uniform in thickness and without cracks. It is also taken that the pavement slab is in full contact with the sub-grade which is assumed to be a dense liquid.

(d) The sub-grade support is in the vertical direction and is proportional to the deflection of the slab. The sub-grade does not possess any shear strength.

Sub-grade support $(P) = k\times$ Deflection of the slab (Δ)

where, k is called the modulus of the sub-grade reaction.

(e) The ratio of pressure to deflection is constant everywhere under the concrete slab.

(f) Calculated load stresses are not very sensitive even to fairly great variations of the modulus of sub-grade reaction (k).

In 1925 and 1926, Westergaard developed the earliest equations to calculate the wheel load stresses at salient locations of a slab.

$$\sigma_{\text{corner}} = \frac{3P}{h^2}\left[1 - \left(\frac{a\sqrt{2}}{l}\right)^{0.6}\right] \tag{8.1}$$

$$\sigma_{\text{interior}} = \frac{0.3162\,P}{h^2}\left[4\log_{10}\left(\frac{l}{b}\right) + 1.069\right] \tag{8.2}$$

$$\sigma_{\text{edge}} = 0.57185\frac{P}{h^2}\left[4\log_{10}\left(\frac{l}{b}\right) + 0.3593\right] \tag{8.3}$$

where,

σ_{corner}	=	stress produced at the corner by the wheel load spread over a circular area
σ_{interior}	=	stress produced on the interior by the wheel load spread over a circular area
σ_{edge}	=	stress produced at the edge by the wheel load spread over a semi-circular area
P	=	design wheel load (i.e., half the single axle load)
h	=	thickness of the concrete slab
a	=	radius of the circular area of the wheel loading
l	=	radius of relative stiffness $= \left(\dfrac{E\,h^3}{12\,k\,(1-\mu^2)}\right)^{0.25}$ (8.4)
E	=	Young's modulus of the cement concrete slab
k	=	modulus of the sub-grade reaction or sub-grade support value (may be obtained from plate load test data)
μ	=	Poisson's ratio of the cement concrete slab (taken as 0.15 for all the equations in the book)
b	=	radius of the equivalent pressure distribution at the bottom surface of the slab

If $a \geq 1.724h$, $b = a$, else, $b = \sqrt{1.6a^2 + h^2} - 0.675\,h$

The above formulae were modified by Westergaard in 1933 and again later based on the field experiments conducted by Teller and Sutherland (1935–1943). In the IRC:58-2002, the following equation of stress due to load at the critical edge region is adopted. It is based on Westergaard's formulae modified by Teller and Sutherland.

$$\sigma_{\text{edge}} = 0.529\frac{P}{h^2}(1 + 0.54\mu)\left[4\log_{10}\left(\frac{l}{b}\right) + \log_{10} b - 0.4048\right] \tag{8.5}$$

To calculate the stress at the corner due to loading, Westergaard's equation (8.1) was modified and the following formulae were recommended by other researchers (Fwa et al. 1996).

By Bradbury (1938): $\sigma_{\text{corner}} = \dfrac{3P}{h^2}\left[1 - \left(\dfrac{a}{l}\right)^{0.6}\right]$ (8.6)

By Kelly (1939): $\sigma_{\text{corner}} = \dfrac{3P}{h^2}\left[1 - \left(\dfrac{a\sqrt{2}}{l}\right)^{1.2}\right]$ (8.7)

By Spangler (1942): $$\sigma_{\text{corner}} = \frac{3.2P}{h^2}\left[1 - \left(\frac{a\sqrt{2}}{l}\right)\right] \tag{8.8}$$

Pickett made a comparative study of the equations recommended by Kelly, Bradbury and Spangler and suggested a formula which has the form of Westergaard's theoretical equation and was found to be more closely matching the larger stress values measured in the Arlington road tests (Moore 1956).

By Pickett (1946): $$\sigma_{\text{corner}} = \frac{4.2P}{h^2}\left[1 - \sqrt{\left(\frac{a}{l}\right)} \times \left(\frac{1}{0.925 + 0.22\left(\frac{a}{l}\right)}\right)\right] \tag{8.9}$$

Based on Westergaard's revised formulae (1948), Ioannides et al. (1985), re-analysed the rigid pavement using the finite element method and recommended the following stress equations.

$$\sigma_{\text{corner}} = \frac{3P}{h^2}\left[1 - \left(\frac{a\sqrt{\pi}}{l}\right)^{0.72}\right] \tag{8.10}$$

For circular area of loading

$$\sigma_{\text{edge}} = \frac{0.803P}{h^2}\left[4\log_{10}\left(\frac{l}{a}\right) + 0.666\left(\frac{a}{l}\right) - 0.034\right] \tag{8.11}$$

For semi-circular area of loading:

$$\sigma_{\text{edge}} = \frac{0.803P}{h^2}\left[4\log_{10}\left(\frac{l}{a}\right) + 0.282\left(\frac{a}{l}\right) + 0.65\right] \tag{8.12}$$

To obtain stresses induced in a slab by dual wheel loads, the equivalent circular area (Figure 8.2) of the dual tyre contact area is calculated to be equal to the contact area of the dual wheel plus the area between them (Huang 2004). The radius of contact area is calculated based on this concept. The equation given in IRC:58-2002 is as follows.

$$a = \left[\left(\frac{0.8521\,P_1}{q\pi}\right) + \frac{S}{\pi}\left(\frac{P_1}{0.5227\,q}\right)^{0.5}\right]^{0.5} \tag{8.13}$$

where,

a = equivalent radius of contact area, assumed circular, for single axle dual wheels
P_1 = load on one tyre
S = centre-to-centre distance of dual tyres (31 cm may taken as the standard value)
q = tyre pressure

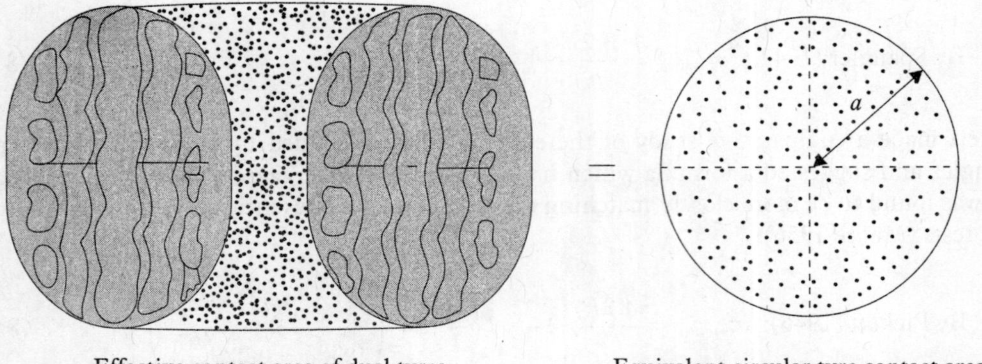

Figure 8.2(a) *Equivalent circular contact area considered for rigid pavement design*

With reference to the original equations of Westergaard (1925; 1926; and 1933), the above modified formulae are empirical since the field test conditions are dependant on the test location and time (Santosh et al. 2006). However, accurate and closed form equations developed based on FEM analysis can be obtained from literature (Ioannides et al. 1985).

Q: *A 40 kN wheel loading is applied on a slab of 240 mm thickness. The radius of the wheel contact area is 150 mm and the radius of the relative stiffness value is 0.96 m. (i) Determine maximum stress when loaded at the corner based on the formula developed by Westergaard and the formula modified by Ioannides et al. (ii) Determine the percentage increase of maximum stress when using the circular loaded area method and the semi-circular loaded area method, using the re-analysed equations of Ioannides et al.*

A: (i) *Corner wheel load stress*

According to Westergaard (equation (8.6)):

$$\sigma_{\text{corner}} = \frac{3 \times 40}{(0.24)^2}\left[1 - \left(\frac{0.15 \times \sqrt{2}}{0.96}\right)^{0.6}\right] = 1241.2\,\text{kPa}$$

According to Ioannides et al. (equation (8.10)):

$$\sigma_{\text{corner}} = \frac{3 \times 40}{(0.24)^2}\left[1 - \left(\frac{0.15 \times \sqrt{\pi}}{0.96}\right)^{0.72}\right] = 1256.9\,\text{kPa}$$

(ii) From equations (8.11) and (8.12):

For circular area of loading:

$$\sigma_{\text{edge}} = \frac{0.803 \times 40}{(0.24)^2}\left[4\log_{10}\left(\frac{0.96}{0.15}\right) + 0.666\left(\frac{0.15}{0.96}\right) - 0.034\right] = 1837.3\,\text{kPa}$$

For semi-circular area of loading:

$$\sigma_{\text{edge}} = \frac{0.803 \times 40}{(0.24)^2}\left[4\log_{10}\left(\frac{0.96}{0.15}\right) + 0.282\left(\frac{0.15}{0.96}\right) + 0.65\right] = 2185.2\,\text{kPa}$$

The semi-circular area of loading method gives 18.9% more value of stress than the circular area of loading.

8.1.2 Warping Stresses

Temperature differential between the top and bottom surfaces of a cement concrete slab is a common phenomenon whether it is day or night. Expansion and contraction of the slab as a result of temperature difference causes geometric deformation—either curling up or down. Warping or temperature stresses will be produced in the slab when these geoetric deformations are completely restrained by its self weight. Two critical conditions of warping stresses in a cement concrete slab are presented in Figure 8.3. Due to curling of the slab, tensile and compressive stresses are produced in its bottom fibres during the day and night respectively. Maximum warping stress is observed at the interior of the slab than towards its edges since the interior part of the slab is more restrained against curling than the edges.

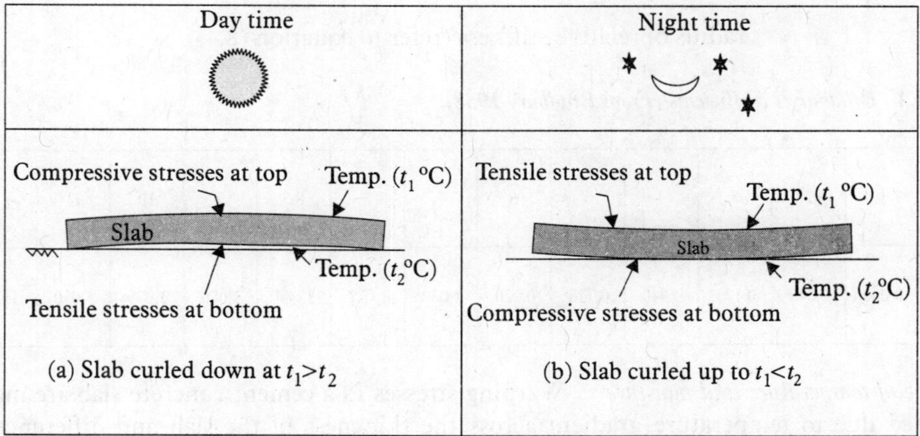

Figure 8.3 *Warping stresses in concrete slab when curling is restrained at different times*

Based on plate theory, Westergaard (1926) developed formulae for calculating the warping stresses in a concrete slab. In 1938, Bradbury modified Westergaard's formulae and developed the following equations for calculating the maximum warping stress at the interior and the edge of the slab having finite dimensions.

$$\sigma_{tx\_\text{interior}} = \frac{E\,\alpha\,\Delta_t}{2\,(1-\mu^2)}\,(C_x + \mu\,C_y) \tag{8.14}$$

$$\sigma_{ty\_\text{interior}} = \frac{E\,\alpha\,\Delta_t}{2\,(1-\mu^2)}\,(\mu\,C_x + C_y) \tag{8.15}$$

$$\sigma_{tx\_edge} = \frac{E\,\alpha\,\Delta_t}{2} C_x \tag{8.16}$$

$$\sigma_{ty\_edge} = \frac{E\,\alpha\,\Delta_t}{2} C_y \tag{8.17}$$

where,

$\sigma_{tx\_interior}$ = Interior warping stress at the slab's mid-span in the x-direction
$\sigma_{ty\_interior}$ = Interior warping stress at the slab's mid-span in the y-direction
σ_{tx_edge} = Edge warping stress at the slab's mid-span in the x-direction
σ_{ty_edge} = Edge warping stress at the slab's mid-span in the y-direction
E = Young's modulus of cement concrete
α = Coefficient of thermal expansion of concrete/ °C
Δt = $(t_1 - t_2)$ °C = Temperature differential between the top and bottom of the slab. The temperature gradient across the depth of the slab is assumed to be linear but in real life, it is non-linear.
μ = Poisson's ratio of concrete slab (≈ 0.15)
L_x and L_y = slab lengths in the x and y directions respectively (refer to Figure 8.1)
C_x = L_x/l } Bradbury's coefficients of warping stress in the x and y directions
C_y = L_y/l
l = radius of relative stiffness (refer to equation (8.4))

Table 8.1 *Bradbury's coefficients (From Bradbury 1938)*

L_x/l or L_y/l	1	2	3	4	5	6	7	8	8.5	9	10	11	≥ 12
C_x or C_y	0.000	0.040	0.175	0.440	0.720	0.920	1.030	1.077	1.084	1.080	1.075	1.050	1.000

Influence of temperature and moisture Warping stresses in a cement concrete slab are mainly developed due to temperature gradient across the thickness of the slab and differences in moisture within the concrete slab. When the bottom surface of the slab is drier than the top, there is downward warping and vice versa (Hatt 1925). Warping of the slab (or slab curling) was also observed by Hveem during an investigation of the performance of concrete pavements in California. He concluded that the combined action of temperature and moisture gradients across the thickness of the slab were responsible for the effect (Hveem 1951). The temperature gradient is not proportional to the thickness of slab (AASHO Road Test. Report 5 1962; Thompson et al. 1987). It was observed from a few field studies that the temperature gradients are non-linear and that the daily fluctuations in temperature is more in the vicinity of the slab surface than at its bottom. Environmental and climatic factors such as air temperature, solar radiation, cloud cover, humidity and precipitation affect the temperature gradient in the concrete slab (Armaghani et al. 1986 and Yu et al. 1998). In addition to this, warping stresses will be more in longer slabs than in shorter slabs as warping results in greater loss of contact along longer slab edges.

The warping stresses determined from the Westergaard–Bradbury equations based on the Winkler foundation model were found to be higher than the full-size experimental results obtained in China. Therefore, the values of stress coefficients were modified by Shi et al. (1993) using the Pasternak foundation model.

Q: *Calculate maximum warping stresses at the edge and interior of a slab of 4.5 m length and 3.5 m width. Take the elastic modulus of concrete as 3×10^4 MPa, radius of relative stiffness as 0.92 m, temperature difference between the top and bottom surface of the slab as 17 °C, coefficient of thermal expansion of concrete as 10×10^{-6} per °C and Poisson's ratio of concrete as 0.15.*

A: $L_x/l = 4.5/0.92 = 4.89$; from Table 8.1, $C_x = 0.6892$

$L_y/l = 3.5/0.92 = 3.80$; $C_y = 0.3870$

The value of C_x is more than C_y. Therefore, maximum stress will be observed in the x-direction. From equation (8.14), maximum stress at the interior is

$$\sigma_{\text{tx\_interior}} = \frac{(3\times 10^4\ \text{MPa})\times(10\times 10^{-6})\times 17}{2\,(1-0.15^2)}(0.6892+0.15\times 0.3870) = 1.949\,\text{MPa}$$

From equation (8.16), maximum stress at the edge is

$$\sigma_{\text{tx\_edge}} = \frac{(3\times 10^4\ \text{MPa})\times(10\times 10^{-6})\times 17}{2}\times 0.6892 = 1.757\ \text{MPa}$$

Thus, the warping stress at the interior is 10.9% higher than at the edge.

8.1.3 Stresses Due to Frictional Forces

Contraction and expansion (movements in the horizontal direction) of the slab takes place due to uniform temperature changes in the slab. The uniform change may be caused due to variation of temperature or moisture content or both. Slab movements are restrained by its self weight caused by the inter-surface frictional forces between the slab and the supporting layer (sub-base or base). For example, when the slab contracts, its movements are restrained by frictional forces and tensile stresses are developed (Figure 8.4) (Sparkes 1939 and 1954). This is the reason cracks are generally formed at the centre of longer slabs.

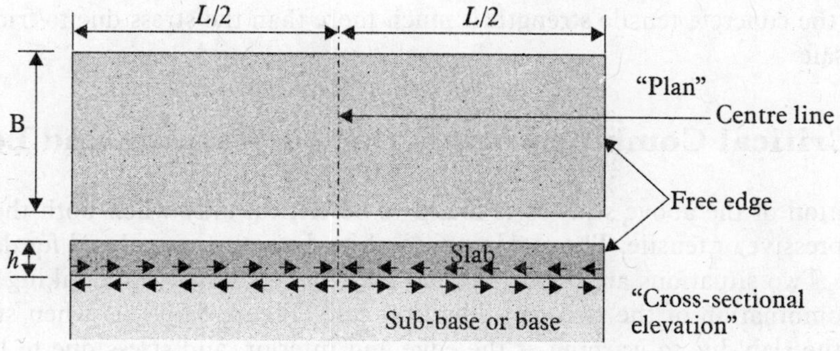

Figure 8.4 *Frictional stresses in the slab*

The maximum movement, with respect to the centre line of the slab, is observed at the free edge region and from there it gradually decreases to zero at the centre line (Kelly 1939). Hence, maximum frictional stress will be developed at the centre of the slab and can be determined by equating the force developed by the slab due to the movement with the frictional resistance offered by the supporting layer on the half length of the slab across its unit widt

$$\sigma_f \times B \times h = \frac{L}{2} \times B \times h \times W \times f$$

On cancelling the common factors, we get,

$$\sigma_f = \frac{W L f}{2} \tag{8.18}$$

where,
- σ_f = Tensile stress in concrete slab due to friction
- W = Unit weight of concrete
- B = Unit width of concrete
- h = Thickness of slab
- L = Length of slab
- f = Average coefficient of friction (often assumed to be $\approx$ 1.5)

The stress due to friction depends on the slab length, unit weight of concrete and coefficient of friction.

Q. *Determine the stress in concrete due to friction between the slab and the sub-base layer and verify its tensile strength adequacy. Use the following data.*
Transverse joint spacing or slab length = 5.0 m
Unit weight of plain concrete = 24.0 kN/m^3
Coefficient of friction = 1.5
Grade of concrete used for slab = M 40

A: By equation (8.18), $\sigma_f = \frac{W L f}{2} = \frac{24.0 \times 5.0 \times 1.5}{2} = 90$ kN/m^2 = 90 kPa

According to IS:456-2000 and IRC:SP:62-2004:
Flexural strength or modulus of rupture, $f_{cr} = 0.7(f_{ck})^{0.5}$ MPa
For, M40 grade of concrete, $f_{cr} = 0.740^{0.5} = 4.42$ MPa = 4420 kPa

Therefore, the concrete tensile strength is much more than the stress due to friction. Hence, the slab is safe.

8.1.4 Critical Combined Stress Due to Warping and Load

A combination of the above stresses is found to be critical only when both the stresses are either compressive or tensile. The maximum combined stress is considered for design of rigid pavements. Two situations are important and need to be studied while taking into account a critical combination of the stresses. The first case (Figure 8.5(a)) is when stresses at the bottom of the slab due to warping at the edge and interior, and stress due to load are both tensile during day time. In the second case (Figure 8.5(b)), the stress at the bottom of the slab due to warping at the corner is compressive but the stress due to load is tensile during night time. As a result, the accumulated stress intensity will be reduced.

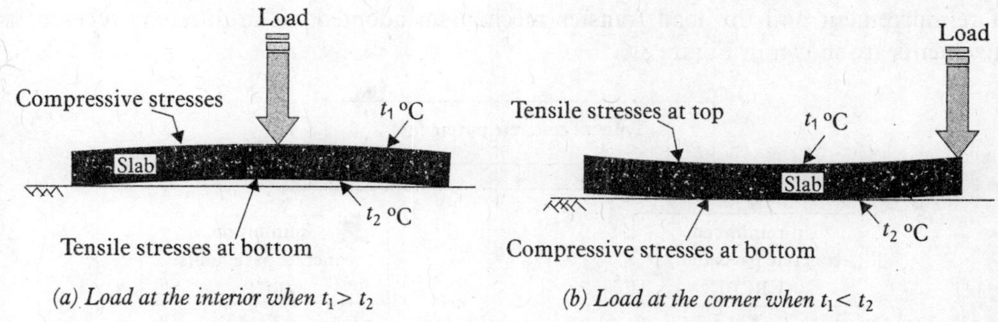

Figure 8.5 *Critical combinations of stresses due to load and warping*

For most places in India, the first case holds good for design of rigid pavements. This is because higher temperature differentials (i.e., temperature difference between the top and bottom fibres of the pavement slab) are observed across the country (in six zones). The temperature differential ranges between 12.5 and 21 °C for slab thickness ranging from 15 to 30 cm (IRC:58-2002). The higher temperature differential causes a greater magnitude of stresses to develop in the slab.

8.2 Software/Charts for Analysis of Rigid Pavements

The software/charts which are commonly used to analyse rigid pavements are listed in Table 8.2.

Table 8.2 *Programs for analysis of rigid pavement*

Name of the Program/chart	Reference/ source	Based on
Influence charts	Pickett and Ray 1951	Theoretical equations derived by Westergaard and Hogg
PCCHWY	Warnes 1972 (used by PCA)	Westergaard's theory
H-51	Packard 1973	
WESLIQUID & WESLAYER	Huang and Wang 1973; Chou 1980	Finite element method with linear deformation response; Winkler foundation method
ILLI-SLAB	Tabatabai and Barenberg 1980; Foxworthy and Darter 1989	
JSLAB	Tayabji and Colley 1984	
N-S	Tang 1993	
KENSLABS	Huang 2004	Finite element method
MSLAB_LOAD and WARP-NONLINEAR	Fwa and Wei 2006	Thick plate model using Winkler foundation

8.3 Types of Rigid Pavements

Concrete pavements may be classified into different groups based on the use of joints, extent of reinforcement and the load transfer mechanism adopted. The different types of rigid pavements are shown in Figure 8.6.

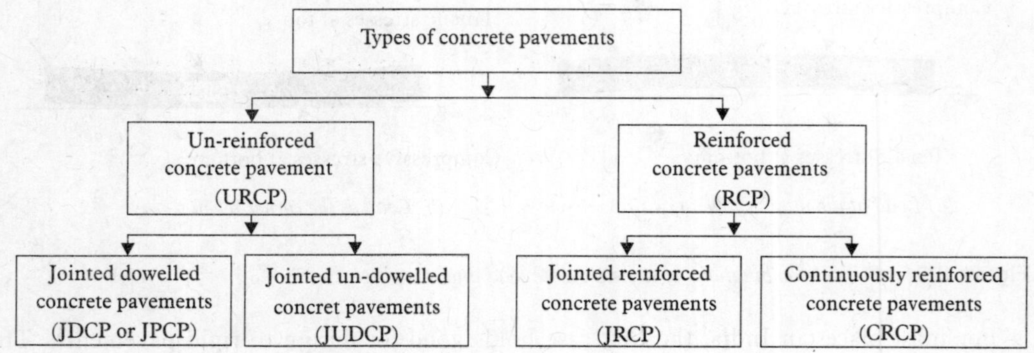

Figure 8.6 *Types of concrete pavements*

Un-reinforced concrete pavements (URCP) are also called plain cement concrete pavements (PCCP). In almost all jointed pavements, load transfer mechanism is implemented using dowel bars placed in transverse joints. Such pavements are called jointed dowelled concrete pavements (JDCP). JDCPs are also termed as jointed plain concrete pavements (JPCP) by a few agencies. They are the most popularly used rigid pavements in India.

Dowel bars may not be used for roads where traffic is very less such as remote rural roads. In such roads, aggregate interlocking of joints should be provided as a low cost means of load transfer. Such pavements are termed as jointed un-dowelled concrete pavements (JUDCP). Load transfer by aggregate interlocking is not effective when the slabs contract and widen the joint. However, tie bars can be placed across longitudinal joints of dual-lane roads to tie up the adjacent slabs at the same level.

Occurrence of cracks in concrete slabs is inevitable due to repeated application of axle loads and weathering action in different seasons. Steel reinforcement in slabs is provided to inhibit widening of cracks and keep the cracked faces in intimate contact. This extends the useful life of the pavement. In jointed reinforced concrete pavements (JRCP), a steel mesh or mat is placed at the middle of each slab. It is not meant for structural strength improvement of the slab but is provided to control crack width. As usual practice of load transfer and tie up of slabs, the dowel and tie bars are placed in transverse and longitudinal joints respectively.

In case of continuously reinforced concrete pavements (CRCP), steel bars are distributed continuously in the longitudinal direction (in the range of 0.5 to 0.7% cross-sectional area of slab) so that construction of transverse joints can be eliminated. Construction of CRCP are preferred in (i) main heavy traffic corridors namely expressways, (ii) adverse climatic conditions and (iii) weak sub-grades. CRCPs can be maintained at low cost because they have less/no joints.

In addition to the above basic types, pre-stressed and concrete-blocks are also used for the construction of pavements.

8.4 Pavement Joints

Joints are provided in concrete pavement at optimal regular intervals to allow shrinkage, contraction, expansion, curl in the up- and downward directions. The slab shrinks due to sudden loss of moisture from fresh concrete before it hardens completely. The rest of the geometric changes take place due to production of warping stresses in the slab caused by variations in temperature and moisture content during different seasons.

The degree to which installing joints brings relief of critical (tensile) stress in concrete slabs by load transfer is called efficiency of the joint action (Teller 1938). Joints should be spaced optimally to maintain structural efficiency, to relieve (tensile) warping stresses and prevent occurrence of cracks during temperature displacements of slab.

Based on the function and purpose of joints, they may be classified into different types (Figure 8.7). The joints provided in the transverse direction are called transverse joints (Figure 8.8(i)). Transverse joints permit the slab to displace in the horizontal direction. Contraction joints allow only contraction whereas expansion joints allow both expansion and contraction. Contraction joints are provided either as (i) dummy joints with saw cuts to a depth of 1/3rd or 1/4th thickness of the slab from the top or as (ii) dowel bars placed at its mid-depth for load transfer. As a guideline, spacing of contraction joints in pavements (URCP) may be taken as 4.5 m and 5.0 m when the thickness of the pavement is up to 25 cm and between 25 to 35 cm respectively (IRC: 15-2002).

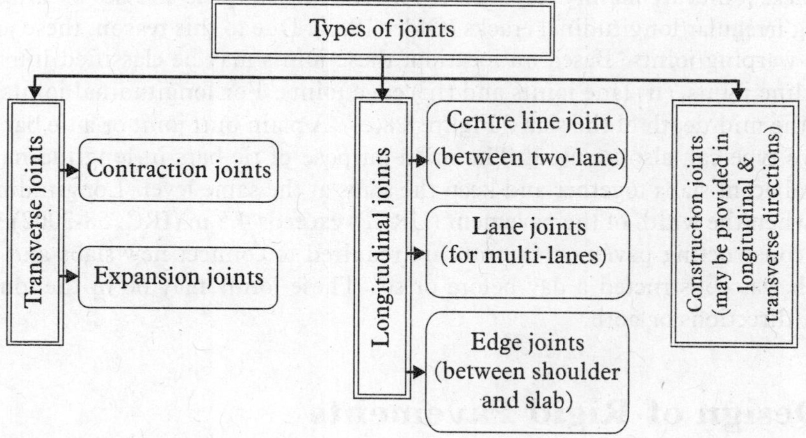

Figure 8.7 *Types of joints in concrete pavements*

For expansion joints, dowel bars with metal caps partially filled with cotton are used (Figure 8.8(b)). Half the length of the dowel bar near the metal cap is lubricated to ease movement of the slab due to temperature variation (Finn 1961). Gap between the joint faces should be filled with a filler and at the top, elastomeric material should be used as a joint-sealant to prevent ingress of rain water and grit. The sealant material must be compressible, elastic and strong enough to resist repeated weathering action. Sealing of joints can be achieved by different methods, viz. (i) by hot pouring bitumen, PVC or modified bitumen, (ii) by cold pouring polysulphide, polyurethane or silicone and (iii) by compression using polychloroprene (Akoto and Nilles 2007).

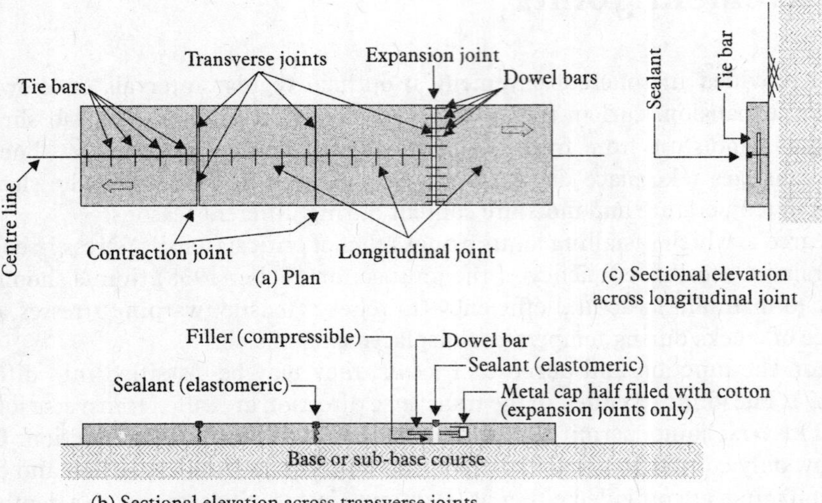

Figure 8.8 *Details of joints used in a dual-lane concrete pavement (not to scale)*

The joints provided in the longitudinal direction are termed as longitudinal joints (Figure 8.8(a)). These joints are mainly responsible for relieving warping stresses by hinge action and preventing irregular longitudinal cracks (Older 1925). Due to this reason, these joints are also known as warping joints. Based on location, these joints may be classified into three types: (i) centre line joints, (ii) lane joints and (iii) edge joints. For longitudinal joints, tie bars are placed at the mid-depth of the slab ((Figure 8.8(c)). A plain butt joint or a tie bar with tongue and groove type can also be used. The main purpose of tie bars in longitudinal joints is to hold the adjacent slabs together and keep the slabs at the same level. Longitudinal joints are required when the width of the pavement (URCP) exceeds 4.5 m (IRC: 58-2002).

While constructing pavements, joints are required to connect new slabs and the end of a slab which was constructed a day before or so. These joints may be in the longitudinal or transverse directions or both.

8.5 Design of Rigid Pavements

Unlike the design of flexible pavements where several changes took place through the years, the design of rigid pavements have followed mechanistic–empirical (M–E) principles from the beginning. In M–E design methods, the slab thickness is determined by considering the fatigue failure of the slab due to damage caused by cumulative axle load passes. The input parameters relate to sub-grade support, material characteristics, traffic loads and climate. Several researchers (Older 1925; Goldbeck 1925; Westergaard 1925; Teller and Sutherland 1935; Spangler 1937; Bradbury 1938; Pickett and Ray 1951; Friberg 1955; Ioannides et al. 1985; and Shi et al. 1993) significantly contributed to thickness design of rigid pavements. However, Westergaard's theory (1925; 1933; and 1948) is the basis on which many modifications took place in the analysis and design of rigid pavements. These modifications have provided reasonably good agreement with the performance of in-service pavements.

The AASHTO method of design of rigid pavement (1993), however, uses empirical principles and serviceability performance concepts. Pavement performance is measured in terms of distresses or damages which are caused due to repetitive traffic loads in different seasons.

A few widely used design methods for rigid pavements are briefly discussed in the following sections.

8.5.1 The Portland Cement Association (PCA) Method

The Portland Cement Association (PCA) method (1984) uses Westergaard theory with finite element analysis (FEM). Design charts were developed based on allowable number of load repetitions related to properties of pavement materials at failures. These were correlated with theoretically calculated maximum edge stress and corner deflection of slabs. The supporting layer and the cement concrete slab are characterised by the (effective) modulus of sub-grade reaction and the characteristic 28 day compressive strength of the cement concrete respectively. The failures of pavement considered are (i) fatigue cracking of slab due to cumulative damage caused by different axle load groups and (ii) erosion or pumping of supporting layer of the concrete slab. In the fatigue analysis, the stress ratio between the maximum stress at the edge when loaded at the outer edge and the flexural strength of concrete is calculated. The computed stress ratio is related to the maximum allowable number of standard axle load repetitions. A fraction value is calculated by dividing the actual repetitions with allowable repetitions of each type of axle group. As a safe design, such fraction values obtained from different axle load groups are cumulated. The value should not be more than one (refer to Miner's fatigue damage rule, discussed in Section 6.3.3). For erosion criterion of the supporting layer (sub-base or base), maximum deflection of the slab corner is considered as critical. The design charts were validated with the performance data of various in-service pavements and road tests. Slab thickness should be derived through the above two failure criteria. Warping stresses due to variations in temperature and moisture are not considered in this method. The rate of increase of slab thickness for decreasing values of the sub-grade's modulus was found to be consistent (Guell 1985).

As the first step of design, a trial slab thickness is assumed and verified with the design criteria. From the next trial onwards, the slab thickness is suitably increased or decreased until the above two design criteria are satisfied. The final design thickness is taken as the thickest value which is obtained using the above two considerations.

The PCA design method has been adopted by Austroads (1992) for the design of slab thickness in which the slab is supported on a cement treated layer.

8.5.2 The AASHTO Design Method of Rigid Pavement (1993)

The AASHTO design method was basically derived from the AASHO road test results. The following equation is recommended to be used for designing the thickness of a concrete slab pavement (AASHTO 1993).

$$\log_{10}(W_{18}) = Z_R S_o + 7.35 \log_{10}(1+D) + \frac{\log_{10}\left[\dfrac{\Delta \text{PSI}}{(4.5-1.5)}\right]}{1 + \dfrac{16.24 \times 10^6}{(1+D)^{8.46}}}$$

$$+(4.22 - 0.32\,p_t)\log_{10}\left(\frac{C_d\,S_c'\,(D^{0.75} - 1.132)}{215.63\,J\left(D^{0.75} - \dfrac{18.42}{(E_c/k)^{0.25}}\right)}\right) - 0.06 \qquad (8.19)$$

where, W_{18} = estimated cumulative 18 kip ESAL during the design period

Z_R = overall standard deviation for a given reliability (refer to Table 7.4)

S_o = combined standard error of the predictions of performance and traffic (an average value of 0.35 may be taken for rigid pavements)

D = thickness of cement concrete slab in inches (the obtained value should be rounded off to nearest half inch)

Δ PSI = design loss of PSI = initial PSI − terminal PSI

p_t = terminal serviceability index (based on the importance of the road, the value ranges from 2.5 and 2.0)

S_c' = modulus of rupture of flexural strength of the cement concrete slab (psi)

C_d = coefficient of drainage (refer to Table 8.3)

J = coefficient of load transfer at joints between adjacent slabs and between the slab and the shoulder (the range is between 2.3 and 4.2; higher values are suggested when the sub-grade is weak and there is high temperature differential in the slab)

E_c = elastic modulus of the cement concrete slab (psi)

k = effective or composite modulus of the sub-grade reaction (pci)

The definitions and significance of W_{18}, Z_R, S_o, ΔPSI, and p_t are similar to the AASHTO design method of flexible pavements (discussed in Section 7.5.1). Selection of the remaining input parameters related to material properties should be average values based on standard deviation and variability. If laboratory tested values of the flexural strength of concrete are not available, a suitable equation may be used (see Section 5.7.3). Drainage coefficients should be selected based on the drainage quality recommended by AASHTO (Table 8.3).

Table 8.3 *Drainage coefficient (C_d) of untreated granular layers of a rigid pavement*

Drainage quality		Percentage of time pavement structure is exposed to moisture levels approaching saturation			
Time required to drain off the water	Subjective rating	< 1%	1 to 5 %	5 to 25 %	> 25 %
2 hours	Excellent	1.25 to 1.20	1.20 to 1.15	1.15 to 1.10	1.10
1 day	Good	1.20 to 1.15	1.15 to 1.10	1.10 to 1.00	1.00
1 week	Fair	1.15 to 1.10	1.10 to 1.00	1.00 to 0.90	0.90
1 month	Poor	1.10 to 1.00	1.00 to 0.90	0.90 to 0.80	0.80
Never drain	Very poor	1.00 to 0.90	0.90 to 0.80	0.80 to 0.70	0.70

From *AASHTO Guide for Design of Pavement Structures, 1993*, [by the American Association of State Highway and Transportation Officials, Washington, DC. Used by permission. Documents may be purchased from the AASHTO bookstore at 1-800-231-3475 or online at http://bookstore.transportation.org

The D value may be determined by trial and error method using equation (8.19) or AASHTO's nomograph of rigid pavement. The nomograph may be observed to be of two parts, the left side of the match line uses values of input parameters related to material characteristics and the right side of it uses values of inputs related to traffic and pavement performance variations. The following example problem explains the design procedure.

Q: *Design the thickness of a cement concrete slab which is to be constructed over a sub-base having effective modulus of sub-grade reaction by considering sub-grade depth up to 10 ft and loss of support due to seasonal variations as 100 pci. Design traffic is 10×10^6 (18 kip) ESALs. Elastic modulus and flexural strength of the cement concrete slab are 5×10^6 psi and 700 psi respectively. Take average values of joint coefficient as 3.5, coefficient of drainage as 1.0, standard deviation as 0.35 and reliability as 95%. Assume that the slab will fail after experiencing the design traffic and reach 2.0 on the loss of present serviceability index.*

A: The chart shown in Figure 8.9 is self-explanatory. Thickness of slab is determined as 11 1/2 inches.

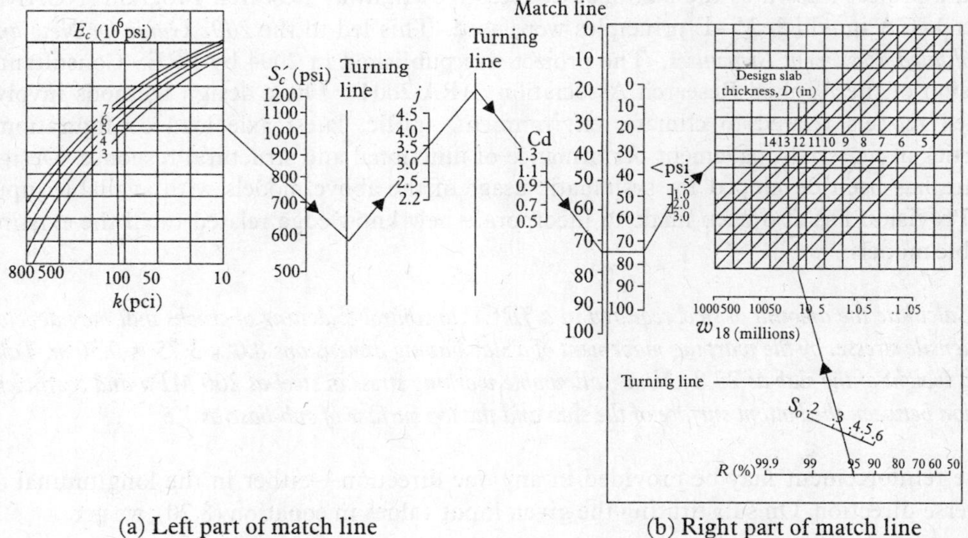

(a) Left part of match line (b) Right part of match line

Figure 8.9 *Example problem*

Source of nomograph: AASHTO Guide for Design of Pavement Structures, 1993. Used by permission. Documents may be purchased from the AASHTO bookstore at 1-800-231-3475 or online at http://bookstore.transportation.org

The AASHTO Design of Reinforcement in Rigid Pavements

The *AASHTO Guide* has made recommendations regarding design of reinforcement for JRCP and CRCP. In JRCPs, this reinforcement is used to control the width of cracks by resisting the tensile stress developed due to frictional forces (as discussed in Section 8.1.3). According to AASHTO (1993), the amount of steel (%) required per metre length in the longitudinal or transverse direction of the slab may be calculated using the following equation.

$$\text{Area of steel } (A_{st})/\text{metre length of slab} = \frac{WLf}{2S} \times 100 \tag{8.20}$$

where,
- W = unit weight of slab (kN/m^3)
- L = length (m) of slab for longitudinal reinforcement or width of slab for transverse reinforcement
- f = coefficient of friction between the bottom of the slab and the top surface of the supporting layer
- S = allowable working stress in steel used for reinforcement (kN/m^2)

In CRCP, the reinforcement requirement depends on minimisation of crack occurrence, restriction of widening of cracks and reinforcement related distress. The detailed analysis of reinforcement in CRCP is available in *AASHTO Guide for Design of Pavement Structures (1993)*

The NCHRP Project 1-37A

To minimise involvement of the empirical component in the *AASHTO Guide*, the AASHTO funded a project known as the National Cooperative Highway Research Program (NCHRP) Project 1-37A in which M–E principles were used. This led to the *2002 Guide for New and Rehabilitated Pavement Structures*. The project was published in 2004 by ERES Consultants, a division of the Applied Research Association (ARA 2004). These design methods involve complex models related to climate, environment, traffic, latest axle load configurations, properties of materials, pavement performance of functional and structural response. Design software has been developed for systematic usage of the above models with available input data. Provision has also been made to incorporate new knowledge related to all the existing available models.

Q: *Calculate the amount of steel required in a JRCP to control widening of cracks that may develop due to tensile stresses by the warping movement of a slab having dimensions 8.0 × 3.75 × 0.30 m. Take the unit weight of the slab as 23.8 kN/m^3, allowable working stress in steel as 200 MPa and coefficient of friction between the bottom surface of the slab and the top surface of sub-base as 1.5.*

A: The reinforcement may be provided in any one direction—either in the longitudinal or transverse direction. On substituting the given input values in equation (8.20), we get,

(i) *In the longitudinal direction*:

$$\text{Area of steel } (A_{st})/\text{metre length of slab} = \frac{(23.8 \times 10^3 \text{ N/m}^3) \times 8.0 \text{ m} \times 1.5}{2 \times (200 \times 10^6 \text{ N/m}^2)} \times 100\,\% = 0.0714\%$$

Or, (ii) *In the transverse direction*:

$$\text{Area of steel } (A_{st})/\text{metre width of slab} = \frac{(23.8 \times 10^3 \text{ N/m}^3) \times 3.75 \text{ m} \times 1.5}{2 \times (200 \times 10^6 \text{ N/m}^2)} \times 100\,\% = 0.0334\%$$

8.5.3 The Indian Roads Congress Design Method of Rigid Pavement (IRC:58-2002)

This design method is based on M–E principles. The design of the rigid pavement comprises three parts, viz. (i) thickness of the slab (JPCP and JRCP), (ii) dowel bars and (iii) tie bars. The details of the design are discussed below.

Design of Slab Thickness

Stresses due to load and warping are calculated using the equations developed by Westergaard and Bradbury. The design process may be divided into three major steps. In the first step, a trial slab thickness is assumed and the stress ratio is calculated by dividing stress due to load at the edge with the flexural strength of concrete. The expected number of standard axle load repetitions (N) for each stress ratio (SR) should be obtained by standard relationships (equations 8.21(a)–(c)) for each group of load. Calculated consumed cumulative fatigue damage developed by different groups of axle load should not exceed one (As discussed in Section 6.3.3. If the above criterion is satisfied, as second and third steps, the adequacy of the flexural strength (or modulus of rupture value) of the slab is checked for (i) total maximum stresses at the edge caused by an axle load group and warping action, and (ii) maximum stress at the corner due to load. The assumed slab thickness is finalised when the flexural strength of the slab is more than the edge and corner stresses. If the above criteria are not satisfied, the assumed slab thickness should be revised (i.e., increased suitably) and the same design procedure (Figure 8.10) followed again. Warping stress at the corner is not considered for design as it is lesser compared to other regions of the slab.

$$\text{If SR} < 0.45, \qquad N_f = \infty \tag{8.21a}$$

$$\text{If } 0.45 \leq \text{SR} \leq 0.55, \qquad N_f = \left[\frac{4.2577}{\text{SR} - 0.4325}\right]^{3.268} \tag{8.21b}$$

$$\text{If SR} > 0.55, \qquad \log_{10} N_f = \left(\frac{0.9718 - \text{SR}}{0.0828}\right) \tag{8.21c}$$

Modulus value of sub-grade reaction (k) may be obtained from the plate load test or it may be obtained from linearly interpolating the relationship given in Table 3.5. If the k value of the sub-grade is less than 6 kg/cm^3, a sub-base layer with or without the cement bounded layer is provided and the k value over the sub-base is termed as the effective k value. The details of the effective k values for bound and unbound sub-base layers can be found in IRC:58-2002.

Critical position of wheel loads Maximum flexural stress in concrete is calculated when tyre imprints of single or tandem axles carrying different loads were placed touching the longitudinal edge of the slab. Lower flexural stresses will occur around the transverse joint when the tyre imprint touches the transverse joint's built-in load transfer devices,viz. dowel bars and/or aggregate inter-lock.

Critical combination of stresses Maximum flexural edge stresses developed due to load and temperature differential is considered as an additive and taken as critical for thickness design of slabs. The effect of moisture change in the concrete slab is not considered in the design of slab thickness (IRC:58-2002).

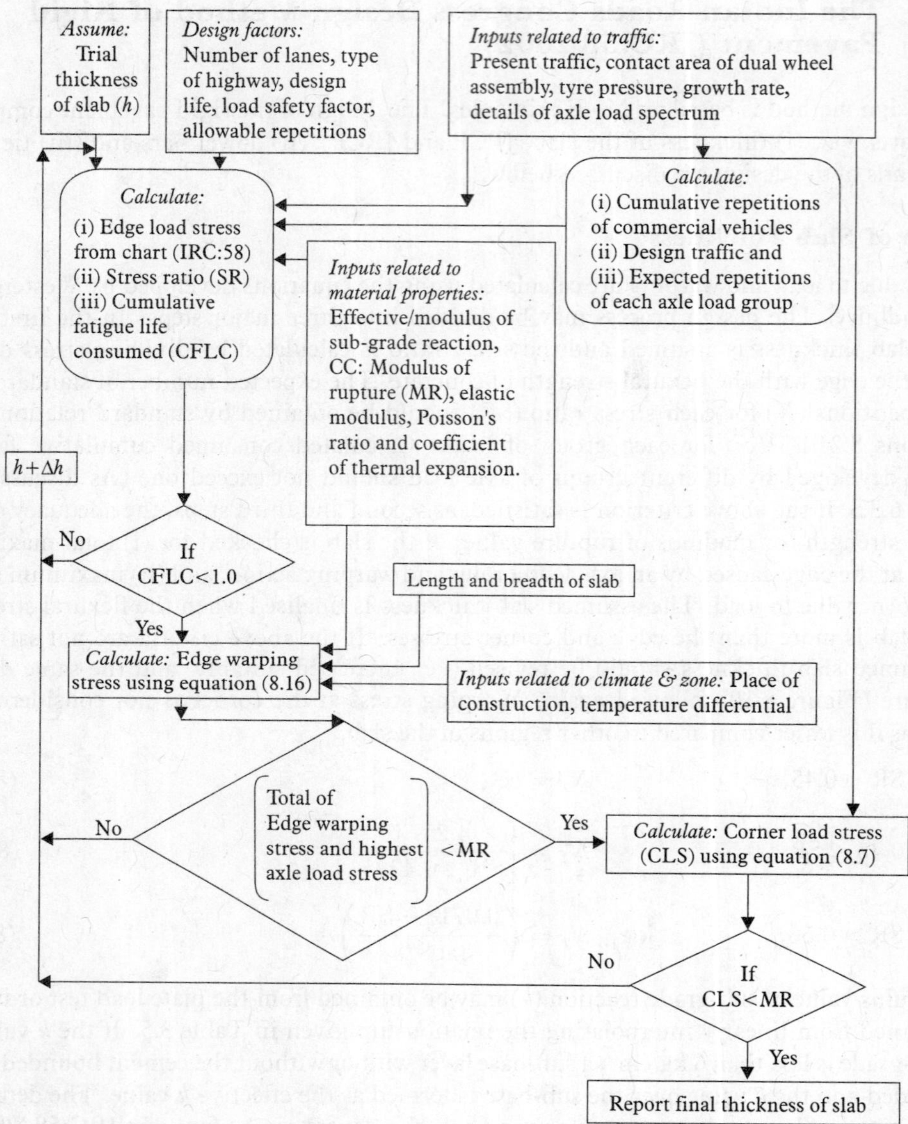

Figure 8.10 *Thickness design of cement concrete slab pavement according to IRC:58-2002*

Flexural stress (FS) due to load at the edge and corner is determined using influence charts developed by Picket and Ray (1951) and equation (8.7) respectively. Equation (8.13) is recommended for calculation of the radius of dual wheel contact area which is substituted in equation (8.7). Edge load stress charts were prepared by IRC for different axle loads of single and tandem axle configurations. Typical charts from IRC:58-2002 is placed as Figure 8.11. Equivalent (or approximate) values of the edge load stress can be calculated using equation (8.5). Warping stress at the edge is calculated using equations (8.16) and (8.17), and the maximum value is selected.

Thickness design of rigid pavement slab based on the corner stress criterion is not considered critical if the load is transferred through dowels or aggregate interlock.

The following example problem explains how the thickness of the slab is arrived at according to IRC.

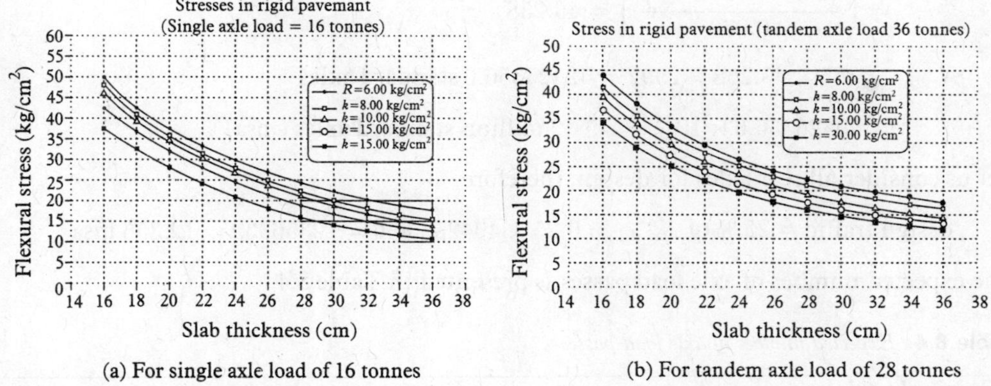

(a) For single axle load of 16 tonnes (b) For tandem axle load of 28 tonnes

Figure 8.11 *Charts for determination of flexural stress at edge due to load (IRC:58-2002)*

Q: *Design the thickness of a cement concrete slab according to the guidelines of IRC for the following input parameters.*

Location: Andhra Pradesh; Road type: National highway; Lanes: Two-lane, two-way; Traffic volume = 2570 commercial vehicles per day (CVPD); Effective modulus of sub-grade reaction = 8 kg/cm²/cm; Grade of cement concrete mix: M40; Poisson's ratio of concrete = 0.15; Coefficient of thermal expansion of concrete = 10×10^{-6} per degree Centigrade; Tyre pressure = 8 kg/cm²; Growth rate of traffic = 7.9%; Design period = 20 years; Number of years from the date of traffic count to the date of opening to traffic = 2 years; Slab width = 350 cm; Spacing of contraction joints = 450 cm. At the given location, axle load survey was conducted and the summarised data is given below.

Load on single axle		*Load on tandem axle*	
Average value of axle load (tonnes)	*% of axle loads*	*Average value of axle load (tonnes)*	*% of axle loads*
20	0.58	36	0.27
18	1.57	32	0.29
16	4.39	28	0.56
14	10.42	24	1.78
12	21.79	20	1.51
10	23.11	16	0.51
Less than 10	31.01	Less than 16	2.21
Total	92.87		7.13

A: *Analysis of design traffic:*

Estimated traffic volume (A) by the construction of road is calculated using equation (6.1).

$$A = 2570(1 + 0.079)^{2.0} = 2992 \text{ CVPD}$$

Cumulative number of standard axle load repetitions (N_{rigid}) in 20 years of design life is calculated using equation (6.3).

TGF = Cumulative traffic growth factor based on geometric growth

$$= \left(\frac{(1+0.079)^{20}-1}{0.079}\right) = 45.258$$

$$N_{\text{rigid}} = 365 \times 45.258 \times 2992 = 49425356.6 \text{ standard axles}$$

$$= 49425356.6 \times 10^{-6} = 49.42 \text{ million standard axles (msa)}$$

Let us consider all rear axles for design, therefore,

$$\text{design traffic} = 25\,\% \text{ of } N_{\text{rigid}} = 0.25 \times 49425356.6 = 12356339 = 12.356 \text{ msa}$$

The expected number of axle load passes is presented in Table 8.4.

Table 8.4 *Expected number of axle load passes*

For single axle			For tandem axle		
Axle load in tonnes (AL)	% of axle loads	Expected no. of load passes (N_E)	Axle load in tonnes (AL)	% of axle loads	Expected no. of load passes (N_E)
20	0.58	71667	36	0.27	33362
18	1.57	193994	32	0.29	35833
16	4.39	542443	28	0.56	69195
14	10.42	1287531	24	1.78	219943
12	21.79	2692446	20	1.51	186581
10	23.11	2855551	16	0.51	63017
Less than 10	31.01	3831701	Less than 16	2.21	273075
Total	92.87 %			7.13 %	

Determination of strength parameters of cement concrete: As the grade of cement concrete mix is M40, the characteristic compressive strength of cement concrete cube after 28 days (f_{ck}) may be taken as 40 MPa. The flexural strength and elastic modulus value of cement concrete can be calculated using the standard relationships given below.

According to IS:456:2000 and IRC:SP:62-2004, using equation (5.16),

$$\text{Flexural strength or modulus of rupture of cement concrete (MR) } f_{cr} = 0.7(40)^{0.5}$$

$$= 4.427 \text{ MPa} = 45.12 \text{ kg/cm}^2$$

According to IS:456-2000 using equation (5.7),

$$\text{Elastic modulus of concrete, } E_s = 5000(40)^{0.5} = 31622.77 \text{ MPa} = 322352.4 \text{ kg/cm}^2$$

Assume Trial thickness of the slab = 33 cm and consider load safety factor (LSF) = 1.2. Table 8.5 gives an analysis of the cumulative fatigue life of the pavement

Table 8.5 *Analysis of cumulative fatigue life of pavement*

Axle type	AL in kg	AL × LSF	Flexural stress (FS) from IRC charts (kg/cm^2)	stress ratio (SR) = FS/MR	N_E	Fatigue life from equation (8.21)(N_f)	Consumed fatigue life $= N_E/N_f$
Single	20	24.0	24.10	0.534	71667	200915	0.356
	18	21.6	21.98	0.487	193994	1533205	0.126
	16	19.2	19.98	0.442	542443	infinite	0.000
Tandem	36	43.2	19.38	0.429	33362	infinity	0.000
Cumulative fatigue life consumed (CFLC) =							0.482

The cumulative value of the fatigue life consumed (CFLC) by the concrete slab having 33 cm thickness is less than one. Hence, the assumed slab thickness is safe against the fatigue criterion.

NOTE If the cumulative value of the fatigue life consumed (CFLC) is greater than one, the value of the assumed thickness should be suitably increased and the above process of calculations is repeated until the criterion is satisfied.

Maximum warping stress at the edge

By equation (8.4), radius of relative stiffness (l) $= \left[\dfrac{322352.4 \times 33^3}{12 \times 8 \times (1 - 0.15^2)}\right]^{0.25} = 105.4$ cm

Bradbury's coefficients for calculating warping stress in the x and y directions (refer to Table 8.1).

$$L_x/l = 450 \text{ cm}/105.4 \text{ cm} = 4.269 \text{ and } L_y/l = 350 \text{ cm}/105.4 \text{ cm} = 3.320$$

The ratio of L_x/l is greater in the x direction than in the y direction. Therefore, maximum warping stress in the edge will occur in the x direction.

From Table 8.1, for $L_x/l = 4$, $C_x = 0.440$ and for $L_x/l = 5$, $C_x = 0.720$; by linear interpolation, we get

$$C_x = 0.440 + \frac{4.269 - 4.0}{5.0 - 4.0} \times (0.720 - 0.440) = 0.440 + 0.07532 = 0.51532$$

For Andhra Pradesh, the temperature differential (Δ_t) = 21°C (from Table 1 of IRC:58-2002)

Maximum warping stress at the edge is calculated by equation (8.16)

$$\sigma_{\text{tx\_edge}} = \frac{322352.4 \times (10 \times 10^{-6}) \times 21}{2} \times 0.51532 = 17.44 \text{ kg/cm}^2$$

Check for total stress at edge due to load and temperature:

Total of edge warping stress and highest axle load stress (from Table 8.5)

$$= 17.44 + 24.1 = 41.54 \text{ kg/cm}^2 < \text{MR } (45.12 \text{ kg/cm}^2)$$

Hence, the assumed 33 cm thickness of the cement concrete slab is safe against total maximum edge stresses due to load and warping.

Stress at corner by wheel load Calculated using equation (8.7).

The 98th percentile of the single axle load is taken as 16000 kg. Therefore, the dual wheel load at one side of the axle is taken as $P_1 = 8000$ kg. Assume that the centre-to-centre spacing between two tires (S) = 31 cm.

Radius of dual wheel contact area (a) is calculated using equation (8.13),

$$a = \left[\left(\frac{0.8521 \times 8000}{8 \times \pi}\right) + \frac{31}{\pi}\left(\frac{8000}{0.5227 \times 8}\right)^{0.5}\right]^{0.5} = 26.51 \text{ cm}$$

$$\sigma_{\text{corner}} = \frac{3 \times 8000}{33^2}\left[1 - \left(\frac{26.51 \times \sqrt{2}}{105.4}\right)^{1.2}\right] = 15.66 \text{ kg/cm}^2$$

The wheel load stress at the corner (15.66 kg/cm^2) is smaller than MR (45.12 kg/cm^2). Hence, the assumed thickness of the cement concrete slab is safe and the design thickness of 33 cm is satisfactory.

NOTE The thickness design of a rigid pavement slab based on the corner stress criterion is considered critical if no load is transferred through dowels or aggregate interlock.

8.5.4 Thickness Design of CC Slab for Rural Roads (According to IRC:SP:62-2004)

This design method is adopted to determine the suitable thickness of a cement concrete slab for serving low volume traffic in remote rural areas. The following are the salient features of the design method (IRC: SP:62-2004).

(i) The minimum wheel load for design of rural roads is considered to be 30 kN (3058 kg) and the minimum tyre pressure 0.5 MPa (5.1 kg/cm^2). However, if there is any possibility of traffic consisting of mini-trucks and buses, a design wheel load of 51 (5200 kg) kN with tyre pressure 0.7 MPa (7.14 kg/cm^2) should be considered.

(ii) Sub-grade strength is denoted in terms of modulus of sub-grade reaction, i.e., k value which can be obtained from plate load test results or CBR values.

(iii) When the design wheel load is considered as 51 kN, a sub-base having a thickness of 150 mm (WBM or equivalent) should be provided. In case of light traffic design wheel load of 30 kN, provide a sub-base of 75 mm thickness (WBM or equivalent). For both cases, increase the k value of the sub-grade by 20 per cent.

(iv) Design life is considered up to 20 years which is assumed based on the performance of such pavements in India.

(v) The CC slab strength is based on it flexural strength. This may be indirectly obtained from compressive strength of CC cubes using equation (5.16) and the target average flexural strength after 28 days can be determined using equation (5.26). The design value of flexural strength should be considered as the strength obtained after 90 days. And its value may be taken as 1.2 times the flexural strength after 28 days. Due to this reason, no heavy traffic should be allowed during the first 90 days after construction.

(vi) The quantity of cementitious material (i.e., cement + fly ash or slag), used in the CC mix, should not exceed 433.2 kg/m^3 and not be less than 316 kg/m^3. Fly ash can be used as partial replacement of OPC (up to 35%), conforming to standard specifications (see Section 5.5.8).

(vii) Take the value of the elastic modulus of concrete to be 3×10^4 MPa (3.06×10^5 kg/cm^2), coefficient of thermal expansion of concrete to be 10×10^{-6} per °C and Poisson's ratio of cement concrete to be 0.15.

(viii) The CC mix should conform to the requirements of the roller compacted concrete pavement or mix design according to IRC: 44.

(ix) For very low volume traffic, rural roads having a single lane width of 3.0 to 3.75 m without longitudinal joints are considered suitable. However, a lane width of 4.5 m should be provided with necessary longitudinal joints at causeways and cross-drainage facilities.

(x) At expansion joints of 20 mm width, provide dowel bars of 25 mm diameter and 500 mm length, placed at 250 mm intervals.

(xi) The thickness design methodology for low volume roads is purely based on stresses due to wheel loading and warping. There is no need to consider wheel load repetitions and the fatigue consumption value since the road is intended to serve a very low volume of traffic in remote rural areas.

(xii) Wheel load stresses at the edge can be calculated using equation (8.5) and at the corner using equation (8.7). The warping stress at the edge can be calculated using equation (8.16). Assume the contact area to be circular. It can be calculated as,

$$a = \left(\frac{\text{Wheel load}}{\text{Tyre pressure} \times \pi}\right)^{0.5}$$

The details of design are shown in the following flow chart (Figure 8.12).

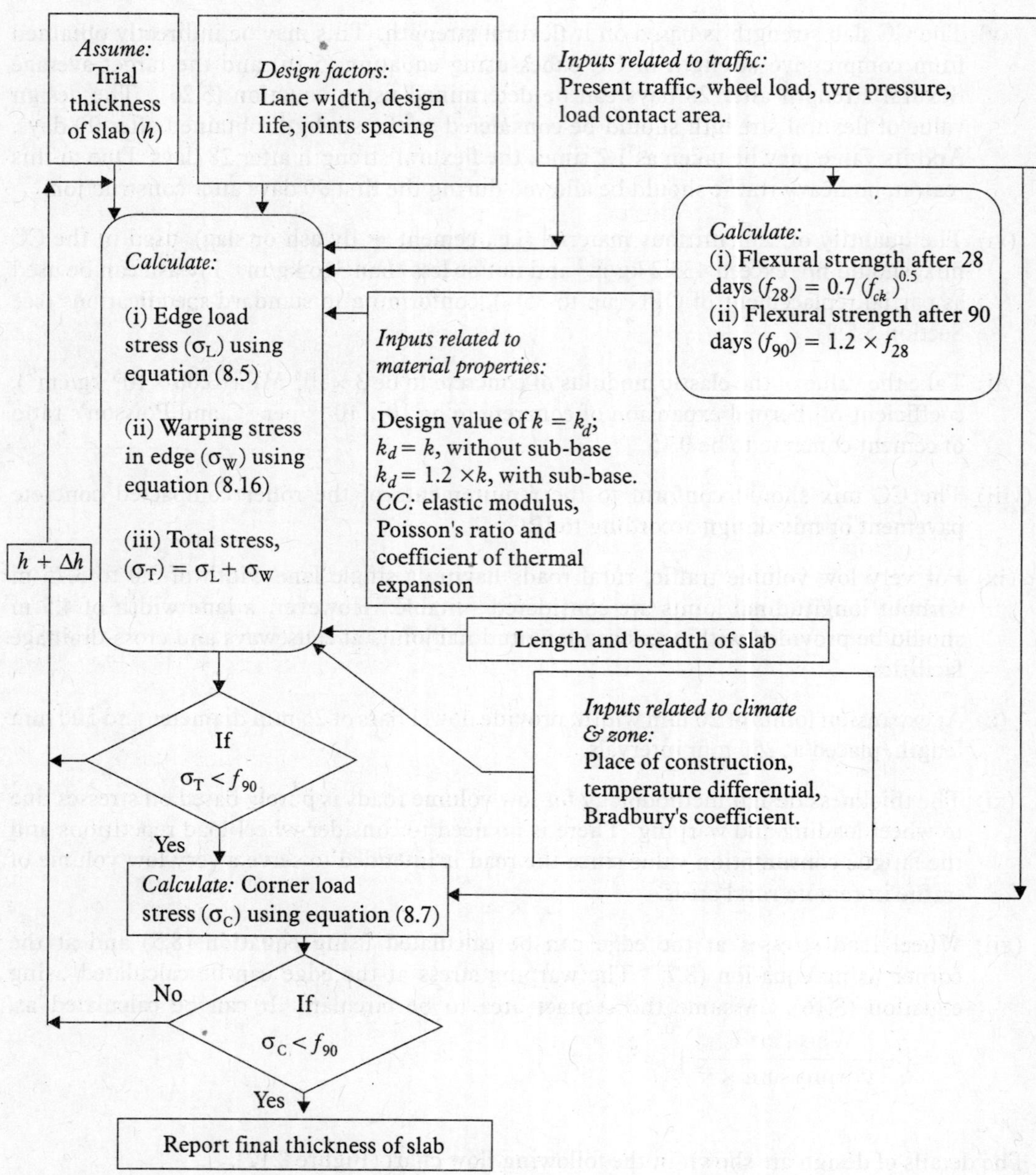

Figure 8.12 *Thickness design of cement concrete slab pavement for rural roads according to IRC:SP:62-2004*

CC pavement slab thickness design using the above method is explained in the following example problem.

Q: *A cement concrete pavement is to be designed for a rural road in a village in Gujarat. Estimated traffic volume is 175 vehicles per day which comprises agricultural tractor trailers/ trailers, heavy trucks, buses and vehicles—both animal-drawn and manually operated. Design the pavement according to the guidelines of IRC:SP:62-2004 for the following input parameters.*

Grade of cement concrete mix: M35; elastic modulus of concrete = 3.06×10^5 kg/cm^2; Poisson's ratio of concrete = 0.15; coefficient of thermal expansion of concrete = 10×10^{-6} °C; tyre pressure = 7.5 kg/cm^2. Assume design period to be 20 years and the slab size to be 350×375 cm. Take the spacing of contraction joints to be 350 cm. Soaked CBR value of the sub-grade soil = 5%. Take its equivalent value of modulus sub-grade reaction, i.e., k to be 4.2 kg/cm^2/cm.

A: As the traffic consists of heavy trucks and buses, let us take wheel load = 5200 kg.

Provide a 150 mm thick WBM layer as the sub-base layer. By considering this sub-base layer, let us calculate the effective k value = $1.2 \times 4.2 = 5.04$ kg/cm^2/cm.

Strength parameters of cement concrete

Grade of concrete = M35 @ 28 day

According to IS:456-2000, using equation (5.7)

Elastic modulus of concrete, $E_s = 5000(35)^{0.5} = 29580 \text{ MPa} = 301636 \text{ kg/cm}^2$

Therefore, flexural strength of concrete, $f_{28} = 0.7 \times (35)^{0.5} = 4.141$ MPa

$$f_{28} = 4.141 \times 10.197 = 42.23 \text{ kg/cm}^2$$

Flexural strength @ 90 day = $f_{90} = 1.2 \times f_{28} = 1.2 \times 42.23 = 50.67$ kg/cm^2

Assume Trial thickness of the slab = 18 cm.

Determination of edge load stress

Using equation (8.4), radius of relative stiffness (l) = $\left[\dfrac{301636 \times 18^3}{12 \times 5.04 \times (1-0.15^2)}\right]^{0.25} = 73.86$ cm

Assume, load contact area is circular, $a = \left(\dfrac{5200}{7.5 \times \pi}\right)^{0.5} = 14.85$ cm

$$b = \sqrt{1.6 \times 14.85^2 + 18^2} - 0.675 \times 18 = 13.87 \text{ cm}$$

Load stress at the critical edge region can be calculated using equation (8.5), on substitution,

$$\sigma_{\text{edge}} = 0.529 \frac{5200}{18^2}(1 + 0.54 \times 0.15)\left[4 \log_{10}\left(\frac{73.86}{13.87}\right) + \log_{10}(13.87) - 0.4048\right]$$

$$= 33.14 \text{ kg/cm}^2$$

Maximum warping stress at the edge

Bradbury's coefficients for calculation of warping stress in the x and y directions (refer to Table 8.1).

$L_{x \text{ or } y}/l = 375 \text{ cm} / 73.86 \text{ cm} = 5.077$

From Table 8.1, for $L_x/l = 5.077$, the value of Bradbury' coefficient by linear interpolation,

$$C_x = 0.720 + \frac{5.077 - 5.0}{6.0 - 5.0} \times (0.920 - 0.720) = 0.7354$$

For Gujarat, assuming a thickness of 18 cm, the temperature differential (Δ_t) = 12.74 °C (from Table 1 of IRC:58-2002).

Therefore, maximum warping stress at the edge is calculated using equation (8.16)

$$\sigma_{tx\_edge} = \frac{301636 \times (10 \times 10^{-6}) \times 12.74}{2} \times 0.7354 = 14.13 \text{ kg/cm}^2$$

Maximum limit of total stress at edge due to warping stress and axle load

$$= 33.14 + 14.13 = 47.27 \text{ kg/cm}^2 < f_{90} \text{ (50.67 kg/cm}^2\text{). OK.}$$

NOTE If the above criterion is not satisfied, the slab thickness should be suitably increased and the above process of calculations is repeated until the criterion is satisfied.

Stress at the corner by wheel load This is calculated using equation (8.7).

$$\sigma_{\text{corner}} = \frac{3 \times 5200}{18^2} \left[1 - \left(\frac{14.85 \times \sqrt{2}}{73.86} \right)^{1.2} \right] = 37.50 \text{ kg/cm}^2$$

At the corner, wheel load stress (37.17 kg/cm^2) is smaller than the value of f_{90} (50.67 kg/cm^2). OK.

Hence, provide cement concrete slab of thickness 18 cm and a WBM layer as a sub-base course of thickness 75 cm.

NOTE No heavy traffic is allowed on the road for the first 90 days of construction since the assumed value of flexural strength (f_{90}) develops only after 90 days.

8.6 Dowel Bars

Dowel bars are placed across transverse joints of concrete slabs at optimum intervals. They act in a group (i) to transfer wheel load by shear resistance from one slab to its adjacent slab thus bringing both slabs into action and (ii) to avoid faulting (or stepping) of slab at joints (Teller 1938). Dowel bars are made of corrosion resistant (epoxy coated) mild steel or stainless steel round bars and embedded mid-depth in the concrete of the slab (FHWA 1990; Odden et al. 2003).

Bearing stress of concrete plays a vital role in holding the dowel bars in position under repeated loading. At joints, the bearing stress on loading concentrate around the periphery of the dowel bars. By this crushing action, minute voids may develop immediately around the contact surface of the bars. This type of failure is termed as *funneling* (Teller 1938). On repeated loading, the size of the voids increases which in turn inhibit transfer of load (or failure of shear transfer takes place). The objective of load transfer at joints by means of dowel bars becomes futile. Therefore, bearing stress in concrete should always be higher than the maximum bearing stress in dowel bars.

8.7 Friberg's Analysis of Dowel Bars

Based on Timoshenko's theory of elastic foundations (Timoshenko and Lessels 1925), Friberg (1940) tried to determine the deflection of a dowel bar which is embedded across the transverse joint of a concrete pavement. He developed equations (8.23a–d) which are based on the following assumptions (Friberg 1940).

- The dowels are not bonded to the concrete. They just fit into the concrete mass. This assumption makes the developed equations directly applicable to long dowel bars.
- The concrete pavement is very stiff compared to the dowel bars.
- The stress and deflections are proportional to the load transferred (P_t) but the locations of maximum moment (x_m) and of the dowel action represented by L_1 and L_2 are independent of P_t (Figure 8.13).

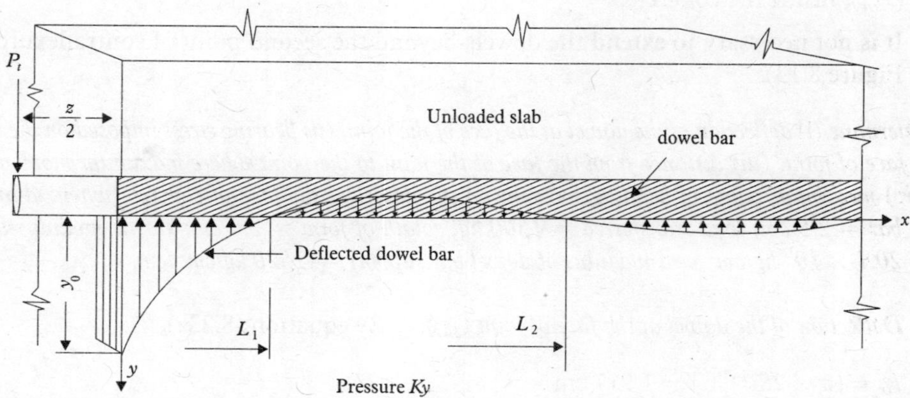

Figure 8.13 *Load and deflection of dowel bar embedded in transverse joint (After Friberg 1940)*

Bearings stress in concrete around dowel bar $= y_o \times K_o$ (8.22)

$$y_o = \text{deflection of dowel at the face of the joint} = \frac{2+\beta z}{4\beta^3 E_o I_o} \times P_t \quad (8.23a)$$

It is a theoretical value of differential deflection.

$$\beta = \text{relative stiffness of an embedded dowel bar (/cm)} = \left(\frac{K_o d_o}{4E_o I_o}\right)^{0.25} \quad (8.23b)$$

$$M_{max} = \text{maximum moment in the dowel bar} = -\frac{P_t e^{-\beta x_m}}{2\beta} \times \sqrt{1+(1+\beta z)^2} \quad (8.24)$$

$$\tan \beta x_m = \frac{1}{1+\beta z} \quad (8.24a)$$

z = width of joint (cm)

where, x_m = maximum moment occurs in the dowel bar

K_o = modulus of dowel support (kg/cm²/cm). Its value ranges between 8310 to 41520 kg/cm²/cm (Grinter 1938 and Friberg 1940). Normally, for the average grade of concrete now in use, a reasonable K_o value may be taken as 41520 kg/cm²/cm (Yoder and Witczak 1975) E_o = elastic modulus of dowel bar (kg/cm²).

I_o = moment of intertia of dowel bar (cm⁴)

P_t = maximum load carried by the dowel bar exactly under load (kg) (refer to Figure 8.13)

It is noted from Friberg's analysis that,

- Considerable change in the value of K_o will not greatly influence the stress distribution since the value of β varies as $(K_o)^{1/4}$.
- The maximum moment occurs at the point where the shear value is zero.
- The maximum moment occurs in the dowel bar at a distance away from the joint face (x_m), inside the concrete.
- It is not necessary to extend the dowels beyond the second point of contraflexure (L_2 in Figure 8.13).

Q: *Determine (i) deflection of the dowel at the face of the joint, (ii) bearing stress imposed on the concrete at the face of joint, (iii) distance from the face of the joint to the point where maximum moment occurs and (iv) maximum value of bending moment on the dowel at the face of concrete when: diameter of dowel bar = 2.5 cm; load transferred = 1500 kg; width of joint = 2.0 cm; elastic modulus of dowel bar = 20.1 × 10⁵ kg/cm² and modulus of dowel bar support =41520 kg/cm²/cm.*

A: (i) *Deflection of the dowel at the face of joint* (y_o): By equation (8.23a),

$$I_o = (\pi \times 2.5^4)/64 = 1.917 \text{ cm}^4$$

$$\beta = \left(\frac{41520 \times 2.5}{4 \times 20.1 \times 10^5 \times 1.917}\right)^{0.25} = 0.2864 \text{ per cm}$$

$$y_o = \frac{2 + 0.2864 \times 2.0}{4 \times 0.2864^3 \times 20.1 \times 10^5 \times 1.917} \times 1500 = 0.01065 \text{ cm}$$

(ii) *Bearing stress imposed on the concrete at the face of the joint (BSC)*: By equation (8.22),

$$\text{BSC} = y_o \times K_o = 0.01065 \times 41520 = 442.2 \text{ kg/cm}^2$$

(iii) *Distance from the face of the joint to the point where maximum moment occurs* (x_m): By equation (8.24a),

$$x_m = \left[\frac{\tan^{-1}\left(\dfrac{1}{1+\beta z}\right)}{\beta} \right] \times \frac{\pi}{180°} = \left[\frac{\tan^{-1}\left(\dfrac{1}{1+0.2864 \times 2.0}\right)}{0.2864} \right] \times \frac{\pi}{180°} = 1.977\,\text{cm}$$

(iv) *Maximum value of bending moment on the dowel bar at the face of the concrete slab*: By equation (8.24),

$$M_{\max} = -\frac{P_t\, e^{-\beta x_m}}{2\beta} \times \sqrt{1+(1+\beta z)^2}$$

$$= -\frac{1500 \times e^{-(0.2864 \times 1.977)}}{2 \times 0.2864} \times \sqrt{1+(1+0.2864 \times 2.0)^2}$$

$$= -\frac{1500 \times 0.56767}{2 \times 0.2864} \times 1.8637 = -2770.5 \text{ kg cm}$$

8.7.1 Deflection of Dowel Bar across a Joint

The support provided by a dowel is evaluated by determining the deflection of slabs across the joint. Deflection across the joint takes place due to the wheel load being transferred by the dowel bar from the loaded slab side to the adjacent unloaded slab side. According to Friberg (1940), the total deflection of the dowel is a function of the following three parameters (Figure 8.14).

1. Deflection of dowel at the joint face or maximum deformation of concrete under the dowel bar (y_o)
2. Slope of dowel at the face of the joint $\left(\dfrac{z}{2}\dfrac{dy}{dx}\right)$ and
3. Deflection in the part of the dowel bar at the joint opening $\dfrac{P_t}{3E_o I_o}\left(\dfrac{z}{2}\right)^3$

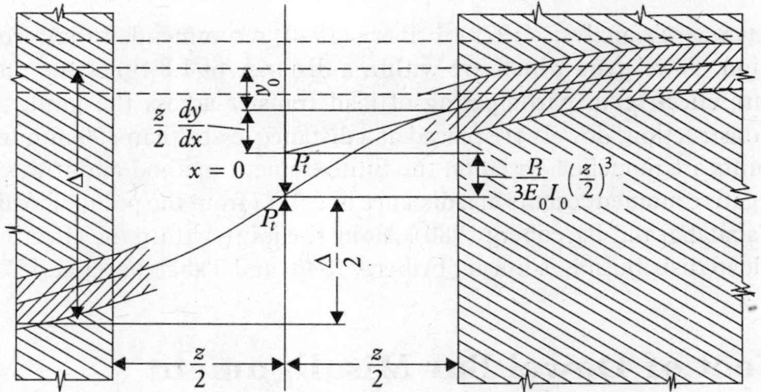

Figure 8.14 *Deflection of a dowel bar across a transverse joint (After Friberg 1940)*

Based on the above quantities and by assuming that the faces of the joint remain parallel, Friberg gives the following formula for calculating the total deflection across the joint (Δ).

$$\Delta = \frac{P_t}{2E_o I_o}\left(\frac{1+(1+\beta z)^2}{\beta^3}+\frac{z^3}{6}\right) \tag{8.25}$$

Q: *Determine the total deflection across a dowel joint when: diameter of dowel bar (d_o) = 2.5 cm; load transferred (P_t) = 1500 kg; width of joint (z) = 2.0 cm; elastic modulus of dowel bar (E_o) =20.1×10^5 kg/cm^2 and modulus of dowel bar support (K_o) = 41520 kg/cm^2/cm.*

A: By equation (8.25),

$$I_o = (\pi \times 2.5^4)/64 = 1.917 \text{ cm}^4; \qquad \beta = \left(\frac{41520 \times 2.5}{4\times 20.1\times 10^5 \times 1.917}\right)^{0.25} = 0.2864 \text{ per cm}$$

$$\Delta = \frac{1500}{2\times 20.1\times 10^5 \times 1.917}\left(\frac{1+(1+0.2864\times 2.0)^2}{0.2864^3}+\frac{2.0^3}{6}\right) = 0.029 \text{ cm}$$

8.7.2 Load Transfer across Transverse Joints

Load transfer across transverse joints (%) is determined from actual deflection measurements. The following relationship was obtained by taking the deflection of the loaded edge of the pavement as equal to the sum of the deflections of the dowel and the adjacent edge of the slab (Friberg 1940).

$$\frac{P_t}{\text{Wheel load }(W)} = \frac{1}{2+\left(\frac{\text{Deflection of dowel}}{\text{Deflection of pavement}}\right)} \tag{8.26}$$

8.7.3 Effective Distance of Load Transfer

Based on Wetergaard's analysis (1925), Friberg (1940) recommended that, from the point of load application, dowel bars which are within a distance of 1.8 times the radius of relative stiffness (l) are effective in participating of load transfer across the joint. In the present practices of construction, dowels are placed at a distance lesser than 300 mm from each other. The dowel joints are modelled based on the finite element method and it was found that the maximum negative moment occurs at a distance of $1.0 \times l$ from the point of loading (Tabatabai et al. 1979; Tabatabai and Barenberg 1980). Along the joint, within the effective distance (i.e., $1.0 \times l$), the load distribution is linear (Friberg, 1940) and Tabatabai et al. 1979, 1980.

8.8 Effect of Dowel Bar Misalignment

It is correct and a desirable practice during construction of transverse joints, to install the dowel bars perpendicular to the cross-section of the pavement. To assure satisfactory functioning of the joints, the dowels should be placed parallel to each other and perpendicular to the joint faces. This facilitates slipping the dowels freely into the concrete.

Misalignment of dowel bars may be classified into two types, viz. (i) horizontal misalignment and (ii) vertical misalignment (Figure 8.15(a) and (b)). When a dowel bar is misaligned in the horizontal plane, the value of K_o apparently becomes the same as the elastic modulus of concrete (Grinter 1938). The vertical misalignment of dowel bars is a common faulty construction practice (Perry 1938). Relative vertical displacement will occur at joints due to vertical misalignment of the dowel bars. The method of determining the relative vertical displacement at an expansion joint is illustrated by the following example problem.

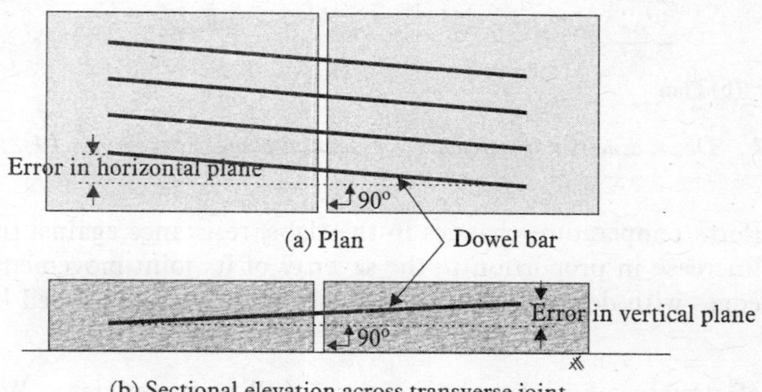

Figure 8.15 *Details of misalignment of dowels in a transverse joint*

Q: *Determine the relative vertical displacement at a joint when 2 cm of vertical error is observed during installation of 50 cm length dowel bars (Figure 8.16). The expansion joint movement is 1.75 cm.*

A: According to Perry (1938), the relative vertical displacement $= \dfrac{2.0}{50.0} \times 1.75 = 0.07$ cm

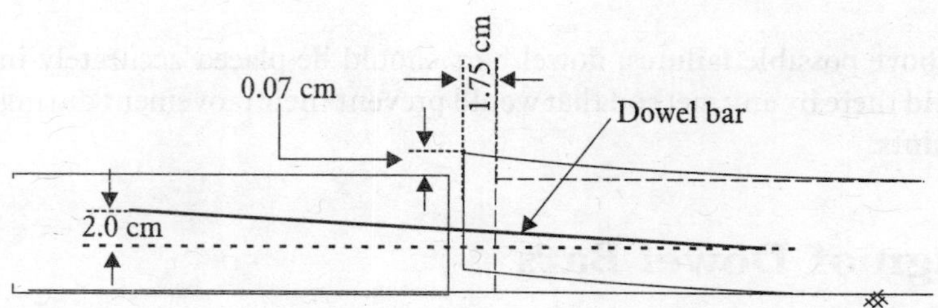

Figure 8.16 *The relative vertical displacement at joint*

The following effects are observed in transverse joints due to faulty installation of dowels (Smith and Benham 1938; Grinter 1938; and Friberg 1940).

- Binding takes place between dowel and concrete. This inhibits movement of slabs when the joints open and close during contraction and expansion of the slab respectively. As a consequence, the dowels will get distorted (Figure 8.17) or bend and funnelling failure will take place in the concrete.

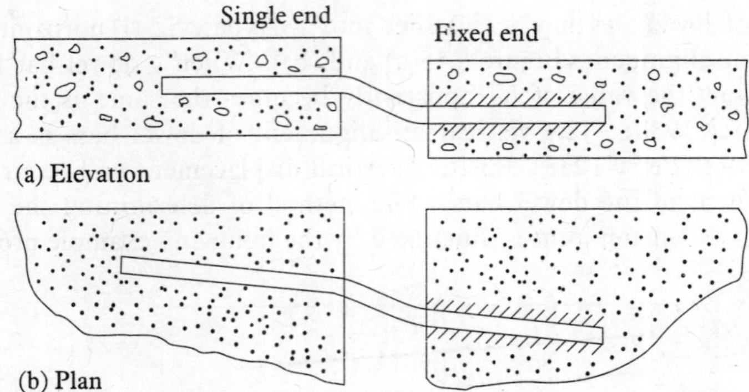

Figure 8.17 *Dowel distortion in horizontal and vertical plane (After Grinter 1938)*

- Due to uniform temperature changes in the slabs, resistance against the movement of joints will increase in proportion to the severity of its joint movement and therefore, pavement edges with dowels will deflect due to such force developed by the frictional resistance.
- Variation of stresses takes place in dowels as well as in concrete. When dowels are misaligned, the stresses produced in dowels and those produced in concrete by wheel loads are essentially alike and result in excessive stresses. In either case, there would be a spalling failure of the concrete. Field tests (Special Investigation A-7) of the Bureau of Materials and Test of the State Commission of Indiana (1938) have established that misalignment in the vertical plane is more serious than misalignment in the horizontal plane since the pavement offers less resistance to spalling failures than to the formation of full depth vertical cracks.
- Ultimately, dowel bars do not aid in transferring load and reducing stresses.

To avoid the above possible failures, dowel bars should be placed accurately in their proper position and held there by any method that would prevent their movement during construction of transverse joints.

8.9 Design of Dowel Bars

A few salient features of dowel design according to IRC:58-2002 are presented below.

Permissible bearing stress of concrete should be greater than the maximum bearing stress in the dowel bar. The bearing stress in concrete and the maximum bearing stress in the dowel bar are calculated using the following equations.

$$\text{Permissible bearing stress in concrete (PBS)} = \frac{(10.16 - d_o)}{9.525} \times f_{\text{ck}} \tag{8.28}$$

where d_o = diameter of dowel bar (cm)

f_{ck} = characteristic compressive strength of cement concrete defined in Section 5.7.1

Equation (8.28) has been adapted from the Committee 325 of the American Concrete Institute (ACI 1956). The bearing stress of concrete around the dowel bar is calculated based on Friberg's analysis using equation (8.22).

The number of dowel bars effectively participating as a group in load transfer is to be determined in a distance equal to 1.0 × radius of relative stiffness (l), which begins from the point of load application close to the edge of the slab (Figure 8.18). Therefore, number of dowel bars in the effective distance (N) $= 1.0 +$ (l/spacing between dowel bars).

When applied wheel load is close to the outer edge of the slab (Figure 8.18), the maximum load will be carried by a dowel bar exactly under the load and no load is carried by a dowel bar which is away from the point of loading at a distance of $1.0 \times l$. Within this effective distance ($1.0 \times l$), the load carried by dowel bars vary linearly. The load transferred across the joint is assumed to be 40%. Installation of dowel bars in slabs is restricted at places where the slab thickness is less than 15 cm.

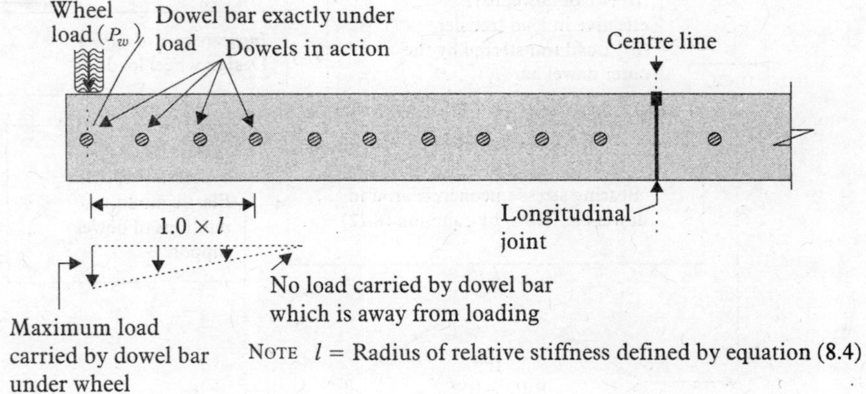

Figure 8.18 *Details of dowel bars participating in load transfer at transverse joint*

The IRC has recommended guidelines for suitable dimensions of dowel bars based on slab thickness. However, for the following conditions, smaller spacing between dowel bars may be assumed.

- To reduce the magnitude of the load carried by dowel bars in the effective length
- For thinner slabs
- When load on axles is heavy or abnormal
- When the sub-grade strength is poor

The design procedure for dowel bars is presented in Figure 8.19 and explained in the following example problem.

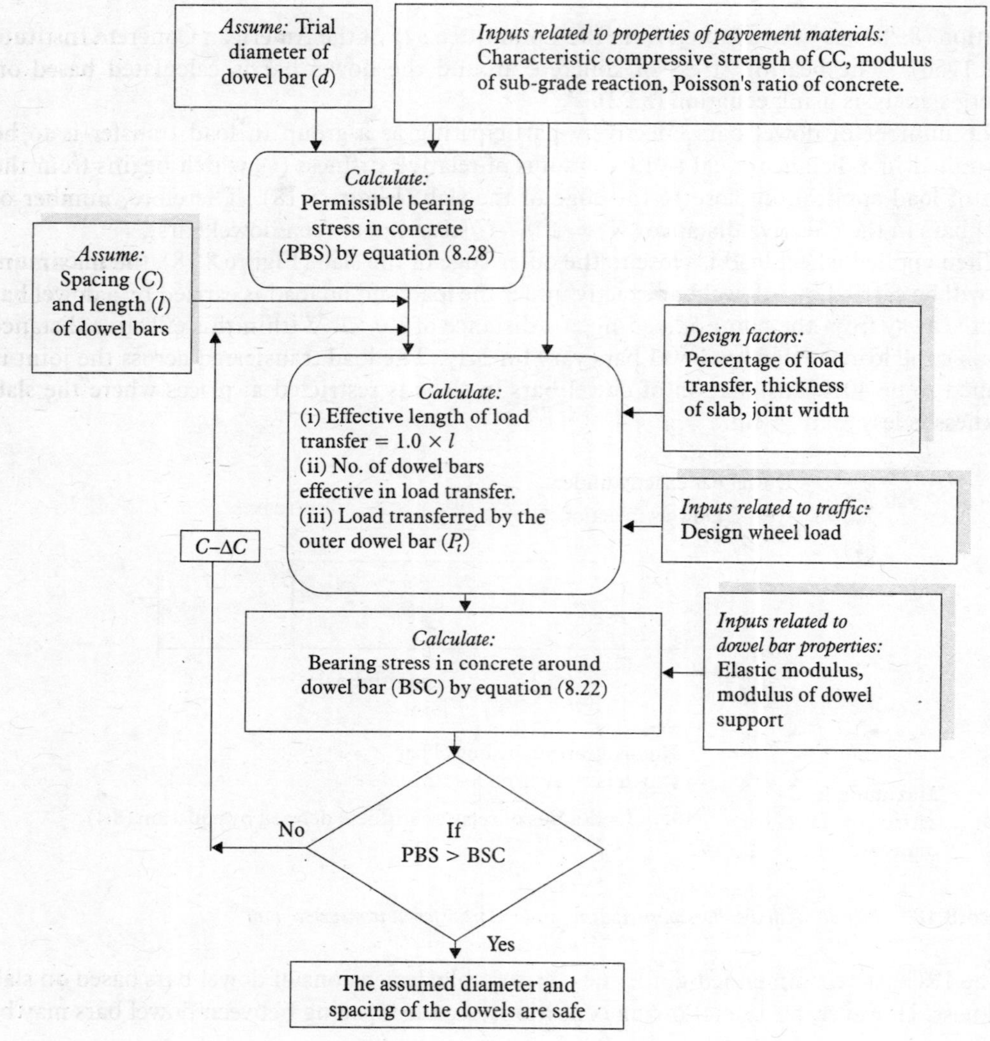

Figure 8.19 *Design of dowel bars according to IRC:58-2002*

Q: *Design dowel bars for the following design inputs: Thickness of slab = 30 cm; design (dual) wheel load = 8000 kg; efficiency of load transfer = 40%; width of joint = 2.0 cm; radius of relative stiffness = 99.4 cm; characteristic compressive strength of cement concrete cube (150 mm) after a 28 day curing = 407.7 kg/cm^2; elastic modulus of dowel bar =20.2×10^5 kg/cm^2 and modulus of dowel bar support = 41520 kg/cm^3.*

A: Assume diameter of dowel bar (d_o) = 3.2 cm, spacing between them (C) = 30 cm, length of dowel bar = 50 cm and the first dowel bar is placed at a distance of 15 cm from the free edge of the pavement. Assumption of the above values may be taken from IRC:58-2002 or by experience.

Permissible bearing stress (PBS) in concrete is calculated by using equation (8.28),

$$\text{PBS} = \frac{(10.16 - 3.2)}{9.525} \times 407.7 = 297.9 \text{ kg/cm}^2$$

Effective distance in which the dowel bars act as a group $= 1.0 \times l = 99.4$ cm

According to IRC, a worst critical loading is assumed as the wheel load is applied 15 cm away from the outer edge and placed exactly over a dowel bar A. The load transfer factors (LTF) are calculated based on the triangular load distribution from the point of loading where the LTF is assumed as one. The other details of the calculation are given in Figure 8.20.

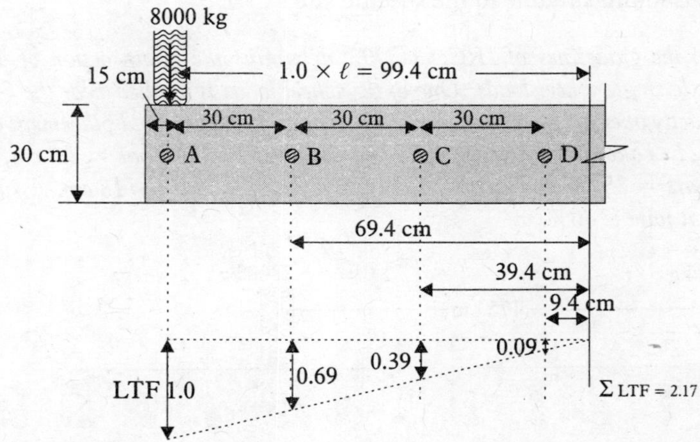

Figure 8.20 *Solution of example problem: Details of load position and LTF*

Sum of TLF = 1.0 + 0.69 + 0.39 + 0.09 = 2.17.
Load transfer efficiency of joint = 40% (given)
Therefore, transferable wheel load = 8000 × (40/100) = 3200 kg

Load carried by dowel bar A = 1.00 × (3200/2.17) = 1474.6 kg	
Load carried by dowel bar B = 0.69 × (3200/2.17) = 1017.5 kg	
Load carried by dowel bar C = 0.39 × (3200/2.17) = 575.1 kg	
Load carried by dowel bar D = 0.09 × (3200/2.17) = 132.8 kg	
	Total = 3200.0 kg

Load carried by the dowel bar A is maximum. Therefore, $P_t = 1474.6$ kg.

Bearing stress in concrete around the dowel bar (BSC) is calculated using equation (8.22).

$$\text{BSC} = y_o \times K_o$$

$$I_o = (\pi \times 3.2^4)/64 = 5.147 \text{ cm}^4$$

$$\beta = \left(\frac{41520 \times 3.2}{4 \times 20.2 \times 10^5 \times 5.147}\right)^{0.25} = 0.2377 \text{ per cm}$$

$$y_o = \frac{2 + 0.2377 \times 2.0}{4 \times 0.2377^3 \times 20.2 \times 10^5 \times 5.147} \times 1474.6 = 0.0066144 \text{ cm}$$

$$\text{BSC} = 0.0066144 \times 41520 = 274.63 \text{ kg/cm}^2$$

Check: BSC (274.6 kg/cm^2) < PBS (297.7 kg/cm^2).

Hence, provide dowel bar diameter = 3.2 cm, centre-to-centre spacing = 30 cm and length = 50 cm. If the above criteria is not satisfied, reduce the spacing or increase the diameter of the dowel bar which is found suitable to the specific site.

Q: *According to the guidelines of IRC:58-2002, determine the group action of dowel bars when loaded by single axle single wheel loads. One of the wheel loads is applied near the free edge of a slab which is placed exactly over a dowel bar (on A). The details of loading and placement of dowel bars are given in Figure 8.21. Take slab thickness = 25 cm; diameter of dowel bar = 2.5 cm; centre- to-centre spacing of dowel bars = 25 cm and radius of relative stiffness of slab = 118 cm. Assume that the load transfer efficiency at joint is 40%.*

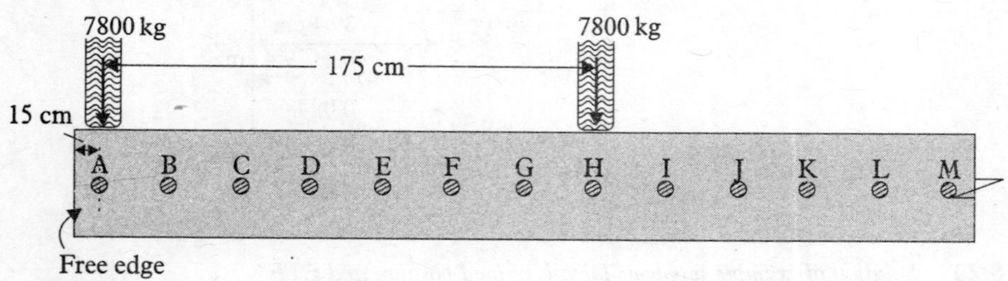

Figure 8.21 *Example problem*

A: Effective distance of load transfer along the joint = $1.0 \times l = 118$ cm

Transferred wheel load (P_t) = 7800 kg × (40/100) = 3120 kg.

Individual load transfer factors (LTF) of dowel bars may be calculated as follows:

Assume that (i) the maximum load is carried by the dowel bar over which the wheel load is applied and that (ii) the triangular load distribution or the loads are linearly proportional from the point of loading.

Consider that the load is above the dowel bar A and that the effective distance of load transfer is between the dowel A and F.

By the dowel bar A = 118/188 = 1.0

By the dowel bar B = (118 – 25)/118 = 93/118 = 0.78

Now, consider that the load is above the dowel bar H and the effective distance of the load transfer is between the dowel H and C.

By the dowel bar E = (118 – 3 × 25)/118 = 43/118 = 0.36

Similarly, LTF by the remaining dowel bars should be calculated as given in Figure 8.22.

Effective number of dowels (acting as a group) when loaded only over A = 1.0 + 0.78 + 0.57 + 0.36 + 0.15 = 2.86

Effective number of dowels (acting as a group) when loaded only over H = (2×2.86) – 1.0 = 4.72, or = (1.0 + 0.78 + 0.57 + 0.36 + 0.15) + (0.78 + 0.57 + 0.36 + 0.15) = 2.86 + 1.86 = 4.72.

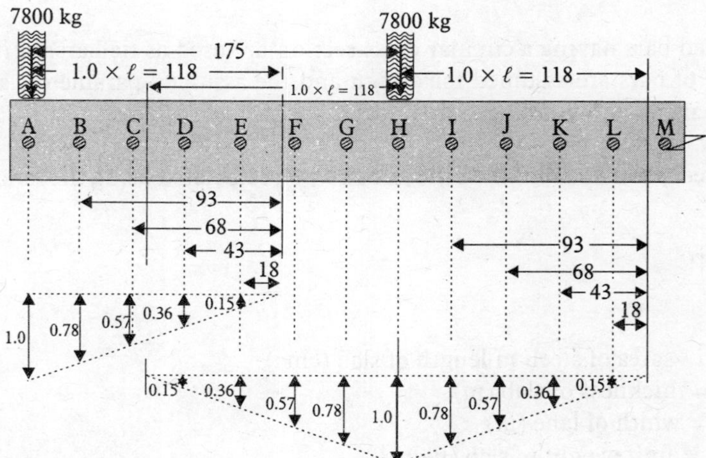

Figure 8.22 *Solution of example problem*

Load transferred by each dowel bar is calculated below.

Dowel bar name	Due to wheel load over	Load transfer factor	Load carried by the dowel bar
A	A	1.0	1.0 ×(3120 kg/2.86) = 1090.9 kg
B	A	0.78	0.78 ×(3120 kg/2.86) = 850.9 kg
C	A	0.57	0.57 ×(3120 kg/2.86) = 621.8 kg
D	A and H	0.36 and 0.15	0.36 ×(3120/2.86) + 0.15 ×(3120/4.72) = 491.8 kg
E	A and H	0.15 and 0.36	0.15 ×(3120/2.86) + 0.36 ×(3120/4.72) = 401.6 kg
F	H	0.57	0.57 ×(3120/4.72) = 376.7 kg
G	H	0.78	0.78 ×(3120/4.72) = 515.5 kg
H	H	1.0	1.0 ×(3120/4.72) = 661.0 kg
I	H	0.78	0.78 ×(3120/4.72) = 515.5 kg
J	H	0.57	0.57 ×(3120/4.72) = 376.7 kg
K	H	0.36	0.36 ×(3120/4.72) = 237.9 kg
L	H	0.15	0.15 ×(3120/4.72) = 99.1 kg
M	H	Nil	Nil

For the given conditions of loading and dowel spacing, the critical load transferred (P_t) by the dowel bar A = 1090.9 kg.

When the sub-grade is weak and the slab is strong, the value of the radius of relative stiffness of slab (l) increases. As the value of l increases, critical load (P_t) transferred by the dowel bar becomes larger because the combined effect of both wheel loads result in increased overlap area of triangularly distributed load. Hence, for design of dowel bars, the value of P_t should be determined by considering the combined effect of both the wheel loads.

8.10 Design of Tie Bars

Plain or deformed bars having a circular cross-section are used as tie bars. Suitable diameter, length and type of bars are assumed for design and the assumed parameters are checked for stresses due to tension and bonding. Salient details of tie bar design according to IRC:58-2002 are placed below.

The area of steel per metre length of the joint may be calculated using the following equation (IRC:58-2002).

$$A_{st} = \frac{hBW}{S} \times f \tag{8.29}$$

where, A_{st} = area of steel/ m length of slab (cm^2)
h = thickness of slab (m)
B = width of lane (m)
W = unit weight of slab (kg/m^3)
S = allowable working stress in steel (kg/cm^2)

To determine the length of the tie bar, its length must be equal to twice the length needed to develop the required bond strength to resist tensile stress in steel. The following equation is recommended by IRC:58-2002.

$$L_{\text{tie}} = \left(\frac{S \times d}{2 \times B_s}\right) \tag{8.30}$$

where, L_{tie} = length of the tie bar (cm)
S = allowable working stress in steel (kg/cm^2)
d = diameter of the tie bar (cm)
B_s = allowable bond stress of concrete; according to IRC, the B_s value for plain and deformed bars is equal to17.5 and 24.6 kg/cm^2 respectively.

The following IRC guidelines are useful during the design of tie bars.

(a) To relieve warping stresses, the diameter of tie bars should be restricted to not greater than 2 cm

(b) To prevent concentration of tensile stresses in tie bars, the centre-to-centre spacing between the tie bars should not be wider than 75 cm.

(c) To make up for incorrect or erroneous placement of tie bars during construction and to compensate loss of bond due to painting, the length of the tie bar calculated using equation (8.30) should be increased by 5 to 10 cm.

Based on the thickness of the slab, standard design values of different tie bars for two-lane pavements with each lane of width 3.5 m are given in Table 9 of IRC:58-2002.

Q: *Determine the suitable diameter, spacing and length of tie bars according to the guidelines of IRC:58-2002 for the following design inputs: thickness of slab = 30 cm; width of lane = 3.50 m; coefficient of friction between the bottom surface of the slab and the top surface of the supporting layer = 1.5; unit weight of cement concrete slab = 2350 kg/cm*^{2}. *Take diameter of dowel bar as 1.6 cm; allowable working stress in steel = 1250 kg/cm*^{2} *and permissible bond stress of tie bars =17.5 kg/cm*^{2}.

A: Area of steel required is calculated using equation (8.29),

$$A_{st} = \frac{0.3 \times 3.5 \times 2350}{1250} \times 1.5 = 2.961 \,\text{cm}^2/\text{m}$$

Cross-sectional area of single tie bar $(A_o) = \pi \times (1.6/2)^2 = 2.01 \,\text{cm}^2$

Spacing of ties bars $= 100 \times A_o/A_{st} = 100 \times 2.01/2.961 = 67.8$ cm

Therefore, provide a spacing of 67 cm centre-to-centre. Length of tie bars is determined using equation (8.30).

$$L_{\text{tie}} = \frac{1250 \times 1.6}{2 \times 17.4} = 57.5 \,\text{cm}$$

Increase the calculated length of the tie bars by 5 and 9 cm to make up for incorrect placement and loss of bond due to paint respectively.

Therefore, $L_{\text{tie}} = 57.5 + 5 + 9 = 71.5$ cm, say 72 cm

8.11 Reinforcement to Control Cracks

The main objective of providing steel reinforcement in concrete slab pavements is to hold the concrete in close contact after a crack forms. It is not intended for structural strength improvement. Reduction of cracks can be accomplished more economically by using steel reinforcements than by adding to the thickness of concrete. The reinforcement should comprise of small steel members closely spaced than by large members widely spaced (Breed 1927).

The amount of reinforcement required according to IRC:58-2002 is the same as that recommended by Goldbeck (1925) and AASHTO (1993) and can be obtained using equation (8.20).

8.12 Concrete Overlays on Existing Bituminous Pavements

Overlaying of cement concrete slabs on existing bituminous pavements is termed as white topping (WT). WT can be considered as the best approach to bituminous pavement rehabilitation in terms of longer serviceability, cost effectiveness and recyclability.

According to the thickness of overlay and its material properties, white toppings can be classified as.

1. Conventional white toppings (CWT)
2. Thin white toppings (TWT)
3. Ultra-thin white toppings (UTWT)

The difference between the toppings are explained in Table 8.6.

Table 8.6 *Details of white topping*

Type of WT	Recommended thickness of CC slab (mm)	Sub-base type	Milling of existing bituminous layer	Degree of bonding between overlay and existing layer	Widely used concrete mix having
1. CWT	200 mm and above (joints with spacing 4 to 4.5 m, according to IRC:58 and IRC:15)	Existing bituminous layer treated as dry lean concrete	Not considered; a whitewash compound may be used to minimise temp. on existing layer	Un-bonded interface (without any composite action)	OPC 33 and above; Grade M40 or above. Coarse agg. max. size: 31.5 mm
2. TWT	Greater than 100 mm but not exceeding 200 mm (joint spacing 0.6 to 1.25 m; constructed according to IRC:15)	Existing bituminous layer having thickness not less than 75 mm (after milling). However, 100 preferred for better performance of pavement	Not required; however, chiselling or milling may be done according to the distress endured	Partially bonded interface	High strength CC with fly ash and fibres. Grade M50. OPC 43 or 53; Coarse agg. max. size: 31.5 mm
3. UTWT	Smaller than or equal to 100 mm (joint spacing same as for TWT)		Desirable up to a mean depth of 25 mm	Bonded interface (the two layers behave as a composite layer)	High strength CC with fibres and mineral admixtures. Grade M50. OPC 43 or 53; Coarse agg. max. size: 25 mm

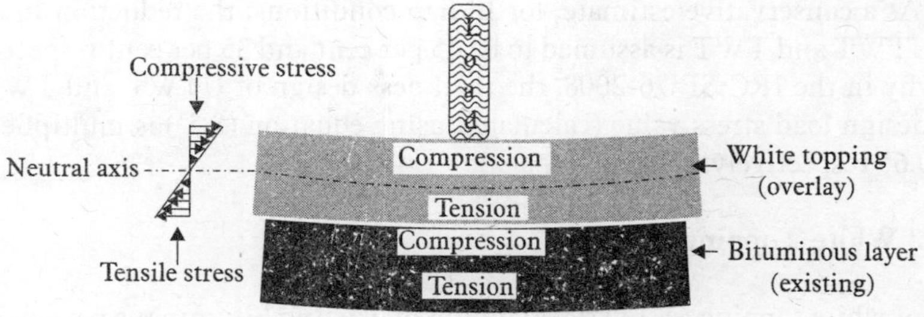

(a) Typical behaviour of layers with unbonded interface

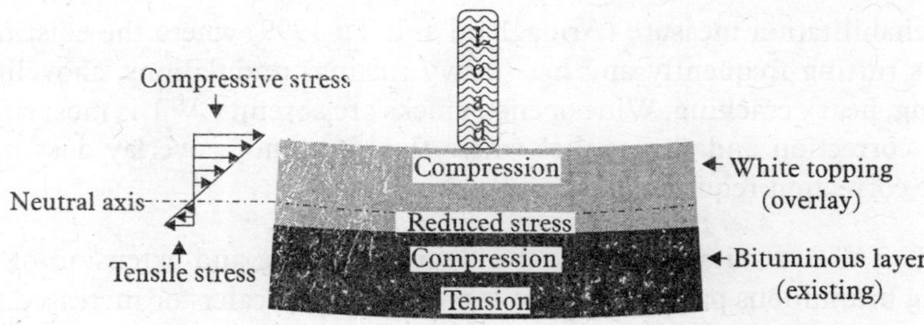

(b) Typical behaviour of layers with bonded layers

Figure 8.23 *Shifting of neutral axis due to composite action of white topping the existing bituminous layer (Elaborated and modified from NCHRP 2004)*

Advantages of UTWT/ TWT There is a considerable reduction of load induced stresses in UTWT and TWT, as compared to CWT. Following are the factors affecting reduction of stresses in UTWT/ TWT (ACPA 2002).

(a) *Effect of bonding between existing bituminous layer and proposed WT:* As the bonding increases, both the layers (i.e., flexible and rigid layers) act as a composite layer. Due to composite action, on loading, the position of the neutral axis shifts downward (Figure 8.23) and the PCC slab area in the compression zone increases and tension zone decreases. This composite action is advantageous since the cement concrete is more capable of withstanding compressive stress than tensile stress. Hence, thickness required for UTWT/TWT is smaller than for CWT.

(b) *Effect of slab size* As the slab size decreases, load induced stresses also decreases. Size of each panel of slab considered for UTWT/TWT ranges from 0.6 to 1.20 m whereas for CWT, sizes ranging from 4.0 to 4.5 m need to be considered.

(c) *Effect of warping* As the slab panel size in terms of area and thickness decreases, warping stress due to frictional resistance and curling stress due to temperature differential, also decreases.

A study on UTWT, conducted by ACPA (2002), reveals that there is about 69 per cent reduction in load induced stresses due to reduced panel size (1×1 m) and bonding effect. However, in general, the ACPA assumes that there is a reduction in stresses of up to 60 per cent for UTWT. As a conservative estimate, for Indian conditions, the reduction in load induced stresses for UTWT and TWT is assumed to be 45 per cent and 35 per cent respectively. This is the reason why in the IRC:SP:76-2008, the thickness design of UTWT and TWT, according to the edge design load stress value (calculated using equation (8.5)) is multiplied by a factor of 0.55 and 0.65 respectively.

Suitability of White Topping

Application of white topping (as overlays) on top of existing bituminous pavement is suitable under the following conditions.

(a) As a rehabilitation measure (Armaghani and Tu 1999) where the existing bituminous layer is rutting frequently and has (heavy rutting) undulations, shovelling, ravelling, bleeding, heavy cracking. Wide opened cracks are absent. CWT is most suitable for such profile correction and also at sites where the bituminous overlay does not easily meet surface correction requirements.

(b) UTWT/ TWT is suitable for structural strengthening and extension of service life of existing bituminous pavement when it is necessary to cater for increased traffic volume and the existing surface is distressed with undulations and minor cracking.

(c) As a maintenance alternative, WT reduces life cycle costs when compared to bituminous overlays during a period of time, particularly in hot climates, as prevailing in India.

(d) At intersections (Speakman and Scott III 1996) and curves where frequent surface distress occurs.

(e) UTWT/ TWT are suitable at underpasses and well-developed urban localities where the level of road surface is restricted to prevent insufficient overhead clearance and surface drainage problems respectively.

(f) UTWT is suitable for shoulders, footpaths, cycle tracks, parking lots, low-volume rural roads and residential streets in urban localities (Cole 1997).

(g) Repairing of a part of a slab or a slab panel area is easy, as done at Great Falls, Montana (NCHRP 338 2004), by removing material from the damaged area along with underlying bituminous layer and replacing it with full depth concrete.

UTWT/ TWT are also suitable as an inlay laid in a trench milled area or in a portion of the existing bituminous pavement at bus-stops, intersections and other such locations.

Design Guidelines (according to IRC:SP:76-2008)

The philosophy of designing a CC white topping on the existing bituminous pavement is similar to the design method of rigid pavements according to the guidelines of IRC:58-2002. Allowable thickness for each type of white topping is given in Table 8.6. The thickness design procedure adopted according to IRC:SP:76-2008 is briefly presented in Figure 8.24. A few other salient features of the white topping design method are given below.

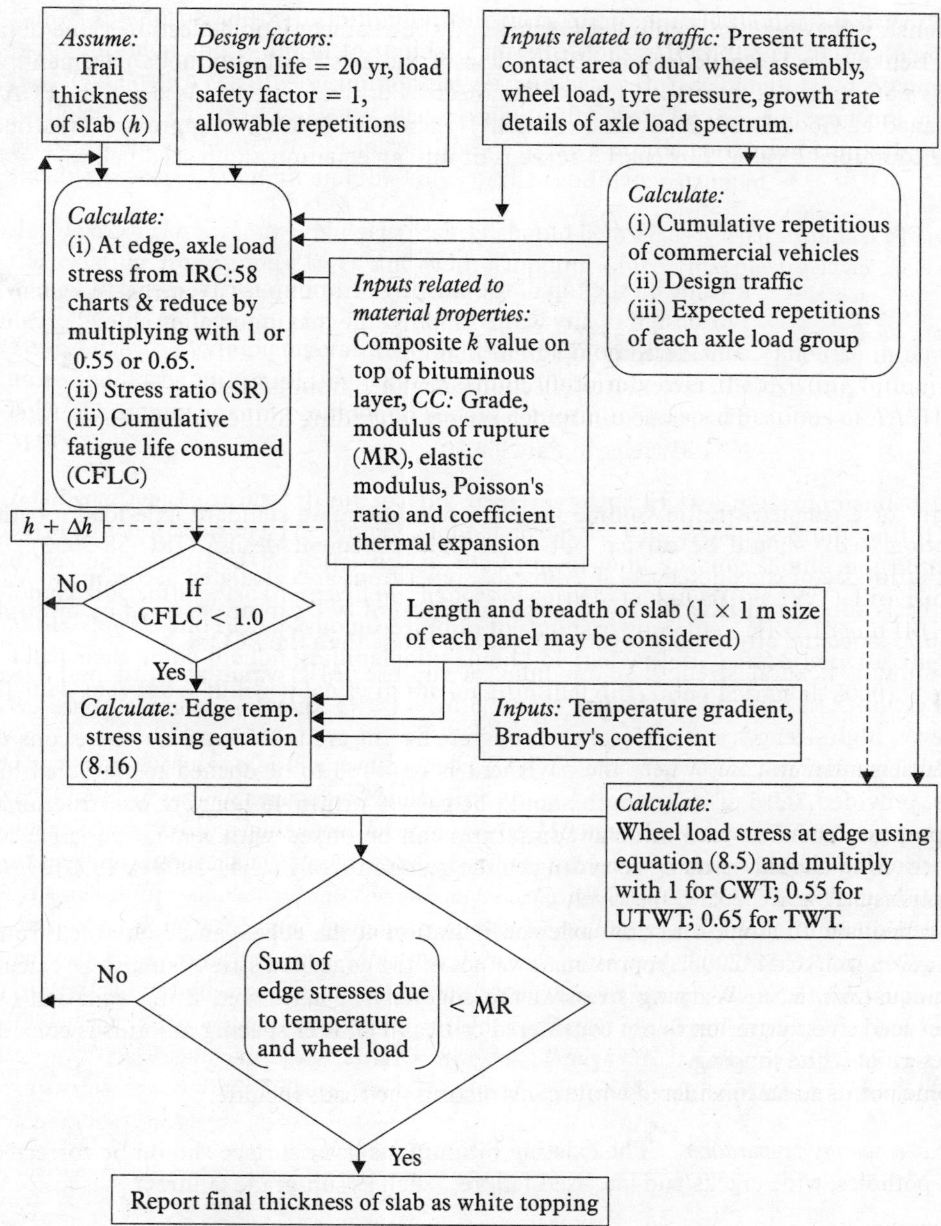

Figure 8.24 *Thickness design of white topping according to IRC:SP:76-2008*

Pavement evaluation: Surface distress condition of the existing bituminous pavement is evaluated along its chainage. Effective or combined k value on top of the existing bituminous pavement is estimated or determined according to IRC guidelines, using (i) two charts of ACPA (2002), by inputting the k value of the sub-grade obtained from the plate load test or indirectly obtained from the CBR value of the sub-grade, when the bituminous pavement consists of the granular base or the cement treated granular base and (ii) a chart showing the relationship between the combined *k* value and the characteristic deflection value obtained from Benkelman beam deflection (BBD) data of the existing bituminous pavement. This chart's data source is from the Corps of Engineers/ Portland Cement Association (PCA) and the Canadian Good Roads Association (CGRA) (Zube et al. 1969). For approximate estimation of the combined *k* value, this chart's curve is fit into an equation and placed below.

$$k_{\text{top}} = 10.05 \times 8.34 \times \log_e(D_c) \tag{8.31}$$

where, k_{top} = k value on the top of the existing bituminous pavement, in kg/cm²/cm. For design of any white topping, the maximum allowable k_{top} value considered is 15 kg/cm²/cm

D_c = Characteristic deflection calculated from BBD data, in mm. This value can be determined according to the guidelines of IRC:81 (refer to Para 9.4.10)

Design (or estimated) traffic volume in terms of cumulative standard axle load repetitions (equation (6.2)) should be carried out as in rigid pavement design (IRC:58-2002). Lane distribution factor considered as 1.0. Allowable repetitions are calculated according to Miner's hypothesis adopted in IRC:58. Fatigue consideration of WT can be obtained by multiplying with 0.75 since the bituminous layer's fatigue life is less than the PCC slab.

Minimum flexural strength or modulus of rupture (MR) value at third point loading (See Section 5.7.3) should not be less than 4.5 MPa ($\approx$ 45 kg/cm²) for grade M40@28 days. However, high strength and performance concrete having grade M50 and above are considered suitable/essential in cases where the pavement is required to be opened to traffic within 72 hours, provided 2/3rd of its strength should be gained within 48 hours of construction. For this purpose, chemical and mineral admixtures can be mixed with cement concrete whose proportioning should be made according to the guidelines of IRC:44-2008 or IS:10262 (refer to Sections 5.11 and 5.10.1 respectively).

Axle loads with single and dual axle configuration at the edge, can be obtained from the chart given in IRC:58-2002. Approximate values of the edge load stress can also be calculated using equation (8.5). Warping stress at the edge can be calculated using equation (8.16). Corner load stress criterion is not considered critical if shorter spacing of joints is considered for design of white topping.

Some points to be considered while constructing the roads include:

(a) *Pre-overlay preparation* The existing bituminous layer surface should be corrected for potholes, wide cracks and localised failures (such as sub-grade failures).

(b) *Milling* To develop composite action of both the layers, milling of the existing bituminous surface to a depth of 25 to 50 mm is done, subject to the condition that minimum thickness (available after milling) required is 75 mm. However, a minimum thickness of bituminous layer (as sub-base course) of 100 mm is desired for better performance of white topped pavements. Milling of the bituminous layer is not essential in the case of CWT but chiselling may be done to make its surface rough which may develop slight bonding action.

(c) *Profile correction* After milling or if the existing bituminous layer thickness is less than or equal to 50 mm, a bituminous macadam or BMD layer as profile correction course should be laid with minimum thickness of 50 mm. It should consist of 60/70 grade bitumen and conform to standard specifications (MOSRT&H 2001). In case of heavily damaged existing bituminous layers with heavy rutting of more than 50 mm and potholes, the engineer-in-charge may economically evaluate the choice of pre-overlay preparations—whether to opt for milling or to lay a profile correction course based on the distress level, strength and thickness of the candidate pavement.

(d) *Avoidance of plastic sheets* No plastic sheet should be used as a separation layer between the existing bituminous layer and white topping since this plastic layer acts as a de-bonding interface.

(e) *Temperature* Laying temperature should not be more than 35°C. The rise in temperature should be minimised by white-washing uniformly over the existing bituminous layer. The white washing compound should conform to the specifications of AASHTO-M148.

(f) *Joints and joints spacing* Joint spacing in terms of panel size is recommended to be between 0.6 to 1.25 m. The widely adopted size is 1×1 m. As a case study on UTWT, it was observed that the panel size in the form of joint spacing should not be taken longer since otherwise there will be chances of corner cracking (Cole 1997). Provision of joints, dowels and tie bars should conform to standard guidelines (IRC:15 and IRC:58). The panels along the longitudinal joint should be tied with tie bars, otherwise, the slab panels may move independently in the longitudinal direction (Tarr et al. 2000).

Q: *Design slab thickness of a thin white topping (TWT) according to the tentative guidelines of IRC:SP:7-2008, for the following input parameters.*

Location: Bihar; existing bituminous layer thickness: 150 mm. The existing bituminous layer has distressed with alligator cracking, block cracking, bleeding, few minor potholes and rutting depth up to 20 mm. Design traffic volume = 1859 commercial vehicles per day (CVPD). Benkelman deflection tests were conducted on the existing bituminous layer after milling to a depth of 25 mm and it was found that the characteristic deflection value was 1.26 mm (after applying all corrections). Grade of cement concrete mix: M 40 having minimum flexural strength as 45 kg/cm^2; elastic modulus of concrete = 3×10^5 kg/cm^2; Poisson's ratio of concrete = 0.15; coefficient of thermal expansion of concrete = 10×10^{-6} per degree Centigrade; tyre pressure = 8 kg/cm^2; growth rate of traffic = 7.5%; design period = 20 years; slab size = 100×100 cm. Take spacing of contraction joints as 100 cm. The axle load survey data is as given below.

Load on single axle		*Load on tandem axle*	
Average value of axle load (tonnes)	*% of axle loads*	Average value of axle load (tonnes)	*% of axle loads*
16	*0.2*	*28*	*0.2*
14	*0.5*	*24*	*0.9*
12	*19.8*	*20*	*1.9*
10	*36*	*16*	*1.8*
Less than 10	*36.2*	*Less than 16*	*2.5*
Total	*92.7*		*7.3*

A: *Analysis of design traffic:*
Cumulative number of standard axle load repetitions (N_{rigid}) in 20 years of design life is calculated using equation (6.3).

$$N_{\text{rigid}} = 365 \times 1859 \times \left(\frac{(1+0.075)^{20} - 1}{0.075} \right) = 29383742 \text{ CVPD}$$

Let us consider traffic on edge as design traffic = 25% of $N_{\text{rigid}} = 0.25 \times 29383742$

Table 8.7 *Expected number of axle load passes*

For single axle			For tandem axle		
Axle load in tonnes (AL)	% of axle loads	Expected no. of load passes (N_E)	Axle load in tonnes (AL)	% of axle loads	Expected no. of load passes (N_E)
16	0.2	14692	28	0.2	14692
14	0.5	36730	24	0.9	66113
12	19.8	1454495	20	1.9	139573
10	36	2644537	16	1.8	132227
Less than 10	36.2	2659229	Less than 16	2.5	183648
Total	92.7 %	–	–	7.3 %	–

Given strength parameters of cement concrete:
Flexural strength or modulus of rupture of cement concrete (MR) value = 45 kg/cm²
Elastic modulus of concrete, $E_s = 3 \times 10^5$ kg/cm²

Determination of modulus of sub-grade reaction of bituminous pavement:
Using the Benkelman beam deflection data, the combined k value on top of the existing bituminous layer can be determined using equation (8.31),

$$k_{\text{top}} = 10.05 - 8.34 \times \log_e(1.26) = 8.12 \approx 8.0 \text{ kg/cm}^2\text{/cm}$$

Assume trial thickness of the slab = 18 cm and consider load safety factor (LSF) = 1.0

The CFLC value is less than one. Hence, the assumed thickness of the slab as TWT is safe against fatigue criterion.

NOTE: If the cumulative value of fatigue life consumed (CFLC) is greater than one, the value of the assumed thickness should be suitably increased and the above process of calculations is repeated until the criterion is satisfied.

Maximum warping stress at the edge:

By equation (8.4), Radius of relative stiffness (l) $= \left[\dfrac{300000 \times 18^3}{12 \times 8 \times (1 - 0.15^2)} \right]^{0.25} = 65.71$ cm

Bradbury's coefficients for calculating warping stress in the x and y directions (refer to Table 8.1)

Table 8.8 *Analysis of cumulative fatigue life of pavement*

Axle type	AL in tones (AL ×LSF)	Flexural stress, (FS) from IRC charts (kg/cm^2)	Flexural stress × 0.65	Check whether total stress =((4)+ σ_{tx_edge}) < 45 kg/cm^2	Stress ratio, SR = (4)/45 kg/cm^2	Expected repetitions N_E	Fatigure life= (N_f) from equation (8.21) $N_{f0.75}$= 0.75×N_f	Cosumed fatigue life = $N_E/N_{f0.75}$
(1)	(2)	(3)	(4)	(5)	(6)	(7)	(8)	(9)
Single	16	41.0	26.65	26.65 + 0.50 = 27.15, OK	0.592	14692	34246	0.429
	14	37.0	24.05	24.05 + 0.50 =24.55, OK	0.534	36730	148550	0.247
	12	32.2	20.93	20.93 + 0.50 =21.43, OK	0.465	1454495	6159232	0.236
	10	27.5	17.87	17.87 + 0.50 =18.37, OK	0.397	2644537	infinity	—
	<10	27.5	17.87	17.87 + 0.50 =18.37, OK	0.397	2659229	infinity	—
Tandem	28	27.5	17.87	17.87 + 0.50 =18.37, OK	0.397	14692	infinity	—
	24	26.0	16.90	16.9 + 0.50 =17.40, OK	0.376	66113	infinity	—
	20	22.5	14.62	14.62 + 0.50 =15.12, OK	0.325	139573	infinity	—
	16	17.5	11.37	11.37 + 0.50 =11.87, OK	0.253	132227	infinity	—
	<16	17.5	11.37	11.37 + 0.50 =11.87, OK	0.253	183648	infinity	—
					Cumulative fatigue life consumed (CFLC) =			0.912

$$L_{x \text{ or } y}/l = 100 \text{ cm} / 65.71 \text{ cm} = 1.521$$

From Table 8.1, for $L_x/l = 1.52$, the value of Bradbury' coefficient by linear interpolation,

$$C_x = 0.000 + \frac{1.521 - 1.0}{2.0 - 1.0} \times (0.040 - 0.000) = 0.02084$$

For Bihar state, the temperature differential $(\Delta_t) = 16.08\,^\circ\text{C}$ (from Table 1 of IRC:58-2002). Maximum warping stress at the edge is calculated using equation (8.16).

$$\sigma_{tx\_edge} = \frac{300000 \times (10 \times 10^{-6}) \times 16.08}{2} \times 0.02084 = 0.50 \text{ kg/cm}^2$$

Check for total stress at edge due to load and temperature :

The 98th percentile axle load is determined as 12 tonnes. However, as a worst condition, let us take the wheel load as $P_1 = 8000$ kg. Assume centre-to-centre spacing between two tyres $(S) = 31$ cm.

Equivalent radius contact area can be calculated using equation (8.13) on substitution,

$$a = \left[\left(\frac{0.8521 \times 8000}{8 \times \pi}\right) + \frac{31}{\pi}\left(\frac{8000}{0.5227 \times 8}\right)^{0.5}\right]^{0.5} = 24.00 \text{ cm}$$

$$b = \sqrt{1.6 \times 24.00^2 + 18^2} - 0.675 \times 18 = 23.15 \text{ cm}$$

Load stress at the critical edge region can be calculated using equation (8.5), on substitution,

$$\sigma_{\text{edge}} = 0.529\frac{8000}{18^2}(1 + 0.54 \times 0.15)\left[4 \log_{10}\left(\frac{65.71}{23.15}\right) + \log_{10}(23.15) - 0.4048\right] = 39.13 \text{ kg/cm}^2$$

Reduced stress for TWT = $0.65 \times 39.13 = 25.43$ kg/cm^2

Maximum limit of total stress at edge due to warping stress and axle load is checked below.

$25.43 + 1.51 = 28.16$ kg/cm^2 $<$ MR (45 kg/cm^2). OK.

Hence, the assumed value of 18 cm as thickness of TWT (cement concrete slab) is safe against the total maximum edge stresses due to load and warping. Therefore, the design thickness of 18 cm is satisfactory.

Exercises

8.1. Determine the crack free length of a slab if its tensile strength is 2.1 MPa, unit weight is 23.2 kN/m^3 and average coefficient of friction is 1.5.

8.2. Determine the percentage difference between corner load stress calculated based on the radius of wheel contact area according to (i) Westergaard's analysis and (ii) the equation recommended by IRC:58-2002 (equation (8.13)). The design parameters are given as: Single axle load =10000 kg; With dual wheel assembly; tyre pressure 8.5 kg/cm^2; spacing between centres of wheels 310 mm, slab thickness = 30 cm.

8.3. State and define different types of rigid pavements.

8.4. State the objectives, functions and different types of joints in concrete pavements.

8.5. Explain why dowel and tie bars are placed in different road joints.

8.6. State the basic requirements of joint sealers and justify.

8.7. What are the different methods of sealing joints and list the materials used?

8.8. Differentiate between AASHTO and IRC methods of rigid pavement design.

8.9. Explain why edge load, edge warping stress and corner load stresses are considered and warping stress at the corner region is not considered in the IRC method of rigid pavement design.

8.10. Draw a flow chart representing the process of analysis for design of rigid pavements according to (i) IRC:58-2002 and (ii) AASHTO 1993.

8.11. What are the salient features of thickness design of concrete slab pavement according to IRC:58-2002?

8.12. State the critical placement of wheel loading and critical combination of stresses considered in IRC:58-2002.

8.13. What are the salient features of the design of cement concrete slab pavement for rural roads according to the guidelines of IRC:SP:62-2004?

8.14. Draw a flow chart showing design method for cement concrete slab pavement for rural roads according to the guidelines of IRC:SP:62-2004.

8.15. State the assumptions made in the design guidelines of CC pavement for rural roads according to the guidelines of IRC:SP:62-2004.

8.16. Draw a flow chart representing the process of analysis for design of dowel bars according to IRC:58-2002.

8.17. State the worst condition of loading considered for design of dowel bars according to IRC-58-2002. Draw figure wherever necessary.

8.18. Determine the actual load transfer by a dowel directly under the load, if the deflection of the pavement edges is 0.02 cm, width of joint = 2.0 cm, elastic modulus of dowel bar = 20.0×10^5 kg/cm^2 and modulus of dowel bar support = 41450 kg/cm^2/cm.

8.19. According to the guidelines of IRC:58-2002, determine group action of dowel bars when there is a single load of 16000 kg. One of the dual wheel loads is applied near the free edge of a slab. Details of loading and placement of dowel bars are given below. Take slab thickness = 24 cm; diameter of dowel bar = 2.5 cm; centre-to-centre spacing of dowel bars = 25 cm and radius of relative stiffness of slab = 122 cm. Assume load transfer efficiency at joint as 40%. Take centre-to-centre spacing between the tyres of the dual wheel to be 31 cm.

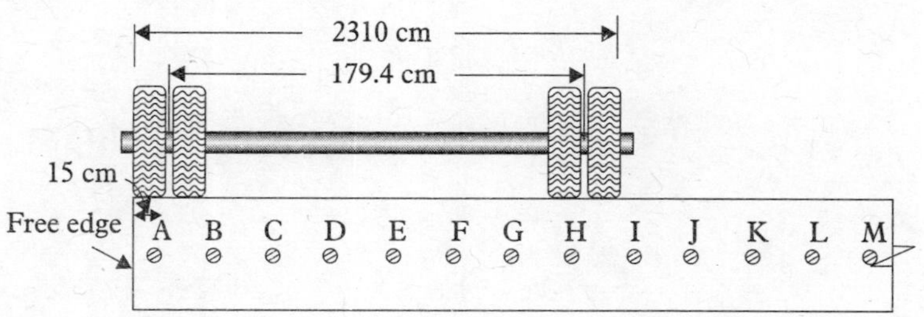

8.20. What do you understand by white toppings? Explain their suitability.

8.21. Explain the salient details of white toppings used to strengthen existing bituminous pavements.

8.22. Draw typical figures showing the presence and absence of composite action of white topping and bituminous layer under loading.

8.23. What are the advantages of UTWT/ TWT compared to conventional CC layers?

8.24. State the different types of white toppings laid as overlays on bituminous pavements.

8.25. What are the salient features of the design method for white topping according to the tentative guidelines of IRC:SP:76-2008?

8.26. What are the salient features related to construction of white toppings according to the tentative guidelines of IRC:SP:76-2008?

8.27. Draw a flow chart showing the design method for white topping according to IRC:SP:76-2008.

8.28. State why load stress at the corners is considered insignificant for thickness design of white toppings according to IRC:SP:76-2008.

9

Structural Evaluation of Pavements

Introduction

Pavement evaluation is carried out to determine the existing condition of pavements in terms of its surface and structural adequacy. The data obtained from such studies are used for deciding the type of maintenance operations required, prioritisation of maintenance works and for establishing a pavement maintenance management system.

Evaluation of the pavement surface condition can be studied with reference to the riding quality in terms of surface roughness, undulations, cracking, potholes and other surface distresses. Such surveys are termed as *functional evaluation* methods.

Diagnosing the existing structural condition of individual layers of pavement as well as examining the overall pavement strength is termed as *structural evaluation* of the pavement. Details of structural evaluation of pavements by different equipment are discussed in the following sections.

9.1 Purpose of Structural Evaluation of Pavements

Structural evaluation of in-service pavements is generally carried out to

- Assess the structural strength
- Estimate the remaining life of a pavement
- Determine the thickness of overlay required
- Establish a pavement management system based on the performance of the road

9.2 Types of Structural Evaluation Methods

Structural evaluation of pavements is generally carried out by two methods: (i) destructive testing (DT) and (ii) non-destructive testing (NDT).

In the destructive testing (DT) method, in situ pavement layers are cut open at different levels of the pavement structure to determine individual layer strengths. Other properties are determined either by in situ testing or by extracting layer samples for testing in the laboratory. As the pavement is cut at different levels and at regular intervals, the road will be heavily damaged. Huge funding would be required to restore such damaged pavements. Due to this reason, destructive testing (DT) techniques have become an unpopular practice and generally abandoned.

In the non-destructive testing (NDT) method, the pavement is not subjected to any kind of damage. Determination of strength parameters of the pavement layers is carried out without disturbing their existing condition. Pavement surface rebound (or elastic) deflections are generally measured by employing different NDT equipment. This is more easy and convenient than directly measuring stresses and strains. Due to this reason, many standard institutions insist on using NDT equipment for structural evaluation of pavements.

However, for physical examination, the pavement may be drilled to collect in situ samples at selected locations along a test section.

9.3 Methods of Structural Evaluation

In the structural evaluation method, the response of a pavement to a test load is observed. While structural response of the pavement can be measured in terms of stresses, strains and deflections, surface deflection is the most common parameter used in almost all pavement evaluation systems, as it is easy to measure. Measurement of surface deflection is rapid, relatively inexpensive and non-destructive. The early full-scale road tests conducted in USA by WASHO and AASHO resulted in correlations between Benkelman beam (BB) deflections and pavement performance under ultimate loading conditions. Since then, efforts have been made and directed by different research groups in different countries to develop deflection-based procedures that can be used to evaluate pavements. Therefore, NDT equipments capable of measuring surface rebound deflections are widely in use today for structural evaluation of pavements.

9.3.1 Desirable Features of the Equipment

Equipment used for structural evaluation of pavements should be able to measure appropriate responses of the pavement subjected to a given loading conditions that are similar to those applied by vehicular traffic. The main features of the loading conditions consist of number of loads, magnitude of load, shape and contact area of load and loading time. Other operational features of the equipment include data acquisition, methodology adopted for calibration and mobility of the equipment. Based on the review of different pavement evaluation equipment, the following desirable features have been identified.

Peak load The testing of highway pavements is usually carried out by applying a peak load corresponding to the standard axle load of 80 kN. Half of this load is applied on to the pavement through a dual wheel set. Therefore, in an equipment having only one loading plate, the load applied through the loading plate will be 40 kN. However, it is desirable to have the flexibility to change the magnitude of peak load within a practical range.

Contact pressure The tyre pressure corresponding to a standard axle is 0.56 MPa (80 psi). However, in practice, tyre pressure of commercial vehicles may vary in the range of 0.7 MPa (100 psi) to 0.84 MPa (120 psi).

Loading time In case of a fast moving truck, the loading time will be in the range of 20 to 30 milli-seconds (ms). It is thus desirable to simulate this loading time during the evaluation of the pavements.

Contact area In the analysis of any pavement system, a circular contact area of load is assumed. The peak load is transferred on to the pavement surface through a circular loading plate having a radius of 300 mm which corresponds to a load of 40 kN and a contact pressure of 0.56 MPa.

Data acquisition system A high speed data acquisition facility is required to collect load and multiple deflection responses over a small duration of time. The facility to store the data as it is acquired is also needed.

Calibration of the system A reliable methodology must be selected to calibrate the sensors. The test results should be reproducible.

Mobility The equipment should be portable and mobile so that it can be conveniently carried to different locations and operated even on heavily trafficked roads.

There are three main categories of structural evaluation methods depending on the method of application of load. They are (a) static loading, (b) steady-state vibratory loading and (c) impulse loading methods.

9.4 Structural Evaluation by Static Loading

Equipments that are in practice for evaluating flexible pavements under this category are (i) the Benkelman beam (BB), (ii) the Lacroix deflectograph (LD) and (iii) the travelling deflectometer (TD). These equipments are very popular because of their low cost and simplicity of operation. The external loads applied are either static or moving at creep speed.

The working principle of the Lacroix deflectograph (LD) is similar to that of BB testing. It can be mechanised with a standard truck and used for rapid measurement of the pavement surface rebound deflections under each of the dual tyres of the rear axle at regular intervals of 3 m distance.

More number of deflection measurements can be taken per day by using LD and TD techniques compared to the BB method.

Structural evaluation of flexible pavements using the Benkelman beam (BB) is presented in the following sections.

9.4.1 Working Principle of the Benkelman Beam (BB)

To measure the response of a flexible pavement in terms of surface rebound deflections under static standard axle truck wheel loading, A. C. Benkelman introduced the Benkelman beam (BB) in 1952. The beam was especially made for the road tests conducted by the Western Association of State Highway Organization (WASHO). The BB method played a major role in the evolution of the overlay design using surface rebound deflections measured under standard axle loads similar to truck traffic loading. The Benkelman beam is a simple, inexpensive and reliable equipment used to assess the structural adequacy of a flexible pavement.

For routine structural evaluation of flexible pavements and overlay design, the BB method is adopted and incorporated by many organisations worldwide, viz. the California Department of Transportation (1979), the Asphalt Institute (1983), TRRL, the AASHTO, CSIR of South Africa, CGRA of Canada, IRC of India and many more.

The details of the BB test as recommended by the IRC:81-1997 are presented below.

The Benkelman beam consists of a probe of slender beam 3.66 m in length. It is pivoted at a distance 2.44 m from the probe point (Figure 9.1). The probe beam is mounted in position by a reference beam of length 2.66 m. The reference beam is equipped with front and rear legs for initial horizontal adjustment using a spirit level. A dial gauge or LVDT is installed on the reference beam 1.22 m away from the pivot and its spindle is in contact with the other end of the probe beam.

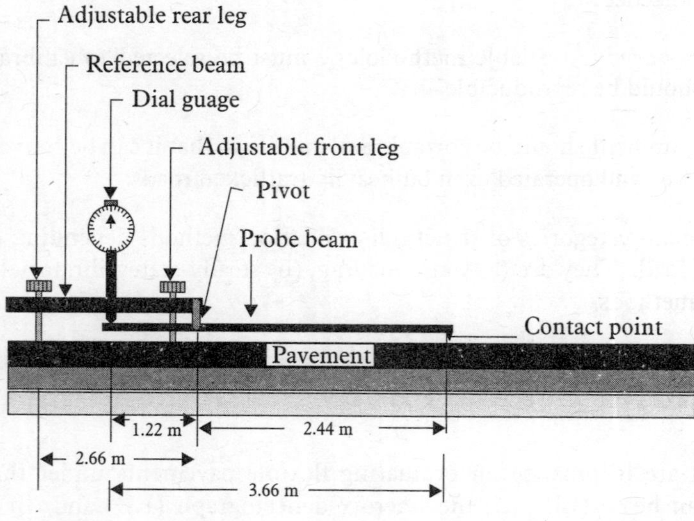

Figure 9.1 *Salient features of a Benkelman beam*

9.4.2 Calibration of BB

Before using the BB, its dial gauge should be calibrated by placing its probe point on a metallic plate of known thickness (Figure 9.2). The reading on the dial gauge should be checked as one-half of the thickness of the metallic plate, since the distance between the pivot to the spindle of the dial gauge is one-half the distance between the pivot and the probe point. While calibrating, the reference beam should be horizontal and there should be no vibrations in the ground. Free movement of the probe beam should be ensured at the pivot.

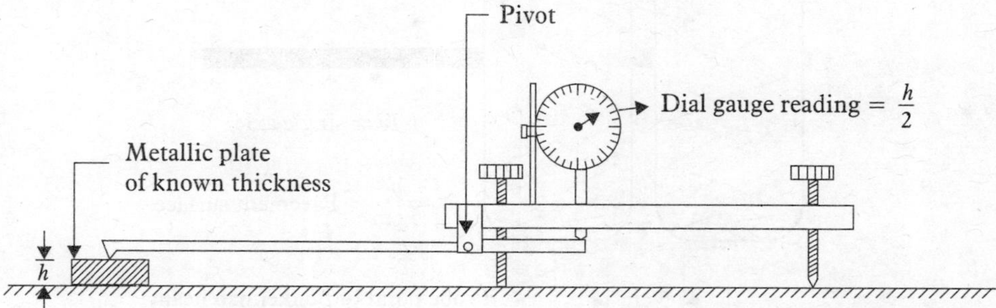

Figure 9.2 *Calibration of BB*

9.4.3 Pavement Condition Survey

The test sections of the pavement are subjectively rated by visual examination of surface distress in terms of cracking and rut depth. The test sections may be classified into the following three types.

Good: No cracks and rut depth less than 10 mm
Fair: No or very little hair cracks and rut depth between 10 to 20 mm
Poor: Considerable cracks on the surface and rut depth more than 20 mm

Additional information such as existing pavement crust thickness, individual layers thickness and prevailing drainage conditions should be recorded separately. The above information should be collected at suitable intervals based upon the condition of the test section and requirement.

9.4.4 Method of Measurement of Rebound Surface Deflections

The Canadian Good Roads Association (CGRA) procedure may be adopted for measurement of pavement surface deflection. Initially, the BB probe point is inserted between the dual tyres of a standing truck's rear axle (Figure 9.3). The standard values of truck rear axle weight and the inflated tyre pressure should be taken as 8170 kg (or 80 kN) and 5.6 kg/cm^2 respectively. During the test, the rear axle load and the tyres pressure should not change beyond a tolerance limit of $\pm$ 1 and $\pm$ 5% respectively (IRC:81-1997).

Proposed test points on the pavement surface are marked at suitable intervals not less than 10 points per section. The intervals should not be greater than 50 m. The points should be marked at a distance (Y) from the pavement edge (0.6 and 0.9 m for single- and double-lane pavements respectively) (Figure 9.4).

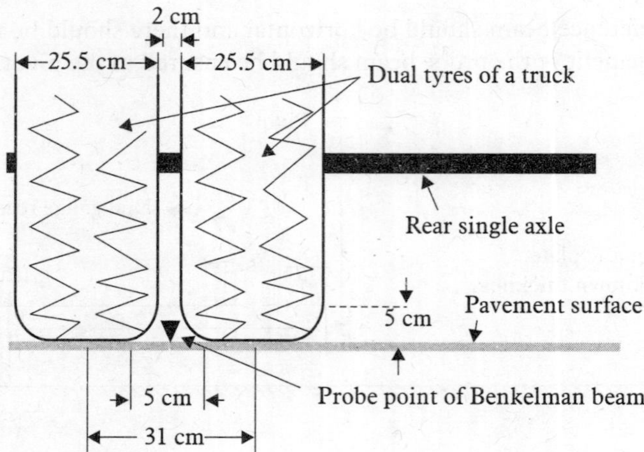

Figure 9.3 *Initial position of the Benkelman beam probe point in between the dual wheels of a truck*

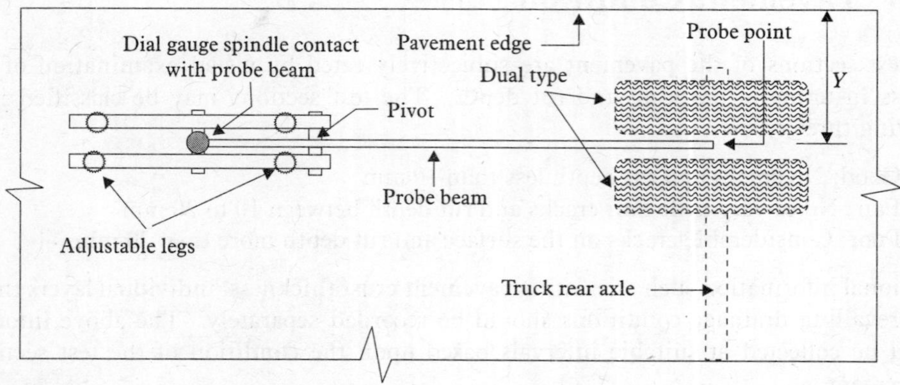

Figure 9.4 *Plan view of Benkelman beam testing when its probe point is inserted in between dual tyres of a truck's rear axle*

Horizontality of the reference beam should be checked and the dial gauge's initial (or first) reading (D_1) recorded when the probe point is deflected under the given standard loading conditions (Figure 9.5(a)). Second reading (D_2) is recorded when the truck is driven at a creep speed ($\leq$ 2 km/h) and stopped 2.7 m from the initial position (Figure 9.5(b)). Finally, the truck is allowed to move further by 9 m and the third reading (D_3) is recorded (Figure 9.5(c)). The above readings should be recorded when the rate of deformation of the pavement is less than or equal to 0.025 mm per minute.

It is observed from Figure 9.5 that initially the pavement surface is deflected under the loading. As the truck moves away, the pavement surface gradually regains its original level. This is the reason why the BB measured surface deflections are termed as rebound or elastic deflections.

Temperature of the bituminous layer should be recorded at its 1/3rd depth as explained in Section 6.3.3 (Figure 6.17). A small pit should be cut from the edge of the pavement up to 50 cm inside the sub-grade and a sample of the sub-grade collected under the BB test point.

The collected soil sample is used to determine the field moisture content of the sub-grade. Individual layer thickness of pavements can be obtained from these cut openings. The holes made in the pavement must be filled with suitable materials and compacted immediately.

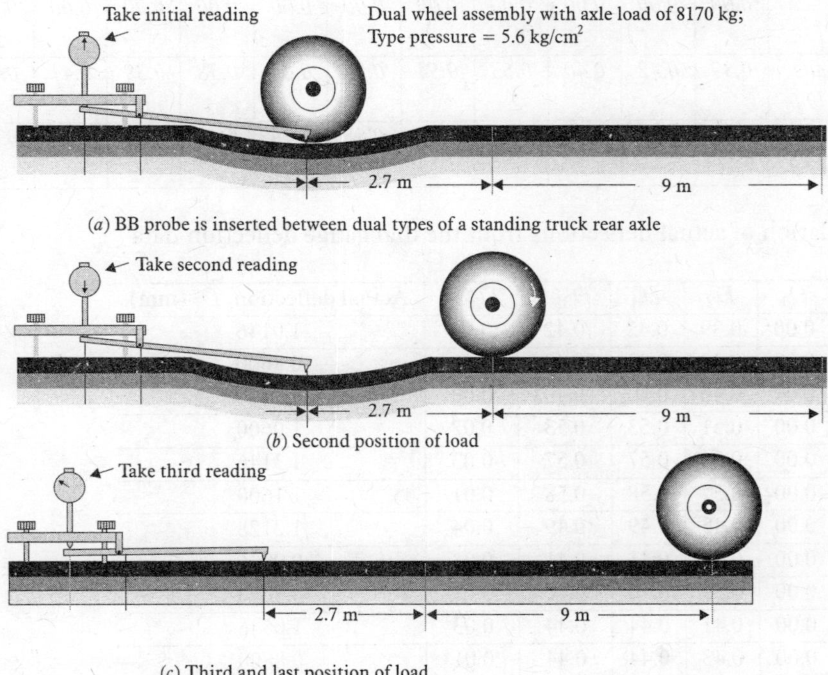

Figure 9.5 *Measurement of pavement surface rebound deflection using Benkelman beam*

9.4.5 Calculation of Deflection Values

The recorded deflections at different positions of load, viz. initial (D_1), intermediate (D_2) and final (D_3) deflections, are used to calculate actual pavement deflections and the standard procedure of IRC:37-1997 is presented in Figure 9.6.

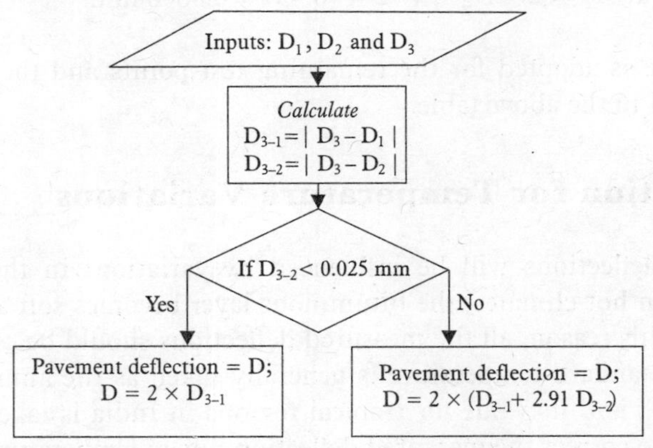

Figure 9.6 *Procedure for calculating the pavement deflection from the BB deflection data*

Q: *Determine the actual deflections from the dial gauge readings (mm) of the Benkelman beam.*

Sl. No.	*1*	*2*	*3*	*4*	*5*	*6*	*7*	*8*	*9*	*10*	*11*	*12*
Initial reading, D_1	*0.00*	*0.00*	*0.00*	*0.00*	*0.00*	*0.00*	*0.00*	*0.00*	*0.00*	*0.00*	*0.00*	*0.00*
Intermediate reading, D_2	*0.39*	*0.42*	*0.40*	*0.53*	*0.54*	*0.57*	*0.45*	*0.38*	*0.39*	*0.41*	*0.43*	*0.48*
Final reading, D_3	*0.42*	*0.43*	*0.40*	*0.43*	*0.57*	*0.58*	*0.49*	*0.41*	*0.40*	*0.44*	*0.44*	*0.51*

A: Calculation of actual deflections from the dial gauge deflection data

Sl.No.	D_1	D_2	D_3	D_{3-1}	D_{3-2}	Actual deflection, D_i (mm)
1	0.00	0.39	0.42	0.42	0.03	1.0146
2	0.00	0.42	0.43	0.43	0.01	0.8600
3	0.00	0.40	0.40	0.40	0.00	0.8000
4	0.00	0.51	0.53	0.53	0.02	1.0600
5	0.00	0.54	0.57	0.57	0.03	1.3146
6	0.00	0.57	0.58	0.58	0.01	1.1600
7	0.00	0.45	0.49	0.49	0.04	1.2128
8	0.00	0.38	0.41	0.41	0.03	0.9946
9	0.00	0.39	0.40	0.40	0.01	0.8000
10	0.00	0.41	0.44	0.44	0.03	1.0546
11	0.00	0.43	0.44	0.44	0.01	0.8800
12	0.00	0.48	0.51	0.51	0.03	1.1946

Using Figure 9.5, actual deflection values are calculated as follows:

For test point 1: $D_{3-2} > 0.025$ mm;
The actual deflection, $D_1 = 2 \times (D_{3-1} + 2.91\ D_{3-2}) = 2 \times (0.42 + 2.91 \times 0.03) = 1.0146$ mm.

For test point 2: $D_{3-2} < 0.025$ mm;
The actual deflection, $D_2 = 2 \times D_{3-1} = 2 \times (0.43) = 0.8600$ mm.

A similar procedure is adopted for the remaining test points and the actual BB deflection values are presented in the above table.

9.4.6 Correction for Temperature Variations

Pavement surface deflections will be influenced by variations in the temperature of the bituminous layer. In hot climates, the bituminous layer becomes soft and deflects more and vice versa. Due to this reason, all the measured deflections should be corrected to a standard temperature. The standard temperature is generally taken as the annual average pavement temperature (AAPT) and its value for tropical regions in India is taken as 35 °C. Equation (6.11) may be used to correct the measured deflection due to temperature variation.

It may be assumed that the relationship between temperature and deflection is linear when the pavement temperature is between 30 to 37 °C. BB testing should be avoided when the climate is very hot like the day time in summer. It is recommended that the tests be conducted in the early morning or evening.

In cold climes and areas of altitude higher than 1000 m above MSL, location-based deflection–performance relationship should be used where the average day temperature is below 20 °C for more than four months in a year.

9.4.7 Correction for Seasonal Variations

The measured deflections are sensitive to the magnitude of strength of the sub-grade. During post-monsoon season, the sub-grade becomes soft (or weak) due to accumulation of moisture in the sub-grade soil. This is the reason, the state (or strength) of the sub-grade immediately after the monsoon season is considered as most critical. It is recommended that the BB testing be conducted during this period to evaluate the weakest condition of the pavement structure.

In case the deflections are measured during dry months, they should be corrected using the following relationship.

$$\text{Corrected deflection} = D_{\text{dry}} \times \text{SCF} \tag{9.1}$$

where, D_{dry} = deflection measured during dry season

Seasonal correction factor (SCF):

$$\text{SCF} = \frac{\text{Maximum deflection measured during the post–monsoon season}}{\text{Minimum deflection measured during the dry season}} \tag{9.2}$$

Factors affecting the value of the seasonal correction factor (SCF) are given below (Jain et al. 1990).

- Sub-grade soil type
- Field moisture of the sub-grade soil
- Plasticity index (PI) of the sub-grade soil
- Annual average rainfall intensity of the test location
- Thickness of the bituminous layer
- Intensity of commercial vehicle traffic

Seasonal correction factors may be taken from the seven charts in IRC:81-1997, using input parameters like sub-grade soil type, PI and annual rainfall data. A typical chart used to obtain the seasonal correction factor is presented in Figure 9.7.

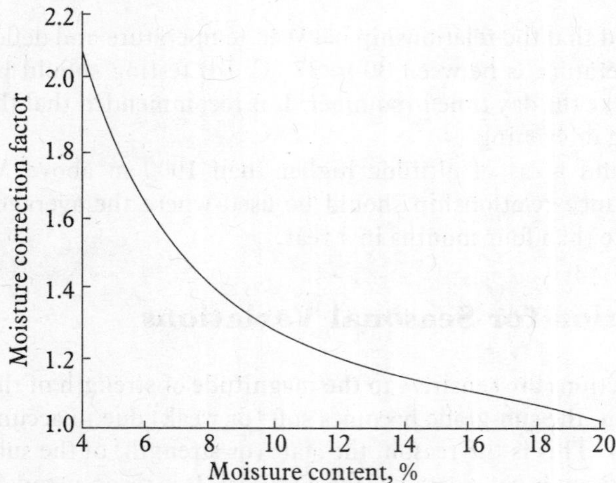

Figure 9.7 *Seasonal correction factor for clayey sub-grade with high plasticity (PI>15) for low rainfall areas (annual rainfall ≤ 1300 mm) (From IRC: 81-1997)*

9.4.8 Traffic Considerations

Design traffic volume in terms of *million standard axles* (msa) should be calculated similar to that determined for the design of flexible pavements. Equation (6.2) can be used. The design period for major highways should be more than 10 years. For other roads, it should be at least 5 years.

9.4.9 Delineation of Homogenous Sub-sections of the Road Stretch

In order to design overlay thickness, as the first step, the BB surveyed length of the road is to be divided into a suitable number of homogeneous sub-sections within which the deflections are statistically similar but different from the adjacent sub-sections. There are many methods to divide the road into homogeneous sub-sections (Ullidz and Peattie 1982; AASHTO 1993). A few widely practiced methods are given below.

AASHTO method In the AASHTO method, the BB deflections are cumulatively added and plotted along the road chainage (on the x-axis). The plotted data points are serially connected with a line and a best fit straight line is drawn considering all the data points. The first homogeneous sub-section is marked from the starting station to where the curve of the data points changes position from one side of the best fit straight line to the other. The remaining homogenous sub-sections can be similarly marked with respect to the position of the curve as and when it crosses the best fit straight line. Such sub-sections are separately considered for design of overlay thickness.

Cu-sum method The sum of the cumulative deviations (Q_i) from the mean value (D_m) of a series of BB deflections are plotted along the road chainage. All the data points are serially connected and a curve will be formed. Several constant gradient lines (or sloped lines) are drawn on the curve and the horizontal distance between each of the gradient lines is treated as a homogenous sub-section. Changes in the slope of the line indicate non-homogeneity of the data points (Ullidz and Peattie 1982). This method is widely known as the *cu-sum method* and is extensively used for delineation of road sections tested by falling weight deflectometers (FWD, explained in Section 9.6). The cu-sum values (Q_i) can be determined as

$$Q_1 = D_m - D_1 \tag{9.3a}$$

$$Q_2 = D_m - D_2 + Q_1 \tag{9.3b}$$

$$Q_i = D_m - D_i + Q_{i-1} \tag{9.3c}$$

$$\textit{Check: } Q_n = D_m - D_n + Q_{n-1} = \text{Zero} \tag{9.3d}$$

where,
Q_i = Cu-sum value at test point i
D_m = Mean value of total deflections
n = Total number of deflections measured in a section of road
Q_n = Last cu-sum value of a section of the road

Field engineer's thumb rule The value of the coefficient of variation (CoV) of deflection data is compared with an index value. For example, when a sub-section has CoV less than 20%, it is termed as a good homogeneous sub-section and when the CoV value exceeds 40%, it is termed as a non-homogeneous sub-section. CoV is evaluated using the following relationship.

$$\text{CoV} = \frac{\text{Standard deviation of the deflections } (s)}{\text{Mean deflection value } (D_m)} \times 100 \tag{9.4}$$

Using the student T-test Finalisation of the sub-sections should be made with additional pavement data such as details of the site condition, CBR or plate load test (PLT) values, surface distress severity and existing thickness details of the pavement. Each sub-section should be statistically tested by determining the statistical significance with the help of the student T-test.

The adjacent sub-sections are then tested and it is verified whether the sub-sections should be treated as different or whether they can be clubbed together. To carry out the student T-test, the following widely used formulae are useful.

$$S_d = \sqrt{\frac{(s_1)^2}{(n_1 - 1)} + \frac{(s_2)^2}{(n_2 - 1)}} \tag{9.5}$$

$$t_{\text{cal}} = \frac{|D_{m1} - D_{m2}|}{S_d} \tag{9.6}$$

where,

S_d	=	Variance of the difference between the means of the two sub-sections
s_1	=	Value of standard deviation of the deflections measured in sub-section 1
s_2	=	Value of standard deviation of the deflections measured in sub-section 2
n_1 and n_2	=	Number of deflection test stations in sub-section 1 and 2 respectively
D_{m1} and D_{m2}	=	Means of deflection measured in sub-section 1 and 2 respectively
t_{cal}	=	Parameter of calculated student T-test value

The t_{cal} value should be compared with the standard value of the student T-test (T_{stand}). The T_{stand} values are determined based on the degree of probability (P). Table 9.1 lists T_{stand} values when the P is assumed to be 0.05 ford a given degree of freedom (DoF).

Table 9.1 *A few values of the* T_{stand} *values*

DoF*	20	21	22	23	24	26	27	29	30	40	60	120	∞
P(0.05)	2.09	2.08	2.07	2.07	2.06	2.06	2.05	2.05	2.04	2.02	2.00	1.98	1.96

* DoF = $(n_1 + n_2 - 2)$

The following procedure may be adopted for checking statistical significance of adjacent sub-sections.

1. When $t_{cal} \leq T_{stand}$, the two means considered are not statistically significant. The deflection data from the two sub-sections are *not different* and the two sub-sections should be clubbed together and treated as one sub-section or section.
2. When $t_{cal} > T_{stand}$, the two means considered are statistically significant. The deflection data from the two sub-sections are *different* and the sub-sections should be treated as different sub-sections for overlay design.

The above methods and the surface distress information are used to delineate a road section into several homogeneous sub-sections for each of which overlay design is carried out separately subject to constructional practicality such as minimum length of sub-section. According to Indian practice, the minimum length of a sub-section is considered to be 1000 m (IRC: 81-1997).

Q: *For design of overlay thickness, Benkelman beam tests were conducted on a flexible pavement. The following 40 BB test stations were placed uniformly at given intervals. Determine homogeneous sub-sections with respect to the serially given test stations using the (i) AASHTO method and the (ii) cu-sum method.*

Test station	*Benkelman beam deflection (mm)*	*Test station*	*Benkelman beam deflection (mm)*	*Test station*	*Benkelman beam deflection (mm)*	*Test station*	*Benkelman beam deflection (mm)*
1	*1.002*	*11*	*0.950*	*21*	*0.777*	*31*	*1.399*
2	*0.915*	*12*	*0.812*	*22*	*0.950*	*32*	*1.364*
3	*0.881*	*13*	*1.123*	*23*	*1.105*	*33*	*1.520*
4	*1.002*	*14*	*0.933*	*24*	*1.192*	*34*	*1.589*
5	*0.984*	*15*	*1.036*	*25*	*1.226*	*35*	*1.520*
6	*0.967*	*16*	*1.192*	*26*	*1.537*	*36*	*1.520*
7	*1.105*	*17*	*0.950*	*27*	*1.347*	*37*	*1.468*
8	*1.123*	*18*	*0.933*	*28*	*1.123*	*38*	*1.589*
9	*1.036*	*19*	*1.174*	*29*	*1.244*	*39*	*1.485*
10	*1.002*	*20*	*0.984*	*30*	*1.295*	*40*	*1.468*

A: (i) *According to the AASHTO method*

Cumulative values of the measured Benkelman beam deflections (BBD) are calculated and given as column 3 of Table 9.2. A curve is plotted using these values and a best fit straight line drawn. Three homogeneous sub-sections (A, B and C) are selected based on the position of the curve along the best fit line (Figure 9.8). The identified test points in each sub-section are given in column 6 of Table 9.2.

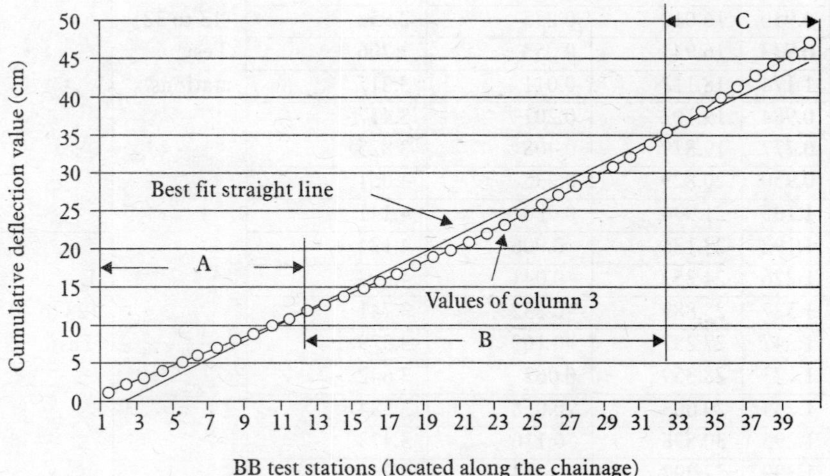

Figure 9.8 *Delineation of the survey section into homogeneous sub-sections based on the AASHTO method*

Table 9.2 *Example problem*

Test station	BBD (mm) D_i	Cumulative values	Deviations from the mean $= D_m - D_i$	Cumulative sum of deviatons (Q_i)	Homogenous sub-section by (6) AASHTO method	Cu-sum method
(1)	(2)	(3)	(4)	(5)		
1	1.002	1.002	0.183	0.183		
2	0.915	1.917	0.270	0.453		
3	0.881	2.798	0.304	0.758	A	
4	1.002	3.800	0.183	0.941	(1 to 12)	
5	0.984	4.784	0.201	1.142	Test	
6	0.967	5.751	0.218	1.360	stations	
7	1.105	6.857	0.080	1.440		
8	1.123	7.979	0.063	1.503		
9	1.036	9.016	0.149	1.651		D
10	0.950	9.965	0.235	1.887		(1 to 22)
11	0.812	10.777	0.373	2.260		Test
12	1.123	11.900	0.063	2.323		stations
13	0.933	12.832	0.253	2.575		
14	1.036	13.869	0.149	2.724		
15	1.192	15.060	–0.006	2.718	B	
16	0.950	16.010	0.235	2.953	(13 to 32)	
17	0.933	16.943	0.253	3.206	Test	
18	1.174	18.117	0.011	3.217	stations	
19	0.984	19.102	0.201	3.417		
20	0.777	19.879	0.408	3.825		
21	0.950	20.829	0.235	4.061		
22	1.105	21.934	0.080	4.141		
23	1.192	23.126	–0.006	4.134		
24	1.226	24.352	–0.041	4.093		E
25	1.537	25.889	–0.352	3.741		(23 to 40)
26	1.347	27.237	–0.162	3.579		Test
27	1.123	28.359	0.063	3.642		
28	1.244	29.603	–0.058	3.584		
29	1.295	30.898	–0.110	3.473		
30	1.399	32.297	–0.214	3.260		
31	1.364	33.661	–0.179	3.080		
32	1.520	35.181	–0.335	2.746		
33	1.589	36.770	–0.404	2.342		
34	1.520	38.290	–0.335	2.007		
35	1.520	39.810	–0.335	1.673	C	
36	1.468	41.278	–0.283	1.390	(33 to 40)	
37	1.589	42.867	–0.404	0.986	Test	
38	1.485	44.352	–0.300	0.686	stations	
39	1.468	45.820	–0.283	0.403		
40	1.589	47.409	–0.404	Q_n=0.000		

(ii) According to the cu-sum method

Deflections mean value (D_m) = 47.409/40 = 1.185225 mm

The cu-sum (Q_i) values are calculated using equation (9.3c) and given in column 5 of Table 9.2. A few example calculations for different test stations are given below.

For test station 1:
From equation (9.3a), $Q_1 = D_m - D_1 = 1.185225 - 1.002 = 0.183$ mm

For test station 2:
From equation (9.3b), $Q_2 = D_m - D_2 + Q_1 = 1.185225 - 0.915 + 0.183 = 0.453225$ mm

For test station 3:

$$Q_3 = D_m - D_3 + Q_2 = 1.185225 - 0.881 + 0.453225 = 0.75745 \approx 0.758 \text{ mm}$$

Similarly, the remaining Q_i values are calculated and a curve is plotted (Figure 9.9). Approximately, two different gradients or slopes of the curve may be identified and two homogenous sub-sections (D and E) are demarcated. Details of the test points belonging to each sub-section are given in column 6 of Table 9.2.

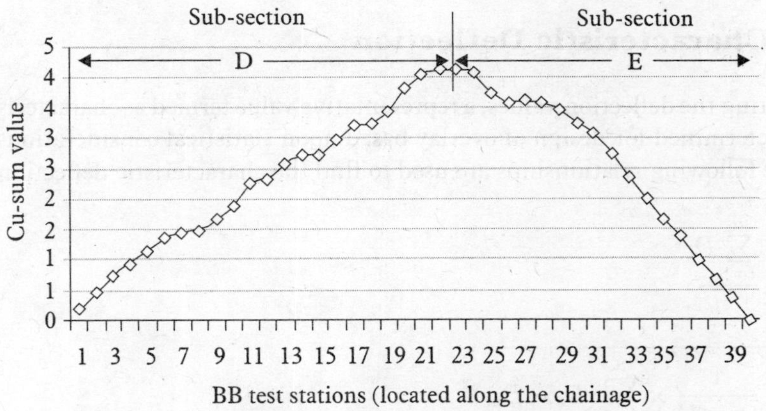

Figure 9.9 *Delineation of the survey section into homogeneous sub-sections based on the cu-sum method*

DISCUSSION: Delineation of the BB survey section by the two methods have given different results. In such a case, statistical significance of the sub-sections should be evaluated by the student T-test method. However, the final number of sub-sections are not decided based upon the results of the above methods only but also by using other data related to minimum length of the sub-sections, pavement surface distress data, existing pavement layers thickness in each sub-section and site conditions.

Q: *Evaluate the statistical significance of the homogeneous sub-section D and E determined above by the cu-sum method.*

A: The following input data is taken from Table 9.2.

Sub-section D test stations: 1 to 22; $n_D = 22$; $D_{mD} = 0.997$ mm; $s_D = 0.215932$ mm
Sub-section E test stations: 23 to 40; $n_E = 18$, $D_{mE} = 1.415$ mm; $s_E = 0.271209$ mm

Calculations for student T-test:

From equation (9.5) and (9.6), we get,

$$S_d = \sqrt{\frac{(s_D)^2}{(n_D - 1)} + \frac{(s_E)^2}{(n_E - 1)}} = \sqrt{\frac{(0.215932)^2}{(22 - 1)} + \frac{(0.271209)^2}{(18 - 1)}} = 0.08091$$

$$t_{\text{cal}} = \frac{|D_{mD} - D_{mE}|}{S_d} = \frac{|0.997 - 1.415|}{0.08091} = \frac{0.418}{0.08091} = 5.16$$

$$\text{DoF} = 22 + 18 - 2 = 38;\ T_{\text{stand}} \approx 2.02.$$

It is noted that $t_{\text{cal}} > T_{\text{stand}}$.

Hence, the results are significantly different for the homogeneous sub-sections D and E. Therefore, the sub-sections D and E should be treated separately for design of overlay thickness. However, for finalisation of the above sub-sections, surface distress data and other relevant data should be duly considered.

9.4.10 Characteristic Deflection

After correcting the deflection values, a representative value termed as characteristic deflection should be determined for design of overlay based upon statistical considerations. In the IRC: 81-1997, the following relationships are used to find the characteristic deflection.

$$D_m = \frac{\sum_{i=1}^{n} D_i}{n} \tag{9.7}$$

$$s = \sqrt{\frac{1}{(n-1)} \times \sum_{i=1}^{n} (D_i - D_m)^2} \tag{9.8}$$

For major highways like NH and SH:

$$D_c = D_m + 2s \tag{9.9a}$$

For all other roads:

$$D_c = D_m + s \tag{9.9b}$$

where,
- D_i = Individual deflections corrected for temperature and seasonal variations
- n = Number of deflections measured in a test section
- D_m = Mean value of the individual deflections
- s = Standard deviation of the deflections
- D_c = Characteristic deflection

9.4.11 Design of Overlay

Overlay thickness of bituminous macadam (BM) can be obtained from the design curves of IRC: 81-1997 (Figure 9.10). Input values required are characteristic deflection (D_c) and design traffic (msa) values.

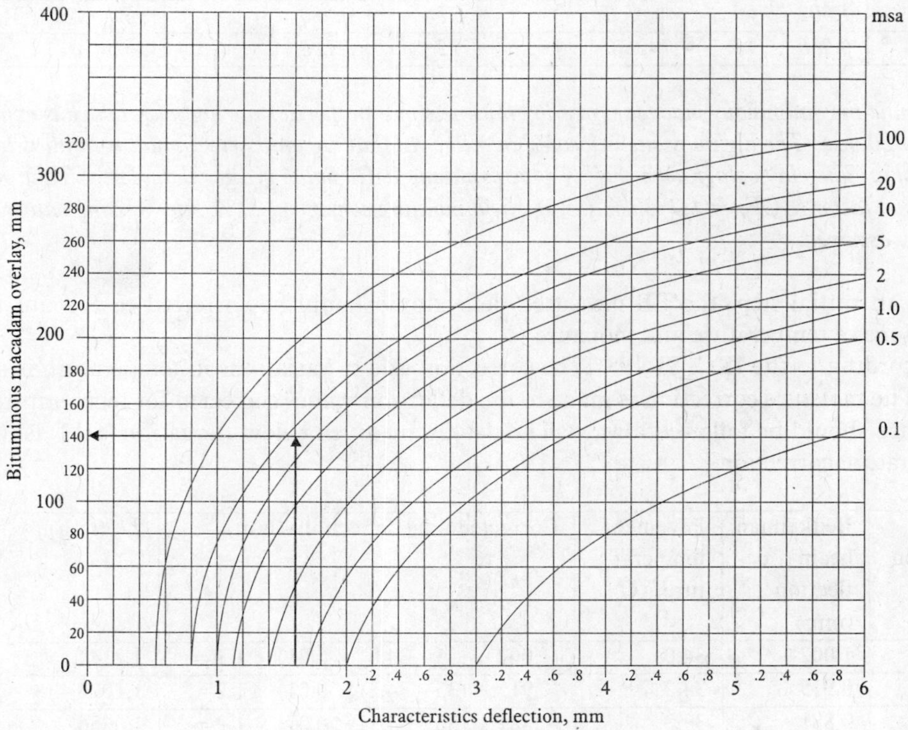

Figure 9.10 *Flexible pavement overlay thickness design curves (From IRC: 81-1997)*

Q: *The following are BB deflections and the bituminous pavement temperatures measured at every test station located at uniform intervals of 50 m. The BB test was conducted using a standard truck with a rear axle weighing 8170 kg having an assembly of dual tyres inflated to a pressure of 5.6 kg/cm²*.

Test station	*Benkelman beam deflection (mm)*	*Pavement temperature (°C)*	*Test station*	*Benkelman beam deflection (mm)*	*Pavement temperature (°C)*
1	*1.002*	*34.0*	*12*	*0.812*	*35.5*
2	*0.915*	*34.2*	*13*	*1.123*	*35.5*
3	*0.881*	*34.3*	*14*	*0.933*	*36.0*
4	*1.002*	*34.6*	*15*	*1.036*	*36.0*
5	*0.984*	*34.6*	*16*	*1.192*	*36.2*
6	*0.967*	*34.9*	*17*	*0.950*	*36.3*

continues . . .

continued

Test station	*Benkelman beam deflection (mm)*	*Pavement temperature (°C)*	*Test station*	*Benkelman beam deflection (mm)*	*Pavement temperature (°C)*
7	*1.105*	*34.9*	*18*	*0.933*	*36.3*
8	*1.123*	*35.0*	*19*	*1.174*	*36.3*
9	*1.036*	*35.0*	*20*	*0.984*	*36.4*
10	*1.002*	*35.0*	*21*	*0.950*	*36.4*
11	*0.950*	*35.0*	*22*	*1.105*	*36.5*

Determine the bituminous macadam overlay thickness of a proposed state highway which is expected to cater to 20 msa. The highway site is located in a low rainfall region where annual rainfall is less than 1300 mm. The clay sub-grade is highly plastic having a PI value greater than 15%. Take seasonal correction factor (SCF) = 1.2 when average field moisture content = 11%. Any missing values may be suitably assumed.

A: As an initial step, the BB measured deflections should be corrected to account for the variations in temperature and moisture.

According to the IRC: 81-1997, the correction due to variations in temperature is applied first. The moisture correction is made to the deflection values corrected for temperature. This sequence should be followed always. The details are given below. Equation (6.11) is used for temperature correction.

Test station	Benkelman beam deflection (mm)	Pavement temperature (°C)	Corrected final deflections (mm)	D_i (mm)
1	1.002	34.0	(1.002 + (35 – 34.0) × 0.01) × 1.2 =	1.2144
2	0.915	34.2	(0.915 + (35 – 34.2) × 0.01) × 1.2=	1.1076
3	0.881	34.3	(0.881 + (35 – 34.3) × 0.01) × 1.2 =	1.0656
4	1.002	34.6	(1.002 + (35 – 34.6) × 0.01) × 1.2 =	1.2072
5	0.984	34.6	(0.984 + (35 – 34.6) × 0.01) × 1.2 =	1.1856
6	0.967	34.9	(0.967 + (35 – 34.9) × 0.01) × 1.2 =	1.1616
7	1.105	34.9	(1.105 + (35 – 34.9) × 0.01) × 1.2 =	1.3272
8	1.123	35.0	(1.123 + (35 – 35.0) × 0.01) × 1.2 =	1.3476
9	1.036	35.0	(1.036 + (35 – 35.0) × 0.01) × 1.2 =	1.2432
10	1.002	35.0	(1.002 + (35 – 35.0) × 0.01) × 1.2 =	1.2024
11	0.950	35.0	(0.950 + (35 – 35.0) × 0.01) × 1.2 =	1.1400
12	0.812	35.5	(0.812 + (35 – 35.5) × 0.01) × 1.2 =	0.9684
13	1.123	35.5	(1.123 + (35 – 35.5) × 0.01) × 1.2 =	1.3416
14	0.933	36.0	(0.933 + (35 – 36.0) × 0.01) × 1.2 =	1.1076
15	1.036	36.0	(1.036 + (35 – 36.0) × 0.01) × 1.2 =	1.2312

continues . . .

continued

Test station	Benkelman beam deflection (mm)	Pavement temperature (°C)	Corrected final deflections (mm)	D_i (mm)
16	1.192	36.2	(1.192 + (35 – 36.2) × 0.01) × 1.2 =	1.4160
17	0.950	36.3	(0.950 + (35 – 36.3) × 0.01) × 1.2 =	1.1244
18	0.933	36.3	(0.933 + (35 – 36.3) × 0.01) × 1.2 =	1.1040
19	1.174	36.3	(1.174 + (35 – 36.3) × 0.01) × 1.2 =	1.3932
20	0.984	36.4	(0.984 + (35 – 36.4) × 0.01) × 1.2 =	1.1640
21	0.950	36.4	(0.950 + (35 – 36.4) × 0.01) × 1.2 =	1.1232
22	1.105	36.5	(1.105 + (35 – 36.5) × 0.01) × 1.2 =	1.3080

From equation (9.2), the mean deflection value, $D_m = 26.484/22 = 1.2038$ mm
From equation (9.3), the value of standard deviation, $s = 0.11394$ mm

As the proposed road is a state highway, the characteristic deflection (D_c) value is calculated from equation (9.4a).

$D_c = 1.2038 + 2 \times 0.11394 = 1.43168$ mm

From Figure 9.10, for a design traffic value of 20 msa and characteristic deflection value of 1.43168 mm, the required thickness of the bituminous macadam overlay is 140 mm.

Equivalent thickness of DBM or BC = 0.7 × 140 = 98 mm when 10 mm thickness of bituminous macadam is assumed equal to 7 mm thickness of DBM or BC.

9.4.12 Limitations of the BB Method

The concept of measuring the rebound pavement surface deflection using a Benkelman beam is associated with the following drawbacks and limitations.

(a) The load applied in the BB method is either static or moving at creep speed, which is not representative of the loads applied on highways by fast moving truck traffic. The low speed of operation of this tool also reduces the feasibility of the method for routine evaluation.

(b) The BB testing requires more manual labour than other NDT equipment.

(c) In this approach, only the maximum surface deflection ($D_{\max}$) of the pavement is measured (Figure 9.11). The profile of the entire deflection bowl is not measured nor is it considered in the design of the overlay thickness according to IRC:81-1997. Two pavements with the same maximum deflection ($D_{\max}$) having different deflection profiles indicate that the strain in asphalt pavement differs with the stiffness of individual layers of the pavement. Therefore, measurement of the entire deflection profile is important to determine the strength properties of individual layers.

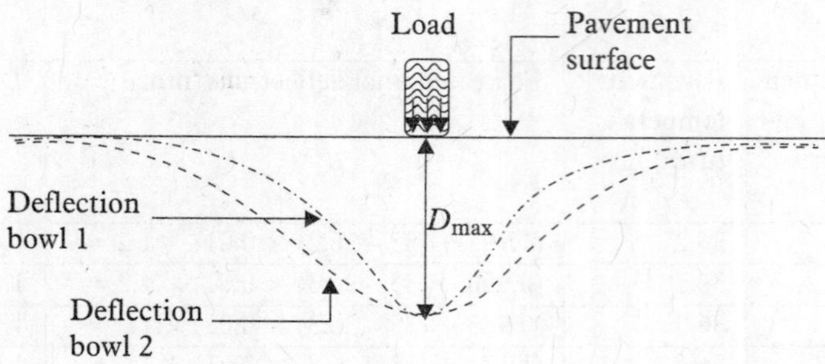

Figure 9.11 *Pavements with same maximum deflection but different deflection profiles*

(d) When the deflection bowl area is wide, the front leg of the BB may fall in the region of deflected bowl (Figure 9.12). The movement of the beam support resting in the deflection bowl can result in erroneous deflection measurements.

(e) The entire deflection bowl may be measured using a mechanised system or a few Benkelman beams placed along the pavement deflection but this method requires more time and labour. The other drawbacks like static loading conditions and erroneous deflection measurement due to deflected front leg remain the same.

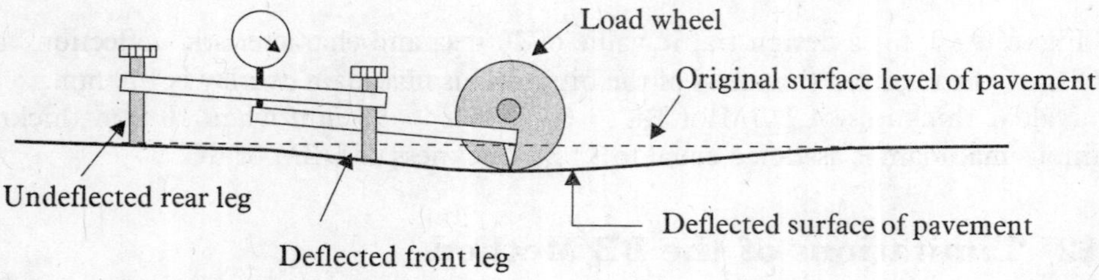

Figure 9.12 *Deflected front legs of BB*

To overcome the above deficiencies of the BB method, other NDT equipment were developed and widely used for structural evaluation of pavements.

9.5 Structural Evaluation by Steady-state Vibratory Loading

Any NDT device that produces a sinusoidal vibration in the pavement with a dynamic force generator is categorised under this group. The most widely known devices are *dynaflects* and various models of the *road rater* (Smith and Lytton 1985). In these devices, a static load is placed over the pavement surface and a steady-state sinusoidal vibration is induced in the pavement with the help of a pulsating dynamic force generator (Figure 9.13). A static weight of 1000 to 2100 lb (4.45 to 9.34 kN) is applied to the pavement through a pair of rigid steel wheels. The dynamic force generator uses a pair of unbalanced flywheels, which rotate in opposite directions at a speed of 8 cycles per second to produce a peak-to-peak force (high to low) equal to 1000 lb (4.45 kN). The surface-deflection is measured using five velocity transducers (geophones) which are placed at the centre of the load and at four radial distances (Figure 9.14). A dynaflect is a trailer-mounted device towed by any standard automobile.

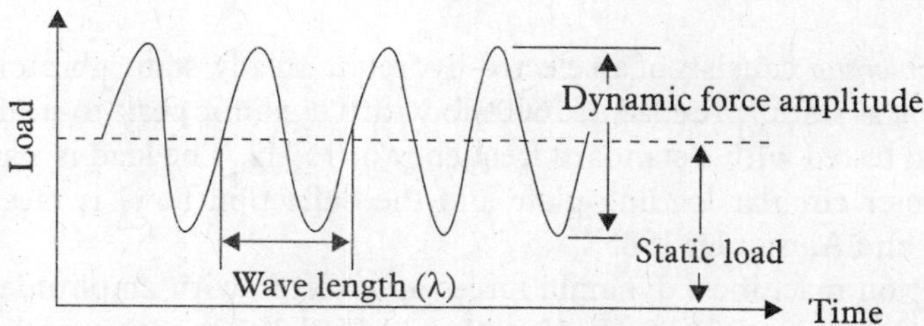

Figure 9.13 *Typical force curve due to steady-state vibratory loading*

Technical limitations of the device include the facts that the peak-to-peak loading is limited to 1000 lb (4.45 kN), the load cannot be varied, and it is difficult to determine the contact area (Smith and Lytton 1985; Tweneboah et al. 1988; Roesset and Shao 1985).

Road raters (RR) are commercially available in three *models as* 400 B, 2000, 2008 (Smith and Lytton 1985). These models vary primarily in magnitude of the load. The models are all trailer mounted. A static load is applied by the weight of the force actuator system and hydraulic pressure acts against the trailer. The deflections are measured using four velocity transducers (Figure 9.15). The technical limitations of this equipment include the facts that the load levels are limited, a heavy static pre-load is required and non-uniform loading configuration is needed.

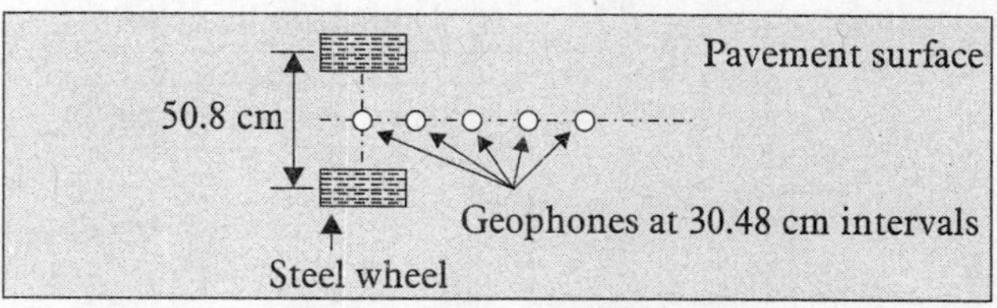

Figure 9.14 *Dynaflect with geophone positions*

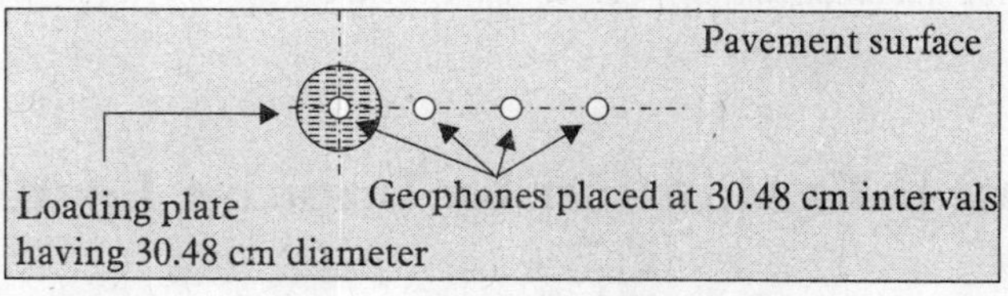

Figure 9.15 *Road rater (RR 2008 model) with geophone positions*

A few salient features of the RR 2008 model (Hoffman and Thompson 1982) are given below.

(a) It has an electronic vibrator capable of generating harmonic loads (peak-to-peak) up to 8000 lb (8 kips or 35.6 kN) at driving frequencies between 6 to 60 Hz.

(b) A pre-load of 5000 lb (5 kips or 22.25 kN) is applied through a plate of 30.48 cm diameter circular loading plate. In some cases, a pre-load of 5800 lb is applied through a plate of 45.72 cm diameter (Smith and Lytton 1985).

(c) Four geophones are used to measure the pavement surface deflection bowl.

A *WES 16-kip vibrator* consists of an electro-hydraulic steady-state vibratory loading system capable of applying a (static) pre-load of 16000 lb with a dynamic peak-to-peak load of 30000 lb at 5 to 100 Hz and tested with a standard frequency of 15 Hz. The load is transferred through a 45.72 cm diameter circular loading plate and the deflection bowl is measured using four geophones (Bush and Alexander 1985).

In other vibration machines, dynamic forces are exerted with amplitudes of up to 500 to 800 lb at frequency levels of 5–60 Hz (Joseph and Hall 1972). Structural properties of the pavement can be determined from observing surface deflections and the propagation of waves. But as frequency is increased beyond the natural frequency of the pavement system, the loads produced are less and the deflection is proportionately less.

Wave propagation technique (Nazarian and Stokoe 1984; Nazarian et al. 1983; Heisey et al. 1982) is another NDT method used for determining moduli and layer thicknesses of pavement systems. The propagation of surface (or Rayleigh) waves through a pavement system is monitored with the help of two receivers located on the pavement surface. The measured velocity versus wavelength data provides a dispersion curve which on inversion gives Young's modulus profiles along with the thicknesses of the layers. This method is also termed as the spectral analysis of surface waves (SASW) method (Figure 9.16).

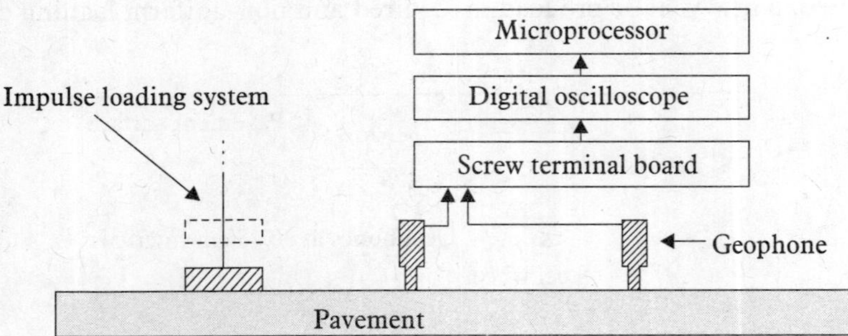

Figure 9.16 *Experimental arrangement for SASW test (elaborated based on Nazarian et al. 1983 and Heisey et al. 1982)*

9.6 Structural Evaluation by Impulse Loading

In this type of loading, a transient impulse force is applied on to the pavement surface and the deflected shape of the surface is measured. Thses equipment are capable of producing load pulses in the range of those applied by wheels of commercial vehicles. Different models of impulse loading equipment which are widely known as falling weight deflectometers (FWD) are available.

9.6.2 Working Principle of the Falling Weight Deflectometer (FWD)

The working principle of an FWD is shown in Figure 9.17 (a, b, c). A typical falling weight deflectometer has an arrangement to drop a pre-determined magnitude of mass over a buffered circular loading plate, which is placed on the surface of the pavement. It can transmit heavier loads on to surface of pavements than any other NDT deflection testing device. The loading range varies depending on the model. Variations in the applied load levels can be achieved by varying (i) the magnitude of the dropping mass and/ or (ii) the height of the drop. The load pulse approximates as a half-sine waveform with variable duration (Figure 9.18). Peak vertical surface deflections of the pavement are measured by velocity transducers, which are kept at different radial distances from the centre of the loading plate. Usually, about six to seven geophones are used to measure the surface deflections. They are normally arranged at a spacing of 300 mm. However, any other spacing may be adopted since there will be no significant effect of geophone configuration on back-calculated moduli values (Mork 1998).

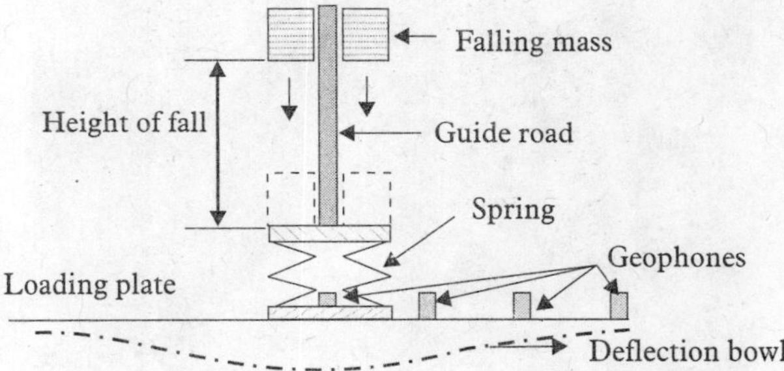

Figure 9.17 *(a) Working principle of a falling weight deflectometer*

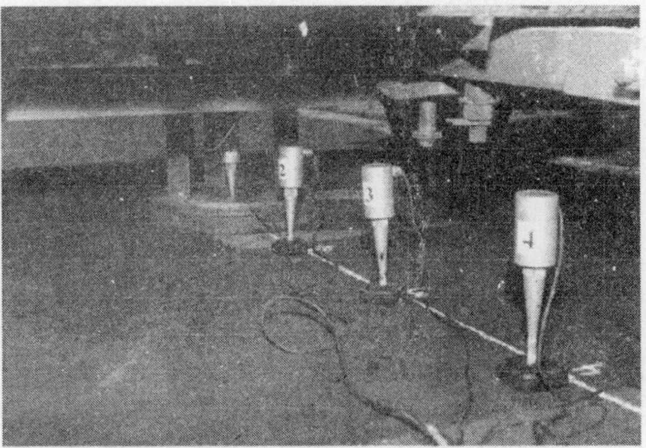

Figure 9.17 *(b) Position of loading plate and geophones during FWD test (Srinivasa 2001)*

Figure 9.17 *(c) A low-cost (IITKGP) FWD test in progress (Srinivasa 2001)*

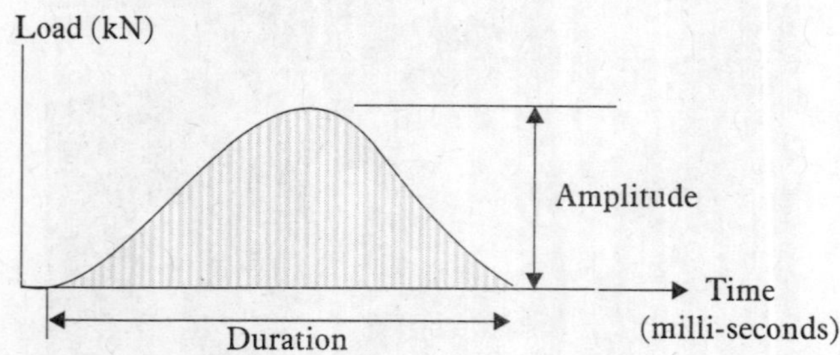

Figure 9.18 *Haversine load pulse*

Q: *Determine the duration of loading time when vehicle speed = 40 km/hr. Assume that the radius of contact area of a single wheel = 150 mm.*

A: Diameter of the contact area = 150 mm × 2 = 300 mm = 0.3 m
Velocity of the vehicle = 40 km/hr × 0.278 = 11.12 m/s

To pass over the 0.3 m distance, the loading duration $= 0.3/11.12 = 0.02698$ seconds
$= 0.0269 \times 1000 = 26.78$ milliseconds
$= 26.78$ ms

9.6.3 Working Principle of a Geophone

Velocity transducers used for measuring surface deflections of pavements are termed as geophones. A coil-magnet system is used for geophone construction (Nazarian and Bush III 1989). The geophone consists of a casing in which a known mass is attached to a coil and vertically suspended in a magnetic field.

Surface wave motion will be induced in the pavement crust when the load is dropped onto the pavement surface. The wave propagates through the pavement system and travels in different directions from the point of loading. The geophones mounted on the pavement surface will pick up the waves due to the relative motion between the coil and the magnet which creates a difference in the electro-magnetic flux in terms of voltage difference. The voltage difference is instantaneously recorded using a microprocessor (Figure 9.19(a)). The surface deflection value can be obtained by multiplying the geophone calibration factor with the value of voltage difference recorded. A typical output from different geophones is presented in Figure 9.19(b).

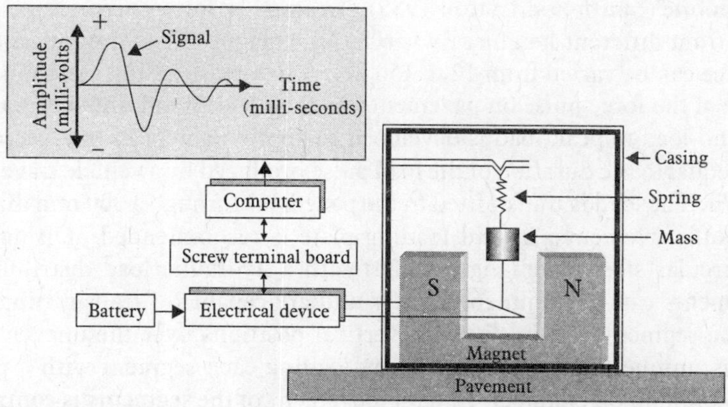

Figure 9.19(a) *Working principle of a geophone*

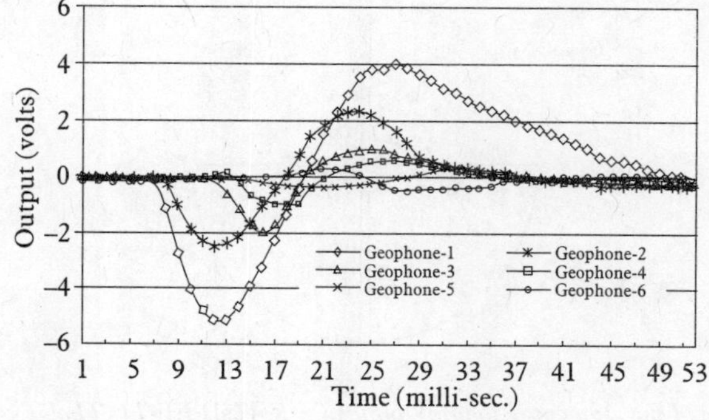

Figure 9.19(b) *Typical output signals from geophones kept at different radial locations (Srinivasa 2001)*

9.7 Models of Falling Weight Deflectometer

Salient features of a few FWD models are presented below.

Dynatest FWD The dynatest model 8000 is trailer-mounted and can be towed by a standard automobile. Impulse force is created by dropping weights from different heights. By varying the drop height and weight, a force in the range of 1500 to 27000 lb (7 to 120 kN) can be developed. The weights are raised hydraulically and released by an electronic signal system. They drop on a rubber buffer system which is different for each weight configuration to produce a load pulse of approximately half-sine waveform. The load is transmitted on to the surface of the pavement through a 300 mm diameter loading plate. It can measure up to 60 test points per hour. In this category, there are other FWD models available. Examples are given below.

- Dynatest 8000 trolley mounted deflectometer (TMD)
- Heavy weight deflectometer (HWD): 6500 to 54000 lb (30 to 240 kN)

Details of the above models of dynatests can be obtained from www.dynatest.com.

KUAB FWD The KUAB FWD is mounted in an encased trailer which can be towed by a standard automobile (Smith and Lytton 1985). An impulse force is created by dropping a set of two weights from different heights. By varying the magnitude of drop mass and its height, the impulse force can be varied from 12 to 150 kN. A two-mass falling system is used to create a smoother rise of the force pulse on pavements with both stiff and soft sub-grade supports. A rise time from no-load to peak-load is developed in approximately 28 microseconds, which is approximately equal to the duration of the load pulse produced by a vehicle travelling at a speed of about 70 km/h. The load is transmitted to the pavement through a 300 mm diameter loading plate. On smooth pavements, a solid loading-plate is recommended. On uneven surfaces, a segmented circular steel plate (Figure 9.20) with a hydraulic load distribution system is used. The segments can move independently and are capable of transmitting uniform load even though the segments are in different vertical positions over the uneven surface of the pavement. This unique feature is achieved by loading each segment with a plunger that is connected to a common oil chamber. Lateral movement of the segments is controlled by using specially designed spherical bearings in each plunger (Tholen et al. 1985).

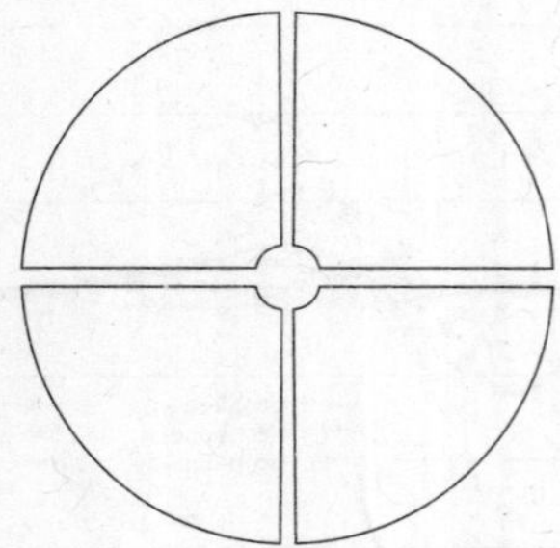

Figure 9.20 *Plan view of the segmented loading plate of a KAUB FWD (Tholen et al. 1985)*

The KUAB FWD is commercially available as KUAB 2m-FWD, where 2m indicates the double mass configuration. The KUAB 2m-FWD models may be classified into the following types based on their loading capability (www.erikuab.com).

- *The KUAB 50 model* Load range of 3,000 to 14,000 lbs force
- *The KUAB 150 model* Load range of 3,000 to 33,000 lbf
- *The largest KUAB 150 model* Load of 66,000 lbf
- *Model 600SP (under development)* A special structural loading device for testing bridges and piers. It can deliver a maximum load of 120,000 lbf.

Phoenix FWD Phoenix FWD is also a trailer-mounted equipment (Smith and Lytton 1985). The set-up and weight are mounted on a pivot so that they can be transported for long distances in the horizontal position. They can be placed upright for testing and travelling. A pre-determined magnitude of mass can be dropped from different heights to develop impact loads of 10 to 120 kN.

LOADMAN This is a portable falling weight deflectometer (PFWD) which was introduced initially by Livneh (1997) and Livneh et al. (1995). The structure of the instrument consists of an aluminum tube (130 mm diameter) containing a free dropping weight of 10 kg. A circular plate (132 or 200 mm diameter) placed at the bottom of the tube is used as the loading surface. The impact loading duration lasts about 10 ms and the device can measure a rebound surface deflection in the range of 0.2 to 5 mm (Siekmeier et al. 2000). The equipment is operated by placing its base on the surface of the pavement layer and then activating the electronic system which drops the weight through 800 mm inside the tube and records all relevant data. Analysis of the test results yields surface deflections and a mean modulus which is a measure of the elastic modulus of the pavement.

Rolling wheel deflectometer (RWD) The RWD can be used to collect deflection of data at a high travelling speed of 90 kmph and it can be operated within traffic streams. The primary output of the RWD is a deflection response that can be converted to a structural index value, SI (ERES 1999).

Another model, a low-cost trolley-mounted FWD was also fabricated at IIT Kharagpur, India (Srinivasa 2001, Srinivasa et al. 1999).

As with any other NDT equipment, the FWD has a few minor drawbacks. Hoffman and Thompson (1982) showed that (i) the deflection pulse generated by the FWD is narrower than that produced by a moving wheel and (ii) the ground accelerations generated by the moving wheel load are typically one-tenth of the FWD induced accelerations. As a result, the inertia of pavement mass affects the impulse load applied by FWD, which is negligible for the moving load. Despite these minor drawbacks, FWD is found to be the best NDT device available till date because of its (i) rapid testing capability, (ii) ability to simulate conditions of loading that is similar to traffic wheel loading and (iii) facility to measure a multi-point deflection basin. Hoffman and Thompson (1982) concluded that deflections under moving wheel loads and the FWD measured deflections are comparable to each other.

9.8 Structural Evaluation of Flexible Pavement Using FWD

Initially, the proposed FWD test points should be marked on the pavement surface along the wheel path at any given suitable interval (Figure 9.21(a) and (b)). The intervals between test points and their layout may be varied based on the requirement of maintenance work. The FWD tests are normally conducted:

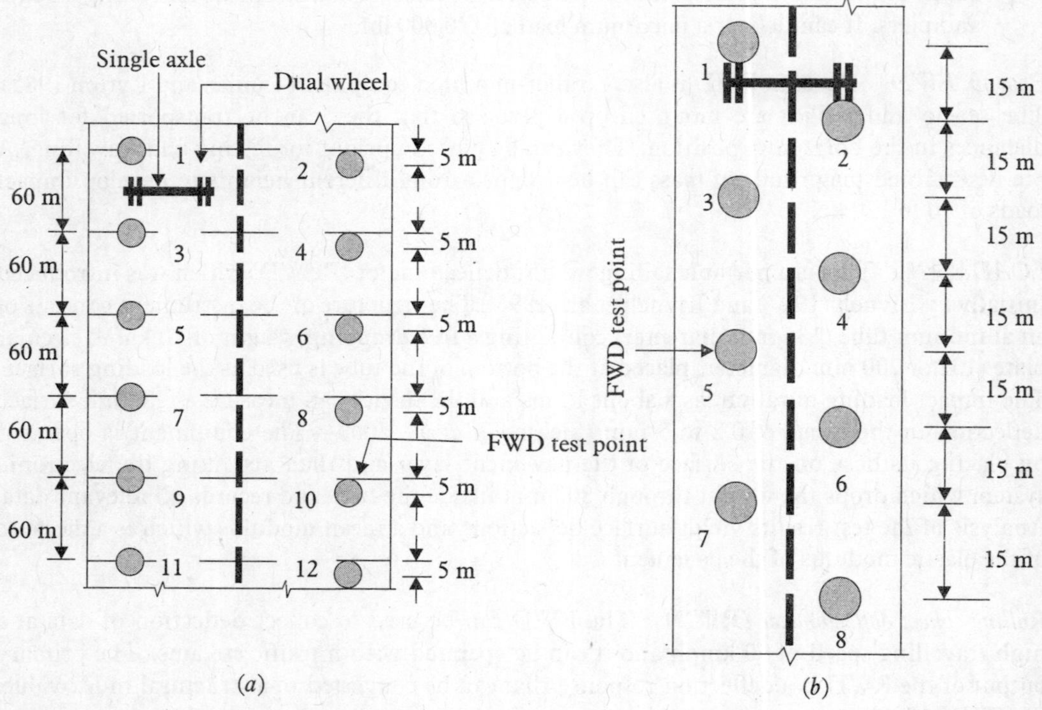

Figure 9.21 *(a) A typical view of FWD test points in a two-line road (b) A typical view of a single-line road with staggered points of FWD tests*

- before and after maintenance work such as overlay and
- in different seasons of a year, the post-monsoon season, especially, is considered as a critical period when the bottom layers are in saturated or moist conditions.

Pavement crust details are obtained by using any one of the following methods

- from the pavement constructional details
- by cutting small pits adjacent to a few test points
- by cutting cores at a few test points using a core cutter (Figure 9.22)
- by using NDT equipment such as ground penetrating radar (Figure 9.23)

Figure 9.22 *Core cutter* **Figure 9.23** *Ground penetrating radar test in progress*

The sub-grade moisture value should be obtained by collecting a sub-grade soil sample under the test point or by using nuclear devices. The temperature of the bituminous layer should be measured by using a thermometer or by using any suitable electronic device.

9.8.1 Deflection Bowl Shape Characteristics

Deflection bowl shape describes many performance features of a pavement and can be related to existing strength (or stiffness) of an individual and overall pavement strength (Stock and Yu 1984; Horak 1987; Van Deusen et al. 1997). As discussed in Section 9.4.11, individual layers stiffness decides the different shape characteristics of the deflection bowl.

To reduce the time required for back-calculation analysis, an appropriate range of pavement layer moduli values may be used as input to GA-based or other back-calculation programs. For such purposes, the following deflection bowl shape parameters (Figure 9.24) are useful. (Khosla and Ali 1989):

Maximum deflection (at $r = 0$ mm) $= D_1$ (9.10a)
Base damage index (BDI) $= D_2 - D_3$ or $D_3 - D_5$ (9.10b)
Surface curvature index (SCI) $= D_1 - D_2$ or $D_1 - D_3$ (9.10c)
Radius of curvature (R) $= r^2/[2D_r(D_1/D_{r-1})]$, $r = 600$ mm (9.10d)
Actual area (cm) $= 30[(D_1 + D_6)/2) + D_2 + D_3 + D_4 + D_5]$ (9.10e)
Normalised actual area (cm) $= (30/D_1) \times [(D_1 + D_6)/2) + D_2 + D_3 + D_4 + D_5]$ (9.10f)
Area (cm) $= (6/D_1) \times [D_1 + D_6 + 2(D_2 + D_3 + D_4 + D_5)]$ (9.10g)
Spreadability $= 100(1 + D_2 + D_3 + D_4 \ldots. + D_n)/(n \times D_1)$ (9.10h)
Area12 $=$ Area/$(150(D_1 + D_2))$ (9.10i)
Area56 $=$ Area/$(150(D_5 + D_6))$ (9.10j)

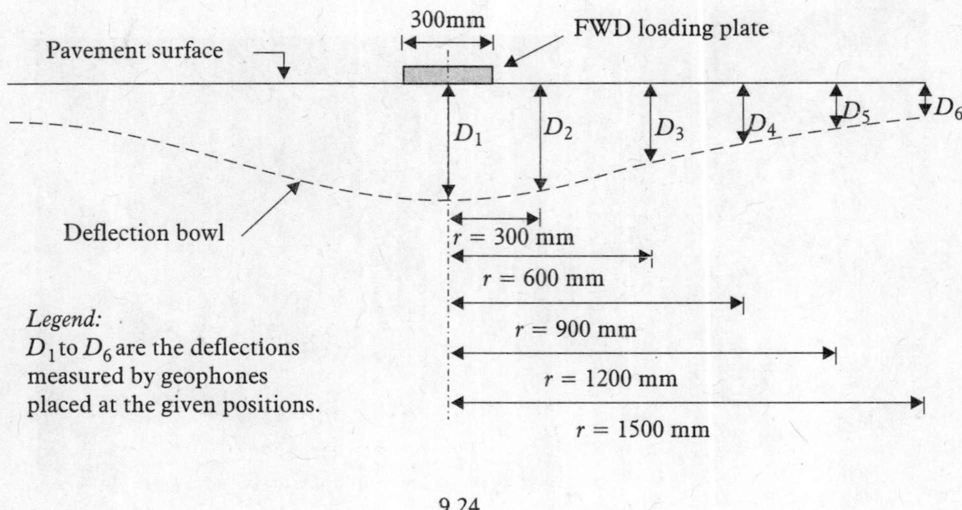

Figure 9.24 *Typical deflection bowl obtained by FWD testing*

The deflection bowl shape parameters are also used to delineate pavement stretches into several homogeneous sub-sections. For more types and details of applications of deflection bowl parameters, the readers are advised to refer to the relevant literature (Kim 2008).

Q: *FWD deflection bowls were measured at 77 test stations which were placed at intervals of 50 m from each other. The bowl shape parameter SCI300, that is, the difference between the geophone deflections measured at 0 and 300 mm radial distance from the centre of the loading plate (i.e., SCI300 = $D_1 - D_2$), was calculated for each deflection bowl and the total surveyed road length of 3.8 km is delineated into two homogeneous sub-sections by the cu-sum method. Salient details of the two homogeneous sub-sections are given below.*

Item values	Homogeneous sub-sections	
	A	B
No. of stations	$n_A = 55$	$n_B = 22$
Mean of SCI300 (mm)	$D_{mA} = 0.377$	$D_{mB} = 0.398$
Standard deviation of SCI300 (mm)	$s_A = 0.065$	$s_B = 0.083$
Length (m)	2700	1100

Evaluate the statistical significance of the above two homogeneous sub-sections. Assume that the site conditions and pavement layer thicknesses are uniform throughout the length of the FWD surveyed road section.

A: *Calculations for the student T-test:*

Let us first evaluate the statistical significance of sub-sections A and B:

From equation (9.5) and (9.6), we get,

$$S_d = \sqrt{\frac{(s_A)^2}{(n_A - 1)} + \frac{(s_B)^2}{(n_B - 1)}} = \sqrt{\frac{(0.065)^2}{(55 - 1)} + \frac{(0.083)^2}{(22 - 1)}} = 0.0201565$$

$$t_{\text{cal}} = \frac{|D_{mA} - D_{mB}|}{S_d} = \frac{|0.377 - 0.398|}{0.0201565} = \frac{0.021}{0.0201565} = 1.041$$

DoF = 55 + 22 − 2 = 75; for probability value = 0.05, $T_{\text{stand}} \approx 2.00$.

It is noted that $t_{\text{cal}} < T_{\text{stand}}$

Hence, the two means (D_{mA} and D_{mB}) are statistically insignificant. Therefore, the two sub-sections should be clubbed and designated as a single section having length 2700 + 1100 = 3800 m.

9.9 Back-calculations of Layer Moduli from FWD Test Data

The surface deflection bowls obtained by FWD tests are taken to estimate the effective moduli of pavement layers. This process is widely known as back-calculation of pavement layer moduli. Effective moduli are the values used as inputs to any theoretical model (FEM or elastic layered theory), which produce theoretical responses (in terms of deflections) that are similar to those measured in the field by FWD testing. A number of back-calculation methods are available in literature and they may be broadly classified as historical methods and microcomputer methods. Historical methods consider a number of simplifications (which are mostly rule based) for a pavement system. For more complex and realistic pavement systems, micro-computer methods are commonly used. Micro-computer methods usually employ an iterative process which starts with an initial set of "seed values" of material properties. The properties (in terms of moduli values) are determined in an iterative way until the values of computed deflection bowl match with the measured deflection bowl. There are different models available in literature in which various optimisation techniques are employed to minimise the errors between the measured and theoretical deflections.

9.9.1 Historical Methods

It is known from literature that the first back-calculation method was a closed form solution for a two-layer system developed by Scrivner et al. (1973). The equation was obtained by using the Burmister's layered theory for surface deflection obtained at a given radial distance. Poisson's ratio values of both layers were assumed as 0.5.

Swift (1972) developed a graphical method for determining the moduli of a two layer pavement system. It was shown that for the same deflection bowl, the deflections measured at given radial distances which are greater than the thickness of the surface layer can produce two different sets of modular ratio. In such cases, expert knowledge is essential to identify the correct solution. Swift (1972) also developed an empirical equation which has the ability to fit measured and calculated deflection bowls of two-layered pavements.

Yih Hou (1977) developed the first closed-form for multi-layer system solution. He suggested that as long as deflection basins are not measured very close to the load, there will be several correct sets of moduli that fit measured deflection basins as there are layers in the pavement. The set of moduli to which a search method converges will depend upon the seed values of the moduli used.

Odemark's (1949) equivalent-layer concept was also used in some back-calculation models to simplify the searching process of the pavement system and thereby facilitate the use of Boussinesq's theory to analyse the pavement. The back-calculation method developed by Ullidtz (1987) is one such case in which this concept was used. It was found that this procedure gives reasonable layer modulus values for pavements in which the layer stiffness decreases with depth. Lytton and Michalak (1979) used a more general form of Odemark's assumptions to convert a multi-layered pavement into a single layer placed over a rigid base.

9.9.2 Microcomputer Methods

With the advent of improved capacity of electronic computers, it is now possible to facilitate computations of deflections of any typical pavement system at various radial distances. Their comparison with measured deflections can be done at high speed. Different sets of layer moduli are used to calculate the values of deflection bowls and match the calculated deflections with measured deflections, within acceptable limits. Almost all microcomputer methods adopt a well-defined procedure which is iterative. A generalised flow chart for microcomputer methods is shown in Figure 9.25.

Salient features of the microcomputer methods are presented below:

Inputs Measured deflections with their corresponding radial distances, layer thicknesses, load and seed moduli.

Deflection calculation Theoretical deflections are calculated using elastic layered theory or finite element method.

Error check The types of error check values used in different back-calculation programs may be broadly classified as (i) sum of squared differences between the measured and calculated deflections, (ii) sum of the absolute differences between the measured and calculated deflections and (iii) squared sum of relative errors (the difference value is divided by the measured deflection before the ratio is squared and summed). If the error checks do not find convergence (i.e., acceptable levels of tolerance), a new search is initiated.

Range of moduli values In order to direct the searching process towards a set of moduli that are considered practical, numerous controls are to be programmed into the system to restrict the search away from unwanted or unreasonable values of the parameters. In most cases, the controls assume the type of pavement system that is to be analysed. For iterative elastic layer back-calculation programs, it is essential for seed value to converge into a definite solution within the pre-selected ranges. The boundary values are to be selected prudently because narrow limits/range may prevent the iteration process until it converges into a correct solution. Similarly, limits that are too broad may allow the program to converge into an incorrect solution (Hall and Mohseni 1991).

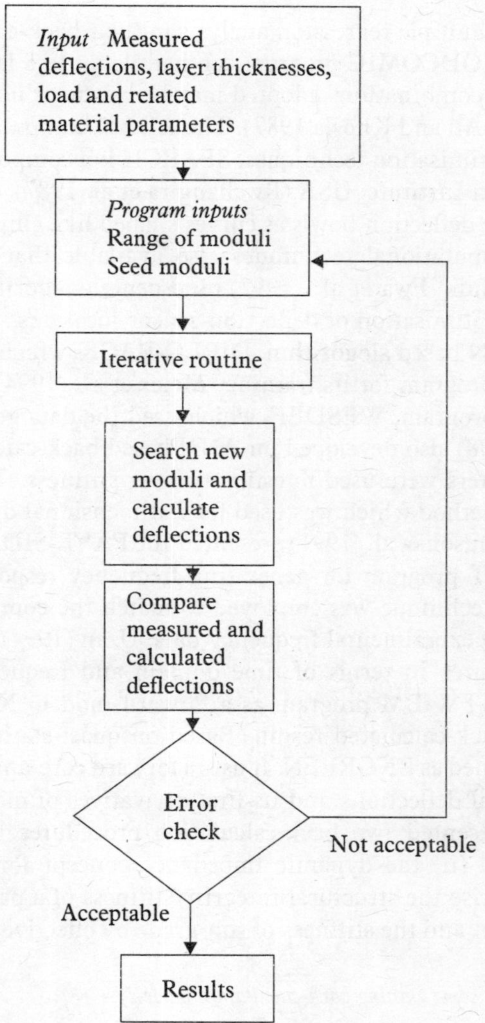

Figure 9.25 *Flow chart for general iterative microcomputer methods*

Search for new moduli There are several techniques available to select the new sets of moduli values. For a 4-layered pavement system, Kilareski and Anani (1982) proposed equations to select new values of moduli. The Hook–Jeeves pattern search algorithm was employed in the MODULUS program of back-calculation (Uzan et al. 1988). Harichandran et al. (1993) used the modified Newton algorithm to develop the MICHBACK program of back-calculation for flexible and rigid pavements. The DEF series programs, namely CHEVDEF, BISDEF and WESDEF developed by USACE (Ullidtz and Coetzee 1995; Bush III and Alexander 1985), employ the gradient search technique. In ELSEDEF series of back-calculation programs and in EVERCALC, CLEVERCALC (Harichandran et al 1993; Lenngren 1991) etc., a successive linear least square approach was used. Regression equations were also used in the LOADRATE back-calculation program (Harichandran et al. 1993). In the MODULUS, regression equations were utilised to identify the depth/location of the stiff layer (Mahoney et al. 1993). Marchionna et al. (1985) also used a multiple regression analysis in their back-calculation program. Using a similar concept, the MODCOMP2 program can handle up to 8 layers of pavement system. In other cases, the layer combinations adopted may be elastic or non-linear stress dependent (Rwebangira et al. 1987; Ali and Khosla 1987). The ADAM computer program (Hossain et al. 1994) uses non-linear optimisation techniques. SEARCH is a computer program developed by the Texas Transportation Institute, USA (Rwebangira et al. 1987), which uses pattern search techniques to best fit the deflection bowls as curves shaped like elliptic integral functions.

There are other computational techniques also available that were used for the back-calculation of layer moduli. Fwa et al. (1997) used genetic algorithms (GA). Kamayama et al. (1998) used GA for optimisation of deflection-sensor locations. Khazanovich and Roesler (1997) developed an ANN based alogorithm, DIPLO-BACK, which used the results obtained from the DIPLOMAT program for its training. Meier et al. (1994) developed another ANN based back-calculation program, WESDEF, which used the data generated by the WESLEA program. Lee et al. (1998) also developed an ANN based back-calculation method in which deflection basin parameters were used to estimate layer stiffness. The ABAQUS program is a finite element based method which was used for 2-dimensional dynamic analysis of 2-layer pavement systems. Magnuson et al. (1991) presented the PAVE-SID back-calculation program that used the SCALPOT program for generating frequency response curves. In this case, a system identification technique was employed to match the computed frequency response functions with the FWD experimental frequency data. Uzan (1994) presented dynamic linear back-calculation procedures in terms of time domain and frequency domain. These two approaches used the UTFWIBM program as a forward model. Newton's method was also used to improve this back-calculated result. Based on quasi-static frequency, Kang (1998) developed a program named as BKGREEN. It uses a forward core-analysis procedure, GREEN, for generating theoretical deflections and its first derivatives of moduli with respect to each layer. Stolle (1996) presented two back-calculation procedures based on (i) approximate elasto-static models and (ii) the dynamic impedance concept for a 2-layer system. Both the procedures characterise the structural integrity/stiffness of a pavement by the equivalent asphalt thickness concept and the stiffness of sub-grade by effective modulus.

Table 9.3 *Salient features of some existing back-calculation models*

Program	Reference	Forward calculation routine	Back-calculation method	Non-linear analys is used	Max. no. of layers considered	Seed[1] moduli
BISDEF	Bush 1985; Lee et al. 1988	BISAR	Iterative	No	3	r
BOUSDEF	Bush 1985; Lee et al. 1988	Odemark	Iterative	Yes	5	r
CHEVDEF	Ullidtz & Coetzee 1995	CHEVRON	Iterative	No	3	r
ELMOD	Ullidtz & Stubstad 1985	Odemark-Boussinesq	Iterative	Yes	4	nr
ELSDEF	Ullidtz & Coetzee 1995	ELSYM5	Iterative	No	3	r
EMOD	Ullidtz & Coetzee 1995	CHEVRON	Iterative	Yes	3	r
EVERCALC	Lee et al. 1988	CHEVRON/	Iterative	Yes	5	g

continues . . .

Table 9.3 *continued*

Program	Reference	Forward calculation routine	Back-calculation method	Non-linear analys is used	Max. no. of layers considered	Seed[1] moduli
FPEDDI	Ullidtz & Coetzee 1995	WESLEA	Iterative	Yes	3	g
ISSEM4	Stubstad & Sharma 1979	BASINPT	Iterative	Yes	4	r
MODCOMP	Irwin 1983	ELSYM5	Iterative	Yes	12	r
MODULUS	Ullidtz & Coetzee 1995	CHEVLAY 2	Database	No	4	r
PADAL	Brown et al. 1987	WESLEA	Iterative	Yes	4	r
WESDEF	Ullidtz & Coetzee 1995	BISTRO	Iterative	No	5	r
MICHBACK	Harichandran et al. 1993	WESLEA	Iterative	No	4	r
BAP	Almedia 2001	CHEVRON	Iterative	No	5	r
DAPS	Rowe & Sharrock 2000	BISTRO	Iterative	No	4	nr
EFROMD2	Al-Suleiman et al. 2000	ELSYS	Iterative	No	12	r
SIDMOD	Wang & Lytton 1993	CIRCLY	Iterative	No	3	r
LOADRATE	Chou & Lytton 1984	BISAR	Regression	Yes	3	r
COMDEF	Anderson 1989	ILLI-PAVE	Iterative	No	3	r
FEAD	Almeida et al. 1991	BISAR	Iterative	Yes	3	r
SID	Wang & Lytton 1993	FENLAP	Iterative	No	4	r
LEAD	Almeida et al. 1994	BISAR	Iterative	No	3	r
FEDPAN	Ong et al. 1991	BISTRO	ANN	No	3	r
No name	Meier & Rix 1994	SAP IV	ANN	No	3	na
DIPLOBACK	Khazanovich & Roesler 1997	WESLEA	GA	No	3	na
NUS-GABACK	Fwa et al. 1997	DIPLOMAT	ANN	No	4	r
No name	Lee et al. 1998	BISAR	Iterative	Yes	2	na
PAVERS	COST 336	ABAQUS	Iterative	No	4	r
CARE	COST 336	WESDEF	Iterative	No	4	r
CANUV	COST 336	WESDEF	Iterative	No	3	r
UMPED	COST 336	OPMEKO	Iterative	No	4	nr
PEDD	COST 336	PAVRAN	Iterative	No	4	nr
MFPDS	COST 336	PAVRAN	Iterative	No	4	g

[1]*r* : required; nr: not required; g: generated; na: not applicable

Table 9.3 presents the salient features of a few back-calculation procedures. It can be observed from the table that most of the methods follow iterative approaches and use the elastic layer theory for the analysis of pavements. Some of the models attempt to adopt the non-linearity of pavement materials. Techniques such as regression analysis, ANN and GA were also used to solve the problem of back-calculation. These methods differ from one another mainly in terms of the pavement systems analysed (i.e., linear or non-linear), the mechanistic model adopted, techniques used for the selection of successive sets of layer moduli in the process of iterations and the convergence criteria.

Comparative study of the performance of various back-calculation software/methods was carried out by different researchers. Each back-calculation method was found to have its own merits and demerits/limitations.

9.9.3 Temperature Correction

Park and Kim (1997) exhaustively summarised the different correction factors proposed by different researchers. The correction for deflection is more complicated than the correction for back-calculated elastic modulus. The general form of the equation can be presented as follows:

$$E_{To} = \lambda_E \times E_T \tag{9.11}$$

where,
- E_{To} = elastic modulus at T_o temperature
- E_T = elastic modulus at T temperature
- λ_E = elastic modulus correction factor

Johnsen and Baus (Park and Kim 1997) recommended the following formula based on the work done by Lytton et al. (Van Deusen et al. 1997).

$$\lambda_E = 10^{-0.0002175(70^{1.886} - T^{1.886})} \tag{9.12}$$

where, T is in °F

Ullidtz (Park and Kim 1997) developed a model based on back-calculated moduli from the AASHO road test deflection data. His correction model is given by:

$$\lambda_E = 1/(3.177 - 1.673 \log(T)) \tag{9.13}$$

where, $T > 1$ °C

Baltzer and Jansen and Kim et al. (Park and Kim 1997) all independently developed a correction model based on statistical analysis of back-calculated moduli and measured AC temperatures. It is of the form:

$$\lambda_E = 10^{m(T_e - 20)} \tag{9.14}$$

where, T_e = effective asphalt concrete temperature and m = a constant.

9.9.4 Selection of Pavement Layer Moduli

The flexible pavement is basically a layered structure which flexes elastically under fast moving vehicles. Typical highway pavements consist of three to four layers containing a bituminous layer, the base, sub-base and the sub-grade. Each layer is characterised by its elastic modulus (E_s), Poisson's ratio (μ) and thickness of layers (h_i). Most of the existing design procedures adopt the elastic layered theory for the analysis of pavements. Elastic moduli, Poisson's ratio and thickness values of different layers of the pavement are taken as inputs to such algorithms. The following sections present a brief review of the different methods adopted in various back-calculation methods/procedures to select the appropriate elastic properties (i.e., moduli values of each layer) based on the FWD test data. Such methods make it possible to accomplish the back-calculation process within a short time by best matching the measured deflection bowl with the calculated deflection bowl.

In addition to the characterisation methods discussed in Chapters 3 and 4, the following relationships are also used by some researchers to back-calculate the pavement layer moduli.

Sub-grade

Even in the past, efforts were made to estimate the sub-grade moduli from surface deflections measured by NDT methods. AASHTO (1993) recommends the back-calculation of the sub-grade resilient modulus value from a single deflection measurement, using the following equation.

$$M_R = \frac{0.24P}{d_r r} \tag{9.15}$$

where, M_R = back-calculated sub-grade resilient modulus value, psi
P = applied load, in pounds
d_r = surface deflection measured at a distance r from the centre of the loading plate, in inches
r = distance from the centre of load, in inches

It is noted that the sub-grade modulus value estimated from equation (9.15) has to be adjusted to be consistent with the modulus values used to represent the AASHTO road test soil.

Roque et al. (1998) developed the following equation to estimate the sub-grade modulus based on the deflections measured using a dual-loading FWD system.

$$\text{Sub-grade modulus (ksi)} = 36.334(D_{x/60})^{-1.015} \tag{9.16}$$

where, $D_{x/60}$ is the FWD deflection in mils (0.001 inch) measured at a distance of 60 inches from the centre of the dual plates.

In ILLI-PAVE analysis (Thompson 1989), the FWD deflections are used to predict the sub-grade modulus using the following equations.

For conventional pavements

$$\log\ E_{Si} = 1.51 - 0.19\,D_3 + 0.27\log(D_3) \tag{9.17}$$

For full depth asphalt concrete pavements

$$\log\ E_{Si} = 24.7 - 5.41 D_3 + 0.31 D_3^2 \tag{9.18}$$

where, E_{si} is the sub-grade soil modulus value (ksi) and D_3 is the FWD deflection (in mils) obtained at 36 inch offset distance.

Molenaar and Van Gurp (1982) developed the following relationship to predict sub-grade soil modulus from the FWD deflections.

$$E_s = 6.514 \times 10^{-3} \times D_2^{-1.00915}$$

where, D_2 is the FWD deflection (in metres) measured at a distance of 2000 mm.

Wimsatt (1999) developed the following regression model:

$$E_s(\text{MPa}) = \frac{0.24 \times (\text{FWD load, N})}{(D_7 \text{ deflection, mm} \times 1828.8)} \tag{9.20}$$

where, D_7 is the FWD deflection measured at a distance of 1828.8 mm from the centre of the load plate.

Granular Materials

Selection of a representative modulus value for granular layers has always been a difficult task due to the fact that the moduli values are stress dependent. For this purpose, the following relationships may be suitably adopted.

Extensive evaluation of in-service pavements led to the development of several empirical relationships which could be used to estimate the value of granular layer modulus from the moduli of underlying layers and the related layer thicknesses. A widely used equation for estimation of the modulus value of the granular layer adopted by Shell (1978) is given as

$$\frac{MR_{\text{gran}}}{MR_{\text{sg}}} = 0.2 \times h_{\text{gran}}^{0.45} \tag{9.21}$$

where, MR_{gran} = MR of the granular base (MPa)
MR_{sg} = MR of sub-grade (MPa)
h_{gran} = thickness of granular layer (mm)

The modulus value of the combined thickness of the base and sub-base layers was assessed to be in the range of 2 to 4 times that of the sub-grade modulus value. Edwards and Valkering (Smith and Witczak 1981) observed from vibratory test results that the modular ratio is approximately equal to 2 and for thick stronger granular layers is about 5. A practical design modular ratio of 3 to 4 was suggested to account for the difficulty of achieving higher compaction values in the field over weak sub-grades. Based on the above results and correlations, provided there was a reasonable agreement to CBR design curves, an expression relating the unbound base thickness (h_2) to modular ratio (R_{mod}) was given as:

$$R_{\text{mod}} = 0.58(h_2)^{0.45} \tag{9.22}$$

where, h_2 is in mm.

For the estimation of base and sub-base moduli, generalised equations were developed by USACE based on the investigations of Barker et al. (1977). The equations are given as:

For base course

$$E_{\text{Rn}} = E_{\text{Rn+1}}\,(1 + 10.52\log(h) - 2.10\log(E_{\text{Rn+1}}) \times \log(h)) \tag{9.23}$$

For sub-base course

$$E_{\text{Rn}} = E_{\text{Rn+1}}\,(1 + 7.18\log(h) - 1.56\log(E_{\text{Rn+1}}) \times \log(h)) \tag{9.24}$$

where, E_{Rn} = elastic modulus of the nth layer
E_{Rn+1} = elastic modulus of the $(n+1)$th layer
h = thickness of the nth layer

Smith and Witczak (1981) carried out extensive analytical investigations on elastic moduli of granular layers provided in flexible pavements. The equation developed for the estimation of moduli of base is given as:

$$\log(E_2) = 1.079 - 0.511\log(h_1) - 0.008\log(h_2) - 0.155\log(E_1) + 0.279\log(E_3) + 0.888\log(c_1) \quad (9.25)$$

where, h_1 = thickness of the asphalt concrete layer in inches
h_2 = thickness of the granular layer in inches
E_1, E_2 and E_3 = modulus values of the asphalt concrete, granular and sub-grade layers (in psi)
c_1 = material constant for the granular layer obtained from repeated triaxial tests

Shook et al. (1982) found that the modular ratio according to Smith and Witczak (equation (9.22)) lies between 2 and 4, same as that predicted by the Shell method. However, the Smith and Witczak equation suggests that the modulus value (E_2) increases as h_1, h_2 and E_1 values decreases, and E_3 and c_1 values (material quality) increases. But this indicates dissimilarity between the results of the USACE and Shell equations. Based on non-linear FEM analysis of pavements with bituminous surfacing and granular bases, Bose (1993) observed that the modular ratio increases as thicknesses of surfacing and base decreases and the sub-grade modulus increases.

As another case to mention, Deen et al. (1971) found that the modular ratio is independent of base course thickness and dependent on the moduli of the asphalt layer and sub-base. This is different from the relationship of Shell and that given by Edwards and Valkering (Smith and Witczak 1981). Similarly, Gerritsen et al. (1987) also found the modular ratio to be very different from that obtained using the Shell relationship.

The DAMA computer program of the Asphalt Institute (1983) used the following equation for estimation of the granular layer moduli (psi).

$$E_{s\ \mathrm{granular}} = c_1 \times (h_{\mathrm{bituminous}})^{-c_2} \times (h_{\mathrm{granular}})^{-c_3} \times (E_{s\ \mathrm{bituminous}})^{-c_4} \times (E_{s\ \mathrm{sub-grade}})^{c_5} \times (K)^{c_6} \quad (9.26)$$

where, h = thickness (inch), c_1 to c_6 = regression constants with the following values: c_1 = 10.447, c_2 = 0.471, c_3 = 0.041, c_4 = 0.139, c_5 = 0.287, c_6 = 0.868, K = a factor representing the type of unbound aggregate layer

AASHTO (1993) recommended the following relationships for the estimation of the E_s value (in psi) of unbound granular materials from CBR values:

$$E_{\mathrm{sgranular}} = 740\ \mathrm{CBR, for}\ \theta = 100\ \mathrm{psi} \quad (9.27)$$

$$E_{\mathrm{sgranular}} = 440\ \mathrm{CBR, for}\ \theta = 30\ \mathrm{psi} \quad (9.28)$$

$$E_{\mathrm{sgranular}} = 340\times\ \mathrm{CBR, for}\ \theta = 20\ \mathrm{psi} \quad (9.29)$$

$$E_{\mathrm{sgranular}} = 250\times\ \mathrm{CBR, for}\ \theta = 10\ \mathrm{psi} \quad (9.30)$$

where, θ is the sum of principal stresses.

Brown et al. (1982) used a stress–path approach by finite element analysis and studied the modular ratio between the granular base and the sub-grade. The modular ratio was found to range from 1.5 to 7.5 with a typical mean value close to 2.5.

Shook et al. (1982) indicated that the granular base modulus varies with traffic loading, modulus value of sub-grade and thickness of asphalt concrete. The modular ratio was found to vary between 1.9 and 6.7.

Freeme et al. (1982) found that any increase in the modulus value of the granular layer laid under a thin surfacing layer results in further increase of the modulus value compared to a thicker surface layer. This may be attributed to the decreased state of stress in the granular layer's increased surface thickness. It was also found that the modulus value of the granular base increases as quality of the material increases.

Similar to the case of sub-grade, attempts were made to estimate the value of the granular layer modulus from the FWD measured surface deflections. Roque et al. (1998) presented the following equation for the estimation of sub-base moduli from deflections measured with a FWD having dual load configuration.

$$\begin{aligned} E_{\text{sub-base}}(\text{ksi}) = {} & 105.81136(h_2)^{-1.0785}\left(D_{x/36} - D_{x/60}\right)^{-6.02523+2.4888/D_{x/60}} \\ & \times[(D_{y/0} + D_{x/12}) - 1.15D_{x/36}]^{2.1609-1.6202/D_{x/60}-5.302/h_2} \\ & \times(D_{x/60})^{3.6706-0.0498h} - 0.686t_2 - 3.0998/(D_{x/60}) \end{aligned} \tag{9.31}$$

where, all thicknesses (h) are in inches and all deflections (D) are in mils (0.001 inch).

Bituminous Layer

The behaviour of bituminous material/mixes is complex. Its properties are visco-elastic and temperature-susceptible. The value of the elastic modulus of the bituminous mix is normally determined by an appropriate test conducted at representative test temperature. Such tests are usually conducted under repeated load conditions in constant stress or strain mode. The modulus of the bituminous mix is influenced by several factors such as test conditions, temperature and other parameters related to the mix. However, the nomographs developed by Shell (Shook et al. 1982) are widely used by different agencies across the world.

Akhter and Witczak (1985) tested a large number of bituminous mix samples and developed a regression equation for estimating asphalt concrete modulus using viscosity, temperature, frequency, volume of air voids, volume of effective asphalt, asphalt content absorbed by weight of total aggregate, percentage by weight of mineral aggregate passing sieve size 0.075 mm and retained on 4.75 mm, 9.5 mm and 19 mm sieves.

The Asphalt Institute (Shook et al. 1982) recommends an equation to estimate the modulus value of a bituminous mix at lower temperatures using parameters related to temperature and penetration values found at 25 °C and 4 °C.

Concluding Remarks

The following observations can be made from a review of related literature.

(a) A number of back-calculation methods are available for determination of effective layer moduli from the FWD deflections. Many of these methods/procedures have drawbacks such as sensitivity to seed moduli and determination of local solutions that are not optimal. However, GA-based methods have the ability to search for the closest global solutions by taking a reasonable computational time. Further, GA-based models with artificial neural networks (ANN) and expert systems can also be used to select ranges of layer moduli and for faster determination of effective moduli.

(b) Different methods are used for the selection of layer moduli. These include laboratory test results, back-calculated values and empirical relationships. The moduli obtained from direct evaluation of in-service pavements or from the standard relationships that estimate effective layer moduli appear to be appropriate as suitable inputs for the analysis of pavements.

(c) Many types of relationships/equations have been developed by different researchers for the estimation of pavement layer moduli. However, the applicability of different relationships popularly used for the estimation of layer moduli should be adequately validated for the prevailing construction practices and climatic conditions.

9.10 An Example Problem of Back-calculation of Layer Moduli

To demonstrate the back-calculation method/procedure, FWD-deflection bowl measurements were taken at a location on National Highway No. 6. The deflections measured during a monsoon season are given in Table 9.4.

Table 9.4 *Details of FWD measured surface deflection bowl*

Sl. No.	Radial distance (cm)	Deflection (mm)
1	0	0.72494
2	30	0.38830
3	60	0.27601
4	90	0.21882
5	120	0.17525
6	150	0.14771

Back-calculation was carried out using a GA-based computer program, BACKGA (Murthy 1999). The main objective in any back-calculation analysis of pavement layer moduli should be to determine a set of pavement layer moduli that produces a deflection basin which closely matches with the measured deflection basin. A typical objective function should minimise the sum of the squared differences of measured and calculated deflections. For our present example, the objective function selected is given by:

$$\text{Minimise object function} = \sum_{i=1}^{n}\left(\frac{D_{mi} - D_{ci}}{D_{ci}}\right)^2 \tag{9.32}$$

where, D_{mi} = measured deflection, D_{ci} = computed deflection

Fitness of the solution is computed using equation (9.33).

$$\text{Fitness} = \frac{1}{1 + \text{Object function}} \tag{9.33}$$

A solution that has a smaller value of object function is considered to be a fitter, and thus a better solution. The flow chart for the algorithm is presented in Figure 9.26.

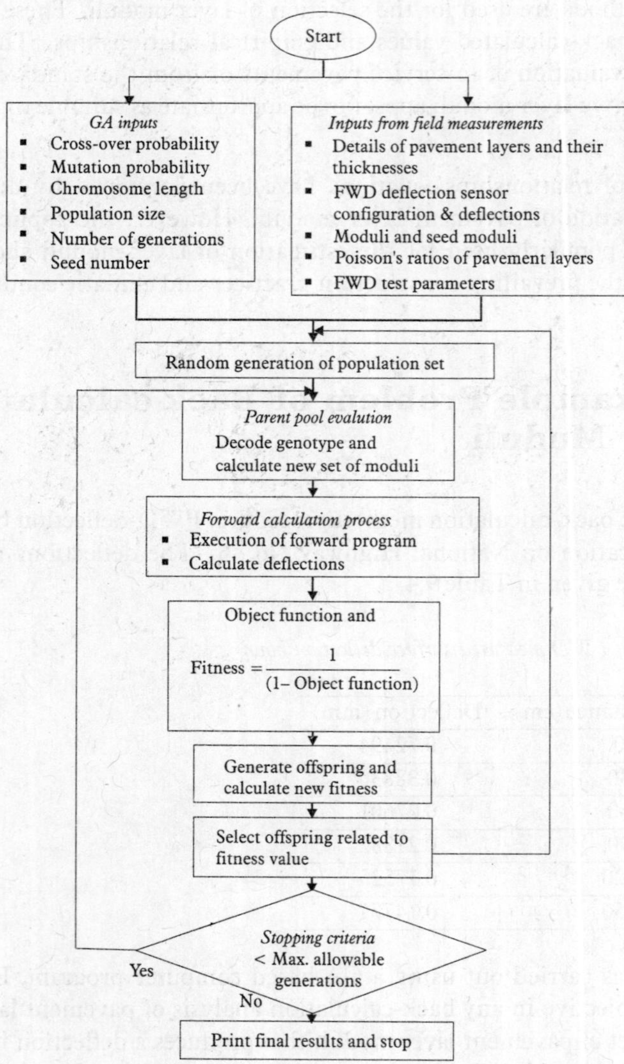

Figure 9.26 *Flow chart for a GA-based back-calculation algorithm*

The following inputs are given to BACKGA.

Main inputs to the program:

- Number of layers = 3
- Poisson's ratio, taken as 0.5 for bituminous layer and 0.4 for other layers.

- Load = 40 kN; circular contact area = 300 mm diameter.
- Surface deflections are measured at 0, 30, 60, 90, 120 and 150 cm radial distances from the centre of the loading plate. The deflections are normalised to correspond to a load of 40 kN.

The ranges of layer moduli and sectional details considered are given in Table 9.5.

Table 9.5 *Pavement structural details*

Layer	Range of elastic modulus (MPa)	Poisson's ratio	Layer thickness (mm)
Bituminous layer	200–1000	0.50	96.0
Granular base course	100–400	0.40	576.0
Sub-grade	25–125	0.40	–

Following are the GA parameters used in the analysis:

population size	=	100
number of generations	=	100
cross-over probability	=	0.81
mutation probability	=	0.10
chromosome length	=	30
seed number	=	0.86620

The difference between the measured and computed (using back-calculated moduli) deflections and expressed by average error (AE) is given by

$$AE = 100 \times \left(\sum_{j=1}^{n} |D_{cj} - D_{mj}|/D_{mj} \right) /ns \tag{9.34}$$

where, D_{mj} = measured deflection at the jth sensor location; D_{cj} = computed deflection for the jth sensor location and ns = number of sensors. The average CPU time taken for the back-calculation of one pavement section in a DEC Alpha 3000 machine is about 21 minutes.

The converging trend of the GA based solution with increasing generations is presented in Table 9.6. The comparison between the measured deflections and the deflections calculated using the back-calculated layer moduli is shown in Table 9.7.

Table 9.6 *Details of GA solutions obtained at different generations*

Gen. no.	Fitness			Best solution obtained so far				
	Max.	Avg.	Min.	E_1 (MPa)	E_2 (MPa)	E_3(MPa)	Fitness	At gen.
1	0.9899	0.9171	0.8407	739.59	193.54	55.362	0.9899	1
2	0.9891	0.9282	0.7922	739.59	193.54	55.362	0.9899	1
3	0.9860	0.9409	0.8639	739.59	193.54	55.362	0.9899	1
4	0.9917	0.9561	0.7982	738.71	213.88	52.302	0.9917	4
5	0.9971	0.9609	0.8589	627.86	213.88	52.302	0.9971	5

continues

Table 9.6 *continued . . .*

Gen. no.	Fitness			Best solution obtained so far				
	Max.	Avg.	Min.	E_1 (MPa)	E_2 (MPa)	E_3(MPa)	Fitness	At gen.
10	0.9966	0.9763	0.8529	627.86	213.88	52.302	0.9971	5
20	0.9977	0.9873	0.9024	611.14	215.484	51.738	0.9976	20
30	0.9977	0.9906	0.9032	563.73	220.327	51.746	0.9985	29
50	0.9978	0.9830	0.8609	563.73	220.327	51.746	0.9985	29
100	0.9978	0.9916	0.9108	563.72	220.347	51.756	0.9985	29

Table 9.7 *Comparison between measured deflections and deflections calculated using back-calculated layer moduli*

Sl. No.	Radial distance (cm)	Measured deflection (mm)	Deflection calculated using back-calculated moduli (mm)	Percent error
1	0	0.72494	0.72310	0.253814
2	30	0.38830	0.38970	0.36055
3	60	0.27601	0.27591	0.036231
4	90	0.21882	0.21781	0.461567
5	120	0.17525	0.17720	1.11270
6	150	0.14771	0.14610	1.089974
			Average error =	0.368343

9.11 Uses of Back-calculated Pavement Layer Moduli

The flexible pavement layer moduli obtained from back-calculation can be used for the following purposes.

(a) To diagnose the structural adequacy of pavements to withstand anticipated traffic loads.

(b) The deflection data obtained from FWD tests are used to prioritise pavement maintenance works where it is necessary to use funds economically.

(c) The back-calculated moduli values and other data related to pavement layers are used to design overlay thickness.

(d) The remaining life of the pavement can be ascertained.

(e) To find out when and how much axle-load restrictions to impose during freeze thaw or post-monsoon season when the pavement is expected to be weak.

(f) To understand the behaviour of pavements under different weather conditions and seasons.

(g) The stiffness (or moduli) of pavement layers and FWD deflections can be related to the pavement performance in terms of fatigue cracking, rutting, frost heave etc.

(h) To determine pavement design criteria or failure criteria.

(i) Characterisation of pavement materials can be ascertained by relating back-calculated moduli to various design parameter values obtained from laboratory testing.

(j) To explain other pavement issues related to non-linear elastic behaviour of bituminous pavements, effect of temperature gradient, climate, drainage conditions and material variability.

9.12 Structural Evaluation of Rigid Pavement Using FWD

Rigid pavement's structural performance is generally related to various distresses such as intensity of cracking, pumping, base/sub-base support, crack stiffness, punch-outs, variations in opening of joints, joint faulting, joint stiffness, load transfer efficiency of transverse joints, and mud-pumping at cracks and joints. In the following sections, we will discuss a few important aspects related to assessment of various rigid pavement performance parameters.

It is noteworthy that the subject knowledge in rigid pavement performance with a mechanistic approach to modelling and design of rigid pavements has significant contributions from various organisations under different research programmess (NCHRP, LTTP, SHRP, FHWA-RD and DOT/FAA/RD) and researchers (Ioannides and Korovesis 1990; 1992; Uzan 1992; Li et al; 1996; 1998; Fwa et al. 1998; 2000; Frabizzio and Buch 2000; Khazanovich et al. 2000; Jiang and Tayabji, 2000).

9.12.1 Back-calculation of Rigid Pavement Material Response Parameters

Mid-slab surface deflection data obtained by conducting an FWD test at 40 kN loading on the mid-slab with seven geophones positioned at given intervals/ configuration (Figure 9.27) is used to back-calculate various values of pavement performance parameters such as radius of relative stiffness (l), modulus of sub-grade reaction (k) and elastic modulus of slab (E_{slab}). The geophone configuration may be taken at regular intervals of 30 cm (Fwa et al. 2000) or any given spacing such as 0, 20.3, 30.5, 45.7, 61.0, 91.4 and 152.4 cm (Frabizzio and Buch 2000) or −30.5, 0, 30.5, 45.7, 61.0, 91.4, 154.2 cm of radial distance from the centre of the loading plate (Jiang and Tayabji 2000). Back-calculation of the above parameters can also be determined by using the deflection basins obtained by conducting FWD tests at the edge centre of the slab and geophones placed along the edge (explained later in Section 9.12.2, Figure 9.30). It is noted that the back-calculated value of the modulus of sub-grade reaction (k) depends on the location of the load application—at the slab interior or near its free edge (Uzan 1992).

Rigid pavement back-calculation techniques may be broadly classified into two types.

I. Procedure based methods

II. Deflection parameter based methods

Procedure based techniques include the following (Ioannides et al. 1989):

(i) Iterative techniques and

(ii) Database techniques

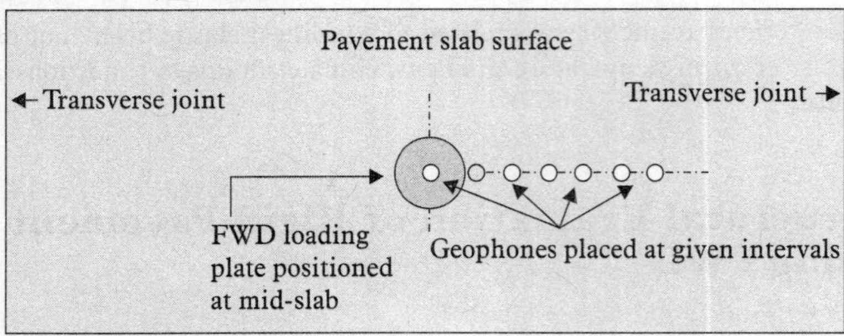

Figure 9.27 *Typical FWD loading position with geophones arrangement for measurement of mid-slab surface deflection basin*

Iterative techniques use an optimised searching procedure linked to a forward analysis of a pavement program to calculate pavement response parameters that best match the measured responses. The measured responses of a pavement may be considered in the form of individual deflections or any deflection basin parameter. In these procedures, a structural analysis computer program or semi-closed form algorithm (Fwa et al. 2000) is called iteratively until the calculated pavement response better matches the measured response.

In *database techniques*, a theoretical model is used to create a database consisting of different sets of deflection basins verses material properties of multiple combinations of pavement structures. Such database can be used to determine pavement material properties by suitably interpolating similar pavement structures to that of the measured response of the pavement. Therefore, back-calculated values will be only confined/ limited to the available database. Because of this, the database should be created by considering all possible multiple combinations of pavement structures. The back-calculation program MODULUS used by Uzan (1992) to determine pavement material parameters utilises the deflection database. The artificial neural network (sNN)-based computer program termed as DIPLOBACK uses a database of deflection basins with pavement properties for back-calculation of composite pavement layer moduli (Khazanovich and Roesler 1997). Similarly, the rigid pavement joint stiffness properties were also predicted using an ANN technique based on dimensional analysis (Ioannides et al. 1996). Other back-calculation programs such as DBCONPAS (Tai et al. 1989) and DATABACKDIPLO (Rufino et al. 2002) can be listed under this category.

The above-mentioned procedure based techniques uses measured deflections or deflection basin parameters. Based on the type of deflection basin parameter used, the rigid pavement back-calculation methods may be further classified into the following types.

1. *AREA methods* These methods use (i) the AREA parameter of the deflection basin (Ioannides 1990) or (ii) the actual area of the deflection basin (Tai et al. 1989; Rufino et al. 2002) or (iii) the normalised actual area of the deflection basin (Crovetti and Tirado-Crovetti 1994).
2. *Best fit methods* These methods closely match (i) the measured and predicted deflection basin (models: BISDEF (Bush and Alexander 1985) and WESDEF (Van Cauwelaert et al. 1989)) or (ii) a few selected measured deflections (Khazanovich and McPeak 1998;

Khazanovich et al. 2000). In this method, all the deflections considered of a basin should be closely matched and if any geophone deflection is erroneous, the back-calculated property of the pavement will be largely affected (Fwa et al. 2000).

3 *Graphical methods* These methods use (i) selected measured deflection ratio (Fwa et al. 1998) or (ii) the value of the deflection basin parameter AREA and maximum deflection (Foxworthy and Darter 1989).

The details of different available existing back-calculation models are given Table 9.8.

Table 9.8 *Salient features of a few existing back-calculation models*

Program or method	Reference	Forward calculation routine	Calculation method*	Procedure followed	No. of measured deflections with their configuration considered
ILLI-BACK	Ioannides and Korovesis 1992; Ioannides 1994	ILLI-SLAB	FEM with plate model; ES or DL with closed-form equations	AREA	4 number @ 0, 30.48, 60.96 and 91.44 cm; With other configurations also
NUS-BACK (2 layers) and NUS-BACK3 (3 layers)	Li Shuo et al. 1996, 1998; Fwa et al. 2000	NUS-DEF2	Panc and Losberg's plate resting on DL or ES; Closed and semi-closed form equations	Best fit	2 number @ 0 and 30 cm or 4 number @ 0, 30, 60 and 90 cm.
ERESBACK2.0	Khazanovich and McPeak 1998	–	DL & ES	Best fit	4 number @ 0, 30.5, 61.0 and 91.4 cm
Graphical solutions	Fwa et al. 1998		Based on NUS-BACK	Graphical	2 number: ratio of deflections measured @ 30 and 0 cm
Graphical solutions (for airfields)	Foxworthy and Darter 1989	ILLI-SLAB	FEM; Different temperatures also considered	AREA	7 number @ 0, 30.48, 60.96, 91.44, 121.92, 152.4 and 182.88 cm

continues

Table 9.8 *continued*

Program or method	Reference	Forward calculation routine	Calculation method*	Procedure followed	No. of measured deflections with their configuration considered
No name (up to 3 layers): A modified version of ERES-BACK2.0	Khazanovich et al. 2000	–	Losberg's plate on elastic solid or DL or ES; Used closed-form equations to predict *l* and *k* values.	Best fit	4 number @ 0, 30.5, 61.0 and 91.4 cm
DBCONPAS	Tai et al. 1989	FEACONS III	FEM; prediction regression equations; deflection basin data bank	Best fit	6 number @ 0, 30.5, 61.0, 91.4, 121.9 and 152.4 cm
No name (for AC overlaid on PCC)	Hall and Darter 1994	Westergaard's interior loading concept	Elastic theory, DL; Closed-form equations; AC modulus can be determined as a function of AC mix temperature	AREA	4 number @ 0, 30.48, 60.96 and 91.44 cm
WESDEF (for airfield pavements with AC, PCC and composite)	Van Cauwelaert et al. 1989	WESLEA	Elastic layers system	Best fit	7 number @ 0, 30.48, 60.96, 91.44, 121.92, 152.4 and 182.88 cm
BAKFAA for airfield pavements (also for AC overlaid on PCC)	www.faa.gov AC No.: 150/5370-11A	LEAF; LEDFAA 1.2	Linear elastic layer theory; Winkler foundation; Closed-form equations	AREA	4 number @ 0, 30.48, 60.96 and 91.44 cm; With other configurations also
DIPLODEF (for AC also)	Kothandram and Ioannides 2001	DIPLOMAT (with an optimisation search routine from WESDEF)	Elastic layer and plate theories; DL, ES	Best fit	
DATABACK DIPLO	Rufino et al. 2002	DIPLOMAT (Khazanovich and Ioannides 1995)	Elastic layer and plate theories; DL, ES; A database approach	Basin actual area or AREA or best fit	4 number @ 0, 30.48, 60.96 and 91.44 cm; With other configurations also

continues

Table 9.8 *continued*

Program or method	Reference	Forward calculation routine	Calculation method*	Procedure followed	No. of measured deflections with their configuration considered
No name	Khazanovich 2000	Westergaard's interior slab loading concept	Analytical closed-form solutions for dynamic loading plate on Winkler foundation	Best fit	3 number @ 0, 60 and 150 cm
No name	Crovetti and Tirado-Crovetti 1994	Westergaard's interior slab loading concept	Direct closed for equations; DL; Correction factors for minimum slab dimension	Normalised actual AREA	4 number @ 0, 30.48, 60.96 and 91.44 cm

* DL: Dense liquid sub-grade model; ES: Elastic solid sub-grade model; FEM: Finite element method; AC: Asphalt concrete.; PCC: Plain cement concrete pavement.

A few additional features of the AREA method used by the ILLI-BACK computer program are listed below (Ioannides 1990; Ioannides and Korovesis 1992; Li et al. 1996).

(a) The ILLI-BACK is the first closed-form analytical rigid pavement back-calculation algorithm developed at the University of Illinois, USA. It uses an FEM based computer program called ILLI-SLAB.

(b) The parameter AREA is determined using deflections measured at four positions with respect to the centre of the FWD loading plate. The AREA parameter is not a true area of the deflection bowl. In fact it is a value expressed in linear units. Based on the FWD geophone configuration, the AREA is determined using trapezoidal rule. Each AREA is normalised with respect to the measured maximum deflection value of the respective deflection bowl in order to eliminate the effects of load magnitude.

(c) The deflection bowl shape parameter AREA can be determined using the following equation.

$$\text{AREA} = \frac{6}{D_1}\,(D_1 + 2D_2 + 2D_3 + D_4) \qquad (9.35)$$

The surface deflections D_1, D_2, D_3 and D_4 are measured respectively at 0, 30.48, 60.96 and 91.44 cm from the centre of the loading plate (Figure 9.28).

(d) The AREA parameter has a unique relationship with the slab radius of relative stiffness (ℓ) in non-dimensional form (Ioannides et al. 1989). From this relationship, the value of modulus of the sub-grade reaction (k value) can be determined from the Westergaard's equation of maximum deflection at the interior loading condition (Westergaard 1926). Once the ℓ and k values are determined, the elastic modulus of the slab can be obtained and the coded algorithm is termed as ILLI-BACK (Ioannides 1990). It is also available with modifications (Ioannides 1994).

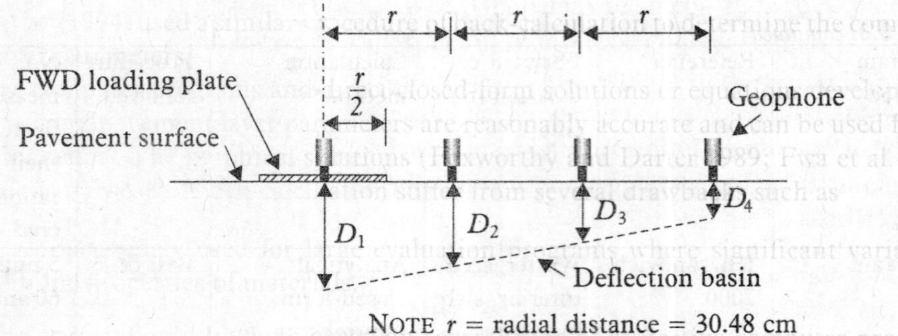

Figure 9.28 *FWD geophone configuration considered for determination of parameter AREA used in ILLI-BACK (elaborated based on Thompson 1989)*

(e) A few analysis concepts of ILLI-BACK were adopted in the 1993 *AASHTO Guide for Design of Pavement Structures*.

Some features of the best fit method used by NUS-BACK are listed below (Li et al. 1996, 1997 and 1998; Fwa et al. 2000).

(a) The NUS-BACK and its different versions were developed at the National University of Singapore.

(b) Closed-form analytical solutions were developed for two support conditions—when a rigid slab is supported on (i) an elastic solid, ES (Boussinesq 1885) and (ii) a dense liquid, DL (Winkler 1867).

(c) To back-calculate two-layer rigid pavement parameters, three semi-closed form iterative procedures which use the above closed-form solutions were developed.

(d) In later versions of NUS-BACK, a closed-form algorithm was incorporated to back-calculate material parameters of pavement slabs resting on a two-layer ES foundation.

(e) In case of two-concrete slabs (such as a concrete overlay on a lean concrete base), model NUS-BACK4 was developed based on the concept of an equivalent slab layer with the assumption of equal flexural rigidity. In this case, the moduli of the two slab layers were back-calculated by trial and error using the values of the modulus of sub-grade reaction, equivalent flexural rigidity and equivalent radius of relative stiffness of the two slabs that are obtained from closed-form equations. During the trial and error iterations, a best match is sought between calculated equivalent flexural rigidity and the equivalent flexural rigidity obtained from deflection measurements.

(f) During the process of back-calculation, a unique reliable feature of NUS-BACK is that it can identify any faulty or erroneous geophone deflection measurements that are inevitable due to the practical problems associated with FWD deflection testing.

Based on research works carried out by Ioannides, Hall and Crovetti at the University of Illinois at Urbana-Champaign, USA, a direct and simple procedure was proposed by Crovetti and Tirado-Crovetti (1994) for back-calculating the k value of a slab supporting layer and the elastic modulus of a PCC slab (E_{slab}). Basically, this procedure uses Westergaard's deflection equation of interior circular loading on a fully supported infinite slab resting on DL and takes account of the minimum slab dimension effect on (i) measured value of maximum deflection (D_1) and (ii) back-calculated value of the radius of relative stiffness (ℓ). The FEM program ILLI-SLAB was used to develop equations of correction factors for adjusting D_1 and l values. The details of the back-calculation procedure proposed by Crovetti and Tirado-Crovetti (1994) are given below.

(a) Mid-slab surface deflections measured at four radial distances, 0, 30.48, 60.96 and 91.44 cm from the centre of the FWD loading plate are used to determine the normalised actual AREA of the deflection basin $= (r/D_1) \times [(D_1 + D_4)/2) + D_2 + D_3]$ (refer to Figure 9.28).

(b) The value of the radius of relative stiffness (l_{est}) of the slab can be estimated using the regression equation developed by Hall (cited in Crovetti and Tirado-Crovetti 1994), which is based on the theoretical deflections calculated using the Losberg model. Hall's equation is given below.

$$\ell_{est} = \left[\frac{\ln\left(\dfrac{91.44 - \text{AREA}}{4603.189}\right)}{-2.069416} \right]^{k_1} \tag{9.36}$$

where, k_1 is a constant value between 4 and 5.

(c) To take account of the effect of limited slab dimensions, the following equations developed by Crovetti and Tirado-Crovetti (1994) can be used to adjust the ℓ_{est} and measured D_1.

Adjusted value of ℓ

$$= \ell_{est} \times \left[1 - 5.2987e^{-2.17612\left(\frac{L}{\ell_{est}}\right)^{k_2}}\right] \tag{9.37}$$

Adjusted value of D_1

$$= D_1 \times \left[1 - 1.06817e^{-0.66914\left(\frac{L}{\ell_{est}}\right)^{k_3}}\right] \tag{9.38}$$

where, L = least slab dimension, i.e., width or length, k_2 and k_3 are the constant values, between 0.4 and 0.5, and 0.8 and 0.9 respectively. The above adjustment equations were also recommended and used by Ioannides (1994).

(d) The k value of the supporting layer of the slab can be determined using Westergaard's interior maximum deflection equation.

$$k = \frac{P}{8D_1\ell^2}\left[1 + \left(\frac{1}{2\pi}\right)\left(\frac{a}{\ell}\right)^2\left(\ln\left(\frac{a}{2\ell}\right) + 0.6727843351\right)\right] \tag{9.39}$$

where, P = load, a = radius of load contact area which may be taken as 15 cm; ℓ and D_1 should be adjusted values.

(e) Elastic modulus of the PCC slab (E_{slab}) can be obtained from Westergaard's equation of the radius of relative stiffness using the values of adjusted ℓ, slab thickness, Poisson's ratio of concrete and estimated k value.

Hall and Darter (1994) used a similar procedure of back-calculation to determine the composite pavement layer parameters.

The above computer programs and direct closed-form solutions or equations developed for back-calculation of pavement layer parameters are reasonably accurate and can be used for the conditions modelled. The graphical solutions (Foxworthy and Darter 1989; Fwa et al. 1998) available for the purpose of back-calculation suffer from several drawbacks such as

(a) They are not widely used for large evaluation programs where significant variability exists in the properties of materials.

(b) Hand plotting should be done based on several runs of respective computer programs with different combinations of input values.

(c) Separate analysis should be carried out for each type of pavement with their different boundary conditions.

(d) Poor interpolation of the results obtained from the graphical charts may be inaccurate.

(e) Obtaining generalised solutions are difficult when there are different loading conditions, deflection sensor configurations and pavement boundary conditions.

(f) Whatever are the limitations of models and analysis procedure adopted in respective computer programs, such limitations will remain the same for the graphical solutions also.

As a concluding remark, the rigid pavement properties determined by different back-calculation techniques and procedures will vary significantly based on the adopted theoretical model of the slab and supporting layers, technique, analysis procedure, number of sensors used, type of deflection basin parameter, slab temperature gradient considerations, conditions assumed for analysis (Uzan 1994), seed moduli and accuracy or quality of measured deflections (Lytton 1989; Stolle and Hein 1989).

Reliability of the back-calculated pavement performance parameters such as modulus of sub-grade reaction and elastic modulus of the slab can be verified or cross-checked with reference to the concerned laboratory test results or correlations with compressive strength test value and construction records. The flexural strength of the concrete can be obtained from correlations between flexural strength and the results obtained from laboratory tests such as tensile splitting strength or compressive strength of concrete since the flexural strength of the concrete cannot be determined from FWD deflection data (Uzan 1992).

9.12.2 Load Transfer across a Crack or Transverse Joint

Structural performance of any rigid pavement is evaluated by determining the load transfer across cracks or transverse joints. The transverse joints may be with or without dowel bars. In case of a transverse joint without dowel bars, the load transfer across the joint takes place by aggregate interlocking. Whatever the type of joint or crack, their performance characteristics are determined in terms of their load transfer efficiency (LTE).

LTE is determined by conducting an FWD test on the side of a crack or transverse joint. In case of transverse joint efficiency testing, the FWD load is applied once on the edge of the approach slab and once on the edge of the leave slab. For both the cases, a geophone is placed at the centre of the loading plate and another geophone is placed on the unloaded slab 30 cm away from the centre of the loading plate. The load transfer tests are preferably conducted early in the morning before the temperature gradient develops (Alexander et al. 1989). Details of how the FWD loading plate is placed on the edge of the leave slab and the position of geophones on either side of a dowel joint are presented in Figure 9.29. The FWD test can also be conducted by placing the loading plate on the approach slab which is adjacent to the joint.

A general observation of the above two tests is that the LTE determined by loading on the leave slab is lower than the LTE value obtained by testing on the approach slab (See Figure 9.29). It may be reasonable to expect that the damage occurring on and under the leave slab is more due to the effect of abrupt (or sudden) application of wheel loads passing from the approach slab to the leave slab thus creating higher stresses on and under the leave slab. This trend may not be consistent because of the variability in temperature of the slab, sub-grade stiffness, sub-grade moisture content, void location and joint faulting.

Typical other loading positions with respect to the joint, viz. (i) at the corner and (ii) at the joint centre may also be considered (Figure 9.30).

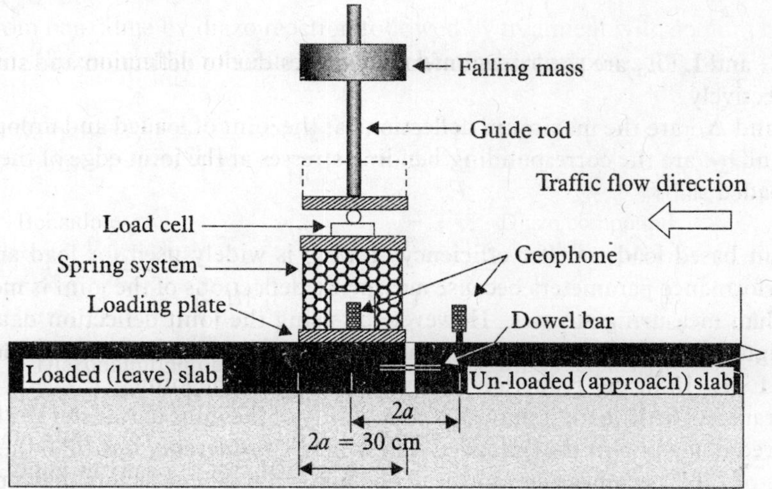

Figure 9.29 *FWD testing of a dowel joint in a cement concrete pavement*

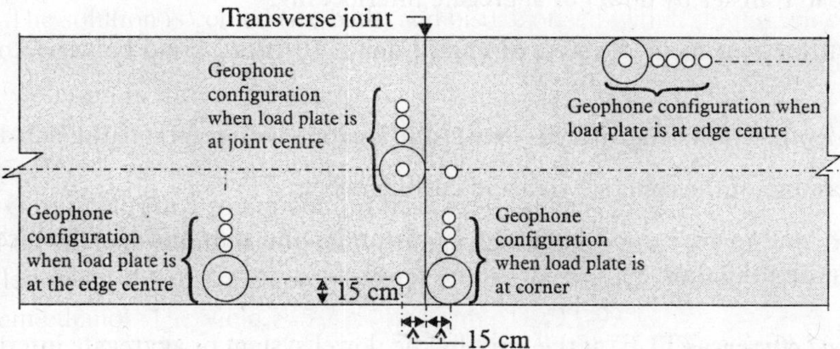

Figure 9.30 *Different typical FWD loading positions with geophone configurations used for structural evaluation of jointed PCC pavements*

9.12.3 Load Transfer Analysis

Load transfer efficiency of a dowel system is an important parameter used to design dowel bars diameter, spacing and length. On one side of the joint, a standard load (40 kN) is applied by using FWD and the resulting deflections of loaded and unloaded slab at the face of the joint are measured. The measured deflections are used for load transfer analysis using the following definitions and formulae.

Load transfer efficiency (LTE) of a joint is its ability to transfer a part of the applied load from the loaded slab to the adjacent unloaded slab. The following formulae can be used to determine LTE of a pavement slab joint tested with FWD (Ioannides and Korovesis 1992).

$$\text{LTE}_\delta = \frac{\Delta_U}{\Delta_L} \times 100 \tag{9.40}$$

$$\text{LTE}_\sigma = \frac{\sigma_U}{\sigma_L} \times 100 \tag{9.41}$$

where, LTE_δ and LTE_σ are the load tranfer efficiencies due to deflection and stress respectively
Δ_L and Δ_U are the maximum deflections at the joint of loaded and unloaded slabs
σ_L and σ_U are the corresponding bending stresses at the joint edge of the loaded and unloaded slabs

The deflection based load transfer efficiency (LTE_δ) is widely used for load analysis rigid pavement performance parameters because measuring deflections of the joint is more easy and convenient than measuring stresses. However, by using the joint deflection data and FWD loading configuration, the value of LTE_σ can be determined using the finite element method. The value of LTE_σ indicates reduction in stress level across the joint.

If a joint transfers little load, it indicates poor ability of the joint to transfer the load and the FWD measured deflection of the unloaded slab will be considerably less than the loaded slab and the value of LTE becomes close to zero. The following salient factors may be considered while determining LTE models.

- Joint load transfer by dowel or aggregate interlocking.
- Joint stiffness, cement concrete strength, dowel stiffness, bond between concrete and dowel.
- Crack depth, width, length, area covered and location with respect to the slab dimensions.
- Temperature of the concrete slab and curling effects.
- Support due to base and sub-grade, voids under the slab and shoulder confinement surrounding the slab.

Transferred load efficiency (TLE) at the joint by the dowel system or aggregate interlocking can be determined by the following equation (Ioannides and Korovesis 1992).

$$\text{Transferred load efficiency, TLE (\%)} = 100 \times P_T/P_a \tag{9.42}$$

where, P_T = transferred total load (N) by aggregate interlocking across the joint or by all dowels of a joint

P_a = applied wheel load (N)

Theoretically, maximum efficiency in the transfer of wheel or applied load is 50% when efficiency of dowel system is assumed to be 100%. For practical considerations of repeated traffic loadings, the efficiency in transfer of load may decrease to 5 to 10% (Yoder and Witczak 1975). In a study, it was observed that for heavy truck traffic, the load transfer efficiency ranges from 35 to 40% (Brown and Bartholomew 1993). Therefore, based on the above two cases, the average value of the load transfer efficiency (LTE) may be taken as 40% and yields $P_t = 0.4$ Pa, where P_t is the maximum load carried by the dowel bar in a joint. This relationship is considered for design of dowel bars according to IRC:58-2002.

Load transfer distribution factor (LTDF) indicates percentage of the total load transferred by a single dowel of a joint and is determined as (Ioannides and Korovesis 1992).

$$\text{LTDF} = 100 \times P_i/P_T \tag{9.43}$$

where, P_i = value of load carried by any single dowel in a joint and

$$P_T = \sum_{i=1}^{n} P_i = \text{total load transferred from the loaded slab to the unloaded slab}$$

For analysis, the value of P_i is taken as equal to P_t and the $\text{LTDF} = 100 \times P_t/P_T$.

Since the analysis of Friberg (1940), many pavement engineers and scientists have been trying to understand load transfer mechanism in concrete pavement and mechanistically model (Tabatabie and Barenberg 1980; Chou 1983; Guo et al. 1995; Shi et al. 1999) it. However, Ioannides and Korovesis (1990; 1992) identified two non-dimensional shear stiffness parameters (AGG/$k\ell$ and $D/sk\ell$) governing load transfer efficiency (LTE$_\delta$) of joints. Such a relationship can be used to back-calculate shear stiffness of a given joint and has evolved as a milestone achievement towards accurate mechanistic modelling of rigid pavement joints. The following are the details of the joint stiffness non-dimensional parameters of a plain cement concrete slab.

For a joint without dowel bars, applied load transfers due to pure shear characteristic of aggregate interlocking mechanism (Ioannides and Korovesis 1990).

$$\text{AGG}_j = \frac{\text{AGG}}{k\ell} \tag{9.44}$$

For a dowel joint (Ioannides and Korovesis 1992), the load transfer taking place due to dowel bars is largely only by shear since the joint gap is relatively small.

$$D_j = \frac{D}{sk\ell} \tag{9.45}$$

where,

AGG_j	=	Non-dimensional stiffness parameter of a joint having no dowel bars
AGG	=	Non-dimensional shear stiffness per unit length of a joint aggregate interlocking
D_j	=	Non-dimensional stiffness parameter of a joint having dowel bars
D	=	Non-dimensional shear stiffness around a dowel bar
k	=	Sub-grade support or modulus of sub-grade reaction, (kg/cm²/cm)
ℓ	=	Radius of relative stiffness of plain cement concrete slab (cm)
s	=	Dowel spacing (cm)

Ioannides and Korovesis (1990; 1992) used a finite element based computer program, ILLI-SLAB and obtained a unique relationship between the non-dimensionless joint-shear stiffness parameters (AGG_j and D_j) and LTE_δ. These relationships hold good for assumed boundary conditions. A few assumptions are given below.

- The plain cement concrete pavement slabs have equal and uniform thickness, flat without any voids under the slab.
- The sub-grade or base support is uniform throughout the length of the joint.
- Load transfer does not take place through the supporting layer, sub-grade or base. The load transfers either by aggregate interlocking when the joint is without dowels or by dowels when the joint is dowelled.
- The LTE of a joint along its length is uniform.
- Primary load transfer mechanism by dowels is largely by shear.

The ILLI-SLAB is based on finite element method and formulated by Tabatabaie, Barenburg and Smith in a report (DOT/FAA/RD-79/4, Vol. II) written in the year 1979. The details related to the joint load transfer mechanism of a plain concrete slab can be obtained from the literature (Ioannides and Korovesis 1992; DOT/FAA/AR-97/7) and a few details are given below.

In case of load transfer by aggregate interlocking mechanism, the AGG_j relates to the ratio D/s, which may be defined as the load transferred per unit length of joint per unit differential deflection of joint. D is the shear stiffness of the dowel supported by the combined action of the dowel concrete interaction (DCI) and shear force in the dowel per unit vertical deflection of the dowel (C). These two stiffnesses are considered as springs in series and summed as follows.

$$D = \frac{1}{\left[\frac{1}{\mathrm{DCI}} + \frac{1}{12C}\right]} \tag{9.46}$$

The formulae used for determining DCI and C may be obtained from literature (Ioannides and Korovesis 1992; DOT/FAA/AR-97/7).

Q: *Calculate (i) the load transfer efficiency of the dowel system and (ii) the differential deflection (DD of the joint), if the deflections of the unloaded and loaded slabs are 0.51 and 1.26 mm respectively.*

A: According to the practice of Alexander et al. 1989, Ioannides and Korovesis (1992) and Odden et al. (2003), load transfer efficiency (LTE) is a ratio between deflections of unloaded slab to loaded slab. LTE is expressed in percentage.

LTE = 100 × (0.51/1.26) = 40.47 %.
DD of joint = 1.26 − 0.51 = 0.75 mm

9.12.4 Detection of Voids and Loss of Support under Corner of Slab or Near a Crack

Loss of support under a slab creates non-uniform distribution of the wheel load stresses which leads to undesirable conditions of concentrated stress zones in the slab. The effect is manifested as cracks or faulting. The loss of support and voids under the slab may occur due to many reasons such mud pumping, densification of the supporting layer, curling up and down of the slab corner and edges.

The void under transverse joints or under an outer corner or edge of a slab can be detected by the NCHRP method using deflection data obtained by applying three different magnitudes of FWD load. From literature it was observed that three load magnitudes were considered by different researchers, viz. 40, 67 and 89 kN (Frabizzio and Buch 2000) and 40, 53.3 or 71.1 kN (Jiang and Tayabji 2000) or four load levels of 21.2, 38.9, 53.0 and 70.7 kN (Chun-Lung and Mang 1994). The FWD loading plate should be positioned at a slab outer corner located near a selected crack (Figure 9.31) or corner and the pavement maximum deflections corresponding to the three levels of load should be measured at standard temperature (preferably during the early morning hours when there is no effect of slab curling). Other loading positions (Figure 9.30) may be considered to detect loss of support or void under the slab.

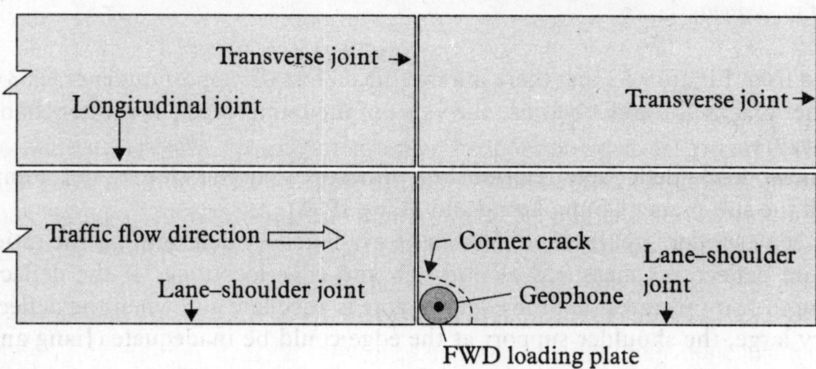

Figure 9.31 *Typical FWD loading position with geophones arrangement for analysis of voids under a slab corner*

A plot should be drawn between measured deflection values on the x-axis and the corresponding load values on the y-axis (Figure 9.32). For each crack, a best fit line should be drawn. These best fit lines should be extrapolated on to the x-axis and the corresponding intercept on the x-axis from the origin is measured for relating possible loss of support under the corner of the slab. The x-intercept represents a "deflection" value under no load. The value of the x-intercept may be compared with the standard support condition or can be treated as a significant loss of support under the slab when the x-intercept is located far away from the origin or when its value is greater than +0.050 mm (Jiang and Tayabji 2000; Crovetti and Darter 1985) or a threshold range of 0.05 to 0.075 mm may be considered (Frabizzio and Buch 2000). A zero or negative value of x-intercept may be treated as no loss of support. The above results may be used with relation to the fault-crack intensity of slab pavements since faulting may indicate possible existence of voids. More details of the testing procedure may be obtained from the investigation conducted by Darter et al. (1985), reported in the NCHRP Report 281 (Frabizzio and Buch 2000) or from procedures developed by Crovetti and Darter (1985).

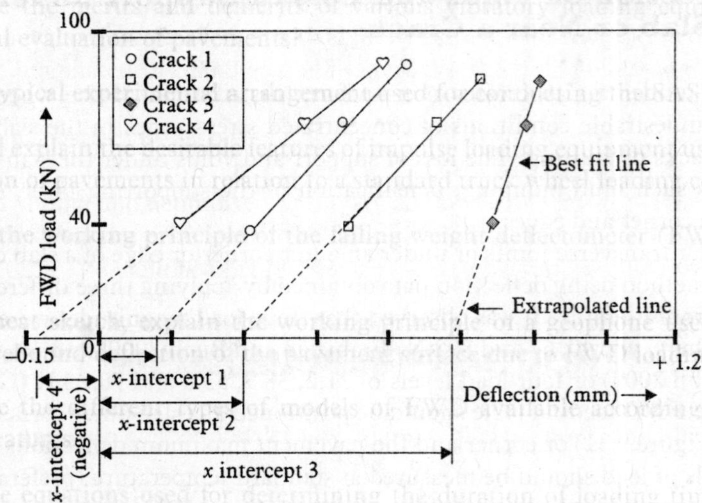

Figure 9.32 *Determination of x-intercepts for detection of voids under slab corner (elaborated based on Frabizzio and Buch 2000)*

It is noted from Figure 9.32 that there is a significant loss of support under crack 3 compared with the other cracks 1, 2 and 4 because the value of the x-intercept 3 is greater than the other x-intercept values.

A non-linear load–deflection relationship indicates that the slab is not completely in contact with the sub-grade (Chung-Lung and Mang 1994).

The slab edge support by the shoulder can be evaluated by determining the ratio between the maximum deflections measured at mid-slab and edge locations. If the deflection ratio value is close to 1, it indicates that the edge support is adequate and when the deflection ratio value is very large, the shoulder support at the edge could be inadequate (Jiang and Tayabji 2000).

The loss of support (k value) under the slab edge and the corner can be back-calculated by using closed-form equations developed by Crovetti and Tirado-Crovetti (1994) based on FWD deflection measurements taken at the slab edge and corner locations or another method of void detection developed by Ricci et al. (1985) at the University of Texas, Austin for the Texas Department of Transportation (Jackson et al. 1994).

Exercises

9.1 Distinguish between functional and structural evaluation of pavements.

9.2 State the purpose of pavement evaluation.

9.3 What are the merits and demerits of destructive and non-destructive methods of structural evaluation of pavements?

9.4 What are the different NDT methods available based on application of test load? Write examples for each test case?

9.5 Compare the working principle of the Benkelman beam, Lacroix deflectograph and the travelling deflectograph.

9.6 With neat sketches, explain the working principle of the Benkelman beam used to measure rebound surface deflection of flexible pavements.

9.7 What are the salient features of the Benkelman beam? Explain with a neat sketch.

9.8 State the need of calibration of the Benkelman beam. What is the standard method of calibration.

9.9 What is the significance of the pavement condition survey for pavement evaluation using the Benkelman beam? Briefly explain the IRC classification types of pavements based on the pavement surface condition data.

9.10 In detail, explain the method of measurement of rebound surface deflections using the Benkelman beam. What are the loading truck standards prescribed according to IRC:81?

9.11 How do we calculate the pavement deflection from the Benkelman beam deflection data?

9.12 Explain the need and details of the corrections required to be made to the BB measured deflection.

9.13 What are the factors affecting the values of seasonal correction factor and temperature correction factor?

9.14 In detail, explain how the design traffic should be determined according to IRC:81.

9.15 Why is there a need to delineate homogenous sub-sections of the BB surveyed road stretch?

9.16 In detail, explain the following methods used for delineating homogenous sub-sections of the BB surveyed road stretch:

(i) AASHTO recommended method, (ii) cu-sum method or the sum of cumulative deviation's method and (iii) the method which uses the coefficient of variation (CoV) of measured deflections.

9.17 Explain in detail how the adjacent homogeneous sub-sections of BB tested road stretches are statistically evaluated using student T-test values.

9.18 What are the limitations of the Benkelman beam test and the measured surface rebound deflection method? Draw figures wherever applicable.

9.19 What is the working principle of the dynaflect used for structural evaluation of pavements? Draw a typical force curve due to steady state vibratory loading.

9.20 Draw the configuration of geophones used for testing with road raters and dynaflects.

9.21 What are the merits and demerits of various vibratory loading equipment used for structural evaluation of pavements?

9.22 Draw a typical experimental arrangement used for conducting the SASW test.

9.23 State and explain the desirable features of impulse loading equipment used for structural evaluation of pavements in relation to a standard truck wheel loading condition.

9.24 Explain the working principle of the falling weight deflectometer (FWD) using a neat sketch.

9.25 With a neat sketch, explain the working principle of a geophone used for measuring vertical rebound deflection of the pavement surface due to FWD loading.

9.26 What are the different types of models of FWD available according to their salient testing features?

9.27 Write the equations used for determining the duration of loading time and height of fall required to produce a desirable impulse load of a FWD when the values of falling mass, spring constant, maximum force exerted on the pavement and acceleration due to gravity are given.

9.28 Explain the need of calibration of FWD sensors such as geophones and load cells.

9.29 State the need of repeatability and reproducibility in FWD measurements.

9.30 What is the significance of linearity of deflections measured with reference to FWD load? Why are linear relationships useful in back-calculation analysis?

9.31 Draw a typical layout of locations of FWD test points in single and dual lane highways. What are the factors influencing the decision of intervals of FWD testing points?

9.32 What are the methods that can be employed to obtain pavement crust details?

9.33 What are the salient points that you can make from the deflection basins measured in different seasons of a year with reference to pavement temperatures and moisture variations?

9.34 Draw a neat sketch showing a deflection bowl with standard notations and write various equations used to express characteristics of the deflection bowl shape. State the uses or applications of deflection bowl shape parameters for evaluation of pavements.

9.35 What do you understand by back-calculation of pavement layer moduli? Write a short note on the historical methods of back-calculation of flexible pavement layer moduli.

9.36 With a flow chart, explain the process of back-calculation of flexible pavement layer moduli using microcomputer methods.

9.37 State the need of temperature corrections applied to (i) the FWD measured deflection bowl and (ii) the back-calculated layer moduli.

9.38 State how the back-calculated moduli are verified and write the widely (a few important ones) used relationships available in literature for estimating the flexible pavement layer moduli.

9.39 How are the latest techniques like artificial neural networks and genetic algorithms useful for back-calculation of flexible pavement layer moduli?

9.40 State the uses and applications of pavement layer moduli back-calculated from the FWD measured deflection bowl data.

9.41 Write a short note on structural evaluation of rigid pavements using FWD. Draw sketches wherever necessary.

9.42 With a neat sketch, show the FWD loading plate position and geophone configuration adopted for back-calculation of rigid pavement material response parameters.

9.43 How are methods of back-calculation techniques used for rigid pavement evaluation classified? Explain each method with suitable examples.

9.44 Write the salient features of the ILLI-SLAB back-calculation program.

9.45 Write the salient features of the NUS-BACK back-calculation program.

9.46 Write the salient features of the ILLI-SLAB back-calculation program developed at the University of Illinois.

9.47 What is the procedure proposed by Crovetti and Tirado-Crovetti for back-calculation of the k value of slab supporting layer and the elastic modulus of the PCC slab (E_{slab})?

9.48 Explain the drawbacks associated with the graphical method of back-calculation of rigid pavement parameters.

9.49 State why the back-calculated rigid pavement parameters may significantly vary. How do you verify back-calculated parameters.

9.50 State the significance of load transfer across a transverse joint used for assessing structural performance of rigid pavements.

9.51 Draw a typical standard layout of the FWD loading plate and geophone configuration adopted for determination of LTE of a transverse joint.

9.52 Write a few important and fundamental equations including non-dimensional parameters proposed by Ioannides and Korovesis for determination of LTE of a transverse joint.

9.53 What are the factors affecting LTE of a joint?

9.54 What are the widely used methods used for detection of voids or loss of support under a slab corner or near a crack? In detail, explain the method recommended by NCHRP.

10

Structural Evaluation of Unbound Granular and Sub-grade Layers Using Dynamic Cone Penetrometer (DCP)

Introduction

The recent trend of pavement design is to adopt mechanistic and empirical ($M-E$) methods. These methods utilise the engineering properties of the pavement layer materials. For this purpose, assessment of strength or stiffness in terms of elastic moduli of granular and sub-grade soil is an important consideration for pavement design as well as quality control during construction. Determination of elastic moduli values of granular/ sub-grade soil using FWD or by a laboratory testing method could be a costly procedure for evaluating low-volume/ unimportant roads. Therefore, deriving a quick, simple and low-cost device involving less skilled personal is an essential necessity to evolve empirical parameters that relate engineering properties of in situ soils. In this regard, the dynamic cone penetrometer (DCP) test has been extensively used by many institutions and agencies around the globe to quickly determine an index value which represents the strength of compacted material of unbound granular and sub-grade layers with reasonable accuracy and at low cost.

10.1 Development of the Dynamic Cone Penetrometer Test (DCPT)

The first DCP known as the Scala penetrometer was developed by Scala (1956) in Australia and used to determine in situ CBR of cohesive soils. The Scala penetrometer consists of a 9.072 kg sliding hammer which drops from a height of 508 mm. The hammer impact energy is transferred through a 15.875 mm diameter steel rod to a cone fitted at its bottom end. The apex angle of the cone is taken as 30° and it penetrates into the soil up to 762 mm.

Later, a modified DCPT was developed by van Vuuren (1969) which was similar to the working principle of the Scala penetrometer. The modified DCP consists of a 10 kg hammer dropping freely from a height of 460 mm. The impulse force is transferred through a 16 mm diameter steel rod to a fitted cone having an apex angle of 30°. The device can be used to test the soil up to 1000 mm depth. van Vuuren developed a relationship between the DCP reading and the CBR value of sub-grade soils in Pretoria and prescribed that the device is suitable for determining CBR values ranging from 1 to 50.

In 1973, the Transvaal Roads Department in South Africa identified a DCP for rapid and routine evaluation of existing highway pavements (Kleyn 1975). Two kinds of cones with apex angles, 30° and 60° were utilised. The DCP consisted of an 8 kg hammer falling from a height of 574 mm. A comparative study between the results obtained using a DCP with 60° cone and 30° cone was reported (Kleyn et al. 1982). In 1982, Kleyn and Savage reported another investigation on sub-grade tested with a 60° cone DCP comprising of an 8 kg dropping hammer falling from a height of 574 mm.

Since then, researchers of many countries like South Africa (Transvaal Roads Department; Kleyn et al. 1982; Bester and Hallat 1977; Kleyn and van Heerden 1983; Wolff et al. 1993), Australia (Smith and Pratt 1983), New Zealand, Zimbabwe and several other countries (Livneh et al. 2000) have extensively used the present version of DCP (Kleyn and Savage 1982) for exercising quality control during construction, design and evaluation of flexible pavements. In the recent past, the DCPT has been adopted for design of flexible pavements and has also been routinely used for assessing in situ strength of unbound granular and sub-grade soil strata in many other countries, viz. USA (Webster et al. 1992, 1994; Grogan and Tingle 1999; FHWA; AASHTO; ASTM D6951 2004; KDOT; MnDOT; WDOT; MDOT; FLDOT; ODOT, INDOT and others), Israel (Livneh and Ishai 1987; Livneh 1991; Livneh et al. 1995, 2000), Ireland (McGrath et al. 1989), UK (TRL 1990), India (Sood et al. 1996; Srinivasa et al. 2001, 2003, 2006; IRC:SP:72-2007; IITR; IITKGP).

In the following sections, we will explain the details and uses of DCPT for pavement engineering.

10.2 The Dynamic Cone Penetrometer (DCP)

The dynamic cone penetrometer (DCP) is a portable equipment that can be used to evaluate unbound granular base, sub-base, sub-grade and also pipeline congested/ narrow trenches where testing with other equipment is difficult and not feasible due to cost, space and time constraints. Because of this, DCPT has gained in popularity in many parts of the world.

The widely used DCP's salient features are presented in Figure 10.1. The basic principle involved in the operation of this apparatus is the measuring of the resistance offered by the pavement layers to the penetration of a standard cone with a diameter of 20 mm (with 60° apex angle)[‡] driven by an 8 kg hammer freely falling through a height of 575 mm (IRC:

[‡] The initial DCP cone apex angle was taken as 30° (Scala 1956; van Vuuren 1969). Later, the cone apex angle was revised to 60° (Kleyn et al. 1982; Livneh and Ishai 1985; Webster et al. 1992). The revised cone angle of 60° was adopted by many standard institutions (FHWA, TRL-UK, ARRB, ASTM, IRC etc.) and formalised as a national standard in different countries.

SP:72-2007). The amount of penetration (in mm) of the cone is generally reported in terms of the average penetration per blow, $DCPI_{60°}$ (mm/blow). This indicates relative shear strength of the material across the depth tested. During penetration of the cone, the shear strength of the material is mainly accrued due to resistance offered by the shear displacement of the soil particles. A greater value of $DCPI_{60°}$ indicates a softer material and vice versa.

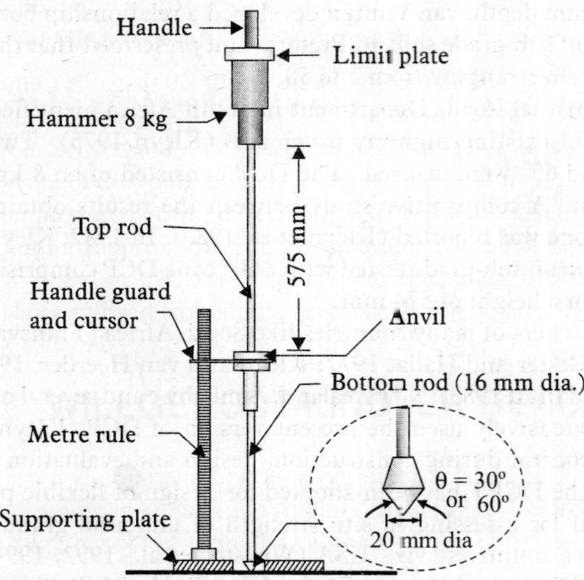

Figure 10.1 *Details of the dynamic cone penetrometer test equipment*

10.2.1 Terminology Used for Indicating the DCP Test Value

In literature, the DCP cone average penetration per blow has been represented in many ways, viz. DCP, DCP index (DCPI), penetration rate (PR), penetration index (PI), $DCP_{\theta°}$. Number of blows required to penetrate a given layer material is represented as DCPN, DCP structural number (DSN), blow rate (BR) and number of blows required to penetrate the given thickness of a layer material (N_{DCP}). In this text, the DCP cone average penetration per blow (in mm/blow) is denoted as $DCPI_{\theta°}$ value, where $\theta°$ denotes apex angle of the cone used.

10.3 Material Testing with DCP

It is convenient and generally recommended to conduct DCP tests during the post-monsoon season because during that time, the accumulation of water content in the granular and sub-grade layers will be more compared to other seasons. The tests are generally conducted along the wheel path, at premature failures or at any selected locations for investigating pavement performance or for exercising construction quality control of granular soil layers.

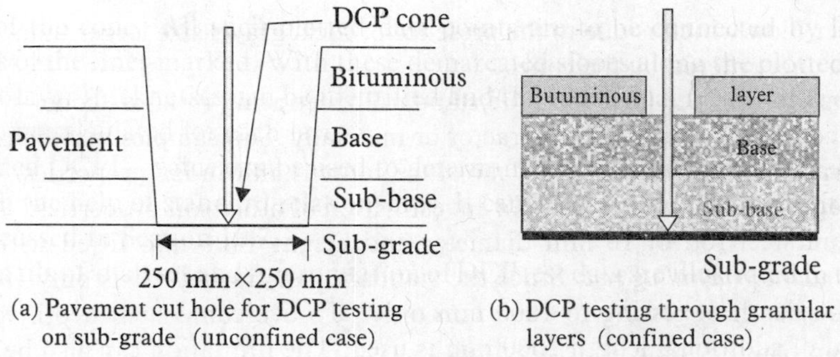

Figure 10.2 *Schematic arrangement for DCP testing on sub-grade and base (modified and elaborated based on Livneh et al. 2000)*

For conducting the DCP test on an existing pavement, a pit is to be excavated in the top (bituminous or concrete) layer with a dimension of about 0.25 m × 0.25 m to the required depth up to (i) base or (ii) sub-grade level. The excavated layer/s material should be removed. Now, the base plate of the DCP is placed in the pit over the sub-grade layer (Figure 10.2(a)) or on the plain surface of the granular base layer (Figure 10.2(b) and 10.4). It should be noted that if the test is intended to be conducted only on the sub-grade, the DCP base plate should be placed over the sub-grade (Figure 10.3).

Figure 10.3 *DCP test in progress (unconfined case)*

Figure 10.4 *DCP test in progress (confined case)*

Just before the start of the test, the initial reading on the DCP scale should be noted by holding the rod vertical with the cone in contact with the surface of the layer material. While one person holds the DCP handle, another person should lift the hammer to the pre-determined height (i.e., 575 mm). The hammer should be allowed to drop freely on to the anvil. For each such blow, the corresponding cumulative penetration value of the cone should be noted. DCP testing should generally be stopped when the cone does not penetrate more than 1 mm per blow which is due to the presence of rock, gravel size larger than 20 mm or due to hard strata encountered by the cone.

After completion of the DCP test, the standard penetrating rod (i.e., cone–rod) should be extracted either with a mechanical extractor or manually. Soil samples may be collected from a few test locations to determine field moisture content and index properties. Collection of such data is optional and can be used for investigation of other soil properties.

The bottom steel rod of 16 mm diameter and height 1000 mm fitted with the cone is called the *standard penetrating rod*. Since the standard penetrating rod is only 1000 mm high, it restricts the depth of testing to 1000 mm only. To overcome such depth restriction, an extension rod of additional length 1000 mm is used. The limitation can also be overcome by using a single rod of 1300 or 1500 mm length in place of the standard penetrating rod (Livneh and Livneh 1994).

As a standard procedure, when the standard penetrating rod has completely penetrated into the soil, an extension rod of 1000 mm length can be screwed on to the standard penetrating rod. In such situations, the total length of the penetrating rod will become 1000 + 1000 = 2000 mm. From an investigation on cohesive and non-cohesive materials in Israel (Livneh et al. 2000), it was found that a multiplying correction factor of 0.2 and 0.1 should be used to correct the CBR values derived from the DCP test results obtained when using a penetrating rod length of 2000 mm and 1500 mm respectively.

It is noted that the DCP test can also be conducted in the laboratory on re-moulded soil or granular material compacted in a steel mould. A mould having an internal minimum diameter of 304.8 mm (12 inches) may be used to significantly eliminate the effect of confinement. Such test details can be obtained from a research work carried out at the University of Illinois at Urbana-Champaign (Ayers et al. 1989). Another method is to construct a test bed of pavement in an open area. Such tests can also be carried out as a prototype model.

10.3.1 Automated and Instrumented DCP

The DCP test can also be carried out with similar specifications and the same procedure by using an electronically operated equipment known as automated DCP (ADCP). The automated DCP, which is mounted on a trolley, is equipped with an electrically operated motor used for lifting and dropping the hammer at given intervals of time. The whole system can be controlled automatically by a laptop computer which records the blow count and penetration readings, extracts the cone–rod after testing, analyses the data and finally gives the results in a standard format.

The iDCP is another version of such a DCP instrument. It is fitted with a load-cell and an accelerometer which electronically records the hammer impulse produced acceleration, velocity and cone displacement histories (Chua and Lytton 1988; Nazarian et al. 2000). Desired outputs can be obtained by analysing the data using standard software packages supplied by the iDCP manufacturer.

10.4 Determination of DCP Index ($DCPI_{\theta^\circ}$) Value

The DCP test data can be represented in different formats (Kleyn 1975; Kleyn et al. 1982). To determine the value of $DCPI_{\theta^\circ}$, a chart is to be drawn with the number of blows vs. cumulative penetration of the cone. All such plotted data points are to be connected by lines and the slope changes of the lines marked. With these demarcated slopes along the plotted data points, the pavement layer thicknesses can be identified and the individual mean value of $DCPI_{\theta°}$ in mm/blow can be calculated for each layer.

The obtained $DCPI_{\theta°}$ value can be used to determine any standard test value, viz. CBR, E_s and UCS with the help of standard relationships. It can also be used for different applications as will be discussed in Section 10.7.

Typical details of analyses and interpretation of DCP test data are illustrated in the following examples.

Q: *A DCP was used for testing a pavement crust down to its granular layers. The cone apex angle was taken as 60°. The following data was obtained from the DCP testing.*

Blow number	*DCP scale reading (cm)*	*Number of blows*	*DCP scale reading (cm)*	*Number of blows*	*DCP scale reading (cm)*
0	9.5 *	13	19.0	26	56.1
1	10.1	14	21.3	27	59.8
2	10.7	15	23.5	28	63.4
3	11.3	16	25.8	29	66.9
4	11.9	17	27.8	30	70.5
5	12.5	18	30.0	31	74.1
6	13.1	19	32.3	32	77.7
7	13.7	20	34.6	33	81.3
8	14.3	21	38.2	34	84.8
9	14.9	22	41.8	35	88.4
10	15.5	23	45.4	36	92.0
11	16.1	24	49.0	37	95.6
12	16.8	25	52.6	38	99.2

*Initial value on the DCP scale just before dropping its hammer

Determine (i) pavement layer thicknesses, (ii) mean $DCPI_{60°}$ value of each layer and (iii) mean CBR value of the layers using the relationship developed by TRL-UK. Draw charts wherever necessary.

A: The following step-wise procedure is adopted for the determination of the above parameters.

i. Determine the value of penetration per blow by deducting the initial value on the scale.
ii. Calculate the cumulative penetration values corresponding to each blow.
iii. Draw a chart using the data of cumulative penetration vs. number of blows (see Figure 10.5).
iv. From the above chart, identify the slope change of the penetration curve and determine the average penetration/blow for each slope change. In Figure 10.5, we can see that there are three different slopes and their corresponding average penetration/blow are 6.1, 22.3 and 35.9 mm/blow respectively from the top to the bottom layer.
v. Layer thicknesses can be obtained from this demarcated slope changes of the penetration curve.
vi. Substitute average penetration/blow values in equation (10.10) as recommended by the TRL-UK, Road Note 8 (1990) and determine the corresponding layer's CBR value. It is

noted that in place of equation (10.10), any other standard equation (from Table 10.1) may be used for converting DCPI to the CBR value.

vii. With the above data, another chart can be drawn which represents variation of the CBR value across the depth (See Figure 10.6).

Blow number	DCP scale reading (cm)	Pen./blow (mm/blow)	Cumulative penetration (mm)	CBR(%)	Remarks
0	9.5	0	0		
1st	10.1	6	6	45.4	Layer 1
2nd	10.7	6	12	45.4	Thickness = 73.0 mm
3rd	11.3	6	18	45.4	Mean values:
4th	11.9	6	24	45.4	$DCPI_{60°}$ = 6.1 mm/blow
5th	12.5	6	30	45.4	CBR = 44.7 %
6th	13.1	6	36	45.4	
7th	13.7	6	42	45.4	
8th	14.3	6	48	45.4	
9th	14.9	6	54	45.4	
10th	15.5	6	60	45.4	
11th	16.1	6	66	45.4	
12th	16.8	7	73	38.6	
13th	19.0	22	95	11.5	Layer 2
14th	21.3	23	118	11.0	Thickness = 178.0 mm
15th	23.5	22	140	11.5	Mean values:
16th	25.8	23	163	11.0	$DCPI_{60°}$ = 22.3 mm/blow
17th	27.8	20	183	12.7	
18th	30.0	22	205	11.5	CBR = 11.3 %
19th	32.3	23	228	11.0	
20th	34.6	23	251	11.0	
21st	38.2	36	287	6.8	Layer 3
22nd	41.8	36	323	6.8	Thickness = 646.0 mm
23rd	45.4	36	359	6.8	Mean values:
24th	49.0	36	395	6.8	$DCPI_{60°}$ = 35.9 mm/blow
25th	52.6	36	431	6.8	
26th	56.1	35	466	7.0	CBR = 6.9%
27th	59.8	37	503	6.6	
28th	63.4	36	539	6.8	
29th	66.9	35	574	7.0	
30th	70.5	36	610	6.8	
31st	74.1	36	646	6.8	
32nd	77.7	36	682	6.8	
33rd	81.3	36	718	6.8	
34th	84.8	35	753	7.0	
35th	88.4	36	789	6.8	
36th	92.0	36	825	6.8	
37th	95.6	36	861	6.8	
38th	99.2	36	897	6.8	

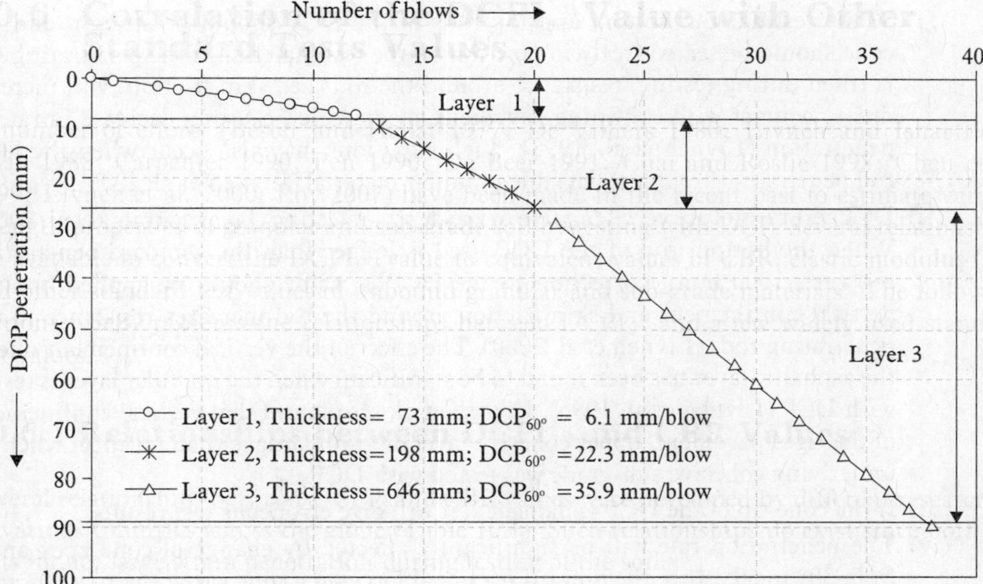

Figure 10.5 *Analysis of DCP test data*

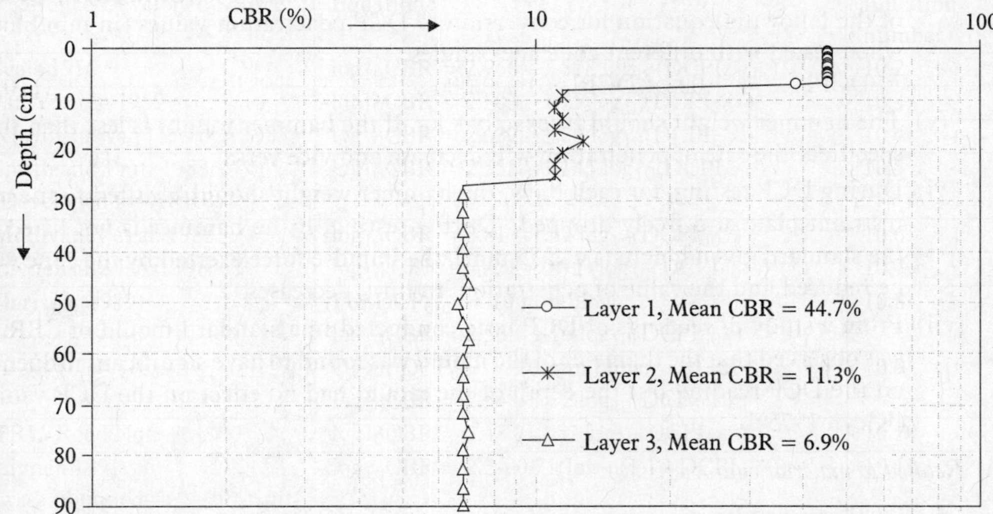

Figure 10.6 *Variation of CBR values across the depth tested*

10.5 Factors Affecting DCP Test Results

The following factors affect the DCP test results.

(a) *Related to the equipment, testing procedure and operation*:

(i) While testing, the bottom and top rods of the DCP should be straight and the cone should be seated freely in position on the test material. If the penetrating rod is tilted during testing, resistance around the rod (i.e., skin friction) will increase due to contact with confining pavement layers which causes a decrease in rate of penetration (Livneh et al. 1995). Such situations may also occur when the DCP rod penetrates through collapsible granular material (Livneh et al. 2000).

(ii) DCP test results are very sensitive to the depth of testing (Jayawickrama et al. 2000). When the bottom rod of the DCP used is longer than the standard penetrating rod (i.e., 1000 mm), correction to the $DCPI_{\theta°}$ value should be applied because vertical confinement and skin friction around the rod increases resistance to the penetrating rod ((Livneh et al. 2000). The effect of the vertical confinement due to the asphaltic layer has been found to be significant when the granular layer is tested with DCP (Livneh et al. 1995). Livneh et al. also found that vertical confinement of the rigid pavement, upper cohesive layer or granular layer had no effect when an underlying cohesive sub-grade was tested with DCP.

(iii) If the cone tip of the DCP is damaged, it will give erroneous test results.

(iv) The penetration rate will be significantly affected by change of cone apex angle from 30° to 60° since the upward frictional force on a cone surface with a 60° apex angle will be greater. A study on this subject reveals that the penetration rates obtained by the DCP with cone apex angle 30° are 10% greater than those obtained with the cone having an apex angle of 60° (Livneh 1991). Livneh suggests the use of the following equation for conversion of DCP penetration values (in mm/blow) when tested with different cone apex angles.

$$DCPI_{30°} = (1.092 \times DCPI_{60°}) + 0.006 \tag{10.1}$$

(v) The hammer weight should be exactly 8 kg. If the hammer weight is less than that specified, the rate of penetration will decrease and vice versa.

(vi) During DCP testing, for each blow, the hammer weight should be lifted to the top restraint plate and freely dropped. During testing, if the hammer is not lifted to the standard given height (i.e., 575 mm), the impulse force exerted by the cone will be reduced and the value of penetration, in turn, decreases.

(vii) From a study of readings of DCP tests conducted in a standard mould of CBR, it was observed that the diameter of the mould was found to have significant influence on the DCP reading but the depth of the mould had no effect on the DCP values (Kleyn 1975).

(b) *Related to material characteristics:*

(i) DCP test results are very sensitive to variations in moisture content present in the test materials (Kleyn 1975; Kleyn and Savage 1982). As the moisture content increases, the penetration rate of DCP also increases and vice versa. Due to this reason, DCP tests are conducted during the post-monsoon season when the granular and sub-grade layers become soft and their minimum strength are recorded.

(ii) DCPI varies with test material composition, soil class, coefficient of curvature, uniformity, density of the layer material and plasticity of the soil (Kleyn 1975; Kleyn and Savage 1982).

(iii) DCPI will be influenced by the intensity of compaction and confinement of granular and sub-grade layers.

10.6 Correlation of the DCPI$_{\theta°}$ Value with Other Standard Tests Values

A number of efforts (Bester and Hallat 1977; De Villiers 1980; Livneh and Ishai 1987; Chau 1988; Carpenter 1990; Pen 1990; De Beer 1991; Chai and Roslie 1998; Chen et al. 1999; Livneh et al. 2000; Roy 2007) have been made in the recent past to estimate various strength properties of granular and sub-grade soil by testing with DCP. Several relationships are available to convert the DCPI$_{\theta°}$ value to equivalent values of CBR, elastic modulus (E_s) and other standard test values of unbound granular and sub-grade materials. The following sections briefly presents the relationships between DCPI$_{\theta°}$ and a few widely used standard test values.

10.6.1 Relationships between DCPI$_{\theta°}$ and CBR Values

Several relationships between DCPI$^{\circ}_{\theta}$ and CBR values were developed by different researchers in various countries across the globe (Table 10.1). Such relationships do exist since both the tests induce large strain penetration during testing of the soil.

Table 10.1 *A few widely used relationships between DCPI$_{\theta°}$ and CBR values*

Reference/Developed/Source	Equation*	Equation number
Scala 1956	$\log_{10}CBR = 2.966 - 1.518 \log_{10}(DCPI_{scala})$	10.2
van Vuuren 1969	$\log_{10}CBR = 2.503 - 1.15 \log_{10}(DCPI_{30°})$	10.3
Kleyn and van Heerden 1983	$\log_{10}CBR = 2.632 - 1.28 \log_{10}(DCPI_{60°})$	10.4
Smith and Pratt 1983 (Developed for ARRB)	$\log_{10}CBR = 2.555 - 1.145 \log_{10}(DCPI_{60°})$	10.5
McElvaney et al. 1985	$\log_{10}CBR = 2.81 - 1.32 \log_{10}(DCPI_{60°})$	10.6
Livneh and Ishai 1987	$\log_{10} CBR^F = 2.2 - 0.71 (\log_{10}(DCPI_{30°}))^{1.5}$	10.7
Harison (1989)	For $DCP_{60°} = 10$ mm/blow: $\log_{10}CBR = 2.56 - 1.16 \log_{10}(DCPI_{60°})$	10.8
	Or for $DCP_{60°} < 10$ mm/blow: $\log_{10}CBR = 2.54 - 1.12 \log_{10}(DCP_{60°})$	10.9
TRL, Road Note 8, 1990	$\log_{10}CBR = 2.48 -1.057 \log_{10}(DCPI_{60°})$	10.10
Livneh 1991 (was obtained by substituting equation (10.1) in equation (10.7))	$\log_{10}CBR = 2.2 - 0.71(\log_{10}(1.1 \times DCPI_{60°}))^{1.5}$	10.11
Webster et al. 1992 (the relationship developed for the US Corps of Engineers)	Overall correlative relationship: $\log_{10} CBR = 2.465 - 1.12 \log_{10}(DCPI_{60°})$	10.12

continues

Table 10.1 *continued*

Reference/Developed/Source	Equation*	Equation number
Ese et al. 1994	$\log_{10} CBR = 2.438 - 1.065 \log_{10}(DCPI_{60°})$	10.13
Webster et al. 1994	For CH soil: $\log_{10} CBR = 2.542 - 1.0 \log_{10}(DCPI_{60°})$	10.14
	For CL soil having CBR<10%: $\log_{10} CBR = 3.538 - 2.0 \log10(DCPI_{60°})$	10.15
Livneh et al. 1995	$\log_{10} CBR^F = 2.14 - 0.69 (\log_{10}(DCPI_{60°}))^{1.5}$	10.16
Nazzai (2003)	$CBR = 1.04 + 2559.44/(-7.35 + DCPI_{60°}^{1.84})$ ‡	10.17
Coonse (1999) at North Carolina State University (Cited in Roy 2007)	$\log_{10} CBR^f = 2.53 - 1.14 \log_{10}(DCPI_{60°})$	10.18

*Note: $DCPI_{60°}$ and $DCPI_{30°}$ are the penetration values in mm/blow of DCP having cone angle 60° and 30° respectively; CBR is the California bearing ratio (%); DCP_{scala} indicates the $DCPI_{\theta°}$ value obtained by using the Scala penetrometer; CBR^F indicates field CBR; and CBR^f indicates the field CBR value of cohesive piedmont residual soil. ‡ The $DCPI_{60°}$ values considered in between 6.31 and 66.67 mm/blow.

The following are a few salient details of the different investigations made for developing relationships between $DCPI_{\theta°}$ and CBR.

(a) Scala (1956) and Kleyn (1975) identified a straight line relationship between the $DCPI_{\theta°}$ and CBR data when plotted on a log–log scale.

(b) Kleyn (1975) studied several factors affecting the readings of DCP tests conducted in a standard mould of CBR. The diameter of the mould was found to have significant influence on the DCP reading due to the confinement effect. The length of the mould had no influence on the reading. For a few types of material tested, the DCP cone resistance observed near the end of the mould was slightly more.

(c) Smith and Pratt (1983) developed a relationship by conducting CBR and DCP in situ tests on natural mottled clay sub-grade in Australian and imported yellow clay with sandstone used for sub-grade.

(d) The US Corps of Engineers (Webster et al. 1992) developed a relationship based on lab CBR values. Many $DCPI_{\theta°}$ – CBR relationships developed by different researchers were compared with this equation and found to be in satisfactory agreement. This relationship has been widely used by many researchers (Webster et al. 1992; Livneh 1995; Siekmeier et al. 2000; and Chen et al. 2001).

(e) Ese et al. (1994) evaluated 23 road sections with a granular base course in Norway and extensively tested the material for determination of laboratory CBR and field $DCPI_{\theta°}$ values. From this data, they developed an equation to convert $DCPI_{\theta°}$ to CBR of the granular base material. They (i) reported that the difference in confining pressure in the laboratory and the field was accounted for in the equation and (ii) suggested that the critical stability value for the gravel base was 2.6 mm/blow.

(f) Nazzal (2003) extensively conducted laboratory CBR and field DCP tests on granular material, clay soil, soil treated with florolite, lime and cement. During the laboratory CBR testing of the materials, the moisture content and compaction level maintained were similar to field conditions. By carrying out non-linear regression analysis of the tests data, an equation was developed. He found that the estimated CBR values by this equation match well with Webster et al.'s (1992) equation when the DCPI$_{60^\circ}$ value is greater than 20 mm/blow.

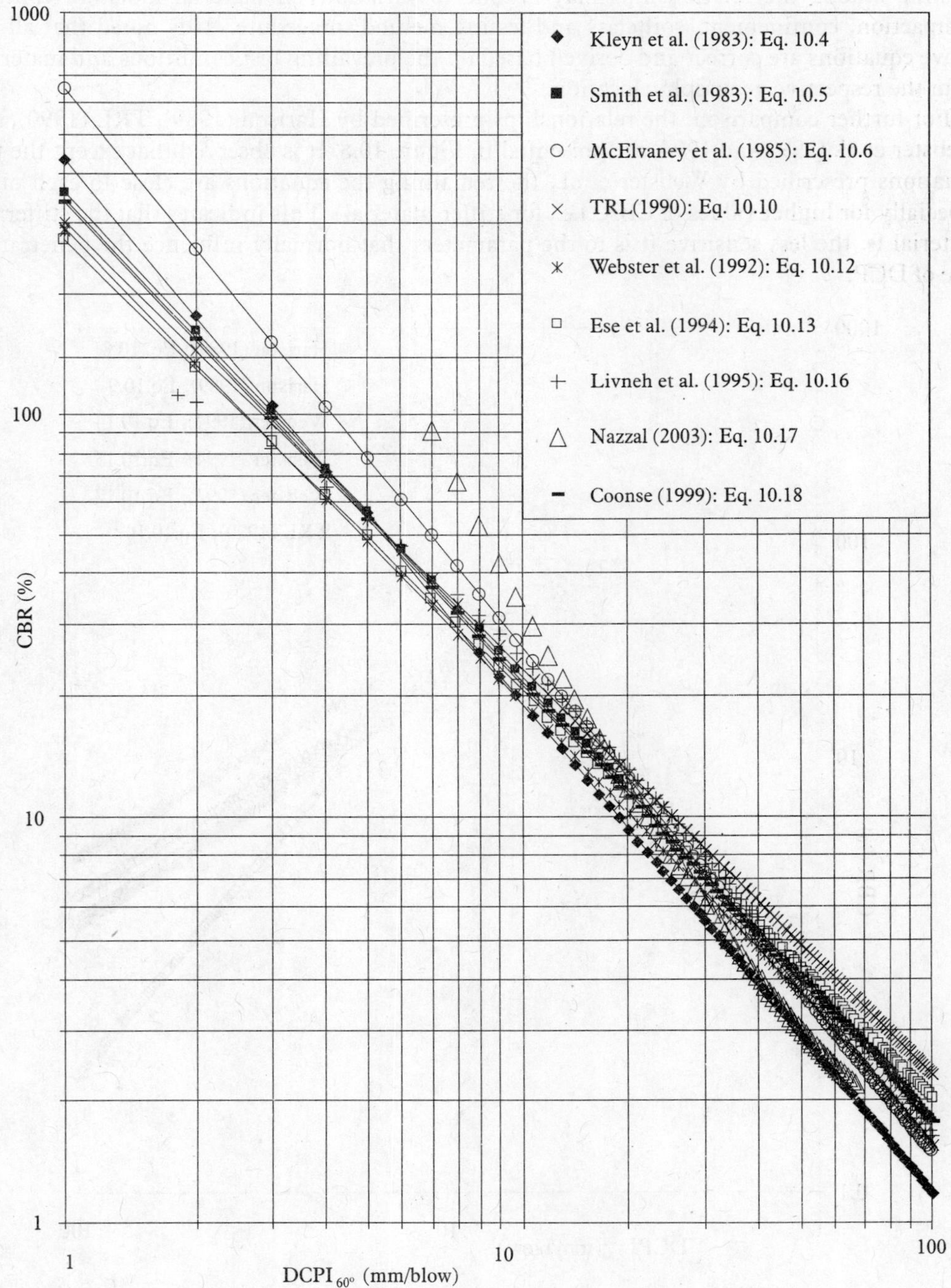

Figure 10.7 *Relationships between DCPI$_{60^\circ}$ and CBR*

A few relations between $DCPI_{60°}$ and CBR are presented in Figure 10.7 and it is observed that except for the relationships prescribed by Nazzal (2003) and McElvaney et al. (1985), all the remaining lines are found to be within a fairly narrow bandwidth. The variations existing among the relationships may be due to variations in material moisture content, compaction, confinement, soil class and testing method/ procedure. It is noted that all the above equations are correct and derived based on the prevailing test conditions and materials from the respective geographic location.

For further comparison, the relationships prescribed by Harison (1989), TRL (1990), and Webster et al. (1992 and 1994) are presented in Figure 10.8. It is observed that except the two equations prescribed by Webster et al., the remaining the equations are close to each other especially for higher values of CBR (i.e., for stiffer material). This indicates that the stiffer the material is, the less sensitive it is to the parameters that normally influence the penetrating rate of DCP.

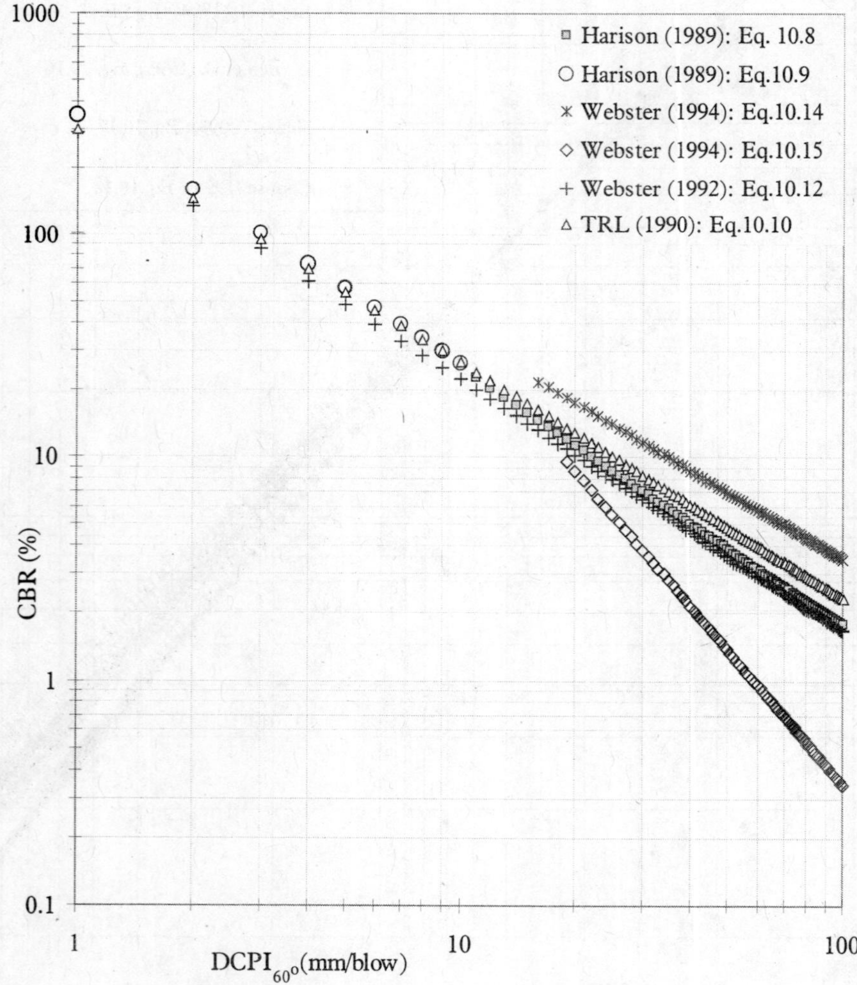

Figure 10.8 *Comparison of a few selected relationships between $DCPI_{60°}$ and CBR*

10.6.2 Relationships between DCPI$_{\theta°}$ and Back-calculated Sub-grade Modulus Values

Correlation of FWD-back-calculated pavement layer moduli with DCPT values can be used for design of flexible pavements. Such models/equations are useful tools to a number of agencies who cannot afford to evaluate the pavement using FWD. Even if an agency has an FWD, it may not be viable to use the same for extensive preliminary investigations. Also, wherever such information is available, the moduli values estimated from DCPI values can be used to check the effective moduli determined from the back-calculation procedure adopted. Such data can also be used to fix a narrow range of layer moduli in procedures of back-calculation where a long iterative process needs to be shortened (See Section 9.10.2).

We will now present different regression-based models used to estimate pavement layer moduli.

Pen (1990) developed the following two relationships from field DCP evaluation.

$$\log(E_s) = 3.250 - 0.89 \log(\text{DCPI}_{60°}) \tag{10.19}$$

where E_s is the sub-grade elastic modulus in MPa obtained from the deflections measured using the PHONIX FWD and,

$$\log(E_s) = 3.653 - 1.17 \log(\text{DCPI}_{60°}) \tag{10.20}$$

where E_s is the sub-grade elastic modulus in MPa back-calculated by the PEACH system.

De Beer (1991) prescribed the following equation to estimate the sub-grade modulus from the DCPI value.

$$\text{Sub-grade elastic modulus (MPa)} = 1176\times(\text{DCPI}_{60°})^{-1.082} \tag{10.21}$$

where the DCPI value, in mm/blow, is obtained with a 60° cone.

To determine the in situ sub-grade modulus, the following equations were prescribed by Chai and Roslie (1998). Relationship between in situ CBR and DCPI:

$$E_s = 17.6 \times (269/\text{BR})^{0.64} \tag{10.22}$$

Based on FWD back-calculated results:

$$E_s = 2224\times(\text{BR})^{-0.996} \tag{10.23}$$

where E_s = sub-grade modulus value (in MPa) and BR = blows/300 mm penetration of a cone having a 60° apex angle.

Chen et al (1999) prescribed the following expression for estimation of sub-grade modulus from the DCPI value based on the structural evaluation of a pavement using FWD.

$$\text{Sub-grade resilient modulus (MPa)} = 338.0\times(\text{DCPI}_{60°})^{-0.39} \tag{10.24}$$

where the $DCPI_{60°}$ value is in the range of 10 to 60 mm/blow.

Livneh (1991) developed the following relationships by correlating the DCPI values with the sub-grade moduli values which were back-calculated from the Benkelman beam deflection data.

$$\log(E_s) = 1.993 + \log(k) - 0.936 \log(DCPI_{60°}) \tag{10.25}$$

$$\log(E_s) = 2.034 + \log(k) - 0.936 \log(DCPI_{30°}) \tag{10.26}$$

where $DCPI_{30°}$ and $DCPI_{60°}$ are DCP penetration values with the cone apex angle as 30° and 60° respectively and k is a factor with a mean value of 14.7.

George and Uddin (2000) developed the following equations for design of flexible pavements based on sub-grade characterisation using DCP (cited in Roy 2007).

For fine grained soils:

$$\log(E_s) = 2.726 - 0.492 \log(DCPI_{60^0}) \tag{10.27}$$

For coarse grained soils:

$$\log(E_s) = 2.372 - 0.475 \log(DCPI_{60^0}) \tag{10.28}$$

where E_s is the sub-grade elastic modulus in MPa; and $DCPI_{60^0}$ is in mm/blow.

Srinivasa et al. (2003) developed the following equation correlating the $DCPI_{60°}$ with the sub-grade modulus back-calculated from FWD deflection bowls.

$$\text{Sub-grade modulus (MPa)} = 357.2 \times (DCPI_{60°})^{-0.645} \tag{10.29}$$

After eliminating outlier data, Chen et al. (2005) prescribed the following equation for estimating the resilient modulus value from DCP penetration values:

$$E_s = 537.76 \times (DCPI_{60^0})^{-0.6645}$$

where E_s = Granular layer resilient modulus (MPa); the $DCPI_{60^0}$ is in mm/blow.

As an indirect approach, Siekmeier et al. (2000) and Chen et al. (2001, 2005) converted the $DCPI_{\theta°}$ value to CBR values by using the relationship developed by Webster et al. (1992). The obtained CBR value is converted to resilient modulus (E_s) value using the following relationship developed at TRL-UK (Lister and Powell 1987).

$$\text{Sub-grade resilient modulus} = 17.6 \times CBR^{0.64} \tag{10.31}$$

The sub-grade resilient modulus values obtained from the above approach has yielded satisfactorily comparable elastic moduli that were determined from back-calculated deflections measured by FWD (Chen et al. 2001, 2005). This procedure must be used with caution because the TRL do not claim to validate the above equation when the CBR value exceeds 12%. As an alternative to the above equation given by TRL-UK, we can use any one of the popular relationships suggested by different researchers with different values (equations (3.51) and (3.52).

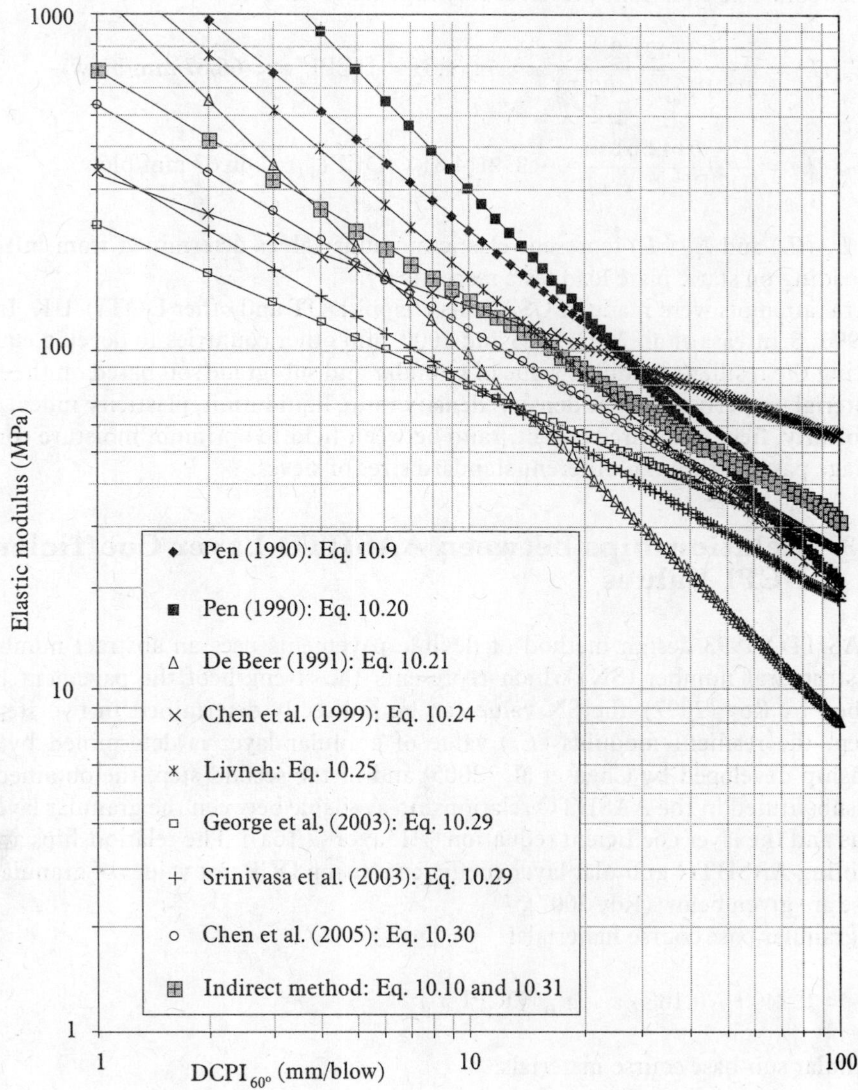

Figure 10.9 *Relationships between $DCPI_{60^\circ}$ to elastic modulus (E_s)*

A few relationships of $DCPI_{60^\circ}$ vs. E_s (elastic or resilient modulus value) are presented in Figure 10.9. It is observed that a wide variation exists among the relationships. Such scatter is not unexpected since the material modulus value varies with respect to many parameters related to the testing methods adopted, moisture content compaction, soil class and confinement conditions. Therefore, before adopting any one of the above relationships, the pavement engineer should conduct a few tests on the given material and compare the obtained test results with the available relationships.

Nazzal (2003) conducted a study to correlate DCP test values with in situ elastic moduli values determined by conducting static plate load tests on untreated and treated granular and sub-grade soil. The equations prescribed by him are given below.

$$E_s(iL) = \frac{17421.2}{\mathrm{DCPI}_{60^\circ}^{2.05} + 62.53} - 5.71 \; (4.81 < \mathrm{DCPI}_{60^\circ} < 66.67 \text{ mm/blow}) \tag{10.32}$$

$$E_s(rL) = \frac{5142.61}{\mathrm{DCPI}_{60^\circ}^{1.57} - 14.8} - 3.49 \; (4.81 < \mathrm{DCPI}_{60^\circ} < 66.67 \text{ mm/blow}) \tag{10.33}$$

where, E_s (iL) and E_s (rL) represent elastic modulus values determined from initial loading and reloading on static plate load tests respectively.

Several attempts were made in USA (Mississippi DOT and other DOTs), UK, India (Sood et al. 1996; Srinivasa et al. 2003, 2003 and 2006) and other countries to develop equations for estimating the resilient modulus value of granular and sub-grade soil based on the DCP value and material properties such as density, density ratio, liquid limit, plasticity index, coefficient of uniformity, field moisture content, ratio between field to optimum moisture contents and percentage passing through different standard sizes of sieves.

10.6.3 Relationships between AASHTO Layer Coefficients and DCPI Values

The AASHTO 1993 design method of flexible pavements uses an abstract number termed as the structural number (SN) which represents the strength of the pavement layers. As prescribed by Roy (2007), the SN value can be indirectly determined in two steps. In the first step, the resilient modulus (E_s) value of granular layer is determined by using the relationship developed by Chen et al. (2005) and in the second step, the obtained E_s value will be substituted in the AASHTO relationship available between the granular layer resilient modulus and the layer coefficient (equation (7.15a) or (7.16a)). The relationships available for determining AASHTO granular layer coefficients using DCP test values of granular base and sub-base are given below (Roy 2007).

For granular base course materials:

$$a_2 = 0.2409 - 0.1655 \times \log_{10} (\mathrm{DCPI}_{60^\circ}) \tag{10.34}$$

For granular sub-base course materials:

$$a_3 = 0.2713 - 0.1508 \times \log_{10} (\mathrm{DCPI}_{60^\circ}) \tag{10.35}$$

where the DCPI_{60° is in mm/blow.

10.6.4 Relationships between DCP and Unconfined Compressive Strength (UCS) of Lime Treated Sub-grade

A reasonably good correlation exists between DCP readings and unconfined compressive strength (UCS) of soil (Bester and Hallat 1977; De Villiers 1980). McElvaney and Djatnika (1991) developed the following regression equations which can be used to determine the UCS of lime soil mixture tested by DCP.

Under-estimation of USC with 50% of probability:

$$\log(\text{UCS}) = 3.56 - 0.807 \log(\text{DCPI}_{60^o}) \quad (10.36)$$

Under-estimation of USC will not exceed 15% of probability with 95% confidence level:

$$\log(\text{UCS}) = 3.29 - 0.809 \log(\text{DCPI}_{60^o}) \quad (10.37)$$

Under-estimation of USC will not exceed 15% of probability with 99% confidence level:

$$\log(\text{UCS}) = 3.21 - 0.809 \log(\text{DCPI}_{60^o}) \quad (10.38)$$

where UCS is in KPa and DCPI_{60^o} is in mm/blow.

In addition to the above relationships, shear strength of granular or cohesion less materials can be determined by using relationships available between the laboratory determined values of DCPI_{60° and the triaxial deviator stress at failure (Ayers et al. 1989).

10.7 Applications of DCP Test Data

The following are potential applications of DCP test results. They can be considered for characterising unbound granular and sub-grade material properties which are useful for design, construction and performance evaluation of pavements.

(a) The DCP can be used for preliminary soil exploration or used for investigating the shallow depth of the sub-grade down to 800 mm which is sufficient for structural evaluation of pavements (Kleyn and Savage 1982).

(b) Quality control of granular base layer compaction can be achieved by limiting the DCP penetration rate (Kleyn et al. 1982; Siekmeier et al. 1998). A typical DCP study was conducted to determine the percentage compaction of soil consisting of gravel and sand with fines less than 10 per cent (Siekmeier et al. 2000). The DCP can also used to evaluate stiffness and construction uniformity of unbound granular and sub-grade layers.

(c) It can be used to check the intensity of compaction of the granular material used for backfill and embankments constructed for different sub-surface and underground utilities, viz. around pipes, sand backfill trenches (Zhang et al. 2004), drain trenches beside pavements (Siekmeier et al. 1998); for evaluating compaction of granular–backfill made for sub-surface drainage, narrow trenches with Proctor compaction and DCP test data (Ford and Eliason 1993).

(d) Based on the DCPI–CBR relationship, the pavement distress level can be predicted (and evaluated) by testing the granular and sub-grade layers (Gabr et al. 2000). The DCP can also be used for performance evaluation of pavement layers.

(e) The thickness of the granular and soil layers can be reliably measured by using the cumulative penetration data of DCP (Livneh 1987). The layer thickness boundaries can be identified when the layers have different strengths (Chua and Lytton 1988).

(f) The DCPT can be used for strength evaluation of stabilised materials (Kleyn et al. 1982) such as lime–fly ash–soil, aggregate–fly ash–soil, aggregate–soil, lime–aggregate–soil, cement–soil etc.

(g) The DCPT results can be used to verify back-calculated unbound granular layer moduli values determined from deflection measurements by PFWD (Siekmeier et al. 1999). It can also be used to verify accuracy of back-calculated resilient moduli when (i) the bedrock is at a shallow depth, (ii) the asphalt concrete layer thickness is thinner than 75 mm (Chen et al. 2001), (iii) when the soil is lime-stabilised (Little 1996) and (iv) no reliable relationship can be established between laboratory and field estimated modulus values (Newcomb 1987).

(h) By conducting a series of experiments in Herfordshire, UK, Huntley (1990) reported that the DCP test results can be used for tentatively classifying soil (Nazzal 2003).

(i) The DCP based design of flexible pavement methods (Kleyn and Savage 1982; Kleyn and van Heerden 1983) can be safely used to design low to medium traffic class pavement crust consisting of thin bituminous surfacing with thick granular base and sub-base courses (Roy 2007).

Therefore, the DCP can be adopted as a low-cost and alternative tool for routine structural evaluation of granular base, sub-base and sub-grade soil.

10.8 Limitations of DCP

The following are the drawback/limitations of the DCPT:

(a) High variability in DCP test results is inevitable due to the presence of well-graded granular material having a grain size coarser than 20 mm. For example, the existing DCPI to CBR conversion equations may be unreliable when DCP tests are conducted on material with very high CBR value (Chen et al. 1999).

(b) The existing relationships between $DCPI_{\theta^\circ}$ to standard test values, viz. CBR, E_s, USC and others may not be applicable to all types of materials since the relationships developed are based on certain in situ conditions especially related to moisture, density, time of testing, effect of vertical confinement, soil class and local conditions.

(c) The DCP based design of the flexible pavement method may be practically explored further for design of thick bituminous surfacing pavements where the design traffic exceeds 10 million ESAL.

Concluding Remarks

The DCPT can be used as a low-cost alternative method of testing unbound granular and sub-grade soil used for construction of earth fills, embankments and pavements. Different relationships are available in literature for converting the DCPI value to a standard test value. It can also be used as the material strength property for design and evaluation purposes. Therefore, pavement engineers should keep in mind the limitations and advantages of the DCPT and that the available relationships may be used with caution since the DCPT results are sensitive to several factors like moisture, compaction, confinement and testing methods adopted.

Exercises

10.1 Enumerate the purpose of DCP testing. State how the test results can be interpreted for (i) structural evaluation, (ii) design, (iii) quality control for construction of earth work, embankments and granular layers and (iv) pavement performance.

10.2 Briefly explain the historical development of the DCP used for pavement evaluation.

10.3 Describe various salient parts of the DCP and explain its working procedure.

10.4 State the terminology used for representing DCP test results.

10.5 State and explain the methods of testing pavement granular and sub-grade layers using DCP.

10.6 What is the need of an extension rod in DCP? Write the related correction factors recommended by Livneh et al.

10.7 Write a short note on automated and instrumented DCP used for pavement evaluation.

10.8 State the different notations used for representing test results of DCP.

10.9 What are the factors affecting test results of DCP?

10.10 State the DCP–CBR equations prescribed by TRL-UK (1990) and Webster et al. (1992).

10.11 List a few salient features of investigations carried out by different researchers for development of the DCP–CBR relationships.

10.12 What is the significance of the relationship between the DCP E_s (modulus value) in the context of M–E based pavement design?

10.13 What do you understand by the indirect approach to the determination of E_s (modulus value) from the DCP value? Write how other existing equations available for estimation of materials strength can be used to determine E_s values.

10.14 Explain how AASHTO recommended layer coefficient values can be determined from DCP test results.

10.15 What are the various applications of DCP test results for pavement engineering?

10.16 State the merits and demerits of using DCP for pavement materials evaluations.

ANNEXURE

The following illustrations of compound curves under different cases (see Chapter 2) are presented here.

Case 1: Simple Compound Curve

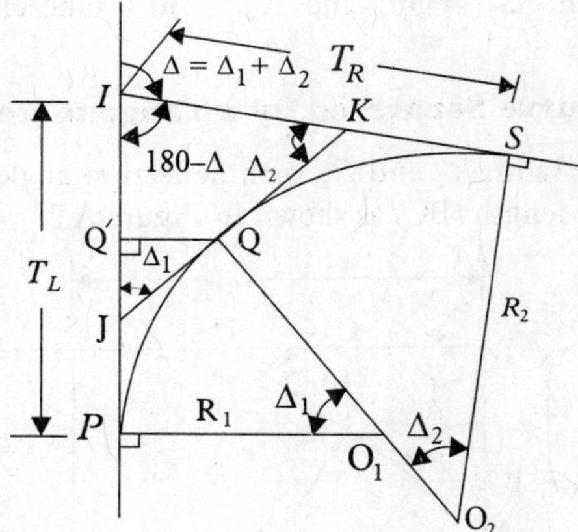

Figure A.1 *A simple compound curve*

The notations used in Figure A.1 refer to the following.

Left side tangent length = PJ = JQ = $R_1 \tan(\Delta_1/2) = T_1$

Right side tangent length = QK = SK = $R_2 \tan(\Delta_2/2) = T_2$

$$T_L = \text{PJ} + \text{JI} \tag{A1}$$

Length of JI can be determined by considering triangle JIQ and applying the sine rule. We get,

$$\frac{\text{JI}}{\sin(\Delta_2)} = \frac{\text{JK}}{\sin(180^\circ - \Delta)} = \frac{\text{KI}}{\sin(\Delta_1)} \tag{A2}$$

The above relationship can be re-written as

$$\frac{\text{JI}}{\sin(\Delta_2)} = \frac{\text{JQ} + \text{KI}}{\sin(180^\circ - \Delta)} = \frac{\text{KI}}{\sin(\Delta_1)} \tag{A2a}$$

where JQ + QK $= R_1 \tan(\Delta_1/2) + R_2 \tan(\Delta_2/2) = T_1 + T_2$

Similarly, for determination of length of T_R

T_R = SK + KI

where SK $= R_2 \tan(\Delta_2/2) = T_2$

From equation (A2a), KI=JI$\times \frac{\sin(\Delta_1)}{\sin(\Delta_2)}$

For setting out the curve, Q and Q' points should be located precisely. They can be determined from the following relationship. From triangle JQ'Q,

$$\frac{\text{JQ}'}{\sin(90^\circ - \Delta)} = \frac{\text{JQ}}{\sin(90^\circ)} = \frac{\text{QQ}'}{\sin(\Delta_1)} \tag{A3}$$

The above relationship can also be written as $\frac{\text{JQ}'}{\sin(90^\circ - \Delta)} = \frac{T_1}{\sin(90^\circ)} = \frac{\text{QQ}'}{\sin(\Delta_1)}$

ASSIGNMENT PROBLEM 1: With reference to Figure A.1, determine the chainages at salient points of a compound curve from the following given values.

R_1 = 650 m; R_2 = 425 m; Δ_1 = 40° and Δ_2 = 30°; take chainage at intersection, as I = 600.00 m.

Case 2: Compound Curve Separated by a Tangent (refer to Figure A.2)

Two circular curves having radii, R_1 and R_2 with deflection angles Δ_1 and Δ_2 respectively, were separated by a straight length (BC) as shown in Figure A.2.

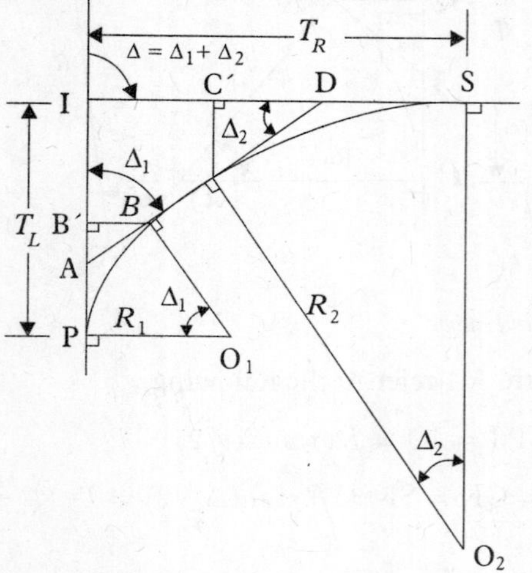

Figure A.2 *Compound curve separated by a tangent*

From Figure A.2, we get,

$$\Delta = \Delta_1 + \Delta_2$$

$$T_1 = \text{PA} = \text{AB} = R_1 \tan(\Delta_1/2) \text{ and } T_2 = \text{CD} = \text{SD} = R_2 \tan(\Delta_2/2)$$

Left side tangent length, T_L =PI = T_1 + AI **(A4)**

The length of AI can be determined from the following relationship by considering triangle AID and applying the sine rule,

$$\frac{\text{AI}}{\sin(\Delta_2)} = \frac{\text{AD}}{\sin(180° - \Delta)} = \frac{\text{DI}}{\sin(\Delta_1)} \quad \textbf{(A5)}$$

where AD = T_1+ length of BC +T_2

To determine the perpendicular offset B'B, consider triangle AB'B,

$$\frac{\text{BB}'}{\sin(\Delta_2)} = \frac{T_1}{\sin(90°)} \quad \textbf{(A6)}$$

Right side tangent length, T_R =SI = T_2+ DI **(A7)**

From equation A5, $\text{DI} = \text{AI} \times \dfrac{\sin(\Delta_1)}{\sin(\Delta_2)}$

To determine the perpendicular offset C'C, consider triangle CC'D,

$$\frac{\text{CC}'}{\sin(\Delta_2)} = \frac{T_2}{\sin(90°)} \quad \textbf{(A8)}$$

ASSIGNMENT PROBLEM 2: With reference to Figure A.2, determine the chainages at salient points of a compound curve from the following given values.

$R_1 = 95$ m; $R_2 = 243$ m; $\Delta_1 = 50°$ and $\Delta_2 = 30°$. These curves are separated by a straight length = 55 m. Take chainage at intersection as $I = 1000.00$ m.

Case 3: Three-Centred Compound Curve

From Figure A.3, we get,

$$\Delta = \Delta_1 + \Delta_2 + \Delta_3$$

The tangent lengths corresponding to the curves,

$$T_1 = \text{PA} = \text{AQ} = R_1 \tan(\Delta_1/2)$$

$$T_2 = \text{QC} = \text{CK} = R_2 \tan(\Delta_2/2)$$

$$T_3 = \text{KE} = \text{SE} = R_3 \tan(\Delta_3/2)$$

Left side tangent length, T_L = PI = PA + AI **(A9)**

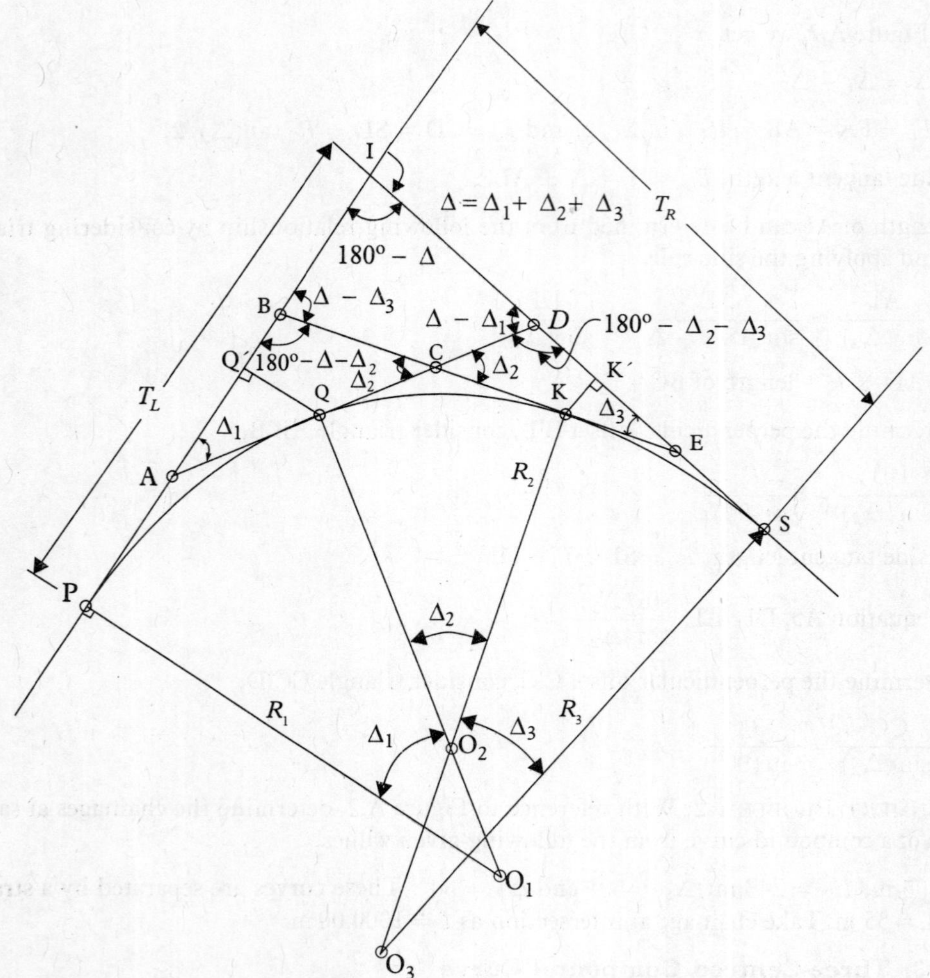

Figure A.3 *A three centred compound curve*

The length of AI can be determined from the following relationship by considering triangle AID and applying the sine rule,

$$\frac{AI}{\sin(\Delta - \Delta_1)} = \frac{T_1 + T_2 + CD}{\sin(180° - \Delta)} = \frac{DI}{\sin(\Delta_1)} \tag{A10}$$

The length of CD can be determined by considering triangle CDE and applying the sine rule.

$$\frac{CD}{\sin(\Delta_3)} = \frac{T_2 + T_3}{\sin(180° - \Delta_2 - \Delta_3)} = \frac{ED}{\sin(\Delta_2)} \tag{A11}$$

To determine the perpendicular offset Q'Q, consider triangle AQ'Q,

$$\frac{QQ'}{\sin(\Delta_1)} = \frac{T_1}{\sin(90°)} = \frac{AQ'}{\sin(90° - \Delta_1)} \tag{A12}$$

Similarly,

Right side tangent length, T_R = SI = T_3+ ED + DI **(A13)**

The lengths of ED and DI can be determined from equations (A10) and (A11) respectively.

To determine the perpendicular offset K'K, consider triangle KK'E,

$$\frac{KK'}{\sin(\Delta_3)} = \frac{T_3}{\sin(90°)} = \frac{EK'}{\sin(90° - \Delta_3)} \quad \textbf{(A14)}$$

$$SK' = T_3 + EK' \quad \textbf{(A15)}$$

Q: *For a given site, it was proposed to align the centre line of a highway with a three-centred compound circular curve. The following data is obtained from field survey:*

Angle of intersection (Δ) = 99°; recommended radii of curve 1, 2 and 3 (from left to right) are 73, 32 and 45 m respectively; minimum lengths of curve 1, 2 and 3 are 35, 22 and 28 m respectively. Adjust the above input parameters of the three-centred compound circular curve so that the (i) minimum radius of any curve should not be less than 30 m and (ii) the ratio of the larger to smaller radii of curves should be less than 2.5.

NOTE: A figure to be drawn with usual notations (draw a figure similar to Figure A.3).

A: The given data is written with the following notations,

$\Delta = 99°$; $R_1 = 73$ m; $R_2 = 32$ m; $R_3 = 45$ m; $L1_{\min} = 35$ m; $L2_{\min} = 22$ m; $L3_{\min} = 28$ m; $R_{\min} = 30$ m; $R_{\max}/R_{\min} = 2.5$; Total length of curves = $L_{\text{total}} = 35 + 22 + 28 = 85$ m.

We know the relationship for determination of length (L) of circular arc having radius (R) and deflection angle = Δ, is $L = \pi R\Delta/180°$.

Deflection angle corresponding to curve 1,

$$\Delta_1 = (L1_{\min}/R_1) \times (180°/\pi) = (35/73) \times (180°/\pi) = 27.47057922°$$

Deflection angle corresponding to curve 2,

$$\Delta_2 = (L2_{\min}/R_2) \times (180°/\pi) = (22/32) \times (180°/\pi) = 39.39084841°$$

Deflection angle corresponding to curve 3,

$$\Delta_3 = (L3_{\min}/R_3) \times (180°/\pi) = (28/45) \times (180°/\pi) = 35.65070725°$$

Therefore, total of $(\Delta_1 + \Delta_2 + \Delta_3) = 102.5121349°$

Error analysis:

Therefore, total error = 102.5121349° – Δ = 102.5121349° – 99° = 3.512134873°

The above error is distributed onto the individual deflection angles proportionately with their length of curves since the deflection angle is proportional to the length of the circular arc.

$$\text{Error in } \Delta_1 = (L1_{\min}/L_{\text{total}}) \times \text{ Total error} = (35/85) \times 3.512134873° = 1.446173183°$$

$$\text{Error in } \Delta_2 = (L2_{\min}/L_{\text{total}}) \times \text{ Total error} = (22/85) \times 3.512134873° = 0.909023144°$$

$$\text{Error in } \Delta_3 = (L3_{\min}/L_{\text{total}}) \times \text{ Total error} = (28/85) \times 3.512134873° = 1.156938546°$$

Check = (Error in Δ_1+ Error in Δ_2+ Error in Δ_3)

Check = $(1.446173183° + 0.909023144° + 1.156938546°) = 3.512134873°$ = Total error; o.k.

Corrections to the deflection angles:

$\Delta_1 = 27.47057922° - 1.446173183° = 26.02440603°$

$\Delta_2 = 39.39084841° - 0.909023144° = 38.48182527°$

$\Delta_3 = 35.65070725° - 1.156938546° = 34.4937687°$

Total of $(\Delta_1 + \Delta_2 + \Delta_3) = 99°$; o.k.

Corrections to radii:

$R_1 = (L1_{\min}/\Delta_1) \times (180°/\pi) = (35/26.02440603°) \times (180°/\pi) = 77.05$ m

$R_2 = (L2_{\min}/\Delta_2) \times (180°/\pi) = (22/38.48182527°) \times (180°/\pi) = 32.75$ m > ($R_{\min} = 30$ m) o.k.

$R_3 = (L3_{\min}/\Delta_3) \times (180°/\pi) = (28/34.4937687°) \times (180°/\pi) = 46.50$ m.

Check: Ratio of $R_{\max}/R_{\min}$ should be less than 2.5.

$R_{\max}/R_{\min} = 77.05/32.75 = 2.35, < 2.5$; o.k.

ASSIGNMENT PROBLEM 3: With reference to Figure A.3, determine the chainages at salient points of a compound curve from the following data.

$R_1 = 77.05$ m; $R_2 = 32.75$ m; $R_3 = 46.50$ m;

$\Delta_1 = 26.02440603°$

$\Delta_2 = 38.48182527°$

$\Delta_3 = 34.4937687°$

Take chainage at intersection, $I = 1050.55$ m.

Case 4: Three-Centred Arcs Separated by Straights

From Figure A.4, we get,

$\Delta = \Delta_1 + \Delta_2 + \Delta_3$

The tangent lengths corresponding to the curves,

T_1 =PA = AJ = $R_1 \tan(\Delta_1/2)$

T_2 =MC = CN = $R_2 \tan(\Delta_2/2)$

T_3 =KE = SE = $R_3 \tan(\Delta_3/2)$

JM = a straight between Arc1 (PJ) and Arc2 (MN).

NK = a straight between Arc2 (MN) and Arc3 (KS).

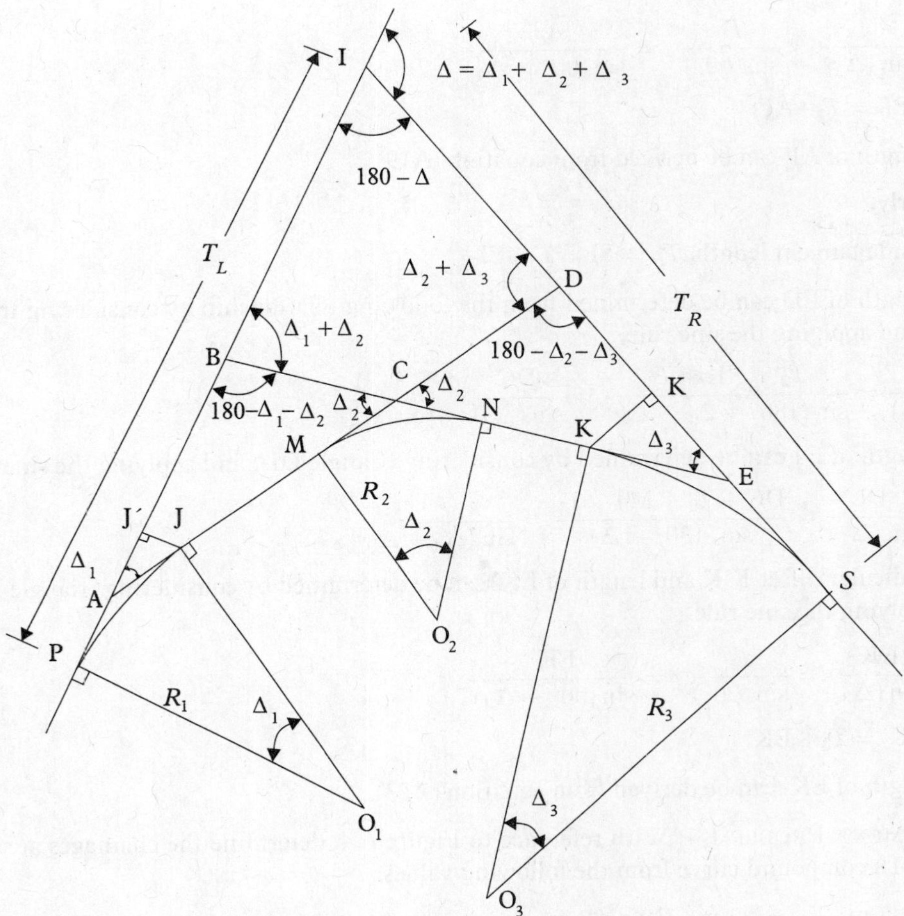

Figure A.4 *Three-centred arcs separated by straights*

Left side tangent length, $T_L = \text{PI} = T_1 + \text{AB} + \text{BI}$ (A16)

The length of AB can be determined from the following relationship by considering triangle ABC and applying the sine rule,

$$\frac{\text{AB}}{\sin(\Delta_2)} = \frac{T_1 + \text{JM} + T_2}{\sin(180^\circ - \Delta_1 - \Delta_2)} = \frac{\text{BC}}{\sin(\Delta_1)} \tag{A17}$$

The length of BI can be determined by considering triangle BIE and applying the sine rule.

$$\frac{\text{BI}}{\sin(\Delta_3)} = \frac{\text{BC} + T_2 + \text{NK} + T_3}{\sin(180^\circ - \Delta)} = \frac{\text{EI}}{\sin(\Delta_1 + \Delta_2)} \tag{A18}$$

The length of BC can be obtained from equation (A17).

Perpendicular offset J'J and length of AJ' can be determined by considering triangle AJ'J and applying sine rule.

$$\frac{\text{JJ}'}{\sin(\Delta_1)} = \frac{T_1}{\sin(90°)} = \frac{\text{AJ}'}{\sin(90° - \Delta_1)} \quad \text{(A19)}$$

$$\text{PJ'} = T_1 + \text{AJ'} \quad \text{(A20)}$$

The length of AJ' can be derived from equation (A19).

Similarly,

Right side tangent length, $T_R = \text{SI} = T_3 + \text{EI}$ (A21)

The length of ED can be determined from the following relationship by considering triangle EDC and applying the sine rule,

$$\frac{\text{ED}}{\sin(\Delta_2)} = \frac{T_2 + \text{NK} + T_3}{\sin(180^0 - \Delta_2 - \Delta_3)} = \frac{\text{DC}}{\sin(\Delta_3)} \quad \text{(A22)}$$

The length of DI can be determined by considering triangle DIA and applying the sine rule.

$$\frac{\text{DI}}{\sin(\Delta_1)} = \frac{\text{DC} + T_2 + \text{MJ} + T_1}{\sin(180° - \Delta)} = \frac{\text{AI}}{\sin(\Delta_2 + \Delta_3)} \quad \text{(A23)}$$

Perpendicular offset K'K and length of EK' can be determined by considering triangle EK'K and applying the sine rule.

$$\frac{\text{KK}'}{\sin(\Delta_3)} = \frac{T_1}{\sin(90°)} = \frac{\text{EK}'}{\sin(90° - \Delta_3)} \quad \text{(A24)}$$

$$\text{SK'} = T_3 + \text{EK'} \quad \text{(A25)}$$

The length of EK' can be derived from equation (A23).

ASSIGNMENT PROBLEM 4: With reference to Figure A.4, determine the chainages at salient points of a compound curve from the following values.

$R_1 = 105$ m; $R_2 = 29$ m; $R_3 = 82$ m; $\Delta_1 = 16°$, $\Delta_2 = 98°$ and $\Delta_3 = 22°$. These curves are separated by two straights having length JM = 35 m and NK=39 m. Take chainage at intersection, $I = 1250.00$ m.

References

1. AASHO Road Test. Report 5. Pavement Research. Highway Research Board. Washington, d.c.1962.

2. AASHO Road Test. Report No. 9, 61-E. Highway Research Board. Washington, d.c. 1962.

3. AASHTO Committee on design. *AASHTO Interim Guide for the Design of Pavement Structures*. 1972.

4. AASHTO.*AASHTO Guide for Design of Pavement Structures*. USA: American Association of State Highway and Transportation Officials (ASHTO). 1986; 1993.

5. AASHTO. *Policy on Geometric Design of Highways and Streets.* Washington, dc: ASHTO. 1984, 1990, 1994, 2001 and 2004.

6. AASHTO. Special Report 61-G: The AASHO road test; Report 7. Washington, d.c.: Highway Research Board, National Research Council.1962.

7. AASHTO. *Standard Specifications for Transportation Materials and Methods of Sampling and Testing: Part II. 7th edition.* Washington, dc: AASHTO.1995.

8. AASHTO. *Standard Specifications for Transportation Materials and Methods of Sampling and Testing: Part 1.* Washington, dc: AASHTO. 2001.

9. Abrams, D. A. Design of concrete mixtures. *Bulletin 1.* Chicago: Structure of Materials Research Lab., Lewis Institute. 1918. Also published in *A Selection of Historic American Papers on Concrete, 1876–1926* (Ed. H. Newlon) by ACI SP-52. 309–330. 1976.

10. ACI 318 Code. Building code requirements for structural concrete, ACI 318-95. Commentary, ACI 318R-95. Farmington Hills, MI: American Concrete Institute. 1996.

11. ACI 435 Code. Control of deflection in concrete structures, Committee 435 Report. Farmington Hills, MI: American Concrete Institute. 1995.

12. ACI, American Concrete Institute Committee 325. Structural design considerations for pavement joints. *Jl. of the American Concrete Institute* 28(1): 1–28. 1956.

13. ACPA. White topping: State of the practice.*Engineering Bulletin EB210.02P*. Skokie, IL: American Concrete Pavement Association. 2002.

14. Ahlborn, G. ELSYM5, Computer program for determining stresses and deformations in five layer elastic systems. University of California, Berkeley. 1972.

15. Ahlvin, R. G. and H. H. Ulery. Tabulated values for determining the complete pattern of stresses, strains and deflections beneath a uniform circular loan on a homogeneous half space. *Bulletin 342*. Highway Research Board, Washington, d.c. 1962.

16. Akhter, G. F. and M. W. Witczak. Sensitivity of flexible pavement performance to bituminous mix properties. *Transportation Research Record No. 1034*. pp.70–79. Transportation Research Board (TRB). 1985.

17. Akoto, B. K. and E. E. Nilles. Repair & restoration of concrete pavements. *Jl. pf the Indian Roads Congress* 68-1: 91–106. 2007.

18. Alexander, D. R., S. D. Kohn and W. P. Grogan. Nondestructive testing techniques and evaluation procedures for airfield pavements. pp. 502–524 in *Nondestructive testing of Pavements and Back-calculation of Moduli, ASTM STP 1026*. Edited by A. J. Bush III and G. Y. Baladi. Philadelphia: American Society of Testing and Materials. 1989.

19. Ali, H. A. and A. Lopez A. Statistical analysis of temperature and moisture effects on pavement structural properties based on seasonal monitoring data. *Transportation Research Record No. 154*. pp.48–55. Washington, d.c.: TRB, National Research Council. 1996.

20. Ali, N. A. and P. N. Khosla. Determination of layer moduli using a falling weight deflectometer. *Transportation Research Record No. 1117*. pp. 1–10. Transportation Research Board. 1987.

21. Allen, J. J. and M. R. Thompson. Significance of variably confined tri-axial testing. *ASCE Journal of Transportation Engineering* 100(TE4): 827–843.1974.

22. Almeida, J. R. de. New University of Lisbon, Portugal, http://www.plan.civil.tohoku.ac.jp/pave/hoso-ml/FWD_ML/FWD438.txt. Accessed on 19-07-2001.

23. Almeida, J. R. de., J. M. Brunton. and S. F. Brown. *Structural Evaluation of Pavements*. (report submitted to the Transportation Research Record). University of Nottingham, 1991.

24. Almeida, J. R. de., S. F. Brown, and N. H. Tom. A pavement evaluation procedure incorporating material non-linearity. pp.218–232 in *Nondestructive Testing of Pavements and Back-calculation of Moduli (Second Volume), ASTM STP 1198*. Edited by Harold L. Von Quintus, Albert J. Bush III and Gilbert Y. Baladi. Philadelphia: ASTM.1994.

25. Al-Suleiman, T. I., N.A. Saeed, and J. Widdup. Towards the development of an improved asphalt overlay design procedure for major roads in Dubai. http://www.arrb.org.au/pubs/suleim00.htm, ARRB Transport Research. Accessed on 16-07-2000.

26. Anderson, M. A data base method for backcalculation of composite pavement layer moduli. pp. 201–216 in *Nondestructive Testing of Pavements and Backcalculation of Moduli, ASTM STP 1026*. Edited by Albert J. Bush III and Gilbert Y. Baladi. Philadelphia: ASTM. 1989.

27. Animesh, D.Analytical design of bituminous pavements based on field performance. Unpublished Ph.D. thesis. Civil Engineering Department, IIT Kharagpur. 1998.

28. ARA Inc., 2004, http://www.trb.org/mepdg/part_12_cover_ack_toc.pdf. Accessed on 17-08-2007.

29. Armaghani, J. and D. Tu. Rehabilitation of Ellaville Weigh Station with ultra-thin white topping. *Transportation Research Record 1654*. pp. 3–11. Washington, dc: Transportation Research Board, National Research Council. 1999.

30. Armaghani, J. M., T. J. Larsen and L. L. Smith. Temperature response of concrete pavements. *Transportation Research Record No. 1121*. pp.23–33. Washington, dc: Transportation Research Board. 1986.

31. Arora, Jitesh. Development of high performance concrete pavements through polymer modification and roller compaction with special reference to cold climatic regions. Seminar on Integrated Development of Rural and Arterial Roads Network for Socio-economic growth. II: III155–160. New Delhi: IRC. 2003.

32. ASCE. Development of CBR flexible pavement design method for airfields: A symposium. *Transactions of the ASCE* vol.115. 1950.

33. Ashraf, M. Roller compacted concrete pavements: Technical and economical benefits. Seminar on Design Construction and Maintenance of Cement Concrete Pavements. III17–25. New Delhi: IRC. 2004.

34. Ashton, J. E. and F. Moavenzadeh. Analysis of stresses and displacements in a three-layered visco-elastic system. *Proc. of the 2nd Inter. Conf. of Struct. Des. of Asphalt Pavements* I: 209–219. 1967.

35. Asphalt Institute. Asphalt technology and construction practices. *Instructors Guide*. Maryland: Asphalt Institute. 1983.

36. ASTM. Standard test method for permeability of granular soils (constant head). Designation No. 2434-68. ASTM Standards Part 19. Philadelphia, PA, 1978.

37. AUSTROADS. *Pavement Design: Guide to the Structural Design of Road Pavements*. Australia. 1992.

38. Awadallah, F. Theoretical analysis for horizontal curves based on actual discomfort speed. *ASCE J. of Transportation Engineering* 131 (11): 843–850. 2005.

39. Ayers, M. E., M. R. Thompson and D. R. Uzarski. Rapid shear strength evaluation of in-situ granular materials. *Transportation Research Record No. 1227*. pp.134–146. Washington dc: Transportation Research Board. 1989.

40. Bagui, S. K. Development of program for mix design of concrete according to IS: 10262-1982.*Journal of Indian Highways* 32(8): 29–52. 2004.

41. Bahadur, J. Basis of road planning. *IRC Journal* XII-V. 1948.

42. Baker, Robert F. (Ed.). L. G. Byrd and D. Grant Mickle (Assoc. Ed.). *Handbook of Highway Engineering*. pp.496–600. New York: Van Nostrand Reinhold. 1975.

43. Bakhmeteff, B. A. *Hydraulics of Open Channels*. New York: McGraw-Hill. 1932.

44. Bakker, R. F. M. Permeability of blended cement concrete in *Use of Fly Ash, Silica Fume, Slag and Other Mineral Byproducts in Concrete middlenameVol SnI*. Edited by V. M. Malhotra. Spec. Pub. SP-79. American Concrete Institute. 1983.

45. Baltzer, S. and J. M. Jansen. Temperature correction of asphalt moduli for FWD measurements. *Proc. of the 4th Int. Conf. on the Bearing Capacity of Roads and Airfields*. Minneapolis, Minnesota. 1994.

46. Barber, E. S. and C. L. Sawyer. Highway subdrainage. *Public Roads* 26(12). 1952.

47. Barker, W. R., W. N. Braston and Y. T. Chou. A general system for the structural design of flexible pavements. *Proc. of 4th International Conference on Structural Design of Asphalt Pavements* Vol. I. pp.209–248.1977.

48. Barksdale, R. D. Laboratory evaluation of rutting in base course materials. *Proc. of 3rd International Conference on Structural Design of Asphalt Pavements*. pp.161–174. 1972.

49. Bergen, A. T. and D. G. Fredlund. Characterization of freeze-thaw effects on subgrade soils. *Symposium on Frost Action in Road, Vol. II*. Organization for Economic Cooperation and Development. Oslo, Norway. 1973.

50. Bester, M. D. and L. Hallat. *Dynamic Cone Penetrometer Correlation (DCP)*. Pretoria: University of Pretoria. 1977.

51. Bishop, A. W. and D. J. Hankel. *The Measurement of Soil Properties in the Tri-axial Test 2nd Edition*. London: Edward Arnold. 1962.

52. Bishop, H. K. Discussion on highway location: Practical considerations by H. K Losh. *Transactions of the ASCE* 96: 477–480. 1932.

53. Blanks, R. F. Modern concepts applied to concrete aggregate. *Transactions of the ASCE* 115 (2403): 403–431. 1950.

54. Bonnaure, F., G. Gest, A. Gravais and P. Uge. A new method of predicting the stiffness of asphalt paving mixes. *Proc. of the Association of Asphalt Paving Technologists* 46. 1977.

55. Bonneson, J. A. Side friction and speed as controls for horizontal curve design. *ASCE J. of Transportation Engineering* 125 (6): 473–480. 1999.

56. Bose, S. and P. K. Jain. Laboratory studies on the use of organic polymers in improvement of bituminous road surfacings. *Highway Research Bulletin 38.* pp.63–79. IRC. 1984.

57. Bose, S. Elastic modulus of granular bases in flexible pavements. Unpublished Ph.D. thesis. Civil Engineering Department, IIT Kharagpur. 1993.

58. Bosscher, P. J., H. U. Bahia, S. Thomas and J. S. Russel. Relationship between pavement temperature and weather data: Wisconsin field study to verify superpave algorithm. *Transportation Research Record no. 1609*. pp.1–11. Washington, d.c.: TRB, National Research Council. 1998.

59. Boussinesq V. J., Application des potentials a letude de lequilibre at du mouvement des solids elastiques avec les notes etendues sur divers points de physique. *Mathematique et Danalyse*. Paris : Gauthier Villars. 1885.

60. Boyce, I. R., S. F. Brown and P. S. Pell. The resilient behaviour of a granular material under repeated loading. *ARRB proceedings*. 8: 1–12. 1976.

61. Bradbury, R. D. *Reinforced Concrete Pavements*. Washington, dc: Wire Reinforcement Inst. 1938.

62. Breed, H. E. Recent developments in concrete pavements, with discussion by A. T. Goldbeck, E. G. Hooper, T. M. Ripley, W.C. Hammatt, R. W. Crum, C. N. Conner, H.C. Boyden, C.R, Hulsart and E. Godfrey E., *Transactions of ASCE* 91(1655):1033–1050. 1927.

63. Brien, D. O. (compiler and editor) *Reference Year Book. 2005*. Penguin India. 2005.

64. Brown S. F. Achievements and challenges in asphalt pavement engineering. Keynote Address. *8th Int. Conf. on Asp. Pavements*. pp. 1–23. Seattle: ISAP. 1997.

65. Brown S. F. and J. M. Gibb. Validation experiments for permanent deformation testing of bituminous mixtures. *Asphalt Paving Technology* 65: 255–290. 1996.

66. Brown S. F. and P. S. Pell. A fundamental structural design procedure for flexible pavements. *Proc. of 3rd International Conference on Structural Design of Asphalt Pavements*. I: 369–381.1972.

67. Brown, S. F and J. M. Brunton. *An Introduction to the Analytical Design of Bituminous Pavements* 3rd Edition. U. K.: Univ. of Nottingham, Dept., of Civil Engg. 1992.

68. Brown, S. F. Achievements and challenges in asphalt pavement engineering. Keynote address. *Proceedings of the 8th Int. Conf. on Asp. Pavements*. pp.1–23. 1997.

69. Brown, S. F. and J. M. Gibb. Validation experiments for permanent deformation testing of bituminous mixtures. *Asphalt Paving Technology* 65: 255–290. 1996.

70. Brown, S. F. Material characterisation for analytical pavement design. pp.41–92 in *Developments in Highway Pavement Engineering 1* edited by P. S. Pell. London: Applied Science Publishers. 1977.

71. Brown, S. F., J. M. Brunton. and P. S. Pell. The development and implementation of analytical pavement design for British conditions. *Proc. of the 5th International Conference on Structural Design of Asphalt Pavements.* Vol. I. pp.3–16. 1982.

72. Brown, S. F., W. S. Tam, and J. M. Brunton. Structural evaluation and overlay design: analysis and implementation. *Proceedings of the 6th International Conference Structural Design of Asphalt Pavements.* pp.1013–1028. 1987.

73. Brown, S.F., K. E. Cooper and G. R. Pooley. Mechanical properties of bituminous materials for pavement design. *Proc. of the Eurobitume Symposium.* pp.143–147. 1981.

74. Brown, V. L. and Bartholomew C. L. FRP dowel bars in reinforced concrete pavements. *Proc. of the International Symposium on FRP Reinforcement for Concrete Structures.* Michigan: American Concrete Institute. 1993.

75. Bruce, G. D. Reaction time in automobile driving. *Journal of Applied Psychology* 20 (3): 355. 1936.

76. Brule, B., Y. Brion and T. Tanguy. Paving polymer blends: Relationships between composition, structure and properties. *Proc. of the Assoc. of Asphalt Paving Techn.* 57: 41–63. 1998.

77. Brunton, J. M. and J. R. d'Almedia. Modeling material non-linearity in a pavement back-calculation procedure. *Transportation Research Record No. 1377.* pp.99–106. Washington, d.c.: TRB. 1992.

78. BS 812. Testing aggregates: Method of determination of the aggregate crushing value. Part 110. London: British Standard Institute.

79. BS: 1377-1990. Methods of test for soils for civil engineering purposes. London: British Standard Institute.

80. Bureau of Materials and Physical Research. PTA (Pavement Technology Advisory)-D4 (Eff.02/2005). A report on performance graded binder materials for hot mix asphalt. Illinois Department of Transportation.

81. Bureau of Reclamation. *Earth Manual.* Denver, USA: Bureau of Reclamation. 1965.

82. Burmister, D. M. Discussion on graphical representation of the mechanical analyses of soils by F. B. Campbell. *Transactions of the ASCE* 104: 156–159. 1939.

83. Burmister, D. M. Graphical distribution of vertical pressure beneath foundations. *Transactions of the ASCE* 103: 301–33. 1938.

84. Burmister, D. M. Stress and displacement characteristics for a two-layer rigid base soil system: Influence diagrams and practical applications. *Proc. of the Highway Research Board* 35: 773–814. 1956.

85. Burmister, D. M. The general theory of stresses and displacements in layered systems. *Jl. of Applied Physics* 16: 84–94; 126–127; 296–302. 1945.

86. Burmister, D. M. The theory of stresses and displacements in layered systems and applications to the design of airport runways. *Proc. of the Highway Research Board* 23: 126–144. 1943.

87. Bush III, A. J. and Alexander. Pavement evaluation using deflection basin movement and layered theory. *Transportation Research Record No. 1022.* pp.16–29. Transportation Research Board. 1985.

88. Bush III., A. J. *Computer Program BISDEF.* U. S. Army Engineer Waterways Experiment Station. 1985.

89. Button, J. W., M. Jawle, V. Jagadam and D. Little. Evaluation and development of a pressure aging vessel for asphalt cement. *Transportation Research Record No. 1391.* pp.11–19. TRB. 1993.

90. Campbell, F. B. Graphical representation of the mechanical analyses of soils. *Transactions of the ASCE.* 104: 150–155. 1939.

91. Cardoso, S. H. and M. W. Witczak. Permanent deformation for flexible airfield pavement design. *Transportation Research Record No. 1307.* pp.111–121. Transportation Research Board. 1991.

92. Carey, W. N. and P. E. Irick. Performance of flexible pavements in AASHO road test. *Proc. of the Int. Conf. Struct. Des. of Asphalt Pavements.* University of Michigan, Ann Arbor, Michigan. 1962.

93. Carlo Bro International. *Recommendations on Road Design Standards. Vol.1: Geometric Design of Rural Roads.* South Africa Transport and Communications Commission. 1990.

94. Carpenter, J. C. Discussion on highway location: Practical considerations by H. K Losh. *Transactions of the ASCE* 96: 480–482, 1932.

95. Carpenter, S. H. Layer coefficients for flexible pavements. *Report No. WF/HRP-08-90.* Madison, Wisconsin: Wisconsin Department of Transportation. 1990.

96. Carse, A. and J. Beehan. Static chord modulus of elasticity of high strength concrete in uniform compression and flexure. *Proc. of the 10th ARRB Conference* 10 (3): 46–56. 1980.

97. Casagrande, A. Classification and identification of soil. *Proc. ASCE.* 73(6): SnPart SnI. 1967.

98. Casagrande, A. Classification and identification of soils. *Transactions of the ASCE* 113(2351): 901–930. 1948.

99. Chadda, H. S. and S. E. Cross. Speed (road) bumps: issues and opinions. *ASCE J. of Transportation Engineering* 111(4): 410–418. 1985.

100. Chai, G. and N. Roslie. The structural response and behavior prediction of subgrade soils using falling weight deflectometer in pavement construction. *Proc. of the 3rd Int. Conf. on Road and Airfield Pavement Technology.* 1998.

101. Chary S. S., Rheology, Academic Books, New Delhi..

102. Chatti, K. and K. K. Yun. SAPSI-M: A computer program for analyzing asphalt concrete pavements under moving arbitrary loads. *Transportation Research Record no. 1539*. Washington, d.c.: Transportation Research Board. 1996.

103. Chau, K. U. Determination of CBR and elastic modulus of soils using a portable pavement dynamic cone penetrometer. *Proc. of the 1st Int. Symposium on Penetration Testing*, ISOPT-1. 1988.

104. Chaubal, A. M. and H. Hans. New generation superplasticizers for high-performance concrete. Seminar on Financing, Implementation and Operation of Highways in 21st Century. II199–202. New Delhi: IRC. 2000.

105. Chen, D. H., D. F. Lin, P. H. Liau and J. Bilyen. A correlation between dynamic cone penetrometer values and pavement layer moduli. *Geotech. Test. Jl.*. 28(1): 42–49. 2005.

106. Chen, D. H., J.N. Wang and J. Bilyen. Application of dynamic cone penetrometer in evaluation of base and subgrade layers. *Transportation Research Record 1764*. pp.1–10. Washington dc: Transportation Research Board. 2001.

107. Chen, J., M. Hossain and T. M. Latorella. Use of falling weight deflectometer and dynamic cone penetrometer in pavement evaluation. *Transportation Research Record 1655*. pp. 145–151. Washington dc: Transportation Research Board. 1999.

108. Childs, L. D, B. E. Colley and J. W. Kapernick. Tests to evaluate concrete pavement sub bases. *Transactions of ASCE*. 124 (2993): 556–587. 1959.

109. Chiu, C. T., M. Tai, B. E. Ruth and G. C. Page. Investigation of laboratory aging process of asphalt binders used in Florida. *Transportation Research Record No. 1436*. pp. 60–69. Washington dc: Transportation Research Board. 1994.

110. Chou, K. M. and R. L. Lytton. Load rating of light pavement structures. *Transportation Research Record 1043*. Washington dc: Transportation Research Board. 1984.

111. Chou, Y. T. Structural analysis computer program for rigid multi component pavement structures with discontinuities: WESLIQUID and WESLAYER. *Technical Report GL–80*. Vicksburg, Miss.: U.S. Army of Waterways Experiment Station. 1980.

112. Chou, Y. T. Subgrade contact pressures under rigid pavements. *ASCE Journal of Transportation Engineering* 103(3): 363–379. 1983.

113. *Chronicle Year Book*. India: Chronicle 2004.

114. Chua, K. M. and R. L. Lytton. Dynamic analysis using the portable pavement dynamic cone penetrometer. *Transportation Research Record No. 1192*. pp.27–38. Washington dc: Transportation Research Board. 1988.

115. Chung-Lung, Wu and Tai Mang. Field testing and structural evaluation of selected concrete pavement sections in Florida. pp. 404–439 in *Nondestructive testing of Pavements and Back-calculation of Moduli, Vol. II, STP 1198*. Edited by H. L. Quintus, A. J. Bush III and G. Y. Baladi. Philadelphia: American Society of Testing and Materials. 1994.

116. CITGO. Power point presentation on performance graded (PG) asphalts. Superpave update for NJDOT/NEAUPG Mechanistic Pavement Design Seminar. Feb.23. Princeton, NJ. 2003.

117. *Civil Services Chronicle*. January 2005.

118. Clayton, C. R. I. and A. W. Jukes. One point cone penetrometer liquid limit test. *Geotechnique* 12(4). 1995.

119. Clement, J. P. *Letter to Editor*. *Journal of ITE* pp. 6–7. March 1983.

120. Cole, L.W. Pavement condition surveys of ultra-thin white topping projects. *Proceedings of the 6th International Purdue Conference on Concrete Pavement Design and Materials for High Performance* 2: 175–187. Indianapolis, Ind. 1997.

121. Collins, A. R. and D. R. Sharp. The design and construction of concrete roads overseas. *Proc. of the Institute of Civil Engineers* 6267: 23–64. 1958.

122. Computer Program DAMA. Pavement structural analysis using multi-layered elastic theory. *Users Manual*. Asphalt Institute. 1983.

123. Cooling, L. F., A. W. Skempton and R. Glossop. Discussion made on a paper titled 'Classification and identification of soils' by A. Casagrande. *Transactions of the ASCE* 113(2351): 966–969. 1948.

124. COST 336. Task Group 1: Summary for FWD back-analysis program questionnaire (as part of the TG1 work program).

125. Coughlin, R. F. and F. F. Driscoll. *Operational Amplifiers and Linear Integrated Circuits*. 4th Edition. New Delhi: Prentice Hall of India Pvt. Ltd. 1991.

126. Craus, J. and A. Polus. Aspects of spiral transition curve design. *Transportation Research Record No. 631*. pp 1–4. Washington, dc: Transportation Research Board. 1977.

127. Crovetti, J. A. and M. I. Darter. Void detection for jointed concrete pavements. *Transportation Research Record No. 1041*. Washington, dc: TRB. 1985.

128. Crovetti, J. A. and M. R. Tirado-Crovetti. Evaluation of support conditions under jointed concrete pavement slab. pp. 455–472 in *Nondestructive testing of Pavements and Back-calculation of Moduli, Vol. II, STP 1198.* Edited by H. L. Quintus, A. J. Bush III and G. Y. Baladi. Philadelphia: American Society of Testing and Materials. 1994.

129. CROW working group. CROW report D06-06. literature survey on existing design methods for flexible pavements. Intermediate Report on the CROW Working Group on Design Tool for Asphalt Pavements Phase 1 and 2.

130. CRRI. Report on the History of Road Development in India. New Delhi: Central Road Research Institute (CRRI). 1963.

131. CRRI. Document on Rural Road Development in India, Vol. II. New Delhi: Central Road Research Institute (CRRI). 1990.

132. CSIR Report. Vehicle overloading management. South Africa. 2001.

133. CSR. *Competition Success Review Year Book 2008*. New Delhi.

134. Currell, G. and A. Dowman. *Essential Mathematics and Statistics for Science*, John Wiley & Sons, Ltd. 2005.

135. D 3282-93. Standard classification of soils and soil–aggregate mixtures for highway construction purposes. ASTM. 1999.

136. Dabbour, E., S. M. Easa and A. O. Abd El Halim. Radius requirements for reverse horizontal curves on three-dimensional alignments. *ASCE J. of Transportation Engineering* 130(5): 610–620. 2004.

137. Dauzats, M. and R. Linder. A method for the evaluation of the structural condition of pavements with thick bituminous road bases. *Proc. of the 5th International Conference on Structural Design of Asphalt Pavements* 1: 387–409. 1982.

138. De Beer, M., Use of the dynamic cone penetrometer (DCP) in the design of road structures. pp.167–183 in *Geotechnics in the African Environment* Vol. 1. edited by Blight et al. Rotterdam: Balkema. 1991.

139. De Jong, D. L., M. G. F. Peutz, A. R. Korswagen. Computer program BISAR: Layered system under normal and tangential loads. External report AMSR.0006.73. Koninklijke Shell Laboratorium, Amsterdam. 1973.

140. De Villiers, P. J. *Dynamic Cone Penetrometer Correlation with Unconfined Compressive Strength*. Pretoria: University of Pretoria. 1980.

141. Deacon, J. A. Load equivalency in flexible pavements. *Proc. of Assoc. of Asphalt Paving Technologists* 38: 465–494. 1969.

142. Deen, R. C., H. F. Southgate and J. H. Havens. Structural analysis of bituminous concrete pavements. *Research Report 305*. Division of Research, Kentucky Department of Highway. 1971.

143. Deme, I. Processing of sand–asphalt–sulphur mixes. *Proc. of the Assoc. of Asphalt Paving Tech*. 43: 465–482. 1974.

144. Denning, J. H. and J. Carswell. Improvements in rolled asphalt surfacing by addition of organic polymers. *Transportation and Road Research Lab. Report 989*. Crowthorne: TRRL. 1981.

145. Despotopoulos, P. T. A new easement curve in highway work. *Civil Engineering and Public Works Review* XLII(495): 378–381. September 1947.

146. Di Benedetto, H., M. N. Partl, L. Franken and C. De La Roche Saint Andre. RILEM TC 182-PEB Performance testing and evaluation of bituminous materials: Stiffness Testing for bituminous mixtures. *Materials and Structures* 34: 66–70. 2001.

147. City Dickinson, E. J. *Bituminous Roads in Australia*. Victoria, Australia: ARRB. 1984.

148. Dickinson, E. J. Performance of thin bituminous pavement surfacings in Australia. *Proc. 11th ARRB Conf.* 11 (3): 35–51. 1982.

149. Dickinson, E. J. The flow and deformation behavior of bituminous binders under pavement service conditions.*Proc. 11th ARRB Conf.* 11 (3): 3–10. 1981.

150. Domke, C. H., M. Liu, R. R. Davison, J. A. Bullin and C. J. Glover. Study of strategic highway research program: Pressure aging vessel procedure using long-term low-temperature aging experiments and asphalt kinetics. *Transportation Research Record No. 1586*. pp.10–15. Washington, dc: Transportation Research Board. 1997.

151. Dormon, G. M. The extension to practice of a fundamental procedure for the design of flexible pavements. *Proc. of the Int. Conf. on the Struct. Des. of Asphalt Pavements.* pp.785–793. Univ., of Michigan, Ann Arbor. 1962.

152. DORTH. Annular Report 2008–2008. Department Of Road Transport & Highways. Ministry of Shipping, Road Transport & Highways Government of India. New Delhi.

153. Duncan, J. M and H. B. Seed. Strength variation along failure surfaces in clay. *Jl. of ASCE* 92(SM6): 81–104. 1966.

154. Duncan, J. M., C. L. Monismith and E. L. Wilson. Finite element analysis of pavements. *Highway Research Record No. 228*. pp.11–17. Washington, dc: Transportation Research Board. 1968.

155. Easa, S. M. and Y. Hassan. Design requirements of equal-arc unsymmetrical vertical curves. *ASCE J. of Transportation Engineering* 124 (5): 404–410. 1998

156. Easa, S. M. Distributing super elevation to maximize highway design consistency. *ASCE J. of Transportation Engineering* 129(2): 127–133. 2003.

157. Easa, S. M. Exact minimum sight distance on sag curve with centered overpass, *ASCE J. of Transportation Engineering* 118(4): 588–592. 1992.

158. Easa, S. M. Lateral clearance needs on compound horizontal curves. *ASCE J. of Transportation Engineering* 119(1): 111–123. 1993.

159. Easa, S. M. Lateral clearance to vision obstacles on horizontal curves. *Transportation Research Record No. 1303*. pp. 22–32. Washington, dc: Transportation Research Board. 1991.

160. Easa, S. M., E. Dabbour and M. Z. A Ali. Three-dimensional model for stop control intersection sight distance. *ASCE J. of Transportation Engineering* 130(2): 261–270. 2004.

161. Edwards, J. M. and C. P. Valkering. *Structural Design of Asphalt Pavements for Heavy Aircraft.* Amsterdam, Holland: Koninklijke/Shell Laboratorium. 1970.

162. Emery, S. J. The prediction of moisture content in untreated pavement layers and applications to design in South Africa. *CSIR Research Report No. 644*. *DRTT Bulletin 20*. Pretoria: CSIR. 1988; 1992.

163. ERES. Rolling weight deflectometer for highway pavements. *Status of Research and Development*. ERES Division, Applied Research Association Inc., Research Sponsored by the US Department of Transportation. 1999.

164. Ese, D., J. Myre, P. Noss and E. Vaernes. The use of dynamic cone penetrometer (DCP) for road strengthening design in Norway. *Proc. of the 4th Int., Conf. on the Bearing Capacity of Roads and Airfields*. pp.343–357. Minneapolis: University of Minnesota. 1994.

165. Fadum, F. F. Discussion made on a paper titled 'Classification and identification of soils' by A. Casagrande. *Transactions of the ASCE* 113(2351): 931–933. 1948.

166. Fadum, F. F. Influence values for estimating stresses in elastic foundations. *Proceedings of the 2nd Int. Conf. on Soil Mechanics and Foundation Eng*. Rotterdam. 1948.

167. Feld, J. Discussion made on a paper titled 'Classification and identification of soils' by A. Casagrande. *Transactions of the ASCE* 113(2351): 946. 1948.

168. Fenwick, J. M. The durability of reinforced concrete. *Queensland Roads* 21 (42):16–18. 1982.

169. FHWA. Concrete pavement joints. T 5040.30. U. S. Department of Transportation, Federal Highway Administration, November 30, 1990. http://www.fhwa.dot.gov/legsregs/directives/techadvs/t504030.htm.

170. FHWA. Evaluation of design consistency methods for two-lane rural highways. Publication No. FHWA-RD-99-173, August 2000. Executive Summary. http://www.tfhrc.gov/safety/ihsdm/pdfs/99-173.pdf, as visited on 17/10/2007.

171. FHWA. Evaluation of joint and crack load transfer. Final Report: FHWA–RD–02–088. October 2003. http://www.tfhrc.gov/pavement/ltpp/reports/02088/02088.pdf.

172. FHWA. Predictive design procedures. *VESYS User Manual, Report No. FHWA-RD-77-154*. Federal Highway Administration. 1978.

173. FHWA. Speed prediction for two-lane rural highways. Publication No. 99-171, August 2000. http://www.tfhrc.gov/safety/ihsdm/pdfs/99-171.pdf, as visited on 17/10/2007.

174. FHWA-TS-80-224. Moulton L. K. and Principal Engineer from TRIAD Engineering Consultants, Inc. Highway subdrainage design. Federal Highway Administration, US Department of Transportation. 1980.

175. FHWA-TS-84-202. Johnson, F. L. and F. F. M. Chang. Drainage of highway pavements. Hydraulics Engineering Circular No. 12. Federal Highway Administration, US Department of Transportation. 1980.

176. Finn, place E. V. *Airports and Airfields, Civil Engineering Reference Book*. 2nd Edition. Edited by J. Comrie J. 4: 115–143. London: Butterworth & Co Ltd. 1961.

177. Flugge, Wilhelm. *Viscoelasticity*. London: Blaisdell Publishing Company, A Division of Ginn and Company. 1975

178. Ford, G. R. and B. E. Eliason. Comparison of compaction methods on narrow surface drainage trenches. *Transportation Research Record No. 1425*. pp.18–27. Washington dc: Transportation Research Board. 1993.

179. Forssblad, Lars. *Vibratory Soil and Rock Fill Compaction.* Solna, Sweden: Dynapac Maskin AB. 1981.

180. Foster, C. R. and R. G. Ahlvin. Stresses and Deflections induced by a uniform circular load. *Proc. of the Highway Research Board* 33: 467–470. 1954.

181. Foster, R. C. Pavement design procedures. *QIP Publication No. 79.* National Asphalt Pavement Association, NAPA., 1965.

182. Foxworthy, P. T. and M. I. Darter. ILLI-SLAB and FWD deflection basins for characterization of rigid pavements. pp. 368–386 in *Nondestructive testing of Pavements and Back-calculation of Moduli, ASTM STP 1026.* Edited by A. J. Bush III and G. Y. Baladi. Philadelphia: American Society of Testing and Materials. 1989.

183. Frabizzio, M. A. and N. J. Buch. Characterization of transverse cracks in jointed concrete pavements (JCPs) using nondestructive test (NDT) methods. pp. 231–245 in *Nondestructive Testing of Pavements and Backcalculation of Moduli: Vol. 3, ASTM STP 1375.* Edited by S. D. Tayabji and E. O. Lukanen. Philadelphia: American Society for Testing and Materials. 2000.

184. Freeme, C. R., J. H. Maree and A. W. Viljoen. Mechanistic design of asphalt pavements and verification using the heavy vehicle simulator. *Proc. of the 5th International Conference on Structural Design of Asphalt Pavements* 1:156–173. 1982.

185. Friberg, B. F. Design of dowels in transverse joints of concrete pavements. *Transactions of American Society of Civil Engineers* 105(2081): 1076–1095. 1940.

186. Friberg, B. F. Stresses in concrete pavements by sector analysis. *Proceedings of the Highway Research Board.* 1955.

187. Fromm, H. J. and G. J. A. Kennepohl. Sulphur asphaltic concrete on three Ontario roads. *Proc. of the Assoc. of Asphalt Paving Tech.* 48: 135–162. 1979.

188. Fuller W. B. and S. E. Thompson. The laws of proportioning concrete. *Transactions of ASCE* 59: 67–143. 1907.

189. Fwa, T. F. and L. S. Tan. Geometric characterization of road humps for speed-control design. *ASCE J. of Transportation Engineering* 118(4): 593–598. 1992.

190. Fwa, T. F. and L. Wei. *Design of Rigid Pavements: The Handbook of Highway Engineering.* edited by T. F. Fwa. CRC Press, Taylor & Francis Group. 2006.

191. Fwa, T. F., C. Y. Tan and W. T. Chan. Back-calculation analysis of pavement-layer moduli using genetic algorithms. *Transportation Research Record No. 1570.* pp.134–142. Transportation Research Board. 1997.

192. Fwa, T. F., K. H. Tan and S. Li. Closed-form and semi-closed-form algorithms for back-calculation of concrete pavement parameters. pp. 267–280 in *Nondestructive Testing of Pavements and Backcalculation of Moduli: Vol. 3, ASTM STP 1375.* Edited by S. D. Tayabji and E. O. Lukanen. Philadelphia: American Society for Testing and Materials. 2000.

193. Fwa, T. F., K. H. Tan. and S. Li. Graphical solutions for back-calculation of rigid pavement parameters. *ASCE Journal of Transportation Engineering* 124 (1): 567–572. 1998.

194. Fwa, T. F., X. P, Shi. and S. A. Tan. Analysis of concrete pavements by rectangular thick plate model. *ASCE Journal of Transportation Engineering* 122(2):146–154. 1996.

195. Gabr, M. A., K. Hopkins, J. Coonse and T. Hearne. DCP criteria for performance evaluation of pavement layer. *ASCE Journal of Performance of Constructed Facilities* 14(4): 141–148. 2000.

196. García, G. A. and L. M. Conesa. (discussion). Unit curve for design of highway transitions by S. K. Rao. *ASCE J. of Transportation Engineering* p.244. May/June, 1997.

197. García, G. A. and L. M. Conesa. Improving steep bends as hairpin curves on mountainous roads (Discussion on this section). *ASCE J. of Transportation Engineering* 118 (6): 882–884. 1992.

198. Gattis, J. L., B. F. Vinsin III and L. K. Duncan. Low-speed horizontal curve friction factors. *ASCE J. of Transportation Engineering* 131(2): 112–119. 2005.

199. Gayakwad, R. A. *OP AMPS and Linear Integrated Circuits.* 3rd Edition. New Delhi: Prentice Hall of India Pvt. Ltd. 2002.

200. Gerritsen, A. H. and R. C. Koole. Seven year's experience with the structural aspects of the *Shell Pavement Design Manual. Proc. of the 6th International Conference on Structural Design of Asphalt Pavements.* Vol. I. pp.94–106. 1987.

201. Ghosh, R. K. and A. K. Garg. Shear stress in concrete pavements: analytical procedure for highway and airfields. *Civil Engineering and Public Works Review* 64(755): 577–582. 1969.

202. Ghosh, R. K., M. R. Chatterjee, M. L. Bhatia and R. C. Bhatnagar. Investigation on sugar mixed concrete for pavements. *Road Research Bulletin 17*. IRC. 1973.

203. Gibby, R. R. Dawson and P. Sebaaly. Local urban transit bus impact on pavements. *ASCE's Jl. of Transportation Engineering* 122(3): 215–217. 1996.

204. Gibreel, G. M., S. M. Easa, Y. Hassan and I. A. El-Dimeery. State of the art of highway geometric design consistency. *ASCE J. of Transportation Engineering* 125(4): 305–313. 1999.

205. Giffin. Discussion on highway location: Practical considerations by H. K Losh. *Transactions of the ASCE*. 96: 485–487. 1932.

206. Glennon, J. C. New and improved model of passing sight distance on two-lane rural highways. *Transportation Research Record No.1195.* pp.132–137. Washington, dc: Transportation Research Board. 1988.

207. Goldbeck, A. T. Highway researches and what the results indicate. *Proc. of the American Road Builders Association*. 1922.

208. Goldbeck, A. T. Researches on the structural design of highways by the United States Bureau of Public Roads. *Transactions of ASCE* .88: 264–300. 1925.

209. Goldbeck, A. T. The design of concrete pavements. *Concrete* 1925.

210. Goldbeck, A. T. The interrelation of longitudinal steel and transverse cracks in concrete roads. *Public Roads*. 1925.

211. Gopal Raju, S. S. S. and V. R. Rengaraju. Use of poly-ethylene waste in stabilization of subgrade soil. *Seminar on Integrated Development of Rural and Arterial Road Network for Socio-economic Growth.* II: 199–208. New Delhi. 2003.

212. Gourley, C. and P. A. K. Greening. Performance of low-volume sealed roads: Results and recommendations from studies in Southern Africa. *TRL Report No. PR/OSC/167/99.* Crowthorn, 1999.

213. Government of India.*Report of the Road Development Committee, 1927 to 1928.* Calcutta: Central Publication Branch. 1928.

214. Greenstein, J. Transition curves for speed changes. *ASCE J. of Transportation Engineering* 102 (No.TE1): 699–713. 1976.

215. Grimer, F. J. and M. A. Ali. The strengths of cements reinforced with glass fibers, *Magazine of Concrete Research* 21(66). 1969.

216. Grinter, L. E. *Transactions of ASCE* 103. p.1157. 1938.

217. Grogan, W. P. and J. S. Tingle. Evaluation of unsurfaced airfield criteria for operation of C-17 aircraft. *ASCE Jl. of Transportation Engineering* 125(1). 1999.

218. Guell, D. L. Comparison of two rigid pavement design methods. *ASCE Journal of Transportation Engineering* 111(6): 607–617. 1985.

219. Guo, H., J. A. Sherwood and M. B. Snyder. Component dowel-bar model for load-transfer systems in PCC pavements. *Journal of Transportation Engineering.* Vol. 121. pp.289–298. 1995.

220. Hall, K. T. and M. I. Darter. Improved methods for asphalt-overlaid concrete pavement back-calculation and evaluation. pp. 83–102 in *Nondestructive Testing of Pavements and Back-calculation of Moduli, Vol. II, STP 1198.* Edited by H. L. Quintus, A. J. Bush III and G. Y. Baladi. Philadelphia: American Society of Testing and Materials. 1994.

221. Hall, T. K. and A. Mohseni. Back-calculation of asphalt concrete-overlaid Portland cement concrete pavement layer moduli. *Transportation Research Record No. 1293.* pp.112–123. Transportation Research Board, 1991,

222. Hall, W. M. Manufacturing concrete of uniform quality. *Transactions of the ASCE* 96: 1336–1358. 1932.

223. Hammons, Michael I. DOT/FAA/AR-97/7. Final report on "Advanced pavement design: Finite element modeling for rigid pavement joints". *Report II: Model Development.* Federal Aviation Administration. 1998.

224. Harichandran, R. S., T. Mahmood, A. R. Raab, G.Y. Baladi. Modified Newton algorithm for back-calculation of pavement layer properties. *Transportation Research Record No. 1384*. pp.15–22. Transportation Research Board. 1993,

225. Harison, J. A. In situ CBR determination by DCP testing using a laboratory–based correlation. *Australian Road Research*. 19(4): 313–317. 1989.

226. Harman, Thomas, John D'Angelo, John Bukowski (the Asphalt Team). *Superpave Asphalt Mixture Design*. Workshop Workbook Version 8.0. U.S. Dept. of Transportation, Federal Highway Administration. Updated 2002.

227. Harwood, D., J. Mason and R. Brydia. Sight distance for stop-controlled intersections based on gap acceptance. *Transportation Research Record No. 1701*. pp.32–41. Washington, dc: Transportation Research Board. 2000.

228. Hassan, Y., S. M. Easa and A. O. Abd El Halim. Design considerations for combined highway alignments. *ASCE J. of Transportation Engineering* 123(1): 60–68. 1997.

229. Hatt, W. K. The effect of moisture on concrete. *Transaction of ASCE* 157: 270–315. 1925.

230. Hawkins, H. G. Jr. How modern headlamp performance impacts sag vertical curve design. *ASCE J. of Transportation Engineering* 133(4): 223–231. 2007.

231. Head K. H. *Manual of Soil Laboratory Testing 1–3*. London: Prentec Press. 1982.

232. Heiner, A. Strength and compaction properties of frozen soils. *Document of the place National Swedish Building Research*. Stockholm, Sweden: Division of Soil Mechanics, Royal Institute of Technology. 1971.

233. Heisey, J. S., K. H. Stokoe II and A. H. Meyer. Moduli of pavement systems from spectral analysis of surface waves. *Transportation Research Record No. 852*. pp.22–31. Washington, dc: Transportation Research Board. 1982.

234. Heukelom, W. An improved method of characterising asphaltic bitumens with the aid of their mechanical properties. *Proc. of the Association of Asphalt Paving Technologies* 42: 62–98. 1973.

235. Heukelom, W. and A. J. G Klomp. Road design and dynamic loading. *Proc. of the Association of Asphalt Paving Technologies* 33: 92–125. 1964.

236. Heukelom, W. and A. J. G. Klomp. Consideration of calculated strains at various depths in connection with the stability of asphalt pavements. *Proc. of the 2nd International Conference on Structural Design of Asphalt Pavements*. pp.277–290. 1967.

237. Hickerson, T. F. *Route Location and Design*. New York: McGraw-Hill Book Co. Inc. 1964.

238. Hicks, R. G. and C. L. Monismith. Factors influencing the resilient response of granular materials. *Transportation Research Record No. 345*. Washington, dc: Transportation Research Board.1971.

239. Hill, R. L., S. L. Sarkar, R. F. Rathbone and J. C. Hower. An examination of fly ash carbon and its interaction with air-entraining agents. *Cement Concrete Res*. 27(2):193–204. 1997.

240. Hinkle, A. H. The engineer's part in making the highway safe. *Transactions of ASCE* 94: 522–529. 1930.

241. Hirsh, M., J. N. Prashker and M. Ben-Akiva. New approach to geometric design of highways. *Transportation Research Record No. 1100*. pp.50–57. Washington, dc: Transportation Research Board. 1986.

242. Hoffman, M. S. and M. R. Thompson. Comparative study of selected nondestructive testing devices. *Transportation Research Record No. 852*. pp.32–42. Washington, dc: Transportation Research Board. 1982.

243. Horak, E. The use of surface deflection basin measurements in the mechanistic analysis of flexible pavements. *Proceedings of the 6th International Conference of Structural Design of Asphalt Pavements*. pp. 990–1001. University of Michigan, U.S.A. 1987.

244. Hossain, M., J. Zaniewski and S. Rajan. Estimation of pavement-layer modulus using non-linear optimization technique. *ASCE Journal of Transportation Engineering*. 120(3): 376–393. 1994.

245. http://training.ce.washington.edu/WSDOT/Modules/04_design_parameters/04-2_body.htm, visited on 14-08-2006.

246. http://www.airporttech.tc.faa.gov/naptf/P-53.pdf. Accessed on 31-03-2008.

247. http://www.cag.gov.in.

248. Huang Tien-Kuen, G. and C. H. Juang. Equivalent single-axle load factor for rigid pavements. *ASCE Jl. of Transportation Engineering* 122 (6): 462–467. 1996.

249. Huang, Y. H. and T. Wang. Finite element analysis of concrete slabs and its implication for rigid pavement design. *Highway Research Record 466*. pp.55–69. Washington, dc: Nat. Res. Council. 1973.

250. Huang, Yang H. *Pavement Analysis and Design*. 2nd edition. Pearson Prentice Hall. 2004.

251. Hubbell, C.C. Circular curve formulas. *Surveying and Mapping* II (3). 1951.

252. Hunting, M. T. Geology in highway engineering. *Transactions of ASCE* 110(2238): 271–297. 1945.

253. Hveem, F. N. Slab warping affects on pavement joint performance. *Proc. of American Concrete Institute* 47: 797–808. 1951.

254. *India 2004, A Reference Annual*. Publications Division. Ministry of Information and Broadcasting. Government of India. New Delhi.

255. *India 2008, A Reference Annual*. Publications Division. Ministry of Information and Broadcasting. Government of India. New Delhi.

256. *India Vision 2020*. The report and background papers. Planning Commission. Government of India. 2004.

257. Indiabudget. http://indiabudget.nic.in/es2007-08/chapt2008/chap94.pdf.

258. Ioannides, A. M. and G. T. Korovesis. Aggregate interlock: A pure-shear load transfer mechanism. *Transportation Research Record No. 1286*. pp.14–24. Transportation Research Board. 1990.

259. Ioannides, A. M. and G. T. Korovesis. Analysis and design of doweled slab on-grade pavement systems. *ASCE Jl. of Transportation Engineering* 118(6): 745–768. 1992.

260. Ioannides, A. M. Concrete pavement back-calculation using ILLI-BACK 3.0. pp.103–124 in *Nondestructive Testing of Pavements and Backcalculation of Moduli: Vol. 2, ASTM STP 1198*. Edited by Harold L. Von Quintas, Albert J. Bush III and Gilbert Y. Baladi. Philadelphia: American Society for Testing and Materials. 1994.

261. Ioannides, A. M. Dimensional analysis in NDT rigid pavement evaluation. *ASCE Jl. of Transportation Engineering* 116 (1): 23–36. 1990.

262. Ioannides, A. M., D. R. Alexander, M. I. Hammons and G. M. Davis. Application of artificial neural networks to concrete pavement joint evaluation. *Transportation Research Record No. 1540*. pp.56–64. Transportation Research Board. 1996.

263. Ioannides, A. M., E. J. Barenburg and J. A. Lary. Interpretation of falling weight deflectometer results using principles of dimensional analysis. *Proc. of the 4th Int. Conf., on Concrete Pavement Design and Rehabilitation*. pp.231–247. place Purdue University. 1989.

264. Ioannides, A. M., M. R. Thompson and E. J. Barenberg. Westergaard solutions reconsidered. *Transportation Research Record No. 1043*. pp.13–23. Washington, dc: Transportation Research Board. 1985.

265. IRC Special Report 15. Ribbon development along highways and its prevention. Indian Roads Congress, New Delhi.1974.

266. IRC. An appraisal of the CBR test. *Journal of the Indian Roads Congress* 45(3). New Delhi: Indian Roads Congress. 1984.

267. IRC. Bituminous roads: Design and construction aspects. *Discussions, Proceedings, Seminar of the IRC*. pp. 45–102. 1994.

268. IRC. Draft approach paper. *Road Development Plan 2000–21*. 1999.

269. IRC. Nagpur Road Plan, Post-war road development in India. In *Proceedings of the Chief Engineers' Conference on Road Development, December 15–18, 1943*.

270. IRC. *Pocket Book for Highway Engineers*. New Delhi: Indian Roads Congress. 2006.

271. IRC. *Road Development Plan for India (1981–2001)*. 1984.

272. IRC. Standard scales and standard sizes of drawings for highway projects. *IRC Journal* XI-I. 1946.

273. IRC: 104-1989. Guidelines for environmental impact assessment of highway projects. New Delhi: Indian Roads Congress. 1989.

274. IRC: 3-1983. Dimensions and weights of road design vehicles. New Delhi: Indian Roads Congress.. 1983.

275. IRC: 35-1970. Code of practice for road markings (with paints). New Delhi: Indian Roads Congress. 1970.

276. IRC: 37-2001. Guidelines for the design of flexible pavements. New Delhi: Indian Roads Congress. 2001.

277. IRC: 38-1970. Design tables for horizontal curves for highways. New Delhi: Indian Roads Congress. 1970.

278. IRC: 39-1986. Standards for road–rail level crossings. New Delhi: Indian Roads Congress. 1986.

279. IRC: 44-2008. Tentative guidelines for cement concrete mix design for pavements, for non-entraining and continuously graded concrete. New Delhi: IRC, New Delhi. 2008.

280. IRC: 52-1981. Alignment survey and geometric design of hill roads. New Delhi: Indian Roads Congress.1981.

281. IRC: 52-2001. Recommendations about the alignment survey and geometric design of hill roads. New Delhi: Indian Roads Congress.2001.

282. IRC: 54-1974. Lateral and vertical clearances at underpasses for vehicular traffic. New Delhi: Indian Roads Congress. 1974.

283. IRC: 58-2002. Guidelines for the design of plain jointed rigid pavements for highways. New Delhi: Indian Roads Congress. 2002.

284. IRC: 66-1976. Recommended practice for sight distance on rural highways. New Delhi: Indian Roads Congress. 1976.

285. IRC: 67-1977. Code of practice for road signs. New Delhi: Indian Roads Congress., 1977.

286. IRC: 69-1977. Space standards for roads in urban areas. New Delhi: Indian Roads Congress.. 1996.

287. IRC: 70-1977. Guidelines on regulation and control of mixed traffic in urban areas. New Delhi: Indian Roads Congress. 1977.

288. IRC: 73-1980. Geometric design standards for rural (non-urban) highways. New Delhi: Indian Roads Congress. 1980.

289. IRC: 76-1979. Tentative guidelines for the structural evaluation of rigid airfield pavements. New Delhi: Indian Roads Congress. 1979.

290. IRC: 81-1997. Guidelines for strengthening of flexible road pavements using Benkelman Beam deflection technique. New Delhi: Indian Roads Congress. 1997.

291. IRC: 86-1983. Geometric design standards for urban roads in plains. New Delhi: Indian Roads Congress. 1983.

292. IRC: 98-1997. Guidelines on accommodation of utility services on roads in urban areas, First revision. New Delhi: Indian Roads Congress.1997.

293. IRC: SP: 23-1983. Vertical curves for highways. *IRC Special Bulletin No. 23.* New Delhi: Indian Roads Congress. 1993.

294. IRC: SP: 42-1994. Guidelines on road drainage. New Delhi: Indian Roads Congress. 1994.

295. IRC: SP: 48-1998. *Hill Road Manual.* New Delhi: Indian Roads Congress. 1998.

296. IRC: SP: 50-1999. Guidelines on urban drainage. New Delhi: Indian Roads Congress. 1999.

297. IRC: SP: 62-2004. Guidelines for the design and construction of cement concrete pavements for rural roads. New Delhi: Indian Roads Congress.2004.

298. IRC: SP: 72-2007. Guidelines for the design of flexible pavements for low volume rural roads. New Delhi: Indian Roads Congress. 2007.

299. IRC: SP: 76-2008. Tentative guidelines for conventional thin and ultra-thin whitetopping. New Delhi: Indian Roads Congress. 2008.

300. IRC: SP: 77-2008. Manual for the design, construction & maintenance of gravel roads. New Delhi: Indian Roads Congress. 2007.

301. IRC: SP:19-2001. Manual for survey, investigation and preparation of road projects. New Delhi: Indian Roads Congress. 2001.

302. IRC: SP:53-2002. Guidelines on use of polymer and rubber modified bitumen in road construction. New Delhi: Indian Roads Congress. 2002.

303. IRC:15-2002. Standard specifications and code of practice for construction of concrete roads. New Delhi: Indian Roads Congress., 2002.

304. Ireson, W. G., C. F. Coombs Jr. and R. Y. Moss. (Ed.). *Hand Book of Reliability and Management.* 2ndEd. McGraw Hill. 1998.

305. Irwin, L. H. *User's Guide to MODCOMP2.* Cornell University, Ithaca, NY: Local Roads Program. 1983.

306. IS: 10262. Indian standard guidelines for concrete mix design. New Delhi: Bureau of Indian Standards. 1998

307. IS: 11196-1985. Specification for equipment for determination of liquid limit of soils by cope penetration method. New Delhi: Bureau of Indian Standards. 1985.

308. IS: 1199-1959. Methods of sampling and analysis of concrete. New Delhi: Bureau of Indian Standards.1999.

309. IS: 1201 to 1220-1978. Methods for testing tar and bituminous materials. New Delhi: Bureau of Indian Standards. 1978; 2002.

310. IS: 1498-1970. Classification and identification of soils for general engineering purposes. New Delhi: Bureau of Indian Standards.

311. IS: 1888. Indian standard method of load test on soils 2nd revision. New Delhi: Indian Standards Institution.

312. IS: 215-1995. Road Tar: Specification. New Delhi: Bureau of Indian Standards. 2000.

313. IS: 217-1988. Specification for cutback bitumen. New Delhi: Bureau of Indian Standards. 1993.

314. IS: 2386 (Part 1)-1963. Methods of test for aggregates for concrete, particle size and shape. New Delhi: Bureau of Indian Standards. 2004.

315. IS: 2386 (Part 3)-1963. Methods of test for aggregates for concrete, specific gravity, density, voids, absorption and bulking. New Delhi: Bureau of Indian Standards. 2002.

316. IS: 2386 (Part 4)-1963. Indian standard method of test for aggregate for concrete. New Delhi: Bureau of Indian Standards. 2005.

317. IS: 2720 (Part 10)-1991. Methods of test for soils, determination of unconfined compressive strength. New Delhi: Bureau of Indian Standards.1992.

318. IS: 2720 (Part 12)-1981. Methods of test for soils, determination of shear strength parameters of soil from consolidated undrained tri-axial compression test with measurement of pore water pressure. New Delhi: Bureau of Indian Standards. 2004.

319. IS: 2720 (Part 13)-1986. Methods of test for soils, direct shear test. New Delhi: Bureau of Indian Standards.1987.

320. IS: 2720 (Part 16)-1987. Methods of tests for soils, laboratory determination of CBR. New Delhi: Bureau of Indian Standards. 2004.

321. IS: 2720 (Part 2)-1973. Methods of tests for soils, determination of water content. New Delhi: Bureau of Indian Standards. 2004.

322. IS: 2720 (Part 28)-1974. Methods of tests for soils, determination of dry density of soils in-place by the sand replacement method. New Delhi: Bureau of Indian Standards.

323. IS: 2720 (Part 29)-1975. Methods of test for soils, determination of dry density of soils in-place by the core-cutter method. New Delhi: Bureau of Indian Standards. 2006.

324. IS: 2720 (Part 30)-1980. Methods of test for soils, laboratory vane shear test. New Delhi: Bureau of Indian Standards. 2004.

325. IS: 2720 (Part 31)-1990. Methods of tests for soils, field determination of California bearing ratio. New Delhi: Bureau of Indian Standards. 2006.

326. IS: 2720 (Part 33)-1991. Methods of test for soils, determination of the density in-place by the ring and water replacement method. New Delhi: Bureau of Indian Standards.

327. IS: 2720 (Part 34)-1972. Methods of tests for soils, determination of the density of soil in-place by rubber balloon method. New Delhi: Bureau of Indian Standards. 2001.

328. IS: 2720 (Part 4)-1985. Methods of tests for soils, grain size analysis. New Delhi: Bureau of Indian Standards. 2004.

329. IS: 2720 (Part 5)-1985. Methods of tests for soils, determination of liquid limit and plastic limit. New Delhi: Bureau of Indian Standards. 2004.

330. IS: 2720 (Part 7)-1980. Determination of water content: Dry density relation using light compaction. New Delhi: Bureau of Indian Standards. 2004.

331. IS: 2720 (Part 8)-1983. Determination of water content: Dry density relation using heavy compaction. *BIS Code*. New Delhi: Bureau of Indian Standards. 2004.

332. IS: 334-2002. Glossary of terms relating to bitumen and tar. New Delhi: Bureau of Indian Standards. 2002.

333. IS: 3812-1981. Specification for fly ash for use as pozzolana and admixture. New Delhi: Bureau of Indian Standards. Reaffirmed in 1999.

334. IS: 456-2000. Indian standard plain and reinforced concrete code of practice. New Delhi: Bureau of Indian Standards. 2000.

335. IS: 516-1959. Methods of tests for strength of concrete. New Delhi: Bureau of Indian Standards.1999.

336. IS: 5816-1999. Splitting tensile strength of concrete: Methods of test. New Delhi: Bureau of Indian Standards. 1999.

337. IS: 6241-1971. Method of test for determination of stripping value of road aggregates. New Delhi: Bureau of Indian Standards.

338. IS: 73-2006. Indian standard paving bitumen: Specifications. New Delhi: Bureau of Indian Standards. 2006.

339. IS: 9214-1979. Indian standard method of determination of modulus of sub-grade reaction (*k* value) of soils in field. New Delhi: Indian Standards Institution. 1980s.

340. Jackson, D. J., M. R. Murphy and A. Wimsatt. Strategies for the application of the falling weight deflectometer to evaluate load transfer efficiency at joints in jointed concrete pavement. pp. 395–403 in *Nondestructive testing of Pavements and Back-calculation of Moduli, Vol. II, STP 1198*. Edited by H. L. Quintus, A. J. Bush III and G. Y. Baladi. Philadelphia: American Society of Testing and Materials. 1994.

341. Jackson, F. H. et al. Concretes containing air-entraining agents. Proceedings. *American Concrete Institute Journal* 40: 509–572. 1944.

342. Jackson, T. J. and R. M. Ragan. Hydrology of porous pavement parking lots. *ASCE's Jl, of the Hydraulics Div.* 100 (12). 1974.

343. Jagadish, R., H. Sharada Bai and S. H. Basavaraj. Modern cement super-plasticizers for durability of concrete structures. *Int. Conf. on Maintenance & Durability of Concrete Structures.* JNT University, Hyderabad. 1997.

344. Jain, P. K. Incorporation of rubber/polymer in bituminous road surfacing. *State of the Art Report.* New Delhi: CRRI. 1988.

345. Jain, S. S., A. K.Gupta and Maj. Jagajit Singh. Analysis of seasonal and temperature correction factors for design of overlays for flexible pavements. *Journal of Indian Roads Congress* 51 (2): 267–299. 1990.

346. James, D. S. and V. R. Everitt. *Introduction to Highway Hydraulics.* Hydraulic Design Series Number 4. Washington d.c..: Federal Highway Administration. 1997.

347. Jameson, G. W., K. G. Sharp and N. J. Vertessy. Full-depth asphalt pavement fatigue under accelerated loading. *Proc. of the 7th Int. Conf. on the Struct. Des. of Asphalt Pavements, Vol. 2.* pp.180–200. Nottingham. 1992.

348. Jarvis, J. R. The off-road testing of road humps for use under Australian conditions. *Proc. of the 10th ARRB Conference Vol. 4.* Traffic Australian Road Research Board. August 1980.

349. Jayawickrama, P. W., A. L. Amarasiri and P. E. Regino. Use of dynamic cone penetrometer to control compaction of granular fill. *Transportation Research Record No. 1736.* Washington dc: Transportation Research Board. 2000.

350. Jeongho, Oh A., Fernando E. G. and Lytton R. L. Evaluation of damage potential for pavements due to over weight truck traffic. *ASCE Jl. of Transportation Engineering.* 133(5): 308–317. 2007.

351. Jervis, W. H. and J. B. Eustis. Accepted procedure for the CBR test: A symposium on development of CBR flexible pavement design method for airfields. *Transactions of the ASCE* 115(2406): 472–484. 1950.

352. Jeuffroy, G and J. Bachelez. Note on a method of analysis for pavements. *Proc. of the 1st International Conference on Structural Design of Asphalt Pavements.* pp.300–309. 1962.

353. Jiang, Y. J. and S. D. Tayabji. Evaluation of concrete pavement conditions and design features using LTPP FWD deflections. pp. 281–294 in *Nondestructive Testing of Pavements and Backcalculation of Moduli: Vol. 3, ASTM STP 1375.* Edited by S. D. Tayabji and E. O. Lukanen. Philadelphia: American Society for Testing and Materials. 2000.

354. Johnson T. C., D. M. Cole and L. H. Irwin. Characterization of frees/thaw granular soils for pavement evaluation. *Proc. of the 5th Int. Conf. on the Struct. Des. of Asphalt Pavements.* pp.805–817. Ann Arbor, Michigan: Univ. of Michigan. 1982.

355. Johnson, A. W. and J. R. Sallberg J. R. Factors influencing compaction test results. *HRB, Bulletin 319.* USA. 1962.

356. Johnson, T. C., D. M. Cole and L. H. Irwin. Characterization of frees/thaw granular soils for pavement evaluation. *Proc. of the 5th Int. Conf. on the Struct. Des. of Asphalt Pavements*. pp.805–817. Univ. of Michigan, Ann Arbor, Michigan. 1982.

357. Joseph, A. H. and J. W. Hall Jr. Nondestructive vibratory pavement evaluation techniques. *Proc. of the 3rd International Conference Structural Design of Asphalt Pavements*. Vol. 1. pp.844–848. 1972.

358. Kadiyali, L. R. Flexible pavement design methodology: The way ahead. *Indian Highways* 34(6): 55–57. 2006.

359. Kallas, B. F. and V. P. Puzinauskas. Flexural fatigue tests on asphalt paving mixtures. Report STP 508. *Proceedings of the Association of Asphalt Paving Technologists* 39: 47–65. American Society for Testing and Materials. 1972.

360. Kallas, B. F. Dynamic modulus of asphalt concrete in tension and tension–compression. *Proc. of the Assn. of Asphalt Paving Technologists* 39: 1–20. 1970.

361. Kamayama S., K. Matsui, A. Kasahara, K. Himeno. and T. Maruyama. Effect of FWD sensor locations on back-calculated layer moduli. *Proc. of the 5th International Conference on Bearing Capacity of Roads and Airfields (BCRA)*. Vol. I. pp.477–486. 1998.

362. Kanchan, P. K., M. N. Nagabushana and P. K. Nanda. Present scenario of overloading of commercial vehicles on Indian roads: Two recent case studies. *Indian Highways* 34(1): 35–42. New Delhi: IRC. 2006.

363. Kandhal, P. S. Quality control requirements for using crumb rubber modified bitumen (CRMB) in bituminous mixtures. *Jl. of Indian Roads Congress* 67-1(522): 99–104. 2006.

364. Kanellaidis, G. Aspects of highway super elevation *ASCE J. of Transportation Engineering* 117 (6): 624–632. 1991.

365. Kanellaidis, G. Human factors in highway geometric design. *ASCE J. of Transportation Engineering* 122(1): 59–66. 1996.

366. Kang, Y. V. Multifrequency back-calculation of pavement layer moduli. *ASCE Journal of Transportation Engineering*. 124(1): 73–81. 1998.

367. Kelly, E. F. Application of the results of research to the structural design of concrete pavements. *Public Roads*. 20. 1939.

368. Kenis, W. J., J. A. Sherwood and T. F. McMohan. Verification and application of the VESYS structural sub-system. *Proc. of the 5th Inter. Conf. of Struct. Des. of Asphalt Pavements* 1: 333–348. 1982.

369. Kerr, H. S. Discussion on highway location: Practical considerations by H. K Losh. *Transactions of the ASCE*. 96: 483-485. 1932.

370. Khayat, K. H. Viscosity enhancing admixtures for cement based materials: An Overview. *Cement and Concrete Composites* 20: 171–188. 1998.

371. Khazanovich, L. and A. M. Ioannides. DIPLOMAT: Analysis program for bituminous and concrete pavements. *Transportation Research Record No. 1482*. pp.52–60 Transportation Research Board. 1995.

372. Khazanovich, L. and J. Roesler. DIPLOBACK: Neural-network-based back-calculation program for composite pavements. *Transportation Research Record No. 1570*. pp.143–150. Transportation Research Board. 1997.

373. Khazanovich, L. and T. J. McPeak. Back-calculation for rigid pavements: Theory and practice. *Proceedings of the International Conference on Computational Engineering*. 1998.

374. Khazanovich, L. Dynamic analysis of FWD test results for rigid pavements. pp. 398–412 in *Nondestructive Testing of Pavements and Backcalculation of Moduli: Vol. 3, ASTM STP 1375*. Edited by S. D. Tayabji and E. O. Lukanen. Philadelphia: American Society for Testing and Materials. 2000.

375. Khazanovich, L., T. J. McPeak. and S. D. Tayabji. LTPP rigid pavement FWD deflection analysis and back-calculation procedure. pp. 246–266 in *Nondestructive Testing of Pavements and Backcalculation of Moduli: Vol. 3, ASTM STP 1375*. Edited by S. D. Tayabji and E. O. Lukanen. Philadelphia: American Society for Testing and Materials. 2000.

376. Khazanovich, Lev and Alex Gotlif. FHWA-RD-02-088. Evaluation of joint and crack load transfer final report. 2003.

377. Khedr, S. A. Deformation characteristics of granular base course in flexible pavement. *Transportation Research Record No. 1043*. pp.131–138. Transportation Research Board. 1985.

378. Khosla, P. N. and N. A. Ali. A mechanistic method for evaluation of layer moduli and overlay design. pp.355–367 in *Non-Destructive Testing of Pavements and Backcalculation of Moduli, ASTM STP 1026*. Edited by A. J. Bush III and G. Y. Baladi. Philadelphia: American Society of Testing Materials. 1989.

379. Kilareski, W. P. and B. A. Anani. Evaluation of in situ moduli and pavement life from deflection basions. *Proc of the 5th International Conference Structural Design of Asphalt Pavements*. Vol.I. p 349. 1982.

380. Kim et al. Temperature correction of deflections and back-calculated moduli. *Transportation Research Record no. 1473*. pp.55–62. Washington, d.c.: TRB, National Research Council. 1995.

381. Kim, R. Y. Assessing pavement layer condition using deflection data (NCHRP 10-48), http://www4.ncsu.edu/~kim/Chapter1.pdf, as visited on 2-07-2008.

382. Kirwan, R. W. and M. S. Snaith. A simple chart for the prediction of resilient modulus. *Geotechnique* 26(1): 212–215. 1976.

383. Kleyn, E. G. and M. J. J. van Heerden. Using DCP soundings to optimise pavement rehabilitation. Paper submitted for Annual Transportation Convention, Johannesburg. *Report LS/83*. Pretoria, South Africa: Materials Branch, Transvaal Roads Department. 1983.

384. Kleyn, E. G. and P. E. Savage. The application of the pavement DCP to determine the bearing properties and performance of the road pavements. *Int. Symposium on Bearing Capacity of Roads and Airfields*. pp.238–246. Trodheim, Norway. 1982

385. Kleyn, E. G. The use of the dynamic cone penetrometer (DCP). *Report No. 2/74*. Pretoria, South Africa: Transvaal Roads Department. 1975.

386. Kleyn, E. G., J. F. Maree and P. F. Savage. The application of a portable pavement dynamic cone penetrometer to determine in-situ bearing properties of road pavement layers and subgrades in South Africa. *The European Symposium on Penetration Testing*. pp.277–282. Amsterdam, Netherlands. 1982.

387. Kleyn, E. G., M. J. J. van Heerden and A. J. Rossouw. An investigation to determine the structural capacity and rehabilitation utilization of a road pavement using the pavement dynamic cone penetrometer. *Int. Symposium on Bearing Capacity of Roads and Airfields*. Trodheim, Norway. pp.1011–1026. 1982.

388. Kludt, K., J.L. Brown, J. Richman and J. L. Campbell. Human factors. *Literature Reviews on Intersections, Speed Management, Pedestrians and Bicyclists, and Visibility*. Publication No. FHWA-HRT-06-034. 2006. http://www.tfhrc.gov/humanfac/pubs/06034/06034.pdf.

389. Kothandram, S. and A. M. Ioannides. DIPLODEF: A unified back-calculation system for asphalt and concrete pavements. *Transportation Research Record No. 1764*. pp.20–29. TRB. 2001.

390. Kulkarni, R. B., R. L. Burns, J. Wright, B. Apper, T. O. Baily and S. T. Noack. Decision analysis of alternative highway alignment. *Journal of Transportation Engineering*. 119 (3): 317–332. American Society of Civil Engineers (ASCE).1993.

391. Kumar, P., S. Chandra and A. K. Maurya. Computer applications in Marshall method of mix design. *Jl. of Indian Highways* 31(10): 25–43. Indian Roads Congress. 2003.

392. Kumar, P., S. Chandra and S. Bose. Strength characteristics of polymer modified mixes. *Int. Jl. of Pavement Engineering* 7(1): 63–71. 2006.

393. Lambe, T. W. Compacted clay: Structure. *Transactions of the ASCE* 125 Part I(3041): 682–706. 1960.

394. Lamm, R. and E. Choueiri. Recommendations for evaluating horizontal design consistency based on investigations in the state of New York. *Transportation Research Record No. 1122*. pp.68–78. Washington, dc: Transportation Research Board. 1987.

395. Lamm, R., E. Choueiri and T. Mailaender. Side friction demanded versus side friction assumed for curve design on two-lane rural highways. pp.11–21. *Transportation Research Record No. 1303*. Washington, dc: Transportation Research Board. 1991.

396. Lamm, R., E. Choueiri, J. Hayward and A. Paluri. Possible design procedures to promote design consistency in highway geometric design on two lane rural roads. *Transportation Research Record No. 1195*. pp.111–122. Washington, dc: Transportation Research Board.1988.

397. Lamm, R., J. C. Hayward and J. G. Cargin. Comparison of different procedures for evaluating speed consistencies. *Transportation Research Record No. 1100.* pp.10–20, Washington, dc: Transportation Research Board. 1986.

398. Lee A. R. and Croney D., British Full-Scale Pavement Design Experiments, Proc., Int., Conf., on the Struct., Des., of Asphalt Pavements, Univ., of Michigan, Ann Arbor, pp.114-136, August 1962.

399. Lee Y. C., Kim Y. R. and Ranjithan S. R. Dynamic Analysis-Based Approach to Determine Flexible Pavement Layer Moduli Using Deflection Basin Parameters. Transportation Research Record No. 1639, Transportation Research Board, pp.36-42, 1998.

400. Lee, A. R. and D. Croney. British full-scale pavement design experiments. *Proc., of the Int., Conf. on the Struct. Des. of Asphalt Pavements*. pp.114–136. Univ., of Michigan, Ann Arbor. 1962.

401. Lee, S. W., J. P. Mahoney and N. C. Jackson. Verification of back-calculation of pavement moduli. *Transportation Research Record No. 1196*. pp.85–95. Transportation Research Board. 1988.

402. Lee, Y. C., Y. R. Kim. and S. R. Ranjithan. Dynamic analysis-based approach to determine flexible pavement layer moduli using deflection basin parameters. *Transportation Research Record No. 1639*. pp.36–42. Washington, d.c.: TRB. 1998.

403. Leisch, J. E. and J. P. Leisch. New concepts in design speed application. *Transportation Research Record No. 631*. pp.4–14. Washington, dc: Transportation Research Board. 1977.

404. Lenngren, C. A. Relating deflection data to pavement strain. *Transportation Research Record No. 1293*. pp.103–111. Transportation Research Board. 1991.

405. Li S., T. F. Fwa and K. H. Tan. Back-calculation of parameters for slab on two-layer foundation system. *ASCE Journal of Transportation Engineering* 123(6): 484–488. 1997.

406. Li S., T. F. Fwa and K. H. Tan. Closed-form back-calculation of rigid pavement parameters. *ASCE Journal of Transportation Engineering* 122 (1): 5–11. 1996.

407. Li, S., T. F. Fwa and Tan Kiang-Hwee. Parameters back-calculation for concrete pavement with two slab layers. *ASCE Journal of Transportation Engineering* 124 (6): 567–572. 1998.

408. Lieberman, E. B. Model for calculating safe passing distance on two-lane rural roads. *Transportation Research Record No. 869*. Washington, dc: Transportation Research Board. 1982.

409. Lipiènik, M. New form of road/railway transition curve. *ASCE J. of Transportation Engineering* 124(6): 546–556. 1998.

410. Lister, N. W. and W. D. Powell. Design practice for bituminous pavements in the United Kingdom. *Proc. of the 6th International Conference on Structural Design of Asphalt Pavements* 1: 220–231. 1987.

411. Little, D. N. Assessment of in-situ structural properties of lime-stabilized clay subgrades. *Transportation Research Record No. 1546*. pp.13–23. Washington dc: Transportation Research Board. 1996.

412. Livneh M. A. Portable FWD for determining in situ asphalt layers moduli. *Proc. of the 5th International RILEM Mechanical Tests for Bituminous Materials Symposium*. 1997.

413. Livneh, M. and I. Ishai. Evaluation of flexible pavements and subsoils using the South African cone penetrometer. *Publication Number 85-301*. Transportation Research Institute. Technion. 1985.

414. Livneh, M. and I. Ishai. Pavement and material evaluation by a dynamic cone penetrometer. *Proc. of the 6th International Conference on Structural Design of Asphalt Pavements*. Vol. 1. pp. 665–674. Ann Arbor, Michigan. 1987.

415. Livneh, M. and N. A. Livneh. Subgrade strength evaluation with the extended dynamic cone penetrometer, *Proc. of the 7th Int., Congress Int., Association of Engineering Geology*. Vol. 1. Lisbon. 1994.

416. Livneh, M. Validation of correlations between a number of penetration tests and in-situ California bearing ratio tests. *Transportation Research Record No. 1219*. pp.56–67. Washington dc: Transportation Research Board.1987.

417. Livneh, M. Verification of CBR and elastic modulus values derived from local DCP tests. *Proc. of the 9th Asian Regional Conference on Soil Mechanics & Foundation Engineering*. Vol. 1. pp.45–50. Bangkok. 1991.

418. Livneh, M., E. Elhabad and N. A. Livneh. Portable falling weight deflectometer (PFWD) for determining pavement moduli. Publication No. 95–097. *J. of the Transportation Research Board.* Haifa: Transportation Research Institute, Technion-Israel Institute of Technology. 1995.

419. Livneh, M., I. Ishai and N. A. Livneh. Effect of vertical confinement on dynamic cone penetrometer strength values in pavement and subgrade evaluations. *Transportation Research Record No. 1473*. pp.1–8. Washington dc: Transportation Research Board. 1995.

420. Livneh, M., N. A. Livneh and I. Ishai. The Israeli experience with the regular and extended dynamic cone penetrometer for pavement and subsoil-strength evaluation. pp.189–213 in *Nondestructive Testing of Pavements and Backcalculation of Moduli: Vol. 3, ASTM STP 1375*. Edited by S. D. Tayabji and E. O. Lukanen. Pennsylvania: American Society for Testing and Materials. 2000.

421. Losh A. R. Highway location: Practical considerations. *Transactions of the ASCE*. 96(1799): 468–476. 1932.

422. Loudon, A. G. The computation of permeability from simple soil tests. *Geotechnique* Vol. 3. 1953.

423. Love, G. D. Sulphur: Potential pavement binder of the future. *ASCE Jl. of Transportation Engg.* 105: 525–533. 1979.

424. Lukanen E. O., C. Han and E. L. Skok Jr. Probabilistic method of asphalt binder selection based on pavement temperature. *Transportation Research Record no. 1609.* pp.1–11. Washington, d.c.: TRB, National Research Council. 1998.

425. Luo, X., R. Salgado and A. Altschaeffl. Dynamic cone penetration test to assess the mechanical properties of the subgrade soil. *Final Report*, FHWA/IN/JTRP-98/13. Purdue University. 1998.

426. Lytton, R. L. and C. H. Michalak. Flexible pavement deflection equation using elastic moduli and field measurements. *Research Report 207-7F.* Texas Transportation Institute, Texas A&M University, College Station. 1979.

427. Lytton, R. L. Back-calculation of pavement layer properties. pp.7–40 in *Nondestructive Testing of Pavements and Backcalculation of Moduli, ASTM STP 1026.* Edited by Albert J. Bush III and Gilbert Y. Baladi. Philadelphia: American Society for Testing and Materials., 1989.

428. Maccarrone, S., G. Holleran and G. P. Gnanaseelan. Properties of polymer modified binders and relationship to mix and pavement performance. *Proc. of the Assoc. of Asphalt Paving Tech*. pp.209–240. 1995.

429. Mackenzie, K. R. and N. G. Fletcher. Structural design of asphalt pavements in australia or the use and misuse equivalencies. *Proc. of the 10th ARRB Conf.* 10(2): 219–231. 1980.

430. Macklin C. Correction made on paper titled 'The vertical curve: A baffling problem' by E. R. Preston Jr. in June 1955. *Civil Engineer* 26(3). 1956.

431. Magnuson, A. H., R. L. Lytton and R. C. Briggs. Comparison of computer predictions and field data for dynamic analysis of falling weight deflectometer data. *Transportation Research Record No. 1293.* pp.61–71. Transportation Research Board. 1991.

432. Mahoney, J. P. and L. M. Pierce. Examination of Washington State Department of Transportation Transfer. Functions for mechanistic–empirical asphalt concrete overlay design. *Tran Transportation Research Record No. 1539.* pp.25–32. TRB. 1996.

433. Mahoney, J. P., B. C. Winters, N. C. Jackson and L. M. Pierce. Some observations about back-calculation and use of a stiff layer condition. *Transportation Research Record No. 1384*. pp.8–14. Transportation Research Board. 1993,.

434. Manorama. *Manorama Year Book 2008*. India.

435. Marchionna, A., M. Cesarini, G. F. Massimo, and M. Malgarim. Pavement elastic characteristics measured by means of tests conducted with the falling weight deflectometer. *Transportation Research Record No. 1007.* pp.46–53. Transportation Research Board. 1985.

436. Marchionna, A., M. G. Fornaci and Malgarini. Evaluation of flexible pavements by overlay design based on FWD tests. *Proc. of the 6th International Conference on Structural Design of Asphalt Pavements* II: 628–637. 1987.

437. Mark, J. G. Concrete and hydraulic cement. US Patent 2,052,586. 1938.

438. Marshal, Stephen. *Urban Pattern Specification*. SOLUTIONS (Sustainability of Land Use and Transport In Outer NeighbourhoodS). Institute of Community Studies, London, 2005.

439. May, R. and M. W. Witczak. Effective granular modulus to model pavement responses. *Transportation Research Record No. 1022*. pp.1–9. Transportation Research Board. 1985.

440. McElvaney, J. and I. Djatnika. Strength evaluation of lime-stabilized pavement foundations using the dynamic cone penetrometer. *Australian Road Research, ARRB* 21(1): 40–52. 1991.

441. McElvaney, J., A Jayaputra and J. Harison. Correlation of CBR and dynamic cone strength measurements of soils. *Proceedings of the 3rd Indonesian Conference on Geotechnics*. Vol. 1. Jakarta. 1985.

442. Mcfadden, G. and T. B. Pringle. Development and scope of investigation: A symposium on the development of CBR flexible pavement design method for airfields. *Transactions of the ASCE* 115(2406): 456–460. 1950.

443. McGovern, E. W. and K. L. Alderton. Development of durable road tar binders from high temperature coke-oven tar. *Proc. of the 6th ARRB Conf.* 6(4): 39–72. 1972.

444. McGrath, P. G. et al. Development of dynamic cone penetration testing in Ireland. *Proc. of the 12th Int. Conf. on Soil Mech. and Found. Engg.* pp.271–276. Rio De Janeiro. 1989.

445. Medina, A. M. F. and A. P. T. Tarko. Speed changes in the vicinity of horizontal curves on two-lane rural roads. *ASCE J. of Transportation Engineering* 133(4): 215–222. 2007.

446. Meier, R. G., and G. J. Rix. Back-calculation of flexible pavement moduli using artificial neural networks. *Transportation Research Record 1448*. pp.75–82. Transportation Research Board. 1994.

447. Metcalf, J. B. Application of full-scale accelerated pavement testing. NCHRP Synthesis 235. Washington, d.c.: Transportation Research Board. 1996.

448. Milligan, V. Field measurement of permeability in soil and rock. State-of- the-art paper. *Proc. of the ASCE conference on In-situ Measurement of Soil Properties* Vol.II. N.C. State University. 1975.

449. Miner, M. A. Cumulative damage in fatigue. *Transactions of ASME, Jl. of Appl. Mech.* 67: A159–A164. 1945.

450. Ministry of Transport and Communication. *Road Development Plan for India (1961–81)*. DoT, Government of India.

451. Mitchell, J. K. and C. L. Monismith C. L. Athickness design procedure for pavements with thin cement stabilized bases and thin asphalt surfacings. *Proc. on the 4th International Conference on Structural Design of Asphalt Pavements*. 1: 409–416.1977.

452. Molenaar, A. A. A. Structural design of pavements, Part III; Design of flexible pavements. Lecture Notes. 2009.

453. Molenaar. A. A. A. and Ch. A. P. M. Van Gurp. A pavement management system for provincial roads in the Netherland. *Proc. of the 5th International Conference on Structural Design of Asphalt Pavements* Vol. 1. pp.485–499. 1982.

454. Monismith C. L. and K. E. Secor. Visco-elastic behavior of asphalt concrete pavements. *Proc. Int. Conf. on the Struct. Des. of Asphalt Pavements*. pp.476–498. Ann Arbor, Michigan: Univ. of Michigan. 1962.

455. Monismith, C. L. and J. A. Deacon. Fatigue of asphalt paving mixtures. *ASCE Jl. of Transportation Engg.* pp.317– 345. 1969.

456. Monismith, C. L. and K. E. Secor. Visco-elastic behavior of asphalt concrete pavements. *Proc., of the Int. Conf. on the Struct. Des. of Asphalt Pavements*. pp.476–498. Univ. of Michigan, Ann Arbor, Michigan. 1962.

457. Monismith, C. L. Evolution of long-lasting asphalt pavement design methodology: A perspective. Distinguished Lecture of the International Society for Asphalt Pavements. Presented at the International Symposium on Design and Construction of Long Lasting Asphalt Pavements. Auburn University, Alabama, USA. 2004.

458. Monismith, C. L., H. B. Seed, F. G. Mitry and C. K. Chan. *Prediction of Pavement Deflection from Laboratory Tests. Proc. of 2nd International Conference on Structural Design of Asphalt Pavements.* pp.109–140. 1967

459. Monismith, C. L., K. E. Secor and E. W. Blackmer. Asphalt mixture behaviour in repeated flexure. *Proc. of the Assoc. of Asphalt Paving Techn.* 30: 188–222. 1961.

460. Moore, J. H. Thicknesses of concrete pavements for highways. *Trans. of ASCE* 121(2834): 1125–1142. 1956.

461. Morales, Pulido Y., S. Rene. Discussion made on a paper titled 'Classification and identification of soils' by A. Casagrande. *Transactions of the ASCE* 113(2351): 960–963. 1948.

462. MORD. *Rural Roads Development Plan: Vision 2025 (Draft)*. Ministry of Rural Development, Government of India. New Delhi, 2006.

463. MORD. *Specifications for Rural Roads*. New Delhi: Ministry of Rural Development (MORD), IRC. 2004.

464. Mork, H. The effect of sensor configuration on the back-calculation of layer moduli. *Proc. of the 5th International Conference on Bearing Capacity of Roads and Airfields*. Vol. 1. pp.467–476.1998.

465. MORTH. *Manual for the Construction and Supervision of Bituminous Works*. New Delhi: IRC. 2001.

466. MORTH. *Pocket Book for Highway Engineers*. New Delhi: Indian Roads Congress. 2002.

467. MORTH. www.morth.nic.in (accessed on February 2, 2006).

468. MOSRT&H. *Pocketbook for Highway Engineers*. New Delhi: IRC. 2002.

469. MoSRTH. *Specifications for Road and Bridge Works*. 4th Edition. New Delhi: Ministry of Shipping, Road Transport & Highways, Indian Roads Congress. 2001.

470. Moulton, L. K. and R. K. Seals. Determination of the in situ permeability of base and subbase courses. Final Report No. FHWA-RD-79-88. Washington d.c.: Federal Highway Administration. 1979.

471. Moulton, L. K. Design of subsurface drainage systems for the control of ground water. Presented at the 58th Annual Meeting of the Transportation Research Board, Washington, d.c.1979.

472. MSRT&H. *Specifications for Road and Bridge Works*. 4th edition. New Delhi: Indian Roads Congress. Reprinted in 2006.

473. Mullis, I. B. Principles applying to highway road-beds. *Transactions of the ASCE* 104(2040): 1381–1401. 1939.

474. Murthy, S. M. Application of genetic algorithms in pavement engineering. M. Tech. Thesis submitted to the Indian Institute of Technology Kharagpur. 1999.

475. NAASRA. *Interim Guide to Pavement Thickness Design*. National Association of Australian State Road Authorities. 1979.

476. NAC. *Prospects for Concrete Pavement for Indian Roads*. Hyderabad: National Academy of Construction, NAC. 2001.

477. Naik, T. R. and S. S. Singh. Fatigue property of concrete with and without mineral admixture. *Concrete Technology: Past, Present and Future*. Edited by P. K. Mehta. Proc. of V. Malhotra Symposium, SP-144: 269–288. Berkley: University of California; Detroit: ACI. 1994.

478. Nair, K. P. The chemistry of bitumen. *Jl. of Indian Highways* 5(4): 26–27. 1977.

479. Nawy, E. G. (Ed-in-chief). *Concrete Construction Engineering Hand Book*. CRC Press. 1997.

480. Nazarian, S. and A. J. Bush III. Determination of deflection of pavement systems using velocity transducers. *Transportation Research Record No. 1227*. p.147. Transportation Research Board. 1989.

481. Nazarian, S. and K. H. Stokoe II. Nondestructive testing of pavements using surface waves. *Transportation Research Record No. 993*. p.67. Transportation Research Board. 1984.

482. Nazarian, S., K. H Stokoe II. and W. R. Hudson. Use of spectral analysis of surface waves method for determination of moduli and thicknesses of pavement systems. pp.38–45. *Transportation Research Record No. 990*. Transportation Research Board. 1983.

483. Nazarian, S., V. Tandon, K. Crain and D. Yuan. Use of instrumented dynamic cone penetrometer in pavement characterization. pp.214–228 in *Nondestructive Testing of Pavements and Backcalculation of Moduli: Vol. 3, ASTM STP 1375*. Edited by S. D. Tayabji and E. O. Lukanen. Pennsylvania: American Society for Testing and Materials. 2000.

484. Nazzal, M. D. Field evaluation of in-situ test technology for *Qc/Qa* during construction of pavement layers and embankments. A thesis submitted to the graduate faculty of the Louisiana State University and Agricultural and Mechanical College in partial fulfillment of the requirements for the degree of master of science in civil engineering. 2003.

485. NCHRP. Guide for mechanistic–empirical design of new and rehabilitated pavement structures. *Final Report, Part 4: Low Volume Roads*. Prepared for NCHRP. TRB. 2004.

486. NCHRP. Project 1-37A. Draft Final Report. Washington dc: National Co-operative Highway Research Program. 2003.

487. NCHRP. Synthesis 338. Thin and ultra-thin white topping: A synthesis of highway practice. National Cooperative Highway Research Program. Washington dc: Transportation Research Board. 2004.

488. NCSA. *Flexible Pavement Design Guide for Highways*. Washington d.c: National Crushed Stone Association. 1972.

489. Nelu, S. and J. Carmel. Concrete chemical admixtures: Perspective and challenges. *Journal of Indian Concrete Institute* 6(4): 23–32. 2006.

490. Neuman, T. R. and J. C. Glennon. Cost-effectiveness of improvements to stopping sight distance. *Transportation Research Record No. 923*. pp.26–34. Washington, dc: Transportation Research Board. 1984

491. Neville, A. M. and J. J. Brooks. *Concrete Technology*. 2nd Indian Reprint. Pearson Education Ltd. 2002.

492. Neville, A. M. *Properties of Concrete*, 4th Indian Reprint. Signapore: Pearson Education Pvt., Ltd. 2005.

493. Newcomb, D. E. Comparison of field and laboratory estimated resilient moduli of pavement materials, *Asphalt Paving Technology* 56: 91–106. Association of Asphalt Paving Technologists. 1987.

494. Nicholson, A. (closure) and S. M. Easa (discussion). Super elevation, side friction and roadway consistency. *ASCE J. of Transportation Engineering* Nov./Dec., pp.569–570. 1999.

495. Nicholson, A. Super elevation, side friction and roadway consistency. *ASCE J. of Transportation Engineering* 124 (5): 411–418. 1998.

496. Nilsson, R. N., I. Oost and P. C. Hopman. Viscoelastic analysis of full-scale pavements: Validation of VEROAD. *Transportation Research Record no. 1539*. pp.81–87. Washington, d.c.: TRB, National Research Council. 1996.

497. Odden, T. D., M. B. Snyder and A.E. Schultz. Performance testing of experimental dowel bar retrofit designs Part 1. Final Report No.MN/RC–2004–17A. Dept. of Civil Engineering, University of Minnesota. 2003.

498. Odemark, N. *Investigations as to the Elastic Properties of Soils Design of Pavements According to the Theory of Elasticity*. Stockholm, Sweden: Staten Vaeginstitat.1949.

499. Older C. Highway research in Illinois. *Transactions of ASCE* LXXXVII(1546):1180–1222. 1924.

500. Older, C. Highway research in Illinois. *Transactions of ASCE*. 88. 1925.

501. Older, C. The Bates experimental road. *Proc. of the American Road Builders Association*. 1922.

502. Oliver, J. W. H. Rubber bituminous digestions: Manufacture and properties. *Program and Papers of the 18th ARRB Reg. Symposium*. 36–53. Traralgon. 1981.

503. Ong, C. L., D. E. Newcomb and R. Siddharthan. Comparison of dynamic and static backcalculation moduli for three-layer pavements. *Transportation Research Record 1293*. pp.86–92. Washington, dc: Transportation Research Board. 1991.

504. Orchard, D. F. Factors influencing the wear of coarse aggregate in the Los Angeles test. *Proc. of 2nd ARRB Conf.* 2(2): 963–80. 1964.

505. Ottesen, J. and R. Krammes. Speed profile model for a design consistency evaluation procedure in the United States. *Transportation Research Record No. 1701*. pp. 76–85. Washington, dc: Transportation Research Board. 2000.

506. Packard R.G. Design of concrete airport pavement. Engineering Bulletin EB050.03P. Skokie, IL: Portland Cement Association. 1973.

507. Palit, S. K., K. Sudhakar Reddy and B. B. Pandey. High performance modified bitumen for pavements. *Int. Seminar on Sustainable Development in Road Transport* I: 107–123. New Delhi. 2001.

508. Pandey, B. B. Recent trends on design of bituminous mix design. *Seminar on Design of Bituminous Mixes*. pp. 45–50. India: IIT Kanpur. 2003.

509. Park, S. W. and Y. R. Kim. Temperature correction of back calculated moduli and deflections using linear visco-elastic and time–temperature superposition. *Transportation Research Record, No. 1570*. pp. 108–117. Transportation Research Board. 1997.

510. Park, S. W. and Y. R. Kim. Temperature correction of back-calculated moduli and deflections using linear viscoelasticity and time-temperature superposition. *Transportation Research Record no. 1570*. pp.108–117. Washington, d.c.: TRB, National Research Council. 1997

511. PCA. *Color and Texture in Architectural Concrete*. SP012.02A. Portland Cement Association. 1995.

512. PCA. *Thickness Design of Concrete Pavements*. Portland Cement Association, PCA. 1984.

513. PCL-208. High performance data acquisition card. *User's Manual*. Dynalog Micro Systems Pvt. Ltd. 1993.

514. Pen, C. K. An assessment of the available methods of analysis for estimating the elastic moduli of road pavements. *Proc. of the 3rd Int. Conference on Bearing Capacity of Roads and Airfields*. Trondheim 1990.

515. Perry, D. J. Discussion on paper titled, Effect of dowel bar misalignment across concrete pavement joints by A. R. Smith and S. W. Benham. *Transactions of ASCE* 103: 1146–1148, 1938.

516. Peterson, J. C. and P. M. Harnsberger. Asphalt aging dual oxidation mechanism and its inter relationships with asphalt composition and oxidative age hardening. Transportation research record no. 1638. *TRB*. pp.47–58. 1998.

517. Pfeiffer, J. Ph. and P. M. Van Doormaal. The rheological properties of asphaltic bitumens. *Journal of the Institute of Petroleum Technology* 22(152): 414–440. 1936.

518. Pickett, G. and G. K. Ray. Influence charts for concrete pavement. *Transactions of ASCE* 116: 49–73. 1951.

519. Ping-Sien, Lin, Wu Yuan-Ting, Huang Tien-Kuen and C. H. Juang. Equivalent single-axle load factor for rigid pavements. *ASCE's Jl. of Transportation Engineering* 122 (6): 462–467. 1996.

520. Planning Commission, Government of India. A report of NTPC. 1980.

521. Planning Commission, Government of India. Documents of different five-year plans.

522. planningcommission.http://planningcommission.gov.in/reports/peoreport/peoevalu/peo_pmgsy.pdf.

523. pmgsy. http://pmgsy.nic.in.

524. pmindia. http://pmindia.nic.in.

525. Poole, A. B. Alkali carbonate reactions in concrete. *Proceedings of the 5th International Conf. on Alkali Aggregate Reaction in Concrete*. Cape Town, South Africa. 1981.

526. Porter, O. J. Development of the original method for highway design: A symposium on development of CBR flexible pavement design method for airfields. *Transactions of the ASCE* 115(2406): 461–467. 1950.

527. Porter, O. J. The preparation of sub-grades. *Proc. of the Highway Research Board* 18 (2): 324–331. Washington dc: Highway Research Board. 1938.

528. Prabhata, K. S. and N. R. Pushpa. Exact equations for critical depth in a trapezoidal canal. Technical note. *ASCE's Journal of Irrigation and Drainage Engineering* 131(5): 474–476. 2005.

529. Price, D.G. The mathematical design of vertical curves for highways. *ICE Engineering Division Papers* No. 8. London. 1942.

530. Prisk, C. W. Passing practices on rural highways. *Proc. of Highway Research Board*. 21: 366–378. Washington dc: Highway Research Board. 1941.

531. Procter, E. R. Design and construction of rolled earth dams. *Engineering News Record* Vol.VIII. 1933.

532. Rada, G. and M. W. Witczak. A comprehensive evaluation of laboratory resilient moduli results for granular material. Paper presented at TRB Annual Meeting. Washington, d.c. 1981.

533. Ragan, R. M. A nomograph based on kinematic wave theory for determining time of concentration for overland flow. Report No. 44. Prepared by the Dept. of Civil Eng., Univ. of Maryland at College Park, Maryland State Highway Administration and FHWA. 1971.

534. Ramachandran, V. S. (Ed.). *Concrete Admixtures Handbook.* New Jersey: Noyes Publishers. 1995.

535. Ramachandran, V. S., V. M. Malhotra, C. Jolicoeur and N. Spiratos. *Superplasticizers: Properties and Applications in Concrete.* Canada: Materials Technology Laboratory CANMET. 1998.

536. Rao, D. V. Personal communication with Prof. Venkateshwar Rao D. Hyderabad, 2008.

537. Rao, S. K. Unit curve for design of highway transitions. *ASCE J. of Transportation Engineering* 121 (2): 169–175. 1995.

538. RDPI. *Road Development Plan for India, 1981 to 2001*. New Delhi: Indian Roads Congress. 1984.

539. RDPV. *Road Development Plan Vision: 2021.* New Delhi: Indian Roads Congress on behalf of the Ministry of Road Transport & Highways, Government of India. 2001.

540. Reddy, K., S, B. Ray, A. Das, B. B. Pandey. Bituminous overlays and pavement rehabilitation. *Journal of Indian Roads Congress* 56(1): 119–141. New Delhi. 1995.

541. Ridgeway, H. H. Infiltration of the pavement surface. *Transportation Research Record no. 616.* Washington, d.c.: Transportation Research Board. 1976.

542. Road Test One. Md Final Report, Special Report No. 4. Washington, dc: Highway Research Board, National Research Council. 1952.

543. Roesset, J. M. and K. Y. Shao. Dynamic interpretation of dynaflect and falling weight deflectometer tests. *Transportation Research Record No. 1022*. pp.7–16. TRB. 1985.

544. Roque, R., B. E. Ruth and S. C. Sedwick. Limitations of back-calculation and improved methods for pavement layer moduli predictions. *Proc. of the 5th International Conference on Bearing Capacity of Roads and Airfields (BCRA)* 1: 409–417. 1998.

545. Rowe, G. M. and M. J. Sharrock. Analysis of falling weight deflectometer test data and the use of analytical pavement design techniques. http://www.abatech.com/Analysis_of_FWD.htm. Accessed on 16-07-2000.

546. Roy, B. K. Geometric design of compound horizontal curves. (Discussion on this section). *ASCE J. of Transportation Engineering* 120(4): 674. 1994.

547. Roy, B. K. Incorporating transition lengths. (Discussion on this section). *ASCE J. of Transportation Engineering* 118 (6): 887. 1992.

548. Roy, B. K. New look at DCP test with a link to AASHTO SN concept. *ASCE Jl. of Transportation Engineering* 133(4): 264–274. 2007.

549. Rufino, D., J. Roesler and E. J. Barenberg. Evaluation of different methods and models for backcalculating concrete pavement properties based on the Denver International Airport data, presented in the 2002 at the Federal Aviation Administration Airport Technology Transverse Conference. 05/2002.

550. Rwebangira, T., R. N. Hicks and M. Truebe. Sensitivity analysis of selected back-calculation procedures. *Transportation Research Record No. 1117*. pp.25–37. Washington, d.c.: Transportation Research Board. 1987.

551. Saal, R. N. S. and P. S. Pell. Fatigue of bituminous road mixes. *Kolloid Zeitschrift* 171(1): 61–71. 1960.

552. Santosh, S. K., T. Srinivas, K. Suresh and B. B. Pandey. Mechanistic design of concrete pavement. *Jl. of the Indian Roads Congress* 67(3): 208–215. 2006.

553. Scala, A. J. Simple methods of flexible pavement design using cone penetrometers. *New Zealand Engineering* 11(2): 34–44. 1956.

554. Schiffman, R. L. General analysis of stresses and displacements in layered elastic systems. *Proc. of the 1st Inter. Conf. of Struct. Des. of Asphalt Pavements*. pp.365–375. 1962.

555. Schrader, Ernest K. in Edward G. (Ed-in-chief)'s *Concrete Construction Engineering Hand Book.* CRC Press. 1997.

556. Scrivner, F. H., C. H. Michalak and W. M. Moore. Calculation of the elastic moduli of a two-layer pavement system from measured surface deflection. *Highway Research Record No. 431*. Washington, dc: Highway Research Board. 1973.

557. Seed, H. B., C. K. Chan and C. E. Lee. Resilience characteristics of subgrade soil and their relation to fatigue failures in asphalt pavement. *Proc. of the Int. Conf. on the Struct. Des. of Asphalt Pavements*. pp.611–636. Ann Arbor: Univ. of Michigan. 1963.

558. Seehra, S. S. Roller compacted concrete for cost-effective pavements in the 21st century. *National Seminar on Challenges for Road Transportation in the 21st Century Leading to Fuel Economy*. pp.107–121. CIRT 2001. Patiala: TIET. 2001.

559. Sharma, B. and P. K. Bora. A study on correlation between compaction characteristics and plastic limit of fine grained soils. *IRC No. 68*. pp.87–104. Highway Research Board. 2003.

560. Shell. *Addendum to the Shell Pavement Design Manual.* London: Shell International Petroleum Company Ltd. 1985.

561. Shell. *Shell Pavement Design Manual: Asphalt Pavements and Overlays for Road Traffic.* London : Shell International Petroleum Company Limited. 1978.

562. Shen, J., S. Amirkhanian and B. Tang. Influence of accelerated aging test temperature on the properties of binders. *Int. Jl. of Pavement Engineering* 7(3): 191–198. 2006.

563. Shergold, F. A. The percentage voids in compacted as a measure of its angularity. *Magazine of Concrete Research* 5 (13): 3–10. 1953.

564. Shi, X. P., T. F. Fwa and S. A. Tan. Three-slab model for concrete pavements. *ASCE Journal of Transportation Engineering* 125(5): 449–455. 1999.

565. Shi, X. P., T. F. Fwa and S. A. Tan. Warping stresses in concrete pavements on Pasternak Foundation. *ASCE Jl. of Transportation Engineering* 119(6): 905–913. 1993.

566. Shifley, L. H. and C. L. Monismith. Test road to determine the influence of subgrade characteristics on the transient deflections of asphalt concrete pavements. *Report No. TE-68-5*. Berkeley: Department of Civil Engineering, Institute of Transportation and Traffic Engineering, University of California. 1968.

567. Shipway, C. H. A study of aggregate crushing test. *Proc. of 2nd ARRB Conf.* 2(2): 981–96. 1964.

568. Shook, J. F. Construction materials control for the ASSHO road test. *Transactions of the ASCE* 126 Part I: 975–990. 1961.

569. Shook, J. F., F. N. Finn, M. W. Witczak. and C. L. Monismith. Thickness design of asphalt pavements: The Asphalt Institute method. *Proceedings of the 5th International Conference on Structural Design of Asphalt Pavements*. Vol. I. pp.17–44.1982.

570. Shukla, R. S. and P. K. Jain. Improvement of waxy bitumen by the addition of synthetic rubbers, polymers and resins. *Highway Research Bulletin 38*. pp.17–28. IRC. 1984.

571. Siekmeier, J., D. Young and D. Beberg. Comparison of the dynamic cone penetrometer with other tests during subgrade and granular base characterization in Minnesota. *Nondestructive Testing of Pavements and Backcalculation of Moduli: 3rd Volume, ASTM SPT 1375*. Edited by S. D. Tayabji and E. O. Lukanen. Pennsylvania: American Society of Testing Materials. 2000.

572. Siekmeier, J., D. Young and D. Beberg. Use of DCP and portable FWD for subgrade characterization in Minnesota. *Proc. of the 3rd Symposium on Nondestructive Testing of Pavements and Backcalculation of Moduli*. SPT 1375. 1999.

573. Siekmeier, J., T. Burnham and D. Beberg. Mn/DOT's new base compaction specification based on the dynamic cone penetrometer. *Proceedings of the 46th Geotechnical Engineering Conference*. Univ. of Minnesota. 1998.

574. Sikdar, P. K. Planning and design of rural roads. In *Proceedings of the National Conference on Rural Roads, 22–24 May 2007*. New Delhi.

575. Sinha, S. Development of roads in India. *The Indian Concrete Journal*.1968.

576. Skempton, A. W. and A. Northley. The sensitivity of clays. *Geotechnique* 2(2). 1952.

577. Skempton, A. W. The colloidal activity of clays. *Proc. 3rd Int. Conf. ISSMFE*. Zurich: ISSMFE. 1953.

578. Skok, E. L. and F. N. Finn. Theoretical concepts applied to asphalt concrete pavement design. *Proc. of the 1st International Conference on Structural Design of Asphalt Pavements*, pp.412–440. 1962.

579. Smith R. E. and R. L. Lytton. operating characteristics and user satisfaction of commercially available NDT equipment. *Transportation Research Record No. 1007*. pp.1–10. Washington, d.c.: Transportation Research Board. 1985.

580. Smith, A. R. and S. W. Benham. Effect of dowel bar misalignment across concrete pavement joints. *Transactions of ASCE* 103(2002): 1133–1144. 1938.

581. Smith, B. E. and M. W. Witczak. Equivalent granular base module prediction. *ASCE* 107(TE6): 635–651. 1981.

582. Smith, D.W.M. General properties of parabolic vertical curves with special reference to road design. *J. of Inst. of C.E.*15 (4).1941.

583. Smith, R. B. and D. N. Pratt. A field study of in-situ California bearing ratio and dynamic cone penetrometer testing for road subgrade investigations. *Australian Road Research* 13(4): 285–294. Australian Road Research Board. 1983.

584. Sood, V. K., S. R. Vijayaraghavan., P. Joshi, Y. V. Rao and S. Kannan. Evaluation of in-situ subgrade strength by dynamic cone penetrometer. Highway Research Board 55: 39–49. Indian Roads Congress. 1996.

585. Sourwine, J. A. A method of analysis of data on frost occurrence for use in highway design. *Public Roads* 11(3): 51–60. 1930.

586. SP: 23-1985. *Hand Book on Concrete Mixes*. New Delhi: Bureau of Indian Standards. 2001.

587. Spangler, M. G. Discussion made on a paper titled 'Classification and identification of soils' by A. Casagrande. *Transactions of the ASCE* 113(2351): 978–984. 1948.

588. Spangler, M. G. Stresses in the corner region of concrete pavements. *Iowa Eng. Exp. Station Bulletin No. 157*. Iowa State University. 1937.

589. Sparkes, F. N. Stresses in concrete road slabs. *Structural Engg.* 17: 98. 1939.

590. Sparkes, F. N. The structural design of concrete roads. *Magazine of Concrete Research* 6(17): 61. 1954.

591. Sparks, G. A., R. D. Neudorf, J. B. Robinson, and D. Good D. Effect of vehicle length on passing operations. *ASCE J. of Transportation Engineering* 119(2): 272–283. 1993.

592. Speakman, J. and H. N. Scott III. Ultra-thin, fiber-reinforced concrete overlays for urban intersections. *Transportation Research Record 1532*. pp. 15–20. Washington, dc: Transportation Research Board, National Research Council. 1996.

593. Specifications and Standards Committee. Horizontal and transition curves for highways. *IRC Journal* XI-3 (paper no: 119). 1947.

594. Specifications and Standards Committee. Vertical curves for highways. *IRC Journal* XVI-1 (paper no: 156). 1951.

595. Spectrum. *Spectrum Hand Book of General Studies 2008.* New Delhi: Spectrum Books (P) Ltd. 2008.

596. Spence, I. M., D. M. Ramsay and R. K. Dir. A conspectus of aggregate strength and the relevance of their factors as the basis for a physical classification of crushed rock aggregate. *Advances in Rock Mechanics*. pp.79084. Washington d.c.: National Academy of Science. 1974.

597. Spiratos N., M. Page, N. P. Mailvaganam, V. M. Malhotra, C. Jolicoeur. *Super-plasticizers for Concrete: Fundamentals, Technology and Practice*. pp. 322. Canada: Supplementary Cementing Materials for Sustainable Development Inc. 2003.

598. Srinivasa K. R., Structural evaluation of pavements using falling weight deflectometer. Ph.D. Thesis submitted to the Indian Institute of Technology Kharagpur, India. 2001.

599. Srinivasa, K. R., A. Kumar and S. Rao. Fabrication of DCP for evaluation of subgrade soil. *Proceedings of the National Conference on Civil Engineering Systems.* Department of Civil Engineering, Osmania University, Hyderabad. 2006.

600. Srinivasa, K. R., K. S. Reddy, M. Mazumdar and B. B. Pandey. Models for estimation of subgrade moduli from DCP tests. *The International Journal of Pavement Engineering & Asphalt Technology* 4(2). United Kingdom. 2003.

601. Srinivasa, K. R., K. S. Reddy, M. Mazumdar and B. B. Pandey. Regression model for estimation of in-situ subgrade moduli from DCP tests, *Indian Highways* 31(7): 5–19. IRC. 2003.

602. Srinivasa, K. R., K. S. Reddy, M. Mazumdar, C. C. Bhattacharya and B. B. Pandey. Pavement evaluation with impulse loading apparatus. *Proceedings of the International Seminar on Highway Rehabilitation and Maintenance*. p III-135 to III-148. New Delhi. 1999.

603. Srinivasa, K. R., K. S. Reddy, M. Mazumdar, C. C. Bhattacharya and B. B. Pandey. Evaluation of subgrade strength using falling weight deflectometer and dynamic cone penetrometer. *National Seminar on Challenges for Road Transportation in the 21st Century.* Department of Civil Engineering. Thapar Institute of Engineering & Technology, Patiala. 2001.

604. Srivastava, P. N. Fact finding survey and highway planning in Utter Pradesh. *IRC Journal* XX-III. 1955.

605. Stanton, T. E. Expansion of concrete through reaction between cement and aggregate. *Proceedings of the ASCE* 66:1781. 1940.

606. Stock, A. F. and J. Yu. Use of surface deflection for pavement design and evaluation. *Transportation Research Record No. 954*. pp. 64–69. Washington dc: TRB. 1984.

607. Stolle, D. and D. Hein. Parameter estimates of pavement structure layers and uniqueness of the solutions. pp.313–322 in *Nondestructive Testing of Pavements and Back-calculation of Moduli, ASTM STP 1026.* Edited by Albert J. Bush III and Gilbert Y. Baladi. Philadelphia: ASTM. 1989.

608. Stolle, D. F. E. Comparison of simplified elastostatic and elastodynamic models for falling weight deflectometer data interpretation. *Transportation Research Record No. 1540.* pp.72–76. Transportation Research Board. 1996.

609. Stubstad R. N., S. Baltzer, E. O. Lukanen, and H. J. Ertman-Larsen. Prediction of AC mat temperatures for routine load/deflection measurements. *4th Int. Conf. on the Bearing Capacity of Roads and Airfields* 401–412. Minn. 1994.

610. Stubstad, R. N., and J. Sharma. Deriving mechanistic properties of pavements from surface deflections. *Proceedings of the International Conference on Computer Applications in Civil Engineering.* 1979.

611. Sudhakar Reddy K., Ray B., Das A., Pandey B. B. Bituminous overlays and pavement rehabilitation. *Journal of Indian Roads Congress* 56(Part 1): 119–141. New Delhi.

612. Sudhakar, R. K. *Analytical Evaluation of Bituminous Pavements.* Unpublished Ph.D. thesis. Civil Engineering Department, IIT, Kharagpur. 1993.

613. Swamee, P. K. Critical depth equations for irrigation canals. *Jl. of. Irrig. Drain. Eng.*119(2): 400–409. 1993.

614. Swift, G. An empirical equation for calculating on the surface of a two-layer elastic system. *Texas Transportation Institute Research Report 136-4.* Texas A&M University. 1972.

615. T 222-81. Standard method of test for non-repetitive static plate load test of soils and flexible pavement components, for use in evaluation and design of airport and highway pavements. *AASHTO Materials Part-II Tests, 17th Edition.* Washington, dc: AASHTO.1995.

616. T 292. Resilient modulus of sub-grade soils and untreated bases/sub-base materials, standard specifications for transportation materials and methods of sampling and testing. Washington, dc: AASHTO. 2001.

617. Tabatabai A. M., E. J. Barenburg and R.E. Smith. Longitudinal joint systems in slipformed rigid pavements Vol.II: Analysis of load transfer systems for concrete pavements. Report No. DOT/FAA.RD–79/4. Washington, dc: Federal Aviation Administration, U.S. Department of Transportation. 1979.

618. Tabatabie, A.M. and E. J. Barenberg. Structural analysis of concrete pavement systems. *Journal of Transportation Engineering* 106 (5): 493–506. American Society of Civil Engineers. 1980.

619. Taber, S. Ice forming in clay soils will lift surface weights. *Engineering News Record* 80(6): 262–263. 1918.

620. Tai, M., K. S. Eom and B. E. Ruth. Development of DBCONPAS computer program for estimation of concrete pavement parameters from FWD data. pp. 291–312 in *Nondestructive Testing of Pavements and Back-calculation of Moduli, ASTM STP 1026*. Edited by A. J. Bush III and G. Y. Baladi. Philadelphia: American Society of Testing and Materials. 1989.

621. TAI, *Thickness Design Manual*.MS 1. 8th Edition. MS 1. USA: The Asphalt Institute. 1970.

622. TAI. *Asphalt Technology and Construction Practices, Instructors Guide*. MS 1. USA: The Asphalt Institute 1983.

623. TAI. *Superpave Mix Design*. 3rd edition. Superpave Series No. 2. MS 1. USA: The Asphalt Institute. 2001.

624. TAI. *Superpave Performance Grade Asphalt Binder Specification and Testing*. 2nd edition. The Asphalt Institute. 1997.

625. TAI. *Thickness Design: Full Depth Asphalt Pavement Structures for Highways and Streets*. Manual Series No. 1. MS 1. USA: The Asphalt Institute. 1991.

626. Taiganidis, J. and G. Kanellaidis. Method for grading design of highways. *ASCE J. of Transportation Engineering* 117(6): 706–712. 1991.

627 Tang, B. Structural evaluation of airfield rigid pavements using falling weight deflectometer. *ASCE Jl. of Transportation Engineering* 119(3): 467–476. 1993.

628. Tarr, S.M., M. J. Sheehan and A. Ardani. Mechanistic design of thin whitetopping pavements in Colorado. *Transportation Research Record 1730*. pp. 64–72. Washington, dc: Transportation Research Board, National Research Council. 2000.

629. Tayabji, S. D. and B. E. Colley. Analysis of jointed concrete pavements. Research Report. Washington, dc: FHWA, Nat. Tech. Information Service. 1984.

630. Taylor, G. D. *Construction Materials*. U.K: Longman Scientific & Technical. 1991.

631. Teller, L. W. and Sutherland E. C. The structural design of concrete pavements, Part II: Observed effects of variations in temperature and moisture on the size, shape and stress resistance of concrete pavement slabs. *Public Roads* 16(9). 1935; October 1936; and April 1943.

632. Teller, L. W. Discussion on paper titled 'Effect of dowel bar misalignment across concrete pavement joints' by A. R. Smith and S. W. Benham. *Transactions of ASCE* 103: 1145–1146. 1938.

633. Terzaghi, K., R. B. Peck and G. Mesri. *Soil Mechanics in Engineering Practice. 3rd edition*. New York: John Wiley & Sons, Inc. 1996

634. The Asphalt Institute. Computer Program DAMA: Pavement structural analysis using multi-layered elastic theory. *Users Manual*. Asphalt Institute. 1983.

635. The National Highways Act. 1956.

636. The National Highways Amendment Bill. 1995

637. Theyse, H. L., M. deBeer and F. C. Overview of the South African mechanistic pavement design method. *Transportation Research Record No. 1539*. pp.6–17. Washington d.c.: TRB. 1996.

638. Theyse, H. L., M. deBeer and F. C. Rust. Rehabilitation design of flexible pavements in South Africa Section 6: Overview of the South African mechanistic pavement design analysis method. *Report RR 93/296*. Department of Transport, Pretoria. 1997.

639. Tholen O., J. Sharma and R. Terrel. Comparison of falling weight deflectometer with other deflection testing devices. *Transportation Research Record No. 1007*. pp.20–26. Washington d.c.: Transportation Research Board. 1985.

640. Tholin A. L. and C. J. Keifer. Hydrology for urban runoff. *Transactions of American Society of Civil Engineers* Paper No. 3061. 125(I): 1308–1355. 1960.

641. Thompson, M. R. and R. P. Elliott. ILLI-PAVE based response algorithms for design of conventional flexible pavements. *Transportation Research Record No. 1207*. pp.145–168. Washington, d.c.: TRB, National Research Council. 1988.

642. Thompson, M. R. ILLI-PAVE based analysis procedures. pp.487–501 in *Non-Destructive Testing of Pavements and Backcalculation of Moduli, ASTM STP 1026*. Edited by A. J. Bush III and G. Y. Baladi. Philadelphia: American Society of Testing Materials. 1989.

643. Thompson, M. R., B. J. Dempsey, H. Hill and J. Vogel. Characterizing temperature effects for pavement analysis and design. *Transportation Research Record No. 1121*. pp.14–22. Washington d.c.: TRB. 1987.

644. Thomson, M. R. Mechanistic–empirical flexible pavement design: An overview. *Transportation Research Record No. 1539*. pp.1–5. TRB.1996.

645. Timoshenko, S. and J. M. Lessels. *Applied Elasticity*. pp.133–141. Westinghouse Technical Night School Press. 1925

646. Timoshenko, S. P. and S. W. Krieger. *Theory of Plates and Shells*. 2nd Edition, McGraw-Hill International Editions. 1983.

647. TRL (Transport Research Laboratory). *A Users Manual for a Program to Analyse Dynamic Cone Penetrometer Data*. Overseas Road Note 8. Department of Transport, UK, 1990.

648. TRRL. *A Guide to Geometric Design*. Overseas Road Note No. 6. Crowthorne. 1988.

649. Tucker, G. R. Amine salts and aromatic sulfonic acids. US Patent 2,141,570. 1936.

650. Turnbull, Appraisal of the CBR method: A symposium on development of CBR flexible pavement design method for airfields. *Transactions of the ASCE* 115(2406): 547–554. 1950.

651. Tweneboah, K. B., B. E. Ruth and W. G. Miley. Dynaflect evaluation of layer moduli in Florida's flexible pavement system. *Transportation Research Record No. 1196*. pp. 96–107. Washington d.c.: TRB. 1988.

652. Ullidtz P. Analytical tools for design of flexible pavements. Keynote address. ISAP. 8th Conference of the International Society of Asphalt Pavements. Seattle. 1997.

653. Ullidtz, P. and K. R. Peattie. Pavement analysis by programmable calculators. *ASCE Journal of Transportation Engineering* 106 (5): 581–597. 1980.

654. Ullidtz, P. and N. F. Coetzee. Analytical procedure in nondestructive testing pavement evaluation. *Transportation Research Record No. 1482*. pp.61–66. Washington d.c.: Transportation Research Board. 1995.

655. Ullidtz, P. and R. N. Stubstad. Analytical–empirical pavement evaluation using the falling weight deflectometer. *Transportation Research Record No. 1022*. pp. 36–44. Washington d.c.:Transportation Research Board. 1985.

656. Ullidtz, P. *Pavement Analysis*. New York: Elsevier Science. 1987.

657. Ullidz, P. and K.R. Peattie. Programmable calculators in the assessment of overlays and maintenance strategies. *Proceedings of the 5th International Conference of the Structural Design of Asphalt Pavements, Vol. I*. Delft. 1982.

658. UNEP. *Environmental Impact Assessment Training Resource Manual. 2nd Edition*. United Nations Environment Programme, Division of Technology, Industry and Economics and Trade Branch. 2002.

659. Uzan J., M. W. Witczak, T. Scullion and R. L. Lytton. Development and validation of realistic pavement response models. *Proc. of the 3rd International Conference on Structural Design of Asphalt Pavements* I: 334–350. 1972.

660. Uzan J., R. L. Lytton and F. P. Germann. General procedure for back-calculating layer moduli. *Proc. of the 1st International Symposium on Nondestructive Testing of Pavements Backcalculation of Moduli*. Baltimore: ASTM. 1988.

661. Uzan, J. Advanced back-calculation techniques. pp. 3–37 in *Nondestructive Testing of Pavements and Back-calculation of Moduli, Vol. II, STP 1198*. Edited by H. L. Quintus, A. J. Bush III and G. Y. Baladi. Philadelphia: American Society of Testing and Materials. 1994.

662. Uzan, J. Characterization of granular material. *Transportation Research Record No. 1022*. pp.52–29. Washington d.c.: Transportation Research Board. 1985.

663. Uzan, J. Dynamic linear back-calculation of pavement material parameters. *ASCE Journal of Transportation Engineering* 120(1): 109–126. 1994.

664. Uzan, J. Influence of the interface condition on stress distribution in a layered system. *Transportation Research Record No. 616*. pp.71–73. Washington, d.c.: TRB, National Research Council. 1976.

665. Uzan, J. Rigid pavement evaluation using NDT: Case study. *ASCE Journal of Transportation Engineering* 118 (4): 527–539. 1992.

666. Vacin, Ota. Investigation of polymer modified asphalt by shear and tensile compliances. Annual Conference Paper of the Transportation Association of Canada. Quebec. 2004.

667. Van Cauwelaert, F. J., D. R. Alexander., T. D. White and W. R. Barker. Multilayer elastic program for backcalculating layer moduli in pavement evaluation. pp.171–188 in *Nondestructive Testing of Pavements and Backcalculation of Moduli, ASTM STP 1026.* Edited by A. J. Bush III and G. Y. Baladi. Philadelphia: American Society for Testing and Materials. 1989.

668. Van der Poel, C. A general system describing the visco-elastic properties of bitumens and its relation to routine test data. *Jl. of Applied Chemistry* 4(5): 221–236. 1954

669. Van Deusen, D, C. Schrader and G. Johnson. Evaluation of spring thaw load restriction and deflection interpretation technique. *Proceedings of the 8th International Conference on Asphalt Pavements.* Seattle, WA. 1997.

670. Van Til, C. J., B. F. McCullough, B. A. Vallerga. and R. G. Hicks. Evaluation of AASHO interim guides for design of pavement structures. NCHRP Report 128. 1972.

671. van Vuuren. Rapid determination of CBR with the portable dynamic cone penetrometer, Reprint from the *The Rhodesign Engineer*. 1969.

672. Vasudevan, R., S. Saravanavel and S. Rajasekaran. Utilization of waste plastics in construction of flexible pavement. *Seminar on Integrated Development of Rural and Arterial Road Network for Socio-economic Growth.* II: 243–257. New Delhi. 2003

673. Vasudevan, R., S. Saravanavel, S. Rajasekaran and D. Thirunakkarasu. Utilisation of waste plastics in construction of flexible pavement. *Jl. of Indian Highways* 34(7): 5–20. Indian Roads Congress. 2006.

674. Venable, W. M. Measuring materials for concrete. *Transactions of the ASCE* 94(1751): 1082–1103. 1930.

675. Venkat Reddy, D. *Engineering Geology for Civil Engineering*. Oxford & IBH Publishing Co. Pvt. Ltd. 1995.

676. Verstraeten, J. Moduli and critical strains in repeated bending of bituminous mixes application to pavement design. *Proc. of the 3rd Inter. Conf. of Struct. Des. of Asphalt Pavements* 1: 729–738. 1972.

677. Verstraeten, J. Stresses and displacements in elastic layered systems, general theory: Numerical stress calculation in four layered systems with continuous interface. *Proc. of the 2nd Inter. Conf. of Struct. Des. of Asphalt Pavements.* pp.277–290. 1967.

678. Vickers B. *Soil Mechanics: Laboratory Work in Civil Engineering.* London: Granada Publishing. 1983.

679. Vreeland, R. P. V. The unsymmetrical vertical parabola. *ASCE J. of Surveying and Mapping* 94(1). 1968.

680. Waltham, Tony. *Foundations of Engineering Geology 2nd edition.* London: Spon Press. 2002.

681. Wang, F. and R. L. Lytton. System identification method for backcalculating pavement layer properties. *Transportation Research Record No. 1384*. pp.1–7. Transportation Research Board. 1993.

682. Wang, Y. and M. P. Cartmell. New model for passing sight distance on two-lane highways. *ASCE J. of Transportation Engineering* 124(6): 536–545. 1998.

683. Wardle, L. J. and B. Rodway. Layered elastic pavement design: Recent developments. *Proceedings of the 19th ARRB Conference*. Sydney, Australia. 1998.

684. Wardle, L. J. Program CIRCLY: A computer program for the analysis of multiple complex circular loads on layered anisotropic media, division of applied geomechanics. Commonwealth Scientific and Industrial Organization, Victoria, Australia. 1977.

685. Warnes, C. E. Structural design of concrete pavement by computer. *ASCE Jl. of Transportation Engineering* 98. 1972.

686. Warren, H. and W. L. Diekmann. Numerical computation of stresses and strains in a multiple-layer asphalt pavement system. Internal report (unpublished). Chevron Research Corporation, Richmond, CA. 1963.

687. WASHO. Special Report 18: The WASHO road test, Part 1: Design, construction and testing procedures. 1954. Special Report 22: The WASHO Road Test, Part 2: Test data, analyses, findings. 1955. Washington, d.c.: Highway Research Board, National Research Council.

688. Wasley, R. J. Uniform flow in a shallow, triangular open channel. *Transactions of American Society of Civil Engineers* Paper No. 3437. 128(I): 633–654. 1963.

689. Waterhouse, A. Stresses in layered systems under static and dynamic loading. *Proc. of the 1st Inter. Conf. of Struct. Des. of Asphalt Pavements*. pp.291–308. 1962.

690. Webster, S. L., R. H. Grau and T. P.Williams. Description and application of dual mass dynamic cone penetrometer. *Instruction Report, GL-92-3*. Army Engineers Waterways Experiment Station. Vicksburg, Miss. 1992.

691. Webster, S. L., R. W. Brown and J. R. Porter. Force projection site evaluation using the electrical cone penetrometer (ECP) and the dynamic cone penetrometer (DCP). *Proc. of the 4th Int. Conf. on the Bearing Capacity of Roads and Airfields*. University of Minnesota. 1994.

692. Westergaard, H. M. Analysis of stresses in concrete pavements due to variations of temperature. *Proc. 6th Annual Meeting of HRB*. pp.201–215. National Research Council, Washington, dc: HRB. 1926.

693. Westergaard, H. M. Analytical tools for judging results of structural tests of concrete pavements. *Public Roads* 14(10): 185–188. 1933.

694. Westergaard, H. M. Computation of stresses in concrete roads. *Proc. of HRB*. 5(Part I): 90–112. National Research Council, Washington, dc: HRB. 1925.

695. Westergaard, H. M. New formulas for stresses in concrete pavements of airfields. *ASCE Transactions* 113. Paper No. 2340: 425–444. 1948.

696. Westergaard, H. M. Stresses in concrete pavements computed by theoretical analysis. *Public Roads* 7(2): 25–35. 1926.

697. Westergaard, H. M. Theory of concrete pavement design. *Proc. of HRB*. Part. I. pp.175–181. National Research Council, Washington, dc: HRB. 1927.

698. Whitlow, Roy. *Basic Soil Mechanics*. Pearson Education Ltd. 2001.

699. Wimsatt, A. J. Direct analysis methods for falling weight deflectometer data. *Transportation Research Record No. 1655*. pp.135–144. Transportation Research Board. 1999.

700. Winkler, E. *Die Lehre von der Elastizitat and Festigkeit* (The Theory of Elasticity and Stiffness). Prague, Czechoslovakia: H. Dominicus. 1867.

701. Wiseman, G., J. Uzan, M. S. Hoffman, I. Ishai and M. Livneh. Simple elastic models for pavement evaluation. *Proc. of the 4th International Conference on Structural Design of Asphalt Pavements* vol.2. 1977.

702. Wistuba, M. R. Lackner, R. Blab and M. Spiegl. Low-temperature performance prediction of asphalt mixtures used for LLP: New approach based on fundamental test methods and numerical modeling. *Int. Jl. of Pavement Engineering* 7(2): 121–132. 2006.

703. Witczak, M. W. and J. Bari. Development of a mater curve (E*) database for lime modified asphaltic mixtures. *Arizona State University Research Project*. 2004.

704. Wolff H., G. D. Van Zyl., P. Paige-Green and S. J. Emery. The development of a structural design catalogue for low volume roads. Ann., Transp., Con., Session 4C. Paper 6, Pretoria. 1993.

705. WSDOT. http://training.ce.washington.edu/WSDOT/Modules/03_materials/03-2_body.htm. 28-09-2006.

706. www.nhai.org. (accessed on February 2, 2006).

707. Yih Hou, T. Evaluation of layered material properties from measured surface deflections. Ph. D. dissertation. University of Utah. 1977.

708. Yoder, E. J. and M. W. Witczak. *Principles of Pavement Design 2nd edition.* New York: John Wiley & Sons, Inc. 1975

709. Yu, H. T., L. Khazanovich, M. I. Darter and A. Ardani. Analysis of concrete pavement responses to temperature and wheel loads measured from instrumented slabs. *Transportation Research Record No. 1639*. pp.94–101. Washington, dc: Transportation Research Board, Washington. 1998.

710. Zhang, Z. J., Y. M. Abu-Farsakh. and L. Wang. Evaluation of trench backfill at highway cross-drain pipes. Submitted to the 83rd Transportation Research Board Annual Meeting, Washington, dc. 2004.

711. Zube, E. D. O. Tueller and J. B. Hannon. Tech Report No. 643449. State of California, Dept., of Public Work, Division of Highway, N& R, USA. 1969.

Index